Actors' &
Performers'
YEARBOOK
2023

Actors' &
Performers'
YEARBOOK
2023

Foreword by Syrus Lowe

methuen | drama

LONDON • NEW YORK • OXFORD • NEW DELHI • SYDNEY

METHUEN DRAMA
Bloomsbury Publishing Plc
50 Bedford Square, London, WC1B 3DP, UK
1385 Broadway, New York, NY 10018, USA
29 Earlsfort Terrace, Dublin 2, Ireland

BLOOMSBURY, METHUEN DRAMA and the Methuen Drama logo are
trademarks of Bloomsbury Publishing Plc

Nineteenth edition published in Great Britain 2023

A catalogue record for this book is available from the British Library.

A catalog record for this book is available from the Library of Congress.

ISBN: PB: 978-1-3502-8826-3
ePDF: 978-1-3503-2228-8
eBook: 978-1-3503-2229-5

Printed and bound in Great Britain

To find out more about our authors and books visit www.bloomsbury.com
and sign up for our newsletters.

Contents

Foreword

I am sitting in my gorgeous hotel room with the Greek sun begging me to join it outside. Due to the pandemic, this is my first holiday in three years but, as is often the case with freelancers, I have to do a couple of hours of work. This same room saw me reposition all the furniture for a ridiculously complicated commercial Zoom audition yesterday. For which I didn't even get a recall.

Today I am marking the last batch of my RADA audition recalls. As a graduate, I have the privilege of sitting on the RADA audition panel. A team of us have independently watched the audition videos. Today, we will agree on which auditionees to put through to the next round. Watching all these young hopefuls, I can't help but think of my own drama school audition process and my subsequent three years of blood, sweat and oat milk lattes.

I graduated from drama school in 2007, on the eve of the financial crash, with many in the film industry worried that they would have to stop making films due to a lack of investment. The financial stability of a generation, for the first time, felt like an incredibly uncertain thing - a pivotal moment in the industry and the world.

Not unlike what we are experiencing now as we enter the new normal - a phrase that landed in our vernacular in the summer of 2020. The world has gone through the most horrendous few years and ours was one of the most impacted industries. It seems almost unthinkable how long our stages were empty, leaving thousands unable to work. Many of our institutions and theatres missed out on vital funding and grants. I despair at the number of actors, especially those who identify as working class, who we might lose due to the pandemic —those who had to leave their profession and find alternative employment. Overnight, friends of mine became delivery drivers, Covid marshals, supermarket workers, hospital porters and Zoom receptionists. Now, with a once-thriving industry only slowly getting back onto its feet and a very real cost of living crisis, I fear that many of these actors will be unable to return to their chosen vocation.

There is an incredible amount of uncertainty out there and I feel we must all remember that we are living through incredibly unprecedented times. We will look back on these years and honestly wonder how on earth we all got through it.

At the same time, I am extremely optimistic and excited about the future and the emerging power actors now have. The actors' new normal has seen two actresses job-sharing a West End role, enabling one of them to return to work as a new mother; a slow but improving Yes or No campaign, intimacy coaches becoming the norm and not something actors have to request; a new industry-wide understanding that representation does matter at every level—as Kamala Harris said, "You can't be what you can't see", and, as I am experiencing now, the ability to self-tape on holiday rather than having to cancel life plans because a casting director decides to grant us an audition.

I think the casting process changed for good during the pandemic and most of these changes have benefited actors. Non-London-based actors were often penalised by having to travel to London on trains during peak hours or even having to stay overnight in hotels to attend in-person auditions. Zoom has revolutionised this and who would have known that a virtual audition would become second nature to so many of us? That includes me, who accidentally left my first Zoom audition six times because the off switch on my phone kept rubbing against the side of my tripod. However, I now have a golden rule for my audition process - self-tapes on the phone and Zoom auditions on the laptop.

I recently recorded an audio series and the conversation in the green room inevitably got onto auditions, self-tapes and Equity's brand-new code of practice. The code says that casting directors should now give you at least three days to record a self-tape and they should not ask you to learn more than six pages. It also states that it is beneficial if you can find someone to read the scenes with you, but it is not an absolute requirement. On more than one occasion, I have been stuck for a reader and trying to find someone took up essential line-learning time. I also know of cases where the need for a reader has impacted people's relationships—situations where one actor is constantly auditioning and the other is not getting any auditions, but has to read in with their partner multiple times a week.

Of course, not all casting directors are following these new guidelines. There is still work to do, but at least we now have a standard to hold them to.

There were a range of experiences during our green room discussion. One actor said that he will always tell his agent when he needs more time to record his self-tapes and that he will only learn a certain number of pages for a first-round audition. This takes confidence, courage and self-belief. I personally will always ask for extensions if I need them. We want to do our best work, which should be under the conditions we need. Those conditions can be very different for different actors. Casting directors must understand that some of us are parents, carers, have a side hustle (if not a few) and that we all have lives. We are not just sitting by our laptops waiting for an email to ping. By having these conversations and sharing stories and experiences, we empower each other to manage our lives as artists.

Talking of side hustles, I think that, post-pandemic, casting directors, agents and producers must understand that most actors need secondary sources of income to support themselves in-between acting engagements. Respecting and accommodating this is the only way the industry will have true diversity and representation. It's the only way to enable so many of those we have lost to come back. I am constantly amazed and inspired by the ingenuity of actors. I have met actors who are also locksmiths, gardeners, personal trainers, dog walkers and tour guides. I have had several side-hustles over the years; I now only support myself in-between acting jobs by working as a corporate role-play actor. Corporate role-play is where people in the business world work with actors on their communication skills by practising conversations. I feel incredibly privileged to use my acting skills to benefit other people. Corporate role-play is a significant and growing part of the acting industry and the subject has its own chapter in this book.

Actors genuinely are some of the most courageous and powerful people. The level of resilience you need to be an actor is unbelievable. The imposter syndrome does not leave you—it gets quieter, but it does not leave you, no matter how "successful" you are. Neither does the uncertainty. I am always astounded when I see in brilliant, older, established actors the fear of not knowing what the next job is. Yes, I found it surprising, but it is reassuring that all of us must embrace the unknown and just trust. Trust our talent, our agents and our individual journeys. Don't compare yourself to your contemporaries and believe that old saying, "What's meant for you won't pass you by."

This book is a brilliant resource to have on your journey. No matter where you find yourself in your career, it can give you a new direction, tactics or focus when you feel a bit lost. I know many of the book's contributors, who are incredibly knowledgeable, sensitive and talented people.

And I will leave you with one of the most impactful things ever said to me in a rehearsal room. These words came from the brilliant voice coach Hazel Holder and I encourage you to remind yourself of them every day: You are enough.

Syrus Lowe trained as an actor at RADA. He has had a successful career in theatre, television, and animation. His most recent work includes *Treason* (Netflix), *Best of Enemies* (Young Vic and West End), *Strike–Troubled Blood* (BBC and HBO), *The Inheritance* (Young Vic and West End), *The Long Song* (Chichester Theatre), *Avenue 5* (HBO) and *Go Jetters* (CBeebies).

Syrus is also a leader in corporate role-play and has worked as a role-play actor in every corner of the economy. In 2016 he created the Corporate Role Play Master Class for Actors. Methuen Drama will publish his book *An Actors Guide to Corporate Role Play* this year. In 2022 he co-founded The Communication Practice. It allows people to practice difficult conversations with actors–and then receive feedback on their communication style.

Syrus' Twitter & Instagram handles are @syruslowedown.

Training
Introduction

This section is largely devoted to those who are 18 and older. This is not to dismiss the fact that there is training (of varying kinds) for those under that age. However, the field is so wide that the confines of this book limit listings only to the major organisations.

Although there is a handful of well-known actors who did not formally train, it is nevertheless very important for today's aspirant to decide whether or not to do so. An ever-increasing number of people want to become actors, so those with 'casting clout' (agents, casting directors and directors) have more and more people to choose from. With such a saturated field, attaining qualifications from a respected training institution becomes a successful way to stand out from the crowd. It is an essential fact that the acting industry works on very tight time-scales and budgets – training allows actors to better acclimate to this high-pressure environment. For instance, an untrained voice may crack after a few days of live performance and be time-consuming and costly for a management to replace (only the larger productions can afford understudies). Or, equally, a fight (in a theatre or on camera) has to be staged so that it (a) looks real, (b) is safe for the participants and (c) can be seen properly by camera and/or audience – actors who've been trained in the essentials of combat will make this staging process much quicker. Unfortunately, nowadays, the industry rarely gives aspirants the opportunity to 'learn on the job': training is vital preparation.

For today's aspiring actor, it is also important to train on a professionally recognised course. The established drama schools are the focus of such training. There are acting-related university degree courses which have a reasonable proportion of vocational training (as well as academic work) and there are numerous part-time, short-term and 'foundation' courses which will give you basic insights into the many crafts involved in acting. However, because of the intense competition, a full-time drama school course of at least a year is likely essential for most people.

For those who have already trained, there are opportunities to learn new skills and refine those already acquired, or simply to keep them in trim when the acting work is not coming in. The latter is very important, as you can be asked to demonstrate your skills at very short notice. Also, the more you can legitimately add to the 'Skills' section of your CV, the more you can enhance your chances of finding work.

Note: It is especially important to **check for the latest information on all fees listed** under all headings in this section. *Actors' and Performers' Yearbook* makes every effort to ensure that such information is correct and up-to-date, but prices are especially liable to ongoing amendment.

Training for the under-18s

The transition from child star to adult actor is a rocky one, and many do not succeed. There are notable exceptions – Emma Watson and Leonardo di Caprio, for instance – but they are the exceptions that prove the rule.

Generally speaking, the best thing for the stage-struck child is to send them to one of the numerous youth theatre groups and drama workshops that exist in almost every town and city. These can be widely found online or on social media, and many are members of the National Association of Youth Theatres – see below. Public productions may be the last priority of such groups – especially for the younger ages – but a terrific amount can be learnt by the young from the theatrical experience. Children in such groups won't learn many of the technical skills necessary to acting, but they will learn a lot of important social skills and the fundamental business of 'interacting' that is so important to an acting ensemble – that it's not just what you can create that matters, but what you can create with other people. Some youth theatres are allied to agencies who will promote their members for professional work, but it is important to note that employment of the under-16s is very strictly regulated.

British Youth Music Theatre

Mountview, 120 Peckham Hill Street,
Loondon SE15 5JT
tel 020 8563 7725
email mail@bymt.org
website www.britishyouthmusictheatre.org
Facebook www.facebook.com/britymt
Twitter @britymt

British Youth Music Theatre (previously Youth Music Theatre UK) is the UK's national company providing musical theatre activities for young people across the UK. It is one of the seven National Youth Music Organisations (NYMOs) supported by Arts Council England; its core programme links young people from local/regional productions into formal training at drama school – so successful auditionees will be talented, with many going on into the creative industries. BYMT has a strong relationship with the UK's largest teaching union, the NASUWT, who are its principal sponsors, and with Trinity College London, who formally assess the activities.

Auditions for young performers take place around the UK in January and February, and successful applicants join the companies of 8 fully staged productions at venues and festivals around the country in the summer holidays.

BYMT's programme includes workshops, courses and projects that help young people develop their skills and abilities in the performing arts. This includes the opportunity to work with artistic teams to create new music theatre. BYMT also creates similar pathways for young writers, composers and musicians as well as those interested in technical theatre. BYMT offer a

wide range of outreach opportunities with schools, youth services and cross-cultural groups.

Training opportunities for graduate directors, assistant directors, assistant MDs, designers and choreographers working alongside its professional staff are also available.

National Association of Youth Theatres (NAYT)

c/o Friargate Theatre, Lower Friargate, York YO1 9SL
tel 0330 229 0820
email info@nayt.org.uk
website www.nayt.org.uk

Founded in 1982, the National Association of Youth Theatres (NAYT) is the development agency for youth theatre practice in England. The organisation supports the development of youth theatre activity through training, advocacy, participation programmes, and information services. Registration is open to any group or individual using theatre techniques in their work with young people, outside formal education. NAYT is an educational charity (No. 1046042) and a company limited by guarantee (No. 2989999).

NAYT responds to enquiries from young people, teachers, parents, carers, youth workers and social services looking for information and advice about youth theatre provision or career or educational opportunities. This free service puts young people in direct contact with youth theatres.

National Youth Arts Wales (NYAW)

Wales Millennium Centre, Bute Place,
Cardiff Bay CF10 5AL

tel 029 2063 6466
email nyaw@nyaw.org.uk
website www.nyaw.co.uk
Facebook www.facebook.com/nationalyouthartswales
Twitter @nyaw_ccic

NYAW represents the National Youth Brass Band of Wales, National Youth Wind Orchestra of Wales, National Youth Choir of Wales, National Youth Dance Wales, National Youth Orchestra of Wales, and National Youth Theatre of Wales (NYTW).

The National Youth Theatre of Wales was founded in 1976 and has since provided opportunities for hundreds of young people, many of whom are now actively involved with the theatre as professional actors, directors, writers, designers and stage managers. The NYTW is aimed at young people aged 16-21 who are drawn from all over Wales. With guidance from its Creative Activist, the youth theatre prepares and rehearses during the summer of each year for a series of high-profile public performances.

In addition, the NYTW spearheads a development programme of workshops and education activities, designed to increase interest and participation in youth theatre.

National Youth Music Theatre (NYMT)

Adrian House, 27 Vincent Square,
London SW1P 2NN
email enquiries@nymt.org.uk
website www.nymt.org.uk

The National Youth Music Theatre offers exceptional opportunities in pre-professional, musical theatre training for talented young people of all backgrounds aged 10-23 years through skill workshops, master classes and residential courses led by industry professsionals, through commissioning and presentation of exciting new work, and – in collaboration with some of the UK's leading creative minds – producing bold, new realisations of major works of the core repertoire.

These opportunities exist for stage performers, musicians, technicians, musical directors, choreographers and designers.

The National Youth Music Theatre represents the very best in work with young people through musical theatre, enabling thousands of youngsters across the UK to develop both their creative and personal potential, leading Andrew Lloyd-Webber to dub it "the best youth music theatre in the world".

National Youth Theatre of Great Britain (NYT)

443-45 Holloway Road, London N7 6LW
tel 020 3696 7066
email info@nyt.org.uk
website www.nyt.org.uk

Founded in 1956 as the world's first youth theatre, the National Youth Theatre of Great Britain is a world-leading youth arts organisation. Delivering free performance opportunities, courses and masterclasses, with a range of funded places, bursaries and fee-waivers, it nurtures and showcases exceptional performers and theatre technicians from Great Britain and Northern Ireland.

Every year the National Youth Theatre visits over 70 arts venues and schools across the UK in the search for young people aged between 14-25 to join their company. The National Youth Theatre also offers a range of digital activities for young people to take part in from home. Once successfully auditioned, members can be involved with ambitious productions both on stage and backstage, as well as developing skills in facilitation and creative leadership. The National Youth Theatre also runs a social inclusion programme featuring long-term engagement with non-mainstream schools, and accredited courses for those not in education or training, as well as many open access projects and community productions.

The National Youth Theatre's world renowned alumni include: Helen Mirren, Daniel Craig, Colin Firth, Rosamund Pike, Daniel Day Lewis, Zawe Ashton, Chiwetel Ejiofor, Orlando Bloom, Catherine Tate, Ben Kingsley, Ashley Jensen, Derek Jacobi, Timothy Dalton, David Walliams, Matt Lucas, Hugh Bonneville, Matt Smith, Adeel Aktar and David Harewood. Backstage NYT graduates have gone on to work in key roles at the world's biggest theatres and events including Olympic ceremonies, award-winning large-scale theatre productions and global tours of the world's biggest music artists. Cultural leaders who started their careers with NYT include Bush Theatre Artistic Director Lynette Linton, Royal Exchange Artistic Director Bryony Shanahan, Brixton House Artistic Director Gbolahan Obisesan, Globe Theatre Artistic Director Michelle Terry, Old Vic Theatre Artistic Director Matthew Warchus and many more.

Scottish Youth Theatre

The Old Sheriff Court, 105 Brunswick Street,
Glasgow G1 1TF
tel 0141 552 3988
email enquiries@scottishyouththeatre.org
website www.scottishyouththeatre.org

Founded in 1977, Scottish Youth Theatre is Scotland's national theatre for and by young people. Using the youth theatre/drama process to develop not only creativity and performance skills but also transferable skills in participants, Scottish Youth Theatre puts particular emphasis on each individual's personal and social development. It offers weekly drama and dance classes for young people aged $2\frac{1}{2}$ to 25, performances for all the family and the flagship Summer Festival, which includes performance and technical theatre courses, open to young people across Scotland aged 8 to 25.

For participants who have shown promise and are interested in a career in any aspect of theatre, film and television, there is Scottish Youth Theatre's high-quality, high-profile project and performance group, SYT Productions.

Scottish Youth Theatre also works in partnership with schools, youth theatres, youth groups and national agencies to deliver tailor-made Special Projects.

Youth Theatre Ireland

7 North Great George's Street, Dublin 1
tel +353 (0) 1 878 1301
email info@youththeatre.ie
website www.youththeatre.ie
Facebook www.facebook.com/YouthTheatreIreland
Twitter @YouthTheatreIrl
Instagram @youththeatreireland

Youth Theatre Ireland is the national development organisation for youth theatre. It supports a network of youth theatres which deliver year-round programmes of drama workshops and performance opportunities to young people aged 12–21 from cities, towns and villages across Ireland.

Youth Theatre Ireland advocates the inherent value and the unique relationship between young people and theatre as an artform, and is committed to extending and enhancing young people's understanding of theatre and to raising the artistic standards of youth theatre across the country. The organisation supports youth drama in practice through an annual programme that includes the National Youth Theatre, National festivals of youth theatres, commissioning new writing, publications, resources, training and other services, as well as research and policy development.

With a membership of 55 youth theatres throughout the country, Youth Theatre Ireland supports the sustained development of youth theatres in partnership with local authorities, youth services, theatres and arts centres. Its productions are of a professional standard and are cast from youth theatres around Ireland. Previous productions include: the world premiere of Carmel Winters' *Salt Mountain* (2015), directed by Jo Mangan; *R.U.R. – Rossum's Universal Robots* by Karel Čapek, directed by Cáitriona McLaughlin (2017); and the world premiere of Dylan Coburn Gray's *Ask Too Much of Me*, directed by Veronica Coburn (2019). For further details about Youth Theatre Ireland's work, please refer to the website.

Arts Emergency

Julie Hesmondhalgh

The crisis in arts education: how working-class artists are being squeezed out of the industry

I had an unexpectedly lovely train journey pre-pandemic. Lucky enough to have managed to reserve a seat at a table in a typically over-crowded carriage, I was planning to shove my earphones in, bury my head in a book and disengage from my fellow passengers. So, when the strangers at my table started to chat to one another – and to me – my heart sank a bit. But it ended up being one of the most interesting and engaging journeys I've ever had.

My cross-country companions were Alan, a middle-aged gay actor; Kate, a young maths teacher at a struggling comprehensive school in West London; and Henry, a Ghanaian-born scientist working in Washington DC. We covered so much in that two hours between London and Manchester: childhood, sexuality, racism, Trump and perhaps inevitably – there being a teacher amongst us – education. Kate talked with sadness about how the new GCSEs were taking their toll on teachers and pupils alike at her school and how she'd been working every evening and weekend to try to get her Year 11s through them. She said that the school was already feeling the effects of the cuts in arts subjects; that although she was a maths teacher, the erosion of subjects that had enhanced her students' creativity and awakened their minds to the wider world was already taking its toll on the mental health of the young people. Henry talked passionately about how, although he was a scientist by trade, it was the arts that gave him joy, that refreshed him and rebooted him after long days at the lab. Music venues, theatres, cinemas: these were his hang-outs of choice. Alan and I both talked about the opportunities that we had taken for granted as we started out in the performing arts – opportunities that no longer exist for young people growing up in towns like ours; from families like ours.

I, along with a dozen of my mates, left my hometown of Accrington at the age of 18 to go to drama school in London, after a brilliant theatre studies teacher at our local Further Education college inspired us all to make a go of it and audition. There were five of us from that course at LAMDA at the same time at the end of the 1980s, all on *full grants* from our Local Education Authority. That FE performing arts course, I found out this week, no longer exists. Neither does the full local authority grant, of course. And nor, I'd venture, does the philosophy that an education in the arts, or a desire to have a career in the arts, is a worthwhile pursuit for people from backgrounds like mine.

There has been an insidious mindset creeping into our national psyche, no doubt massively exacerbated by the prohibitive costs of higher education tuition fees, that some-how a career in the arts is pie-in-the-sky and unrealistic, and that an arts or humanities degree or drama/art school training is not worth the investment. God forbid that anyone should be enthusiastic about learning for learning's sake and want to study philosophy or classics, never mind acting or dance because of a personal passion for the subject, without wondering and worrying about how to make that choice economically viable in the long term. As Nicky Morgan, the then Conservative Education Minister famously said in 2014, 'Arts subjects limit career choices', warning young people that studying arts at higher education could 'hold them back for the rest of their lives'.

The majority of educationalists, of course – even those working in Science and Maths subjects like my travelling companion Kate – would disagree. The study of the arts, and in particular the performing arts, are partly encouraged in top public schools, I'm sure, because of the confidence, social skills and interpretative thinking that develop as a result. The wealthy have never been discouraged from indulging their passion for music, film, painting, theatre and dance. A government report in November 2017 recorded that the creative industries were indeed thriving with the '£92bn sector growing at twice the rate of the economy' (**www.gov.uk** *Creative industries' record contribution to UK economy*, 29 November 2017).

But it appears that a huge swathe of the population, namely the state educated, the less well-off, the working class, for whom the decision to saddle oneself with over £27,000 debt at the start of their adult life is a major consideration, are being massively disincentivized to engage with the arts and humanities, from school onwards. It starts with funding cuts and continues as arts subjects are moved into a more theoretical and less practical curriculum framework at GCSE level. The controversial English Baccalaureate and its exclusion of arts is seen by many as the nail in the coffin of any meaningful creative education. Drama, art, dance and music at school have often been the only access young people have had to learning those skills.

There are, luckily, amazing organisations picking up the pieces and attempting to fill the gaps that current government policy is leaving. There is hope. Groups of people are crowdfunding to create bursaries to allow students from less privileged backgrounds to access arts and performance degrees. Theatres and art spaces are investing in outreach work to pull hard-to-reach communities into their buildings through youth theatre and specialised groups. Teachers and directors are setting up free training programmes, and watching their talented students overcome sometimes unbelievably challenging personal circumstances to thrive and succeed in an arts industry that they have been told is not for them: organisations like Alt, Nottingham-based Talent First and the mighty Arts Emergency.

Set up in 2011 by comedian Josie Long and campaigner Neil Griffiths, the Arts Emergency philosophy and aim are simple and effective: to create an 'Alternative Old Boys' Network'; to open up the same opportunities naturally afforded to those privileged few, who grow up with those school and family connections firmly in place, to everyone. They have pulled together an enormous number of experts and practitioners from a vast array of specialised areas and connected them with young people from backgrounds that have meant they have little access to the arts. Free talks and events are regularly made available, and when the scheme spread to the North a couple of years ago I became involved as a supporter and speaker in schools and colleges.

There is an incredibly successful mentoring scheme that I have witnessed first-hand as my husband, the writer Ian Kershaw, has been a mentor for over a year now. His first mentee, a sparky seventeen-year-old aspiring writer and the first in her family to access higher education, won't mind me saying that she thrived under the programme. Together, they saw theatre, attended talks by leading writers, met people in the industry and visited studios and rehearsal rooms. She grabbed the opportunity she was offered to write for a local theatre-in-education tour and did work experience at CBBC. She is now at university studying English with a creative writing pathway as part of her BA.

Maisie (not her real name) was clear about what she wanted to do from the off and Arts Emergency enabled her, creating networks that simply don't ordinarily exist for people like her. But sometimes the work they do is about opening up unknown worlds to their participants. Another young person might, for example, be passionate about, and fascinated by, films and filmmaking, but have no access to the world of the studio floor or editing suite or post-production house. He or she might be a fantastic and naturally gifted vision mixer or a sound recordist, but unless they're given the opportunity to experiment in these roles, they'll never know. As Arts Emergency say: 'You can't be what you can't see.'

The working-class artists who were encouraged and supported by the state from the 1950s through to my generation growing up in the 1980s and early 1990s, who are now part of the cultural landscape of the UK as writers, actors, directors, dancers, visual artists, musicians, directors, etc. are the last of their kind. Or could be, if we don't act to change the current climate of exclusion. A culture without diversity is a sick one. If our future artists only come from a narrow stratum of society (the most well-off and privately educated) then who will be left to tell the stories of the rest of us? Who will hold a mirror to our world and ask the important questions about how we live now? Because art exists not only to entertain, but to reflect and inform and inspire. At its best, it can be transcendent and transformative and completely democratic; in that it is, or should be, available to us all, regardless of where we're from and who we are. The more diverse our culture, the wider the world of the stories we experience, the richer we all are for it. Perhaps most importantly, it creates, as I experienced on that Pendolino train a few weeks back, a point of connection in an increasingly isolating and fractured world.

Arts Emergency, Unit W3, 8 Woodberry Down, London N4 2TG, **info@arts-emergency.org**

Julie Hesmondhalgh was born and grew up in Accrington, Lancashire. She trained at LAMDA and set up Arts Threshold Theatre in the early 90s. She co-runs Take Back Theatre Collective in Manchester. Her *Working Diary* was published in 2019. She is best known for playing Hayley in Coronation Street from 1998-2014. She has worked extensively in theatre, TV and radio.

Levelling the playing field: actors from working- and benefit-class backgrounds

David Mumeni, actor and founder of Open Door
Interview by Rob Ostlere

David Mumeni is a performer, writer and acting teacher, and the artistic director and founder of Open Door, a charity supporting young people who want to apply for drama school but face financial barriers. Open Door offers an eight-month part-time intensive course, with successful acting and production arts applicants receiving free auditions and financial support for interviews, as well as mentoring and a range of other help. David trained as an actor at Drama Centre and has gone on to work extensively at the highest levels of the industry. Here he talks about the need for organisations like Open Door, makes the case for drama school training and shares advice for students and those in the first few years of their careers.

What were you seeing in the industry that led you to create Open Door?

It was about addressing inequality by making sure that everyone who wanted to go to drama school got their fair go. Part of that was making the audition process affordable for young people from working- and benefit-class backgrounds, and also finding talent from places outside London.

As well as finding these young people, mentoring them and supporting them financially with applications, you've also been working directly with the schools to make changes

Yes, for example getting a wider intake of people by pushing the drama schools to do more auditions across the country. Or pushing to change the audition panels, making sure they're diverse in all the different ways, be it class or race or gender. We also looked at the way the panels sometimes behaved. It's not about having to be super, super nice but if you don't create a space that allows someone to be comfortable they're just not going to do their best work. I've also been talking to the schools which don't redirect actors in the first round. What we've seen with some of our young people we mentor – who maybe haven't had access to youth theatres or good drama departments at school – is that they can transform and be amazing simply by asking them the right questions: "What's this speech about for you? How do you relate to it? What do you want? Who are you speaking to?" You're expecting all these young people to all come in at the same level and they're not. You have to give redirection in the first round.

And the drama schools have taken all this on?

Not as urgently as we'd like. There's a lot of work that still needs to be done but some have been really responsive. The auditions have changed. The schools are looking at the curriculums and the classes they teach. I think Sarah (Frankcom) taking over LAMDA is really exciting. She has the artistic side but also used to work in a school and helped set up a lot of the youth provisions in Manchester. It's good that someone understands where young people are coming from, especially those from outside London.

You've previously made the case brilliantly for drama schools

Well, you do learn there! Acting is a skill, and you get the chance to practice doing that every day. Whereas if you go straight into the industry, you're not necessarily going to do that much acting, especially to start with. Even if you did a couple of plays and a week on a TV series that's only sixteen or seventeen weeks' acting. And that's in a good year!

And you've done a lot of myth-busting. One idea that comes up is that the schools are too expensive, but you've managed to get all these great students in from lower income backgrounds

With the schools we work with there is no such thing as too expensive because the big ones all have student finance. Affordability is only a problem with schools that don't have that; although the privately-run drama schools do offer bursaries and DaDAs (Dance and Drama Awards), it can still be a struggle. With the loans – it is a debt, of course it is – but you're only going to pay that back if you earn enough. Also, with most of these big schools there's massive bursary funding to assist with living costs. And we've highlighted the issue at schools where they might need more.

And students get a lot for their money, relatively

People are paying nine grand a year to go to an amazing university but they're doing three or four hours a week contact-time in a lecture hall full of people. Drama school, you get triple that in a day with some of the best teachers in the country in a room of sixteen to twenty people. And then you get a showcase at the end!

With Open Door you've given advice to students about changes in the industry, especially casting and how that impacts choosing material for their showcases

With showcases, I say to the students worrying about type-casting that agents are going to assume you can do different stuff and are going to try to put you up for as much as possible. So just show you, rather than worrying about, "What do I need to present to be signed?" Present good acting. Rather than trying to fit yourself into some archetype, pick pieces that might be challenging when you're working on them but that when you perform you can do them with some ease. That sort of thinking applies throughout your third year. Your main focus has to be on acting to the best of your ability, being a nice person when you chat to people, and hopefully things will happen for you.

What about auditioning advice?

It's the same thing we tell the Open Door young people when they audition; you've got no control over what this panel thinks. One panel might like you, one panel might not. Your job is to go, "This character is connecting with this character, I'm playing this objective. I'll do my interview, show you what I'm actually like and then leave. If you don't like it, you don't like it". There's power in that. That's some of the work we do at Open Door. It takes eight months to get a young actor to a place of confidence where they realise they have no control over what people think. All you can say is, "I did the best job I could do in the circumstances that were given and in the time I had".

Talking about the industry more widely now, how do people balance having an awareness of inequalities without letting that preoccupy them and hold them back?

It's really hard to quantify why you are where you are in your career. If I think about my mixed-race background, perhaps it's got me this far because I'm a little bit different to other people but it might have limited me in all these other ways. The point is it's really hard to be sure of whether something doesn't happen for you because of your class, your race or your accent or whatever. Of course, that's not to deny that those barriers aren't there. But if you go around thinking everything you don't get is because of that, I don't think that's a healthy way to look at it. Wherever you can, separate the two: "Have I not got this because the industry is tough?" or "Have I not got it because of a barrier?" Sometimes it might be very clear, and I've felt that. But I've come up against these barriers and I've done OK so my thought is let me try and help others with solutions.

And actors can take positive steps themselves to address inequalities?

When I started Open Door people said to me, "You're creating these actors but there's no work for them". I feel like it's a little bit different now and I don't have that fear. Of course, there are still a lot of the same types of writers working but people are breaking through and people do want to hear original stories and original voices. But if that work isn't being made for you, you can create it. And that doesn't mean you have to write it. I've known lots of people who wanted to change agents for example, and put on a show to do that. They've not been able to write something but they've said I'm going to get my friend to write it, and I'm going to get my director-friend to direct it, and another actor in to play this part and develop it. And sometimes that play goes on further: to Edinburgh, another theatre, into TV development.

It's important to balance focusing on the problem and the solutions?

We have to find ways of using the passion and the anger, putting it into some sort of positive action that is effective. We need tangible solutions, schemes and work: be it writers' programmes, or things like Sabrina Mahfouz creating a scheme for ethnic minority theatre critics, or something like Open Door. Next, we need to start supporting new voices in producing; to see more diversity among the people in charge.

To find out more about Open Door and to apply, go to **www.opendoor.org.uk**. You can support the charity's work by following them on social media **@opendoorpeople** and donating at **www.opendoor.org.uk/donate**

Rob Ostlere is the author of *The Actor's Career Bible*, published by Bloomsbury, a practical guide to building an acting career based on in-depth interviews with over seventy-five industry experts. He trained at National Youth Theatre and RADA and has since worked widely across television, theatre and film. *The Actor's Career Bible* is available at **www.bloomsury.com**. You can also find out more **@actorscareerbible** on Instagram, at **www.actorscareerbible.com** and on the book's YouTube channel. Rob can be found via **@robostlere** on social media, where there is more information about his latest acting and writing work.

Drama schools

Currently there is a core of established drama schools which belong to an organisation called the Federation of Drama Schools (**www.federationofdramaschools.co.uk**) which was formed after the closure of Drama UK in 2016. The nineteen drama schools which are members of the Federation all run courses that were formerly accredited by Drama UK, offering practice-based, vocational training courses, quality assured by experienced professionals. Upon graduating from any of these schools you will be eligible for Spotlight and Equity membership. There are also, of course, well-respected courses that are not part of the Federation of Drama Schools.

It is important to check the current funding arrangements for each course you intend applying for. Don't simply rely on what arrangements were in place last year, as things have a habit of changing. Almost all of the drama schools offer a three-year BA degree in acting – in spite of the fact that there is little or no written component to the courses, let alone formal, written exams. Historically, the schools took the 'degree' route to help students get funding on the same basis as those following conventional academic courses. Degree status actually means very little in the acting profession, and courses with degree status are not necessarily better than those without it. Funding for some accredited one- and two-year courses is available, but not with the same frequency as for three-year courses.

It is worth spending time checking through all the courses listed below – also, read through the *Guide to Professional Training in Drama and Technical Theatre*, which although slightly out of date is very helpful. Look at the online prospectuses for any school that you feel could be viable for you – and read each one thoroughly. Important considerations include whether you could be eligible for funding whether student loan, scholarship or DaDA award for your fees and maintenance. Central London is significantly more expensive to live in than out of London schools.

Above all, it's important to try to assess which schools and courses you feel would suit you best and to apply, via UCAS **www.ucas.ac.uk** or **www.cukas.ac.uk**, to as many as you can afford the audition fees and travel costs for. Some schools offer means-tested audition fee waivers. Don't forget to factor in the cost of overnight accommodation, if necessary. The plain truth is that competition for places is so intense, that you need to audition for as many places as feasible. Every time you do another audition you will learn more about the techniques of auditioning than any book or class can teach you. It is important to appreciate that many people take two or three years of auditioning, and sometimes more, before they get places. If you are determined to become a professional actor, you have to take rejection in your stride – learn from it, and keep on trying until you succeed.

Finally, carefully check the application deadlines, funding details and audition specifications of each school to which you intend to apply – there are some considerable variations. See the Checklist following the listings given below. Many schools will have audition guidelines and advice for applicants on their website.

Notes:

• For general information on funding for fees and maintenance loans, see **www.gov.uk/browse/education/student-finance**.

• Places on some courses are currently funded through Dance and Drama Awards (DaDAs). These were introduced in the late 1990s, and provide funding for about two-thirds of successful applicants. For more details, check each relevant school's prospectus and website – also look at **www.gov.uk/dance-drama-awards**.

• For the latest details on member of the Federation of Drama Schools please see FDS website **www.federationofdramaschools.co.uk**.

* denotes membership of the Federation of Drama Schools

ArtsEd*

14 Bath Road, London W4 1LY
tel 020 8987 6666
email info@artsed.co.uk
website www.artsed.co.uk
Principal Dr Julie Spencer *Deputy Principal* Yewande Akindele

ArtsEd is one of the UK's leading drama schools, offering outstanding conservatoire training on the BA (Hons) courses in Acting and Musical Theatre. In 2019, they were awarded TEF Gold, the highest rating from the Teaching Excellence and Student Outcomes Framework and were recently placed sixth in *The Telegraph*'s list of British universities with the best graduate prospects. ArtsEd was ranked as the top school for overall student satisfaction in the 2018 and 2019 National Student Survey.

Degree courses are validated by City, University of London. Dance and Drama Awards are available, linked to the Level 6 approved Trinity College London diplomas and ArtsEd also awards bursaries from its own funds. Applications for courses and awards should be made direct to the school.

Acting courses:

• BA (Hons) Acting/Level 6 Diploma in Professional Acting (3 years). Applicants must be aged 18 or over.
• BA (Hons) Musical Theatre/Level 6 Diploma in Musical Theatre (3 years). Applicants must be aged 18 or over.
• MA Acting (1 year postgraduate). Applicants must be aged 21 or over.
• Foundation Musical Theatre – Cert HE (1 year). Applicants must be aged 18 or over.
• Foundation Acting – Cert HE (1 year). Applicants must aged 18 or over.
• Part-time Foundation Musical Theatre (2 terms). Applicants must be aged 18 or over.
• Part-time Foundation Acting (2 terms). Applicants must be over 18 or over.

Bath Spa University

Newton Park, Newton St Loe, Bath BA2 9BN
tel 01225 875875
email admissions@bathspa.ac.uk
website www.bathspa.ac.uk
Head of Comedy Pat Welsh

Specific course on comedy. The undergraudtae degree in Comedy at Bath Spa responds to the increasing employment opportunities for comedy writers and performers in the entertainment sector. The course covers stand-up, sitcom, panel show, street performance, physical comedy, sketch, high comedy and satire. The programme is postponed for the academic year 2022-23.

The Birmingham Theatre School

The Old Fire Station, 285-287 Moseley Road, Highgate, Birmingham B12 0DX
tel 0121 440 1665
email info@birminghamtheatreschool.co.uk
website www.birminghamtheatreschool.com
Principal Chris Rozanski

Full-time acting courses:

• HND Performing Arts/Theatre Acting (2 years). Applicants must be aged 18 or over with BTEC level 3 or A level qualifications.
• BTEC Extended National Diploma in Performing Arts (Acting) (2 years). Applicants must be aged 16 or over.
• Professional Acting Diploma (1 year). Applicants must be aged 18 or over.
• Part-Time Evening Acting Diploma. Termly.
• Acting for Beginners. Autumn, spring and summer terms, 11 weeks per term.

The Bridge Theatre Training Company

Admin:The Bridge at Cecil Sharp House,
2 Regent's Park Road, London NW1 7AY,
Courses: Held in the Camden area
tel 020 7424 0860
email admin@thebridge-ttc.org
website www.thebridge-ttc.org
Joint Artistic Directors Mark Akrill, Judith Pollard

The Bridge is a non-profit organisation which provides intensive training for a professional acting career. Courses include comprehensive career guidance, and a graduating season of public productions in London theatres, with a West End showcase in front of agents, directors and casting directors.

Bridge students receive training in acting, singing, dance, improv, Shakespeare,combat and much more.

Bridge students also study screen acting and will record a video showreel.

Full-time acting courses:

• Professional Acting Course (2 years). Applicants must be aged 18 or over.
• Professional Acting Course (1 year postgraduate/post-experience). Applicants must be aged 21 or over, with a university degree or significant relevant experience.

Bristol Improv Theatre

50 St Paul's Road, Bristol BS8 1LP
mobile 07936 617158
email hello@improvtheatre.co.uk
website https://improvtheatre.co.uk
Twitter @BITheatre

A gentle introduction to the world of improvisation. Offers introductory through to advanced courses in improv. There is currently no wheelchair access.

Bristol Old Vic Theatre School*

1-3 Downside Road, Clifton, Bristol BS8 2XF
tel 0117 973 3535
email enquiries@oldvic.ac.uk
website www.oldvic.ac.uk
Facebook www.facebook.com/BOVTS
Twitter @BOVTS
Instagram @bovtsbristol
Principal Fiona Francombe *Artistic Director* Jenny Stephens

All courses are entirely vocational and are validated by the University of the West of England.

Applications for all full-time courses are through UCAS. All applicants are auditioned – please see our website for details of the relevant selection process.

• BA Hons Professional Acting (3 years).
• MA Screen Acting (1 year, 38 weeks).
• MFA in Professional Acting (1 year, 40 weeks, for international students).
• Summer Foundation Course in Acting (10 weeks) – apply directly to the School.

City Lit

1-10 Keeley Street, Covent Garden, London WC2B 4BA
tel 020 7492 2542
email drama@citylit.ac.uk
website www.citylit.ac.uk/courses

The Acting Diploma (Level 3) is an intensive year-long course that provides students with a thorough foundation in actor training.

Working with industry professionals and experienced teachers, candidates will develop skills in actor's voice, movement and physicality. Students will hone their craft across a range of specialisms, from classical training through to screen performance. Students will perform in a full-scale theatre production at the end of the course.

The course timetable is designed to fit around part-time employment.

Applicants for the course will ideally have completed a full Level 2 Foundation in Drama course or equivalent (at least one years' actor training).

Entry is by audition. Please prepare 2 2-minute monologues (one classical, one contemporary) and be prepared to attend a 3-hour workshop. No audition fee. Auditions from April for September course start.

Students can apply for an Advanced Learner Loan from Student Finance England for up to £2,225 of the fees for this course. For more information contact the Drama department at drama@citylit.ac.uk.

The Comedy School

14-15 Gloucester Gate, London NW1 4HG
tel 020 7486 1844
email LTL@TheComedySchool.com
website www.thecomedyschool.com
Facebook www.facebook.com/keithpalmerthecomedyschool
Twitter @comedyschooluk
Founder Keith Palmer

Founded in 1998. The only arts organisation of its kind in the UK which works with comedy in many different settings. Based in Camden, London. Offers workshops and intensive 6-week courses on improv, clowning, comedy acting for TV, compère hosting, stand-up, puppetry and much more. Bookings taken on their website.

Court Theatre Training Company

The Courtyard Theatre, Bowling Green Walk, 40 Pitfield Street, London N1 6EU
tel 020 7739 6868
email info@courttheatre.org.uk
website www.courttheatre.org.uk
Principal/Director Tim Gill

The Court Theatre Training Company site has wheelchair access and provides support for students with learning support needs.

Full-time acting courses:

• BA (Hons) Acting (2 years) – Taught on a 2-year accelerated program, this distinctive course is specially designed for the practical training of actors resident within the professional environment of a working theatre and is taught by working practitioners in the field. The course fee is £10,800 per academic year. Applicants must be aged 80+ and hold 80 UCAS entry points on entry. Mature students up to any age are accepted with no UCAS point requirement. Public funding is available via the Student Finance Company. Applications should be made directly via the website or via UCAS throughout the year.

Cygnet Training Theatre*

CYGNET THEATRE

Cygnet Theatre, Friars Gate, Exeter EX2 4AZ
tel (01392) 277189
email info@cygnettheatre.co.uk
website www.cygnettheatre.co.uk
Principal Rosalind Williams *Artistic Director* Alistair Ganley

Cygnet offers 3-year full-time training based in its own studio theatre alongside a 1-year foundation course and post-graduate options. Ensemble training: delivering technical skills in acting, voice, movement, singing, TV, film and recorded media, through dedicated workshops, one-to-one tutorials, and an ongoing commitment to public performance and touring.

Functions as a small touring company, drawing its members from all over the UK and abroad. Successful applicants demonstrate talent, flexibility, maturity, awareness and self-discipline. Applicants must be aged 18 or over. Professional Acting Certificate; ATCL & LTCL as appropriate. Stage Combat (BADC) exams.

The Dorset School of Acting

Lighthouse, 21 Kingland Road, Poole,
Dorset BH15 1UG
tel (01202) 922675
email admin@dorsetschoolofacting.co.uk
website www.dorsetschoolofacting.co.uk
Co-founders & Principals James Bowden, Laura Roxburgh

The 1 year diploma course in Acting & Musical Theatre has a 100% success rate in placing students at reputable drama schools for further training or into professional work. It is designed to provide a real insight into the rigours of drama school training, giving classes in acting, dance, voice and singing, tutorial sessions, theatre visits and business advice. It does not expect applicants to be strong in all disciplines when they audition.

Acting courses offered:

• 1 Year Diploma in Acting & Musical Theatre (30 weeks) – the qualification gained is Trinity ATCL Level 4 in Drama & Speech. Applicants should be aged 16+. Applications should be made directly to the school by the middle of August.
• Fully funded 2-year vocational sixth form for students aged 16-19 (level 3) in Acting (60 weeks) – the qualification is an extended diploma equivalent to 3 A levels. The course is designed to give students a strong foundation in the fundamentals of the performing arts industry with an acting bias. Applications should be made directly to the school by the middle of August.

Drama Studio London (DSL)*

1 Grange Road, London W5 5QN
tel 020 8579 3897
email admin@dramastudiolondon.co.uk
website www.dramastudiolondon.co.uk
Facebook www.facebook.com/dramastudiolondon/
Twitter @Drama_Studio
Instagram @dramastudiolondon
Director of DSL Emma Lucia Hands

Drama Studio London (DSL) provides full time, professional acting training, for the profession by the profession, for adults with passion and talent. For more information and to apply, visit the website or contact **admissions@dramastudiolondon.co.uk**. Diploma students have the option of taking the Trinity College London National Certificate in Professional Acting, along with their DSL Diploma.

• 1 Year PGDip/MA in Professional Acting validated by University of West London (UWL)
• 2 Year MFA in Professional Acting with Independent Production, validated by UWL
• 3 Year BA (Hons) in Professional Acting, validated by UWL
• Short part-time evening courses and summer school

East 15 Acting School*

Loughton Campus: Hatfields, Rectory Lane, Loughton IG10 3RY
tel 020 8508 5983
email east15@essex.ac.uk
Southend campus: Elmer Approach, Southend-on Sea SS1 1LW
tel (01702) 328200
website www.east15.ac.uk
Facebook www.facebook.com/east15actingschool
Twitter @E15actingschool
Instagram @E15actingschool

Full-time acting courses: All BA courses are 3 years. Deadline for applications end of May, but ideally end of April.

• BA Acting, BA Acting (International), BA Acting and Community Theatre, BA Acting and Contemporary Theatre, BA Acting and Stage Combat, BA Physical Theatre

• BA World Performance

All acting courses require a successful audition. For additional academic requirements see course details on the website.

Other full-time undergraduate courses:
• Certificate of Higher Education in Theatre Arts (1 year)
• BA Stage and Production Management (3 years)
• BA Creative Production
• MA Acting (1 year). Selection for this course is based upon experience and potential. All applicants must be over the age of 21; there is no upper age limit. Applicants must hold a BA degree (normally at least a 2:1) or have suitable previous life, professional or academic experience.
• MA/MFA in Acting (International)
• MA/MFA Theatre Directing (1 year)
• MA Advanced Professional Theatre Practice (1 year)

Please see the website for details of the above courses.

École Internationale de Théâtre Jacques Lecoq
57 Rue du Faubourg Saint-Denis, 75010 Paris
tel +33 (0) 1 4770 4478
email contact@ecole-jacqueslecoq.com
website www.ecole-jacqueslecoq.com
Facebook www.facebook.com/ecole.jacqueslecoq
Instagram @ecolejacqueslecoq
Principal Mrs Pascale Lecoq

Founded in Paris in 1956, with the aim of producing a young theatre of new work, generating performance languages which emphasise the physical playing of the actor. Focuses on art theatre, but with the view that theatre education is broader than the theatre itself: "It is a matter not only of training actors, but of educating theatre artists of all kinds." Provides as broad and durable a foundation as possible for every student. Also offers part-time courses. See also the company's entry under *Short-term and part-time courses* on page 39.

Full-time acting courses:
• Professional Course (Certificate – Master Level; 2 years). No public funding available. Applications should be made direct to the school from November to June (generally after June there is a waiting list). Applicants must be aged 21+ with initial theatre training and stage experience.

Federation of Drama Schools

FEDERATION OF DRAMA SCHOOLS

London
email info@federationofdramaschools.co.uk
website www.federationofdramaschools.co.uk
Twitter @fdsdramaschools

The FDS brings together established UK drama school training providers as a group to develop

discussion, resources and projects which support and promote accessible, high-quality professional performers training, and to communicate to prospective students the range of training options available within the drama school contexts. FDS aims to provide current and relevant information to prospective performers, staff, parents and the industry, to ensure a pipeline of talent continues to emerge from drama schools to shape and inform the contemporary performance industries.

Fourth Monkey
The Monkey House, 97-101 Seven Sisters Road, London N7 7QP
tel 020 7281 0360
email office@fourthmonkey.co.uk
The Bamboo House, 9 Portland Square, Bristol BS2 8ST
tel 0117 942 2723
email bamboohouse@fourthmonkey.co.uk
website www.fourthmonkey.co.uk
Facebook www.facebook.com/FourthMonkeyTC
Twitter @FourthMonkeyTC
Instagram @fourthmonkey
Artistic Director Steven Green *Director of Training* Charleen Qwaye

Established in 2012 to provide innovative and inclusive industry responsive training courses. Works to develop and empower the next generation of professional actors and creative theatre makers and challenge the status quo of traditional conservatoire training.

Accredited training courses:
• BA (Hons) Acting (2 year accelerated degree)
• CertHE Acting & Theatre Making (One year foundational course)
• MA Collaborative Theatre (One year full-time or two year part-time course)

Fourth Monkey has Centres of Excellence in London and Bristol which host the Young Actors Company and offer extensive professional developmeny opportunities and short courses. Fourth Monkey is also a critically acclaimed Ensemble Theatre Company renowned for its visually stunning and compassionate storytelling.

The Free Association, London
113 Southgate Road, London N1 3JS
email hello@thefreeassociation.co.uk
website https://thefreeassociation.co.uk/
Twitter @FAImprov

The Free Association's London and Amsterdam schools are formulated around the FA syllabus – a huge (ever growing) book, meticulously written and designed to help you learn everything from the fundamentals of long-form improv through to advanced moves, forms and techniques. There are six levels in total, in a structured path. Work your way up through the levels, adding to your skill set so we consistently produce "complete" performers in the FA's long-form style. Taster 2.5 hour class costs £20.

The Giles Foreman Centre for Acting

Studio Soho,
2A Royalty Mews (entrance between Quo Vadis/
Barrafina & Firezza), Dean Street, London W1D 3AR
tel 020 7437 3175
email info@gilesforeman.com
website www.gilesforeman.com
Director Giles Foreman

An exciting professional acting studio housing some of the country's top coaches in the disciplines of screen- and theatre-acting, movement, voice, improvisation, on-camera, Meisner technique, movement psychology and character analysis – directing and text analysis.

Comprises 2 easy-access, large, bright, air-conditioned studios plus changing room, chillout area and kitchen, and props store. (Wheelchair-accessible, entrance lift and step-free studio facilities.) Plus separate daylight-studio and meeting-rooms. Wi-Fi throughout. Offers the opportunity for professional actors to develop their skills through regular acting classes and workshops, and to create projects in both film and theatre. Specialised intensive masterclass short courses offered by internationally renowned practitioners from all over the world. Due to its location at the heart of the the UK film, TV and theatre industry, also offers many opportunities to meet casting directors, directors and producers through industry showcases, casting-network and Q&A evenings.

Professional coaches available to prepare actors for auditions and self-tapes, and develop characters for projects they have secured.

Full-time courses:
• Post-Graduate-Equivalent Intensive Diplomas in Acting and Directing (15 months). One subsidised scholarship available. Applicants should be aged 20 or over. PCDL registered.
• Foundation ATCL Diploma (two terms, evening and weekend-mode). Validated by Trinity College London. Applicants should be aged 17 or over.

GSA, Guildford School of Acting*

University of Surrey, Stag Hill Campus,
Guildford GU2 7XH
tel (01483) 684040
email gsaenquiries@gsa.surrey.ac.uk
website www.gsauk.org
Facebook www.facebook.com/gsauk
Twitter @the_gsa
Instagram @guildfordschoolofacting
Head of GSA Dr Catherine McNamara

Guildford School of Acting was founded in 1935 and is part of the University of Surrey. GSA is a vibrant community of performers, performance makers,

creative practitioners and technicians graduating from a wide variety of programmes each year. From 1964 onwards has concentrated on the vocational training of actors and stage managers.

Full-time acting courses: Applications for undergraduate courses should be made via UCAS. Applications for the BA (Hons) Theatre (conversion by distance learning) and for Foundation and Postgraduate courses should be made direct to the University of Surrey.

• Foundation Acting (1 year).
• Foundation Musical Theatre (1 year).
• BA (Hons) Acting (3 years). Applicants must be aged 18 or over, with 3 A levels.
• BA (Hons) Musical Theatre (3 years). Applicants must be aged 18 or over, with 3 A levels.
• BA (Hons) Actor Musician (3 years). Applicants must be aged 18 or over, with 3 A levels.
• BA (Hons) Theatre Production. Applications must be aged 18 or over, with 3 A levels.
• BA (Hons) Actor Musician (3 years) Applicants must be 18 or over, with 3 A levels.
• BA (Hons) Theatre Production (3 years). Applicants must be 18 or over, with 3 A levels.
• BA (Hons) Theatre (1 year on-line learning conversion programme).
• MA in Acting (1 year) Applicants must be aged 21 or over.
• MA in Musical Theatre (1 year). Applicants must be aged 21 or over.
• MA Stage and Production Management (1 year). Applicants must be aged 21 or over.

Guildhall School of Music & Drama*

Silk Street, Barbican, London EC2Y 8DT
tel 020 7628 2571
email registry@gsmd.ac.uk
website www.gsmd.ac.uk
Vice Princiapl and Director of Drama Orla O'Loughlin

Full-time acting courses:

• BA (Hons) Acting (3 years). We aim to produce actors who are flexible and versatile, able to move with confidence between classical and contemporary theatre, film, television and radio. There is a generous staff-student ratio and a high number of teaching hours, with students receiving 35–40 hours of contact time each week. Applicants must be 18 years old at the start of the course with a minimum of 2 A-level passes or equivalent.
• Entrance for the course is by audition. Applications should be made direct to the School as early as possible. We encourage applicants from a wide range of ages and backgrounds to audition, and our students are selected on merit by audition which means it is not necessary to have any previous acting experience.

Hoopla, London

The Miller, 96 Snowsfields Road, London Bridge,
London SE1 3SS

email classes@hooplaimpro.com
website www.hooplaimpro.com
Twitter @hooplaimpro

Hoopla are the founders of the UK's first improv comedy club. Fun, friendly improv classes and shows at London's first improv theatre and biggest improv comedy school. Open to all and offers half-price or free places on improv classes to students, the unemployed or people on lower incomes. Works with a number of schools and charities to help make improv available to everyone. Various 6–8 week courses are available.

International School of Screen Acting
The Old Lab, 3 Mills Studios, Three Mills Lane, London E3 3DU
tel 020 8709 8719
email enquiries@screenacting.co.uk
website www.screenacting.co.uk
Facebook www.facebook.com/screenactingUK
Twitter @ScreenActingUK
Instagram @ScreenActingUK
Key contact Raminta Asakaviciute

Founded in 2002, ISSA is the leading specialist screen acting school in the UK. It runs as a full-time drama school dedicated to preparing actors for today's TV and film industry. Based within 3 Mills Studios, the school is at the heart of a creative and successful media village.

Full-time acting courses:
• One Year Full Time Intensive Screen Acting
• Two Year Screen Acting

Italia Conti Academy*
47 Church Street West, Woking, Surrey GU21 6DG
email acting@italiaconti.co.uk
website www.italiaconti-acting.com
Course Leader Acting Courses Bradley Leech

A member of FDS, the Academy offers a 3-year BA (Hons) Acting Degree, validated by the University of East London, as well as a 1-year CertHE Introduction to Acting course which is in preparation for full-time actor's training. Italia Conti Academy is a world-renowned centre for actor training. Its graduates populate the performance industries and it is this commercial edge that makes the BA (Hons) Acting course unique. It is one of the country's leading vocational acting courses with an emphasis on professional development and employability.

Full-time acting courses:
• BA (Hons) Acting (3 years). Applicants must be aged 18 or over with 5 GCSEs (grade C or above), including English and maths, and 2 A levels (grade E or above) or equivalent.
• CertHE Introduction to Acting (1 year). Applicants must be aged 18 or over with 5 GCSEs (grade C or above), including English and maths.

LAMDA (London Academy of Music & Dramatic Art)*
155 Talgarth Road, London W14 9DA
tel 020 8834 0500

email enquiries@lamda.ac.uk
website www.lamda.ac.uk

LAMDA (London Academy of Music & Dramatic Art) is a world-leading conservatoire, providing exceptional vocational training in the dramatic arts. LAMDA prepares actors for sustainable careers in the industry. You can see our alumni at the National Theatre, the RSC, Shakespeare's Globe, on London's West End, on Broadway and on big and small screen worldwide.

In 2021 LAMDA was granted full degree awarding powers. Students joining the Academy on full-time courses will have their qualifications awarded in LAMDA's name. LAMDA has a range of scholarships and bursaries available to ensure that the most talented students can access training, regardless of their financial circumstances. Committed to recruiting on talent alone, LAMDA auditions and/or interviews everyone who submits an application by the advertised deadline, providing they meet the age requirements for the training. Does not ask applicants for specific academic qualifications; asks only for talent, passion and a commitment to learn.

Full-time acting courses:
• BA (Hons) Professional Acting (3 years). Minimum entry age is 18. Admission is by audition and interview.
• MFA Professional Acting (2 years). Minimum entry age is 18, but due to the experience necessary for this course, most students will be 21 and over and hold a first degree in a relevant subject.
• MA Classical Acting for the Professional Theatre (1 year). This course is for international students with a BA or BFA degree or equivalent. Students without this qualification must demonstrate a comparable level of knowledge and experience gained in a professional company or vocational drama school. Admission is by audition and interview.
• Foundation Diploma (1year). Minimum entry age is 18. Admission is by audition and/or interview dependent on experience and career intent. This course is not validated by a higher education institution; it is part of LAMDA's own range of non-accredited diplomas.
• LAMDA Semester Diploma in Classical Acting (14 weeks). Minimum entry age is 18 and admission is by application only. International applicants may apply to LAMDA directly or through their home university or college.

Please visit **www.lamda.ac.uk** for further details, application deadlines and fees, as well as information on all other LAMDA courses.

The Liverpool Institute for Performing Arts (LIPA)*
Mount Street, Liverpool L1 9HF
tel 0151 330 3000
email admissions@lipa.ac.uk
website www.lipa.ac.uk
Facebook www.facebook.com/LIPALiverpool

Twitter @LIPALiverpool
Instagram @lipaliverpool
Principal & *Chief Executive Officer* Professor Sean McNamara

LIPA offers a Foundation Certificate in Acting, BA (Hons) Acting, BA (Hons) Acting (Screen & Digital Media), MA in Acting (Company) and MA Professional Practice: Theatre and Darama Facilitation.

Full-time acting courses:

• Foundation Certificate in Acting (1 year). This highly practical course aims to provide the skills, tools and knowledge to stand out from the crowd and improve your chances of securing a place at one of the top drama schools. Apply direct to LIPA.
• BA (Hons) Acting (3 years). Offers training that prepares actors for rehearsal, performance, production, interdisciplinary creation and industry engagement. Working with traditional and innovative approaches, you expand your psychological and physical processes to hone your acting methodology. Validated by Liverpool John Moores University. Apply to LIPA via UCAS and a LIPA application form.
• BA (Hons) Acting (Screen & Digital Media) (3 years). LIPA's intensive and practical training prepares actors to work across established mediums and emerging digital story-telling platforms. Also learning off-camera skills (including scriptwriting and filmmaking techniques) enables the student to create a digital portfolio. Validated by Liverpool John Moores University. Apply to LIPA via UCAS, followed by an online LIPA form.
• MA Acting (Company) (1 year). On this course you will create original ensemble work to perform and tour as a professional company, supported by funding from us. You will also receive advanced training to further your technical skills and approach. Apply direct to LIPA.
• MA Professional Practice: Theatre and Drama Facilitation. Enables students to maintain professional practice while working toward elevating their facilitation career to a more specialised or strategic level. Apply direct to LIPA.

Liverpool Theatre School/Liverpool Central Studios

35 Sefton Road, Liverpool L8 5SL
tel 0151 728 7800
email info@liverpoolcentralstudios.com
website https://liverpoolcentralstudios.com/liverpooltheatreschool
Facebook www.facebook.com/LiverpoolTheatreSchool
Twitter @LTSchool
Instagram @liverpooltheatreschool

Performing arts centre based in the heart of Liverpool offering the highest standard of training from beginners' classes to full-time professional training. Aims to produce musical theatre performers, dancers and actors that have the skills, knowledge and attitude to be successful in an increasingly demanding profession. Application form can be downloaded online and sent to **auditions@liverpoolcentralstudios.com**.

Courses offered

• Diploma in Professional Acting Course (Level 6)
• BTEC Level 3 Extended Diploma in Musical Theatre
• Diploma in Professional Musical Theatre (Level 6) (three year course)
• Diploma in Professional Dance – Contemporary Dance (Level 5)

London School of Dramatic Art

4 Bute Street, London SW7 3EX
tel 020 7581 6100
email enquiries@lsda-acting.com
website www.lsda-acting.com
Facebook facebook.com/LSDA.Acting
Twitter @LSDA_Acting
Instagram @lsda_acting
Principal Jake Taylor *Administrator* Emeline Touzet

Offers a range of comprehensive courses designed to develop individual creative talents, and to provide a thorough grounding in all aspects of performance as part of a student's preparation for a working life as an actor. There is currently no wheelchair access to the main building or training rooms: if this affects applicants who would like to know when these spaces become accessible, please let the school know. All auditions are free and no international student fees are charged. No formal qualifications are required as the training is vocational: "We look more at potential and at levels of creativity."

Full-time courses:

• Advanced Diploma in Acting (1 year). No public funding available. Applications should be made to the school by the end of September. Applicants must be aged 18 or over.
• Foundation Diploma in Acting (1 year). No public funding available. Applications should be made direct to the school by the end of September. Applicants must be aged 18 or over.

London School of Musical Theatre

83 Borough Road, London SE1 1DN
tel 020 7407 4455
email info@lsmt.co.uk
email auditions@lsmt.co.uk
website www.lsmt.co.uk
Facebook www.facebook.com/LondonSchoolMusicalTheatre
Twitter @TheLSMT
Instagram @thelsmt
Principal & *Course Producer* Adrian Jeckells

Full-time courses:

• Musical Theatre Diploma Course (1 year). Age range for entry is 18-35.

London Studio Centre (LSC)

Artsdepot, 5 Nether Street, Tally Ho Corner,
North Finchley, London N12 0GA
tel 020 7837 7741
email info@londonstudiocentre.ac.uk
website www.londonstudiocentre.org
Facebook www.facebook.com/LdnStudioCentre
Twitter @LdnStudioCentre
Director Nic Espinosa *Dean of Studies & Programme
Leader* Robert Penman

London Studio Centre is a professional dance
conservatoire accredited by the Council for Dance,
Drama and Musical Theatre (CDMT).

Courses include:

• BA (Hons) Theatre Dance (validated by Middlesex
University)
• Foundation Course
• LSC Diploma
• Foundation Degree Professional Dance
Performance (validated by the University for the
Creative Arts)
• Saturday Associate Programmes

LSC's facilities include state-of-the-art dance and
drama studios and access to fully equipped theatres.

LSC graduates are regularly seen performing on stage
in London's West End and in international dance
companies.

Manchester School of Theatre at MMU*

School of Theatre, Cavendish Street,
Manchester M15 6BG
website www.theatre.mmu.ac.uk
Programme Leader BA (Hons) Acting David Salter

Full-time acting courses:

• BA (Hons) Acting (3 years full-time). Applicants
must be aged 18 or over with 3 A levels or equivalent.
Applications should be made through UCAS by
January.
• BA (Hons) Drama and Contemporary Performance
(3 years, full-time; 6 years, part-time). Applicants
must be 18 or over with 3 A levels or equivalent.
Applications should be made through UCAS.

Mountview*

120 Peckham Hill Street, London SE15 5JT
tel 020 8881 2201
email enquiries@mountview.org.uk
website www.mountview.org.uk
Facebook www.facebook.com/mountviewldn
Twitter @mountviewLDN
Instagram @mountviewldn
Principal Abigail Morris

Full-time acting courses: Applications for the
courses listed below should be made direct to the
school.

BAs validated by the University of East Anglia and
Trinity College London. Applicants must be aged 18

or over at the start of the course. Entry is based on
performance at audition, previous formal academic
qualifications are not essential. Dance and Drama
Awards are available for a significant number of
students.

• BA (Hons) Acting (3 years).
• BA (Hons) Actor Musicianship (3 years).
• BA (Hons) Musical Theatre (3 years).

MAs validated by the University of East Anglia.
Applicants must be aged 21 years or over at the start
of the course. Students who do not hold an
undergraduate degree will need to undertake an
access assignment to establish suitability for
undertaking the MA.
• MA Performance – Acting (1 year).
• MA Performance – Musical Theatre (1 year).

The MTA (The Musical Theatre Academy)

Bernie Grant Arts Centre,
Town Hall Approach Road, Tottenham Green,
London N15 4RX
tel 020 8885 6543
email info@theMTA.co.uk
website www.theMTA.co.uk
Facebook @theMTAonline
Twitter @theMTAonline
Instagram @theMTAonline
Principal Annemarie Lewis Thomas

The MTA run the UK's first accelerated learning
programme for multi-disciplinary performers,
meaning that their students are industry ready in 2
years as opposed to the more traditional 3. The acting
component of the musical theatre course is split 50/
50 between stage and screen acting. The college only
employs working professionals ensuring that students
are taught current and relevant industry thinking.
The college has received industry plaudits for its work
and is extremely successful at gaining students agent
representation on completion of the course, with
nearly three-quarters of graduates still in the industry
carving out careers.

Oxford School of Drama*

Sansomes Farm Studios, Woodstock,
Oxford OX20 1ER
tel (01993) 812883
email info@oxforddrama.ac.uk
website www.oxforddrama.ac.uk
Facebook www.facebook.com/
TheOxfordSchoolofDrama
Twitter @oxford_drama
Instagram @oxford_drama
Principal Edward Hicks

The smallest of the drama schools, it has a 94%
employment rate and an 'Outstanding' Ofsted rating.
Provides a significant number of Dance and Drama
Awards and Advanced Learning Loans for its 1- and
3-year courses. Also offers its own Hardship fund

which is distributed each year to students on full-time courses at the school. Students not in receipt of a DaDA are prioritised for funding. The Sir John Gielgud Charitable Trust currently supports the school and, in addition, students have also won the Laurence Olivier Bursary, the Spotlight Prize, the Alan Bates Award and the BBC Carleton Hobbs bursary award.

Full-time acting courses: Applications for the courses listed below should be made direct to the school by 31 May.

• Three Year Acting Course. Applicants must be aged 18 or over.
• One Year Acting Course. Applicants must be aged 21 or over.

RADA (Royal Academy of Dramatic Art)*

62-64 Gower Street, London WC1E 6ED
tel 020 7636 7076
email enquiries@rada.ac.uk
website www.rada.ac.uk
Facebook www.facebook.com/RoyalAcademyofDramaticArt
Twitter @RADA_London
Instagram @royalacademyofdramaticart
Principal Niamh Dowling

RADA offers vocational training for actors, stage managers, designers and technical stage craft specialists.

Full-time undergraduate and postgraduate courses:
• BA (Hons) in Acting
• MA Theatre Lab
• Foundation Course in Acting (non-HE)
• Foundation Degree (FdA) in Technical Theatre and Stage Management
• BA (Hons) in Technical Theatre and Stage Management (progression year)
• Postgraduate Diploma (PgDip) in Theatre Costume

RADA training is practical, intensive and rigorous, and offers the highest level of teaching with unparalleled links to the industry, and an impressive track record of graduate employment as award-winners and leaders in their field. Across theatre, film, television and radio, graduates are employed as actors, directors, writers, producers; lighting, sound, costume and prop designers, scenic artists; stage managers and production managers.

Also creates opportunities for the wider community to enagage with training through short courses and widening participation and outreach work.

Rose Bruford College*

Lamorbey Park, Burnt Oak Lane, Sidcup DA15 9DF
tel 020 8308 2600
email enquiries@bruford.ac.uk
website www.bruford.ac.uk
Instagram @rosebruford, @brufordstudents

Principal and CEO Clarie Middleton

Full-time acting courses: Applicants for the BA degree courses listed below must be over the age of 18 with the equivalent of a minimum of 2 A levels at grade C or above. BA Applications should be made through UCAS and MAs through the college website.

• BA (Hons) Acting (3 years)
• BA (Hons) Actor Musicianship (3 years)
• BA (Hons) American Theatre Arts (3 years)
• BA (Hons) Contemporary and Popular Performance (3 years)
• BA (Hons) European Theatre Arts (3 years)
• BA (Hons) Theatre and Social Change (3 years)
• MA Actor and Performer Training
• MA Actor Musicianship
• MA Theatre for Young Audiences (1 year)

Royal Academy of Music

Musical Theatre Department, Marylebone Road, London NW1 5HT
tel 020 7873 7373
website www.ram.ac.uk/mth
Head of Musical Theatre Daniel Bowling MMus

Students are enrolled at the Royal Academy of Music, an institution of world renown, training students for more than 190 years. Students study for University of London degrees. Fellow students include instrumentalists, composers, jazz and commercial musicians, pianists and opera singers.

Full-time acting courses:

• MA Musical Theatre Programme (1 year). Aimed at graduates, mature students and experienced performers wishing to undertake a career in musical theatre. The course provides an intensive training in singing, acting, movement and voice to students of postgraduate (or equivalent) level. Includes extensive one-to-one tuition with expert tutors and industry showcase, projects for invited industry guests and public performances.
• Postgraduate certificate Musical Theatre (1 year).

Royal Birmingham Conservatoire*

Jennens Road, Birmingham B4 7XG
tel 0121 331 5901
email conservatoire@bcu.ac.uk
website www.bcu.ac.uk/conservatoire/acting
Head of School Stephen Simms *Admissions* Karen Edmunds

Full-time acting courses:

• BA Applied Theatre
• BA Stage Management
• BA Acting
• MA/MFA Acting
• MA/MFA Professional Voice Practice

The Royal Central School of Speech and Drama*

ROYAL CENTRAL
SCHOOL OF SPEECH & DRAMA

UNIVERSITY OF LONDON

University of London, Eton Avenue,
London NW3 3HY
tel 020 7722 8183
email enquiries@cssd.ac.uk
website www.cssd.ac.uk
Principal Josette Bushell Mingo OBE

Scholarships/Bursaries Central has a range of scholarships and bursaries available for students on its undergraduate and postgraduate programmes. Visit the website for further details.

Undergraduate courses:

BA (Hons) Acting – three specialist courses:

• Acting
• Acting Collaborative and Devised Theatre
• Acting Musical Theatre

BA (Hons) Contemporary Performance Practice - three specialist courses:
• Drama, Applied Theatre and Education
• Experimental Arts and Performance
• Writing for Performance

BA (Hons) Theatre Practice – 9 specialist courses:
• Costume Construction
• Design for Performance
• Lighting Design
• Production Lighting
• Prop Making
• Scenic Painting for Stage and Screen
• Set Construction for Stage and Screen
• Sound Design and Production
• Stage Management and Technical Theatre

All applications for undergrdauate courses should be made via UCAS by 25 January 2023.

Postgraduate courses:

All MA courses below are for those holding an undergraduate degree or who have relevant professional experience. Two-year MFAs are also available in many of the subjects below. All postgraduate applications should be made through the website.
• Acting Classical
• Acting Contemporary
• Acting for Screen
• Actor Training and Coaching
• Applied Theatre
• Advanced Theatre Practice
• Creative Producing
• Drama and Movement Therapy

• Music Theatre
• Movement: Directing and Teaching
• Scenography
• Voice Studies: Teaching and Coaching
• Writing for Stage and Broadcast Media

Royal Conservatoire of Scotland*

100 Renfrew Street, Glasgow G2 3DB
tel 0141 332 4101
email hello@rcs.ac.uk
website www.rcs.ac.uk
Facebook www.facebook.com/rcsofficial
Twitter @RCStweets
Instagram @rcsofficial
Principal Jeffrey Sharkey

RCS is Scotland's national Conservatoire, based in the heart of Glasgow. Offers the very best education and opportunities to students from across the world, and each year welcomes students from more than fifty countries. RCS is consistently recognised as one of the world's top performing arts education institutions by QS World Rankings (2016–2021), cementing its position as a global leader in performing arts education.

Full-time acting courses: Applications for the undergraduate courses listed below should be made via **www.ucas.com/ucas/conservatoires** by 26 January 2023. Applications for postgraduate courses listed below should be made via **www.ucas.com/ucas/conservatoires** by 31 March 2023. Please email admissions@rcs.ac.uk for more information.

Courses available:

• BA Acting (full-time, 3 years)
• BA Performance in BSL and English (full-time, 3 years)
• BA Musical Theatre (full-time, 3 years)
• BA (Hons) Contemporary Performance Practice (full-time, 4 years)
• Professional Graduate Diploma in Musical Directing (full-time, 1 year)
• MA Musical Theatre - Performance/Musical Directing (full-time, 1 year)
• MA Classical and Contemporary Text - Acting/Directing (full-time, 1 year)
• MFA Classical and Contemporary Text - Acting/Directing (full-time, 16 months)

Royal Welsh College of Music and Drama*

Castle Grounds, Cathays Park, Cardiff CF10 3ER
tel 029 2039 1361
email admissions@rwcmd.ac.uk
website www.rwcmd.ac.uk

Full-time acting courses:

• BA (Hons) Acting (3 years). Applicants should normally be at least 18 years old by the time of enrolment. There is a range of support in place to help cover the cost of tuition, the details of which will depend on where the student normally lives. Applications should be made through UCAS.

• BA (Hons) Musical Theatre (3 years). Applicants should normally be at least 18 years old by the time of enrolment. There is a range of support in place to help cover the cost of tuition, the details of which will depend on where the student normally lives. Applications should be made through UCAS.

• MA in Acting for Stage, Screen and Radio (4 terms – September until January). Applicants should normally be at least 21 years old by the time of enrolment. Applications should be made directly to the college.

• MA in Musical Theatre (3 terms – January until December). Applicants should normally be at least 21 years old by the time of enrolment. Applications should be made directly to the college.

The School of the Science of Acting

First Floor, Dwell House, 637 Holloway Road, London N19 5SS
tel 020 7272 0027
email info@scienceofacting.com
website www.scienceofacting.com

Full-time acting courses: No public funding is available for the courses listed below, but students may apply for a limited number of scholarships. There are daytime and evening courses.

• Three Year Acting Course. Offering a BA (Hons) in Acting accredited by Kingston University. Applicants must be aged 18 or over.

• Two Year Acting Course. Applicants must be aged 18 or over.

• One Year Acting Course. Applicants must be aged 18 or over.

• Three-year Evening Courses. "One to One" sessions, workshops and other training also available.

The International College of Musical Theatre (ICMT)

68 Wallis Road, Hackney Wick, London E9 5LH
tel 020 7253 3118
email info@theicmt.com
website www.theicmt.com
Principals/Directors Kenneth Avery-Clark, Christie Miller

Courses offered:

• One Year Full-Time Professional Development Musical Theatre Programme

• 2 Year Full-Time Professional Development Musical Theatre Programme

• One Year Level 4 Diploma in Musical Theatre Foundation Course

• 3 Month Top-up Musical Theatre Course

• Two Year Accelerated BA (Hons) Musical Theatre Performance

Specific academic requirements apply for the BA (Hons) program. Entry is by audition only. Applicants must be skilled in at least 2 of the 3 disciplines: acting, singing, dance. Train for a week in New York (one year course).

Welcomes candidates with disabilities and will consider each on a case-by-case basis, according to the strength of their audition. Please note that current premises are not wheelchair accessible.

Checklist of drama school deadlines, audition requirements, audition fees and funding systems

Using this section

Following the continued uncertainty caused by Coronavirus, many schools were still re-evaluating their application procedures at the time of writing. As a result, we advise you use the information listed here as a starting point, and double-check all details on schools' websites and application forms. If you're still unsure, each school's site lists contact details for their admission departments. Read all application information sent to you by schools as carefully as possible.

Audition fees

Almost all schools offer the chance to apply for free or supported audition fees. For example, Guildhall offer a Supported Application Scheme available to eligible participants, and Central's website says, "Many UK-based applicants may be eligible for a free audition." Check if you are eligible via the schools' websites and application forms. The following are details for applications and initial auditions for three-year acting courses at the various schools listed.

Filmed auditions

Each of the schools requiring a filmed audition offer guidelines to applicants. Again, check these carefully. Here are some general pointers:
• the aim is simply to be seen and heard clearly, so don't worry about producing a studio-quality tape
• a smartphone is fine for filming your audition; you don't need a specialist camera
• film with a plain background behind you; a wall, door or blind, for example. White and pale/pastel colours work best; if possible, avoid very bright and very dark colours
• try to film in a quiet room, to minimise background noise
• light (via a window, room-light or lamp) should come from in front you. Light coming from behind you will create shadows
• unless instructed otherwise, film in landscape
• your phone should be placed at eye-line height
• you can keep your phone still by wedging it in place (with books, for example). If you have the budget, high-street pound and saver shops sell small tripods, normally under £5.

Unless otherwise stated, details were correct at time of going to press. However, † by the name of the drama school indicates that we were unable to obtain any up-to-date details of their courses for 2023; ‡ provisional course details.

School	Definition of 'Classical'	Definition of 'Modern/Contemporary'	Other Parameters	Audition Fee	Funding System	Application Deadline
ArtsEd	Speech preferably written in verse. Welcomes unheard pieces from around the globe	Post 1990. Welcomes unheard pieces from around the globe	No longer than 2 mins each	£45	DaDA or student loans	March (deadline may be extended)
Royal Birmingham Conservatory	Elizabethan/Jacobean. They provide a list of suggestions	Guidance says, "You should be able to demonstrate your knowledge of contemporary repertoire"	No longer than 2 mins each. Verse and chorus of an accompanied song (no longer than 2 mins)	£35	Student loanVia UCAS Conservatoire – 26th January 2023	
Bristol Old Vic Theatre School†	BOVTS no longer specify when either speech should be written. Contrast, however, is important, for example by performing a classical and contemporary speech, a comedy and drama, or two very different characters	BOVTS no longer specify when either speech should be written. Contrast, however, is important, for example by performing a classical and contemporary speech, a comedy and drama, or two very different characters	Speeches should not exceed 2 mins.	Preliminary audition is via Zoom: £25	Student loan	Via UCAS.– 28th February 2023
Royal Central School of Speech and Drama†	Two classical speeches are required, with a list of suggestions from Shakespeare and Jacobean writers.	After 1960	Two-minute time limit for all pieces. Two memorised songs also required, though a trained singing voice is not required for admission. (If you do not wish to sing, you will not be made to do so.)	£55	Student loan	Via UCAS – mid January

School	Definition of 'Classical'	Definition of 'Modern/Contemporary'	Other Parameters	Audition Fee	Funding System	Application Deadline
Drama Studio London	Shakespeare or one of his contemporaries	Post-1955	No longer than 2 mins for each. Initial auditions carried out over Zoom. 3 mins talking to camera about yourself, your motivations, your likes and your acting experience etc. 2 mins some full body video shots with movement (dance or physical theatre). Can be set to music or words or silence	£47.50	Student loan	No set deadline
East 15	Shakespearean or other ElizabethanJacobean playwright	Post-1990	No longer than 90 seconds for each	£55	Student loan	Via Ucas – deadline subject to change, so check website
Guildford (GSA)†	Written before 1800	Post-1950	A Shakespeare sonnet	£45	DaDA/ Maintained	Mid-January – via UCAS
Guildhall School	Verse (blank or rhymed) from a play by Shakespeare or another Elizabethan/Jacobean playwright (for example, Jonson, Marlowe, Webster)	Post-1956	No longer than 2 mins each. Applicants should prepare two contrasting monologues which may come from different eras, but this is not a requirement. A short unaccompanied song of your own choice, in English for second, and final rounds only. This is to assess your ability to perform and interpret a song rather than your singing ability	£Student loan	Third week of January	

School	Definition of 'Classical'	Definition of 'Modern/ Contemporary'	Other Parameters	Audition Fee	Funding System	Application Deadline
Italia Conti	Shakespeare piece from supplied list on the website	1970-present day	Applicants will be requested to submit a self-tape with the following; Identification – name, UCAS number and programme you are applying for; Speech 1 – Shakespear Speech; Speech 2 – Contemporary Speech - A piece from a modern play of your choice; Voice Exercises – 6 exercises as per the audition pack; Singing Audition - 'Happy Birthday', or any short extract from any song that you know unaccompanied; and 'About me'. See audition pack for further instruction.	£45	Student loan	Via UCAS – mid-January
LAMDA†	Elizabethan/Jacobean	Modern from 1970 to today	One speech at the initial audition. They advise preparing a contemporary speech but applicants can use classical should they wish. No longer than 2–3 mins in length.	UK/EU auditions first round: £12; recall audition £48	Student loan	Early March
LIPA‡	Asks for a verse speech of your choosing. Examples given: Classical poetry; twentieth century poetry; spoken word; Shakespeare; Elizabethan; Jacobean; Restoration	Post-1960	2 min devised piece. All pieces have 2 min time limit	£45 – may be subject to an increase for 2021	Student loan	Via UCAS – mid-January
Manchester School of Theatre†	Shakespeare blank verse	After 1970	And a contrasting speech from any published play. No longer than 2 mins each	£45	Student loan	Via UCAS – 15 March

School	Definition of 'Classical'	Definition of 'Modern/ Contemporary'	Other Parameters	Audition Fee	Funding System	Application Deadline
Mountview‡	Blank verse prior to 1800. Shakespeare and his contemporaries, Elizabethan, Jacobean, ancient Greek, Roman, Restoration or international equivalent periods	After 1997	No longer than 2 mins each	£35 early bird fee £45 standard fee	DaDA	Mid-February
Oxford School of Drama	Elizabethan/Jacobean (16th/ 17th century)	20th or 21st century	No more than 2 mins each. Second piece must be a contrasting (a different subject, theme or emotion) speech from the classical piece chosen.	£15 for First Round audition by self-tape is paid on application. £30 recall fee.	DaDA and Advanced Learner Loans	May 2023
RADA‡	Elizabethan/Jacobean	After 1960	Second classical speech may be required; a song in recall	£36 for applications received on or before 13 December; £76 for applications received after 13 December	Student loan	End February
Rose Bruford	Shakespearean/Jacobean/ Elizabethan etc	Approximately 1960 onwards	Approx 90 seconds	£55	Student loan	Via UCAS – mid-January
Royal Conservatoire of Scotland	Shakespeare – preferably in verse	Of your own choice	You can choose a classical and a contemporary piece, or two contrasting contemporary pieces	£55	Student loan	Via UCAS conservatoires 15 January
Royal Welsh College of Music and Drama‡	Elizabethan/Jacobean period. There is a list of speeches *not* to be used	From 1956	You can choose a classical and a contemporary piece, or two contrasting contemporary pieces	£35	Student loan	Via UCAS Conservatories – 15 January

Notes:

- When only 'Classical' is specified, this can mean anything written before about 1800.
- When only 'Modern' or 'Contemporary' is specified, you should be fine with anything written after 1945 – and speeches written between 1900 and 1945 have often proved acceptable in this category.
- 'Verse' is sometimes specified – this doesn't mean that it necessarily needs to rhyme. In fact, some schools specify 'blank' (i.e. non-rhyming) verse.
- You'll find various definitions in the 'Classical' column – "Shakespearean/ Jacobean", "Elizabethan/Jacobean", "Shakespeare/Contemporaries". Strictly, these all imply slightly different (but overlapping) periods in history. In practice, anything written between about 1560 and 1640 should be fine.

- All schools ask that there is sufficient contrast between 'Classical' and 'Modern/ Contemporary' speeches.
- See individual schools' websites for more detailed audition requirements and advice.
- UCAS & CUKAS (**www.cukas.ac.uk**) fee (where appropriate) is in addition to each school's audition fee.
- Musical Theatre & other specialist courses usually have additional audition requirements.
- Also see *Effective audition speeches* on page 153.

What are drama schools looking for?

Geoffrey Colman

A lifelong contract

Many drama school applicants underestimate the fact that becoming an actor is about signing a sort of lifelong and extraordinary contract that contains the most incredible clause – one that requires the artist to metaphorically go to places both dark and light, to represent, live and die for us. Seven times a week or in fourteen takes. To successfully navigate such challenges one must possess a licence, for to 'go there' is not something that everybody can or wants to do. Not everybody has the talent. Not everybody is prepared to dedicate the years of preparation required to become an actor. Alas, many also underestimate the phenomenal personal responsibility of such an undertaking and delude themselves that it can be achieved by just wanting it very much – like a child wants ice-cream. I have not found this to be the case.

With the ongoing accusations of institutional racism and cultural elitism that the wider cultural sector continue to address, the drama school has also had to confront its now historic idea of training, and think again, very seriously, about how it can be something more than just a place for a few hand-picked individuals. As the enormity of the 2020 global pandemic became desperately apparent, the operational challenges faced by many drama schools in the UK - how to train its talented students online, remotely, far away from their world-famous studios; were superseded by longer-held, ethical questions about what tradition, in the light of 'Black Lives Matter' and 'Me Too' even meant - and certainly what it looked like. Whilst classes and rehearsals temporarily moved onto zoom, the sector set about reimagining its curriculum in the longer term. A post-pandemic return, never again legitimizing discourses that had historically reproduced particular forms of classed, 'raced' and gendered exclusion. The conservatoire always, famously, aspired to the idea of industry 'nearness' but its historic enactment of this was formed by a profession awash with poor practices, received normative paradigms, prejudices and general professional 'truths' handed down as performance rules or lineage. The training sector has responded with urgent forcible change, and whilst their historic studios may remain the same, the environment in which professional training now happens is both alert to its past failings and hugely ambitious of real long-lasting positive change.

The professional or conservatoire sector comprises schools that subscribe to, and are measured by, a set of overarching industry-approved principles held by the Federation of Drama Schools (FDS) **www.federationofdramaschools.co.uk**. The core principles state that the selection process is by audition, and that training will be professionally aligned, intensive, and delivering at least 900 hours of practical contact teaching a year. Many thousands apply to the FDS schools each year, for a precious few places. Of course, conservatoire training is not for everyone. There are many university drama departments where the courses, whilst not offering 30+ professional contact hours per week, do offer a vast range of performance-related academic disciplines that can be studied both theoretically and practically. Such programmes, though perhaps less specialist, do offer the student excellent opportunities to act, write, and direct whilst developing their own individual performance interests and skills.

Recent years have seen emerge a vast catalogue of non-professional diploma and degree-awarding courses offering performance-related study and preparation. Often curated by established conservatoires, such courses give the less experienced performer invaluable insight into the ways of the conservatoire system, and are particularly useful when considering whether professional actor training is a viable option.

What are you looking for? Do your research

Despite the existence of excellent regulating bodies such as the Quality Assurance Agency – which sets important benchmarks for the delivery of training, published student surveys and the names of famous alumni – across the conservatoire drama schools there is significant variation in terms of funding (including tuition top-up fees), quality of training, award outcomes (certificate, diploma, degree), and most certainly graduate employment prospects, which differ from school to school. So never mind the question about what are drama schools looking for – what are *you* looking for? Most candidates have such a limited, almost passive, expectation about what drama schools want at audition, and of the actual training itself. The first task is, therefore, not to perfect some extraordinarily well-honed accent or radical audition monologue interpretation, but rather, many months prior to this process, to undertake a sleeves-rolled-up systematic approach to a lot of very necessary research into the sector itself. If you are going to commit three years of your life to something, you really should find out what that something is!

All drama schools and university drama departments publish their entry requirements in either a glossy prospectus or more typically on a website, but, as such, these only really describe required entry criteria, a brief course outline and, in the case of some drama schools, a list of suggested classical audition speeches. Drama schools require potential students to audition, whilst it is not unusual for the university sector to offer some, but not all, candidates an interview and workshop. Entry requirements and selection criteria vary from institution to institution, but in general terms, the university sector is looking for well-qualified students with excellent A-level or equivalent qualifications. The conservatoire sector, on the other hand, bases its selection much more on audition success than exam grades, and is looking for 'evidence of ongoing commitment to acting' (such as having played featured roles in youth theatre production companies), 'evidence of a trainable voice and body', 'evidence of intellectual, emotional and physical skills', and so on. These competencies are all there waiting on the audition panellist's check list. There is not a section that refers to 'tingle factor' or 'star quality' because this is only found on the fame TV panellist's laminated sheet. Equally, there isn't an additional sub-criteria requirement listing particular body types to balance future casting designs not yet discussed.

The choice of audition speech preoccupies many candidates who unearth an astounding range of two-minute extracts – often inappropriately sourced from internet material that disallows any creative placement of their own heart and mind. Don't obsess about contrasting this or the other. Just select an extract from a play that is simple, clear, unfussy and – most important of all – one that allows for you to enter its world without a fight (and most certainly without the need to show that you are entering it). People do bring much worked-upon accents, props, shouts, peculiar moves, glances and screams, as though volume alone will do the trick. This should be avoided. Remember, too, that audition panellists experience the gamut of human suffering in two-minute chunks. But emotion in itself is not the gold medal if it is false, inappropriate or showy (especially without real context). The audition day is not merely there to equip the candidate with a jolly site tour or a space within which to recite a contrasting classical and contemporary speech. It might even, just possibly, offer some sort of snatched insight into how the course might be taught. To enter the world of drama school depends upon something far more fundamental than a set of well-worn, clichéd, seen-it-in-the-movies assumptions.

Both the conservatoire and university sector see the value of Open Day events – and so should you. The real answers required are sometimes just a little bit more abstract. Open Days afford a terrific and all-important onsite 'experience' of the building, its community of staff and students, and general but –nevertheless important – 'feel' of the place. Training institutions have rightly been questioned about how they construct their communities and, in particular, what they are doing to increase diversity. A recent parliamentary enquiry into access and diversity in the performing arts concluded that, despite many positive initiatives, drama schools needed to reform. One long-held perception that is difficult to dispel is that the whole audition process is very expensive. Whereas university drama departments accept applications via a centralised UCAS system, drama schools also ask for an additional fee. Many of the conservatoires within the Federation of Drama Schools now offer audition-fee waivers – offering free or heavily subsidized auditions to those facing the greatest barriers to attending.

If possible, attend a few plays or musicals performed by final-year students from different schools or departments as this can be extremely useful in that it demonstrates a very public slice of the quality of teaching and professional guidance offered. Once started, this level of cultural forensic work will certainly enable you to identify at least where you would like to study. But why do you want to become an actor? This is the real question that you must ask. Not so that you can decorate your application form or personal statement with incredible, but quite useless, prose (as often audition candidates do), but rather, align all future coordinates to it. You will need to refer to this answer for the rest of your life.

Audition actively, with clarity and commitment

It was the jaded theatre producer Emmanuel Azenberg who pessimistically described how successful entry into the ranks of the professional Broadway musical chorus required an alarming, but necessary, process of becoming a kind of *fabulous invalid* – a gradual giving up of self and becoming unable to do or cope with anything other than being in the chorus itself – never really knowing who deals the cards – and, in fact, never really knowing what the game is in the first place! Having been involved with drama school auditions for many years, I would suggest that his observation might just as well apply as a cautionary tale to those many thousands of audition candidates that approach the day with all-too-little consideration for the task and commitment ahead.

The craft of acting is not limited to a single method or approach; it is joyfully promiscuous. But for every actor we witness on our screens or in the theatre itself we also encounter a different sort of promiscuity. Some actors are famously trained and some are just famous, possessing a peculiar, but much desired, cultural tag. The 'celebrity' is often 'untrained', but connected to the performance industry by events that afford measurable charisma, enigma or sensation. As such celebrities may not in the short term need a drama school training, but rather, a constant stream of tabloid stories showing hasty late-night retreats from exclusive bars and restaurants. Such activities can (and occasionally do) open doors and give entry into the industry – but the hinges that hold them are tissue-thin – and the doors will not always remain permanently open!

Training

Look diligently before you leap

Training is not casual, but quite conservative and very ordered indeed. One class follows another and then another. How do you fit into this delightful regime? It can be repetitive and exhausting. The panel will look for signs of someone who can cope with this or not. A professional training is a physical, emotional, muscular assimilation of many processes. Learning lines is not the issue – but learning the difficult routine and discipline of acting can be. The audition is as much about assessing this point as to whether a given Juliet or Hamlet is believable.

Like many momentous occasions in life the drama school audition can be so very memorable. Like the first day of the school summer holidays or the first page of a new novel or even your first kiss. For there to be a first day at drama school is an achievement in itself. And yet to audition is to be part of an occasion mixed with both excitement and fear. Excitement in that all the waiting and preparation is over – but also fear regarding what happens if a place is not offered. To be an acting student at a conservatoire drama school is not to be part of something that is either casual or meaningless. But success in the current climate is now also measured by other indictors. Most students juggle outside work commitments with a very heavy workload of study and somehow exist on far less money than is possible. Drama school training is impacting – it marks all those who experience it. Yes every move, every gesture and vocal shift is catalogued for later dissection. But this is why to be trained is not to take an unfathomable leap in the dark. Sacrifices will have to be made and we must ensure that in the new funding climate becoming an artist will not render a fearful voiceless future to all but a privileged few.

What drama schools want is to restore the helplessness of our own lives through the long productive and meaningful careers of future artists like you. Don't take an unfathomable leap. Only if you're utterly convinced should you sign the training contract – but prepare for this moment with diligence, care and humility. Good luck!

Geoffrey Colman works as a professional acting coach having been is Head of Acting at The Royal Central School of Speech and Drama for many years.

It's warm up north

Adelle Hulsmeier

Training

Overcoming the stigma that suggests the North East of England offers limited opportunities to actors, both trained and un-trained, is difficult. At a time when travel and movement is significantly restricted, this article is timely in putting some of the more progressive opportunities offered in the North East of England on the map. It offers an overview of some of the exciting and progressive opportunities that are currently offered in this region, particularly Newcastle and Sunderland, hopefully helpful to today's aspirant actors when thinking about the extent of opportunities that may exist 'closer to home' or that may be worth re-locating for.

Sunderland Culture, Sunderland

Sunderland Culture, of which the Music, Arts and Culture (MAC) Trust, the University of Sunderland and Sunderland City Council are the founding partners, is a new organisation which was created to bring together Sunderland's most important cultural assets and activities.

This cultural initiative enjoys the benefits of the National Glass Centre, the Northern Gallery of Contemporary Art, Sunderland Museum and Winter Gardens, the Sunderland Empire, a 400-seat venue the Auditorium at the Fire Station, and music venue The Peacock.

The new and exciting Auditorium at the Fire Station which sits in Sunderland's Music, Arts and Cultural quarter, is the city's newest cultural venue. It offers dance classes, theatre workshops and a heritage centre. Live Theatre's Live Tales and DanceCity also operate from the venue. The Fire Station Auditorium is a versatile performance space which offers a year-round programme of live music, theatre, dance and comedy in a spectacular new state-of-the-art 550 seated or 800 standing capacity space. The auditorium provides a fantastic opportunity to bring artists, shows and performances to the city that have not been able to visit Sunderland before.

Live Theatre, Newcastle

Live Theatre has an international reputation as a new writing theatre. As well as producing and presenting new plays, there are extensive artistic opportunities for anyone looking to develop their acting skills from ages 11+.

The Elevator Programme supports the early career development of independent artists in the North East and across the UK. It incorporates writing courses and script developmental opportunities, bursaries and space for companies to develop new work.

Elevator is an annual festival which allows artists to present new theatre in Live Theatre's venue. Since 2014 Elevator has launched 25 brand new plays, worked with 17 associate artists and awarded 16 bursaries.

Every year, Live Theatre select emerging theatre artists/companies to be their associate artists, benefiting from exclusive opportunities and support such as mentoring and development time and space.

For young people Live Theatre offers the largest free youth theatre in the region, open to ages 11-25. Over 3 terms you can develop skills in stage craft, develop a new play to perform and explore scripts that have been produced and performed at Live Theatre. Young people aged 11-25 can also join the Wordplay group to explore the world of spoken word.

Arts Award is a national accredited qualification designed to grow young people as artists and arts leaders. Live Theatre often works in partnership with organisations such as The Prince's Trust as well as its own Youth Theatre members, and Live Theatre's plays, post-show talks and workshops can support young people to achieve Arts Award. Students taking Arts Award at Live Theatre have a 100% pass rate.

Creative Careers Week offers work experience for ages 14-18. 10 students are offered experience placements where they are introduced to the creative production, development, and finance and marketing departments within Live Theatre. Students can also work as a collective to creatively devise a 10 – 15 minute performance throughout the week.

Volunteer roles at Live Theatre are varied and available in Live Tales (a children and young people's writing centre) and in other areas of Live Theatre's work. They include supporting and encouraging children and young people to write, illustrating their stories or leading tours of the buildings. All volunteers receive ongoing training and support, a programme of social events and some discounts at Live Theatre. There are volunteering opportunities at Live Theatre, Newcastle, and The Fire Station, Sunderland.

Project A, Newcastle Theatre Royal, Newcastle

Project A is a 1 year actor training programme, delivered from within Newcastle's Theatre Royal. Delivery takes place over 3 terms and 18 students are accepted on the programme each year. They have access to the main house auditorium, visiting professionals, studio theatre, rehearsal room and dedicated training space.

Over 90% of Project A's graduates are working professionally or gaining agent representation within 6 months of graduation.

The course is full time and students are expected to attend between 25-45 hours a week. In term 1 you develop performance skills in relation to character creation and vocal and physical development. Term 2 is delivered by associate specialists and covers areas such as business, Shakespeare, Meisner and screen. The final term is the production term which takes students into an intensive rehearsal process, culminating in a showcase performance at the Theatre Royal.

Alphabetti Theatre, Newcastle

Alphabetti is a fringe venue in Newcastle that creates, produces, and programmes original work from emerging artists in music, theatre, comedy and poetry.

While they predominantly programme original work across the performing arts, if you've got an idea that doesn't quite sit in that section, they advise you still get in touch.

Northern Stage, Newcastle

Northern Stage is the largest producing theatre company in the North East of England. Northern Stage Filmmakers is a course for 16-25 year olds in partnership with My Life Productions, Woodhorn Museum and The Heritage Lottery Fund. During the course you can learn all aspects of filmmaking, including acting, directing, writing, producing, camera, sound and editing. The group produce a 30-minute documentary and a 15-minute fictional film (based on the true stories of the documentary) premiered at Northern Stage and Alnwick Playhouse.

Specialist Work Placements are open to Further Education and Higher Education Students, as well as bespoke professional placements for people already in the industry or seeking to learn more. The placements are open for 6 weeks a year and are tailored to meet the needs of the applicant.

NORTH training programme supports the development of North-East based performers and theatre companies. It comprises of actor training, small-scale touring and company development. Applicants must be 20+ at the time the course begins.

For younger creatives there are opportunities in their young company (open to 16-21 year olds covering three different programmes; the collective, the ensemble and the team) and open stages courses (weekly drama sessions for ages 5-7, 8-11 and 12-15).

A play in 10 weeks tops up knowledge and skills of the rehearsal process. The workshops cover working with script, character development, devising and performing.

North East-based theatre companies and individual theatre-makers can also apply to NORTH to support company development. Successful applicants could receive 1 week R&D time in the Byker rehearsal space, 1 day with the associate director of Northern Stage, 6 essential skills workshops and 4 hours with a member of the Northern stage staff who can support ideas.

Each year Northern Stage will produce a small-scale touring production, featuring emerging North East actors.

Curious Monkey, Newcastle

Curious Monkey is an international award winning theatre company based in Newcastle and founded by artistic director Amy Golding. They offer volunteer placements for students or graduates looking for experience working within a professional theatre company, and from time to time they run bespoke internships for people who are interested in working in theatre.

Troupe is open to 14–21 year olds with a care background or living in supported accommodation. It offers a unique opportunity to get involved in theatre by seeing shows and shadowing professionals. The programme offers monthly theatre trips to one of Newcastle's cultural venues, accompanied by short workshop on the performances viewed, a Q&A before the performance, a backstage tour, and a chance to meet the artists involved in making the show. This programme offers opportunities to undertake master classes and workshops with professional artists that explore different theatre skills, ranging from stand-up comedy to lighting, set design or sound recording. There is also the opportunity to shadow artists on theatre projects and work alongside Curious Monkey's creative teams, gaining experience of different roles within theatre.

Curious Monkey welcome people seeking sanctuary in the UK through the Arriving project. The Arriving project is a place where people seeking sanctuary in the North East of England can be creative, can have new experiences and feel welcome. It's a place to meet up with friends and make new friends, through monthly trips to the theatre, and involvement with events and projects that are led by Curious Monkey's creative team – from yoga to salsa to creating theatre to writing a book. Curious Monkey also support Arriving group members who want to develop their skills in the performing arts to work one on one with artists in areas they show a particular interest in. The group are also involved in volunteering at events and projects to gain experience in different public facing roles, put their many varied skills to good use, practise English in different settings and be part of the Curious Monkey team.

Care about Care offers a creative conversation for those who work in, make decisions about or have experience of the care system through involvement with performance festivals in the North East which feature immersive theatre, spoken word, rap, dance, performances, virtual reality films, an interactive podcast, storytelling, workshops, open space discussion and debate.

Final thoughts

There is a plethora of opportunities for emerging and training artists to engage with. It will always be important to ensure that you are honing and updating your skills, and the aforementioned opportunities offer a broad range of exciting things to get involved with. They come with networking opportunities, access to industry professionals and chances to work in exciting theatre venues. Establish how proactive you want to be and pursue the opportunities that are available to you – weekends, evenings, holidays – there are opportunities available all year round, and experiences available that are diverse and exciting, which you may wish to pursue. Remember: this is not limited to London, it's warm up North too!

Important links

Sunderland Culture: **https://sunderlandculture.org.uk**
Live Theatre: **www.live.org.uk**
Project A: **www.theatreroyal.co.uk/taking-part/project-a**
Alphabetti Theatre: **www.alphabettitheatre.co.uk**
Northern Stage: **www.northernstage.co.uk**
Curious Monkey: **https://curiousmonkeytheatre.com**

Adelle Hulsmeier is a Senior Lecturer and Programme Leader at the University of Sunderland. Her career trajectory is characterised by her conviction to embed the notion of social change as an integral part of teaching and learning. Adelle has managed the Faculty of Arts and Creative Industries' collaborative relationship with Northumbria Police; a successful project that runs annually and as an embedded element within the Screen, Media and Performance programmes. In tandem with this, she also strategically leads an academic partnership with Live Theatre, Newcastle *(Live)*; which allows students to experience teaching and learning in an operational and professional theatre venue, extending the reach of HE beyond the parameters of a classroom environment.

Short-term and part-time courses

This section lists both 'taster' opportunities for drama school aspirants, and further training for professional actors.

Pre-drama-school courses

Competition for drama school places seems to be growing even more ferocious, and many applicants will enhance their chances if they go on a pre-drama-school course. You may, for example, have done A level Drama, but the actual acting training on such courses is often limited – generally geared more towards the exam-passing university entrant than auditioning for drama school. Whatever your acting background, a 'taster' course (for just a week, for instance) can give you a good idea of what further help/training you need in order to prepare you properly for drama school auditions.

Additional skills

As well as the organisations listed below, there are periodic 'one-off' workshops around the country. These are usually 'trailed', and sometimes advertised, in The Stage. Equity occasionally subsidises such enterprises (some, away from the major cities), so it is worth checking with your local Branch/Organiser. Actors Centres are not just places to sharpen up your existing skills and develop new ones, but also great meeting places for actors to exchange ideas and information.

Academy of Creative Training

8/10 Rock Place, Brighton, East Sussex BN2 1PF
tel (01273) 818266
email info@actbrighton.org
website www.actbrighton.org
Principal/Director Janette Eddisford

All classes are in the evenings and at weekends to allow students to undertake actor training whilst maintaining their domestic and financial commitments. Monthly payment options are available by arrangement. Entry onto long courses is via audition or attendance on an intensive workshop of 8 evenings held monthly throughout the year and designed as an introduction to actor training. Students embarking on the Diploma in Acting are eligible to audition for a bursary. Range of short courses and Summer Schools. The school operates an equal opportunities policy that includes disabled students, but there is limited access to the dance studio and washroom facilities.

Courses offered:

• ATCL Diploma in Acting (2 years). For students aged 18+.
• Intensive Foundation Course (1 year, 10 hours per week). For students aged 16+.
• Creative Playground (10 weeks of 3 hour Masterclasses, runs each term)
• Introduction to Playwriting (2 terms)

Academy of Performance Combat (APC)

email info@theapc.org.uk
website www.theapc.org.uk

APC is dedicated to bringing combat in any form, in any media into the 21st century. "We are absolutely committed to safer, more exacting techniques than any other organisation." Please see the website for more details of courses and qualifications offered.

ArtsEd*

14 Bath Road, London W4 1LY
tel 020 8987 6666
website www.artsed.co.uk

Courses offered:

• Post-Diploma BA (Hons) in Musical Theatre or Acting (3-years). Validated by City University.
• Foundation in Musical Theatre or Acting (1-year full-time).

EXCELerate Part-Time Courses in Acting or Musical Theatre. 3 evenings per week running over 3 terms.

Part-time evening and holiday courses for children and 17+ years:
• Various courses in acting and musical theatre disciplines, including stage, screen, voice, dance and audition technique, are offered for varying skill levels throughout the year.

For full details on all courses offered at ArtsEd, please visit **www.artsed.co.uk**.

The Birmingham Theatre School

The Old Fire Station, 285-287 Moseley Road,
Highgate, Birmingham B12 0DX
tel 0121 440 1665
email info@birminghamtheatreschool.co.uk
website www.birminghamtheatreschool.com
Principal Chris Rozanski

Courses offered:

• Full-time Professional Acting Courses.
• Two-year full-time Btec Extended Diploma in
Performing Arts Acting (fully-funded places for 16 to
18 year olds).
• One-year full-time Professional Acting Diploma
(18+ fees apply).
• Part-time Professional Diploma (Evenings &
Weekends). Applicants must be aged 18 years or
over.
• Acting for Beginners (11 weeks). Covers the basics
of character creation, voice, improvisation and
performance discipline for acting beginners. Students
participate in all aspects of the creative process, from
basic exercises to final presentations. Classes take
place in the evening.

The Bloomsbury Alexander Centre

Bristol House, 80ᴀ Southampton Row,
London WC1B 4BB
tel 020 7404 5348
email info@bloomsburyalexandertechnique.com
website www.bloomsburyalexandertechnique.com
Director Natacha Osorio

The centre specialises in teaching the Alexander
Technique. Teachers are available for private lessons,
with discounts available for students and actors.
There are ongoing introductory workshops and
courses, as well as vocal work for actors with
experience of the AT. The introductory course runs
for 4 weeks (1.5 hours a week) and costs £120. Also
home to the Bloomsbury Voice Centre, offering the
varied expertise of several voice coaches. *Note for
disabled actors*: "Our premises are on the ground
floor with 3 steps in the hall leading to our door on
the ground floor."

Boden Studios

99 East Barnet Road, New Barnet, Herts EN4 8RF
tel 020 8447 0909
email info@bodens.co.uk
website www.bodens.co.uk

Established in 1975. A part-time performing arts
school offering 1 full scholarship each year.

British Academy of Dramatic Combat

email info@badc.org.uk
website www.badc.co.uk
Facebook www.facebook.com/
BritishAcademyOfDramaticCombat
Twitter @BADC_UK

Instagram @badc_uk

The BADC is the longest established dramatic combat
organisation in the UK. BADC teachers offer courses
across the UK for performers to train in dramatic
combat for all forms of performance media.
Upcoming courses and workshops are listed on our
website, for all levels of experience, covering a variety
of armed and unarmed weapon systems.

The British Academy of Stage & Screen Combat

c/o Sedulo, 505 Albert House, 256-260 Old Street,
London EC1V 9DD
email info@bassc.org
website www.bassc.org
Facebook www.facebook.com/TheBASSC
Twitter @TheBASSC
Instagram @TheBASSC

Founded in 1993 with the aim of improving the
standards of safety, quality and training of stage
combat, and promoting a unified code of practice for
the training, teaching and assessing of stage combat
within the United Kingdom.

All BASSC teachers have undergone a rigorous
training programme and the examining members of
the BASSC are highly qualified, experienced
professionals with a tradition of working in theatre
throughout the UK, including the National Theatre,
RSC, Royal Opera House, The Royal Court, Donmar
Warehouse, Liverpool Everyman, Theatre Royal York
and Newcastle, and Shakespeare's Globe; as well as on
television and film productions such as: *Vikings*
(Seasons 1-6), *Vikings: Valhalla, American Patriot,
Anna Karenina, Ironclad, The Eagle, Hammer of the
Gods, Troy, Stardust, The Last Legion, Sherlock
Holmes, Sherlock Holmes: A Game of Shadows* and
Lockwood & Co.

BASSC teachers train students in stage combat at
numerous drama schools, universities and colleges

including: RADA, the Royal Central School of Speech and Drama, the Royal Birmingham Conservatoire, Drama Studio London, Young Actors Theatre Islington, Italia Conti, ArtsEd and Acting Coach Scotland. They also teach students outside of drama courses at independently run classes and workshops including the annual British National Stage Combat Workshop. Teachers run classes and workshops in the USA, Germany, Spain and Ukraine.

Since its formation the BASSC has established a reputation as the invigorating driving force behind stage combat in the United Kingdom, and is respected, both nationally and internationally, as the leading provider of professional-level stage combat training.

As a result of this, British Equity, in 1997, recognised the BASSC's Advanced Certificate as a valid qualification for entry onto the Equity Fight Directors' Training Scheme, and in 2001 the BASSC was appointed by the Equity Council for the training and assessment of Fight Director candidates applying to join the Equity Fight Directors' Register.

The BASSC now has training schemes in place which allow for development from Actor/Combatant to Certified Teacher, as well as assessment and training of Fight Directors for the Equity register.

City Lit
Keeley Street, Covent Garden, London WC2B 4BA
tel 020 7492 2542
email drama@citylit.ac.uk
website www.citylit.ac.uk

The college offers an eclectic mix of disciplines such as acting, movement, voice, musical theatre, teaching, media, mime, circus, stage fighting, magic, comedy, dance, self-presentation, debating, accents, sight-reading and pronunciation for speakers of other languages, etc., which develop vocational, social and personal skills.

There are various small grants that might cover travel, books or child-care. Contact The City Lit for a prospectus and visit **www.citylit.ac.uk/dramaschool.**

Drama Studio London (DSL)*
1 Grange Road, London W5 5QN
tel 020 8579 3897
email admin@dramastudiolondon.co.uk
website www.dramastudiolondon.co.uk
Managing Director Emma Lucia Hands

Courses offered:
• Acting Summer School
• Adult Evening Acting Beginners Course (10 weeks)
• Adult Evening Acting Intermediate Course (10 weeks)
• Writing for the Stage and Screen

East 15 Acting School*
Loughton Campus: Hatfields, Rectory Lane, Loughton IG10 3RY

tel 020 8508 5983
email east15@essex.ac.uk
Southend Campus: Elmer Approach, Southend-on-Sea SS1 1LW
tel (01702) 328200
website www.east15.ac.uk
Facebook www.facebook.com/east15actingschool
Twitter @E15actingschool
Instagram @E15actingschool
Director Chris Main *Key contact* Laura Collins (Executive Assistant)

For more information about Undergraduate and Postgraduate trainging, please visit **www.east15.ac.uk.**

Applicants must be aged 17 years or over.

École Internationale de Théâtre Jacques Lecoq
57 Rue du Faubourg Saint-Denis, 75010 Paris
tel +33 (0) 1 4770 4478
email contact@ecole-jacqueslecoq.com
website www.ecole-jacqueslecoq.com
Principal Mrs Pascale Lecoq

Founded in Paris in 1956, with the aim of producing a young theatre of new work, generating performance languages which emphasise the physical playing of the actor. Focuses on art theatre, but with the view that theatre education is broader than the theatre itself: "It is a matter not only of training actors, but of educating theatre artists of all kinds." Provides as broad and durable a foundation as possible for every student. As well as the part-time courses listed below, offers a 2-year full-time Professional Course resulting in a Master Level Certificate. See also the company's entry under *Drama schools* on page 15. As a movement school, all classes require a great degree of physical movement, so applicants must be physically fit.

Courses offered:
• LEM (1 season October-June). 7 hours per week. Entry by file.
• Introductory Course (1 season October-June). 5 hours per week. Entry by file.
• Workshops online on the website.

Fourth Monkey Actor Training Company
The Monkey House, 97-101 Seven Sisters Road, London N7 7QP
tel 020 7281 0360
email office@fourthmonkey.co.uk
website www.fourthmonkey.co.uk

A training provider with a difference, offering full- or part-time ensemble-based contemporary rep training and professional performance opportunities.

Courses offered:
• BA (Hons) Acting (2 years accelerated). 2 year, full-

Training

time actor training programme, 40 hours a week. Based in London and includes a second year spent predominantly working as a professional rep company, concluding at the Camden Fringe. Applicants must be aged 18 and over. Performance experience and A-level qualifications or similar desirable but not compulsory.
• Year of the Monkey. One year course, full-time actor training programme, 22-40 hours a week variable, concluding at the Camden Fringe Festival. Applicants must be aged 18 and over. Performance experience and A-level qualifications or similar desirable but not compulsory.
• MA Collaborative Theatre. One year course full-time, 2 years part time. Applicants must be 18 or over, academic qualifications not essential.

Accepts applications from all areas of society; the only factor impacting suitability on any training programme is the presence of talent, a desire to learn, enthusiasm to develop and a willingness to work as an ensemble company member.

The Giles Foreman Centre for Acting

Studio Soho,
2A Royalty Mews (entrance between Quo Vadis/ Barrafina & Firezza), Dean Street, London W1D 3AR
tel 020 7437 3175
email info@gilesforeman.com
website www.gilesforeman.com
Director Giles Foreman

An exciting professional acting studio housing some of the country's top coaches in the disciplines of screen- and theatre-acting, movement, voice, improvisation on-camera, Meisner technique movement psychology and character analysis, directing and text analysis.

Comprises 2 easy-access, large, bright, air-conditioned studios plus changing room, chillout area and kitchen, and props store. (Wheelchair-accessible, entrance lift and step-free studio facilities.) Plus separate daylight-studio and meeting-rooms. Wi-Fi throughout.

Courses offered (many run throughout the year):
All ages from 17+

• Complete Beginners/Introduction to Acting (10 weeks: 3 hours per week). Open entry.
• Intermediate Acting (12 weeks: 4 hours per week). Entry by application.
• Advanced Acting (12 weeks – 4 hours per week). Entry by application.
• Professional Acting (12 weeks: 4 hours per week). Entry by interview/audition.
• Movement (10 weeks: 2 hours per week). Entry by application.
• Voice (10 weeks: 2 hours per week). Entry by application.
• On-Camera (10 weeks: 3 hours per week). Entry by application.
• Meisner Technique (10 weeks: 3 hours per week). Entry by application.

Other courses offered:
• Meet the Industry Evenings (2 hours), September-July. Application via Spotlight or relevant CV.
• Workshops on specialised subjects (12 hours over 2 days). Application by appropriate previous study and/or performing experience.

GSA, Guildford School of Acting*

Stag Hill Campus, Guildford GU2 7XH
tel 01483 684040
email admissions@surrey.ac.uk
website www.gsauk.org
Twitter @the_gsa
Instagram @guildfordschoolofacting
Head of GSA Dr Catherine McNamara

Courses offered:

• Singing in the Theatre (1 week). A summer course designed for students over the age of 17 who wish to improve their singing. Other disciplines relating to the voice will also be explored. Entry is in July.
• Musical Theatre (2 weeks). Culminating in a performance in the Bellairs Playhouse, this course is open to students aged 17 or over and takes place in July/August.
• Audition Techniques (1 week). Course takes place in August and is geared towards students aged 17 or over.
• Intensive Musical Theatre Dance for Beginners (1 week). An intensive course to discover what your body is capable of doing. Explore the foundations of tap, jazz and ballet and get guidance and expert advice on what you need to work on and hopefully gain the confidence to compete in a dance class situation. The course takes place in August and is open to students 17 years and over.
• Acting for Camera (1 week). The course takes place in August and is open to students 17 years and over.

Other summer schools: Courses are offered at a reasonable cost and provide either a stimulating refresher course or an introduction to basic theatre training. There is no audition procedure, and everyone is welcome. All courses are staffed by members of the GSA faculty.

July/August:
• Youth Theatre (9 days).
• Musical Theatre (2 weeks).
• Intensive Musical Theatre Dance (5 days).
• Intensive Musical Theatre Acting (5 days).
• Intensive Musical Theatre Singing (5 days).
• Audition Technique (2 x 5-day sessions).
• Directing a Musical (5 days).
• Acting for Camera (5 days).

For further information or to download an application form, please refer to the website, or telephone or email (**gsasummerschool@gsa.surrey.ac.uk**) for a brochure.

Guildhall School of Music & Drama*

Silk Street, Barbican, London EC2Y 8DT
tel 020 7628 2571

email shortcourses@gsmd.ac.uk
website www.gsmd.ac.uk

Guildhall School of Music & Drama is a vibrant, interntaional community of musicians, actors and production artists in the heart of London. Offers Short Courses and Summer Schools, online and in person, open to a wide range of ages and abilities in drama, music and production arts.

Courses offered: Summer Schools include:

• Acting Summer Schools for ages 12-15, 16-17 and 18+
• Stage management
• Prop making

Evening courses include:
• Introduction to Acting Practice, Levels 1 and 2
• Improvisation
• Approaching Text: The Actor's Work at Home
• Creative Writing
• Shakespeare: An Experiential Workshop, Levels 1 and 2

Course spaces are limited, early booking is encouraged. New courses and programme dates are added regularly. Check the website or contact via email for more information.

The Impulse Company

Classes in central London
mobile (07525) 264173
email Lyn@impulsecompany.org
website www.impulsecompany.org
Principal & Director Scott Williams *Key contact* Lyn A Dade

Established for over 20 years in the UK, Scott Williams' Impulse Company provides Meisner-rooted core training for the adult actor within a supportive and positive atmosphere. It also offers occasional short courses, a summer rehearsal and performance programme, and workshops in New York.

Principal course offered:

• Modular Year course. 3 self-contained 8-week terms. Entry is by interview, in April, October and January each year. 8+ hours per week.
• Second Year Rehearsal & Performance course. 3 self-contained 11-week rehearsal and performance periods per year. Entry is by completion of the Year course, or by invitation. 7+ hours per week.

International School of Screen Acting

3 Mills Studios, Three Mill Lane, London E3 3DU
tel 020 8709 8719
website www.screenacting.co.uk
Facebook www.facebook.com/screenactingUK
Twitter @ScreenActingUK
Instagram @ScreenactingUK

Founded in 2002, offers full-time training specifically in television and film acting, taking a holistic

approach to creativity in relation to students' personal development.

Courses offered:

• 1-year Intensive Screen Acting. Fast, full-time intensive course focusing on equipping the student actor with the means to encompass the challenges of a demanding industry. Audition requried.
• 2-year Screen Acting. In-depth screen actor training preparing actors for the intense demands of the industry. Audition required.
• 'Crash Course'. A week-long course offered at various times throughout the year. No audition required.
• Summer Course. A selection of 2-day and 5-day courses. Check the website for updates.

LAMDA (London Academy of Music & Dramatic Art)*

155 Talgarth Road, London W14 9DA
tel 020 8834 0500
email enquiries@lamda.ac.uk
website www.lamda.ac.uk

Courses offered: Short-term courses are offered in the following areas:

• Shakespeare Summer School (8 weeks). Students 18+.
• Shakespeare at LAMDA (4 weeks). Students aged 17+.
• Acting for Audio/Building a Home Studio. Students aged 18 +.
• Self-taping for Professional Actors. Students aged 21+.
• Audition Coaching. Students aged 16+.
• Introduction to Actor Training. Students aged 16+.
• Introduction to Screen Acting (2 weeks). Students aged 16+.

For more information on all LAMDA's courses, including fees and deadlines, please visit the website.

London School of Dramatic Art

4 Bute Street, London SW7 3EX
tel 020 7581 6100
email enquiries@lsda-acting.com
website www.lsda-acting.com
Facebook www.facebook.com/LSDA.Acting
Twitter @LSDA_Acting
Instagram @lsda_acting
Principal Jake Taylor *Administrator* Emeline Touzet

Offers a range of comprehensive courses designed to develop individual creative talents, and to provide a thorough grounding in all aspects of performance as part of a student's preparation for a working life as an actor. There is currently no wheelchair access to the main building or training rooms: if this affects applicants who would like to know when these spaces become accessible, please let the school know. All auditions are free and no international student fees are charged. No formal qualifications are required, as the training is vocational: "We look more at potential and at levels of creativity."

Part-time 18+ acting courses:

• Diploma in Acting (2 years, 7.5 hours per week). Entry is by audition.
• Access to Acting (5 weeks, 4 hours per week)

Short-term 18+ acting courses:

• Introduction to Drama School (2 weeks in July)
• Introduction to Drama School (2 weeks in August)
• Screen Acting (1 week in September)
• Audition Techniques (1 week in September)

Manchester School of Acting

14-32 Hewitt Street, Manchester M15 4GB
tel 0161 238 8900
email info@manchesterschoolofacting.co.uk
website www.manchesterschoolofacting.co.uk
Key contact Mark Hudson

High-profile acting school offering part-time training for actors.

Method Acting London

32 Woodfield Road, London W9 2BE
tel 020 7622 9742 *mobile* 07764 680232
email main@methodacting.co.uk
website www.methodacting.co.uk
Principal & Director Sam Rumbelow

Within the specifically defined and well-established structure of the classes, a grounded, conscious understanding of the craft of acting is facilitated and the powerful creativity of thoughts, impulses and emotions is unlocked. Entry is after a detailed talk and discussion of the class and the applicant, conducted by phone.

Part-time/short-term 16+ acting courses:

• Main Method Studio Intensives, Fri–Sunday 10–6 pm, 8 units spaces through the year
• Online Method, 3 weeks of classes twice a week, 5 units through the year
• Voice & Movement Classes, 4 Weeks online and in studio
• Audition Coaching Drama School/Industry
• Role Coaching Stage and Screen

Michael Chekhov Studio London

48 Vectis Road,
London SW17 9RG (Administration Office)
mobile 07968 691016
email info@michaelchekhovstudio.org.uk
website www.michaelchekhovstudio.org.uk
Director Graham Dixon

Founded in 2003, the MCSL provides actors (and directors) an opportunity to explore Michael Chekhov's unique approach to the art of acting. Many drama trainings are based upon 'closed systems' that look inside one's own psychology to create a character, but Chekhov created an 'open

system' that permits actors to enter an objective creative world immediately using an increased ability to imagine and sense. Yearly programs of workshops and intensives on the basic techniques of Chekhov leading to more advanced work including ensemble initiatives and private coaching on the Chekhov approach to the art of acting and directing.

Morley College

North Kensington Centre: Wornington Road, London W10 5QQ; *Chelsea Centre*: Hortensia Road, London SW10 0QS; *Waterloo Centre*: 61 Westminster Bridge Road, London SE1 7HT
tel 020 7450 1889
website www.morleycollege.ac.uk

Offers part-time acting classes from entry-level to advanced. Classes are led by specialist acting tutors with extensive professional experience. An Access Hardship Fund and concessionary fees are available to some students.

Courses offered: A range of evening and part-time acting skills courses are available. Some courses require tutor approval.

• Acting level 1, 2 and 3
• Acting: The Company
• Specialised courses: Physical Theatre, Directing, Playwrighting, Voice, Devising, Puppetry
• Drama skills such as Confidence through Acting and Public Speaking, and including courses for actors with moderate learning disabilities
• HND in Performing Arts

Mountview*

120 Peckham Hill Street, London SE15 5JT
tel 020 8881 2201
email enquiries@mountview.org.uk
website www.mountview.org.uk
Facebook www.facebook.com/mountviewldn
Twitter @mountviewLDN
Instagram @mountviewldn
CEO & Artistic Director Abigail Morris

Courses offered:

• Foundation Acting (2 terms). Part time, 7.5 hours of classes per week. Entry is by audition.
• Foundation Musical Theatre (2 terms). Part time, 7.5 hours of classes per week. Entry is by audition.
• Foundation in Acting for Stage & Screen Performance (2 termss). Full time. 30 hours of classes per week. Entry is by audition.
• Foundation Musical Theatre (2 terms). Full time. 30 hours of classes per week. Entry is by audition.
• Acting Bootcamp (3 weeks), Course takes place in July/August. No audition required.
• Musical Theatre Bootcamp (3 weeks). Course takes place in JulyAugust. No audition required.

The Oxford School of Drama*

Sansomes Farm Studios, Woodstock,
Oxford OX20 1ER

tel 01993 812883
email info@oxforddrama.ac.uk
website www.oxforddrama.ac.uk
Facebook www.facebook.com/
TheOxfordSchoolOfDrama
Twitter @Oxford_Drama
Instagram @oxford_drama
Principal Edward Hicks

The Oxford School of Drama provides professional actor training in the form of Three Year, One Year and Six Month Foundation courses. The Three Year and One Year courses are accredited by Trinity College, London and are recognised by industries around the world and boast successful alumni including writers, directors, filmmakers and actors, Claire Foy (*The Crown*) and Jude Owusu (*To Kill a Mockingbird*) are two recent examples. Entry is by audition only, please visit **www.oxforddrama.ac.uk/apply** to find out more.

Pineapple Dance Studios

7 Langley Street, London WC2H 9JA
tel 020 7836 4004
website www.pineapple.uk.com

Pineapple offers more classes than any other studio throughout Europe, and the widest variety of dance styles. The philosophy behind the creation of the Pineapple Dance Studios was to break down the elitist barriers surrounding dance, making it available to everyone – from the absolute beginner to the advanced and the professional dancer. Everybody is welcome: Pineapple offers classes for all levels and all ages. Approx. 250 classes per week, ranging across 40 styles from classical ballet to street jazz, hip hop to Salsa, Egyptian dance to Bollywood grooves.

The Questors Theatre Ealing

12 Mattock Lane, London W5 5BQ
tel 020 8567 0011
website www.questors.org.uk

Provides part-time training for actors in the context of a working theatre. Financial support is available from a private trust fund for a limited number of students.

Courses offered:

• Acting: Foundation and Performance (2 years). 6 hours of classes per week. Entry is by audition.

Royal Academy of Dramatic Art (RADA)*

62-64 Gower Street, London WC1E 6ED
tel 020 7636 7076
email enquiries@rada.ac.uk
website www.rada.ac.uk
Instagram @royalacademyofdramaticart
Director Edward Kemp

Courses offered:

• Singing Academy for Actors. Online: 5 day course to improve singing techniques from a musical and dramatic perspective. Age 16+. No audition.
• Fundamentals of Acting. Online: 4-week online training programme suitable for anyone interested in learning the basics of acting, particularly those thinking about going to drama school. Age 18+. Entry by audition.
• Elements of RADA Workshops. Online: a chance to explore key subjects taught at the Academy: voice, movement, contemporary text, classical text and improvisation. Age 20+. No audition.
• Scene Study for Actors. Online: 10 weeks.
• Explore the work and ideas of Constantin Stanislavski, Uta Hagen and Sanford Meisner to clarify and develop your own approach to acting. Age 20+. No audition.
• The RADA Contemporary Drama Summer School (5 days). This course provides the opportunity to work on modern or contemporary texts. Students work in groups led by a director, with support from a voice and a movement instructor. Other playwrights talk about their work during special evening sessions, describing their experience of working with actors and what they expect from them, following presentations of excerpts from their plays by RADA graduates. Students present rehearsed material and receive feedback from the director and the voice and movement teachers on the last day of the course. Students below the age of 18 are not normally accepted; there is no upper age limit.
• Numerous other courses throughout the year. Please check the website.

Richmond Drama School

RACC, Parkshot, Richmond TW9 2RE
tel 020 8891 5907
email info@rhacc.ac.uk
website www.RHACC.ac.uk

Courses offered:

Richmond Drama School has an exceptional reputation for outstanding teaching and a strong history of placing students in top CDT drama schools; these include RADA, Central, Drama Studio, ALRA and Stella Addler (New York) amongst others. Many previous students, who have not desired an academic pathway, have been able to step straight into the professional industry.

Courses offered:

• Foundation Year in Acting
• Audition Techniques
• Stage Combat
• Improvisation
• Many more

Rose Bruford College*

Lamorbey Park, Burnt Oak Lane, Sidcup DA15 9DF
tel 020 8308 2600

Training

email enquiries@bruford.ac.uk
website www.bruford.ac.uk
Instagram @rosebruford, @brufordstudents
Principal and CEO Clarie Middleton

Courses offered:

• Acting Summer School (2 weeks). Designed for participants over the age of 18 (16+ for non-residential students). This programme includes classes, rehearsals and workshops on voice, movement, acting and improvisation.
• Acting Advanced Intensive (12 weeks). Designed for professionals who want additional training.
• MA Collaborative Theatre (full time, 13 months). Designed for professional practitioners to develop their practice as a researcher through experiential learning.
• MA Theatre for Young Audiences (part or full time). Designed to work and study with leading TYA figures.

The Royal Central School of Speech and Drama*

ROYAL CENTRAL
SCHOOL OF SPEECH & DRAMA

UNIVERSITY OF LONDON

64 Eton Avenue, London NW3 3HY
tel 020 7722 8183
email short.courses@cssd.ac.uk
website www.cssd.ac.uk

Central offers a range of practical on-line and in-person short courses in:

• Acting
• Voice
• Movement
• Writing
• Communication
• Design and Production
• Youth Theatre

Short courses are delivered all year round, led by industry professionals and are suitable for all abilities.

The School of the Science of Acting

First Floor, Dwell House, 637 Holloway Road, London N19 5SS
tel 020 7272 0027
email info@scienceofacting.com
website www.scienceofacting.com

Courses offered:

• 6 Month Intensive Acting Course.

Seven Dials Playhouse

1A Tower Street, Covent Garden, London WC2H 9NP

tel 020 3841 6600
email boxoffice@sevendialsplayhouse.co.uk
website www.sevendialsplayhouse.co.uk
Facebook www.facebook.com/SevenDialsPlayhouse
Twitter @7DialsPlayhouse
Instagram @7dialsplayhouse
Chief Executive Amanda Davey

Founded in 1978, formerly The Actors Centre. Seven Dials Playhouse runs workshops and courses from its venue in the heart of the West End. The Centre boasts five studios, a Green Room Cafe and Bar, and incorporates the Tristan Bates Theatre. Their members-only professional workshop programme is unrivalled and covers all aspects of performance and business skills development for the working actor. Membership is assessed and approved against a professional criteria that demands a level of training, experience and/or affiliation with recognised industry bodies. Membership comes with a host of of benefits including access to the building, studio/theatre hire discounts, perks, free opportunities and access to workshops and courses in the quarterly programme. Seven Dials Playhouse also runs workshops and courses for non-members, programmed throughout the year and on a bespoke basis.

Regular workshops include Acting, Screen Acting, Shakespeare, Auditioning, Improvistion, Voice, Dialect, Voiceovers, Stage Combat, Physical Theatre, Musical Theatre, Writing and Career Advice. In addition, members can book individual sessions to work on Audition Technique, Accents, Marketing/Branding, Voice and Singing.

Please see the website for more information.

Theatre Royal Haymarket Masterclass Trust

Theatre Royal Haymarket, London SW1Y 4HT
tel 020 7389 9660
email info@masterclass.org.uk
website www.masterclass.org.uk
Twitter @Masterclasstrh
Patrons Dame Judi Dench, Sir David Hare, Maureen Lipman CBE, Elaine Page OBE

Masterclass is a theatre charity based at the Theatre Royal Haymarket that opens doors to young people from all backgrounds, aged 16-30, who are interested in the performance industry. The programme provides workshops and talks with leading actors, directors, designers and writers working in theatre today, alongside unique performance experiences, apprenticeship opportunities and community projects.

Previous Masters have included Danny DeVito, Simon Callow, Mike Leigh, Alan Rickman, Joanna Lumley, Idris Elba, Bradley Cooper and Damian Lewis. For details of forthcoming events, consult the website.

Theatre Workout Ltd

Kemsing Road, London SE10 0LL
tel 020 8144 2290
email enquiries@theatreworkout.com
website www.theatreworkout.com
Facebook www.facebook.com/theatreworkout

Twitter @theatreworkout
Director Adam Milford

Theatre Workout is the centre for education in London's West End offering CPD workshops, summer schools, short courses and other bespoke training.

Private tutors and coaches

Acting Coach Scotland
Unit 34, 6 Harmony Row, Govan Workspace,
Glasgow G51 3BA
tel 0141 440 1272
email hello@actingcoachscotland.co.uk
website www.actingcoachscotland.co.uk
Facebook www.facebook.com/ActingCoachScotland
Twitter @hello_acs
Instagram @Weareactingcoachscotland
Principal Nick J. Field

Established in 2008, with the aim of making high
quality professional training available to all. Acting
Coach Scotland offers 3 full-time courses: a unique
drama school preparation HNC in acting; a unique
professional HND in acting and performance, and a
bespoke 1-year full time diploma in stage and screen
performance. Staff are working actors, producers,
writers, directors and other specialists. No
scholarships are currently available.

There are no specific academic requirements for
entrance, acceptance is by audition and interview.
Applicants should be 17 years or older. The average
age of the students is 25. Application should be made
directly to the school.

Intensive training in acting, improvisation, acting for
camera, voice, accents and performance psychology.
Students experience many public performances, and
the PD/HND courses include a 3-week run at the
Edinburgh Fringe, and considerable acting for camera
training. Students who complete the PD/HND course
are entitled to Graduate Membership of Spotlight.

Applications from applicants with disabilities are
welcome. Successful candidates with disabilities will
have a full needs assessment before the course begins.

Antonia Doggett
1 Brading Crescent, Wanstead E11 3RT
mobile 07814 155090
email antoniadoggettcontact@gmail.com
website www.antoniadoggett.co.uk

Specialises in audition preparation, cold reading, text,
Shakespeare, voice, LAMDA/Trinity examinations,
one to one, courses and workshops. Charges £35 per
hour and prefers payment by PayPal or electronic
transfer. Is happy to provide material for private
students to use, and to answer minor follow-up
queries after a lesson.

Teaches in east London, or happy to travel elsewhere
in London or client's home for longer classes. Has
been coaching for 18 years and previously trained
with Teatr Piesn Kozla, Poland, assistant director for
Stathis Livathinos, National Theatre of Greece.

Audition Doctor
South East London
mobile 020 357 8237

email tilly@auditiondoctor.co.uk
website www.auditiondoctor.co.uk
Twitter @auditiondoctors

A bespoke service that provides invaluable help for
auditions, whether you are a professional actor
dealing with confidence issues or a Drama School
applicant. Charges £80 per hour. Students bring their
own material to work from. Answers minor follow-
up queries at no extra charge. Teaches from home
(wheelchair accessible). The nearest station is
Borough on the Northern Line, around a 4-minute
walk away. "I have been, and continue to be, a
professional working actor for the last 20 years, and
have been teaching for the last 5. With my sanity
intact and an unbridled passion for the business, I am
perfectly placed to give up-to-date assistance,
direction and information in an ever-changing
profession." Audition Doctor has been listed in the
top 10 Acting Coaches on the Acting in London
website

Barbara Berkery
London N19
email barbaraberkery@hotmail.com
website www.barbaraberkery.com

Specialises in accents, voice and text. Details of fees
and discounts are available upon enquiry. Happy to
provide material for private students to use, and to
answer minor follow-up queries at no extra charge.
Teaches from home and/or studio, both of which are
wheelchair accessible. Main teaching location is 10
minutes' walk from Holloway Road tube (bus routes
17, 43, 271 and 263). Further details are available
from IMDb. Has taught hundreds of actors/aspiring
actors over a period of 30 years, and possesses
extensive experience both as an actress and as a
director. Works with her Associates at Vox Barbarae.

Ross Campbell
Private Studios, West London and Surrey
mobile 07956 465165
email rosscampbell@ntlworld.com
website www.rosscampbelle.biz;
www.dailysingingtips.com;
www.thesingersportal.com
Facebook www.facebook.com/rosscampbelluk;
www.facebook.com/SingingAnExtensiveHandbook
Twitter @rosscampbelluk

Specialises in singing and acting techniques, audition
preparation, college entrance and related
examinations and diplomas. Charges £80 per hour. Is
happy to provide material for private students to use
and to answer minor follow-up queries after a lesson.

Teaches in a private studio at home in Surrey and a
private London studio. The nearest stations are West

Brompton and Barons Court (a 7-minute walk). Has taught many actors, singers and triple threat performers for 30 years, and has professionals in every West End show on a continuous basis. Ross is a professor at the Royal Academy of Music London; Fellow of The Royal Society of Arts; author of *Singing: An Extensive Handbook for all Singers and Their Teachers*; Director and Head of Singing and Musical Theatre at Musical Theatre UK (MTI); Consultant to Musical Theatre UK Ltd; Patron and Chief Advisor to the CEO of International Performing Arts and Theatre Ltd; former Head of Music and Singing at Guildford School of Acting/University of Surrey (GSA); and a consultant to Musical Theatre Poland (MTP). He is also an award-winning author for the ABRSM.

Mel Churcher

mobile 07778 773019
email melchurcher@gmail.com
website www.melchurcher.com
website www.actinganddrama.com

Teaches by Zoom. More details are available from www.imdb.com and from own websites.

Has taught thousands of actors and aspiring actors over 30 years. Has worked as an actor and theatre director; taught at most major UK drama schools and at the Actors Centre; coached on more than 50 films; run national and international workshops; and authored 2 books: *A Screen Acting Workshop plus DVD* (Nick Hern Books, 2011), and *Acting for Film: Truth 24 Times a Second* (Virgin Books, 2003). Holds an MA in Performing Arts (Middlesex) and in Voice Research (CSSD). "I am happy to help with most aspects of auditioning and working in theatre and film. I can advise on understanding the differences between film and theatre, film technique and building confidence and overcoming nerves."

MJ Coldiron

54 Millfields Road, London E5 0SB
mobile 07941 920498
email mcoldiron@mac.com

Offers audition coaching for professional and aspiring actors; advice about theatre and performance training in the US and the UK; and coaching in acting technique, public speaking and presentation skills. Charges £50 per hour, £130 for 3 sessions. Occasional group workshops. Can provide material for clients and is happy to receive minor follow-up queries. Teaches from home studio, with the nearest rail station being Hackney Central Overground. Has taught hundreds of aspiring actors over 30 years: please make contact for more details. Advises clients: "The theatrical profession is very demanding and is not to be sought for fame or fortune. It is also very competitive and you must work hard, but if you have talent, desire and discipline I can help you to improve your technique and gain in confidence."

The Confident Voice

School of Philosophy and Economic Science Building, 11-13 Mandeville Place, London W1V 3AJ
mobile 07976 805976
email neville@speakwell.co.uk
website www.speakwell.co.uk
Tutor Neville Wortman

At present online via Zoom. One-to-one hour tuition includes audition technique and voice. Services include coaching in elocution, communication techniques and self-awareness; also the establishment of confidence and natural performance. Neville specialises in dialogue, Shakespeare, musical comedy and lyrical interpretation. Fee details are available on application.

Bridget de Courcy

19 Muswell Road, London N10 2BJ
email singinglessons@bridgetdecourcy.co.uk
website www.bridgetdecourcymusic.co.uk

Taught singing at the Actors Centre, Covent Garden for 19 years.

Jane de Florez, LGSM PGDip MBACP DipPsych

West Kensington/Barons Court, London W14
tel 020 7602 0741 *mobile* 07931 714411
email janedeflorez@gmail.com
website www.singingteacherwestlondon.com

Specialises in singing technique, repertoire, performance, auditions. Charges £40 per hour. Is happy to provide material for private students to use, and to answer minor follow-up queries at no extra charge. Teaches from a large home studio, which is 5 minutes' walk from West Kensington and Barons Court tube stations. Has taught hundreds of actors and aspiring actors for the past 25 years, and now sees at least 10 pupils each week who are performers or aspiring performers. Teaches a strong, versatile technique that is suitable for all types of music. Specialist in acting through song. Most students go into classical, musical theatre and cabaret.

Prue Gillett Actor Training

Gloucestershire
email prue@pruegillett.com
website www.pruegillett.com

Specialises in the Meisner Technique, Received Pronunciation and Accent Reduction. Charges from £120 per 3-hour session for group classes, and £40 per hour for private sessions. When possible, will provide material for students' use, and will answer minor follow-up queries at no extra cost. Teaches one-to-one online and from home near Cirencester, Gloucestershire. Workshops at drama schools and other locations are arranged on request. Please see website for further details.

John Grayson

2 Jubilee Road, St Johns, Worcester WR2 4LY
mobile 07702 188031

email johngraysonvoiceartist@outlook.com
website www.johngraysonvoiceartist.com

Actor, singer and voice artist specialising in coaching audition speeches, voiceover for actors, and public speaking and presentation for business people. Teaches via Zoom etc, or from home. Nearest station Worcester Foregate Street (good service from Birmingham), then a 10–15 minute walk. Can provide material if needed. Happy to receive follow up queries.

Martin Harris

17 Groveland Road, Wallasey, Merseyside CH45 8JX
tel 0151 637 1481 *mobile* 07788 723570
email martin@auditioncoach.co.uk
website www.auditioncoach.co.uk

Specialises in audition technique and selection and direction of audition pieces. Offers group acting classes as well as one-to-one tuition for aspiring and professional actors. Also teaches sight reading and gives advice about CVs, agents and jobs. Charges £30 per hour. Accepts payment with cash or cheque, or via Internet banking.

Is happy to provide material for private students to use, and will answer minor follow-up queries at no extra charge. Teaches on-line at home or at the client's home (with a small extra charge).Wallasey Grove Road is the nearest train station. The home/ office is next to the station. Has taught more than 200 actor clients over 10 years. Trained as an actor at Birmingham School of Acting, and has worked as an actor and director since 1995. Currently also Artistic Director of Rocket Theatre.

Daniel Hoffmann-Gill

London
mobile 07946 433903
email danielhg@gmail.com

Specialises in actor confidence-building, improvisation technique, removing actors' blocks, audition technique, casting technique and various practitioner-centred methods such as Guskin, Meisner, Lecoq and Donnellan. Has been a professional actor for more than 24 years, working in film, TV and theatre, and has taught actors for over 21 years. Focuses on one-to-one work, aimed at enabling the actor to do themselves and their imagination justice – also, on practical assistance in audition technique and how to do the very best you can in any casting situation, "no matter how bizarre". Uses real casting briefs and exercises, for students to try out their ideas.

Has previously taught at the Royal Central School of Speech and Drama, East 15, the Actors Centre, the National Theatre, as well as for numerous London agents. References from previous students are available on request. Charges £50 per hour, with special packages available for long-term work or working towards drama school entry: these are

tailored on an individual basis, so please email for details. Works from home or from the client's home, and occasionally uses performance spaces, depending on the project. All locations used are wheelchair-accessible. Has taught around 300 actors. Advises clients that "hard graft and positive attitude go a long way in a tough, tough industry".

Jennifer Jane Hooker

Based in Central London
mobile 07725 977146
email coaching@jjhooker.com
website www.jjhooker.com

Specialises in character work, scene breakdown, emotional and sensory work, and audition technique. Teaches both known actors and new students with emphasis on practical work – proven results in both drama school entry and auditions. Trained with Susan Batson of Susan Batson Studios, NYC, who sends her actors to JJ when they are in Europe. Certified practitioner of Core Competency Coaching, an effective technique to get rid of fears and judgements that stop us from reaching our true potential. Can provide material for use by private students.

Mark Hudson

MSA, 14-32 Hewitt Street, Manchester M15 4GB
tel 0161 238 8900
email mark@manchesterschoolofacting.co.uk
website www.manchesterschoolofacting.co.uk

International film, television and theatre - acting, dialogue and dialect coach.

Charlie Hughes-D'Aeth

Based in Brighton, London and online
email chdaeth@aol.com
website https://charliehughesdaeth.co.uk

Freelance text and voice coach. Currently voice coach at the Old Vic and consultant on RSC's *Matilda the Musical*. Offers coaching on practical voice technique for business and theatre/musical theatre. Also works with people living with Long Covid.

Desmond Jones

3 Merton Avenue, London W4 1TA
tel 020 8747 3537
email enquiries@desmondjones.com
website www.desmondjones.com

Specialises in physical audition techniques and mime and physical theatre. One of the founders of physical theatre; has run his own School of Mime and Physical Theatre for 25 years, with expertise in all aspects of movement. Charges are negotiable, with various packages and discounts available; please make contact for more information. Will provide clients with occasional worknotes and is happy to answer minor follow-up queries. Teaches out of home (a 3-minute walk from Turnham Green station, bus routes 94, 27, H91, 191, 267), or the home of the client – whichever is more suitable. Has taught more than 2,500 aspiring actors over 40 years. Advises clients: "Do it now!"

Lawrence Lambert

c/o The Actors Centre, 1A Tower Street,
London WC2H 9NP
email lawrielambo@yahoo.co.uk

Audition, creating character, improvisation, text and voice. Specialist in Method Acting. Work detail can be for beginners, professionals or individuals returning to the profession. Charges £30 per hour, with a discount for block bookings. Happy to provide material for private students to use and to answer follow-up queries after a lesson.

Will teach at home, at the client's home or at the Actors Centre; all are wheelchair-accessible. Nearest tube/railway station is Arsenal (home) or Leicester Square (Actors Centre). Bus route is 19.

Is currently teaching Acting for Film at the Met Film School, Ealing, and Introduction to Acting at the City Lit, Holborn. Has taught professional actors and aspiring actors for over 30 years. Experienced in stage, television and feature film, and is an East 15 acting school graduate. "I cater for all types of experience – from novice to seasoned professional."

Marj McDaid

Stoke Newington, London N16
tel 020 7923 4929 *mobile* 07815 993203
email marj@voicings.co.uk
website www.voicings.co.uk

Specialises in voice for speech and singing (Estill method – safe techniques for shouting, screaming, etc.), character work, and accents (especially Irish and American). Discounts can be arranged when a number of sessions paid for in advance. Prefers cash or interbank transfer. Is happy to provide audition speeches (not songs) for private students to use, and will answer minor follow-up queries at no extra charge. Teaches from home, which is 10 mins from Dalston or Stoke Newington (overground) and not far from Highbury & Islington tube. Bus routes include 67, 73, 76, 149, 243, 393 and 476. Has taught hundreds of actors and aspiring actors over 20 years.

Martin McKellan

mobile 07425 204070
email leomckellan@yahoo.com
website www.martinmckellan.com

Specialises in auditions, acting classes and all aspects of voice work (accent and dialogue a particular area of expertise). Rates are negotiable and offers are available; please make contact for full details. Is happy to provide material for private students to use, and to answer minor follow-up queries at no extra charge. Will teach from home, from a client's home

or at another location. Covent Garden is the nearest tube station, 3 minutes' walk away. Has taught thousands of actors and aspiring actors over the past 15 years, and has extensive experience as a freelance acting/voice coach working in the West End and in Regional Theatre and for both film and television.

Alison Mead

9 Victoria Road, Chislehurst BR7 6DE
tel 020 3601 7022 *mobile* 07770 672589
email alison.mead49@gmail.com
website www.alisonmead.com

Currently teaching Meisner Techniques at Rose Bruford School of Performing Arts, Alison specialises in audition technique, accent work, sight reading, acting through song, acting for camera, Shakespeare, character building and Stanislavski techniques. Charges are negotiable, but there is a basic rate of £40 per hour for private tuition (£60 for 2 hours). Sessions can be also be shared by two people for £60 per hour. Alison is happy to provide material for private students to use, and to answer minor follow-up queries after a lesson.

Teaches at home, which is wheelchair-accessible or is happy to travel to student's home for a small extra charge. The nearest station is Elmstead Woods, 20 minutes from London Bridge. Trains to Bickley from Victoria run twice per hour and take 25 minutes. Also offers workshops for schools and further education designed specifically to meet the students' needs. She has taught many actors and aspiring actors for over 25 years. Alison has taught Drama and Theatre Arts at degree level, A-Level and GCSE. She has adjudicated at 6 drama festivals for both adults and young people and runs her own theatre company, AMProductions. "Make sure this is the career for you and that it is what you want above all else."

Robin Miller

London
mobile 07957 627677
email robinjenni@hotmail.com
website www.mandy.com/uk/actor/robin-miller;
www.spotlight.com/profile/0632-4531-6660

Specialises in audition speeches, accents and dialects. Charges £25 per hour (special packages negotiable; preferred payment methods are cash or cheque), and is happy to answer minor follow-up queries at no extra charge. Teaches at home – no steps up to the house. Nearest station is St Margaret's, 12 minutes away, or Twickenham, 10 minutes away. Bus routes are H22, H37, 110 or 267. Also teaches at the client's home. Has 30 years' experience in the acting profession as an actress, writer, workshop leader, teacher and director; please see Spotlight and Mandy for further details. Advises actors that "choosing the right speech is incredibly important".

Frances Parkes

Suite 5, 3rd Floor, 1 Harley Street,
London W1G 9QD

tel 020 8542 2777
email frances@maxyourvoice.com
website www.maxyourvoice.com

Group and one-to-one forums and coaching online. Voice and speech coaching, including accents, dialects and dialogue. Coaches actors in TV/film and auditions for the pilot season. Charges £35 for a 30 minute one-to-one online session.

Teaches at The Actors' Centre, Spotlight, Diorama and Harley Street which are wheelchair accessible. Trained at the Guildhall on the professional acting course, and RADA. "Use your inspiration to fuel your work and your commitment to learn your craft."

Richard Ryder

London and Madrid
mobile 07967 352551
email richervoice@gmail.com
website www.richardrydervoice.com
website www.theaccentkit.com

Specialises in accents, voice and text coaching. Charges £75 per hour, online only. Happy to provide material for private students to use, and to answer minor queries at no extra cost. Has more than 20 years' teaching and coaching experience, at the RSC, National Theatre, West End theatre, TV and film. You can download The Accent Kit app for iPhone and Android.

Rebecca Semark

Epping, Essex
mobile 07956 850330
email rebecca@semark.biz
website www.semark.biz

Specialises in audition technique, monologues and voice technique. Tuition for stage and drama school entrants includes singing and LAMDA exams. Also coaches public speaking for older students and adults. Teaches from home, online via Zoom or Skype. The closest station is Epping on the Central Line, which is a 5-10 minute walk. Has taught many performers, actors and aspiring actors for over 25 years. Has worked extensively in theatre and television as an actress and in many plays, musical theatre and television. Please call for an informal chat to discuss your needs.

Ros Simmons

120 Hillfield Avenue, Crouch End, London N8 7DN
tel 020 8347 8089
email ros@rossimmons.co.uk
website www.rossimmons.co.uk

Coaching Rates:

• 1 hour individual coaching session £85.00

There is a reduction to this rate for a commintment of 3 or more sessions. Due to Covid restrictions, presently teaches online via Skype or Zoom.

Specialises in accents and dialects, voice and auditions, as well as Spoken English skills for those with English as a second language. Provides full accent breakdowns and is happy to answer minor follow-up queries.

Has taught around 1,000 actors and aspiring actors, in drama schools and privately, over a period of 20 years. Trained as an actor at the Polytechnic School of Theatre in Manchester, and has worked extensively in theatre, film, TV and radio.

Giles Taylor

mobile 07973 960681

Specialises in Shakespeare, general acting technique and audition technique. Is a verse specialist, but works too on prose texts – classical and modern. Charges £50 per session which lasts for 90 minutes.

"I have been an actor for over 30 years and a Shakespeare consultant for over 15, training actors, students and directors, either in production, workshop or privately."

Paul Todd

3 Rosehart Mews, London W11 3JN
tel 020 7229 9776

Specialises in singing, acting, piano, music theory and voice. Happy to provide material for students to use, and to answer minor follow-up queries at no extra charge. Teaches from home, the nearest tube stations are Notting Hill/Bayswater/Queensway around 8-9 minutes away. Bus routes are 7, 23, 27, 28, 31 and 328. More details about services offered are available from Forward Talent/Yellow Pages. Has taught many actor/singers and aspiring actor/singers over 40 years. Has extensive experience as Musical Director at numerous theatres around the UK, including Theatre In The Round, Scarborough and The Royal National Theatre. Advises: "Get on with it. Get the right teacher. Do it."

Anne Wittman

North London
email info@spokenstates.com
website www.spokenstates.com

Specialises in coaching British and other non-US actors in a range of American dialects for audition and performance. Also works with accent correction for foreign speakers who would like to attain greater clarity of speech and to correct or soften their existing accent towards General American. Coaches RP for both native and foreign speakers; also coaches acting for audition and performance. Enjoys working with poets and other writers on presentation of their own material at readings.

Charges £75 per hour and a half session, £100 for two hours. Happy to provide material for private students to use, and to answer minor follow-up queries at no extra cost. Teaches from home (wheelchair accessible), but is also connected with various institutions. Nearest tube stations are Finsbury Park or Highgate: the most direct route to the main teaching location is the W3 or W7 bus from Finsbury Park. Has taught at least 500 actors since 1994. Further details are available from the website – also see Anne's article on dialect published in the 2013 edition of *Contacts*, under Drama Training.

Training

An actor's toolkit

Compiled by Simon Dunmore

You need to organise the following essential items before you even get your first interview, let alone an agent and/or your first job. You should start planning for all these in good time, before the end of your training – ready for your first public production.

1 Join Equity! You can join (very cheaply) as a student member (see **www.equity.org.uk/about-us/join-us**) and, for a small extra fee, reserve your professional name: details of how to go about this are on the website.

2 A good, strong professional name. If you can't (or don't want to) use your real name, it's important to select an alternative that you're completely comfortable with.

3 Well-designed headed paper. Beatrice Warde, the passionate typography expert, said, "Typefaces are the clothes words wear." Find a typeface that 'dresses' your professional name well.

4 Secure and reliable telephone and Internet connections for professional use. *Note*: It is very important that your outgoing message and email address sound professional and not like hangovers from your adolescence.

5 A reliable computer with printer. *Tip*: Laser printers provide a much crisper quality when printing text – and laser toner is much cheaper, per page, than ink.

6 An up-to-date copy of *Actors' and Performers' Yearbook*. *Tip*: It is worthwhile not only reading the rest of this book to get a feel for how different parts of the profession function, but also reading through websites.

7 A good set of photographs and sufficient copies. See Angus Deuchar's article and the introduction to Photographers and Repro Companies starting on page 360.

8 A well-laid-out and up-to-date CV. *Notes*: It's important to ensure that all spellings of proper names (directors, play titles, etc.) are correct. Also, to understand how to convert your CV into Portable Document Format (PDF) for email transmission.

9 A good standard letter that you can adapt for individual circumstances, and use in emails, etc.

10 Half-a-dozen (or more) varied audition speeches. See my *Effective Audition Speeches* article on page 153.

11 Half-a-dozen (or more) varied audition songs.

12 A mental list of things (not just acting ones) you could talk about in order to respond to the almost inevitable question(s), "What have you been doing recently?" and/or "Tell me a bit about yourself."

13 An entry in Spotlight – details at **www.spotlight.com/join**. *Note*: Entry into *Spotlight* is strictly limited to professionally trained and/or professionally experienced performers, and applications are always vetted.

14 A reasonable selection of clothes for interviews and auditions. Essentially, you need to feel comfortable and appropriately dressed for each individual circumstance … and you will face a wide variety of such circumstances.

15 An up-to-date passport – jobs which require travelling abroad at short notice are becoming more frequent.

16 A budget. The costs of the above can accumulate quite quickly – before you've earned a penny. And there are many other minor things not listed: postage; Equity entry fee and annual subscription; subscriptions to *The Stage* and other professional publications; travel costs to interviews, and so on. All the above items can easily add up to much more money than you might think: you need to calculate your potential professional expenses and budget for them. *Notes*: Although many of the above are allowable against tax (see Philippe Carden's article *Tax & National Insurance for Actors* on page 399), don't forget to include your potential tax bill! Also, at the outset of your career, consider carefully the cost-effectiveness of items like personal websites, showreels, etc. These are only worthwhile if you have sufficient high-quality material that makes you look 'professional'.

17 Sources of non-acting income that are flexible enough for you to drop at 24 hours' notice. At an educated guess, only about 10 per cent of the profession earn a living *solely* from acting. And, even for those, incomes can be incredibly variable – £200 one year to over £20,000 the next.

18 A working knowledge of the nation's transport systems (especially London's): you will often not know where you might be required for audition/interview (even work) until very late in the day. *Tip*: As a general rule it is wise to double your estimated travelling time to allow for the almost inevitable foul-ups.

19 A great deal of patience, persistence, determination, cunning and resourcefulness.

20 A stoical source of solace for the bad times. *Tip*: Find another activity that absorbs you as much as acting does.

21 A copy of my *An Actor's Guide To Getting Work* for reading on the loo (published by Methuen).

General points:

(a) Can you organise yourself? Acting can be an instant business. For days/weeks/months/years nothing happens, and then a few minutes/hours/days/weeks/months/years later it can *all* be happening. You must always be ready, but not constantly on tenterhooks. In spite of the popular image of the chaotic, dizzy actor, you have to be personally organised or you could significantly harm your employment prospects.

(b) As an actor you are your own business. You are not only your own work-force, but also your publicity and public relations office, accountancy division, transport manager, and – above all – your managing director. Of course, you may well have an agent, an accountant, etc., but none of these people can do anything unless you give them clear direction. You are finally responsible for your success or failure in the business.

Simon Dunmore directed productions for over 30 years – nearly 20 years as a resident director in regional theatres and latterly working freelance. In that time there were more than 200 productions (of all styles, colours, shapes and sizes) including several Drama School Showcases, Maugham's *Home and Beauty* and new plays about sex, WB Yeats' up-and-down relationship with Maud Gonne, one set inside a pyramid, and another about Bismarck. Favourites included: *The Promise* (Alexei Arbuzov), *Antigone* (Jean Anouilh), a seven-handed version of *Antony & Cleopatra* and too many others to mention. He also taught acting, and worked in many drama schools and other training establishments around the country. He wrote several books: *An Actor's Guide to Getting Work* (fifth edition, 2012), the *Alternative Shakespeare Auditions* series, and was formerly the Consultant Editor for *Actors' Yearbook*.

Agents and casting directors
Introduction

Actors have probably existed since before the invention of writing; actors' agents have only been around since the invention of the telephone, just over a century ago. Prior to this, work-seeking actors had to make themselves known in person to potential employers. Actors would 'catch a ride' with one of the touring companies in the hope of proving themselves to the manager – and then being put on the payroll. Others would pay managers to let them play small parts, in the hope of being noticed. All this meant a lot of hard work and/or expense (let alone the time needed to earn their living by other means) for the pre-electronic-age actor. The invention of actors' agents seemed to fill a vital gap.

In the 1970s, a number of actors, dissatisfied with the (by then) traditional agent system, formed the first co-operative agencies (see page 85). This simple idea – with all members taking turns to 'man' the office – took a while to become established. Nearly forty years later, the best 'co-ops' have as much professional credibility as their conventional counterparts.

It used to be the case that only the biggest companies used casting directors. The administrative burden inherent in running such a company (let alone directing productions) meant that assistance in the casting process became essential. The 1990s saw a rise in the use of casting directors and in the number of freelancers working on short-term contracts: most of the latter work in a wide variety of fields.

The simple fact is that a significant proportion of properly paid acting work is 'brokered' by casting directors and agents.

Agents and casting directors have very distinct functions – just look at the upcoming listings! The term 'casting agents' is used to describe walk-on agents who take the responsibility for casting walk-ons/extras in television and film. They have client bases comprising lots of different types, and on request can supply a suitable crowd for any occasion. Thus they fulfil the roles of both agent and casting director for non-speaking parts that don't need to be auditioned.

Agents

A good agent understands contracts, knows the current rates in every field of work and – most importantly – has plenty of professional contacts and access to far more casting information than most individuals can ever possess. Directors and casting directors rely on the agents they know and trust to help with the filtering process of whom to interview. A good agent will work hard at promoting each of their clients; in return, they charge commission on every contract they negotiate – generally 10-20 per cent (plus VAT, if appropriate). A good agent will also (a) have only as many clients as they can reasonably handle, and (b) ensure that they have a good range of ages and types of actors in order to cover as many casting opportunities as possible.

Use the listings that follow to (a) target your submission as accurately as possible (for example, by writing to a specific, named person – unless advised otherwise), (b) check for any details that could inform the content of your letter, and (c) find out whether each would be interested in any extras, like a showreel. Time spent checking such details can save money and enhance your chances of being noticed more than the next person. Unless you have a good collection of professional credits, it is generally best to write to agents when there's an opportunity for them to see you performing in something.

If you are invited to meet an agent, that is often a good sign. You should approach the occasion in much the same way as you would an interview for a production. The major difference is that you should be prepared to ask (reasonable) questions – rates of commission, for instance.

When seeking representation, it can be a good idea to target only those agencies that you think might suit you. For instance, might you feel lost in a large agency, but feel more comfortable with a smaller one? On the other hand, some larger agencies have huge 'clout' and can be the first 'port of call' for the casting of prestigious productions.

When you've been taken on by an agent, it is important to establish how your working relationship will function. Be clear about any areas of work that you don't want to be suggested for, discuss your availability for auditions and interviews, agree how much promotion you should do for yourself, and so on.

These listings only contain agents who represent adult actors – there are many others who represent children, models, extras and so on.

PMA following an agency's name denotes membership of the Personal Managers' Association, the leading professional body of talent agencies in the UK. It was set up more than 70 years ago with the intention of encouraging good practice among agents through better communication between agents and from agents to the industry.

42 PMA
Palladium House, 1-4 Argyll Street,
London W1F 7TA
tel 020 7292 0554
email info@42mp.com
website www.42mp.com
Partner Kate Buckley, assisted by Bea Marston
Managers Ness Evans, Molly Cowan, Molly Wansell, Harrison Davies, Kelly Byrne, Ellie Martin-Sperry, Sibella Dowad, Elle Cairns

Established 2013. Main areas of work are theatre, TV and film. Represents actors, directors, casting directors, writers and producers. Welcomes performance notices nationwide given a week's notice. Welcomes letters, CVs and photographs sent by email and show reels. Represents actors with disabilities.

A&J Artists
56 Park Avenue, Enfield EN1 2HW
tel 020 8004 3367
email info@ajartists.com
website www.ajartists.com
Managing Director Jo McLintock *Key contact* Jo McLintock

Established in 1984. 2 agents represent actors. Areas of work include theatre, musicals, television, film and commercials.

Will consider attending performances with a minimum of 2 weeks' notice. Accepts submissions (with CVs and photographs) from actors previously unknown to the company if sent by email. Invitations to view individual actors' websites are also accepted.

Chris Abakporo
47 Chatsworth Road, Stratford, London E15 1RB
mobile 07494 018583
email chrisabak@hotmail.co.uk
Agent Chris Abakporo

Established in 2010. Areas of work include TV, film and commercials. Welcomes CVs and photographs sent by email. Also accepts showreels and invitations to view actors' websites.

Access Artiste Management Ltd
The Bloomsbury Building, 10 Bloomsbury Way, London WC1A 2SL
tel 020 3916 0270
email mail@access-uk.com
website www.access-uk.com
Manager Sarah Bryan

Established in 1999. Areas of work include theatre, musicals, television, film, commercials and corporate. Also represents directors, musical directors, choreographers, composers, playwrights and musical works.

Will consider attending performances in Greater London and elsewhere with 1 month's notice. Accepts submissions (with CVs and photographs) from professional actors previously unknown to the company. Showreels, voicereels and details of individual actors' websites should only be sent upon request. Welcomes enquiries from disabled actors.

Actors Direct Ltd
Number 5, 651 Rochdale Road, Manchester M9 5SH
tel 0161 277 9360 / 020 7206 2759
email info@actorsdirect.org.uk
website www.actorsdirect.org.uk

Established in 1994. Personal management. Sole representative of approximately 60 actors. Areas of work include theatre, musicals, television, film, commercials, corporate and voice-overs.

Will consider attending performances if given 2 weeks' notice. Accepts submissions (with CVs and photographs) from actors previously unknown to the company if sent by post or email. Also accepts showreels and voicereels.

Actors International Ltd
5 West Court, Enterprise Road, Maidstone ME15 6JD
tel 020 7118 2278
email mail@actorsinternational.co.uk
website www.actorsinternational.co.uk
Facebook www.facebook.com/actorsintl
Twitter @ACTORSINTL
Agents Caroline Taylor, Lee Thomas

Established in 2000. 2 agents represent around 70 actors. Areas of work include theatre, musicals, television, film, commercials and corporate.

Will attend showcases/performances within Central London given as much notice as possible. Accepts email submissions ONLY; no postal submissions will be considered.

AFA Associates
Unit 101A, Business Design Centre, 52 Upper Street, London N1 0QH
tel 020 7682 3677 *mobile* 07904 962779
email afa-associates@hotmail.com
Agent Rhiannon Mosson

Established in 2009. Works in theatre, film, TV, commercials, corporate, musicals and promos.

Welcomes performance notices within the Greater London area if given at least 7 days' notice. Accepts approaches from actors by post and email, and welcomes showreels and invitations to view individual actors' websites. Represents actors with disabilities.

The Agency | Dublin
25 Leeson Street Lower, Dublin D02 XD77, Republic of Ireland
tel +353 1 661 8535
email office@theagency.ie
website www.theagency.ie
Directors Karl Hayden

The Agency has been representing Ireland's foremost acting talent for stage and screen since its establishment over 30 years ago. In that time its multi-award-winning clients have appeared in numerous productions worldwide, and the company continues to set the standard for excellence in acting.

AHA Talent Ltd PMA
2 Percy Street, London W1T 1DD
tel 020 7250 1760
email mail@ahatalent.co.uk
website www.ahatalent.co.uk
Twitter @AHActors
Agents Kirsten Wright, Mark Price, Darren Rugg, Kevin Brady, Chloe Brayfield, Amy Clarke *Assistants* Seetal Kaur, Eloise Mace

6 agents represent around 200 actors and creatives working in theatre, musicals, television, radio, film,

commercials, computer games, corporate role-play and voice-overs. Creative clients include designers, directors, theatre makers, choreography, heads of departments and composers.

Will consider attending performances within Greater London given 2-3 weeks' notice. Welcomes submissions (with CVs, photographs, showreels, voicereels and sae) from actors previously unknown to the agency by post or mail. Does not accept email applications or invitations to view an actor's website. *Commission*: 10-15% depending on the medium.

All Talent Agency Ltd

4/1 161 West Street, Glasgow G5 8BN
tel 0141 418 1074 *mobile* 07971 337074
email info@alltalentagency.co.uk
website www.alltalentagency.co.uk

Established in 2005. 2 agents represent 50-60 actors. Also represents other skills within the profession.

Will consider attending performances in Central London and Glasgow with at least 2-3 weeks' notice. Accepts submissions (with CVs and photographs) from actors previously unknown to the company; postal submissions preferred. Invitations to view showreels or voicereels and individual actors' websites also accepted, and follow-up calls welcomed. Welcomes enquiries from disabled actors. *Commission*: 15%.

Anita Alraun Representation

1A Queensway, Blackpool,
Lancashire FY4 2DG (correspondence address)
tel (01253) 343784
Sole Proprietor & Agent Anita Alraun

1 agent represents 20 actors. Areas of work include theatre, musicals, film, television, commercials, radio drama, corporate and some voice-overs.

Accepts submissions (with CV, photograph and SAE – essential for reply) by post only from trained/ experienced actors previously unknown to the company. Emailed submissions will not be considered. Please do not send showreels or voicereels unless requested. *Commission*: Radio 10%; Theatre 12.5%; Film and TV 12.5%; Commercials 15%.

Jonathan Altaras Associates Ltd PMA

53 Chandos Place, London WC2N 4HS
tel 020 7812 6461
email info@jaalondon.com
Agents: Wim Hance, Helen Filmer

Established in 1991. Areas of work are theatre, musicals, TV, film, commercials, corporate and voice-over.

Welcomes performance notices in the Greater London area, given as much notice as possible. Welcomes letters with CVs, photographs, showreels, voice tapes with sae. Invitations, CVs, photographs,

showreel link by email. No follow-up phone calls please. Does not currently represent actors with disabilities but is open to the idea of representing disabled actors.

ALW Associates

1 Grafton Chambers, Grafton Place,
London NW1 1LN
tel 020 7388 7018
email alw_carolpaul@talktalk.net

Established in 1977 as Vernon Conway Ltd. Sole representation of 50 actors. Areas of work include theatre, television, film and commercials.

Will consider attending performances at venues within Greater London and occasionally elsewhere with 1 week's notice. Accepts submissions (with CVs and photographs) from actors previously unknown to the company, sent by post or email. Also accepts invitations to view individual actors' websites. Showreels and voicereels should only be sent on request. *Commission*: Theatre and Radio 10-12.5%; Film and TV 12.5%; Commercials 15%.

Amber Personal Management Ltd

Colony, 9 Piccadilly Place, Manchester M1 3BR
tel 0161 228 0236
email info@amberltd.co.uk
website www.amberltd.co.uk
Twitter @ambermgmt
Agents Sally Sheridan, Jasmine Parris, Estelle Jenkins

Works in theatre, musicals, television, film, commercials, corporate and voice-over. 3 agents represent 90-100 actors. Will consider attending performances in Manchester, Leeds, Liverpool and London if given a minimum of 2 weeks' notice.

Welcomes applications via email at **apply@amberltd.co.uk**. Encourages enquiries from actors with disabilities. Spotlight Link CVs preferred. *Commission*: Recorded Media (TV/Film/Commercial) 15%; Theatre, Musicals, Corporate 10%.

The American Agency

14 Bonny Street, London NW1 9PG
tel 020 7485 8883
email americanagency@btconnect.com
Agent Ed Cobb

Areas of work include theatre, musicals, television, film, commercials, corporate and voice-overs. 2 agents represent 80 actors.

Will consider attending performances within the Greater London area. Accepts submissions (with CVs and photographs) from actors previously unknown to the agency if sent by post or email. Invitations to view individual actors' websites, showreels and voicereels are also accepted. Welcomes enquiries from disabled actors. *Commission*: Theatre 10%; Other 15%.

Angel & Francis Ltd PMA

2-6 Boundary Row, London SE1 8HP
tel 020 7439 3086

email submissions@angelandfrancis.co.uk
Twitter @AngelFrancisLtd
Director Kevin Francis *Senior Agent* Ryan Dixon

Established in 1976. 2 agents represent about 80 actors and leading TV/film casting directors and creatives. Areas of work include theatre, television, film and commercials. *Commission*: 10-12.5%.

Christopher Antony Associates
Building 3, 566 Chiswick High Road,
London W4 5YA
tel 020 8994 9952
email info@christopherantony.co.uk
website www.christopherantony.co.uk
Agents Chris Sheils, Kerry Walker

Christopher Antony Associates has been operational since 2006. Offers a personal management service specialising in musical theatre. As theatre agents, represents a small and diverse list of artistes in the West End, UK tours and overseas.

APM Associates
Elstree Film Studios, Shenley Road,
Borehamwood WD6 1JG
tel 020 8953 7377
email apm@apmassociates.net
website www.apmassociates.net
Twitter @apmassociates
Managing Director Linda French

APM Associates represent clients in all fields of the entertainment industry, including television, film, theatre, musical theatre, commercials and dance.

APM welcomes applications from both experienced performers and graduates of accredited drama schools via email, together with a Spotlgiht Profile link. *Commission*: Brochure and specimen contract available upon offer of interview.

ARG (Artists Rights Group Ltd) PMA
4A Exmoor Street, London W10 6BD
tel 020 7436 6400
email comiskey@argtalent.com
website www.argtalent.com
Agents Sue Latimer (assisted by Sarah Spahovic), Claire Cominsky (assisted by Katherine Darke), Tiffany Grayson

Established in 2001. Represents approximately 60 actors, as well as presenters and production in the areas of theatre, musicals, film, TV and corporate.

Welcomes performance notices UK wide, ideally with a week or more notice. Please send letters (with CV and photographers), CVs, showreels and photographs by email.

The Artists Partnership PMA
21-22 Warwick Street, London W1B 5NE
tel 020 7439 1456
email email@theartistspartnership.co.uk
website www.theartistspartnership.co.uk

Managing Director Roger Charteris *Agents* Alice Coles, Kimberley Donovan, Annalisa Gordon, Emily Hayward-Whitlock, Miranda Hefferman, Saskia Mulder, Leigh Rodda, Zoe Stoker, Robert Taylor, Lottie Champness, Harry Wilson, Sarah Vignoles

Represents actors, directors, writers, experts and speakers for theatre, television, film, commercials, voice-overs, speaking and literary opportunities.

Jonathan Arun Group (JAG) PMA
37 Pearman Street, London SE1 7RB
tel 020 7840 0123
email info@jag-london.com
website www.jag-london.com
Twitter @_jag_london
Instagram @_jag_london
Agents Jonathan Arun, Max Latimer, Rachel Chambers, Maria Girod-Roux (Commercials)
Assistant Vena Dacent

Established in 2007. Main areas of work are theatre, film, television, musical theatre, commercials and American TV/film. Will consider attending performances if given at least 3 weeks' notice.

Please approach the agency by email only, with Spotlight link and showreel. Tries to respond to all, but if interested in taking further will always respond within 2 weeks.

Asquith & Horner (Joined with Elspeth Cochrane PM)
The Studio, 14 College Road, Bromley BR1 3NS
tel 07770 482144
email asquith@dircon.co.uk
Senior Partner Anthony Vander Elst *Partner* Helen Melville

Established 1989 and lately joined with Elspeth Cochrane Personal Management (established 1960). 2 agents represent 30 actors. Also represented are directors, choreographers, presenters, singers, dancers and commercial models. Areas of work include theatre, musicals, television, film, commercials, corporate and voice-overs.

Will consider attending performances at venues within Greater London and elsewhere, but requests as much notice as possible. Accepts submissions (CVs and photographs) from actors previously unknown to the company; also accepts showreels and voicereels, and invitations to view actors' websites. "Unsolicited enquiries should always be accompanied by an appropriately stamped and addressed envelope for return of answer, photo, voicereel, etc." Please avoid sending large email files without prior warning.

Associated International Management (AIM) PMA
Suite 11, 25-27 Heath Street, London NW3 6TR
tel 020 7831 9709
email info@aimagents.com
website www.aimagents.com

Key contacts Stephen Gittins, Alexander Clarkson, Jonathan Clarkson-Wild

An international management established in 1984. Agents represent around 60 actors. Areas of work include theatre, television, film and commercials.

Will consider attending performances within the Greater London area with at least 3 weeks' notice. Accepts submissions (with CVs and photographs) from actors previously unknown to the agency if sent by post, but not by email. *Commission*: 12.5%.

BAM Associates (UK) Ltd

Benets, Dolberrow, Churchill, Bristol BS25 5NT
tel (01934) 852942 *mobile* 07501 720047
email casting@ebam.tv
website www.ebam.tv

Represents 80 actors. Areas of work include television, film, commercials, theatre, musicals, corporate, radio and voice-overs.

Welcomes emailed submissions from actors seeking representation. *Commission*: Theatre 10%; Mechanical Media 15%.

Gavin Barker Associates Ltd PMA

2D Wimpole Street, London W1G 0EB
tel 020 7499 4777
email assistant@gavinbarkerassociates.co.uk
website www.gavinbarkerassociates.co.uk
Managing Director Gavin Barker *Associate Director* Michelle Burke *Agent* Chris Davis *Junior Assistant* Phil Mennell

Established in 1998. 3 agents represent 80 actors and a handful of creatives. Areas of work include theatre, musicals, television, film, commercials, corporate and voice-overs. Also represents directors and choreographers.

Will consider attending performances at venues in Greater London given at least 3 weeks' notice. Accepts submissions (with CVs and photographs) from actors previously unknown to the company if sent by email. Follow-up calls are not welcome. Happy to receive showreels and voicereels. "We do not currently represent any disabled actors, but would consider each applicant on a case by case basis." *Commission*: 10-15%.

Becca Barr Management

First Floor, 37 Foley St, London W1W 7TN
tel 020 3137 2980
website www.beccabarrmanagement.co.uk
Facebook www.facebook.com/Beccabarrmanagement
Twitter @BeccaBarrmgmt
Instagram @beccabarrrmanagement

BBM represents an eclectic mix of talent ranging from presenters to experts, actors, social influencers and content creators.

Accepts submissions by email (with CVs and photographs). Showreels and voicereels are also welcome. Query via online form.

Becky Barrett Management PMA

7-10 Adam Street, London WC2N 6AA
tel 020 3773 9590
email info@bbm.agency
website www.beckybarrettmanagement.co.uk
Facebook www.facebook.com/BBMAgents
Twitter @BBMAgents
Managing Director Becky Barrett *Agents* Danielle Crockford, Tracey Andrews

Established in 2014. Main areas of work are theatre, film, TV and commercials. BBM offers a personal management service with a strong focus on triple threat performers. The company represents 120 actors.

Welcomes applications from both experienced performers and new graduates from accredited schools. Please send submissions to representation@bbm.agency including your Spotlight link and showreel links. *Commission*: Theatre 12.5%; television commercials and all other entertainment activites 15%.

EBA (Eamonn Bedford Agency)

1st Floor, 28 Mortimer Street, London W1W 7RD
tel 020 7734 9632
email info@eamonnbedford.com
email enquiries@eamonnbedford.com
website www.eamonnbedford.com
Agents Eamonn Bedford, Charlie Cox, Katie McCord

Established in 2012. 3 agents represent 100 clients. Areas of work include theatre, film and TV.

Accepts CVs with photographs from those seeking representation, via email. *Commission*: TV and Film 12.5%, Theatre 10%.

Olivia Bell Management PMA

191 Wardour Street, London W1F 8ZF
tel 020 7439 3270
email xania@olivia-bell.co.uk
Managing Director Xania Segal *Agents* Robin Hudson, Gavin Mills, Antony Read, Harriet Kingdon, Julie Gordon, Ellie Nelson

Established in 2001. 7 agents represent 130 actors. Areas of work include theatre, musicals, television, film and commercials.

Will consider attending performances at venues within Greater London with a minimum of 1 week's notice. Accepts submissions (with CVs and photographs) from actors previously unknown to the company if sent by post. Invitations to view individual actors' websites and showreels or voicereels are also accepted. *Commission*: 12.5–20%.

Jorg Betts Associates PMA

2 John Street, London WC1N 2ES
tel 020 3405 4546
email agents@jorgbetts.com

Established in 2001. Areas of work include theatre,

Agents and casting directors

musicals, television, film, commercials and corporates. Also represents directors, casting directors, choreographers and presenters.

Accepts submissions (with CVs and photographs) from actors previously unknown to the company if sent by post.

Rebecca Blond Associates PMA

69A Kings Road, London SW3 4NX
tel 020 7351 4100
email info@rebeccablond.com
Agent Rebecca Blond

Established in 1991. 2 agents represent around 60 actors in all areas of acting work; also represents directors.

Welcomes performance notices for shows within Greater London with 2 weeks' notice. Welcomes representation enquiries (with CV and photographs) by post or email, as well as showreels and invitations to view individual actors' websites. Does not welcome follow-up calls. *Commission*: Varies.

Bloomfields Welch Management PMA

Working From Southwark, The Hoxton Hotel, Colombo Street, London SE1 8DP
tel 020 7659 2001
email submissions@bloomfieldswelch.com
website www.bloomfieldswelch.com
Twitter @bwmgt
Director Emma Bloomfield *Agents* Barnaby Welch, Clare Partridge

Established in 2004. Areas of work include theatre, musicals, television, film, commercials and corporate. 3 agents.

Will consider attending performances anywhere, given at least 2 weeks' notice. Accepts submissions (with CVs and photographs) from actors previously unknown to the company if sent by email, but not by post. Invitations to view individual actors' websites, showreels and voicereels are also accepted. Welcomes enquiries from disabled actors.

Blue Star Associates

7-8 Shaldon Mansions, 132 Charing Cross Road, London WC2H 0LA
tel 020 7836 6220
email bluestar.london.2000@gmail.com
Director Keith Hopkins *Associate Director* Joshua Lawson

Established in 2007 (formerly Barrie Stacey Promotions, established 1960). Works in theatre, musicals, pantomime, television, film and commercials. Around 70 actors represented. Will consider attending performances in the Greater London area.

Welcomes letters (with CVs and photographs) sent by post or email. Does not represent actors with disabilities. *Commission*: Theatre 10%; TV/Film 15%.

Sandra Boyce Management PMA

125 Dynevor Road, London N16 0DA
tel 020 7923 0606
email info@sandraboyce.com
Agent Sandra Boyce (MD)

2 agents represent 50 actors in all areas of acting work; directors also represented.

Welcomes performance notices if given at least 2 weeks' notice, and is prepared to travel within the Greater London area. Happy to accept letters (by post, enclose SAE) with CVs and photographs from individuals previously unknown to the company, but does not welcome follow-up calls. Encourages approaches from disabled actors. Also welcomes showreels and voicereels.

Michelle Braidman Associates Ltd PMA

2 Futura House, 169 Grange Road, London SE1 3BN
tel 020 7237 3523
email info@braidman.com
website www.braidman.com
Twitter @TeamBraidman
Agents Michelle Braidman, Nicola Whitworth, Rebecca Kirby

Established in 1983. A leading international theatrical agency representing actors, directors and creative talent.

Submissions should be sent electronically to **representation@braidman.com**.

British Talent Agency®

website www.britishtalent.net

Established in 2009. Main areas of work include: film, TV, commercials, documentary, video games, all forms of theatre, musical theatre, dance cruises, resorts, voice over, presenting, modelling, events, corporate, webisodes, apps and new media. Represents professional actors, singers, dancers, writers, directors, presenters, comedians, models, recording artists and bands throughout the world including across the UK, USA, EU and Canada, and as far afield as the Middle East and Australia.

Welcomes contact by actors previously unknown to the agency, if made by website contact form with cover note and links to Spotlight and/or IMDb. No attachments. Please visit our website and read our contact policy before approaching. "Invitations to shows are always welcome."

BROOD PMA

49 Greek Street, London W1D 4EG
tel 020 7998 7861
website www.broodmanagement.com
Twitter @broodlondon
Main Agent Brian Parsonage-Kelly

Represents 60 actors and personalities. Clients work throughout the industry from Hollywood to Fringe, corporates to cruises and soaps to commercials.

Prospective clients please visit the website, apply by email only to **broodapplication@aol.com**.

Brown, Simcocks & Andrews LLP PMA

504 The Chandlery, 50 Westminster Bridge Road, London SE1 7QY
tel 020 7953 7484/020 7953 7494
email info@bsaagency.co.uk
website www.brownsimcocksandandrews.co.uk
Partners Carrie Simcocks (retired), Kelly Andrews

Established in the 1970s. Areas of work include theatre, musicals, television, film, commercials and corporate. Not taking new clients.

The BWH Agency Ltd PMA

85 Great Portland Street, 1st Floor, London W1W 7LT
tel 020 7734 0657
email info@thebwhagency.co.uk
website www.thebwhagency.co.uk
Agents & Company Directors Joe Hutton, Bill Petrie, Lisa Willoughby, Andrew Braidford *Agent* Holly Davidson *Assistants* Nicole Robinson, Oliver Campbell *Accountant* Maddie Burdett-Couts

Established in 2004, main areas of work are theatre, musicals, TV, film, commercials and radio. Welcomes submissions by email only, CVs, photographs and showreels.

Paul Byram Associates (THE AGENCY) PMA

Suite B0079, The Long Lodge, 265-269 Kingston Road, Wimbledon SW19 3FW
tel 020 3137 3385
email contact@paulbyram.com
website www.paulbyram.com
Senior Agent Paul Byram *Agent* Jason Jenkins

Established in 2010 main areas of work are TV, theatre, film, commercials, corporate and musicals. Represents 50 actors, as well as casting directors and directors. Charges commission on a sliding scale.

Welcomes perfomance notices within central London and Fringe venues with 2 weeks' notice; will occasionally go further afield with greater notice. All contact via the company website contact page or, worst case, via email only. No post please. Represents actor with disabilities.

CAM (Creative Artists Management) PMA

55-59 Shaftesbury Avenue, London W1D 6LD
tel 020 7292 0600
email reception@cam.co.uk
website www.cam.co.uk
Twitter @CAM_London
Agents Michael Wiggs, Dawn Green, Peter Brooks, Samantha Boyd, Bex Elliff, Lucy Doyle; *Assistants* Alex Scanlan, Lucinda Francis, Caitlin O'Farrell, Kev Reddington

Founded in 1988. Main areas of work include film, television, theatre, musical theatre, commercials, corporate and voice over. Represents about 280 actors; also represents directors. Welcomes performance notices if given about a week's notice, mainly in London, but will consider travelling further afield depending on show/venue/agent availability. Welcomes CVs and photos, and showreels sent by email. Follow-up phone calls not necessary. *Commission*: varies depending on contract.

Carey Dodd Associates PMA

78 York Street, London W1H 1DP
tel 020 7993 4992
email agents@careydoddassociates.com
email applications@careydoddassociates.com
Agents Christopher Carey, Samantha Dodd *Assistant* Megan Check

Jessica Carney Associates PMA

4th Floor, 23 Golden Square, London W1F 9JP
tel 020 7434 4143
email assistant@jcarneyassociates.co.uk
website www.jessicacarneyassociates.co.uk

Established in 1950. Areas of work include: theatre, television, films, commercials and musicals. Also represents technicians and craftspeople.

Cannot consider actors for representation unless they can be seen in performance (not showcase) within Greater London (requires 2-3 weeks' notice), or possess good mainstream TV credits. Only accepts submissions if sent by email to **representation@jcarneyassociates.co.uk**. Emails should contain a link to their Spotlight CV and showreel. *Commission*: TV/Film 12.5%; Theatre 10%; Commercials 15%.

CBL Management PMA

20 Hollingbury Rise, Brighton BN1 7HJ
mobile 07956 890307
email enquiries@cblmanagement.co.uk
website www.cblmanagement.co.uk
Facebook www.facebook.com/cblmanagement
Twitter @cblmanagement
Agents Claire Carpenter, Beth Eden, Linda Edwards

Established in 2007. 3 agents represent 90 artistes. Works in theatre, musicals, television, film, commercials, corporate and voice-over.

Welcomes CVs and photographs by email only.

CDA Ltd PMA

22 Astwood Mews, London SW7 4DE
tel 020 7937 2749
email cda@cdalondon.com
website www.cdalondon.com
Agents Belinda Wright, Laura Gibbons

2 agents represent 60 actors.

Will consider attending performances at venues

within Greater London with 3 weeks' notice. Accepts submissions (with CVs and photographs) from actors previously unknown to the company if sent by post. Showreels, voicereels and invitations to view individual actors' websites are also accepted. *Commission*: Variable.

Centre Stage Agency

7 Rutledge Terrace, South Circular Road, Dublin 8
tel +353 1 453 3599
website www.centerstageagency.com

Founded 1994, areas of work include theatre, television, film, musicals, voice-over, commercial and web-based work.

Will consider attending performances at venues in Dublin with 1 weeks' notice. Accepts submissions (with CVs and photographs). Showreels are also welcome. Query via the form on the website. *Commission*: 10-15%.

Esta Charkham Associates

16 British Grove, Chiswick, London W4 2NL
tel 020 8741 2843
email office@charkham.net
website www.charkham.net

Established in 2010. Areas of work include theatre, film, TV, radio, voice-over and comedy.

Will consider attending performances at venues in the Greater London area with at least 2 weeks' notice. Accepts submissions via email to **representation@charkham.net** with a covering letter. Does not accept follow-up calls.

Sharry Clark Artists

tel 020 8349 9824; Welsh office (01792) 401112
email info@petercharlesworth.co.uk
email sharryclarkartists@gmail.com
website https://sharryclarkartists.wordpress.com
Facebook www.facebook.com/SharryClarkArtists
Twitter @SharryCArtists
Director Sharry Clark

Does not welcome unsolicited contact – including performance notices – from actors previously unknown to the company.

Claypole Management

Kemp House, 152-160 City Road,
London EC1V 2NX
tel 020 3693 3830
email info@claypolemanagement.co.uk
website www.claypolemanagement.co.uk

Established in 2000. Areas of work include: theatre, musicals, television, film, commercials and corporate.

Will consider attending performances. Welcomes Spotlight, Casting Network and Mandy links to showreels via email. Also welcomes invitations to view individual actors' websites, showreels or Spotlight links. Happy to receive applications for representation from disabled actors.

Clic Agency

Bangor, Gwynedd
mobile 07979 713381
email clic@btinternet.com
website www.clicagency.co.uk
Facebook www.facebook.com/groups/168535334204/
Twitter @clicagency
Proprietor Helen Pritchard

Established in 2008. Represents around 50 actors from all over the UK. Also carries out casting for productions being filmed in North Wales.

Accepts submissions (with CVs and photographs) from actors previously unknown to the company, sent by email. Encourages enquiries from disabled actors and welcomes showreels, voicereels, follow-up calls and invitations to view individual actors' websites. *Commission*: Varies, but not more than 15%.

Elspeth Cochrane Personal Management

Now amalgamated with Asquith & Horner. See the company's entry under *Agents* on page 59.

Cole Kitchenn Personal Management Ltd PMA

See the entry for InterTalent Rights Group on page 70 .

Shane Collins Associates

Flat 31 The Courtyard, 154 Goswell Road,
London EC1V 7DX
tel 020 7253 1010
email info@shanecollins.co.uk
website www.shanecollins.co.uk
Agent Shane Collins

Established in 1986, the agency represents around 85 actors working in all areas of the industry.

Will consider attending performances within Greater London given as much notice as possible. Accepts submissions from actors previously unknown to the company sent to **submissions@shanecollins.co.uk**.

Conway Van Gelder Grant PMA

3rd Floor, 8-12 Broadwick Street, London W1F 8HN
tel 020 7287 0077
email info@conwayvg.co.uk
Agents John Grant (*Assistants* Alice Smith, Deborah Charlton and James Evans), Nicola van Gelder (*Assistants* Rachael Swanston and Clarissa Efthymiades), Nicholas Gall (*Assistant* James Evans), Kat Oliver (*Assistant* Georgie Davies), Greg Herst

5 agents represent actors working in all areas of the industry.

Will consider attending performances within Greater London and occasionally elsewhere, given 3-4 weeks' notice. Accepts submissions by email from actors previously unknown to the agency, along with invitations to view an actor's website. Showreels and voicereels should only be sent if requested after initial contact has been made. Follow-up telephone calls and emails are not welcomed. *Commission*: Varies according to contract.

Howard Cooke Associates (HCA) PMA

19 Coulson Street, London SW3 3NA
tel 020 7591 0144
Managing Director/Senior Agent Howard Cooke

HCA is now a personal management company and is open to existing clients only.

Cooper Searle Personal Management Ltd

3rd Floor, 207 Regent Street, London W1B 3HH
tel 020 7183 4851
mobile 07538 561441 / 07795 261662
email admin@coopersearle.com
website www.coopersearle.com
Twitter @CooperSearle
Instagram @coopersearlepersonalmanagement
Theatrical Agency Director Emily Rose *Agent* Paul Rose

Established in 2010. Represents around 60 clients. Main areas of work are theatre, musicals, television, film, commercials, corporate and stills.

Will try to attend performances if it is possible and welcomes approaches from actors. Will always see clients perform. Applications should be via email containing actor's Spotlight link and any other relevant material or links.The agency considers every application based on performance ability and marketability. *Commission*: 12.5-20%.

Lou Coulson Associates Ltd PMA

96 Webber Street, London SE1 0QN
tel 020 7734 9633
email lou@loucoulson.co.uk
website loucoulson.co.uk
Agents Lou Coulson, Tom Reed, Megan Wheldon, Anne-Rose Yuill, Amy Higgins, Victoria Davidson, Louise Bedford *Assistants* Kim Wiles, Harry Shepherd-Smith, Hannah Barker, Nicola Arnold

Represents actors working in all areas of the industry and has strong relationships with US agencies and managers.

Will consider attending performances within Greater London and occasionally elsewhere, given notice. Accepts postal submissions (with CVs, photographs and sae to ensure reply) from actors previously unknown to the agency, along with invitations to view an actor's website. Showreels should only be sent if requested after initial contact has been made. Follow-up telephone calls and emails not welcome. *Commission*: varies according to contracts.

Coulter Hamilton (CHR) PMA

Glasgow office: The Pentagon Centre, Washington Street, Glasgow G3 8AZ

tel 0141 204 4058
email info@coulterhamiltonrae.com
London office: Suite B01, Parkhall Business Centre, 40 Martell Road, London SE21 8EN
tel 020 7139 5027
website www.coulterhamiltonrae.com
Twitter @coulterhamrae
Instagram @coulterhamiltonrae
Agent & Managing Director Julie Hamilton *Agent & Partner* Gary Rae *Young Performers* Gary Hamilton *Office Manager* Fran Bloomer *Assistant* Ally Saxon

Coulter Hamilton Rae is one of the UK's leading talent agencies, focusing exclusively on performers and creatives in all media, with offices in London and Glasgow. Areas of work include theatre, television, film, commercials, corporate and voice-overs.

Accepts submissions (with CVs and photographs) from actors previously unknown to the company if sent by email. Showreels and voicereels are also accepted. *Commission*: 7.5-15% (sliding scale).

Lizanne Crowther Management Ltd PMA

57 Trinity Rise, London SW2 2QP
tel 020 3764 5334
email mail@lcm.limited
website www.lcm.limited
Twitter @lcm_limited
Instagram @lcm_limited
Agent Lizanne Crowther

Represents 85 actors.

Accepts submissions by email from actors previously unknown to the company. Send a covering letter, CV and headshot by email with the subject 'Representation' or send hard copies with an sae if you want your headshot to be returned.

Curtis Brown Ltd PMA

Haymarket House, 28-29 Haymarket, London SW1Y 4SP
tel 020 7393 4400
email info@curtisbrown.co.uk
website www.curtisbrown.co.uk
Agents Tiffany Agbeko, Debi Allen, Lara Beach (*Assistant* Ashleigh Hall); Kate Buckle, Jacquie Drew (*Assistants* Emma Power and Madeleine Newman-Suttle); Oriana Elia (*Assistants* Jack Collins and Isabelle Whitaker); Mary Fitzgerald and Lucy Johnson (*Assistant* Inez Baxter); Sophie Holden, Cordelia Keaney, Alistair Lindsey-Renton and Helen Clarkson (*Assistants* Emma Bennett and Ronan McCabe); Sarah MacCormack and Emma Higginbottom (*Assistant* Josh Byrne); Charlene McManus (*Assistant* Jessica Lax); Adam Maskwell, Grant Parsons, Joe Powell, Kate Staddon (*Assistants* Abigail Millar and Isabelle Sweetland); Frances Stevenson and Jessica Jackson (*Assistant* Emily Hughes); Sam Turnbull, Olivia Woodward (*Assistant* Alex Sedgley).

One of Europe's oldest and largest independent literary and media agencies. Established over 100 years ago, there are now more than 20 agents within the Book, Media, Actors and Presenters Divisions, 5 of whom represent actors. Also represents writers, directors, playwrights and celebrities.

Submissions should be sent by post and addressed to 'Actors Agents'. They should include a covering letter with email address, CV, photograph, showreel (if actor has one) and sae for the return of the showreel. Tries to respond within 4-6 weeks. Does not meet potential clients before viewing their work. Does not accept emailed submissions. *Commission*: 12.5-15%.

David Daly Associates
London office: 586 King's Road, London SW6 2DX
tel 020 7384 1036
email agent@daviddaly.co.uk
Manchester office: 16 King Street, Knutsford WA16 6DL
tel 01565 631999
email north@daviddaly.co.uk
website www.daviddaly.co.uk
Twitter @DavidDalyAssoc
Agents David Daly, Rosalind Bach (London); David Daly, Mary Ramsay (Manchester)

An established actors' agency bringing over 30 years of experience to the entertainment industry.

CDM Ltd PMA
Fourth Floor, 80-81 St Martin's Lane, London WC2N 4AA
email mgattrell@cdm-ltd.com
website www.cdm-ltd.com
Managing Director Michael Gattrell

Areas of work are theatre, musicals, TV, film, commercials and corporate. 3 agents represent 140 actors; directors, choreographers, designers and musical directors are also represented.

Will consider attending performances within Greater London and elsewhere, given as much notice as possible. Welcomes letters (with CVs and photographs) from actors previously unknown to the agency, sent by post or email. Does not welcome follow-up calls. Accepts showreels, voicereels and invitations to view individual actors' websites. Encourages applications from actors with disabilities.

Davis Bishop Associates
Cotton's Farmhouse, 28 Whiston Road, Cogenhoe, Northamptonshire NN7 1NL
tel (01604) 891487
email admin@cottonsfarmhouse.org
Agents Lena Davis, John Bishop

Established in 1986. Areas of work include theatre, musicals, television, film, commercials, corporate, voice-overs. Also represent other skills within the profession.

Will consider attending performances in Greater London with plenty of notice. Accepts submissions

(with CVs and photographs) from actors unknown to the company. Follow-up calls and email submissions are not welcomed. *Commission*: 10-20%.

Denton Brierley PMA
12-18 Hoxton Street, London N1 6NG
tel 020 3866 5747
email info@dentonbrierley.com
Instagram @dentonbrierley
Agents Suzy Brierley, Gavin Denton-Jones, Sofe Goodwin, Simon Grant Jones

Four agents represent actors working in all areas of the industry. Will consider attending performances within Greater London, given 2 weeks' notice. Accepts email submissions (with Spotlight CVs, photographs and showreels) from actors previously unknown to the agency. *Commission*: varies according to contract.

Devine Artist Management
email manchester@devinemanagement.co.uk
website www.devinemanagement.co.uk

Works in all areas. A paperless office which only accepts applications by email. Prefers to view showreels via a link. Does not welcome follow-up calls. Only represents actors with a disability and encourages applications from such individuals.

Diamond Management PMA
31 Percy Street, London W1T 2DD
tel 020 7631 0400
email agents@diman.co.uk
website www.diamondmanagement.co.uk
Agents Lesley Duff, Jean Diamond, Clare Partridge

Established in 2003. Main areas of work are TV, theatre, commercials and film; also represents directors, MDs, writers and costume designers.

Welcomes letters (with CVs and photographs), follow-up phone calls, CVs and photographs sent by email, showreels, voice tapes and invitations to view actors' websites. Represents actors with disabilities. *Commission* 12.5%.

DQ Management
10 Argyll House, Marlborough Drive, Bushey, Herts. WD23 2PS
tel (01273) 721221 *mobile* 07713 984633
email dq.management1@gmail.com
website www.dqmanagement.com
Senior Partners Peter Davis, Kate Davis

Established in 2003. Areas of work include theatre, musicals, television, film, commercials and corporate. 2 agents represent 80 actors.

Will consider attending performances within the Greater London area and elsewhere with at least 2 weeks' notice. Accepts submissions (with CVs and photographs) from actors previously unknown to the company if sent by post. Invitations to view individuals' websites, showreels or voicereels are also accepted. Welcomes enquiries from disabled actors. *Commission*: Theatre 10%; West End 12.5%; TV/Film/Commercials 15%.

Kenneth Earle Personal Management

214 Brixton Road, London SW9 6AP
tel 020 7274 1219
email kennethearle@agents-uk.com
website www.kennethearlepersonalmanagement.com

Established in 2000. 3 agents represent around 40 actors. Areas of work include theatre, musicals, television, film, commercials, corporate and voice-over.

Accepts submissions (with CVs and photographs) from actors previously unknown to the company if sent by post or email. No telephone calls. Please include any showreels, voicereels, demos, links, websites and invitations. *Commission*: 15%.

Emptage Hallett PMA

Cardiff Office: 2nd Floor, 3-5 The Balcony, Castle Arcade, Cardiff CF10 1BU
tel (02920) 344205
email cardiff@emptagehallett.co.uk
London Office: 3rd Floor, 34-35 Eastcastle Street, London W1W 8DW
tel 020 7436 0425
email mail@emptagehallett.co.uk
website www.emptagehallettcardiff.co.uk
website www.emptagehallett.co.uk
Twitter @EHCardiff, @emptagehallett
Instagram @emptagehallet
Cardiff Office: *Agents* Gemma McAvoy, Alexa Flynn; London Office: *Directors* Michael Emptage, Michael Hallett, Sarah Highland *Agents* Hannah Wilkinson, Laura Nassim *Voiceover Agent* Jody Salt

Cardiff Office: Founded in 1999, main area of work is theatre, TV, film, commercials, voice-over, videogames and corporate. Represents around 90 actors, and also directors, presenters, writers, fight directors and casting directors. Charges standard PMA rates. Will make every effort to attend performances in Cardiff and surrounding areas. Happy to receive emails with links to view showreels, voicereels and Spotlight CV link. Committed to providing equal opportunities for all irrespective of colour, race, religion or belief, ethnic or national origins, gender, marital or civil partnership status, disability or age.

London Office: Represents an exclusive list of actors, writers and casting directors working in film, television and theatre. Welcomes representation enquiries which include a covering email and a link to their Spotlight CV and showreel, contact **submissions@emptagehallett.co.uk**. Writers should email **writers@emptagehallett.co.uk**.

The Jane Estall Agency

37 Madeira Drive, Hastings TN34 2NH
mobile 07703 550006

email thejaneestallagency@gmail.com
website www.thejaneestallagency.webeden.com
Owner/Director Jane Estall

Established in 2010. Represents around 25 actors. Areas of work include theatre, musicals, TV, film, commercials, corporate and voice-over. Also represents stand-up comedians and chaperones.

Will consider attending performances, given 1 week's notice. Welcomes submissions (with CVs and photographs) from actors previously unknown to the agency, sent by post and email; also accepts showreels, voice tapes and invitations to view individual actors' websites. Represents actors with disabilities.

Paola Farino

109 St George's Road, London SE1 6HY
tel 020 7207 0858
email info@paolafarino.co.uk
website www.paolafarino.co.uk

Established in 2007. Sole agent, works in theatre, TV, film, commercials, corporate and photography. Will consider attending performances within Greater London. Prefers to receive performance notices and all other approaches by email – include Spotlight PIN. "Check website first to see if there is anybody else represented with a similar MO."

Feast Management Ltd PMA

tel 020 7354 5216
email office@feastmanagement.co.uk
website www.feastmanagement.co.uk
Agents Helen Seagriff, Lisa Stark

2 agents represent actors. Areas of work include theatre, musicals, television, film, radio, commercials, corporate and voice-overs.

Will consider attending performances in the London area if plenty of notice is given. Accepts submissions by email from actors previously unknown to the company.

Kerry Foley Management Ltd

mobile 07747 864001
email kerry@kfmltd.com
website www.kfmltd.com
Twitter @KFM_Agency
Director Kerry Foley

Established in 2011. Main areas of work are theatre, musicals, television, film, commercials and corporate. Also represents creatives, including directors, musical directors and choreographers. Will consider CVs and photographs sent by email. Agency is open to all actors on their merits.

James Foster Ltd

7 Bell Yard, London WC2A 2JR
tel 020 7434 0398
email info@jamesfosterltd.co.uk
website www.jamesfosterltd.co.uk
Twitter @JamesFosterLTD

Managing Director/Senior Agent James Foster

Originally Jeremy Brook Limited and Jean Clarke Management (established in 1995). Areas of work include theatre, musicals, television, film, commercials, corporate and radio.

Will consider attending performances in Greater London with at least 3-4 weeks' notice. Accepts submissions from actors previously unknown to the agency by email (see website for further details). Showreels, voicereels and invitations to views an actor's website are also accepted, but follow-up calls and emails are not welcome.

Julie Fox Associates

tel London 020 3092 1512 North (01270) 780880
email agent@juliefoxassociates.co.uk
website www.juliefoxassociates.co.uk
Agents Julie Fox, Corrine Murray

Agency works in all areas of live and recorded media. 2 agents represent 50 actors; directors and casting directors also represented. Accepts email approaches only (letters, CVs, showreels or links to Spotlight).

Hilary Gagan Associates PMA

187 Drury Lane, London WC2B 5QD
tel 020 7404 8794
email hilary@hgassoc.co.uk
Agent Hilary Gagan

3 agents represent approximately 100 actors. Areas of work include theatre, musicals, television, film, commercials, corporate, voice-overs. Also represents directors and choreographers.

Will consider attending performances in Greater London with at least 2 weeks' notice. Accepts submissions (with CVs and photographs with name on back of photograph) from actors previously unknown to the agency (include sae). Invitations to view individual actors' websites, showreels and voicereels are also accepted. Follow-up calls are welcomed, as are enquiries from disabled actors. *Commission*: 7.5–15%.

Gardner Herrity PMA

24 Conway Street, London W1T 6BG
tel 020 7388 0088
email info@gardnerherrity.co.uk
Key contacts Andy Herrity, Nicky James

Areas of work include feature films, television, theatre, video games, voice overs and radio drama.

Will consider attending performances within the Greater London area with at least 3 weeks' notice. Accepts submissions if sent by email representation@gardnerherrity.co.uk. Welcomes enquiries from disabled actors. *Commission*: 10%.

Garricks PMA

Angel House, 76 Mallinson Road,
London SW11 1BN

tel 020 7738 1600
email info@garricks.net
Key contact Megan Willis

Established in 1981. Areas of work include theatre, television, film, commercials and corporate.

Will consider attending performances at venues within Greater London and elsewhere. Accepts submissions (with CVs and photographs) from actors previously unknown to the company, sent by post or (preferably) email. Invitations to view individual actors' websites are also accepted. *Commission*: TV, Film and Theatre 10%; Commercials 15%.

Gilbert & Payne Personal Management

Room 404, 4th Floor, Linen Hall,
162-168 Regent Street, London W1B 5TB
tel 020 7734 7505
email ee@gilbertandpayne.com
Director Elena Gilbert *Key personnel* Elaine Payne

Established in 1996. 2 agents represent 50 actors. Areas of work include theatre, musicals, television, film, commercials and corporate, with a particular emphasis on musical theatre. Also represents choreographers.

Will consider attending performances at venues in Greater London with a minimum of 1 week's notice. Accepts submissions (with CVs and photographs) from actors previously unknown to the company if sent by post. Follow-up telephone calls are also accepted. *Commission*: Theatre 10%.

Global Artists PMA

6th Floor, 41-44 Great Queen Street, Covent Garden, London WC2B 5AD
tel 020 7839 4888
email info@globalartists.co.uk
website www.globalartists.co.uk

A personal management company representing professional actors and actresses. Areas of work include theatre, musical theatre, television, film, commercials and corporate. Also represents a limited number of theatre designers, choreographers, directors and musical directors.

Accepts submissions from actors previously unknown to the company, sent by post or email. Does not welcome telephone enquiries.

Gordon & French PMA

12-13 Poland Street, London W1F 8QB
tel 020 7734 4818
website www.gordonandfrench.co.uk
Agents Kate Bryden, Christina Cooke, Donna French

Established in 1972. Main areas of work are theatre, TV, film commercials and voice-over. Represents 70 performers.

Accepts requests for respresentation by post or email; the email address for submissions is
representation@gordonandfrench.co.uk. If applying

by post and would like material returned please enclose an sae. Every representation request is read but owing to the volume of material received the company is only able to respond to those submissions it would like to pursue. The company only caters for voice work for their existing clients and therefore are unable to accept these representation requests.

Grantham-Hazeldine Ltd PMA

Suite 427, The Linen Hall, 162-168 Regent Street, London W1B 5TE
tel 020 7038 3737
email agents@granthamhazeldine.com
website www.granthamhazeldine.com
Agents Gina Rowland, Nicholas Errington

Established in 1984. The agents represent actors and creatives. Areas of work include theatre, musicals, television, film, commercials, corporate and voice-overs. Also represents writers and stunt co-ordinators.

Accepts submissions (with CVs, photos and showreel) from actors previously unknown to the company if sent by email. *Commission*: Radio 10% plus VAT; Theatre 12.5% plus VAT; TV and Film 15% plus VAT.

Louise Gubbay Associates

17-19 Station Road West, Oxted, Surrey RH9 8FE
mobile 07803 551466
email louise@louisegubbay.com
website www.louisegubbay.com
Twitter @lgaagency
Managing Director Louise Gubbay

Founded in 2006. Works in theatre, musicals, television, film and commercials.

Welcomes CVs from professionally trained actors only, by email. *Commission*: Varies.

Hall James Personal Management

12 Melcombe Place, London NW1 6JJ
tel 020 3036 0558
email info@halljames.co.uk
website www.halljames.co.uk
Directors Sam Hall, Stori James

Established in 2006. Areas of work include musicals, television, film, commercials and corporate. 2 agents represent around 50 actors; also represents theatre directors and choreographers.

Welcomes performance notices and letters (with CVs) from individual actors previously unknown to the agency, as well as showreels. *Commission*: 10%

Hamilton Hodell Ltd PMA

20 Golden Square, London W1F 9JL
tel 020 7636 1221
email info@hamiltonhodell.co.uk
website www.hamiltonhodell.co.uk
Agents Christian Hodell, Christopher Farrer,

Alexander Cooke, Madeleine Dewhirst, Sian Smyth, Joshua Woodford

The agency represents actors, working in leading roles in film, television, theatre and radio productions.

The Harris Agency Ltd

71 The Avenue, Watford, Herts WD17 4NU
tel 01923 211644 *mobile* 07956 388716
email theharrisagency@btconnect.com
Agent Sharon Harris

Established in 1977. Welcomes emails with Spotlight links from actors previously unknown to the agency. Also accepts follow-up calls, showreels, voicereels, and invitations to view individual actors' websites/shows. Encourages enquiries from actors with disabilities. *Commission*: Theatre 10%; TV, Film, Commercials 15%.

Harvey Stein Associates Ltd

tel 020 7175 7937
email info@harveystein.co.uk
website www.harveystein.co.uk
Managing Director Lois Harvey

Established in 2015, with 1 agent and 1 assistant, managing a small client list working throughout the industry. Happy to receive respresentation requests by email, but no large files, just links.

HATCH Talent Ltd PMA

113 Shoreditch High Street, London EC1 6JN
tel 020 3950 6333
email info@hatchtalent.co.uk
website www.hatchtalent.co.uk
Agents Vic Murray, Michael Ford, Becky Williams, Lucy Nooshin *Agent's Assistants* Olu Abulude, Mia Pavey, Sophie Cotton

Established in 2017. Currently representing over 150 clients. Areas of work include theatre, TV, film and radio; also represents presenters, comedians and writers. Welcomes CVs, photographs and showreels sent by email. Committed to a policy of equal opportunity.

Hobsons

2 Dukes Gate, London W4 5DX
tel 020 8995 3628
email voices@hobsons-international.com
website www.hobsons-international.com
Drama Agent Christina Beyer *Commercial Agent* Linda Sacks

Areas of work include representation of voice-over artists in theatre, musicals, television, film, commercial and corporate.

Will consider attending performances at venues within Greater London given 2 weeks' notice. Accepts submissions (with CVs and photographs) from actors previously unknown to the company if sent by post. Showreels are also accepted.

Jane Hollowood Associates Ltd
17/113 Newton Street, Manchester M1 1AE
tel 0161 237 9141
email info@janehollowood.co.uk
website www.janehollowood.co.uk
Agents Jane Hollowood, Cat Grose, Janine Bardsley

Established in 1998; 3 agents represent approx. 100 actors working in many areas of the industry.

Will consider attending performances across the country, depending on diary commitments and provided that 2-3 weeks' notice is given. Accepts email submissions (with CVs, Spotlight links and photographs) from actors previously unknown to the agency. Follow-up telephone calls are unwelcome. *Commission:* Theatre 10%; Radio, Role-play and Voice-overs 12%; Television, Film and Commercials 15%.

Nancy Hudson Associates PMA
49 South Molton Street, London W1K 5LH
tel 020 7499 5548
email agents@nancyhudsonassociates.com
website www.nancyhudsonassociates.com
Twitter @NHALtd
Director & Agent Nancy Hudson

Established in 1999. 2 agents represent 80 actors. Areas of work include theatre, television, film, commercials, radio, corporate and voice-overs.

Welcomes submissions by email with Spotlight link.

Hunwick Associates PMA
3F1, 44 Howe Street, Edinburgh EH3 6TH
tel 0131 225 3860
email office@hunwickassociates.com
website www.hunwickassociates.com
Agent Maryam Hunwick

Personal management agency established in 1999. 1 agent represents actors in all media including several BAFTA and BIFA award-winning stage, screen and television artists.

Will consider attending performances at venues within Greater London and in Scotland given 4 weeks' notice. Accepts submissions (with CVs and photographs) from actors previously unknown to the company. Will also accept showreels. *Commission:* Theatre 10%; TV and Broadcast Media 12.5%; Commercials 15%.

IAMBE Productions Ltd
376 London Road, Hadleigh, Essex SS7 2DA
mobile 07834 584977
email admin@iambeproductions.com
website www.iambeproductions.com
Twitter @Acts4events

Established in 2015. Areas of work include theatre, film, corporate and festivals.

Will consider attending performances, though this is dependent on client. Accepts submissions by email

(with CVs and photographs) and links to showreels. Happy to consider applications for representation from disabled actors. *Commission:* Varies.

Icon Actors Management
Tanzaro House, Ardwick Green North,
Manchester M12 6FZ
tel 0161 273 3344
email info@iconactors.net
website www.iconactors.net
Agent Kirstie Jones

Established in 2000. Areas of work include theatre, musicals, television, film, commercials, corporate and voice-overs.

iD Agency Limited
6 Paramount Court, 41 University Street,
London WC1E 6JP
mobile 07528 381833
email info@theidagency.co.uk
website www.theidagency.co.uk
Company Director Barbara Adie

Established in 2011. Works in theatre, musicals, TV, film, commercials, corporate and presenting. 2 agents represent 30 clients (actors and presenters).

Will consider attending performances in London. Actors should send Spotlight link via the form on the website **www.theidagency.co.uk**. *Commission:* 12.5%, 20% for commercial.

IDAMOS Agency
1 Frederick Court, London E18 1LE
tel 020 3318 0244
email idamosagency@gmail.com
website www.idamos.com
Director Liz Isaac *Head Agent* Phillip Barnes

Established in 2012, IDAMOS represents actors with unique skills in a variety of performance fields, including theatre, musicals, film, TV, commercials, corporate and voice-over. 2 agents represent 55 actors.

Will consider attending performances at venues within Greater London with 2 weeks' notice. Accepts submissions (with CVs and photographs), and also happy to receive showreels, voicereels and invitations to view individual actors' websites, all via email.

Identity Agency Group (IAG) PMA
20 Noel Street, London W1F 8GW
tel 020 3915 3980
email casting@iagtalent.com
website www.iagtalent.com
Agents in theatre, film and TV Femi Oguns (CEO), Ikki El-Amriti, Jonathan Hall, Julianna, Nina Malone

Established in 2006. Full respresentation with IAG is by invitation only. Does not accept submissions via email or post.

Imperial Personal Management Ltd
102 Kirkstall Road, Leeds LS3 1JA
tel 0113 244 3222

email katie@ipmcasting.com
website www.ipmcasting.com
Managing Director Katie Ross

Established in 2007. 4 agents represent 30-50 actors working in television and film; also has a subsidiary company, IPM Crew. Recommends Imperial Photography (**info@ipmcasting.com**).

Welcomes performance notices within the Greater London and Northern areas (within 50 miles of the company's postcode), and prefers 1 month's notice if possible. Welcomes letters (with CVs and photographs) from individual actors previously unknown to the agency, sent by post or email. Accepts follow-up telephone calls, showreels and voicereels, and welcomes invitations to view individual actors' websites. Encourages enquiries from actors with disabilities. *Commission*: 10-15%.

Inclusive Talent

Kinettles, Grange Road, Duxford, Cambs. CB22 4WF
tel 07841 990611
email agent@inclusivetalent.co.uk
website www.inclusivetalent.co.uk
Twitter @incTalentUK
Instagram @inclusivetalentuk

Agency that represents people of all ages, with or without disabilities as well as Neurodiverse performers. Runs regular open casting in London and around the country.

Independent Talent Group Ltd PMA

40 Whitfield Street, London W1T 2RH
tel 020 7636 6565

Areas of work include theatre, musicals, television, film, commercials, corporate and voice-overs. Also represents directors, writers, technicians and presenters.

Will consider attending performances at venues within Greater London. Please see the website for up-to-date submission policies. *Commission*: 12.5%.

Inter-City Casting

27 Wigan Lane, Wigan,
Greater Manchester WN1 1XR
tel 01942 321969
email intercitycasting@btconnect.com
Agent Caroline Joynt

Established in 1983. 2 agents represent approximately 60 actors. Areas of work include theatre, musicals, television, film, commercials and corporate.

Will consider attending performances at venues in Manchester and Liverpool. Accepts submissions (with CVs and photographs) from actors previously unknown to the company if sent by post. Showreels, voicereels and invitations to view individual actors' websites also accepted. Recommends the photographer Michael Pollard (see entry under *Photographers and repro companies* on page 367). *Commission*: 10-12.5% plus VAT.

International Actors London and Irish Actors London (IAL)

Penthouse 11, Bickenhall Mansions,
London W1U 6BR
tel 020 7125 0539
email ialagents@gmail.com
website www.ialagency.com
Key contact John Riordan

Established in 2011. Works in theatre, TV, film and commercials. 2 agents represent ethnically diverse and international actors based in the UK.

Will consider attending performances within the Greater London area, given 2-4 weeks' notice. Actors should apply by emailing their Spotlight link, which should have their showreel attached. Welcomes applications from actors with disabilities. *Commission*: Theatre 10%; Voice-over, Commercial Theatre 12.5%; TV, Film, Commercials 15%.

InterTalent Rights Group PMA (incorporating Cole Kitchenn Management Ltd)

1st Floor, Malvern House, 15-16 Nassau Street,
London W1W 7AB
tel 020 7427 5681
email actors@intertalentgroup.com
website www.intertalentgroup.com

Managing Directors & Agents Alex Segal, Oliver Thomson (*Assistant* Caitlin Rae Boyle), Ashley Vallance (*Assistant* Bex Severn), *Agents* Brooke Kinsella, Sam Day *Associate* Alexandra MacMillan

For submission: go to the 'contact' section on the website. Prospective clients: Scripted: send CVs for respresentation to actors@intertalentgroup.com; Unscripted: alex@intertalentgroup.com. Cannot always guarantee a reply.

JB Associates

PO Box 173, Manchester M19 0AR
tel 0161 249 3666
email info@j-b-a.net
website www.j-b-a.net
Proprietor John Basham

Established in 1996. 2 agents represent 65 actors. Areas of work include theatre, musicals, television, film, commercials, corporate and voice-overs.

Will consider attending performances at venues in the North and occasionally elsewhere, given 3-4 weeks' notice. Accepts submissions (with CVs and photographs) from actors previously unknown to the company preferably by email. Will also accept showreels, voicereels and invitations to view individual actors' websites. *Commission*: Theatre 10%; TV 15%.

Jeffrey & White Management Ltd PMA

7 Paynes Park, Hitchen, Hertfordshire SG5 1EH
tel 01462 429769

email info@jeffreyandwhite.co.uk
Partners Gemma Towersey, Ellie Goodhew

Established in 1986. 2 agents represent 70 actors. Areas of work include theatre, musicals, television, film, commercials and corporate.

Will consider attending performances given as much notice as possible. Accepts submissions (with CVs and photographs) from actors previously unknown to the company if sent by post or email. *Commission*: Theatre, Film and TV 12.5%; Commercials 15%.

Mark Jermin Management

Venue No. 1, 995A Carmarthen Road, Fforestfach, Swansea SA5 4AE
tel (01792) 45855
email info@markjermin.co.uk
website www.markjerminmanagement.co.uk
Agents Mark Jermin, Charlotte Jones, Andrew Phillips

Established in 2007. Areas of work include theatre, musicals, television, film, commercials, corporate and voice-overs.

Will consider attending performances at venues within London, Manchester and south and west Wales, given 2 weeks' notice. Accepts submissions by email (with CVs and photographs) for actors unknown to the agents. Also accepts unsolicited CVs (with photgraphs), via email. Happy to receive invitations to view actors' websites and to consider applications for representation from disabled actors. *Commission*: Negotiable.

Johnston & Mathers Associates Ltd

PO Box 3167, Barnet, London EN5 2WA
tel 020 8449 4968
email Johnstonmathers@aol.com
website www.johnstonandmathers.com
Key personnel Dawn Mathers, Suzanne Johnston

Established in 2001. Areas of work include theatre, musicals, television, film, commercials and corporate. A small agency of around 40 actors.

Will consider attending performances within the Greater London area with at least 1 month's notice. Accepts submissions (with CVs and photographs) from actors previously unknown to the company if sent by email. Invitations to view individual actors' websites are accepted, as are showreels and voicereels. Welcomes enquiries from disabled actors.

JPA Management PMA

30 Daws Hill Lane, High Wycombe, Bucks HP11 1PW
tel (01494) 520978
email agent@jpaassociates.co.uk
website www.jpaassociates.co.uk
Agent Marylyn Phillips

Established in 1995; part of JPA Associates. Main areas of work are theatre, TV, film and commercials. Represents over 40 actors. Welcomes CVs and

photographs sent by email. Has a diverse and full-inclusive cast list. *Commission*: 10%-15%.

JWL (Jewell, Wright Ltd)

Soho Works, The Tea Building, 56 Shoreditch High Street, London E16JJ
tel 020 3865 0932
email agents@jwl-london.com
website www.jwl-london.com
Twitter @JewellWrightLtd
Director/Agent Jimmy Jewell *Assistant (Screen)* Eva Lottie Harris *Assistant (Stage)* Sabrina Carter

Established in 2005. Main areas of work are theatre, musicals, television, film, commercials and radio. 3 agents represent 100 actors.

Will attend performances in Greater London only, if given at least 2 weeks' notice. Welcomes letters (with CVs and photographs, plus showreel) from individual actors previously unknown to the company if sent by email. Actively encourages enquiries from actors with disabilities. *Commission*: Theatre 15%; Television/Film 15%; Commercials 17.5%.

Roberta Kanal Agency

82 Constance Road, Twickenham, Middlesex TW2 7JA
tel 020 8894 7952 *mobile* 07726 915874
email roberta.kanal82@gmail.com
Director Roberta Kanal

Established in 1972. Please email with photo and basic details. All emails will be scknowledged. No phone calls please.

Keddie Scott Associates PMA

154-160 Fleet Street, London EC4A 2DQ
tel 020 3490 1050
email info@keddiescott.com
website www.keddiescott.com
Managing Director Fiona Keddie-Ord (*Assistants* Jonathan McHardy and Richard Vincent) *Scottish Book* Paul Harper (*Assistant* Tamsin Pollock - *email* scotland@keddiescott.com) *Northern Book* Anthony Williams (*Assistant* Sue Avanson - *email* north@keddiescott.com)

Established in 2003. Works in all areas of the performing arts industry, including TV, film, commercials, theatre, musical theatre (small-, mid- and large-scale) and corporate assignments of every nature. Please note that KSA operates on a Personal Exclusive Management basis.

Steve Kenis & Co PMA

Flat 8, 69 Drayton Gardens, London SW10 9QZ
tel 020 7434 9055
email sk@sknco.com
Agents Steve Kenis, Karen Holmes

Founded in 2000. 2 agents represent 14 actors, as well as writers, directors and technicians. *Commission*: 10%.

Kew Personal Management

PO Box 765, Redhill, Surrey RH1 9HB
mobile 07876 457402
email info@kewpersonalmanagement.com
website www.kewpersonalmanagement.com
Company Manager Kate Winn

Works in theatre, musicals, TV, film, commercials, corporate, voice-over and presenting.

Will consider attending performances in the Greater London area. Accepts emails from actors previously unknown to the company. Accepts showreels, voicereels and links to Spotlight pages. Also represents children. Happy to accept submissions from disabled actors.

LA Management

10 Fair Oak Close, Kenley, Surrey CR8 5LJ
tel 020 7183 6211
email lee-ann@lamanagement.biz
website www.lamanagement.biz
Actors' Agent/Talent Director Lee-Ann Robathan

Established in 2006. Main areas of work are television, film, commercials, corporate, theatre and radio. Also represents presenters, singers and voice-over artists. Will see actors perform, but requires 1 week's notice.

Welcomes letters with follow-up calls, emails, showreels and voicereels. LA Management is open to representing all actors, with or without disabilities.

Laine Management

PO Box 178, Manchester M30 3BL
tel 0161 789 7775
email info@lainemanagement.co.uk
website www.lainemanagement.co.uk
Company Director Samantha Rigby

Areas of work include theatre, television, film, commercials and corporate.

Will consider attending performances at venues in Manchester and the surrounding area with 2-4 weeks' notice. *Commission*: 15%.

Langford Associates Ltd

Vicarage House, 58-60 Kensington Church Street, London W8 4BD
tel 020 8878 7148
website www.langfordassociates.com
Key personnel Barry Langford, Simon Hayes

Established in 1987. 1 agent represents 40-45 actors. Areas of work include theatre, television, film, commercials, corporate and voice-overs.

Will consider attending performances at mainstream venues within Greater London, given 2 weeks' notice. Accepts submissions (with CVs and photographs) by post or email. Email submissions should include no more than 1 small image (emails with multiple attachments will be deleted unread). 'Name' actors

seeking representation may ring and speak to Barry Langford in complete confidence.

"Always happy to receive details by post and will regularly meet with new actors. Include an sae if actors wish details to be returned. Do not send unsolicited showreels. 10x8in photographs are preferable, and it is suggested that the photo is updated every 18 months, and that actors are listed on Spotlight."

Nina Lee Management PMA

tel 020 3842 2639
email nina@ninaleemanagement.com
website www.ninaleemanagement.com
Agent Nina Lee

Areas of work include theatre, TV, film, commercials, corporate and radio.

Welcomes performance notices, each one will be considered on its individual merits. Accepts submissions by email (with CVs and photographs).

Lime Actors Agency & Management Ltd

Nemesis House, 1 Oxford Court, Bishopsgate, Manchester M2 3WQ
tel 0161 236 0827
email georgina@limemanagement.co.uk
Director Georgina Andrew

Established in 1999. 1 agent represents 70 actors. Areas of work include theatre, musicals, television, film, commercials, corporate and voice-overs. Also represents musical directors.

Will consider attending performances at venues within Greater London and elsewhere given 4 weeks' notice. Accepts submissions (with CVs and photographs) from actors previously unknown to the company if sent by post. Follow-up telephone calls, showreels, voicereels and invitations to view individual actors' websites are also accepted.

Eva Long Agents

Norwood House, 9 Redwell Road, Wellingborough NN8 5AZ
mobile 07736 700849
email EvaLongAgents@yahoo.co.uk
Key personnel Eva Long

Established in 2003. 1 agent represents 40 actors. Areas of work include theatre, musicals, television, film, commercials, corporate and voice-overs.

Will consider attending performances within the Greater London, Midlands and East Anglia areas, with at least 1 month's notice. Prefers to receive submissions (with CVs and headshots) by email, rather than by post. Showreels, voicereels and invitations to view individual actors' websites are also accepted. Welcomes enquiries from disabled actors. *Commission*: 15%.

Gina Long (Longrun Artistes)

71-75 Shelton Street, Covent Garden, London WC2H 9JQ

Agents and casting directors

tel (01843) 639747 *mobile* 07748 723228
email longrunartistes@icloud.com
website www.longrunartistes.com
Twitter @longrunartistes
Founder/Director Gina Long

Established in 2005. Works in theatre, musicals, TV, film, commercials, corporate, voice-over and dance. 2 agents represent 120 clients. Will accept unsolicited applications from actors previously unknown to the agency, as hard copy (with photographs).

Lovett Logan Associates PMA

London office: Henry Wood House,
2 Riding House Street, London W1W 7FA
tel 020 7495 6400
email london@lovettlogan.com
Scottish office: 15 Carlton Road, Edinburgh EH8 8DI
tel 0131 478 7878
email edinburgh@lovettlogan.com
website www.lovettlogan.com
Twitter @LovettLogan

Established in 1981. Areas of work include theatre, musicals, television, film, radio, commercials, corporate and voice-overs.

Will consider attending performances at venues in Greater London and Scotland (handled by Scottish office) with 2-3 weeks' notice. Accepts submissions (with CV, photo, showreel link) from actors previously unknown to the company if emailed to **representation@lovettlogan.com**. Invitations to view individual actors' websites are also accepted.

LSW Promotions

PO Box 31855, London SE17 3XP
tel 020 7793 9755
email londonswo@hotmail.com
website www.londonshakespeare.org.uk
Executive Director Bruce Wall *Development Associate* James Croft

Established in 1998. 2 agents represent 20 actors. Areas of work include theatre, musicals, television and film.

Will consider attending performances at venues within Greater London and elsewhere, given 2 weeks' notice. Accepts submissions (with CVs and photographs) from actors previously unknown to the company, sent by post or email. Invitations to view individual actors' websites are also accepted. *Commission*: 10% donation to charity (LSW Prison Project).

MacFarlane Chard Associates PMA

113 Kingsway, London WC2B 6PP
tel 020 7636 7750
email enquiries@macfarlane-chard.co.uk
website www.macfarlane-chard.co.uk
Twitter @MacFarlaneChard
Agents (actors) John Setrice, Philip Bird

Founded in 1994. Works in all areas. Agents represent 120 actors, as well as directors, writers, producers, technicians and authors.

Will consider attending performances in London, given as much notice as possible. Welcomes emails from Spotlight registered actors previously unknown to the agency and encourages enquiries from actors with disabilities. Does not welcome follow-up calls. *Commission*: Varies.

MacFarlane Doyle Associates

Flat 1, 24 Brackley Road,Chiswick, London, W4 2HN
tel 020 3600 3470
email enquiries@macfarlanedoyle.com
website www.macfarlanedoyle.com
Agents Ross MacFarlane, Niei Morgan, Alys Drew

Established in 2009. Main areas of work are theatre, musicals, television, film, corporate, commercials and voice-overs. Each agent represents around 20 actors; directors and choreographers are also represented.

Welcomes performance notices and will travel to any area, given 3 weeks' notice. Prefers submissions by email. Represents actors with disabilities. *Commission*: Theatre, TV & Film 15%; Commercials 20%.

Management 2000

11 Well Street, Treuddyn, Flintshire CH7 4NH
tel (01352) 771231
email jackey@management-2000.co.uk
website www.management-2000.co.uk

Established in 2000. 1 agent represents 30 actors. Areas of work include theatre, musicals, television, film, commercials, corporate and voice-overs.

Accepts submissions (with CVs and photographs) from actors previously unknown to the company if sent by post. Follow-up telephone calls, showreels and voicereels are also accepted. *Commission*: 10-15%.

Marcus & McCrimmon PMA

tel 020 7323 0546
email info@marcusandmccrimmon.com
website www.marcusandmccrimmon.com
Twitter @marcandmcc
Agents Sam James, Clive Marcus

Founded in 1999, an independent talent agency with a focus on creating and developing careers. Main areas of work are stage, musical theatre, TV, film and commercials.

Markham, Froggatt & Irwin PMA

4 Windmill Street, London W1T 2HZ
tel 020 7636 4412
email admin@markhamfroggattirwin.com
website www.markhamfroggattirwin.com
Twitter @MFandI_Talent
Agents: Film, TV and Theatre Alex Irwin, Jonty Brook, Anna Dudley, Richard Gibb, Tom Christensen, Isabella Riggs *Commercials, Voice and Radio* Tig Teague

Works in theatre, musicals, television, film, commercials, corporate and voice-overs.

Scott Marshall Partners PMA

Holborn Studios, 49/50 Eagle Wharf Road,
London N1 7ED
tel 020 7637 4623
email info@scottmarshall.co.uk
website www.scottmarshall.co.uk
Twitter @smpagency
Agents Amanda Evans, Manon Palmer, Craig Sills,
Adrianna Tsigara, Chloe Storey, Sarah Mowat

Areas of work include theatre, musicals, television,
film, commercials, corporate and voice-overs. Also
represents directors (theatre and TV) and creatives.

Accepts submissions (with CVs and photographs)
from actors previously unknown to the company if
sent by email only to
submissions@scottmarshall.co.uk. No postal
submissions accepted.

McEwan and Penford PMA

Studio 11.B.1 The Leather Market, Weston Street,
London SE1 3ER
tel 020 3735 8278
email hello@mcewanandpenford.com
website www.mcewanandpenford.com
Agents Aileen McEwan, James Penford, Perry Juby

Established in 1988, the agency represents actors
working in theatre, musicals, television, film and
commercials. Actors will consider short film work if
paid; submit a CV and script with enquiries.

Cannot accept postal submissions. Only attach one
small image to emails. Please don't send show-reels as
files, pefers links to Spotlight, Vimeo, etc. Due to a
high number of submissions the company will only
respond if it wishes to take things further. Please give
as much notice as possible for invitations to
performances; unlikely to be able to travel outside of
London.

McLean-Williams Ltd PMA

Unit F22B, Parkhall Business Centre,
40 Martell Road, Dulwich, London SE21 8EN
tel 020 3567 1090
email info@mclean-williams.com

Established in 2002; agency representing clients
working in theatre, musicals, television, film,
commercials and corporate role-play.

Will consider attending performances within Greater
London given 2 weeks' notice. Welcomes
submissions (with CVs, photographs, showreels and
voicereels) from actors previously unknown to the
agency. Will also accept follow-up telephone calls,
emails and invitations to view an actor's website.

Bill McLean Personal Management

23B Deodar Road, London SW15 2NP
tel 020 8789 8191

Established in 1972. Will consider attending
performances in Greater London with sufficient

notice. Accepts submissions (with CVs and
photographs) from actors previously unknown to the
company if sent by post. Follow-up telephone calls
are also accepted. *Commission*: Theatre 10%; TV
12.5%; Commercials 15%.

McMahon Management

28 Cecil Road, London W3 0DB
tel 020 8752 0172
email mcmahonmanagement@hotmail.co.uk
website www.mcmahonmanagement.co.uk
Twitter @McMahonMgmt
Agent Thomas McMahon *Assistant Agent* Brian
Morse

Established in 2009. Works in theatre, TV,
commercials, corporate and film. Will consider
attending performances within London and Greater
London given 2 weeks' notice. Welcomes letters (with
CVs and headshots) from individuals previously
unknown to the agency; these can only be returned
with an appropriate sae. Happy to receive email
requests with Spotlight link included. Does not
welcome follow-up phone calls. *Commission*: Theatre
12.5%; TV, Film, Commercial and Corporate 15%.

MCS Agency

47 Dean Street, London W1D 5BE
tel 020 7734 9995
email info@mcsagency.co.uk
Key contact Fay Carnell

Established in 1994. 2 agents represent actors. Areas
of work include theatre, musicals, television, film,
commercials and voice-overs. Also represents
presenters.

Will consider attending performances at venues
within Greater London with 2 weeks' notice. Accepts
submissions (with CVs and photographs) from actors
previously unknown to the company if sent by post.
Showreels, voicereels and invitations to view
individual actors' websites are also accepted.
Commission: 15-20%.

Middleweek Newton Talent Management PMA

Cromer Studios, Holy Cross Church Crypt,
98 Cromer Street, London WC1H 8JU
tel 020 3394 0079
email agents@mntalent.co.uk
website www.mntalent.co.uk
Agents Lucy Middleweek, Ileana Cillario, Olivia
Jaggers

Established in 2013. Areas of work include theatre,
television, film and commercials.

Accepts submissions by email (with CVs and
photographs). Also welcomes showreels and
invitations to view individual actors' websites.

Milburn Browning Associates PMA (MMB Creative)

The Old Truman Brewery, 91 Brick Lane,
London E1 6QL

tel 020 3582 9370
email michele@mmbcreative.com
Managing Director Michele Milburn *Agents* Malcolm
Browning, Tara Lynch, Nicola Bailey-James

Milburn Browning Associates became part of the
umbrella group MMB Creative in 2016, which
included a literary agency and a new voice-over
agency, Fuller Voices with Becky Fuller as MD also
joined MMB Creative. Manages a select client list
providing a first-rate service and offers the clout and
reputation that only comes with decades of
experience and proven success.

MLA Talent (formally Mike Leigh Associates)

International House, 24 Holborn Viaduct, London,
EC1A 2BN
tel 020 7017 8757
email mikeleigh@mlatalent.com
website www.mlatalent.com
Agents Mike Leigh

Established in 2007. Works in all areas except voice-
over. 2 agents represent 60 actors; also represented
are presenters, comedians, DJs and writers.
Recommends the photographer Steve Ullathorne
(**steve@steveullathorne.com**).

Will consider attending performances within Greater
London given 1 month's notice. Welcomes letters
(with CVs and photographs) from actors previously
unknown to the agency if sent by post, but not by
email. Will accept showreels, voicereels, and
invitations to view individual actors' websites.
Commission: 15%.

Morello Cherry Ltd

tel 020 7993 5538 *mobile* 07886 846938
email apply@mcaa.co.uk
website www.mcaa.co.uk

Established in 2007. 1 agent represents 35 actors.
Areas of work include film, television, SVOD, theatre
and commercials.

Correspondence by email/telephone only. Accepts
submissions via email with links to online CV,
footage and images; requests no large file downloads.
Commission: Standard Equity rates.

Lee Morgan Management

Pennine Place, 2A Charing Cross Road,
London WC2H 0HF
tel 020 3196 1740
email lee@leemorgan.biz
website www.leemorgan.biz

Established in 2005. Represents clients working in
musicals, television, film and commercials.

Welcomes performance notices in the London areas,
given 2 weeks' notice. Is happy to receive letters (with
CVs and photographs) from individual actors
previously unknown to the agency, sent by email.

Accepts showreels and voicereels, and encourages
enquiries from actors with disabilities.

MR Management PMA

67 Great Titchfield Street, London W1W 7PT
tel 020 7636 8737
email info@mrmanagement.net
website www.mrmanagement
Agents Mark Pollard, Ross Dawes

Established in 2001. Main areas of work are theatre,
musicals, TV, film and commercials. Also represents
directors, presenters and writers. Welcomes CVs and
photographs sent by email, showreels and voice tapes.
Open to clients with disabilities but not currently
representing any disabled actors. *Commission* 10-
12.5% Theatre, 15% Film and TV.

Mrs Jordan Associates PMA

4 Old Park Lane, London W1K 1QW
tel 020 3151 0710
email apps@mrsjordan.co.uk
website www.mrsjordan.co.uk
Associates Seán D. Lynch, Guy Kean

Established in 2008. Areas of work include stage,
television, film, commercials, corporate and voice-
overs. Represents some regionally based actors. Does
not represent walk-ons, extras, models or under-16s.
2 principal agents plus associates represent around 85
actors.

Will consider attending performances but would
need to meet in advance. Unsolicited applications
accepted by email only. Spotlight link imperative.
Very happy to consider applications from actors with
disabilities. Check website's New Applicants page for
advice before you email us. *Commission*: 10-15%.

MSFT Management PMA

The Pink Studio, 1 Gilbert Street, Enfield EN3 6PD
tel 07917 157748
email msftmanagement@gmail.com
website www.msftandmanagement.com

A fast-growing personal management agency
representing multi-skilled artists, dedicated to the
progression of their clients. MSFT Management is
specifically looking for mid-career actors to join the
London-based agency.

Requirements: actors must be registered with
Spotlight, have a showreel and ideally be a member of
Equity to apply for representation.

Elaine Murphy Associates

Suite 1, 50 High Street, London E11 2RJ
tel 020 8989 4122
email elaine@elainemurphy.co.uk
Director Elaine Murphy

Established in 1990. Employs 2 agents. Areas of work
include film, TV, theatre, musicals, television,
commercials, corporate and voice-overs.

Will consider attending performances within Greater London with plenty of notice. Accepts submissions (with Spotlight link) from actors previously unknown to the agency; showreels, voicereels and invitations to view individual actors' websites are also accepted.

Nelson Browne Management Ltd PMA

65-69 Shelton Street, London WC2H 9JQ
mobile 07796 891388
email enquiries@nelsonbrowne.com
website www.nelsonbrowne.com
Company Director Mary Elliott Nelson

Established in 2007. 2 agents represent 80-90 actors working in musicals, television, film, commercials, corporate and voice-over; also represents directors and actor/musicians.

Welcomes performance notices within the Greater London area, given 2 weeks' notice. Welcomes submissions from actors previously unknown to the agency by email with Spotlight link or links to showreels. Encourages enquiries from actors with disabilities. *Commission*: Theatre 10%; TV and Film 15%.

Northern Lights Management

Unit 20, Riverview, Ripponden HX6 4BL
tel 01422 382203
email office@northernlightsmanagement.co.uk
website www.northernlightsmanagement.co.uk
Twitter @NLightsActorsM
Agents Maureen Magee, Angie Cowton

Established in 1996. Represents Northern and Northern-based actors. Areas of work include theatre, musicals, television, film, commercials, corporate and voice-overs.

Accepts submissions (with CVs and photographs) from actors previously unknown to the company by email, but no large attachments. Links to showreels are also accepted. Telephone calls are not accepted.

Nyland Management

mobile 07902 246157
email casting@nylandmanagement.com
website www.nylandmanagement.com

2 agents represent 60 actors. Areas of work include theatre, musicals, TV, film, commercials, motion capture, corporate, role-play, promotions and voice-overs.

Accepts submissions from Spotlight members. Email only.

Otto Personal Management Ltd

Hagglers Corner, 586 Queen's Road, Sheffield S2 4DU
tel 0114 372432 *mobile* 07587 133212
email admin@ottopm.co.uk

Established in 1985. 41 actors. Areas of work include theatre, musicals, television, film, commercials, corporate and voice-overs.

Will consider attending performances at venues in the UK with approximately 1 month's notice. Accepts submissions (with CVs and photographs) from actors previously unknown to the company, sent by post or preferably by email. Will also accept showreels, voicereels and invitations to view individual actors' websites. *Commission*: 10-13%.

Paling and Jenkins

80-91 St Martin's Lane, London WC2N 4AA
tel 020 7043 2451
email enquiries@palingandjenkins.co.uk
website www.palingandjenkins.co.uk/welcome
Twitter @palingjenkins
Editor Agents Steven Paling, Debbie Jenkins, Dan Taylor

Focuses on personal management with an emphasis on getting to know clients as individuals and helping develop careers. 3 agents represent 110 actors. Areas of work include theatre, musical theatre, film, television and commercials. Welcomes applications via email with CV and photo.

Pan Artists Agency

Cornerways, 34 Woodhouse Lane, Sale M33 4JX
tel 0161 969 7419
email panartists@btconnect.com
website www.panartists.co.uk

Established in 1973. Accepts submissions (with CVs and photographs, "which must be up to date") from actors previously unknown to the company, sent by post or email. Postal submissions must be accompanied by an sae.

Paul Pearson – London Theatrical

18 Leamore Street, London W6 0JZ
tel 020 8748 1478
email agent@londontheatrical.com
website www.londontheatrical.com
CEO Paul Pearson *Head of Media* Chris Read

Established in 2009. 2 agents represent 35 clients. Main areas of work are film, television, theatre and commercials.

Only accepts CVs and photographs sent by email. Has an equal opportunities policy. *Commission*: 15%.

Pelham Associates PMA

19 Pelham Square, Brighton BN1 4ET
email agent@pelhamassociates.co.uk
website www.pelhamassociates.co.uk
Agents Peter Cleall, Dione Inman

Established in 1993. Areas of work include theatre, musicals, television, film, commercials, corporate and voice-overs.

Will consider attending performances at venues within Greater London and elsewhere, given at least 2 weeks' notice. Accepts submissions (with CVs and photographs or Spotlight link) from actors previously unknown to the company if sent by email. *Commission*: 12.5%

Pemberton Associates Ltd
50 Liverpool Street, London EC2M 7PY
tel 020 7224 9036
website www.pembertonassociates.com
Twitter @PembertonAssocs

Established in 1989. 3 agents represent 150 clients. Areas of work include theatre, musicals, television, film, commercials, corporate and voice-overs.

Will consider attending performances at venues in the North West, with 2-3 weeks' notice, if looking for new clients. Accepts submissions (with CVs and photographs) from actors previously unknown to the company if sent by post.

Frances Phillips PMA
89 Robeson Way, Borehamwood, Herts. WD6 5RY
tel 020 8953 0303 *mobile* 07957 334328
email frances@francesphillips.co.uk
website www.francesphillips.co.uk

Established in 1983 and representing 50 actors aged 16 and upwards. Areas of work include theatre, musicals, television, film, commercials, corporate and voice-overs. Submissions by email only considered if Spotlight View PIN number and date of birth details are included. CVs and photos will be requested at a later date if required.

Piccadilly Management
23 New Mount Street, Manchester M4 4DE
tel 0161 212 8522 *mobile* 07930 834891
email info@piccadillymanagement.com
website www.piccadillymanagement.com
Agent Peter Foster

Established in 1985. Main areas of work include television, theatre, stage, commercials, corporate and voice-overs. Represents around 50 actors.

Welcomes approaches from actors previously unknown to the company, sent by post or email. Accepts invitations to view individual actors' websites and welcomes enquiries from actors with disabilities.

Janet Plater Management Ltd
Floor D, Milburn House, Dean Street,
Newcastle upon Tyne NE1 1LF
tel 0191 221 2490
email info@jpmactors.com
website www.jpmactors.com

Established in 1997. 1 agent represents approximately 65 actors. Areas of work include theatre, musicals, television, film, commercials, corporate and voice-overs. Extras department has over 800 extras in the North East region.

Will consider attending performances with a few weeks' notice. Accepts submissions (with CVs and or photographs or Spotlight link) from actors previously

unknown to the company if sent via email. Links to showreels welcome; if applying by email no large attachments. *Commission*: Maximum of 15%.

Morwenna Preston Management
tel 020 8835 8147
email info@morwennapreston.com
website www.morwennapreston.com
Twitter @MorwennaPreston
Instagram @morwennaprestonmanagement

Three agents represent actors for theatre, musicals, television, film and commercials.

Welcomes performance notices 4 weeks in advance, and is prepared to travel within the Greater London area. Welcomes letters (by email) from individuals previously unknown to the company. Does not welcome follow-up calls. Welcomes showreels and invitations to view individual actors' websites. *Commission*: 12.5%.

Price Gardner Management (PMA)
BM 3162, London WC1N 3XX
tel 020 7610 2111
email info@pricegardner.co.uk
website www.pricegardner.co.uk
Contact Sarah Barnfield

Television, film, theatre, musical theatre, commercials, radio, voice-over and corporate. Submissions can be made via the website contact form or via email.

Principal Artistes
Suite 1, 57 Buckingham Gate, London SW1E 6AJ
tel 020 7637 2120 *mobile* 07881 623708
email info@principalartistes.co.uk
Twitter @PrincipalArtist

Established in 1993. 2 agents represent 60 actors. Areas of work include theatre, musicals, television, film, commercials and corporate.

Will consider attending performances at venues in Greater London with at least 1 week's notice. Accepts submissions (with CVs and photographs) from actors previously unknown to the company if emailed to **enquiries@principalartistes.com** or uploaded to the website **www.principalartist.com**. If sent by post please ensure it bears the correct posage. *Commission*: Theatre 10%; Other 15%.

Qtalent PMA
1st Floor, Kean Street, Covent Garden,
London WC2B 5PN

Qtalent, which was incorporated with International Artistes, have over 50 years' experience and know-how in the British entertainment industry. This combined management resource now forms a unique and powerful force in the fields of film, television and theatre in the UK and beyond. Qtalent are part of Qdos Entertainment, which is one of the largest entertainment groups in the UK. Together they represent a diverse client base, including numerous high-profile performers and actors.

Accepts submissions via email with CVs and headshots. For further information on how to apply, please visit: **www.qtalent.co.uk**.

RBM Actors

3rd Floor, 1 Lower Grosvenor Street,
London SW1W OEJ
tel 020 7976 6021
email info@rbmactors.com
website www.rbmactors.com
Agent Richard Bucknall

Works mainly in theatre, television, film and commercials. 2 agents represent around 30 actors, and comedians/writers.

Will consider attending performances within Greater London, given 2-3 weeks notice. Welcomes letters (with CVs and photographs) from individual actors previously unknown to the company, sent by post only, but not follow-up calls. Accepts showreels and voicereels, as well as invitations to view individual actors' websites. Encourages enquiries from actors with disabilities. "We advise you to contact us when you are appearing in something. We don't represent actors we don't know or haven't seen."

Redeeming Features

Unit 1 Fairmule House, 27 Waterson Street,
London E2 8HT
tel 020 3740 3338
email artists@redeemingfeatures.co.uk
website www.redeemingfeatures.co.uk
CEO and Founder Nathanael Wiseman *Head of Talent* Danielle Whiteman *Head of Development* Isabel Pastor *Casting Director* Andrew Fawn *Agent* Donovan Simmons and Zack Miller *Assistant Agent* Georgina Lest

Redeeming Features is an award-winning film and television production company with a boutique talent agency; an offshoot of a production company with an understanding of the realities of the industry from the point of view of scheduling, budgeting, casting and shooting.

Main areas of work are stage, film, TV, online, commercials, shorts, music videos and emerging platforms.

Will consider attending performances within Greater London, given as much notice as possible. Can only represent actors who have a head shot and showreel, and are on Spotlight. *Commission:* around 20% across the board.

Redroofs Associates

26 Bath Road, Maidenhead, Berkshire SL6 4JT
tel 01628 674092
email agency@redroofs.co.uk
website www.redroofs.co.uk

Established in 1947, the agency only represents Redroofs graduates and current students. It does not, therefore, welcome performance notices or representation enquiries from actors unknown to the school. Areas of work include theatre, musicals, television, film, commercials, corporate and voice-overs. *Commission:* 15%.

Redrush Talent

37 Main Street, Killinchy, County Down BT23 6PN
tel 02891 878 146 *mobile* 07803 594961
email janice@redrushtalent.com
website www.redrushtalent.com
Founder and Agent Janice Rush *Assistant* Louise Statham

Founded in 2009, 1 agent represents 10 actors and also represents presenters and writers. Main areas of work include film, theatre, musicals, TV, commercials, corporate and voice-over.

Will consider attending performances at venues within Greater and Central London, given at least 1 weeks' notice. Accepts submissions (with CVs and photographs) from actors previously unknown to the company if sent by email. Showreels, voicereels and invitations to view individual actors' websites are also accepted. Redrush are happy to consider applications for representation from disabled actors. *Commission:* 15%.

The Regan Talent Group

Aberdare House, Cardiff Bay, Cardiff CF10 5FJ
tel (02920) 473993
email hello@reganmanagement.co.uk
website https://regantalentgroup.co.uk
Twitter @Regantalentgroup
Editor Agents Leigh-Ann Regan, Debi Maclean, Ffion Evans, Geraint Hardy

Established in 2001. Represents actors, presenters, writers, directors, producers and content creators. Represents Welsh language actors. Approach agency by email: representation@reganmanagement.co.uk include a cover letter, showreel and Spotlight link.

Lisa Richards Agency PMA

108 Upper Leeson Street, Dublin 4
tel +353 1 637 5000
email info@lisarichards.ie
website www.lisarichards.ie
Managing Director Lisa Cook *Agents (Actors)* Lisa Cook, Richard Cook, Jonathan Shankey, *(Voice-over)* Lorraine Cummins *(Literary)* Faith O'Grady *(Comedy)* Ami Burke, Christina Dwyer *(Corporate)* Eavan Kenny

Established in 1989, originally a theatrical agency but now provides representation for actors, comedians, voice-over artists, authors, playrights, directors and designers.

Welcomes performance notices if sent 3 weeks in advance, and is prepared to travel around Ireland.

Welcomes letters (with CVs and photographs) from actors previously unknown to the company if sent by post, but not by email; does not welcome follow-up calls. Happy to receive showreels and invitations to view individual actors' websites. Welcomes enquiries from disabled actors. Submission guidelines on site for authors. Also operates a London office.

Rossmore Management PMA

Golden Cross House, 8 Duncannon Street, London WC2N 4JF
tel 020 7258 1953
email agents@rossmoremanagement.com
website www.rossmoremanagement.com

Established in 1993. 2 agents and an assistant represent 70 actors. Areas of work include theatre, musicals, television, film, commercials, radio and voice-overs.

Will consider attending performances at venues within Greater London. Accepts submissions (with CVs and photographs) from actors previously unknown to the company by email. Please include sae. *Commission*: Theatre and Radio 10%; Film, TV and Commercials 15% plus VAT.

Royce Management

121 Merlin Grove, Beckenham BR3 3HS
tel 020 8650 1096
email office@roycemanagement.co.uk
website www.roycemanagement.co.uk

Established in 1980. 2 agents represent 50-60 actors. Areas of work include theatre, musicals, television, film, commercials, corporate and voice-overs.

Will consider attending performances at venues within Greater London with a minimum of 1 weeks' notice. Accepts submissions with a link to actors' Spotlight page by email. No attachments.
Commission: Commercials 15%; All other work 10%.

Saraband Associates

PO Box 2493, Ilford, Essex IG1 8JW
tel 020 8551 9193

Areas of work include theatre, musicals, television, film and commercials.

Will occasionally consider attending performances at venues in Greater London, given 1 month's notice. Accepts submissions (with CVs and photographs) from actors previously unknown to the company if sent by post. An sae should be included with CVs and photographs. *Commission*: Varies.

Savages Personal Management

67 Queens Wharf, Riverside Studios, 2 Crisp Road, London W6 9NE
tel 020 7348 7875
email info@savagespm.co.uk
website www.savagespm.co.uk
Facebook www.facebook.com/savagespm.co.uk

Twitter @SAVAGESLondon
Agents Justin Savage, Lindsey Milligan

Established in 2016. Areas of work are theatre, film, TV, musicals, commercials, corporate presenting and events. Represents approximately 80 actors, presenters, directors and writers. Will consider attending performances, given 3 weeks' notice. Welcomes enquiries from artists not previously known to the company by email with a link to a showreel and Spotlight page only. Cannot consider artists without a showreel or a Spotlight entry. Will try to respond to all applications. Represents actors with disabilities and from every sphere of life. *Commission*: theatre 12.5%, plus VAT; everything else 15% plus VAT.

Scream Management

MediaCity UK, The Greenhouse, MediaCity UK, Salford M50 2EQ
tel 0161 850 1996
1st Floor, 11 Goodwins Court, Covent Garden, London WC2N 4LL
email info@screammanagement.com
website https://screammanagement.com/contact
Twitter @screamtalent98

Established in 1998. Represents young actors for TV, film, commercials, voice overs and stage. See website to book auditions and attend workshops.

SDM (formerly Simon Drake Management)

14 Ivor Court, Gloucester Place, London NW1 6BJ
tel 020 7183 8995 / 020 7183 9013
email admin@simondrakemanagement.co.uk
website www.simondrakemanagement.co.uk
Agent Simon Drake

Established in 2007. Works in theatre, musicals, TV and film. Unsolicited approaches should be made via email only, giving Spotlight PIN.

Dawn Sedgwick Management

3 Goodwins Court, London WC2N 4LL
tel 020 7240 0404
email dawn@dawnsedgwickmanagement.com
website www.dawnsedgwickmanagement.com
Key contact Dawn Sedgwick

Established in 1992. 3 agents represent 15 actors. Areas of work include theatre, television, film, commercials, corporate and voice-overs. Also represents presenters, comedians and writers.

Accepts submissions (with CVs and photographs) from actors previously unknown to the agency if sent by post, but not by email. Showreels, voicereels and invitations to view individual actors' websites are also accepted. Welcomes enquiries from disabled actors. *Commission*: 15%.

Select Management

PO BOX 748, London NW4 1TT
mobile 07956 131494

email mail@selectmanagement.info
website www.selectmanagement.info
Agent Venetia Suchdev

Established in 2008. Areas of work include theatre, TV, film, commercial, voice over, print, modeling, corporate, dance and presenting.

Will consider attending performances at venues within Greater London with at least 1 week's notice. Accepts CVs and photographs if sent by email. Also welcomes voice tapes and showreels or invitations to view individual actors' websites as well as applications for representation from disabled actors. *Commission*: 20%; no commission on any work obtained by actors themselves.

Sharkey & Co. Ltd PMA

44 Lexington Street, London W1F 0LW
tel 020 7287 1923
email info@sharkeyandco.com
website www.sharkeyandco.com
Agent Simon Sharkey

Established in 2012, main areas of work are theatre,TV, film, musicals, cabaret, radio, commercials, voice-over, talking books and corporates. Represents 85 actors. Does not represent children.

Welcomes CVs and photographs sent by email with links to showreels and websites. Welcomes perfomance notices with a minimum of two weeks' notice, Greater London preferred. *Commission* Feature films and Commercials 15%; everything else 12.5%.

Shepherd Management Ltd PMA

3rd Floor, Joel House, 17-21 Garrick Street, London WC2E 9BL
tel 020 7420 9350
email info@shepherdmanagement.co.uk
Agents: Drama Christina Shepherd, Sandra Chalmers, Jeanette Hunter, James Beresford *Commercials* Karen Hough *Associate Agent* Clare Thomas

5 agents and 2 junior agents represent 120 actors, 1 director and 1 designer. Areas of work include theatre, musicals, television, film, corporate and voice-overs.

Will consider attending performances within Greater London given as much notice as possible. Showreels and voicereels will also be accepted. Emails and follow-up telephone calls are not welcomed.

Shepperd-Fox PMA

5 Martyr Road, Guildford GU1 4LF
mobile 07710 237144
email info@shepperd-fox.co.uk
website www.shepperd-fox.co.uk
Twitter @shepperdfox
Agents Jane Shepperd

A boutiquw theatrical agency representing a select list of clients in theatre, TV, film, musical theatre, commercials and radio.

Rebecca Singer Management

16 Albert Street, Banbury OX16 5DG
tel 01295 261494 *mobile* 07801 259963
email office@rebeccasingermanagement.com
website www.rebeccasingermanagement.com
Twitter @rsm_office
Agent Rebecca Singer

Established in 2016, after 23 years with the Richard Stone Partnership. Main areas of work are theatre, musicals, TV, film, commercials, corporate work, radio and audiobooks. Does not do commercial voice-overs. Represents 50 actors and one fight director, and would be happy to represent actors if they move in to directing.

Welcomes performance notices, prefereably with a month's notice. Happy to travel within the London area if a theatre is accessible by public transport. Welcomes CVs and photographs sent by email, showreels and voice tapes. Would happily represent actors with disabilities. *Commission*: 12.5%.

Sandra Singer Associates

21 Cotswold Road, Westcliff-on-Sea, Essex SS0 8AA
tel (01702) 331616
email sandrasingeruk@aol.com
website www.sandrasinger.com
Key personnel Sandra Singer, Aimiee Singer

Main areas of work are with leads and featured artists for feature films, film, television, commercials and musical theatre. Specialises in artistes under 25 years of age, but is also a boutique agency of established artistes.

Accepts applications by email. No zip files, jpgs, or emails with large files unless requested. Showreels should only be sent on request.

Camilla Storey Management

1 Knightsbridge Green, London SW1X 7NE
mobile 07540 690676
email info@csmagt.com
Twitter @CamStoreyMagt
Instagram @csm.agency
Agent Richard Johnson *Assistant Agent* Flora Cheley

Areas of work include TV, film, theatre, commercials, corporate, musicals and pantomimes.

Accepts submissions by email (with CVs and photographs), and also welcomes showreels.

Smart Management

PO Box 64377, London EC1V 1ND
tel 020 7837 8822
email smartmanagement@btconnect.com
Agent Mario Renzullo

Established in 2000. Areas of work include theatre, musicals, television, film, commercials, corporate and radio. Contact by post/email.

Will consider attending performances given 1 month's notice.

Stanton Davidson Associates PMA

St Martin's House, 59 St Martin's Lane,
London WC2N 4JS
tel 020 7581 3388
email contact@stantondavidson.co.uk
website www.stantondavidson.co.uk
Twitter @SDALondon
Agents Geoff Stanton, Roger Davidson

Agency represents approximately 100 clients, actors,
singers, producers, directors, designers, composers
and musical directors. Areas of work include theatre,
musical theatre, opera, film, television, radio,
commercials, corporate and voice-overs.

Will consider attending performances both in and
outside of Greater London, but request as much
notice as possible. Accepts submissions from actors
previously unknown to the company, preferably by
email with a limited number of small attachments. If
you can't resist the temptation to send a CV and
photograph by post, please include an appropriately
sized envelope for their return.

Stevenson Withers Associates PMA

Studio 7c, Clapham North Arts Centre,
Voltaire Road, London SW4 6DH
tel 020 7720 3355
email talent@stevensonwithers.com
website www.stevensonwithers.com
Twitter @StevensonWither
Agents Natasha Stevenson, Jennifer Withers, Lindsay
Kutner, Tom Norcliffe *Assistants* Perry Antoniou,
Jamie Nash

3 agents represent over 100 actors. Areas of work
include theatre, musicals, television, film,
commercials, corporate and voice-overs. Actors
should approach the company by email.

Stirling Management Actors Agency

490 Halliwell Road, Bolton, Lancashire BL1 8AN
tel 01204 848333
email admin@stirlingmanagement.co.uk
website www.stirlingmanagement.co.uk
Agents Glen Mortimer, Karen Mortimer, Nathan
Wedge

Established in 2008. 3 agents represent 80-100 actors
and performers.Also agency for 40-60 children. Areas
of work include theatre, TV, film, commercials,
corporate, voice-overs and photo shoots. Also
represents cruise-ship singers and entertainers.

Will consider attending performances at venues in
the north west given at least 1 weeks' notice, though
preferably more. Accepts submissions by email (with
CVs and photographs). Asks that Spotlight links and
showreels be included if available. *Commission:*
Theatre 10%, TV, film and commercials 15%, Voice-
over and photoshoots 20%.

Stiven Christie Management

1 Glen Street, Tollcross, Edinburgh EH3 9JD
tel 0131 228 4040
email info@stivenchristie.co.uk
website www.stivenchristie.co.uk
Proprietor Douglas Stiven

Founded in 1983 (and incorporating The Actors
Agency of Edinburgh). Agency represents actors for
theatre, musicals, television, film, commercials,
corporate and voice-overs.

Katherine Stonehouse Management

Ealing Studios, Ealing Green, London W5 5EP
tel 020 8758 8452
email hello@katherinestonehouse.co.uk
website www.katherinestonehouse.co.uk
Agent Katherine Stonehouse

Established in 2009. Specialises in film, TV, theatre,
musical theatre, commercials, voice-over, social
influencer commercial partnerships and non-fiction
writing.

The Talent Agency Ltd

Fairways, Deans Lane, Walton-on-the-Hill,
Tadworth, Surrey KT20 7TS
mobile 07808 921286
email info@thetalentagencyltd.co.uk
Managing Director Mike Smith *Producer* Daryl Smith
Consultant Sally James

A management company established in 1974 and
covering all aspects of clients' career and long-term
development; represents around 10 actors. Areas of
work include television, film, commercials, corporate
and voice-overs. Also represents radio and TV
presenters and sports stars.

Will consider attending performances at venues in
Greater London and elsewhere, given 2-3 weeks'
notice. Accepts submissions (with CVs and
photographs) from actors previously unknown to the
company, sent by post or email. Also accepts
showreels and voicereels. Invitations to view
individual actors' websites are only accepted if sent
via email. Submitted CVs should be as complete as
possible, and separate clearly professional experience
from student productions. Applicants should always
state if they have yet to acquire a professional role.
Commission: 15-20% according to press, accountancy
and PR agreements.

Tavistock Wood PMA

Tavistock Wood, 45 Conduit Street,
London W1S 2YN
tel 020 7494 4767
email info@tavistockwood.com
website www.tavistockwood.com
Agents Angharad Wood, Charles Collier, Bella
Wingfield, Grace Cavanagh-Butler, Jethro Thompson

Specialist boutique agency and management company representing around 100 clients across the fields of acting, writing and direction. The agency is now well known for an approach which places a strong focus on pan-European talent. Accepts submissions, (with CVs and photographs), from actors previously unknown to the company by post only – these should be accompanied by a covering letter and a sae.

TCG Artist Management Ltd
Garden Studios, 65-69 Shelton Street,
Covent Garden, London WC2H 9HE
tel 020 7240 3600
email info@tcgam.co.uk
website www.tcgam.co.uk

TCG Ltd provides actors for work in all areas of the entertainment industy including feature films, TV, radio and theatre.

Katie Threlfall Associates PMA
13 Tolverne Road, London SW20 8RA
tel 020 8879 0493
email info@ktthrelfall.co.uk
Twitter @KTThrelfall
Agent Katie Threlfall

Founded in 1996 as Hillman Threlfall; changed its name to Katie Threlfall Associates in 2006. 1 agent represents 90 actors in theatre, musicals, television, film, commercials and corporate.

Will attend performances at venues within Greater London if given 1 month's notice. Accepts submissions (with CVs and photographs) from actors previously unknown to the company. Welcomes showreels and invitations to view individual actors' websites. "Address letters correctly to the agent. Only write in if you have a showreel, or with an invitation to a show: we do not take on or meet people whose work we do not know." *Commission*: Commercials 15%, Television 12.5%, Theatre 10%.

Tildsley France PMA
tel 020 8521 1888
email info@tildsleyfrance.co.uk
website www.tildsleyfrance.co.uk
Agent & Company Director Alex France *Company Director* Kathryn Kirton

Established in 2003 as Janice Tildsley Associates and relaunched as Tildsley France Associates in 2017. Areas of work include television, film, commercials and theatre.

Please check website for information before approaching for representation. *Commission*: 10-15%.

TMG London
Adam House, 7-10 AdamStreet, The Strand,
London WC2N 6AA

tel 020 7437 1383 *mobile* 07866 589905
email tanya.greep@googlemail.com
Proprietor Tanya Greep *Key personnel* Natalie Elliott

Established in 1981. 2 agents and 1 assistant represent 70-80 actors. Areas of work include theatre, musicals, television, film, commercials, corporate and voiceovers.

Will consider attending performances at venues within Greater London with 2 weeks' notice if an actor is playing a substantial role. Accepts submissions by email. Showreels and voicereels should only be sent on request. *Commission*: 12.5%.

TTA (Top Talent Agency)
19-25 Salisbury Square, Hatfield,
Hertfordshire AL9 5BT
tel 01727 855903
email admin@toptalentagency.co.uk
website www.toptalentagency.co.uk
Director & Head Agent Warren Bacci *Child & Teen Division* Toni Thorpe *Head of Adults' TV, Film & Theatre* Leoni Morris *MT Division* Mel Cursons *Adult Junior Agent* Fran Wright *Adult Commercial Division* Jakes James *Head of HR & Director* Andy Musgrove *Head of Finance* Nicola Tomlin

Established in 2008. 7 agents represent 300 actors (children and adults). Areas of work include theatre, musicals, television, film, commercials, corporate and voice-overs.

Will consider attending performances with 1 week's notice. To be considered for representation, please apply through the Top Talent website, **www.toptalentagency.co.uk**, and go to the 'join us' page. *Commission*: 15% for adults and 23% for child actors. Can represent disabled actors.

United Agents PMA
12-26 Lexington Street, London W1F 0LE
tel 020 3214 0800
email info@unitedagents.co.uk
website www.unitedagents.co.uk
Agents Jess Alford, Sophie Austin, Julia Charteris, Kate Davie, Charlotte Davies, Lorna Fallowfield, Sean Gascoine, Olivia Homan, Lindy King, Kitty Laing, Thea Martin, Stephanie Moore, Lucia Pallaris, Helen Robinson, Dallas Smith, Lisa Toogood, Maureen Vincent, Kirk Whelan-Foran, Ruth Young *Commercials* Sarah Armitage, Joanna Scaratt, Carly Peters *Television Writers/Performers and Presenters* Duncan Hayes *Voices* Kate Davie, Rebecca Haigh

Established in 2007. Represents about 500 actors. The agency also represents writers, directors, producers, designers and other creatives.

"We now only accept submissions by email. Please email your CV and headshot to **submissions@unitedagents.co.uk** and expect a reply within 4-6 weeks. Any physical submissions will not receive a response."

Urban Talent

Nemesis House, 1 Oxford Court, Bishopsgate, Manchester M2 3WQ
tel 0161 228 6866
email liz@nmsmanagement.co.uk
Key contact Liz Beeley

Urban Talent represents 30-50 actors. Areas of work include theatre, television, film, commercials, corporate and voice-overs. Also represents presenters.

Will consider attending performances at venues in the North West with 2 weeks' notice. Accepts submissions (with CVs and photographs) from actors previously unknown to the company, sent by post or email. Also accepts invitations to view individual actors' websites. *Commission*: 15%.

UVA Management

Pinewood Studios, Pinewood Road, Iver Heath, Bucks SL0 0NHL
tel 0845 370 0883
email info@uvamanagement.com
website www.uvamanagement.com
Head agent Wayne Berko

Established in 2004. Main areas of work are theatre, musicals, television, commercials and corporate. 2 agents represent around 8 actors; also represents presenters.

Welcomes letters (with CVs and photographs) from actors previously unknown to the company if sent by post or email, but prefers not to receive invitations to view individual actors' websites. Does not accept showreels or voicereels. Welcomes enquiries from actors with disabilities. *Commission*: Theatre 10%; TV and Film 13%.

Roxane Vacca Management PMA

61 Judd Street, London WC1H 9QT
Twitter @roxanevacca
Instagram @roxanevaccamanagement
Agents Dane Millard, Roxane Vacca

2 agents represent 52 actors. Does not welcome performance notices, but will accept letters (with CVs and photographs) from individual actors previously unknown to the agency if sent by post. Also accepts showreels, voicereels and invitations to view individual actors' websites. *Commission*: Film & TV 12.5%; Theatre 10%; Commercials 15%.

VisABLE People Ltd

93 High Street, Evesham WR11 4DU
tel 020 3488 1998 *mobile* 07729 738317
email office@visablepeople.com
website www.visablepeople.com
Facebook www.facebook.com/visablepeople
Twitter @visablepeople
Instagram @visablepeople
Agents Louise Dyson MBE

Founded in 1994, VisABLE is the world's first agency representing only disabled people for professional engagements. It represents artistes with a wide range of impairments and in every age group, including children. 2 agents represent around 150 artistes in all areas of acting, including presenting.

Does not welcome performance notices. Happy to receive applications from disabled actors via VisABLE website only. Showreels should always be via a link sent by email. Also happy to receive invitations to view individual actors' websites. Recommends the London photographer Richard Bailey. *Commission*: 10%-17.5% (commercials: 20% agency fee).

VSA Ltd PMA

187 Drury Lane, London WC2B 5QD
tel 020 7240 2927
email info@vsaltd.com
website www.vsaltd.com

VSA has a long and very fine heritage as an agency, having been created by the theatrical agent and impresario Vincent Shaw back in the 1950s. Since then the agency has maintained its position as a top theatrical management looking after many successful artists, including the legendary Jessie Matthews, as well as giving many industry leaders such as Bill Kenwright an opportunity to get started in the industry.

Andy Charles took over the agency in 2002, after working alongside Vincent Shaw as his head agent, and today runs VSA with fellow agent and business partner Tod Weller. Their combined experience of the industry from both sides of the fence ensures an in-depth understanding of the demands of an ever-changing business, as well as an empathy and insight into the daily challenges of an artist's life. "Our continued success depends on our relationships with our clients and with casting professionals – relationships we nurture and never take for granted; friendly, professional and very personal management is paramount to all that we do."

Suzann Wade

9 Wimpole Mews, London W1G 8PB
website www.suzannwade.com
Founder Suzann Wade

Areas of work include theatre, musicals, film, TV, commercials, corporate, animation, computer games and voice-over. Talent agency and personal management.

No direct emails or follow-up calls, representation interest via website contact form only. Encourages enquiries from disabled actors, American and Asian actors based in the UK, linguists and high-physicality actors.

Waring & McKenna Ltd PMA

17 South Molton Street, London W1K 5QT
tel 020 7836 9222

email info@waringandmckenna.com
website www.waringandmckenna.com
Twitter @waringandmckenna
Instagram @WaringMcKenna
Agents Daphne Waring, John Summerfield, Richard Carey, Alice Coombes, Liz Ekberg

Established in 1993. 5 agents represent approximately 100 actors. Areas of work include film, TV, theatre, commercials, corporate and voice-overs both nationally and internationally.

Will consider attending performances at venues within Greater London and occasionally elsewhere, given at least 1 month's notice. Accepts submissions (with CVs and photographs) from actors previously unknown to the company, email preferable. Follow-up telephone calls are also accepted. Showreels and voicereels should only be sent on request. *Commission*: Theatre and Radio 10%; TV and Low-Budget Films 12.5%; Commercials, Voice-overs and Feature Films over £4 million 15%.

WGM Atlantic Talent & Literary Group

5 Chancery Lane, London WC2A 1LG
tel 020 3637 2064
email hello@wgmatlanticgroup.com
website www.wgmtalent.com
Facebook www.facebook.com/wgmtalent
Twitter @WGMAtlantic
Instagram @wgmatlantictalent
Agents Madeleine Cotter, Guy Howe, Greg Morton, Sophie Lucas, Hugo Midwinter

Established in 2015, the main areas of work are TV, film and theatre. Represents 70 actors, as well as writers and creatives.

Welcomes performance notices when given 2 weeks' notice. WGM Talent accepts letters (with CVs and photographs) sent by email, as well as voice tapes and invitations to view actors' websites from actors not previously known to the company. *Commission*: 12%.

Williamson & Holmes

5th Floor, Sovereign House,
212-224 Shaftesbury Avenue, London WC2H 8PR
tel 020 7240 0407
email info@whlondon.co.uk
website www.whlondon.co.uk
Agents Jackie Williamson, Hugo Harrison, Carolyn Floyd, Charlotte Watts

Established in 2005. Areas of work include theatre, musicals, television, film, commercials and corporate.

Will consider attending performances at venues within Greater London with 2 weeks' notice. Accepts submissions from actors only with a link to Spotlight page. *Commission*: Theatre 10%; TV/Film/Commercials/Radio 15%.

Willow Personal Management

151 Main Street, Yaxley, Peterborough PE7 3LD
tel 01733 240392

email office@willowmanagement.co.uk
website www.willowmanagement.co.uk
Director Peter Burroughs

Established in 1995. 1 agent represents more than 150 actors. Specialises in the representation of short actors (under 5ft) and tall actors (over 7ft). Areas of work include theatre, musicals, television, film, commercials, corporate and voice-overs.

Accepts submissions (with CVs and colour photographs) from actors previously unknown to the company if sent by email. *Commission*: 15%.

Wintersons PMA

59 St Martin's Lane, London WC2N 4JS
tel 020 7836 7849
email info@nikiwinterson.com
website www.nikiwinterson.com
Agents Niki Winterson, Lawrence James, David O'Hanlon and Shauna Kiernan *Chief Operations Officer* Alasdair Cameron *Financial Executive* Mithra Harding *Assistants* Dom Valentino, Aleks Rusic

Established in 2011. Main areas of work are theatre, TV, film, commercials and corporate. Represents 100 actors. Also represents directors, writers and casting directors. Welcomes performance notices and will attend whenever possible within London. Welcomes letters, CVs via email with Spotlight links only. Please do not attach images or large files to emails.

Felix de Wolfe PMA

20 Old Compton Street, London W1D 4TW
tel 020 7242 5066
email info@felixdewolfe.com
website www.felixdewolfe.com
Twitter @felixdewolfe
Instagram @felixdewolfe
Agents Caroline de Wolfe, Wendy Scozzaro, Rob Hughes, Dom Scozzaro

Areas of work include film, television, theatre, musicals, commercials, corporate and radio. Also represents directors, producers and writers.

Accepts submissions via the contact page on the website: **www.felixdewlofe.com**. *Commission*: Variable.

Edward Wyman Agency

23 White Acre Close, Thornhill, Cardiff CF14 9DG
tel 029 2075 2351
email wymancasting@yahoo.co.uk
website www.wymancasting.co.uk
Managing Director Judith Gay

Areas of work include television, film, commercials, corporate, photo shoots and voice-overs.

Accepts submissions from actors previously unknown to the company. Application forms can be downloaded from the website. All submissions should include CVs and photographs and a valid DBS certificate. Welsh actors are particularly welcome. Most work South Wales-based. *Commission* 15%.

CO-OPERATIVE AGENCIES

Before making an approach, it is important to understand what being a member of one of these entails, and to be clear about your reason(s) for wanting to join. Many Co-ops have clear details for applicants on their websites.

21st Century Actors Management
tel 07496 413 929
email 21centuryactors@gmail.com
website www.21stcenturyactors.co.uk

Co-operative management established in 1992. Areas of work include theatre, musicals, television, film, commercials and corporate. Members are expected to work 3 days in the office per month.

Will consider attending performances at venues in and around London. Accepts submissions (with Spotlight CVs) from actors previously unknown to the company if sent by email. Actors requesting representation should write stating why they wish to join a co-operative, and outlining their casting type and skills. *Commission*: Theatre, TV, Commercials and Film 10%.

1984 Personal Management Ltd
Suite 508, Davina House, 137 Goswell Road, London EC1V 7ET
tel 020 7251 8046
email info@1984pm.com
website www.1984pm.com
Twitter @1984pm_actors

Co-operative management (CPMA member) representing 23 actors. Areas of work include theatre, musicals, television, film, commercials, and corporate. Members are expected to work 4 days in the office per month unless paying commission.

Accepts emails (with CVs, photographs or link to Spotlight CV). Please see website Apply section for further details.

Actors Alliance
Unit 3.28, Chester House, Kennington Park, 1-3 Brixton Road, London SW9 6DE
tel 020 7407 6028
email actors@actorsalliance.co.uk
website www.actorsalliance.co.uk

One of the longest running co-operatives, established in 1976. Managed by a membership of actors acting as agents for each other; members must be subscribed to Spotlight and Equity membership is encouraged. Areas of work include London/West End/touring regional theatre, musicals, TV, VOD, cinema-release features and indepentent films, commercials, corporates and voice-overs. Members are expected to work in the office at least 1 day a week and attend a monthly meeting unless acting professionally.

Applicants must be based in London and, given a minimum of 2 weeks' notice, agents will endeavour to attend an applicant's performance in Greater London. Welcomes applications via email providing links to showreels and CV. See www.actorsalliance.co.uk for more details.

Actors' Creative Team
7 Bell Yard, London WC2A 2JR
tel 020 8050 7462
email office@actorscreativeteam.co.uk
website www.actorscreativeteam.co.uk
Twitter @ActorsCreativeT
Instagram @actorscreativeteam

Founded in 2001, this co-op agency finds work for its members, and also runs in-house training to develop, explore and maintain performance skills. Clients regularly work in theatre, musicals, television, film, commercials and corporate projects. Members are expected to work 3 days in the office each month and to attend fortnightly meetings. Welcomes performance notices for events, given at least 2 weeks' notice. Accepts emails from actors seeking representation, see the website for more details. Prospective clients need to include their reasons for choosing a co-operative agency in a covering email. *Commission*: Theatre up to 10%; Recorded media up to 12.5%.

The Actors File
Unit 5ᴮ, The Co-op Centre, 11 Mowell Street, London SW9 6BG
tel 020 7661 4033
email office@theactorsfile.co.uk
website www.theactorsfile.co.uk
Twitter @The_Actors_File

Established in 1983. Co-operative management representing 25-30 actors. Areas of work include theatre, musicals, television, film, commercials, corporate and voice-overs. Members are expected to work approx. 3 days in the office per month and to attend business meetings.

Will attend performances at venues in Greater London and occasionally elsewhere. Accepts submissions by post or email which include CV, photograph and covering letter detailing interest in a co-op. Will also accept showreels.

The Actors' Group
Swan Buildings, 20 Swan Street, Manchester M4 5JW
tel 0161 834 4466
email enquiries@theactorsgroup.co.uk
website www.theactorsgroup.co.uk
Twitter @TheActorsGroup1

Established in 1980. Co-operative management representing actors. Member of CPMA and Co-operatives UK.

Areas of work include stage, television, film, commercials, radio, voice-overs, roleplay and corporate. Members are expected to carry out various office duties.

Will consider attending performances at venues in the North with 2-4 weeks' notice. Accepts submissions (by email) from actors previously unknown to the co-operative. Will also accept follow-up telephone calls, showreels, voicereels and invitations to view individual actors' websites.

Actors Network Agency

55 Lambeth Walk, London SE11 6DX
tel 020 7735 0999
email info@ana-actors.co.uk
website www.ana-actors.co.uk
Twitter @anaactors
Instagram @anaactors

Established in 1985. Co-operative personal management representing 35-40 actors. Areas of work include theatre, musicals, television, film, commercials, corporate and role-play. Members are expected to work up to 4 days in the office per month.

Will consider attending performances at venues in Greater London and occasionally elsewhere, given as much notice as possible. Accepts submissions (link to Spotlight entry or CV and photograph together with any showreels) via email. *Commission*: 10%; Commercials 12.5%.

Actorum Ltd

Unit 5, 11 Mowll Street, London SW9 6BG
tel 020 7636 6978
email info@actorum.com
website www.actorum.com

Co-operative management representing 35 actors. Operates on the principle of collective self-determination in the entertainment business with each actor working 4 days a month in the office when not working professionally.

Will consider attending performances at venues in Greater London and elsewhere, given 4 weeks' notice. All applications sent to **newaps@actorum.com**. Showreels, voicereels and invitations to view individual actors' websites accepted. *Commission*: Theatre 10%; TV, Commercials and Film 15%.

Alpha Actors

8 Woodberry Down, London N4 2TG
tel 020 7241 0077
email alpha@alphaactors.com
website www.alphaactors.com
Facebook @AlphaActors
Twitter @AlphaActors
Instagram @alphaactors

A co-operative agency established in 1983, Alpha Actors currently represents 28 actors working in theatre, musicals, television, film, commercials and corporate work. Members are expected to work on average a total of 4 days in the office each month.

Welcomes submissions by email or by post with letter, CV and photograph, and will consider attending performances within Greater London, given as much notice as possible.

Arena Personal Management Ltd

139 Collingwood Road, Surrey SM1 2QW
tel 020 3488 1373
email info@arenapmltd.co.uk
website www.arenapmltd.co.uk

A hybrid co-operative of working and client members representing 20 London and southeast actors. Areas of work include theatre, musicals, television, film, commercials, corporate and voice-overs. Working members are expected to work one day in their home office per week and benefit from some preferred consideration for doing so.

Will consider attending showcases at venues in Greater London given 3-4 weeks' notice and if invited personally by an actor interested in a co-operative agency. Accepts submissions (with CVs and photographs) from actors previously unknown to the company by email only. Will also accept follow-up telephone calls, showreels, voicereels and invitations to view individual actors' websites. *Commission*: rates dependent on member status with both considered attractive.

AXM (Actors Exchange Management Ltd)

Unit J302, J Block, Biscuit Factory,
100 Clement's Road, London SE16 4DG
tel 020 7837 3304
email info@axmgt.com
website www.axmgt.com
Twitter @AXMgt

Established in 1983. Co-operative management currently representing 18 actors. Areas of work include theatre, musicals, television, film, commercials, corporate and voice-overs. Members are expected to work 3-4 days in the office per month.

Will consider attending performances at venues in Greater London given sufficient notice. Accepts submissions (with CVs and photographs or Spotlight links) from actors previously unknown to the company if sent by email. Showreels and voicereels should only be sent on request following an interview. *Commission*: Variable depending on work type.

Bridges: The Actors' Agency Ltd

Studio S12, Out of the Blue Drill Hall,
36 Dalmeny Street, Edinburgh EH6 8RG
tel 0131 554 3073
email admin@bridgesactorsagency.com
website www.bridgesactorsagency.com
Facebook @bridgesactorsagency.com
Twitter @bridgesactorsagency

Instagram @bridgesactorsagency

Established in 2008. At present the only co-operative agency active in Scotland. Areas of work include theatre, television, film, commercials, radio and corporate. Members are expected to contribute to the running of the office, and to attend meetings; therefore all prospective members must be based a commutable distance from Edinburgh or Glasgow.

Accepts submissions via emails: include a CV and headshot. Will also accept showreels, voicereels and invitations to view individual actors' websites. Welcomes invitations to attend performances and showcases.

Entry to the agency is via audition after a selection process. If successful, a stakeholder donation of £100 is required to join the agency which is refundable when memership is terminated. Prospective members must also be registered with Spotlight. *Commission*: Non-Electronic 10%; Electronic 12%.

Castaway Actors Agency

13 Upper Baggot Street, 2nd Floor,
Dublin 4 D04 W7K5, Republic of Ireland
tel +353 1 671 9264/9059
email castawayactors@gmail.com
website www.castawayactors.com

Established in 1988. A co-operative agency representing actors and providing top talent to the Irish and international entertainment industry for 30 years. Structured on a co-operative basis, members play an integral part in the running of all aspects of the agency and are expected to fulfil office duties throughout the year. Members are expected to fulfil office duties throughout the year. Areas of work include theatre, musicals, television, film, commercials, corporate and voice-overs. Accepts submissions with CVs, headshot and a cover letter from Dublin-based actors at **applicationsforcastaway@gmail.com.**

CCM

c/o 802 Garratt Lane, Tooting, London SW17 0LZ
tel 020 3697 1961
email casting@ccm.com
website www.ccmactors.com
Lead contact Lucy Aley-Parker *Administrator* Mike Anfield

Established in 1993. Co-operative management representing up to 30 actors. Areas of work include theatre, film, television, musicals and commercials. Currentlyworking from a virtual office.

Members will consider attending performances, with notice. The agency accepts letters and emails (with photographs and CVs – hard-copy submissions preferred) from actors previously unknown to the membership, and will also accept invitations to view actors' personal websites. Entry to the agency is via audition, which prospective members will be invited

to attend. Actors must be aware of how co-operatives work, and their role within them. Please see our website for application procedure. Information is available from Equity and Spotlight. A Training Fee of £250 (in 2 instalments) is required to join the agency. Prospective clients must also be registered in Spotlight.

Central Line

11 East Circus Street, Nottingham NG1 5AF
tel 0115 941 2937
email agents@thecentralline.co.uk
website http://thecentralline.co.uk
Facebook www.facebook.com/centralactors
Twitter @centralactors

Co-operative management agency established in 1984. Areas of work include theatre, musicals, television, film, commercials, corporate and voice-overs. Also represents directors. Members are expected to work in the office as and when appropriate.

Will consider attending performances at venues in Greater London and elsewhere. Accepts submissions (with links to Spotlight) from actors previously unknown to the company, sent by email only. Will also accept follow-up telephone calls, showreels, voicereels and invitations to view individual actors' websites. *Commission*: 8-15%.

Circuit Personal Management Ltd

Suite 1.7, Universal Square, Devonshire Street,
Manchester M12 6JH
tel 0330 995 0069
email circuitpm@outlook.com
email circuitrepresentation@gmail.com
website www.circuitpm.co.uk
Twitter @CircuitPM
Instagram @Circuitinsta

Established in 1988; member of CPMA. Co-operative management primarily representing actors in the North West area. Areas of work include theatre, musicals, television, film, commercials, corporate and voice-overs. Members are expected to work approximately 4-5 days quarterly in our Manchester office and to attend monthly meetings.

Will consider attending performances at venues within the operating area, preferably with 3-4 weeks' notice. Accepts submissions from actors (with CVs and photographs) sent by post or email. Will also accept follow-up telephone calls. *Commission*: Theatre 10%, Radio and Voiceover 10%, Film 14%.

City Actors Management

tel 020 7793 9888
email info@cityactors.co.uk
website www.cityactors.co.uk

City Actors is one of London's leading co-operatives, established in 1981. Employs full-time lead agent Nikki Everson. The agency has helped actors secure work mainly in film, TV, theatre and commercials, with companies such as the RSC, the National and the BBC.

Membership of the agency provides support, training and a wealth of knowledge to actors at every stage of their career. To apply email **applications@cityactors.co.uk**, sending details of a current production and/or a showreel, a headshot and CV or Spotlight link, and explaining your interest in joining and being part of a co-operative.

Crescent Management
London
tel 020 8987 0191
email mail@crescentmanagement.co.uk
website www.crescentmanagement.co.uk

Established in 1991, the agency has 20–25 members working in theatre, musicals, television, film, commercials and corporate drama. Members are expected to work 2-3 days in the office each month.

Will consider attending performances within Greater London given 2 weeks' notice. Accepts submissions (Spotlight link and headshot) from actors previously unknown to the agency: please read the advice on how to apply given on the website. Will also accept follow-up telephone calls, showreels, voicereels and invitations to view an actor's website. *Commission*: Theatre 10%; Television 12.5%; Film 15%.

Denmark Street Management
4th Floor, Silverstream House, 45 Fitzroy Street, London W1T 6EB
tel 020 7459 4902
email mail@denmarkstreet.net
website www.denmarkstreet.net

Established in 1985. Accepts submissions via the 'apply' link on the website only (applicants must be members of Spotlight) from actors previously unknown to the company. Showreels and voicereels should only be sent on request. Applicants should state why they would like to join a co-operative. We are an agency committed to diversity and inclusiveness without regard to age, sex, ethnicity, disability, race, colour, national origin, sexual orientation, gender identity. *Commission*: 10% for all work.

Direct Personal Management
c/o Yorkshire Dance, 3 St Peter's Building, St Peter's Square, Leeds LS9 8AH
tel 0113 266 4036
email office@directpm.co.uk
St John's House, 16 St John's Vale, London SE8 4EN
tel 020 8694 1788
website www.directpm.co.uk
Facebook www.facebook.com/DirectPersonalManagement
Twitter @DPMActors
Instagram @DPMActors

Established in 1984 (formerly Direct Line Personal Management). Co-operative management normally representing 20 to 30 actors. Areas of work include theatre, musicals, television, film, commercials, corporate, role-play and voice-overs. Members are expected to work 2 days in the office each month.

Will consider attending performances at venues within Greater London and elsewhere, with 1 month's notice. Accepts submissions (with CVs and photographs) from actors previously unknown to the company, sent by post or email. Follow-up telephone calls, showreels, voicereels and invitations to view individual actors' websites are also accepted. "Please consult our website before applying. Every applicant's enquiry is read and replied to." *Commission*: 5–15%.

Frontline Actors' Agency
30-31 Wicklow Street, Dublin 2, Republic of Ireland
tel +353 1 635 9882
email contact@frontlineactors.com
website www.frontlineactors.com
Facebook www.facebook.com/FrontlineActorsAgency
Twitter @FrontlineActors
Chair Rory Mullen

Established in 2000. Main areas of work are theatre, television, film, commercials, corporate and voice-overs. Co-operative agency with 24 actor members who are expected to work approximately 1 week per quarter in the office. Will attend performances in Ireland only, given 2 weeks' notice.

Welcomes letters (with CVs and photographs), showreels and invitations to view actors' websites. Encourages submissions from actors with disabilities.

IML
Estate Offices, Horseferry Road, London SW1P 2EH
tel 020 7587 1080
email info@iml.org.uk
website www.iml.org.uk

Founded in 1980, Independent Management is one of the oldest co-operative agencies representing professional actors. Has a consultant agent, and members work in the office 1-2 days a month.

Areas of work include theatre, musicals, television, film and commercials.

Apply via email with CV and showreels, also accepts invitations to see work. See website for more details.

Inspiration Management
3.3 Hoxton Works, 128 Hoxton Street, London N1 6SH
tel 020 7012 1614
email mail@inspirationmanagement.org.uk
website www.inspirationmanagement.org.uk

Established in 1986, Inspiration is a co-operative actors' agency. Areas of work include theatre, television, film, commercials, corporate, audio and role-play. Members work 36 days in the office per year, when not engaged in professional acting work, and attend meetings once a month.

Actors can apply to join by email, with details of their shows where applicable, and are encouraged to consult the website prior to applying. Successful applicants will be invited to interview and audition. *Commission*: 10% across the board.

NorthOne Management
53 Lambeth Walk, London SE11 6DX
tel 020 7735 5061
email actors@northone.co.uk
website www.northone.co.uk
Twitter @N1Management
Lead Agent Kaitlin Reynell

Established in 1987. Co-operative management representing up to 30 actors. Areas of work include theatre, television, film, commercials and corporate. Members are expected to work 2-3 days in the office per month (hybrid working optional).

Will consider attending performances at venues within Greater London given at least 1 weeks notice. Accepts submissions via their website application form from actors previously unknown to the company, with an explanation of why they wish to be representd by a co-operative agency. Will also accept follow-up telephone calls, showreels and voicereels. Prefers to hear from actors when currently performing. Administration and technical skills are advantageous. Applicants must be on Spotlight. *Commission*: 10%.

Oren Actors Management
Chapter Arts Centre, Market Road, Cardiff CF5 1QE
tel 02920 233321
email info@orenactorsmanagement.co.uk
website www.orenactorsmanagement.co.uk
Facebook www.facebook.com/OrenActorsManagement
Twitter @Oren_Actors
Instagram @oren_actors

Established in 1985. Co-operative management representing 20-25 actors. Areas of work include theatre, musicals, television, film, commercials, corporate and voice-overs. Members are expected to work 4 hours in the office per week when not in commissionable work.

Will consider attending performances at venues in Greater London, Cardiff, South West England and Wales given 2 weeks' notice. Accepts submissions (with CVs and photographs) from actors previously unknown to the company. Will also accept follow-up telephone calls, showreels, voicereels and invitations to view individual actors' websites. Applicants are asked to state clearly why they have approached a co-operative. *Commission*: Theatre 8%; Mechanical Media 10%.

Performance Actors Agency
137 Goswell Road, London EC1V 7ET
tel 020 7251 5716

email info@performanceactors.co.uk
website www.performanceactors.co.uk
Key personnel Lionel Guyett

Established in 1984. Co-operative management representing 30+ actors. Areas of work include theatre, musicals, television, film, commercials, corporate and voice-overs. Members are expected to work 3-4 days a month in the office.

Will consider attending performances at venues within Greater London and occasionally elsewhere. Accepts submissions by email from actors previously unknown to the company. Will also accept showreels and voicereels. "We only recruit new members when specific categories are required. Call or email first." *Commission*: 10%.

RbA Management Ltd
Office A, 2nd Floor, Building 2, 360 Edge Lane, Liverpool L7 9NJ
tel 0151 708 7273
email info@rbamanagement.co.uk
website www.rbamanagement.co.uk

Established in 1995, RbA is a co-operative management representing up to 20 actors. Areas of work include theatre, musicals, television, film, radio, commercials, corporate and voice-overs. Members are expected to contribute 5 working days in the office every 2-3 months.

Will consider attending performances at venues in the North West (Manchester, Liverpool, North Wales) and nationally with 3-4 weeks' notice. Accepts brief, straightforward submissions (with CVs and photographs along with a covering letter) from actors previously unknown to the company if sent by post or email. Showreels, voicereels and invitations to view individual actors' websites are also accepted. *Commission*: 15%.

Rogues & Vagabonds Management
Deptford Lounge, Giffin Street, London SE8 4RJ
tel 020 7254 8130
email rogues@vagabondsmanagement.com
website www.vagabondsmanagement.com
Twitter @RandVManagement

Co-operative management representing 28-30 actors. Areas of work include theatre, television, film, commercials and corporate. Members are expected to work in the office 3 days per month.

Will consider attending performances anywhere, if given at least 3-4 weeks' notice. Accepts submissions (with CVs and photographs) from actors previously unknown to the company if sent by post or email to joinrogues@gmail.com. Showreels, voicereels and invitations to view individual actors' websites are also accepted. Welcomes enquiries from disabled actors. *Commission*: Less than £300, no commission; Over £301, 10%; Over £600, 15%.

Rosebery Management Ltd
87 Leonard St, London EC2A 4QS
tel 020 7684 0187

email admin@roseberymanagement.com
website www.roseberymanagement.com
Twitter @roseberymgmt
Instagram @roseberrymgmt

Established in 1984. Represents 45 actors in theatre, musicals, television, film, commercials, corporate work and voice-overs. Rosebery has a full-time Lead Agent. For applicantions email **roseberyapplications@gmail.com**.

Stage Centre Management Ltd
tel 020 3978 0080
email info@stagecentre.org.uk
website www.stagecentre.org.uk

Established in 1982. London-based co-operative management agency. Areas of work include theatre, musicals, television, film, commercials and corporate. Members are expected to work from home on behalf of the agency 1 day per week when not acting (there is no physical office); this commitment is flexible and can be discussed on application.

Will consider attending performances at venues within Greater London and elsewhere, given at least 2 weeks' notice. Accepts submissions from actors previously unknown to the company. Will also accept follow-up communications, showreels, voicereels and invitations to view individual actors' websites. Applicants should not apply if they are unable to provide visible evidence of their work (e.g. performance notice, showcase or showreel).
Commission: 10-15% depending on job.

Being an agent
Howard Roberts

There are a number of unfortunate stereotypes of agents, and – particularly among younger actors – misconceptions about an agent's role. Whilst popular belief would have us all enjoying long lunches between bouts of shark-like behaviour, the truth is somewhat more akin to that of any other hard-working facilitator.

What does an agent do?
There is no definitive job description for an agent; you will find that different agents have different styles, and work in different ways. Broadly speaking, however, we can divide the agent's role into four broad aims, as follows:
• to maintain contacts across the industry, in order to secure work for their clients – most commonly in terms of obtaining casting information;
• to negotiate fees on behalf of those clients, in order to maximise rewards for the artist, and to ensure that those fees are paid;
• to manage the artist's diary in order not to miss the next job opportunity; and
• to advise the artist on their career choices and options.

Bear in mind that your agent is working for you all the time, even when you might not be earning. It is for this reason that you pay them commission for all performing work in which you are engaged whilst they represent you.

When you see agents at showcases and first nights, or when you hear that an agent is coming to your production, remember that this is usually after they have already worked a full day in the office. Attending these events is a key part of their business: it is their opportunity to network, to keep abreast of new developments and new performers, and to maintain good relationships – for example, with a casting director. The job of an agent can be immensely rewarding, but those rewards come as a result of long hours and hard work.

How do I get an agent?
Sadly, anyone can call themselves an agent, because there are no entry restrictions to the profession. In this book, you will find more than 50 pages listing agents: some of them belong to the Personal Managers' Association (PMA), a body that requires members to have at least three years' trading in the industry prior to joining. However, many other established and reputable agents choose not to belong to the PMA. So take advice. Talk to other performers, to casting directors and to established industry advisers like John Colclough, and endeavour to establish a shortlist of suitable contacts.

A phone call or an email may establish whether an agency is currently considering new clients. Don't be too disheartened if they say that their list is full – persevere with other approaches. And do be careful with emailed requests: many agents now find themselves inundated with email traffic from actors seeking representation, and could choose not to respond.

If an agency asks you to send in your details, check what they require: this will usually be a current CV, a clear 10x8in head shot and a covering letter. See if they want a DVD showreel, or a CD voicereel, but be careful of sending these unsolicited. I would suggest that you always send a correctly stamped and addressed envelope with your submission, as this will make it easier for the agent to respond.

The CV should contain your relevant professional experience, details of where you trained, and any other marketable skill(s) you may possess (for example, a clean driving licence, sports at which you are proficient, languages you might speak, musical instruments you can play, whether you can safely ride a horse, and anything else that might add to your performance).

Photographs should be clear and as up to date as possible. Remember, on the Spotlight site your photo will appear slightly smaller than a passport photo, so you want the best possible definition, at the smallest size. You are in an image-led profession, and your picture is likely to be the first point of contact. Always go to a professional photographer, but be careful of spending too much money on photos until you have an agent; chances are, they might want something different. And always put your contact details on the back of your photo; in a busy office it can get separated from your letter and CV.

Keep your letter businesslike: check to whom you are writing, date the letter and spell their name correctly. Finally, ensure that you use the correct postage: it will not improve your chances if the agent has to pay a surcharge on your letter. Of course, the agent might be happy to receive an emailed submission, using your Spotlight PIN number to access your details. Always ensure that your Spotlight entry is up to date with your correct playing age, latest credits and full list of marketable skills.

Interviews

Turn up on time – never late, but not too early either. Check where you are going in advance so that you don't arrive flustered. You are going to see a busy person, who may be in a position to help your career, so treat the meeting seriously. If you fail to attend at the agreed time, they may think that you will treat castings in a similar manner.

Before 'the day', have your questions ready and prepared in your mind. How long have you been established? How many agents work here? How many clients do you represent? What are your commission rates? (It is unusual for these to be higher than 15% – and be very wary of any agency who would charge you for enrolment.) Are you VAT registered? (If so, remember that this means you will be paying VAT on top of your commission.) Where would you fit in with this agency, and would you clash with any of their existing clients?

This is all information that you need to glean – but at interview, do be careful *how* you ask your questions. Some agents might be more reticent than others; you will need to carefully judge the mood and tone of the meeting. The agent might want to make it clear that they are interviewing you, and not the other way round. Remember, agents will vary in their style and way of working: you must be sensitive and able to adapt.

Offers of representation

Agencies come in all shapes and sizes. Larger, well-established West End concerns certainly have the attraction of the star names they represent, and if they offer you a place it could work for you. They will have the first look at film scripts, and the international cachet. However, what are sometimes referred to as the 'boutique agencies' might also be advantageous: with them, you are likely to have direct access to the principal partners, and you are more likely to be important to them. Smaller agencies have the motivation to secure as much work as possible for their clients, for as much time as possible. They will not want 'passengers'.

If you do get an offer, or offers, of representation, take time to think about it, and *always* seek advice. This is an important decision. Remember that you are entering into a business relationship, not looking for a new best friend. Of course, the best sort of actor to be is a working actor, and so the agency that works best for you is the one that helps you to keep working, irrespective of its size and location or how long it has been established.

Contracts

A contract should place your business relationship on a professional basis, clearly stating not just commission rates, but also such important issues as the required notice period for terminating your agreement. Don't be afraid of being contractually committed, but neither should you ever sign a contract on the spot. Take it away and get a second opinion, be it from another performer, from Equity, or from someone with specialist knowledge.

Problems?

How often do agents hear actors complain that their agent never puts them up for anything – or that they are not seen, even though they are ideal for a part? The harsh reality is that it is a buyer's market. You face vast amounts of competition for every job, and despite your agent's best efforts, the casting director still might not want to see you.

If you really do feel that the actor-agent relationship is not working, the first person you should talk to is your agent! Try to work out if there has been any misunderstanding about your skills, or playing age, or photo; often such issues can easily be resolved by honest discussion.

If there are irreconcilable differences, then try hard to part amicably. It's a small profession, and agents do talk to one another. Attempt to secure new representation before you move, but first check any obligations you have to your existing agent in terms of period of notice, or ongoing work, or work for which you have been submitted.

And finally ...

Always try and work with your agent. Establish how proactive they want you to be. If there are areas of work you do not wish to pursue, make sure that you let your agent know. Always ensure that you keep your agent fully aware of your availability – weekends and holidays included.

Remember: actors face huge amounts of competition, and it is the agent's job to improve the odds in a client's favour. It is a very tough profession, and experience often indicates that you have to work very hard just to be lucky.

Howard Roberts MSc is a partner in Sandra Griffin Management Ltd. He has been an actors' agent for more than 20 years, initially as an assistant and then as a co-director. Prior to this he was a lecturer in Economics and Politics in Further Education. He lives in West London.

Agents and casting directors

CPMA: the Co-operative Personal Management Association

Almost all actors' co-operative agencies belong to the Co-operative Personal Management Association (CPMA), which was created in 2002 to promote co-op agencies in the profession, encourage the highest professional standards, and represent the interests of co-op agencies to outside bodies, such as Equity and Government departments.

Actors represented by co-operative agencies run the agency themselves, through a democratic structure, and work as unpaid agents for each other. Some co-ops employ a co-ordinator or administrator (who is not an actor). Co-op agencies are non-profit-making, and any surplus funds are put back into the business. Co-op agencies began in the UK in 1970, since when many more have been established and thrive. Co-ops access the same casting information as conventional agents and suggest actors for jobs, negotiate contracts and fees, take commission on jobs, and recommend and promote their clients to casting directors (CDs) and others. There is often a fee to join a co-op, which is refunded when you leave. Other, non-refundable, fees may be charged, and there could also be a voluntary monthly levy to cover office costs, co-ordinator's fees, etc. Co-op members work in the office (typically two to four times a month), attend business meetings (usually monthly) to discuss aspects of running the agency, oversee the work of other co-op members (often with CDs), and consider the work of applicants.

Belonging to a co-op has many advantages: ·

• You quickly learn how the industry works, which can be very useful for newcomers and those returning to the profession.

• You are in contact with many industry professionals, which could help you get work.

• You are supported by other actors in the agency, some of who will have a lot of experience.

• You know which jobs you have been suggested for, and can monitor them.

• You have more influence over how you are represented, and can be more pro-active in your career.

• You can say which type of work you will or won't do, without fear of being asked to leave the agency.

• Usually, more than one person decides whom to suggest for a job. Many CDs acknowledge that co-ops often know their clients much better, and can sell them with honesty and confidence.

• Co-ops have smaller lists of clients, tend to avoid clashes, and commission rates are lower.

However, you should be aware that there can be drawbacks to being part of a co-op. As with conventional agents, standards vary; a co-op is only as good and professional as its members. Can you be sure that other members are working as hard for you, as you are for them? Continuity can also be a problem, with so many people involved. Although co-ops with a co-ordinator may have an advantage in this respect, measures such as detailed note-taking and not changing negotiators on a contract still need to be taken. And CDs tend to send breakdowns for major TV and film roles to the top agencies in the industry – although other parts will be sent to good co-ops.

To join a co-op you need to be a good agent (not just a good actor), committed, reliable and keen to support fellow actors. You must be prepared to get on the phone, talk to CDs, and sell your clients with knowledge and conviction, making intelligent and credible suggestions for roles. Consider, too, your personal commitments, such as doing non-acting jobs to earn money, and expenses, such as travel to and from the office, and joining/ training fees.

If you are thinking of applying to a co-op, first ask if applications are being considered – and if so, how they should be submitted. Check CVs and photos on the agency's website to identify potential gaps. Co-ops usually want to see an applicant's work, so send a showreel or details of the show you're in (they tend not to go to drama school shows or showcases, unless someone has expressed interest).

To find out more about the agency, talk to current and former members. You might want to know when the agency was established; if any ex-members have returned; the extent of their contacts with CDs and with theatres; the range of casting information they receive; and whether they belong to the CPMA, which has a code of conduct (Equity particularly welcomed the creation of the CPMA for this reason). If the co-op is interested in your application, you will be interviewed by all available members. If offered a place, you will usually have a three- to six-month trial period. After discussion to see how both sides feel, you may then be offered full membership.

Please visit **www.cpma.coop** for further information.

Agents and casting directors

Voice-over agents

This section lists agencies that specialise in voice-overs. Check the details of how each wishes to be approached, and refer to the 'Showreel, Voicereel and Website Services' section for more about getting a voicereel (or 'voice demo') made. Some of the larger conventional agencies have their own voice-over departments – generally for their existing clients only.

Ad Voice
40 Whitfield Street, London W1T 2RH
tel 020 7323 2345
email info@advoice.co.uk
website www.advoice.co.uk
Key personnel Susan Barritt

2 agents represent clients working in television and radio commercials, documentaries, corporate, animations and audiobook recordings. Submission via **info@advoice.co.uk**.

Bespoke Voice Agency
Third Floor, 8-12 Broadwick Street,
London W1F 8HW
tel 020 7287 1070
email voices@bespokeagency.co.uk
website www.bespokevoiceagency.co.uk
Agents Kate Pulmpton, Hayley Ori

Areas of work include animated film, commercials, documentary, audio books, gaming and camapigns. *Commission*: 15%.

Calypso Voices
27 Poland Street, London W1F 8QW
tel 020 7734 6415
email calypso@calypsovoices.com
website www.calypsovoices.com
Manager Jane Savage

2 agents represent 80 clients for voice-over work. Areas of work include television and radio commercials, documentaries, animation, corporate, audio books and on-air promotions.

Damn Good Voices
218 Chester House, 1-3 Brixton Road,
London SW9 6DE
mobile 07702 228185; 079809 549887
email casting@damngoodvoices.com
website www.damngoodvoices.com
Facebook www.facebook.com/damngoodvoices
Twitter @damngoodvoices
Instagram @damngoodvoices
CEO Simon Cryer *Junior Agent* Georgia Hill *Assistant* Stefan Newton

Established in 2010, Damn Good Voices is a voiceover agency representing award-winning UK and US voice talent, working across all media including TV, film, radio, online, gaming, animation and corporate.

Represents over 300 actors and singers. Represenation requests should be made via the website only. Go to Representation in FAQs on the website. All submissions for representation are tracked and responded to personally. Submissions by email will not be accepted. *Commission*: 15%

Hamilton Hodell Ltd
20 Golden Square, London W1F 9JL
tel 020 7636 1221
email info@hamiltonhodell.co.uk
website www.hamiltonhodell.co.uk
Head of Voice and Commercials India Sinclair, Joseph Crawford

Main areas of work are television, film, commercials and audio books. 2 agents in the Voice and Commercials department and 5 in the Acting department represent around 200 clients in total.

Welcomes letters (with CVs) from individual actors previously unknown to the agency, sent by post only. Will accept follow-up telephone calls, unsolicited voicereels, and invitations to view individual actors' websites. Currently represents, or plans to represent, actors with disabilities. *Commission*: 15%.

Hobsons
2 Duke's Gate, Chiswick, London W4 5DX
tel 020 8995 3628
email voices@hobsons-international.com
website www.hobsons-international.com
Managing Director Donna Lampton

Welcomes submissions for representation by email. Voice showreels and CV to **voices@hobsons-international.com**.

Inter Voice Over
85 Great Portland Street, 2nd Floor,
London W1W 7LT
tel 020 7262 6937
email info@intervoiceover.com
website www.intervoiceover.com
Casting Director Liliane Goudriaan

Established in 1998. Main areas of work are voice-over, voice acting, television, film, commercials and corporate videos. Welcomes voice demos by email to **casting@intervoiceover.com**.

Lip Service
53A Brewer Street, London W1F 9UH
tel 020 7734 3393

email bookings@lipservice.co.uk
Managing Director Alex Mactavish

Four agents solely represent over 100 clients and a number of foreign clients. Areas of work include television, film, commercials and audio books.

Accepts submissions (with CVs and voicereels) from individual actors previously unknown to the company, sent by email or post. Please enclose an sae for their return.

Rabbit Vocal Management
27 Poland Street. 3rd Floor. London, W1F 8QW
tel 020 7287 6466
email info@rabbitvocalmanagement.co.uk
website www.rabbitvocalmanagement.co.uk
Head of Rabbit Vocal Management Amy Howell

Representing 200 artists. Covers all areas of voice work including TV and radio, commercial, documentaries, audio books, promos and continuity, and animation.

Accepts submissions (with CVs) from actors previously unknown to the agency if sent by email but not by post. Invitations to view individual actors' websites are also accepted. Represents disabled actors.

Red 24 Voices
1st Floor, Kingsway House, 103 Kingsway, London WC2B 6QX
tel 056 0386 5556
email paul@red24presenters.com
website www.red24artists.com
Managing Director Paul Weedon

Main areas of work are television, commercials and radio. Represents over 50 clients. Recommends the company The Showreel for the production of voicereels.

Welcomes letters (with CVs) from individual actors previously unknown to the agency, sent by post or email. Will accept unsolicited voicereels and invitations to view individual actors' websites. *Commission*: 20%.

Rhubarb Voices
1st Floor, 1A Devonshire Road, Chiswick, London W4 2EU
tel 020 8742 8683
email enquiries@rhubarbvoices.co.uk
website www.RhubarbVoices.co.uk
Key contact Johnny Garcia

Leading UK voice talent agency with experience casting voices into all platforms of the spoken word, including commercials, continuity and promos, corporate pieces, animation, games, ADR/lip-sync and more. Represents around 90 exclusive UK and North American artists, and more than 100 foreign-language artists.

Actors seeking representation should email their CV (including any voice-over work to date), a photo and an MP3 showreel. Please note that the agency prefers not to receive follow-up calls.

Shining Management Ltd
PO Box 1045, Chislehurst BR7 9AR
tel 020 7734 1981

email info@shiningvoices.com
website www.shiningvoices.com
Twitter @ShiningVoices
Instagram @shiningmanagement
Agents & Co-directors Jennifer Taylor Cave, Clair Daintree

2 agents represent 80 clients. Areas of work include voice-overs for television, film, commercials, computer games, animation and audio books.

Accepts emailed submissions ONLY to **shiningvoices@gmail.com**. "Please do not ring with submission enquiries." *Commission*: 15%.

Talking Heads
Argyll House, All Saints Passage, London SW18 1EP
tel 020 7292 7575
email voices@talkingheadsvoices.com
website www.talkingheadsvoices.com

Areas of work include commercials, television, film, animation, corporate videos, audio books and foreign voices.

Accepts submissions (with CVs and voicereels) by email or post. Invitations to view websites are also accepted. *Commission*: 15%.

Sue Terry Voices Ltd
1st Floor, 35 Great Marlborough Street, London W1F 7JF
tel 020 7434 2040
email sue@sueterryvoices.com
website www.sueterryvoices.com
Managing Director Sue Terry

8 agents represent around 400 actors working in voice-overs only. Does not welcome unsolicited approaches by actors without performing agents. *Commission*: 15%.

Tongue & Groove
PO Box 173, Manchester M19 0AR
tel 0161 249 3666
email info@tongueandgroove.co.uk
website www.tongueandgroove.co.uk
Producers Bev Ashworth, John Basham

2 agents represent 50 clients. Areas of work include voice-overs for television, commercials and audio books.

Accepts submissions (with CVs and voicereels) from individual actors previously unknown to the company if sent by post. Also accepts voicereels and invitations to view individual actors' websites.

Vocal Point
16 Manette Street, London W1D 4AR
tel 020 7419 0700
email enquiries@vocalpoint.net
website www.vocalpoint.net
Agent Ben Romer Lee

Areas of work include television, commercials and audio books. 2 agents represent approximately 85 clients.

Agents and casting directors

Accepts submissions from actors previously unknown to the company. Invitations to view individual actors' websites are also accepted. Follow-up calls are not welcomed. *Commission*: 15%.

VoiceBank Ltd

PO Box 825, Altrincham, Cheshire WA15 5HH
tel 0161 973 8879
email elinors@voicebankltd.co.uk
website www.voicebankltd.co.uk
Director Elinor Stanton

Works in all areas: musicals, television, film, commercials, audio books and radio. Represents 42 clients.

Welcomes unsolicited voicereels and invitations to view individual actors' websites. Does not currently represent any actors with disabilities, but "this would not be a barrier to joining the company".

Voice Shop

First Floor, 1ᴀ Devonshire Road, London W4 2EU
tel 020 8742 7077
email info@voice-shop.co.uk
website www.voice-shop.co.uk
Key contact Maxine Wiltshire

3 agents represent 42 clients working in television, film, commercials and audio-book recording.

Welcomes emails with MP3 audio samples from new actors, but prefers not to receive follow-up telephone calls or voicereels. All audio samples should contain appropriate material, and be professionally produced. *Commission*: 15%.

Voice Squad

76 Park Avenue North, London NW10 1JY
tel 020 8450 4451
email voices@voicesquad.com
website www.voicesquad.com
Director Neil Conrich

4 agents represent more than 1,300 clients. Areas of work include television, film, commercials and audio books.

Accepts submissions (with CVs and voicereels) from individual actors previously unknown to the company if sent by email.

Voicebank, The Irish Voice-Over Agency

39-40 Upper Mount Street, Dublin 2 D02 PR89, Republic of Ireland
tel +353 1 235 1020
email voicebankvoices@voicebank.ie
website www.voicebank.ie
Company Manager & *Owner* Deborah Pearce

Voicebank are a voice-over agency only and represent actors, comedians and presenters for all aspects of voice work. Main areas of work include commercials, animations, games, audiobooks, corporate work, television, film and radion. 2 agents and 2 assistant agents represent more than 300 artists.

Artist submissions accepted by email only: include CV, Spotlight link and demo reels of no longer than 2 minutes, as mp3 or wav files. Only likely to consider representing experienced voice-over talent and professionals in either acting, comedy or broadcasting. May also consider young newcomers to the industry who demonstrate a capability and confidence that is appropriate for the competitive nature of this industry. *Commission*: Varies.

The Voiceover Gallery

1st Floor, 44 Berwick Street, London W1F 8SE
tel 0161 881 8844
email info@thevoiceovergallery.co.uk
77 Blythe Road, London W14 0HP
tel 020 7987 0951
email info@thevoiceovergallery.co.uk
website www.thevoiceovergallery.co.uk
London: *Director* Marylou Thistleton-Smith *Voice Agent* Roddy Norris; Manchester: MD: Jason Thorpe *Vendor Manager* Hannah Ralph *Agency Manager* Judith Summerton *Voice Agent* Katie Berkes

Areas of work include corporate, documentary, new media, television and radio advertising. 3 agents represent 60 English voices and multiple foreign voices.

For all representation enquiries and instructions for submissions to the agency, visit the 'Our Services' section of the website, and click on 'Artist Services'. *Commission*: 15%.

VSI (Voice & Script International)

Aradco House, 132 Cleveland Street, London W1T 6AB
tel 020 7692 7700
email info@vsi.tv
website www.vsi.tv

1500 foreign-language and English-speaking voice-over clients. Areas of work include voice-overs for television, film, corporate and commercials.

Accepts submissions (with CVs) from individual actors and presenters previously unknown to the company, sent by post or email (**voices@vsi.tv**). Also accepts voicereels and invitations to view individual actors' websites. "We only use mother-tongue foreign-language speakers."

Yakety Yak All Mouth Ltd

3rd Floor, 25 D'Arblay Street, London W1F 8EJ
tel 020 7430 2600
email hello@yaketyyak.co.uk
website www.yaketyyak.co.uk
Proprietor Jolie Williams

5 agents represent 200 clients. Areas of work include voice-overs for television, film, commercials, animation and audio books.

Books are currently closed, but submissions can be sent to **submissions@yaketyyak.co.uk** in MP3 format. *Commission*: 15%.

Agents and casting directors

Presenters' agents

Jeremy Hicks Associates Ltd
15 Arlington Road, London NW1 7ER
email info@jeremyhicks.com
website www.jeremyhicks.com
Agents Jeremy Hicks, Sarah Dalkin, Charlotte Leaper
Agents' Assistant Julie Dalkin

Represents presenters, writers and chefs.

Commission: 15% (10% for scriptwriters)

Red 24 Presenters
First Floor, Kingsway House, 103 Kingsway,
London WC2B 6QX
tel 07770 433673
email paul@red24presenters.com
website www.red24presenters.com
Managing Director Paul Weedon

Welcomes letters (with CVs and showreels) from
individual presenters previously unknown to the
company, sent by post or email, and accepts
invitations to view individuals' websites.

Sandra Singer Associates
21 Cotswold Road, Westcliff-on-Sea, Essex SS0 8AA
tel (01702) 331616
email sandrasingeruk@aol.com
website www.sandrasinger.com

2 agents represent approximately 40 main clients.
"We are a specialist boutique agency representing
some of the best talent in the UK for Acting and
Musical Theatre." Also a leading Young Performers
agency. Email requests in the first instance regarding
representation. *Commission*: 10% Stage; 20% Screen.

Triple A Media
Suite 23, 264 Lavender Hill, London SW11 1LJ
tel 020 7228 9007
email info@tripleamedia.com
website www.tripleamedia.com
Owner/Agent Andy Hipkiss

Established in 2007. Areas of work include television,
radio and corporate. Also represents a number of
other media professionals, including DJs, presenters
and experts. Member of the Personal Managers
Association (PMA).

Accepts submissions by email (with CVs and
photographs), and welcomes showreels. Happy to
represent actors with disabilities.

Jo Wander Management
111 Coppergate House, Whites Row, London E1 7NF
tel 020 7199 6324
email jo@jowandermanagement.com
website www.jowandermanagement.com
Managing Director Jo Wander

1 agent represents 15-20 presenter clients.

Welcomes letters (with CVs and showreels) from
individual presenters previously unknown to the
agency, sent by post or email; will accept invitations
to view individuals' websites.

Agents and casting directors

Casting directors

Essentially, casting directors take on the 'nitty-gritty' work involved in the casting process – it is usually the director, and sometimes the producer, who actually 'directs' the casting decisions. The crucial thing to remember is that each one is employed by someone else. Some casting directors are employed on a full-time basis; a significant number work freelance and can be as concerned about where their next job is coming from as you are. Therefore, if one gets you to meet their director-employer, it is important that you live up to that casting director's expectations: carefully absorb any brief that they give you. If you suddenly decide to take a radically different approach, they will be put into a difficult position with that director-employer.

Fundamental to the job of being a casting director is a wide knowledge of all kinds of actors. Therefore a good one will have seen as many productions as possible. An empathetic, intuitive and imaginative casting director has immeasurable value to both actors and director.

You should approach casting directors in much the same way as you would agents: however, it's even more important that there's something they can see you in. It's also important to remember that they are more project-oriented than talent-oriented. In other words, whilst an agent is looking for talent to add to their client list, a casting director is usually concentrating on specific talent for a specific project. Research what the casting director is currently casting, and target them accordingly. You can keep reasonably up to date with the activities of some casting directors by looking at the website of the Casting Directors Guild (CDG) – **www.thecdg.co.uk**.

Agents and casting directors

Pippa Ailion CDG

Unit 62A, Eurolink Business Centre, 49 Effra Road, London SW2 1BX
tel 020 7492 0709
email enquiries@pippaailioncasting.co.uk
Casting Directors Pippa Ailion CDG, Natalie Gallacher CDG *Assistant* Richard Johnston

Established in 1991, main areas of work are musical theatre and theatre. Casts on a case-by-case basis. Most recent productions: *Come From Away*, *Tina The Musical*, *The Lion King* and *The Book of Mormon*.

Welcomes performace notices within London given 4 weeks' notice. Welcomes CVs and pohotgraphs sent by email.

Dorothy Andrew Casting CDG

Kings Cottage, 409 Kings Road, Ashton-Under-Lyne, Lancashire OL6 9EX
tel 0161 344 2709
email dorothyandrewcasting@gmail.com

Casts mainly for television, film and commercials.

Will accept postal submissions (with CVs and photographs) from actors previously unknown to the company, but unsolicited emails and showreels are not welcomed. "When writing, make your letter short and to the point. Always include a photograph (10x8in b&w) and a CV. Only send in a showreel if requested."

Shaheen Baig Casting CDG

tel 020 7272 0522
email info@shaheenbaigcasting.com
website www.shaheenbaigcasting.com
Twitter @sbaigcasting

Recent film work includes *Lady Macbeth*, *God's Own Country*; Carol Morley's *The Falling*; Ben Wheatley's *Free Fire*; Paddy Considine's *Journeyman* and the debut features of Stephen Merchant *Fighting with My Family* and Idris Elba *Yardie*. Shaheen has also worked on several acclaimed television projects including *Marvellous*, *Peaky Blinders*, *Black Mirror* (for Channel 4); *Guerrilla*, *National Treasure*, *Damilola: Our Loved Boy*; Philip K. Dick's *Electric Dreams* for Channel 4/Sony & Amazon, and Shane Meadows' *The Virtues* for Channel 4.

Amy Ball CDG

See the entry for the Royal Court Theatre under *Producing theatres* on page 143.

Briony Barnett Casting CDG

11 Goodwin's Court, London WC2N 4LL
tel 020 7836 3751
email briony@brionybarnettcasting.co.uk

Recent credits include, theatre: the Oliver award-winning *Handbagged*; the Olivier-nominated *The House That Will Not Stand* and *A Wolf in Snakeskin Shoes* starring Lucian Msamati (all for Tricycle Theatre). Film credits include *The Knot* and *Common People*. TV credits include the BBC Drama series *Dickensian*.

BBC Drama Series Casting

See the entry for BBC (Drama Production) under *BBC network television* on page 288.

Lesley Beastall Casting

41E Elgin Crescent, London W11 2JD
tel 020 7727 6496
email assistant@lbcasting.co.uk
Casting Director Lesley Beastall

Works in commercials and film. Recent credits include: The Racers (Ladbrokes); ASDA Christmas 2019, Tale of Two Cities (BT).

Does not welcome performance notices or unsolicited submissions by actors previously unknown to the company, but will accept invitations to view individual actors' websites. Any such approach should be made by email only.

Rowland Beckley

See the entry for BBC (Drama Production) under *BBC network television* on page 288.

Leila Bertrand Casting CDG

97 Edenham Way, London W10 5XA
tel 020 8964 0683 *mobile* 07976 187638
email leila@leilabcasting.com

Leila Bertrand has been a casting director for over 15 years. Casts across theatre, film, TV and commercials. Credits include, theatre: *Macbeth* at Arcola Theatre, Wilton's Music Hall and international tour; film: *Sea Monster* (dir. Mark Walker) BAFTA nominee.

Actors should send headshots and CVs by post.

Lucy Bevan CDG

Ealing Studios, Ealing Green, London W5 5EP
tel 020 8567 6655
email office@lucybevancasting.com

Main areas of work are film and television. Credits include: *The Batman* (2022), *Death on the Nile* (2022), *Venom: Let There Be Carnage* (2021), *Belfast* (2021) and *Cruella* (2021).

Sarah Bird CDG

PO Box 32658, London W14 0XA
tel 020 7371 3248
email sarah@sarahbird.com

Casts for film, television, theatre and commercials. Casting credits include: *You Don't Have To Say You Love Me*, directed by Simon Shore (Samuelson Productions); *Ladies in Lavender*, directed by Charles Dance (Scala Productions); *Fortysomething* (Carlton TV); and *Calico*, directed by Edward Hall (Sonia Friedman Productions).

Nancy Bishop Casting

WAC ARTS Building, 213 Haverstock Hill, London NW3 4QP
email info@nancybishopcasting.com
website www.nancybishopcasting.com

Nancy Bishop has worked on over 100 feature films and TV shows, casting hundreds of actors in the UK, Europe and the USA, and retaining close relationships with producers and directors. Her credits include *Borat: Subsequent Moviefilm*, *Mission Impossible IV*, *Snowpiercer*, *The Romanoffs* and *Anne Frank: The Whole Story*. Awards include an CS Artios Award for best casting of a comedy and an Emmy Award. She has also written three books about on-camera casting techniques, publlished by Bloomsbury, the most recent is *Auditioning for Film and TV: A post #metoo guide*.

Nicky Bligh CDG

mobile 07968 788561
email nicky@nickyblighcasting.com
Twitter @nickybligh

Covers TV and film, especially comedy. Has worked for numerous TV channels: BBC, SKY, Channel 4 and Comedy Central; and, production companies such as Tiger Aspect, Hat Trick and Universal Films. TV credits include *Bad Education*, *Psychobitches* and *Mrs Brown's Boys*.

Siobhan Bracke CDG

Basement Flat, 22A The Barons, St Margaret's, Middlesex TW1 2AP

Main area of work is theatre. Theatre credits include: Head of Casting for the RSC (1986-91); Shakespeare's Globe for Mark Rylance; Lyric Hammersmith for Neil Bartlett; Hampstead Theatre for Tony Clark/ Lucy Bailey; Cheek By Jowl for Declan Donnellan; Chichester – *Nicholas Nickelby* for Philip Franks; *I Am Shakespeare* for Mark Rylance; *When We Are Married* for Ian Brown; West Yorkshire Playhouse. Television credits include: *A Doll's House* and *Measure for Measure* for David Thacker; *Buddha of Suburbia* and *Persuasion* for Roger Michell.

Will consider attending performances at venues in Greater London and occasionally elsewhere, given as much notice as possible (preferably 4-5 weeks). Accepts submissions (with CVs and photographs) from actors previously unknown to the casting director if sent by post. Does not welcome email enquiries.

Andy Brierley CDG

email andy@andybrierley.com
Twitter @AndyBCasting

Andy has worked in casting for over a decade across a wide range of television, film and theatre projects such as *The Scandalous Lady W* and *Remember Me* (starring Michael Palin) for the BBC; *Top Boy* and *Run* (starring Olivia Colman) for Channel 4; and *Our Town* (Almeida Theatre). Recent credits include *Silent Witness* (2018) and *The Tunnel* (2017–18).

Aisha Bywaters Casting

email info@aishabywaters.com
website www.theb-side.co.uk/management/aisha-bywaters/

Will attend theatre in Greater London area with 4 weeks' notice. Accepts submissions from actors via email only.

Candid Casting

email submissions@candidcasting.co.uk
website www.candidcasting.co.uk
Facebook www.facebook.com/candidcasting
Twitter @candidcasting
Casting Director Amanda Tabak CDG

Main areas of work are television and film. See website for further details.

Cannon, Dudley & Associates

Dean Hill, Dean Street, East Farleigh ME15 0HT
tel 01622 720740
email cdcasting@blueyonder.co.uk
website www.facebook.com/cannon.dudley
Casting Director Carol Dudley CDG, CSA *Casting Associate* Helena Palmer

Main areas of work are film, theatre and television. Recent credits include: *The Third Mother – Mother of Tears* (dir. Dario Argento); *Master Harold and the Boys* (dir. Lonny Price); and theatre productions for Hampstead, Edinburgh and the West End.

Will consider attending performances at venues in Greater London given as much notice as possible. Accepts submissions (with CVs and photographs) from actors previously unknown to the casting director if sent by post. Does not welcome email enquiries. CVs which are not submitted for specific projects or with reference to current shows or television performances cannot be kept for future reference. Telephone enquiries about current casting projects or progress of mailed submissions are not welcomed.

John Cannon CDG

BBC Elstree, (Rm N202) Neptune House, Eldon Avenue, Borehamwood WD6 1NL
tel 020 8228 7122
email john.cannon@bbc.co.uk

Currently Casting Director for *Eastenders*.

Other recent television credits include: *Holby City*, *Silent Witness*, *Mr Stink*, *Gangsta Granny*, *The Boy in the Dress*, *Grandpa's Great Escape*, *Big School*, *WPC*

56, *32 Brinkburn Street*, *The Coroner*, *Shakespeare and Hathaway*, *Father Brown* and *The Sister Boniface Mysteries* – all BBC. Previously Resident Casting Director for the Royal Shakespeare Company.

Welcomes performance notices with at least 2 weeks' notice. Also happy to receive emails (or letters) from actors, as well as invitations to view individual actors' websites or online showreels. Please contact via BBC only, not via social media.

See also the entry for BBC (Drama Production) under *BBC network television* on page 288.

Anji Carroll CDG

email anji@anjicarroll.tv

Has been responsible for casting over 50 plays for the New Vic Theatre, including the award-winning *Snow Queen* and *Around the World in 80 Days* (Royal Exchange run, UK tour and transfer to New York and Miami); *The Jungle Book* (UK tour); *The Worst Witch* (UK tour and West End transfer); *Pippi Longstocking* (Royal and Derngate, Northampton); *The Beauty Queen of Leenane* (co-production with Queens Theatre Hornchurch); *Peter Pan* (Hull Truck Theatre); *Before the Party, Echos End, Aladdin* (Salisbury Playhouse); *The Ladykillers* (New Wolsey Theatre); and *The Lost Boy, Alice in Wonderland* (Theatre in the Quarter).

Television credits include: BBC2's comedy drama series *The Cup*; *The Bill* (over 50 episodes); *The Sarah Jane Adventures: Invasion of the Bane*; 2 series of *London's Burning* (32 episodes) and *The Knock* (4x90-minute episodes). Film credits include: *LUCY 2.0*; *Papadopoulos and Sons*; *West Is West*; *Mrs Ratcliffe's Revolution*; *Out of Depth* and *The Jolly Boys' Last Stand*. Also various drama-documentaries, including BBC 4's political drama series *Number Ten*.

Suzy Catliff CDG

email soosecat@mac.com

Casting director and theatre director. Casts for television, film and theatre. Co-author of *The Casting Handbook* published by Routledge. Recent casting credits include: for theatre: Changeling Theatre: *The Winter's Tale*; *Nell Gwynne*; *Measure for Measure*; *Blithe Spirit*; *Hamlet*. Television: *Departure* - 6-part drama series; UK associate *The Murdoch Mysteries*; *Frankie Drake*. UK casting on *Primeval New World* and final two series of *Primeval UK* (ITV); *Silent Witness* (Series IX & X); *Blitz* (Channel 4); *D-Day* (BBC 1); *Sir Gadabout* (ITV); *Casualty* (3 series); *Ny-Lon* (associate). For film: *A Bunch of Amateurs*, *Stormbreaker*, *The Swimming Pool*, *Sense and Sensibility*, and *The English Patient* (associate).

Urvashi Chand CDG

Cinecraft, 69 Teignmouth Road, London NW2 4EA
tel 07980 213050
email urvashi@chandcasting.com
website www.chandcasting.com

Main area of work is film. Recent credits include: *Daylight Robbery* (dir. Barry Leonti), and *Red Mercury* (dir. Roy Battersby).

Will consider attending performances within the Greater London area and elsewhere with at least 2 weeks' notice. Accepts submissions (with CVs and photographs) from actors previously unknown to the agency, by email. Showreels, voicereels and invitations to view individual actors' websites are also accepted.

Charkham Casting

16 British Grove, London W4 2NL
tel 020 7927 8335
email charkhamcasting@btconnect.com
Casting Directors Beth Charkham, Gary Ford

Areas of work include theatre, musicals, television, film and commercials. Recent credits include: *Charlie and the Chocolate Factory*, *Silent Witness* and *The Bill*.

Andrea Clark Casting

email andrea@aclarkcasting.com
website www.aclarkcasting.com
Twitter @AndCasting
Casting Director Andrea Clark

Works mainly in film, television and commercials.

Accepts showreels, links and invitations to view individual actors' websites or links to view Spotlight, Mandy, Backstage or IMDb pages. Emails with multiple or very large attachments can't be viewed. "When an actor has an agent, I prefer contact to be made via the agent."

Sam Claypole

email contact@samclaypolecasting.com
website www.samclaypolecasting.com
Casting Director Sam Claypole

Established in 2005. Works in film, TV, theatre, corporate and commercials. Recent credits include: *The Infernal Machine* (Paramount), *Lagging* Series 2 (BBC) and *Dead Canny* (UKTV).

Welcomes Spotlight, Casting Network, Mandy links to showreels, invitations to view actors' websites and performance notices via email.

Ben Cogan

See the entry for BBC (Drama Production) under *BBC network television* on page 288.

Jayne Collins CDG

The Price Building, 110 York Road,
London SW11 3RD
tel 020 7223 0471
email info@jaynecollinscasting.com
website www.jaynecollinscasting.com

Areas of work include theatre, musicals, television, film and commercials.

Will consider attending performances within the Greater London area and elsewhere, given at least 1

week's notice. Accepts submissions (with CVs and photographs) from actors previously unknown to the company if sent by post, but not by email. Welcomes showreels.

Alistair Coomer

See the entry for the National Theatre under *Producing theatres* on page 139.

Anna Cooper

Donmar Warehouse, 41 Earlham Street,
London WC2H 9LX
tel 020 7240 4882
email acooper@donmarwarehouse.com

Currently Casting Director at the Donmar Warehouse. Anna was previously a freelance casting director. She started work at the Almeida Theatre in 2003 and then worked independently – largely in theatre.

Recent theatre includes: *A Number* (Nuffield, Southampton/Young Vic); *Tonight at 8.30*, *The Hudsucker Proxy* (Nuffield, Southampton) and *Multitudes* (Tricycle). As Associate to Toby Whale, TV includes: *Capital*, *Doc Martin*, *Arthur and George*, *Atlantis*; film includes: *The Lady in the Van* and *Belle*.

Irene Cotton Casting

25 Druce Road, Dulwich Village, London SE21 7DW
tel 020 8299 1595
email irenecotton@btinternet.com
Director Irene Cotton CDG

Recent credits include: *Jungle Tribes*; *Charlotte's Song*; Oscar-winning short 2016 *Stutterer*; *Above the Clouds*; *This is Axiom*; *A Thousand Leaves*; *Americus* (RAI Feature); *The Little Mermaid* (Feature); *Done 4* , *Jobs Dinner* (Malcrazo Films); *The Little Black Book* (Park Theatre); *Dirty Dancing* (Aldwych Theatre and tour), *Long Lonely Walk* (film), *Why We Went To War* (Channel 4), *The Bill* (ITV); *The Countess* (Criterion Theatre, London); *Bang Bang* (dir. John Cleese and Nicky Henson); *Panorama* (BBC); and *Caffe Latte* commercial (Home Productions). Welcomes performance notices as far in advance as possible, and is prepared to travel to performances within Greater London. Does not welcome any other unsolicited form of approach, including CVs, photographs, showreels or invitations to view individual actors' websites. Advises actors to make contact only to inform the casting director "when their work can be seen – TV, film or stage".

Kahleen Crawford Casting CDG

Film City Glasgow, Govan Town Hall,
401 Govan Road, Glasgow G51 2QJ
tel 0141 425 1725
email casting@kahleencrawford.com
website www.kahleencrawford.com
Casting Directors Kahleen Crawford, Danny Jackson, Caroline Stewart

Main areas of work include film, TV and commercials. Recent productions include: *Outlaw King* (dir. David Mackenzie); *The Miniaturist* (dir. Guillem Morales); *I, Daniel Blake* (dir. Ken Loach); *Under the Skin* (dir. Jonathan Glazer) and *45 Years* (dir. Andrew Haigh).

Welcomes CVs and photographs from actors previously unknown to the casting director (of a reasonable file size), if sent by email. Happy to receive invitations to view productions in London, Glasgow and the surrounding areas, provided 1 week's notice is given. Also accepts links to online showreels. Only grants a general interview in special circumstances.

Crocodile Casting

9 Ashley Close, Hendon, London NW4 1PH
mobile 07900 148487 or 07900 243458
email crocodilecasting@gmail.com
website www.crocodilecasting.com
Casting Directors Tracie Saban, Claire Toeman

Established in 1996 with the aim of constantly accessing new faces and fresh talent. The company casts for commercials, corporates and feature films. Sometimes holds general auditions to meet new actors and models. Also runs regular worshops.

Sarah Crowe Casting CDG

92-96 De Beauvoir Road, London N1 4EN
tel 020 7286 5080
email info@sarahcrowecasting.co.uk
website www.sarahcrowecasting.co.uk
Twitter @scrowecasting

Sarah has worked extensively in both TV and film specialising in comedy. Her credits include *The Death of Stalin* and *The Thick of It*, both directed by Amando Iannucci; and *Rev* (dir. Peter Cattaneo).

Gary Davy CDG

13 Islington High Street, Angel, Islington, London N1 9LQ
tel 020 7253 3633
email casting@garydavy.com
email office@garydavy.com

Casts for film and television. Casting credits include: Small Axe (BBC/Amazon); *The Tourist* (BBC/HBO); *The Man Who Fell to Earth* (Showtime/P+); *You Don't Know Me* (BBC); *Baptiste* (BBC); *Marcella* (ITV); *The Frankenstein Chronicles* (ITV); *The Enfield Haunting* (SKY); *Alex Rider* (Amazon/IMDBTV); and UK casting on *Band of Brothers* (HBO/BBC).

Film casting credits include: *Woman in Gold*, Steve McQueen's *Hunger*, *The Sweeney*, *Revenger's Tragedy*, *The Proposition*, *44 Inch Chest* and *Streetdance 3D*.

Stephanie Dawes CDG

13 Nevern Square, London SW5 9NW
tel 07802 566642
email stephaniedawes5@gmail.com

Works in television and voice-over. Recent credits include: *Saved*, *Blue Murder*, *Stockwell* and *Britannia High* (all ITV1).

Gabrielle Dawes CDG

PO Box 52493, London NW3 9DZ
tel 020 7435 3645
email gdawescasting@gmail.com

Freelance Casting Director and Creative Associate for Jonathan Church Productions. As an Associate of Chichester Fesitval Theatre 2006–16 she cast over 45 prodictions.

Theatre includes: *The Norman Conquests*, *All About My Mother*, *New Voices 24-Hour Plays* (Old Vic); *Cat on a Hot Tin Roof*, *Three Days of Rain*, *Treasure Island* (West End); Rupert Goold's *Macbeth* (Chichester/West End/Broadway); *Wallenstein*, *The Grapes of Wrath*, *Separate Tables*, *Hay Fever*, *Aristo*, *Funny Girl*, *The Circle*, *Taking Sides/Collaboration* (and West End); *Hobson's Choice*, *The Waltz of the Toreadors*, *Twelfth Night* (all Chichester); *The English Game* (Headlong Theatre); *The Elephant Man* (Sheffield); *As You Like It* (Watford).

As Deputy Head of Casting at the National Theatre 2000–2006, award-winning productions included *Caroline, or Change*; *His Dark Materials*; *Elmina's Kitchen*; *The Pillowman* and *Coram Boy*.

Television credits include: Harold Pinter's *Celebration* and *Elmina's Kitchen* by Kwame Kwei-Armah. Films include *Perdie* (BAFTA award for Best Short Film) and *The Suicide Club*.

Recent casting includes TV development for Hat Trick Productions on *Whatever Happened to Zimraan* by Alistair Beaton; Season Casting Associate for the 2017 Theatre Royal Bath Summer Season.

Paul De Freitas CDG

16 Wimpole Mews, London W1G 8PE
tel 020 7486 5407
email info@pauldefreitas.com
website www.pauldefreitas.com

Main areas of work are film, television and commercials. Casting credits include: *Dog Boy* (BBC2); *Lazarus & Dingwall* (BBC2); *Bernard & The Genie* (Talkback/Attaboy); *The Princess Academy* (Weintraub Productions); and *What Larry Says* (Platypus Productions).

Kate Dowd Casting CDG

Lyric Hammersmith, Lyric Square, King Street, London W6 0QL
tel 020 7828 8071
email kate@katedowdcasting.com

Credits include: film *Mad Max*, *The Bourne Identity*, *Eye in the Sky* and *The Hurricane Heist*; TV series *The Assets*, *Galavant* and *Still Star-Crossed*.

Carol Dudley CDG, CSA

See entry for Cannon, Dudley & Associates.

Julia Duff CDG

1st Floor, 11 Goodwins Court, London WC2N 4LL
tel 020 7863 5557
email julia@juliaduff.co.uk

Casts mainly for television. Casting credits include:
*New Tricks, Hotel Babylon, Secret Diary of a Call Girl,
Persuasion, Monarch of the Glen,* and *The Amazing
Mrs Pritchard.*

Maureen Duff CDG

PO Box 47340, London NW3 4TY
email info@maureenduffcasting.com

Main areas of work are film and television. Credits
include: Film: *Closing The Ring, The Habit of Beauty,
The Flying Scotsman*; TV: *Miss Scarlet & The Duke* S1-
3, *Vera* S4–11, *The Fall* S1-3, *The History of Mr Polly,
Tom Brown's Schooldays, Poirot* (several), *Marple*
(several).

Jennifer Duffy CDG

11 Portsea Mews, London W2 2BN
tel 020 7262 3326
email casting@jennyduffy.co.uk

Main areas of work are film and television. Credits
include: *Life 'n' Lyrics* (Fiesta Productions, BBC
Films, Universal); *Wallace & Gromit: The Curse of the
Wererabbit* (Aardman/Dreamworks); *Macbeth* (BBC)
and *Dunkirk* (BBC2, Huw Wheldon BAFTA Award
2005).

Irene East Casting CDG

40 Brookwood Avenue, Barnes, London SW13 0LR
tel 020 8876 5686
email IrnEast@aol.com

Main areas of work are theatre and film. Casting
Director for Love and Madness Productions. Theatre
credits include: *Bunny's Vendetta* (Derry); *Aristocrats*
(Letterkenny); *Richard III* (Riverside and Tower of
London); *Fool for Love, Macbeth, Ajax* (dir. Jack
Shepherd); *A Skull in Connemara, The Tempest* and
The Playboy of the Western World. Features include:
Begin (dir. Jack Shepherd), *A Distant Mirage* (dir.
Harbajan Verdi), *A Small Dot on the Landscape* (dir.
Alice D. Cooper), *If You Can Hear Me* (dir. Jesse
Lawrence) and Bertolt Brecht's *Fleischhacker* (dir.
Phoebe Von Held).

Will attend performances at venues in Greater
London and occasionally elsewhere, given a couple of
days' notice. Please, no showreels unless requested.

Daniel Edwards CDG

tel 020 7078 7451 or 020 7096 8936
email daniel@danieledwardscasting.com
Twitter @dedwardscasting

Daniel worked as an actor for over 20 years in film,
TV and theatre (under the name Danny Edwards)
before moving into casting in 2005. Casts
independently as well as being Casting Associate to

Kate Rhodes James. Recent TV credits include: *Mr
Selfridge* (2015–16), *Him* (2016), *Ripper Street* (2016),
Line of Duty (2017), *Born to Kill* (2017).

EJ Casting

PO Box 63617, London W9 1AN
tel 020 7564 2688 *mobile* 07891 632946
email info@ejcasting.com
Director Edward James

Casts for theatre, musicals, film, commercials and
corporate work. Casting credits include: *Into the
Woods* and *Sweet Charity* (theatre); commercials for
AOL, Lloyds Bank, Sony BMG, Universal Music, and
Cadbury's Fingers; and *Air on a G String* (film).

Will consider attending performances at venues in
Greater London and occasionally elsewhere. Accepts
showreels containing work that has been broadcast.
Due to the overwhelming number of CVs sent, is
unable to accept general enquiries. "Please only send
an application if it is a performance notice or in
response to a specific breakdown."

ET Casting Ltd.

86-90 Paul Street, London EC2A 4NE
tel 020 3010 3030
email info@etcasting.com
website www.etcasting.com
Casting Director Emily Tilelli *Casting Associates* Zita
Zutic-Konak

Established in 2011. Main areas of work are
commercials, digital content, stills and feature films.
Recent credits include: *Paul Dood's Deadly Lunch
Break* (feature film) and *Tucked* (feature film). Will
consider attending performances in the Greater
London area, with a minimum of 3 weeks' notice.

Welcomes CVs and photographs sent by email,
showreels and voice tapes, and invitations to view
individual actors' websites.

Richard Evans CDG

10 Shirley Road, London W4 1DD
tel 020 8994 6304
email richard@evanscasting.co.uk
website www.evanscasting.co.uk
website www.auditionsthecompleteguide.com

Main areas of work are theatre, musicals, television,
film and commercials. Casting credits include: *The
Rat Pack – Live From Las Vegas* (theatre).

Will consider attending performances at venues in
Greater London and occasionally elsewhere, given
sufficient notice. Requests 1-2 weeks before the
opening night for theatre productions, and 2-3 days
prior to transmission for television shows. Accepts
follow-up telephone calls after a production has
opened. Welcomes submissions (with CVs and
photographs) from actors previously unknown to the
casting director if sent by post, and email enquiries
with links to Spotlight page, online showreel, etc.
(but no large attachments).

Advises actors to: "Be specific, find out what people cast and their current projects, suggesting yourself for particular roles whenever possible. When inviting casting personnel to see your work, always ensure that the part you are playing is worth them coming to see, and offer complimentary tickets. Unless a part is very specific or hard to cast, we usually only invite artists in to audition whose work we have seen or have met, as this enables us to speak honestly and accurately about them to the creative teams with whom we are working. It is worth keeping in touch when you have something to say as your career progresses especially if you have met or know someone."

Susie Figgis

19 Spencer Rise, London NW5 1AR
tel 020 7482 2200

Recent credits include: *A Boy Called Christmas* (2021), *Blinded by the Light* (2019), *Dumbo* (2019), *Bohemian Rhapsody* (2018) and *The Guernsey Literary and Potato Peel Pie Society* (2018).

Sally Fincher CDG

tel 020 8347 5945
email sallyfincher@btinternet.com

Main area of work is television. Credits include: *Murder In Suburbia, Sweet Medicine, Barbara, Kiss Me Kate, Outside Edge* and *The Upper Hand*.

Rachel Freck CDG

tel 020 8673 2455
email casting@rachelfreck.com

Credits include: film *Confetti, The Mask of Cain*, and *Housewife*; TV series *Little Dorrit, The Office, Toast, Mrs Wilson, W1A, Quacks* and *Howards End*.

Fruitcake London

Studio 125, 77 Beak Street, London W1F 9DB
tel 020 7993 5165
email casting@fruitcakelondon.com
Casting Director Andrew Mann

Casts mainly for TV commercials and digital media. Casting credits in 2012 include: commercials for San Miguel, Vauxhall, Sky TV, M&S and Nike; and pop promos for Chase & Status, Paulina Rubio and Ayumi Hamasaki.

Will consider attending performances at venues in Greater London given 2 weeks' notice. Accepts submissions (with CVs and photographs) from actors previously unknown to the casting directors if sent by post. Does not welcome email enquiries.

Caroline Funnell

Areas of work include theatre and musicals. Will consider attending performances within the Greater London area with at least 2 weeks' notice. Artistic Director of Sixteenfeet Productions.

Credits includes: English Theatre Frankfurt; New Victoria Theatre, Stoke; Casanova Lyric Theatre; Hammersmith; regional theatres; and freelance work.

Martin Gibbons Casting

Manchester & London
email info@martingibbons.com
website www.martingibbons.com
Casting Director Martin Gibbons CDG, Alex Wheeler

Established in 2011. Main areas of work are film, television, commercials, theatre, music videos, corporate and voice-over. Will consider attending performances in Manchester and London.

Welcomes CVs and photographs sent by email, as well as showreels and voice tapes.

Tracey Gillham CDG

tel 020 3778 0441
email tracey@traceygillhamcasting.co.uk
email michelle@traceygillhamcasting.co.uk
website www.traceygillhamcasting.co.uk
Associate Michelle Cavanagh

Main areas of work are film and television. For recent credits, please see Spotlight or the CDG website.

Nina Gold CDG

117 Chevening Road, London NW6 6DU
tel 020 8960 6099
email info@ninagold.co.uk
Casting Directors Nina Gold, Robert Sterne

Main areas of work are film, television and commercials. Recent film credits: *The Man Who Would be King* (2018); *The Little Stranger* (2018); *Mamma Mia! Here We Go Again* (2018); Recent TV credits: *Chernobyl* (2019); *Brexit* (2019); *King Lear* (2018); *Succession* (2018); *Patrick Melrose* (2018). Other casting credits include: *Vera Drake*, directed by Mike Leigh (Thin Man Films); *The Life and Death of Peter Sellers*, directed by Stephen Hopkins; *The Jacket*, directed by John Maybury (Warner Bros); *Daniel Deronda*, directed by Tom Hooper (BBC TV); *Amazing Grace* and *Rome* both directed by Michael Apted; *Starter for Ten* directed by Tom Vaughan; *The Illusionist* directed by Neil Burger; and *Brothers of the Head* directed by Keith Fulton and Louis Pepe.

Jill Green CDG

WAC Arts, 213 Haverstock Hill, London NW3 4QP
tel 020 3405 0222
email office@jillgreencasting.org
website www.jillgreencasting.org
Twitter @JGreenCasting

Casts for theatre and musicals, as well as workshops and readings. Casting credits include: Theatre: *Dear Evan Hansen* (Noel Coward); *Jersey Boys* (Trafalgar Theatre/Prince Edward Theatre/Piccadilly Theatre/UK and Ireland tours); *Crazy For You* (Chichester Festival); *101 Dalmations* (Regents Park Open Air); *Bedknobs and Broomsticks* (UK tour); *The Lion King*

(2015-2023 UK and Ireland tour); *Touching the Void* (Duke of York's Theatre/Old Vic/tour); *War Horse* (New London Theatre/ 2015-2020 tours); *Hairspray* (London Coliseum); *The Lion, the Witch and the Wardrobe* (Bridge Theatre/West Yorkshire Playhouse); *The Curious Incident of the Dog In The Night-Time* (Gielgud Theatre/Piccadilly Theatre/ 2015-2019 tours); *Beautiful - The Carole King Musical* (Aldwych Theatre/UK and Ireland tour); *Lazarus* (Kings Cross Theatre); *Kinky Boots* (Adelphi/ UK and Ireland tour); *Aladdin* (Prince Edward); *Young Frankenstein* (Garrick); *Jane Eyre* (National Theatre/ UK tour 2017); *La Strada*; *Show Boat* (New London Theatre/Crucible Theatre, Sheffield); *The Scottsboro Boys* (Garrick/Young Vic); *The Producers* (Theatre Royal Drury Lane/ UK tour); *Contact* (Queens Theatre); *Fosse* (Prince of Wales); Film: dancers for *Paddington 2* and *Beyond the Sea*.

Will consider attending performances within Greater London and occasionally elsewhere, given a minimum of 4 weeks' notice. Accepts email submissions (with Spotlight links, footage/CVs and photographs attached) from actors who are currently appearing in a production or wish to submit for a specific role whilst the company is casting. Does not welcome blanket mailings, unsolicited emails or showreels (unless an sae is enclosed for their return).

David Grindrod CDG

4th Floor, Palace Theatre, Shaftesbury Avenue, London W1D 5AY
tel 020 7437 2506
email dga@grindrodcasting.co.uk

Casts for musicals and films. Film credits: Dance casting *Nine*, Ensemble casting *Mamma Mia!* and *The Phantom of the Opera*. West End casting: *Chicago*, *Mamma Mia!*, *Ghost*, *Hairspray*, *Love Never Dies*, *Sister Act*.

Will consider attending performances within Greater London and possibly elsewhere, given as much notice as possible. Does not welcome unsolicited submissions from actors. Casting breakdowns are released via Spotlight, therefore actors should only write in with reference to specific productions.

Angela Grosvenor CDG

66 Woodland Road, London SE19 1PA
tel 020 8244 5665
email angela.grosvenor@virgin.net

Established in 1990. Main areas of work include TV and film. Recent credits include: The *Tractate Middoth*, *Topsy and Tim* and *The Cafe*.

Welcomes invitations to productions to view actors for consideration, and casting interviews can be arranged dependent on the situation.

Louis Hammond CDG

tel 020 7610 1579
email louis@louishammond.co.uk

Main areas of work are theatre, television and film.

Casting credits include: *Barber Shop Chronicles* (Roundhouse/UK tour/BAM New York); *Beautiful Thing*, *Macbeth* (Bristol Tobacco Factory); *Kanye the First*, *Heroine* (High Tide); *The Sugar-Coated Bullets of the Bourgeoisie* (Arcola/High Tide); The 5 Plays Project (Young Vic); *Inkheart* (HOME Manchaester); *The Distance* (Sheffield Crucible/Orange Tree Richmond); *Romeo and Juliet* (Sheffield Crucible); *Creditors* (Young Vic); *Harrogate* (High Tide Festival); The Fun Fair (HOME Manchester); Primtime, *Creditors* (Young Vic); *Romeo and Juliet* (Sheffield Crucible); *The Funfair* (HOME Manchester); Primtime, *Violence and Son*, *Who Cares*, *Fireworks* (Casting Associate at the Royal Court); *Romeo and Juliet* (HOME, Manchester); *Amadeus* (Chichester Festival Theatre); *The History Boys* (Sheffield Crucible); *The Winter's Tale* (Open Air Theatre, Regents Park); *Driving Miss Daisy* (UK); *Rough Cuts/International Residencies* (Royal Court); *The Resistible Rise of Arturo Ui* (Liverpool/ Nottingham); *Batman Live* (World Arena Tour). Film – *Mirrormask* and *Arsene Lupin*. TV – *The Bill* (Head of Casting).

Hammond Cox Casting

86 Long Lane, London EC1A 9ET
tel 020 7734 3335
email office@hammondcoxcasting.com
website www.hammondcoxcasting.com
Casting Directors Michael Cox, Thom Hammond

Established in 2012. Works in film, commercials, music video and theatre. Recent credits include: Beady Eye (Music Video); Robinsons (Commercial) and *Flight of the Pompodour* (Short Film).

Gemma Hancock CDG

North Lodge, Weald Chase, Staplefield Road, Cuckfield, West Sussex RH17 5HY
email gemma@hancockstevenson.com
website www.hancockstevenson.com

Main areas of work are theatre, television and film.

Julie Harkin Casting CDG

17 Remington Street, London N1 8DH
tel 020 7336 0433
email info@julieharkincasting.com

Specialises in TV and film. Recent TV credits: *War and Peace*, *Cuffs*, *Fortitude*, *Utopia*, *Misfits*, *Kiri* and *Informer*. Film credits: *War Book*; *Monsters*, *Dark Continent*, *The Woman in Black*, *Angel of Death*, *The Scouting Book for Boys*, *Eden Lake*, *Beast*, *The Titan*, and *The Ritual*.

Accepts links to view CVs, and online profiles or showreels via email. Welcomes performance notices via email, if given 2 weeks' notice.

Judi Hayfield CDG / Judi Hayfield Ltd

6 Richmond Hill Road, Gatley, Cheshire SK8 1QG
mobile 07919 221873

Former Head of Casting for Granada.

HB Casting

mobile 07957 114175
email hannah@hbcasting.com
Casting Director Hannah Birkett

Previously awarded British Arrows, a CDA and a Film Craft Cristal for best casting. Areas of work include television, film and commercials.

Will consider attending performances with one week's notice via email. Accepts CVs and photographs via email only.

Serena Hill

22A Whitehall Gardens, Acton W3 9RD
mobile 07425 710707
email serenahillcasting@gmail.com

Serena Hill joined Trafalgar Entertainment as the Casting Director in 2019. She began her Casting Director career at the Royal Court Theatre before moving to the National Theatre as Head of Casting under the successive artistic directorships of Richard Eyre, Trevor Nunn and Nicholas Hytner. She then took up the position of Casting Director at Sydney Theatre Company for artistic director Robyn Nevin, followed by co-artistic directors Cate Blanchett and Andrew Upton, and finally Kip Williams. As a freelance casting director in the UK, Serena worked on BBC Television Film's *Heading Home*, written and directed by David Hare, and *Tumbledown* by Charles Wood, directed by Richard Eyre. As a freelance director in Australia Serena has worked on the Australian productions of *War Horse* for the National Theatre/Global Creatures (2013), *Les Misérables* for Cameron Mackintosh/Michael Cassel Group (2014) and the adult cast of *Matilda the Musical* for the Royal Shakespeare Company and Louise Withers Associates (2015). Recent UK credits include: *Dealing with Clair* by Martin Crimp (Orange Tree Theatre and English Touring Theatre); *Macbeth* at Chichester Festival Theatre; *To Kill A Mockingbird* for Sonia Friedman Productions; and Anything Goes for Trafalgar Productions.

Accepts links to view actors' CVs, on-line profiles, and showreels via e-mail.

Lotte Hines CDG

mobile 07793 966457
email lotte@lottehinescasting.com

Lotte was the Deputy Casting Director at the Royal Court between 2007 and 2014.

Subsequent credits include: *The Glass Menagerie* (Headlong), *Brenda* (Hightide Festival), *La Musica* (Young Vic) and *The Weir* (The Lyceum, Edinburgh).

Polly Hootkins Casting CDG

mobile 07545 784294
email phootkins@clara.net
website www.thecdg.co.uk
Key personnel Polly Hootkins

Prefers all submissions (CVs, photographs, showreels, etc.) via email.

Julia Horan CDG

Horan & Hines, 26 Falkland Road,
London NW5 2PX
tel 020 7267 5261 *mobile* 07967 356869
email julia@horanandhines.com

Julia has worked at the Young Vic, Royal Court, Almeida, Donmar and extensively in the West End and internationally. Recent theatre casting credits include: *All About Eve* (West End), *The Jungle* (Young Vic/NewYork/San Francisco), *The Doctor* (Almeida/Adelaide/West End) and *Harry Potter and the Cursed Child* (West End/Broadway). Film credits include *The Exceptions*. Film and TV credits include *Together, The Exception* and *The Trial*.

Will consider attending performances within the Greater London area and elsewhere. Accepts submissions (with CVs and photographs) from actors previously unknown to the casting director, via email only.

Juliet Horsley

See the entry for the National Theatre under *Producing theatres* on page 139.

Amy Hubbard CDG

tel 020 3567 1210
email amy@amyhubbardcasting.com
Twitter @amyhubcast
Casting Director Amy Hubbard

Amy is an award-winning casting director with extensive experience on both blockbuster features (*Lord of the Rings, The Hobbit*) and TV series (*Homeland*). Recent credits include, film: *Dark River, Mary Shelley, The Man Who Invented Christmas*; TV: *Hatton Garden*.

Dan Hubbard CDG

tel 020 3874 5270
email dan@danhubbardcasting.com
Casting Director Dan Hubbard *Casting Associate* Claire Robinson

Film credits include: *The Bourne Ultimatum, The Bourne Supremacy, Six Days, Captain Phillips*; TV credits include: *American Odyssey, Downtown Abbey*.

Accepts actor submissions by email only. Will accept invitations to performances in the London area, availability permitting.

Hubbard Casting

47 Bedford Street, London WC2E 9HA
tel 020 7631 4944
email ros@hubbardcasting.com
email john@hubbardcasting.com
Casting Directors John Hubbard, Ros Hubbard

Known for films: *The Da Vinci Code* (2006), *Lara Croft: Tomb Raider* (2001), *The Mummy* (1999).

John Hubbard's recent credits include, film: *Hurricane*, 2018.

Ros Hubbard's recent credits include films: *The More You Ignore Me* (2018), *Journey's End* (2017), *Interlude in Prague* (2017) and *The Time of Their Lives* (2017).

Isabella Odoffin Casting CDG

email office@isabellaodoffin.com
website https://isabellaodoffin.com
Twitter @isabellaodoffin
Instagram @isabellaodoffincasting

Isabella Odoffin is a London-based Casting Director with over a decade of experience in casting. She works across film, television and theatre. See her website for open casting calls.

Janis Jaffa Casting

London W12
email janis@janisjaffacasting.co.uk

Works mainly in TV, film and commercials.

Will consider attending performances within Greater London. Welcomes emails (with CVs and photographs attached) from individual actors previously unknown to the agency. Will accept showreels and invitations to view individual actors' websites by email.

Jina Jay CDG

Facebook www.facebook.com/JinaJayCasting
Twitter @jinajaycasting

Known for films and TV. Recent credits include: *Halo* (2019), *The First Lady* (2022), *Dune* (2021), *Enola Holmes* (2020) and *Black Mirror* (2016-19).

Lucy Jenkins (Jenkins McShane Casting)

74 High Street, Hampton Wick,
Kingston on Thames KT1 4DQ
tel 020 8943 5328
email lucy@jenkinsmcshanecasting.com

Casts mainly for film, television, theatre and commercials. Casting credits include: *Babyfather* (BBC); *The Bill* (television); *Top Dog* (short film) and *Emma* (theatre).

Victor Jenkins Casting CDG

The Casting Office, 81 Rivington Street,
London EC2A 3AY
Twitter @verbalictor

Known for TV. Recent credits include: *The Undeclared War* (2022), *Fleabag* (2016-19), *Unforgotten* (2015-19), *Humans* (2015-18) and *Broadchurch* (2013-17).

Priscilla John Casting CDG

tel 020 8741 4212
email priscilla@priscillajohn.com
Casting directors Priscilla John, Orla Maxwell, Francesca Bradley

Casting directors working on diverse and exciting film and international TV projects. Priscilla leads the team with a wealth of experience including the Royal Court Theatre in the 1970s, Granada TV, and an independent career casting for David Lean, Steven Spielberg, Gore Verbinski, Terence Davies and Andrei Tarkovsky. Always on the hunt for new UK talent, the team are passionate theatregoers attending West End and graduate shows.

Sam Jones CDG

mobile 07941 960998
email sam@samjonescasting.co.uk

Previously Head of Casting for the RSC, the Almeida Theatre and, for the first 6 years of its life, National Theatre Wales. Currently a member of the Casting Directors' Guild and the International Casting Director Network, and is an Honorary Fellow of the Royal Welsh College of Music and Drama. During her career she has worked with both regional and international theatre producers and in the West End, including with Sir Peter Hall, Terry Hands, Steven Berkoff, Luc Bondy, Patrice Chereau, Emma Rice, Moira and Fiona Buffini, Polly Teale, Shared Experience, Told By An Idiot, Manchester International Festival (co-production with 59 Productions and Ballet Rambert), the Royal Court, Hampstead Theatre, Old Vic and Yong Vic. Recent TV and film work includes: *The English*, *Black Earth Rising*, *The Long Call*, *The Trick*, *Ridley Road*, *Wanderlust*, *Life*, *NW*, *Don't Forget the Driver*, *The Lost Honour of Christopher Jeffries*, *To Provide All People* and *The Hollow Crown*.

Sue Jones CDG

24 Nicoll Road, London NW10 9AB
tel 020 8838 5153
email sue@suejones.net

Main areas of work are film, television, theatre and commercials. Casting credits include: *The Virgin of Liverpool*, starring Ricky Tomlinson and Imelda Staunton (MOB Films); *The Sound of Thunder*, with Ed Burns, Ben Kingsley and Catherine McCormack; *The Origins of Evil* (CBS/Alliance Atlantis); *Messiah* and *Coriolanus* (both plays directed by Stephen Berkoff); *The Vicar* (BBC television); and *The Politician's Wife* (Channel 4).

Kastwork

tel 020 7580 6101
email emma@kastwork.com
website www.kastwork.com
Director Emma Ashton

Areas of work include television, film and commercials. Recent credits include: *Brother* (commercial for Bacon, Copenhagen); *Galaxy* (commercial for RSA, London); *Hostel 1 & 2* (for International Production Co.).

Will consider attending performances in Greater London with at least 1 week's notice. Invitations to showcases are also welcomed. Accepts submissions (with CVs and photographs) from actors previously unknown to the company; invitations to view individual actors' websites are also accepted.

Kate and Lou Casting

PO Box 397, Wallington, Surrey SM5 9EL
tel 020 323 1952 mobile 07976 252531
website www.kateandloucasting.com
Facebook www.facebook.com/kateandlou
Twitter @kateandloucast

CDA award winner. Casts for film, drama, commercials, still photography, online content and short films. Recent credits include: National Lottery Advert – Michael Gracey, Argos Christmas Advert 2019 – Traktor, This Time Away – Magali Barbe.

Welcomes performance notices. Will accept emails (with CVs and photographs) from individual actors previously unknown to the company, and unsolicited CVs and photographs, sent via email. Does welcome showreels or invitations to view individual actors' websites.

Anna Kennedy Casting

8 Rydal Road, London SW16 1QN
email anna@kennedycasting.com
website www.annakennedycasting.com

Welcomes performance notices, for productions within the Greater London area, with 2 weeks' notice. Will accept letters, but not emails, with CVs and photographs from individuals previously unknown to the casting director; also welcomes showreels and invitations to view actors' websites.

Beverley Keogh CDG

29 Ardwick Green North, Ardwick,
Manchester M12 6DL
tel 0161 273 4400
email beverley@beverleykeogh.tv

Main areas of work are television, film and commercials. Casting credits include: The Village, In The Flesh, Last Tango in Halifax, Scott & Bailey and The Mill.

Accepts submissions (with CVs and photographs) from actors previously unknown to the casting director, sent by post or email.

Kharmel Cochrane Casting

Studio 111, 65 Alfred Road, London W2 5EU
tel 020 3735 9640
email office@kharmelcochrane.co.uk
website http://kharmelcochrane.com
Twitter @KharmelCochrane

Kharmel first cut her cast teeth as a Casting Director on the acclaimed Daniel Wolfe music video Time to Dance starring Jake Gyllenhaal and Callum Turner. She followed up with award-winning films such as Lilting (2014) and the Bafta award-winning Home

(2016). Recent credits include The Witch, The End of the F**king World and The Lighthouse. Main areas of work include film and TV, commercials, music videos, shorts. Get in touch via email.

Belinda King Creative Productions

157 Clarence Avenue, Northamptonshire NN2 6NY
tel 01604 720041
email casting@belindaking.com
website www.belindaking.com
Instagram @belindakingprod
Casting Director Joe Finn

An award-winning production company and producers of shows at sea. Partnerships and projects include Seabourn, Sir Tim Rice, Color Line, Princess Cruises, Holland America Line and Silja Line. International casting with auditions worldwide including London, New York and Sydney.

Casting: lead vocalists, contemporary dancers, commercial dancers.

Suzy Korel CDG CDA

mobile 07973 506793
email suzy@korel.org

Casting predominantly for theatre.

Karen Lindsay-Stewart CDG

PO Box 2301, London W1A 1PT
email asst@klscasting.co.uk

Known for Harry Potter and the Philospher's Stone (2001); Penny Dreadful (2014–16). Main areas of work are television and film. Recent films: Eternal Beauty (2017); How to Talk to Girls at Parties (2017); The Secret of Marrowbone (2017). Other casting credits include: Sylvia, Harry Potter and the Chamber of Secrets, and Cambridge Spies.

Will consider attending performances at venues in Greater London with sufficient notice. Accepts submissions (with CVs and photographs) from actors previously unknown to the casting director if sent by post, but does not welcome email enquiries. Do not send sae(s) for replies.

Kay Magson Casting CDG

PO Box 175, Pudsey, Leeds LS28 7LN
tel 0113 236 0251
email kay.magson@btinternet.com
Casting Director Kay Magson

Recent credits include: Grease (Curve and national tour); Terrible Thames/Billionaire Boy (Birmingham Stage Co); West Side Story, The Music of Andrew Lloyd Webber, The Color Purple (all for Curve where she is an Associate Artist); Rock 'n' Roll pantos at Theatre Clwyd and Liverpool Everyman each year; Oliver Twist (Leeds Playhouse and Ramps on the Moon); Maggie May for Leeds Playhouse where she is an Associate. Casts regularly for Derby Theatre and Storyhouse including Grosvenor Park Open Air Theatre.

Will consider attending performances within the Greater London area and elsewhere, with at least 4 weeks' notice. Accepts submissions (with CVs and photographs) from actors previously unknown to the casting director, via email only.

Carolyn McLeod
56 Bloomsbury Street, London WC1B 3QT
tel 020 7209 0050
email info@cmcasting.co.uk
website www.carolynmcleodcasting.com
Facebook www.facebook.com/carolynmcleodcasting
Twitter @CarolynMCasting

Main areas of work are film and television. Recent projects include: Independent features: *Boiling Point*, with Stephen Graham, *Sweetheart, Villain, The Ballad of Billy McCrae, A Gift From Bob* and *Red Sandra*. Other projects include, for Netflix: *Afterlife of the Party, The Princess Switch: Switched Again, The Knight Before Christmas, A Christmas Prince: I, II & III, The Princess Switch* and *The Saint*. Along with film for the BBC, ITV, Hallmark, SyFy Channel, Disney and TV series *Weapons of Choice*.

Given sufficient notice will consider attending performances at venues in and around Greater London. Will accept emailed broadcast or show notifications, also emailed submissions from actors previously unknown to the casting director. Showreels, voicereels and invitations to view individual actors' websites are also accepted, but receipt may not be acknowledged.

Anne McNulty CDG
email mcnulty19@gmail.com

Former Resident Casting Director for Donmar Warehouse. Now working as a freelance casting director, mainly in theatre. See Anne's article on page 116 for advice on casting for the stage.

Sooki McShane (Jenkins McShane Casting)
mobile 07940 591612
email sooki@jmcasting.net
website www.jmcasting.net

Works mainly in theatre, film and television. Casting credits include: *Barbeque 67* (BBC Radio 4); *The Play That Goes Wrong* (UK tour); *La Cage Aux Folles* (directed by Jez Bond); *Beauty and the Beast* (Mercury Theatre); *Red Riding Hood* (Liverpool Everyman); and *Edge of Justice* (directed by Jake L Reid).

Thea Meulenberg Casting
Keizersgracht 116 Amsterdam
mobile 0031 6547 98109
email info@theameulenberg.com
website www.theameulenberg.com
website www.kftv.com/thea-meulenberg-casting
Facebook www.facebook.com/
TheaMeulenbergCasting

Casting Directors Laurens Meulenberg, Sevina Stapert-Meulenberg

Established in 1980. Works in TV, film, commercials, corporate, print and photography. Provides casting solutions to the highest level of craftsmanship and creativity. Worldwide clients from USA, Dubai, India, the UK, Germany and the Netherlands.

Hannah Miller
See the entry for the Royal Shakespeare Company under *Producing theatres* on page 144.

Stephen Moore CDG
email stephen@stephenmoorecasting.co.uk
website www.stephenmoorecasting.co.uk
Twitter @StephenRMoore

Main areas of work TV, film and theatre. Recent credits include, for TV: *Holby City* (BBC1); *Father Brown* (BBC1); *Shakespeare and Hathaway* (BBC1); *Doctors* (BBC1). For theatre: *Loot* (dir. Michael Fentiman); *The Boys in the Band* (dir. Adam Penford); *Monster Raving Loony* (dir. Simon Stokes).

Will consider attending performances in Greater London with a few weeks' notice. Welcomes CVs, photographs and links to showreels sent by email.

National Theatre Casting Department
South Bank, London SE1 9PX
020 7452 3336
email casting@nationaltheatre.org.uk
website www.nationaltheatre.org.co.uk/about-the-national-theatre/casting

See the entry for the National Theatre under *Producing Theatres*, page 139

James Orange Casting CDG
Linear House, Peyton Place, Greenwich, London SE10 8RS
tel 020 3393 2612
email casting@jamesorange.com
Casting Director James Orange

Established in 2007. Casting Director for Cameron Mackintosh Ltd 2010–14. Recent projects include: *An American in Paris* (West End), *On the Town* (Regents Park), *The Addams Family* (UK tour), *Strictly Ballroom the Musical* (West Yorkshire Playhouse and Toronto), *Shirley Valentine* (UK tour).

Accepts submissions (with CVs and photographs) from actors previously unknown to the casting director, via email only. Does not accept invitations to attend performances.

Helena Palmer
Freelance casting director working in theatre, film and TV. Casting work has spanned more than 20 years and has included working at the Royal Exchange Theatre, Manchester, the National Theatre and most recently the Royal Shakespeare Company.

Has worked on a wide range of classical and contemporary plays and with directors including Maria Aberg, Michael Boyd, Philip Breen, Gregory Doran, David Farr, Polly Findlay, Simon Godwin, Rupert Good, Iqbal Khan, Blanche McIntyre and Prasanna Puwanarajah. Has also worked on a variety of UK, US and European film and TV productions. Recent projects include: *The Fever Syndrome* directed by Roxana Silbert (Hampstead Theatre), *The Mirror and the Light* directed by Jeremy Herrin (Gielgud Theatre), *Blackmail* directed by Anthony Banks (Mercury Theatre) and *Antigone* directed by Dawn Walton.

Will attend theatre performance with a suitable amount of notice. Email submissions only.

Theo Park Casting

Unit 2, Oakford Yard, 2ᴀ Oakford Road, London NW5 1AH
tel 020 7419 1159 *mobile* 07949 566906
email theo@theoparkcasting.com

Recent films include: *The Current War* (2017); *Action Point* (2018); *Calibre* (2018); *The Spy Who Dumped Me* (2018); *Overlord* (2018) *Darkness Visible* (2019); *The Hustle* (2019); *Frankie* (2019). Recent TV includes *Vanity Fair* (mini-series 2018).

Susie Parriss Casting

1 Leamington Avenue, Morden SM4 4DQ
tel 020 8543 3326
email susieparrisscasting@gmail.com
website www.susieparrisscasting.com

Known for *Naked* (1993); *Secrets and Lies* (1996); *Hugo* (2011); and *Endeavour* (2012–19).

Recent TV includes: *Goodnight Sweetheart* (1993–2016); *Lewis* (2006–15); *Whitechapel* (2012); *Poldark* (2015–18); *Agatha Raisin* (2016–18) and *Victoria* (2016–19).

Simone Pereira Hind Casting CDG

Summerhall, Summerhall Place, Edinburgh EH9 1PL
tel 0131 290 2526
email anna@sphcasting.com
website www.simonepereirahind.com

Works primarily in film, TV and theatre. Most recent credits include: *Munich: The Edge of War* (Netflix), *Granite Harbour* (BBC), *The White Card* (Soho Theatre) and *Outlander* season 7 (Sony and Starz).

Is able to attend performances in Edinburgh, Glasgow and sometimes London. Accepts CVs with photographs and showreels via email only. Happy to receive enquiries from actors previously unknown, particularly those based in Scotland. She is not always able to respond though may keep details on file for future reference.

Kate Plantin CDG

4 Riverside, Lower Hampton Road, Sunbury on Thames TW16 5PW
tel 01932 782350

email kate@kateplantin.com
website www.kateplantin.com
Key Contact Kate Plantin

Established in 2000. Main areas of work include: theatre, film, television, corporate and commercials. Recent castings include: Theatre: *The Dog Walker* (dir. Harry Burton); *The Rubenstein Kiss* (dir. Katherine Farmer); *A Belly Full* (dir. Marcia Cash); *Other People's Money* (dir. Joe Harmston); *Sexy Laundry* (dir. Phoebe Barran). Film: *The Stranger in Our Bed* (dir. Giles Alderson); *The Pebble and the Boy* (dir. Chris Green); *Break* (dir. Michael Elkin); *The Bromley Boys* (dir. Steve M. Kelly) and *Tango One* (dir. Sacha Bennett). Television: *Andy and the Band* Series 1 and 2 (dir. Matt Holt).

Will consider attending performances at venues outside of London given 3 weeks' notice and 2 weeks' notice if within Greater London. Accepts submissions by email (with CVs and photographs). Also welcomes showreels and invitations to view actors' websites.

Gilly Poole CDG

11 Goodwins Court, London WC2N 4LL
tel 020 7379 5965
email gilly@crowleypoole.co.uk

Known for: *Titanic* (1997), *A Knight's Tale* (2001).

Recent credits include, TV: *Killing Eve* (2018), *The Durrells* (2016–2018); *Trollied* (2012–18), *The White Princess* (2017), *Indian Summers* (2015–16), *Outnumbered* (2007–16); theatre: *Sunny Afternoon* (Hampstead Theatre 2014, West End 2014–16).

Carl Proctor CDG

15ʙ Bury Place, London WC1A 2JB
tel 020 7681 0034 *mobile* 07956 283340
email carlproctorcasting@gmail.com
website www.carlproctorcasting.com

Casts mainly for film and television. Casting credits include: *Son of God* (dir. Christopher Spencer); *Blood Creek* (dir. Joel Schumacher); *Shadow of the Vampire* (dir. E. Elias Merhige); *The Wedding Date* (dir. Clare Kilner); *Mrs Palfrey at the Claremount* (dir. Dan Ireland); and *Twelfth Night* (dir. Trevor Nunn).

Asks that actors only contact by email. CVs and photographs are no longer kept on file as these details are available on Spotlight Interactive.

Andy Pryor CDG

PO Box 77788, London SE5 5NE
tel 020 4541 4390
website www.andypryor.co.uk

Casts mainly for film and television. Casting credits include: *Doctor Who* (2005-2023); *Gentleman Jack* (2019-2022); *It's a Sin* (2021); and *The A Word*.

Leigh-Ann Regan Casting (LARCA) Ltd

Aberdare House, Mount Stuart Square, Cardiff, CF10 5LR
mobile 07779 321954
email leigh-ann@larca.co.uk

Areas of work include television, film, commercials and theatre. Recent credits include: 21-part drama series for S4C/Fiction Factory (Ypris); 4 years casting *Caerdydd* for S4C/Fiction Factory.

Will consider attending performances in Greater London and elsewhere with at least 1 week's notice. Accepts submissions (with CVs and photographs) from actors previously unknown to the casting director.

Nadine Rennie

See the entry for the Soho Theatre under *Producing theatres* on page 145.

Simone Reynolds CDG

email simonemreynolds@gmail.com

Main areas of work are film, television, theatre and commercials. Casting credits include: *The 39 Steps* (Olivier Award for Best Comedy); *The Vicar of Dibley* (TV); *The Politian's Wife* (BAFTA and Emmy Awards, TV); *Love of my Life* (film); *Happily Ever After* (film); *Jack and Sarah* (film); *Shining Through* (film).

Will consider attending performances at venues in Greater London and elsewhere, given as much notice as possible. Accepts postal submissions (with CVs and photographs) from actors previously unknown to the casting director, but does not welcome email enquiries. Advises actors to: "Keep CVs clear (separate out the part from the director and venue) and keep covering submissions brief."

Kate Rhodes-James CDG

78 Kingston Road, Teddington TW11 9HY
tel 020 8943 3265 *mobile* 07967 077256
email office@krjcasting.com

Kate trained as an actress. After three years she decided it wasn't for her. She assisted the casting on *The Young Indiana Chronicles* and then assisted Debbie McWilliams on three Bond films. Her first solo project was *Cold Feet* (ITV) and then *The Lakes* (BBC). Recent credits include, film: *Their Finest* (2016); TV: *Sherlock* (2010–17), *A Discovery of Witches* (2018), *Bodyguard* (2018).

Vicky Richardson CDG

email vrichardson.casting@gmail.com

Previously Casting Associate at the Donmar Warehouse. Since becoming a freelance casting director, she has worked with the National Theatre, Royal Exchange (Manchester), Nuffield Theatre (Southampton), The Orange Tree and Cleanbreak.

Danielle Roffe Casting

71 Mornington Street, London NW1 7QE
email danielle@danielleroffe.com
website www.danielleroffe.com

Works in film and television. Recent credits include: *The Upside of Anger*, *She's Gone*, and *Holy Cross*.

Welcomes performance notices and is prepared to travel within Greater London. Does not welcome unsolicited CVs, photographs or showreels, but is happy to receive invitations to view individual actors' websites.

Jessica Ronane CDG

See the entry for the Old Vic under *Producing theatres* on page 141.

Annie Rowe CDG

tel 020 8354 2699 *mobile* 07734 809597
email annie@annierowe-casting.com
Twitter @AnnieRoweCasts

Established in 2009. Main area of work: short and feature film, theatre.

Happy to receive performance notices, given 2 weeks' notification. Showreels and invitations to view actors' websites welcome by email only. Please submit via Spotlight link for a specific job, rather than unsolicited.

Neil Rutherford Casting

mobile 07960 891911
email neil@neilrutherford.com
website www.neilrutherford.com

A casting director since 2000, working mainly in theatre in the West End and internationally, having been Head of Casting at ATG until 2012 and now freelance.

Welcomes CVs and letters (with photographs) via email. Also happy to receive casting interview enquiries and production invites via the same method.

Jane Salberg

86 Stade Street, Hythe, Kent CT21 6DY
tel 01303 239277
email janesalberg@aol.com

Works in theatre and musicals. Recent credits include: UK Casting Director for Jean Ann Ryan (Cruise Musicals); *Horrid Henry Live and Horrid* (UK tour); and *The Wizard of Oz* (Royal Festival Hall).

Prefers not to receive performance notices or unsolicited submissions, but will consider invitations to view individual actors' websites.

Ginny Schiller CDG

9 Clapton Terrace, London E5 9BW
tel 020 8806 5383
email casting@ginnyschiller.co.uk
website www.ginnyschiller.co.uk

Main area of work is theatre, but has also cast for television, film, radio and commercials. Recent work includes: *The Starry Messenger* (Wyndhams); *Admissions* (Trafalgar); *The Cherry Orchard* (BOV and Royal Exchange); *Richard II* (Almeida); *The Father* and *Bad Jews* (Ustinov, West End and tours); multiple West End transfers or original productions, over 20 shows at the Rose Theatre Kingston, 30+ for Theatre Royal Bath, and the Ustinov Studio seasons 2011-2019.

Accepts links to view actors' CVs and online profile or showreel via email. Welcomes performance notices via email, if given 2 weeks' notice.

Nadira Seecoomar CDG

tel 020 8892 8478
email nadira.seecoomar@gmail.com

Known for *The Inbetweeners 2* (2014), *The Inbetweeners Movie* (2011), *My Summer of Love* (2004), *Jump Tomorrow* (2001).

Recent credits include, film: *The Festival* (2018); TV: *The Windsors* (2016–18), *People Just Do Nothing* (2017), *Ill Behaviour* (2017), *White Gold* (2017), *Chewing Gum* (2017)

Select Casting Ltd

PO Box·748, London NW4 1TT
mobile 07956 131494
email info@selectcasting.co.uk
website www.selectcasting.co.uk
website http://pro.imdb.com/name/nm3052115/
Twitter @selectcasting
Casting Venetia Suchdev

In 2004 Select Casting Ltd started up as an in-house extras agency for an already established production house. It gained independent status as a casting agency as well as an extras agency for actors and background supporting artistes in 2007. Select Management was established in 2008 to look after a handful of professional actors, dancers, presenters and models who are registered on Spotlight.

Initially specialising in the Bollywood market it quickly progressed to more regional film productions by film-makers from other regions in the Indian subcontinent. Also offers services to film-makers from the Middle East and Russia and a wider global market, allowing production companies to make one call and fulfil all their requirements for an international cast and crew globally.

Provides line production services and full accounting packages (including tax credits and day-to-day cash flow services etc).

Recent filmography: Bollywood films include: *Bhagam Bhag, Namastey London, Salaam-E-Ishq* and *Patiala House*; Russian films include: *Platon*; Middle Eastern productions include: *El Malik Farourk (King Farouk)*; Hungarian-US productions include: *Magic Boys*; Chinese productions include: *Vanguard, Dual Crisis, Triumph in the Skies II, Passage of my Youth, Impman 4, Finding Mr Right 2, Flying Tiger 2*; British feature films include: *Keith Lemon - The Film* and *Kick, Robot Overlords*; Canadian TV series: *The Frankie Drake Mysteries*. Has also worked on several music videos, commercials, idents and promos etc.

Phil Shaw

Suite 476, 2 Old Brompton Road, South Kensington, London SW7 3DQ
tel 020 8715 8943
email philshawcasting@gmail.com

Main areas of work are theatre, television, film and commercials. Casting credits include: Originating Co-Exec Producer: *Wire in the Blood* (ITV pilot); *Deckies* (Channel 4 series pilot); *Days in the Trees* (BBC Radio); *The Bill* (Thames TV); *Body Story* (BBC TV doc/drama series); *Romans 12:20* (BAFTA nominated; Grand Jury Prize, ARPA, Los Angeles); *Winter Fiction* (NFTS); *The Killing of Sister George* (Oldham Coliseum); *The Turn of the Screw* (No. 1 tour); *Billy Liar; The Chalk Garden; People Are Living There* (King's Head Theatre); *Cock & Bull Story* (Old Red Lion); *Enjoy* (Watford Palace); *Angels in America* (Lyric, Hammersmith); *The Last Post* (BAFTA nominated; Grand Prize, Berlin Film Festival); *Italian Movies* (Indiana Productions, feature - UK casting). Currently in development: *Albion* (US/UK TV drama series) and *Deadly* (UK/Canada TV drama series written/directed by Neil LaBute).

Will consider attending performances at Central London venues, and also West End, NT and RSC understudy runs, given a minimum of 2 weeks' notice. Accepts postal submissions (with resume/photograph), emailed Showcards and performance notices, but does not welcome unsolicited showreels or email enquiries (unless a performance notice).

Michelle Smith CDG

220 Church Lane, Woodford, Stockport SK7 1PQ
tel 0161 439 6825
email michelle.smith18@btinternet.com

Specialising in film, television and commercials. Recent TV casting credits include: *Reg* (BBC1), *Common* (BBC1), *Moving On* (BBC). Recent film credits include: *The Messenger, Electricity, The Violators* and *Lies We Tell*.

Suzanne Smith CDG

99 Leighton Road, London NW5 2RB
tel 020 7278 0045
email suzanne@suzannesmithcasting.com

Works in film and television. Credits include: *Shadow and Bone; Good Omens; To Olivia; Carnival Row* and *Outlander*.

Emma Stafford

tel 0161 833 4263
email assistant@emmastafford.tv
website www.emmastafford.tv

Areas of work include television, film and commercials. Recent credits include: *200 Magazine*, Co-op Bank, Robinsons, *If I Were a Butterfly*.

Will consider attending performances within the North West area with at least 2 weeks' notice. Accepts letters (with CVs and photographs) from actors previously unknown to the agency; will also accept CVs and photographs sent by email, and view showreels.

Helen Stafford

14 Park Avenue, Enfield, London EN1 2HP
tel 020 8360 6329
email helenstaffordcasting@gmail.com

Casts in film and theatre, in both the UK and the USA. Recent credits include: Films: *The Phantom Warrior*, *The Bezonians*, *Righteous Villains Original Gangster*, *Smoking Guns aka A Punter's Prayer* and *Red Devil* (now *Red Rage*); Theatre: New York Broadway production transfers to London West End.

Will consider seeing actors perform in Central and Greater London, with 1 week's notice.

Robert Sterne

See the entry for Nina Gold CDG under *Casting directors* on page 106.

Gail Stevens & Rebecca Farhall Casting

First Floor Studio Office, 119 Roman Road, London E2 0QN
email office@gailstevenscasting.com

Main areas of work are television, film and commercials. Casting credits include: *Pistol*, *Zero Dark Thirty*, *Slumdog Millionaire*, *Trainspotting* and *Babylon*.

Sam Stevenson CDG

email sam@hancockstevenson.com
website www.hancockstevenson.com

See entry for National Theatre in *Producing theatres* on page 139.

Syson Casting

tel 020 7287 5327

Recent feature films and TV credits include: *Holmes & Watson: The Abandoned Case* (2022); *Wonder Woman 1984* (2020); *The Alienist* (2018-20); *Terminator: Dark Fate*; and *Aladdin* (2019).

Amanda Tabak CDG

See the entry for Candid Casting under *Casting directors* on page 102.

Topps Casting

The Media Centre, 7 Northumberland Street, West Yorkshire HD1 1RL
tel 01484 511988
email nicci@toppscasting.co.uk
website https://casting.niccitopping.com
Twitter @niccitopping
Casting Director Nicci Topping

Works in television, film and commercials. Recent work includes Gucci pre-fall 2017 campaign; Disney; Facebook; Paul McCartney music promo; Louis Tomlinson promo; *Black Prince* (feature film); *Dusty and Me* (feature film); CDA Award Best Short Film Casting: *The Big Day*; John Lewis Christmas 2018: #EltonJohnLewis.

Welcomes performance notices within Greater London and elsewhere (Manchester, Leeds, Sheffield)

if given 2 weeks' notice. Accepts letters (with CVs & photographs) from individual actors previously unknown to the agency, sent by post or email.

Jill Trevellick CDG

92 Priory Road, London N8 7EY
tel 020 8340 2734
email jill@jilltrevellick.com

Main areas of work are film and television. Casting credits include: *Downton Abbey*; *Save Me*; *The Victim*; *Apple Tree Yard*; *The Hour*; *Merlin*; *Fish Tank*; *What We Did On Our Holiday*; *The Hamburg Cell*.

Anne Vosser

156 Lower Farnham Road, Aldershot, Hampshire GU12 4EL
tel 01252 404716 *mobile* 07968 868712
email anne@vosser-casting.co.uk
website www.vosser-casting.co.uk

Main areas of work are theatre and musicals. Casting credits include: *What The Butler Saw*, *Zorro*, *Taboo*, *Fame*, *Saturday Night Fever*, *Footloose*, *Never Forget* (all in the West End).

Fiona Weir CDG

2nd Floor, 138 Portobello Road, London W11 2DZ
tel 020 7727 5600
Twitter @FWCASTING

Recent credits for film and TV include: *Wednesday* (2022); *Fantastic Beasts: The Secrets of Dumbledore* (2022); *Judy* (2019); *Room* (2015); *Brooklyn* (2015).

Matt Western

mobile 07740 70207
email matt@mattwestern.co.uk
website www.mattwestern.co.uk

Main areas of work are film, television and commercials. Recent casting credits include: Film: *Three Acts* (2018), *The Holly Kane Experiment* (2017), *Susu* (2017), *Golden Years* (2016), *Boys Will Be Boys* (2016); TV: *Missing* (series 1, 2014 and series 2, 2016).

Jeremy Zimmermann Casting

tel 020 7478 5161
email info@zimmermanncasting.com

Main areas of work are film and television. Casting work includes: *Willow*, *Keeping Mum*, *Dog Soldiers* and *Hellboy*.

Will consider attending performances at venues in Greater London and elsewhere. Accepts email submissions (with CVs and photographs) from actors previously unknown to the casting director, but does not welcome postal submissions. Invitations to view individual actors' websites are also accepted.

Casting for the stage

Anne McNulty

If the essence of acting on stage is the gathering of a group of people to share a story, then the work of a casting director is to guide and support the director in meeting and choosing the actors to make up that group. The director will have ideas and expectations and it's my job to share the widest possible range of acting talent to achieve the cast. The choice is wide open until we have seen all our actors.

The play, the director, the venue, the timescale, the salary – these are the first things to take into consideration when I am approached to work with a director on a play. We will both read the script in depth. We produce a breakdown describing each of the roles and I may send this out to agents via a Spotlight link; it will depend on size of cast and if the director has strong initial ideas. I will check CVs and perhaps go straight to an offer for the key roles in a production.

I will also compile a list of actors for each of the roles based on my knowledge of their work, details from their agents and their CVs. We will also receive individual submissions and will read these too. The decisions about who and how many actors to meet will depend on the director's schedule and who we feel is suitable. We will also be speculative if there is a credit that interests us on an actor's CV, or if we have seen a review that describes a particular actor who we like the sound of. It is not necessary to have an agent to be considered for casting but sometimes if may be a stipulation that the actor has some professional experience. It all depends on the role and the director.

I may work with an assistant and between us we will book rooms, liaise with the director about the text you should prepare, fix the meetings and read in, if required.

You will be invited to audition because you have been singled out as a potential for the role and one of a small group being met. A fixed time has been allocated for your meeting and you need to use it to show your skills. Please don't make excuses. You should have been given enough time to prepare, but if you are called in at short notice then do all you can and share that in the meeting.

Know the story of the play. The internet can offer a precis for existing texts, and if it is a new play you may be sent the script – if not, interpret what you can from the sides you are sent. It is vital to prepare well and bring your sense of the character into the meeting. You are coming into the room to get the job, so a sense of who you are as a person and as a company member is important. Expect to be asked a question about any shows you have seen lately, or if you have a favourite writer or actor, who they are and why you chose them.

If the role requires an accent then prepare in that accent and also be ready to use your own accent. The director could ask you to give an extreme interpretation of the character to see how far you can stretch in trying something. Do think about how you dress, as being too relaxed and informal can suggest you're not taking the meeting seriously. Shorts and flip-flops simply do not work.

One other crucial piece of advice is to listen carefully and be succinct. The urgency and nerves of wanting to do a good audition can mean you don't hear properly or reply quickly, meaning you may not hear everything that the director has said. Often, this clarity is vital and you can always ask for them to say it again. If you are asked if you have any questions, it usually means 'do you understand?' and it is not an opportunity to stall or to ask the director how they see the part.

You may meet directors who are less forthcoming and simply want you to work on the text. They may give you a note but will not really engage in chat. Don't be alarmed, they will be considering your work just the same and that is their style.

If the meeting does not lead to you getting the role, your work and the inspiration you offered will be recorded by the team and hopefully they will think of you for future projects. You may feel you are totally right for a role but there are many considerations in balancing a company, casting a family, the siblings – even twins! Also, the relationship of the parents, best friend, rival or lover, will decide how the choice is made. I always feed back to agents and actors after their auditions. This can take time but gives you an indication of how it went so you can use that in the future.

When I am in the midst of a casting, the priority will always be the meetings. I will give you as much information as possible, to ensure that your meeting can be open, investigative and a time to really work the text. Make the most of it.

My other source of insight is to see as many shows as I can – every evening and sometimes on the weekend. I will go to regional productions and shows on tour, to watch as many actors, interpretations and styles of direction and production, as they give me lots of information. I cover many of the drama school shows and share the progress of new graduates as they find their first jobs in theatre. I will also see all the current television and films – so there's plenty of input going into each new casting.

I think William Shakespeare sums it up perfectly: 'the readiness is all'. Keep it simple, prepare well and good luck.

Anne McNulty, CDG, is originally from Manchester and moved to London in 1986 to work for a charity, then joined the Young Vic in 1990 as PA to the Artistic and Administrative Directors. This was where she met Sam Mendes and joined the Donmar Warehouse as Casting Director, plus administrative support, in May 1992. After working with both Michael Grandage and Josie Rourke, she left in 2012 to pursue a freelance career and to work in drama schools, with a particular interest in audition workshops.

Casting for musical theatre

David Grindrod

The process of producing/casting a musical can be a very long and costly affair. Everyone is looking for the next *Phantom of the Opera* or *Mamma Mia!*; years of work can go into the production you see on stage today. Workshops have now become a necessity in order to see if a show 'has legs', without spending too much money. In consultation with the producer and creative team, I will assemble a group of actors who may not be totally right for the roles but who work well in a workshop situation. If the green light is given after the workshop presentation, the casting process – in conjunction with everything else – begins.

A casting breakdown is drawn up: this consists of all the details required by agents and artists about the characters, vocal ranges, etc. plus the proposed dates of the production. Open calls are sometimes organised for specific roles, but normally the breakdown gets sent to agents via the Spotlight link, which reaches 500 agents/representatives at the touch of a button.

There is always a 'wish list' of actors whom producers would like in their production, but the bulk of submissions will come through agents, in the form of photos and CVs. Unsolicited mail is also received; sometimes it is difficult to keep all this on file due to sheer number of submissions. Either I or my associates will also attend college shows and presentations to look for specific talent.

When preparing your photos and CVs, always remember that these are the calling cards with which you promote yourself! A good photograph is not 'artistic' (i.e. showing a face half in shadow); rather, it should always present a good full face that really does look like you. Your CV should ideally be just one page stapled to the back of your photograph. It should include all relevant details (*not* forgetting contact details) to show your skills. Make this information clear and precise. If you feel that you are suitable for musical casting, be very accurate and truthful about your vocal range: don't make it complicated – basically, tenor or soprano, with the top of your range noted. We can normally tell your style by the shows you have appeared in.

The audition process normally begins with artists performing two contrasting songs that show range and personality. Make an effort to pick a song that is suitable for the show – not pop, for example, when you are up for Rogers & Hammerstein. Nerves will take over; therefore, don't sing the song you learnt yesterday, but perform something tried and tested (something you would be happy singing naked in Trafalgar Square!). When we ask, "Have you got something else?" we don't want the answer, "My agent said you only wanted two songs,"; have your book of audition pieces with you and give us the chance to choose an alternative. Actors often ask whether I have favourite songs that I like to hear – or songs that I don't: I only really mind when they come in with completely the wrong song for the production.

If an actor is successful, they will receive a call-back for a dance/movement call. This normally causes concerns, but actually it is not usually that specific; we only want to see whether a person is happy with his/her body. If the audition is for a major dance show, hopefully you will know your limitations, and either not audition at all, or be ready to throw yourself into the routine. Again, be honest: then you won't upset the creative team.

Further recalls take place with music and script from the show: the musical supervisor or associate director normally takes these calls. If you come in for the musical supervisor, come back with music prepared and your own song. *Always* bring your own song – it's a good reminder for the team. In addition to any script you are asked to read, you may get asked for a speech: have a couple of acting pieces prepared, and again, nerves will take over, so make sure you know them properly. Remember that these speeches are also to allow the director to assess how well you can respond to direction, and how readily you can take a note.

The culmination of the casting process – 'the finals' – is the most nerve-wracking experience, even for a highly experienced artist. Bring everything with you that you have been given. You may not get *asked* for everything, but have it just in case. You may have been asked to dress in a certain way; always put some thought into that, as directors can be blinkered at times ... I have known artists to arrive with a couple of outfits and ask me to pick one! The panel will consist of the whole creative team and the producers. At this stage I can't do any more for you – though hopefully I can keep the atmosphere in the room happy and 'up'. Stay calm, don't change anything that you have been told, and audition to the best of your abilities.

Now the wait to see if you have the role. Always remember that you have got this far in the process because you can sing and act far better than anyone else. In the end, the decision could come down to height, look, hair colour; funnily enough it may not have anything to do with your singing/acting skills at this point. And you may not get an instant answer; you may have to wait until other meetings have taken place. You may get put on 'hold': normally that means you are not first on the list, but if somebody above you declines the offer you may move up. If you are lucky, the phone call will come with a straight offer. How exciting is that ... Contractual details are then advised and, if all that is agreed, your date for first rehearsal is given. Always remember that you are a small part of the bigger picture – a small part of the jigsaw puzzle that goes together to form: The Musical.

David Grindrod founded David Grindrod Associates (DGA) with Stephen Crockett in January 1998, after 20 years' experience in the theatre in various roles ranging from assistant stage manager to general manager. Current West End casting includes *Chicago, Evita, The Lord of the Rings, Mamma Mia!* (worldwide), *Spamalot, The Sound of Music.* Films include *The Phantom of The Opera.* DGA are also casting consultants for *On The Town* and *Kismet* at the English National Opera, and belong to the Casting Directors Guild of Great Britain.

Agents and casting directors

Woman in a brown skirt

Sophie Stanton reflects on the Donmar Warehouse's pioneering commitment to providing more opportunities for female actors in its all-women Shakespeare Trilogy, which helped her to land her most significant roles to date: Falstaff in the Donmar's *Henry IV* and Mrs Rich in the RSC'S revival of *The Fantastic Follies of Mrs Rich* by Mary Pix.

I mourned my training when it ended. I consider myself fortunate that I did, but it was painful. Perhaps that's why for many years I compulsively enrolled on courses in whatever subject piqued my interest at the time.

On the cartoon course, perhaps a couple of years out of drama school, I titled one project, 'The Seven Stages of Wan'. It's a portrait of an actress as she journeys through her career from early childhood to old age, sans everything. I revisit it now with one question in mind – how prophetic was I in those early years?

The first three frames are self-explanatory: 'I wanna be Mary' depicts a child of nursery school age in the school nativity (I was always a shepherd in ours); 'I wanna be picked', aged fourteen she's auditioning for a production of Romeo and Juliet – we did *A Midsummer Night's Dream*. I was Puck. We also did The Mikado. I played Koko, the Lord High Executioner. A pattern was emerging. 'I wanna be unpicked' sees the young drama student suffering 'first-term fatigue syndrome' at the fictitious Deptford Academy of Dramatic Art, (DADA)… Whilst training, I played a wealth of older ladies – drunks, eccentrics, powerhouses of motherhood – and was all the better for it as a young mind at the very start of a career. Of course, there was no way I was going to get an agent from it, but I was truly stretched in most disciplines and, therefore, ironically, in my creative prime upon graduation.

The first couple of years were paltry. I played a mouse, Pimple, someone who'd been abused on *The Bill*. The worst corpse of my entire life occurred in a 'reminiscence show' we inflicted on older members of the community round various care homes, when one woman screamed, 'Oh, shut up! You are getting on my nerves' in the middle of my solo. Which rather hit the nail on the head and drove it into my heart. But it got me my Equity card.

'I wanna work' was the frame I saw myself in at the time of drawing the cartoon. Our female protagonist sits in a coffee shop with a male actor friend sharing a conversation she has had with her agent, desperate to get a job *of any description*. Both are smoking (how times have changed). She asks how his career is going. 'Well, great. But then, I'm a boy' is the response. (Or have they?) We fast-forward to the middle-aged actress outside a Winnebago. 'Love, I'm a bloody joke,' she says on the phone, 'I've got two sodding lines and some business with a rhino! It would be *nice* to play Lady M before it's too late, frankly!' In a letter to my former self I might comment that this insight into life for an actress of a certain age is uncanny. To which, my former self would undoubtedly reply, 'That's not me being insightful, it's the truth.' Which of course it is, unless you are exceptionally lucky. Or unless you get cast as a man. I wonder what I would have felt had I known then that I'd wait twenty-odd years to play a major role and that that major role would be an old fat bloke. I'm sure the old fat bloke bit of the equation wouldn't have been an issue having cornered the market in shepherds, traditionally male fairies, executioners and old ladies. But the wait?

And so to Falstaff in the Donmar Warehouse's all-female Shakespeare Trilogy (St Ann's Warehouse, New York, 2015; Donmar King's Cross, 2016). In one, rare twenty-four-hour period, I landed two smashing theatre jobs and was on a 'pencil' (they do fall through, don't ever trust a pencil) for a TV series that has so far run to three seasons and would no doubt have made a healthy dent in my mortgage. But it had been too long since I'd played a part I'd really had to work at. There is a rose called Falstaff. It is unmissable in a border – bold, broad, robust, its petals seem infinitesimal and it's almost the colour of electricity, at once mesmerising and repellent. Its lust for the world strikes me as so enormous that all that energy simply cannot last. Which is probably all I need to say about the role. It undoubtedly changed the landscape for me as an artist. You cannot turn that down. It just doesn't come around very often if you're a bird.

Don't get me wrong: many of the roles I have played have been absolute gems – in *Mercury Fur*, *England People Very Nice*, *Dying for It*, *Beautiful Thing*, *Ding Dong the Wicked*, *Nut*, *Ink*, *Made in Dagenham: The Musical* – in bastions of new writing: the Almeida, the Royal Court, the National, the Bush. Just too, too many to mention, providing exceptional material with which to carve out a notably varied career. But, still, a lot of them amount to cameos as they're in relief of the male protagonist, which is often all we can expect as 'character actresses'.

Falstaff gave me no choice but to step up as an artist. To stride out, to claim space and make noise unapologetically in a manner which is simply foreign to us as both women and as female actors. It was a language that I had barely spoken since childhood, in fact, when I had been permitted to play the noisy parts in school plays. I took inspiration from John Travolta strutting through the streets of NYC to the sound track of 'Staying Alive' – just feeling great about himself. I studied men who walk only in straight lines, taking for granted that the rest of us will step aside. I dropped my voice an octave and hit maximum volume. And, of course, I embraced the male spread. Falstaff gives it large.

Women, to this day, tend to be written small. Even the female juvenile lead is often written with a bias towards making the bloke-part look tender when he falls in love with her (which isn't a terribly progressive representation of men either, might I add, we must fight for both genders). Obviously, I get cast as the juve lead's mum or just that woman who's complaining in a shop. I call them the 'brown skirt parts'.

God forbid they should dress you in anything interesting; you might upstage the lead. Yesterday's conversation with a costume designer – 'I'm going to make you downbeat, muted. In contrast to, you know, *the politicians*.' The film is about the politicians, need I say, all male.

Unsurprisingly, Falstaff was the best possible preparation for the biggest female role I have played to date – Mrs Rich in *The Fantastic Follies of Mrs Rich*, an adaptation of Mary Pix's lost play *The Beau Defeated* of 1700 (RSC, Stratford, 2018). Mrs Rich is writ large, oh, yes she is. The delicious absurdity of her social pretension, the enormity of her wit, her kitsch, her pain and her glory, the cabaret, the vaudeville demanded by the writing – none of it could I draw on from having played the brown-skirt parts. All of my references were male. I spent a lot of time researching the work of drag queens. We just don't have permission to display as women. At best, it is not female tradition. At worst it is unsavoury. I had four soaring solos written by Grant Olding scored for four saxophones aspiring to be a string quartet (not since I was heckled by an old lady had I sung solo), I was gifted endless innuendos, ad libs, exquisite soliloquies and audience collusion. I learnt the harpsichord, how to vogue, wolf whistle, had costumes made which really should be behind glass at the Victoria and Albert museum and finally – finally — I got to perform my first professional sword fight. That part was Falstaffian.

God forbid this swathe of women in significant male roles should be relegated to a thing of the past because look at where it can lead. It would be nice not to have to play a man in order to fulfil an epic role of a lifetime, but those female roles are painfully rare. Women have to be represented bigger – not just more, but bigger. We cannot let this work fade. Do not go gentle into that good night. Thank you, Mr Dylan Thomas. I shall try very hard not to.

In the penultimate frame of my cartoon, our now older protagonist has indeed won the part of Lady M, but it's too late as her memory has gone and she suffers a mammoth dry in the 'dashed the brains out' speech. Two walk-on actors mutter bitchy comments behind her. It's bleak. And finally, we come to 'Dribble Hall; retirement home for dear old thesps'. We find the elderly woman at what is possibly her final Christmas, being entertained by Naff Theatre Company. Her face is full of loss, *wan*, but there's a soupçon of defiance left about the eyes. She says to herself, 'And so it came to pass'... This, the last frame, is again titled, 'I wanna be Mary'.

Perhaps this has answered my question. Perhaps I should've been delighted to know that I'd play an old bloke in twenty or so years because evidently in my mid-twenties I was already resigned to a life of artistic frustration simply because of my gender.

When the time comes, if I reach an age when I can expect to spend time somewhere like Dribble Hall, I do hope I have wits enough not to be saying, 'I wanna be Mary.' Mary's a dull part. Mary's basically there to give birth to one of the lead guys. Mary is Woman-in-a-Brown-Skirt. I hope, in my dotage, that I'm aiming higher than Mary. I wanna be saying, I dunno, 'I wanna be the Angel Gabriel.' Or I wanna be...!

God?

Now, God's a good part.

Sophie Stanton graduated from RADA in 1991 and has worked extensively in British theatre, television, film and radio ever since. She also sometimes writes and occasionally directs. Her first play *Cariad* was published in 2007. She is currently working on her second play with the generous support of the Arts Council England. Amongst other things.

Theatre
Introduction

Theatres and theatre companies/managements exist in all kinds of different forms, and paid opportunities for live performance are not restricted to putting on productions. The days of the permanent repertory company are almost gone, but there is a much wider diversity of work available. The larger companies/managements often use casting directors (see page 100), who should usually be your first port of call. However, it can be worth exploiting any personal contacts that you may have.

For all approaches, it is important to send your submissions to the person named – unless you have a personal contact.

Active listening in a community of nomads

Cherrelle Skeete, co-founder and Artistic Director of Blacktress UK
Interview by Joan Iyiola

Cherrelle Skeete is an actress, writer, cultural curator and consultant. She is co-founder and Artistic Director of Blacktress UK, a network and support group for Black womxn actors and creatives providing a platform to grow and connect through community. Cherrelle works across theatre, television and film and was on the 2019/2020 Soho Theatre Writers Lab. Cherrelle believes storytelling is a necessary tool to activate understanding, build bridges and heal ourselves so we can all move towards our own freedom.

How have you used community practices in your work as an artist?

I think community is the ultimate dialogue, a dialogue of active listening in the hope that no one gets left behind. I have to mention 'community' because no person is an island and I didn't just turn up here. It took a group of people to make various decisions and who said different things to support me and remind me who I am. To me, community is liberation, strength, a place to really learn. I've found a lot of solace in different communities. Your community is your chosen family, it's the place where you learnt your craft at different points. It might be the place where you learnt that you were actually good at something or where you felt seen for the first time when other parts of society weren't seeing you. It's a space that's about everybody who's responsible for taking care of it, a space that's cultivated, with a sense of community, similarities based on what that community is setting out to do. There'll be a certain demographic within that community, with similar cultural interests. I think it's something we as artists do. We're always looking for our tribe. When you're auditioning for something, you're looking for your tribe. Everyone involved is involved in a sense of community, it's everywhere.

Off the back of that, can you give us an overview about Blacktress, your reasons for setting it up and the work that you have created with this wonderful group?

Blacktress has been going for four years. I'm a co-founder and I run it alongside my partner, Shiloh Coke. It's a network, support group, and we're curators. The work is Black women and femme-centered. We do Spark workshops, we ran a festival of Black women-led work early in its formation called the Blacktress Season. We've curated specific events, which again are Black-women-centred, but they're open to all. We have socials where we're celebrating women who may not necessarily be recognised within the mainstream and we'll see them first and celebrate them. This was a space cultivated out of many conversations I'd heard, women saying they felt alone, isolated, didn't feel seen or heard. So, we create a safe space which is often about healing. I believe those who've suffered most deserve the greatest victories and I think we're so victorious. Yes, I'm the founder but I'm not the sole custodian of that space. Every single person holds everybody's story, everybody's physical and spiritual being's space with a sense of care and thoughtfulness, consideration, compassion, curiosity and the ability to just listen.

What might you want to say to the graduating actors and performers of this year about the importance of this act of self-care?

Firstly, it's really important to spend some time on your own to get to know who you are – who you are without the noise, the industry stuff. Just strip back and learn so you can identify when you're feeling low and also identify what you need to get back to a place where you feel balance. Because the word self-care has been thrown around a lot, it's become this almost overused buzzword. I think what I'm going to start using is 'balance'. To get back to a place of balance. The first thing I say to graduates is find your tribe, you were put together with other people within your year group by circumstance. They may be your tribe, but you may also need to reconnect with yourself and find your people. Speak about your experiences, they're valid. Use this wonderful thing the internet and reach out to people. We're all in it together, literally. There's no wrong way of doing it, they're all just experiences. Affirm your experiences for yourself by writing them out. I encourage everyone to journal, but if you don't like to write, maybe scrapbook. Do it for self first and then everything else will come from that in terms of connecting with people and you'll attract the right people who might be your future collaborators. That's the whole point: you want to be making art with people who respect you, respect the dignity of life, and you can be on the same page in terms of how you want to make art.

We're seeing a lot of anti-racism pledges from theatres and companies at the moment. What does leadership in this space look like to you?

If you look at your team of people who you work with and the building that you might work in and you see that there are opportunities being opened up, maybe think about what you would usually do and then challenge yourself to do something slightly different. Bring in someone who wouldn't necessarily be within that environment that you've created. If you're actively wanting change, as an artist, a venue, an organisation, then bring in people to do that. I think what we're asking for post-lockdown is actually human kindness and it's not passive. It's a loving action. Create that space, even give up space. A lot of what we're doing is about the dismantling of the powers that be, speaking truth to power, which is not always easy.

In order for us to sit in this space where we can all sit together, it's 'I do something for you, you do something for me' and we're constantly going, making offerings of kindness in the space to find out what our collaborative power is.

The relationship is reciprocal. That's why I said community is for me the biggest dialogue, not one-sided. When you have community leaders, the pyramid is upside down and you as the leader are at the bottom. Because you're answering to people at the top and that's your community and it's actually about being of service. I want to create more spaces where we're doing more reimagining, talking about what we need, what are the active measures that we need to do. Do we need to ringfence tickets to make sure that we've got audience members? We can't be using the same tactics as before. We've got to up our game. If that wasn't working, let's try something else. We're very fortunate in the arts to lead on that because we are the people literally creating with our tools, our hands, our talent, the people that we come across. So, every kind of process that we're going into with our storytelling, you literally get to reset and restart again how you want this ship to run.

Theatre

I think that's amazing. You know, in theatre you build this incredible relationship with people over the course of five months and then that's it! Then you start again with these nomadic people, but I think there's something so beautiful about that.

That's beautiful, our imagination is our superpower.

I think the most powerful thing that we have as a people, as Black people, as human beings, as creatives, whoever you are, is our imagination. In terms of culture, culture is a collection of concepts. There has to be a dialogue, we can't just have one concept all the time. The exchange has to be happening back and forth constantly and the concept grows, then we all agree and eventually that becomes a culture. There's a repetition of concepts that everybody agrees on. So, if we're saying that we want to keep reimagining, we've got to keep talking to each other, listening – actively listening – and, from that, take action.

You incorporate activism in your artistry. How would you encourage others to do the same?

Everyone is responsible for their own activism but, firstly, it's to be active. It's a movement of love, corny as that sounds. We're actually wanting to say, can we stop hurting each other, live peacefully, be kind, make space for those we're pushing out. When the theatres closed, obviously it was very sad, but we have to think about what happened to all of us, how these spaces function and if they're functioning in a way that's serving us as a people. Let's re-evaluate our core values and what we need. Remember, those spaces belong to the people. Our taxes fund those buildings so we have to hold them accountable. Let's start with self, what do I need? What can I do to achieve the things I need to get me balanced? What spaces and environments for the people of certain communities they're meant to be serving are going to give them balance? Does the environment we're creating and cultivating support that? Re-evaluating and reconnecting, these are brilliant places to begin. This period and returning has to be about us opening these spaces in a way that introduces different things, making these spaces more accessible for everybody. To serve the community, serve spaces where dialogues can be had and that requires everybody, everybody speaking and knowing what that they need.

For more information about Blacktress go to **www.blacktress.co.uk** or follow them on Twitter **@blacktress**. Follow Cherrelle directly at **www.cherrelleskeete.com** or **@cherrelleskeete** on Instagram.

Dramaturg at HOME

Petra Jane Tauscher

The growth in the number of visible dramaturgs in British theatre in the last 25 years has been remarkable. Their emergence in this country has often been greeted with suspicion, particularly in and around the new theatre writing community, which is far larger here than in most other European countries. Some playwrights thought being assigned a dramaturg by a commissioning theatre was an unhelpful control mechanism, an infringement of their creativity. Some artistic directors associated dramaturgs with the American prevalence of work-shopping plays in development with actors (28 workshops in the case of Tony Kushner's *Angels in America*) as risible and other playwrights saw dramaturg-led workshops as excuses for theatres not committing to the production of more new plays. This was to dismiss out of hand the enhancement that positive support from an informed specialist, the dramaturg, and actors' creativity can bring to the writing process.

The British resistance to this principle is partly understandable given the traditional under resourcing of theatre here in comparison with many other European countries, and its success in new theatre writing drawn from a very rapid turnover in the initial presentation of new product with on average four-week runs, and the same amount of time, or less, for rehearsal. It is interesting to note the rise of work-shopping in the more commercially lucrative musical theatre sector. *Made in Dagenham* received four major workshops over a couple of years. On the continent new productions can rehearse for six months and stay in the repertoire for several years. The German premiere production of Mark Ravenhill's *Shopping and Fucking* began its life at the Baracke in January 1998, then transferred to the Schaubühne, where it remained in the repertoire for over a decade. Nevertheless the original resistance to dramaturgs in Britain demonstrated a lack of understanding of their wider responsibilities beyond support to new writing. In fact the breadth of the field of dramaturgy is such that any one dramaturg's relationship to it at any one time is akin to any one doctor's relationship to the whole of medicine. However, unlike doctors, dramaturgs can shift between different aspects of dramaturgy fairly readily, particularly if they are, like myself at HOME in Manchester, employed full time by one theatre company. To make the function of my role more clear my job title is Creative Producer and Dramaturg.

In my role as creative producer I am concerned with making things happen, such joint productions with other theatre companies; liaising with potential visiting companies; relating to other theatre-makers across Greater Manchester and helping to manage programmes within the building such as the assistant directors we nurture on lengthy placements from the two-year MA in Directing at Birkbeck College, University of London. As dramaturg, in addition to our own productions, there is only time for me to be deeply involved in one or two other productions at a time, though I can give notes to any production visiting HOME. For his first production in the new building Artistic Director Walter Meierjohann asked playwright Simon Stephens to adapt Odon von Horvath's *Kasimir and Karoline* into a local contemporary setting, *The Funfair*. The play, set in 1929 just after the worldwide financial crisis, had a strong resonance with current times. The three of us put a lot of work into ensuring the translation of every sentence was correct and relevant and Simon managed to stay faithful to the original at the same time as making the play very much his own. Next season, I am working with writers on two key projects: Ibsen's *Ghosts* in a new version by David Watson directed by Polly Findlay, and with 59 Productions on an adaptation of Paul Auster's novella, *City of Glass* by Duncan Macmillan which opens here and transfers to the Lyric, Hammersmith in London and then New York.

Much of my work with the director and writer is in the preparation of a piece, but the role of dramaturg during a production is often underestimated. The production dramaturg acts as a partner to the director throughout a process, which always throws up questions, surprises and change! My involvement is strongest at the start and at the end of the rehearsal process. In rehearsals actors are encouraged to approach me to seek support, particularly on creating back stories and other psychological aspects of their character. In 'tech' rehearsal – particularly with a show that has high visual ambition - a director's focus has to be on the technical team. Occasionally actors may feel they have 'lost' the director, and having bonded with the dramaturg over the early work, it is useful that I am present to address their concerns in those long tech days when nerves are bubbling before an opening. Likewise the preview period is key in the director/dramaturg relationship as this is the critical period where there is so much to digest. Directors' notes are technical and for the actors and contain much detailed observation. The dramaturg feeds their own notes to the director and always has the whole piece in mind. Is the rhythm of the play correct? Is the story clear? What are we saying with this play? Is the original conceptual ambition of the piece coming through? Where are the audience confused or bored? What can be changed?

It has helped my work as a dramaturg that I trained for three years at the prestigious Ernst Busch Theatre Academy in Berlin, extending my study abroad year from reading Modern Languages at Oxford. Not long after the fall of the Berlin Wall, I arrived from Oxford with a very academic approach to theatre making. When I was cast as Queen Elizabeth I in Schiller's *Mary Stuart* I spent a lot of my pre-rehearsal preparation time on the eighteenth-century German cultural and philosophical context in which Schiller was writing. I remember reading a great deal of Immanuel Kant. I had to learn how not to let all that interesting work block my own creativity. My fellow student, Nina Hoss (now one of Germany's most celebrated actors on stage and screen), cast opposite me as Mary, spent much of her preparation time contemplating and simulating the spatial dynamics of the rooms that the two queens would have occupied. I learnt fast the importance of a sensual, physical way into material alongside the more cerebral. It is from this training perhaps that I discovered a love of theatre that understands and utilizes space, and how the visual tension of the stage supports an actor and a story as well as adding layers of possibility. Interestingly the first three months of actor and director training at the Ernst Busch is improvisation without words. This was the foundation of theatre training for me, and an experience I cannot recommend enough to young actors and directors fresh from the verbal world of schools and universities. It was here I learnt to observe and articulate observation with precision, which is perhaps the most important skill of production dramaturgy.

It was at Ersnt Busch that I encountered my first dramaturg, as the Head of the school; Dr Klaus Voelker was an eminent dramaturg who had worked as the resident dramaturg in major producing houses in Germany and Switzerland and with Samuel Beckett in France. The role always intrigued me, and in my first professional years as a member of the Peter Stein Ensemble and then at the Berlin Ensemble, I began to understand the different functions and the variety of the role within an organization. In the UK the dramaturg is often seen as a new name for a literary manager. That is certainly one aspect of a dramaturg's responsibility, but on the continent a dramaturg is key in planning ahead, co-curating seasons, discovering directorial, design and acting talent, nurturing relationships and generally supporting the vision the artistic director has for a building.

HOME was formed in 2012 by merging two arts institutions, one which had already lost its original building, the Library Theatre, and one which was to lose its larger cinema, Cornerhouse (also an art gallery, bookshop and cafe). The wonderful award winning new building has two theatre spaces – a 450-seat theatre – and a fully flexible studio space for 150, five cinemas showing independent films and a large gallery. The central staircase of the whole building was designed deliberately to bring the audiences of the different art forms into direct contact, with the hope that it would help create in all of them an interest in what the other audiences were enjoying.

It is a thrilling place for a dramaturg, with exciting challenges. Over the last year the theatre team has worked successfully on establishing a new identity for the theatre work as well as developing a relationship with the other art forms and the different audiences. Traditionally in Britain there is an odd lack of overlap between audiences for film and theatre and this is something we are working on. Already in one year we see the cinema and visual arts audiences investing in our theatre work – perhaps attracted by the visual sophistication of much of the work in the programme, by companies such as 1927, Philippe Quesne, Peeping Tom, Hofesh Shechter. We are creating a new audience beyond traditional theatre-goers. This is key to the future and we look to ways to connect our audiences. Much of my programming time is in co-curating festivals which bring the art forms together. For example every April our Viva Festival celebrates Spanish and Latin American theatre, film and art. The theatre work in the festival is a mix of invited international companies and newly commissioned work. This year we were able to provide a residency for Cuban playwright, Abel Gonzalez Melo and we staged the UK premiere of his first, 2006, success *Chamaco* (*Kiddo*) alongside a newly commissioned work *Weathered* (both plays were cast with local actors). I am currently working with the other departments on a 2017 Russian season to coincide with the centenary year of the Russian Revolution.

An interest in international work connects all our art forms and is a key part of HOME's identity. In theatre we look to ways to connect the international and local. An example of this is our collaboration with the Irish theatre company ANU productions. The first project, *Angel Meadow*, was an immersive piece in an abandoned pub as part of our site-specific season in 2014, giving tiny fractions of audiences very close encounters and experiences with actors in confined spaces. Angel Meadow no longer exists. It was a part of the old Ancoats' district of inner Manchester. In the nineteenth century Angel Meadow was a steaming sordid hell on Earth at the centre of the industrial world. Small groups of audience were moved through the old Ancoats pub, layered with the various lives of people who had passed through the doors of Angel Meadow: lodgers in a night asylum, working men in a pub, dead bodies laid out for an inquest and scuttling gangs fighting for their territory. They not only saw the world of Irish immigrants, they heard it, touched it, and tasted it, encountering landlords, butchers, devils and angels along the way, moving in an instant from present-day Ancoats to its violent, sordid past, and back again, and even inhabiting both at once.

Theatre

Angel Meadow became a sell-out success and the team decided to invite ANU back this year to mark the 20th anniversary of the bombing of Manchester by the Provisional IRA. The bomb, the largest detonated in mainland Britain since the Second World War, devastated the city centre and injured 212 people. We were not aiming to forefront the political historical analysis and context, but to capture the impact on Mancunians lives 1996, and their reflections two decades later. *On Corporation Street* was based on a hundred testimonies from those involved and collected by Manchester's Mighty Heart Theatre. The testimonies were performed by the cast, word for word, copy in hand, in Manchester Town Hall at the end of May in front of a small audience. It was a powerful collection of reminiscences given further status through public performance. ANU's production, cast with Irish and Manchester actors, distilled those stories and reactions to their essentials, preserving recognisable elements of the original wording and enhancing these through sensitive and imaginative performance to give a heightened sense of reality and considerable time for reflection. We housed the production inside HOME itself with an audience moving around the building and scenes taking place in back corridors, storage spaces and surreal small rooms built into our studio. The show's audience was a fascinating mix of theatre lovers who came for the immersive promenade experience and Mancunians drawn by the material who had never experienced theatre other than from a seat.

Funding has now materialized to fully equip the facilities within our smaller, second theatre space, and we are planning a more focused and responsive programming policy for it. We have already christened the space with a number of exciting pieces of theatre that have emerged on the scene (*The Beanfield, Beyond Caring*), but the new fully flexible seating creates great opportunities. This will include two festivals of new work: the two-week-long Orbit festival in October will bring together leading emerging UK theatre companies; and Push in January–February, which will be specifically for theatre-makers from Greater Manchester building on the success of the former Re:play festival of the Library Theatre. Nurturing emerging companies and artists is an essential part of what we do. We have a full development programme alongside our produced work and we use every opportunity to provide young theatre-makers with space and dramaturgical support. Now that our second space is fully operational, our collaborative programmes and projects with emerging local and national writers, directors and companies will increase. Our second year feels as challenging and exciting as our first!

After graduating from Oxford, **Petra Jane Tauscher** spent her first professional years in Europe: three years with Peter Stein, then at the Berlin Ensemble as an assistant director. Upon returning home to the UK, she had an opportunity to work in film and later became Head of Drama Development for Atlantic Productions, alongside her work as a freelance dramaturg for theatre. Petra joined HOME's theatre team in 2013 as creative producer and dramaturg. She co-curated the site-specific and opening season, and has been the resident production dramaturg for all HOME-produced shows until 2018. From late 2019, Petra has been Director of the International Youth Arts Festival, Kingston upon Thames.

Producing theatres

Included in this section are the national and regional building-based companies that mount their own productions – sometimes in co-operation with others, and sometimes sending out tours. (Almost all also receive touring productions.) The majority are subsidised by the national and regional Arts Councils (and use Equity's regional theatre contract), but a few are not (and use Equity's commercial theatre contract), and a few have their own contractual arrangements. Almost all have websites which can be very useful for keeping track of their activities. A little extra insight into a theatre – beyond that listed on the following pages – might just tip the balance in your favour.

In real terms, rates of pay are better than they were a decade and more ago, but they are still only 'adequate' – especially if you are incurring the extra costs of living away from home. However, rehearsing and performing a production in such a theatre can be an exhilarating experience. A well-run theatre has a wonderful 'family' atmosphere, and in the close-knit working environment you can often make connections which sustain for many years afterwards – as well as contacts who might be useful in years to come. It is well worth checking each theatre's 'casting procedures' very carefully as there are significant variations between them. It is also worth familiarising yourself with their programmes of productions via The Stage and/or their websites.

Abbey Theatre Amharclann na Mainistreach
26/27 Lower Abbey Street, Dublin 1,
Republic of Ireland
tel +353 1 878 7222
email info@abbeytheatre.ie
website www.abbeytheatre.ie
Artistic Director Caitriona McLaughlin *Executive Director* Mark O'Brien *Casting Director* Sarah Jones
Production details: The Abbey Theatre produces an ambitious annual prgramme of Irish and international theatre across its two stages and on tour in Ireland and internationally. The Abbey Theatre is committed to building the Irish theatre repertoire, through commissioning and producing new Irish writing, and re-imagining national and international classics in collaboration with leading contemporary talent.

Casting procedures: The Abbey Theatre is the only theatre in Ireland with a full time in-house casting department dedicated to seeking out new and emerging talent, as well as keeping abreast of the continued work and development of previously established actors from all over the country and abroad. The Abbey Theatre holds general auditions bi-annually. The casting department attends performances throughout the year, nationally and internationally, as well as drama school showcases in Dublin and London.

Almeida Theatre
Almeida Street, London N1 1TA
tel 020 7359 4404
email info@almeida.co.uk
website www.almeida.co.uk
Artistic Director Rupert Goold
Production details: A small room with an international reputation. The Almeida makes brave new work that asks big questions of plays, of theatre and of the world around us. It brings together the most exciting artists to take risks; to provoke, inspire and surprise audiences; to interrogate the present, dig up the past and imagine the future. Stages approximately 6 productions each year.

Casting procedures: Productions are cast by external freelance casting directors on a project-by-project basis. Uses the TMA/Equity Subsidised Rep contract and subscribes to the Equity Pension Scheme. Actively promotes the use of inclusive casting.

Alphabetti Theatre
St James Blvd, Newcastle upon Tyne NE1 4HP
tel 0191 261 9125
email admin@alphabettitheatre.co.uk
website www.alphabettitheatre.co.uk
Facebook www.facebook.com/AlphabettiTheatre
Twitter @Alphabetti
Instagram @Alphabetti_theatre
Editor Artistic Director Ali Pritchard

Alphabetti Theatre is an 80 seat theatre based in Newcastle upon Tyne. They believe great art should be for everyone not just those who can afford it. They create, produce and programme new, original work from emerging artists across the performing arts,

Theatre

championing work in music, theatre, comedy and poetry. They create opportunities for both artists and audiences to experiment, evolve and discover; providing space for theatre companies, writers, directors, poets, comedians and musicians. Email for details.

Arcola Theatre

24 Ashwin Street, London E8 3DL
tel 020 7503 1645
email production@arcolatheatre.com
website www.arcolatheatre.com
Artistic Director Mehmet Ergen

Production details: Founded in 2000 by Artistic Director Mehmet Ergen and Executive Producer Leyla Nazli, Arcola Theatre is now one of the most respected arts venues in the UK, "blazing a trail in artistic excellence and innovative management from the outset". Housed in a converted factory in Hackney, Arcola is a favourite of established theatre literati as well as young, upwardly mobile innovators. London's largest theatre studio, it has become well known for the variety of its programming, from new writing to classic drama, music and comedy.

Arcola has staged work by some of the best living actors, writers and directors, including productions by William Gaskill, Timberlake Wertenbaker, Ariel Dorfman, Sean Holmes, Dominic Domgoole, Max Stafford-Clark and Frank McGuinness, among others. 2 studio theatres and 4 other spaces suitable for rehearsals and other events.

Yvonne Arnaud Theatre

Millbrook, Guildford, Surrey GU1 3UX
tel 01483 440000
website www.yvonne-arnaud.co.uk
Facebook www.facebook.com/GuildfordYAT
Twitter @YvonneArnaud
Programming & Producing Manager Tom Hurley

Production details: The Yvonne Arnaud Theatre is a busy producing and presenting house, creating shows in Guildford and touring nationally. On both the main stage and in the Mill Studio an eclectic mix of classical and contemporary work by new, lesser-known and established writers is staged.

The Creative Learning department offers an exciting mix of activities for young people and adults all year round. The Yvonne Arnaud opened the 80-seat Mill Studio in 1993, to provide a venue for work that would not otherwise be seen in Guildford, championing unheard voices and diverse storytelling.

Belgrade Theatre

Belgrade Square, Coventry CV1 1GS
tel 024 7625 6431
email admin@belgrade.co.uk
website www.belgrade.co.uk
Facebook www.facebook.com/
BelgradeTheatreCoventry

Twitter @BelgradeTheatre
Instagram @belgradetheatre
CEO Laura Elliot *Creative Director* Corey Campbell

Production details: Recent productions include: *Kerbs* (co-produced with Paines Plough); *Nothello*; *May Queen* (co-produced with Paines Plough) and 'legendary' annual pantomimes.

Birmingham Repertory Theatre

Centenary Square, Broad Street, Birmingham B1 3AH
tel 0121 245 2000
email info@birmingham-rep.co.uk
website www.birmingham-rep.co.uk
Facebook @BirminghamRep
Twitter @TheRepBirmingham
Artistic Director Sean Foley *Associate Directors* Madeleine Kludje, Iqbal Khan

Production details: Birmingham Rep is the only producing theatre in the UK's Second City and the oldest building-based theatre company in the UK. It has an unparalleled pioneering history and has been at the forefront of theatre in the UK for over 100 years. Its mission is to create artistically ambitious, popular history for, by and with the people of Birmingham and the wider world.

The Rep stages multiple productions in the House each year, and two in the Studio and Door. They also run Outreach, Community and Education programmes.

Casting procedures: "The play's director, a casting director and sometimes a producer handle casting for all Main House and Studio productions. We currently make use of freelance casting directors, specific to each production, administered by the producers."

Birmingham Stage Company (BSC)

Suite 228, 162 Regent Street, London W1B 5TB
tel 020 7437 3391
email office@birminghamstage.com
website www.birminghamstage.com
Facebook www.facebook.com/birminghamstage
Twitter @birminghamstage
Instagram @birminghamstage
Actor & Manager Neal Foster

Production details: Founded in 1992, the BSC stages 5 shows each year, 4 of which tour nationally. Produces a range of plays with particular emphasis on its family shows, which visit 60 venues around the UK. Recent productions include: David Walliams' *Demon Dentist*, *Gangsta Granny* and *Billionaire Boy* (West End) and *Horrible Histories* (West End, UK tour). Offers TMA/Equity approved contracts and subscribes to the Equity Pension Scheme.

Casting procedures: Uses freelance casting directors and sometimes holds general auditions. Casting breakdowns are published on the website. "Do as

much research as you can before submitting."
Actively encourages applications from disabled
actors.

Bridge Theatre

3 Potters Field Park, London SE1 2SG
email info@bridgetheatre.co.uk
website www.bridgetheatre.co.uk
Artistic Director Nicholas Hytner

Production details: Founded by Nicholas Hytner and
Nick Starr in 2017, the Bridge is the first theatre run
by London Theatre Company. Commissions and
produces new shows, as well as occasionally staging
classics. Actors who have appeared on the stage
include Maggie Smith, Ben Whishaw, Laura Linney,
Jim Broadbent and Gwendoline Christie. The new
900-seat adaptable auditorium is designed to answer
the needs of contemporary audiences and theatre-
makers and respond to shows with different formats
(end-stage, thrust stage and promenade). It is the first
wholly new theatre of scale to be added to London's
commercial sector in 80 years and draws local and
international visitors. Productions have included:
Young Marx, Julius Caesar, Nightfall, Allelujah! and *A
Midsummer Night's Dream.*

Bristol Old Vic

King Street, Bristol BS1 4ED
0117 987 7877
email admin@bristololdvic.org.uk
website www.bristololdvic.org.uk
Artistic Director Nancy Medina

Production details: Bristol Old Vic is a theatre
company founded in 1946 and based in a complex
which includes the unique Theatre Royal, opened in
1766 – the oldest theatre auditorium in the UK,
which many think the most beautiful. Bristol Old Vic
is also unique in its close working relationship with
the Bristol Old Vic Theatre School.

The Bush Theatre

7 Uxbridge Road, London W12 8LJ
tel 020 8743 3584
email info@bushtheatre.co.uk
website www.bushtheatre.co.uk
Facebook www.facebook.com/bushtheatre
Twitter @bushtheatre
Artistic Director Lynette Linton *Associate Director*
Daniel Bailey *Producer* Oscar Owen *Assistant Producer*
Nikita Karia

Production details: Founded in 1972, the Bush
specialises in developing and producing new writing
from the widest range of perspectives. Stages 10
productions a year, totalling around 289
performances. Also tours productions, although the
bulk of performances are at the Bush itself. Up to 8
actors are employed on each production, and the
company offers TMA/Equity approved contracts.
Recent productions include: *Guards at the Taj* and
HIR.

Casting procedures: Employs freelance casting
directors and does not hold general meetings or issue
public casting breakdowns. Welcomes letters and
emails from actors previously unknown to the
company. Does not welcome showreels or invitations
to view actors' websites. Actively encourages
applications from disabled actors and promotes the
use of inclusive casting.

Chichester Festival Theatre

Oaklands Park, Chichester PO19 6AP
website www.cft.org.uk
Facebook www.facebook.com/chichesterfestivaltheatre
Twitter @ChichesterFT
Instagram @ChichesterFT
Artistic Director Daniel Evans *Executive Director* Kathy
Bourne

Production details: Chichester Festival Theatre is
one of the UK's flagship theatres, renowned for the
exceptionally high standard of its productions as well
as its work with the community and young people.
The Festival Theatre seats 1,300, the bold thrust stage
design makes it equally suited to epic drama and
musicals; the Minerva Theatre seats 300 and is noted
for premieres of new work alongside intimate
revivals. The annual Festival season runs from April
to November, during which productions originated
at Chichester reach an audience of over 230,000 and
frequently transfer to London as well as touring
nationally and internationally. Year-round
programming continues through the winter with
high-class touring productions.

Casting procedures: Casting is done on a
production-by-production basis.

Citizens Theatre

Gorbals, Glasgow G5 9DS
tel 0141 429 5561
email info@citz.co.uk
website www.citz.co.uk
Artistic Director Dominic Hill *Production
Administrator (Casting & Contracts)* Jacqueline Muir

Production details: Internationally renowned
producing theatre, producing work in Glasgow and
on tour as well as a pioneering year-round Citizens
Learning and TAG programme for participants of all
ages. Stages 7 productions a year, and undertakes 2
tours per annum. Offers TMA/Equity approved
contracts.

Casting procedures: Does not use freelance casting
directors. Holds limited general auditions once a year
in June, and specific casting for individual shows as
and when required. Welcomes emails from actors
(with CVs and photographs), which should be
submitted to **jackie@citz.co.uk.**

Coliseum Theatre

Fairbottom Street, Oldham OL1 3SW
tel 0161 624 1731

Theatre

email mail@coliseum.org.uk
website www.coliseum.org.uk
Artistic Director Chris Lawson

Production details: A producing theatre making up to 6 shows each year, with additional co-productions, incoming tours and one-off special events. Also runs Learning and Engagement programmes (contact Olivia Race). Recent productions include: *The Jungle Book*, *Aladdin* and *Beryl*.

Casting procedures: Does not use freelance casting directors. Casting breakdowns are available from the website. Welcomes letters and email submissions for specific roles (with CVs and photographs). Also accepts invitations to view individual actors' websites. Offers TMA/Equity approved contracts and subscribes to the Equity Pension Scheme. Will consider applications from disabled actors to play characters with disabilities.

Contact Theatre

Oxford Road, Manchester M15 6JA
tel 0161 274 3434
email programming@contactmcr.com
website www.contactmcr.com
CEO & Artistic Director Keisha Thompson

Production details: Since re-opening in 1999, Contact has emphasised its work with young adults (aged 13-30), putting participation at the heart of its ethos and activities. Contact is also one of the most culturally diverse theatres in the country; it was awarded the inaugural ECLIPSE award for cultural diversity, as well as the Arts Council's ART04 Award Northwest for 'outstanding achievement in the arts'.

Contact has striven to rewrite the rulebook on what 'theatre' can be and presents a range of artforms, including theatre, dance, live art, cabaret, spoken word, circus, comedy and music. The huge variety of participatory work with young people is integrated as closely as possible with the company's 'professional' programme which is comprised of in-house productions and touring theatre.

Casting procedures: Uses freelance casting directors and does not advertise casting breakdowns publicly. Welcomes letters (with CVs and photographs) from actors, but warns that it is unable to reply to unsolicited submissions. The theatre prefers not to receive showreels, emails and invitations to view actors' websites. Offers TMA/Equity approved contracts. Actively encourages applications from disabled actors and promotes the use of inclusive casting.

Curve

60 Rutland Street, Leicester LE1 1SB
tel 0116 2423560
email contactus@curvetheatre.co.uk
website www.curveonline.co.uk
Artistic Director Nikolai Foster *Director of Production* Andy Bartlett

Production details: A new state-of-the-art theatre designed by world-renowned architect Rafael Vinoly. Has 2 auditoria, one with 750 seats and the other providing a 350-seat flexible smaller space. "A stunning glass façade encloses a magnificent foyer and mezzanine walkway, with views onto the café, bars, dressing rooms and workshop areas. The stage is placed at street level between the 2 auditoria."

Casting procedures: Uses both in-house and freelance casting directors. Holds general auditions; actors may write in for casting breakdowns as soon as productions are announced. Does not welcome unsolicited approaches by post or by email, showreels, or invitations to view individual actors' websites. Offers Equity-approved contracts as negotiated through TMA. Actively encourages applications from disabled actors and promotes the use of inclusive casting.

Derby Theatre

15 Theatre Walk, St Peter's Quarter, Derby DE1 2NF
tel 01332 593939
website www.derbytheatre.co.uk
Twitter @derbytheatre
Artistic Director Sarah Brigham

Production details: Derby Theatre has a long and rich history of delivering high-quality drama to audiences. Previously Derby Playhouse, Derby Theatre, which sits at the heart of the city, is now owned and run by the University of Derby. The theatre is rooted in the local community but international in its outlook, producing and presenting performances working with the best local, regional and national talent, as an Arts Council England National Portfolio Organisation.

In 2012 Derby Theatre was awarded strategic funding by Arts Council England to develop a new model for regional theatre in the 21st century. From 2013, under the new artistic directorship of Sarah Brigham, who works alongside General Manager Gary Johnson, the theatre is transforming from a traditional producing house to an organisation of training, mentorship and artistic excellence. Its aim is to be an examplar – a new way of looking at the role and responsibility of theatre to its community. Derby's focus will ensure that each part of the theatre's process will be open to public learning opportunities, building the organisation's ability to take artistic risks by bringing creatives and audiences along on a creative path via the co-production of narratives.

Stages 6 productions annually in the Main House, and also works in youth theatre and TIE. Offers Equity-approved contracts as negotiated through UK Theatre, and subscribes to the Equity Pension Scheme. Recent productions include (from 2013): *Cooking with Elvis*, *The Seagull*, *Kes* and *The Odyssey*.

Casting procedures: Uses freelance casting directors. Actors are invited to email enquiries to casting@derbytheatre.co.uk. Welcomes letters (with

CVs and photographs) from individual actors previously unknown to the company, sent by post or email, and accepts showreels as well as invitations to view actors' websites and visit productions. Applications from disabled actors are actively encouraged.

Donmar Warehouse

41 Earlham Street, London WC2H 9LX
tel 020 7240 4882
website www.donmarwarehouse.com
Artistic Director Michael Longhurst *Casting Director* Anna Cooper CDG

Production details: Independent producing house located in Covent Garden. The building originally served as a vat room and hop warehouse for the local brewery. In 1961 it was purchased by Donald Albery and converted into a rehearsal studio for the London Festival Ballet, which he formed with ballerina Margot Fonteyn. The theatre takes its name from them.

In the 1990s the Donmar was redesigned. The current theatre space retains the characteristics of the former warehouse while incorporating a new thrust stage. Recent productions include: *The Prime of Miss Jean Brodie, Aristocrats, Measure for Measure, Sweat, Sweet Charity* and *Appropriate.*

Casting procedures: Casting breakdowns are not publicly available. Offers TMA/SOLT/Equity approved contracts.

The Dukes

Moor Lane, Lancaster LA1 1QE
tel 01524 598500
email ask@dukeslancaster.org
website www.dukeslancaster.org
Director Joe Sumison *Theatre Secretary* Jacqui Wilson

Production details: A producing theatre with an independent cinema. Stages several home-produced shows each year in the main house (313 seats) and 1 in the studio (178 seats), with a focus on contemporary drama and outdoor, site-specific productions. Also runs a Youth Arts programme. Recent productions include: *The Life And Times Of Mitchell & Kenyon, No Fat Juliets, Sabbat* and *Robin Hood* (outdoor walkabout production).

Casting procedures: Does not use freelance casting directors. Casting breakdowns are obtainable through the website, postal application (with sae) and Spotlight. Welcomes letters (with CVs and photographs) but not email submissions. Showreels and invitations to view individual actors' websites are also accepted. Offers TMA/Equity approved contracts. Actively encourages applications from disabled actors and promotes the use of inclusive casting.

Dundee Rep and Scottish Dance Theatre Ltd

Tay Square, Dundee DD1 1PB
tel (01382) 227684

website www.dundeerep.co.uk
Joint Chief Executive & Artistic Director (Dundee Rep) Andrew Panton *Executive Director and Joint Chief Executive* Liam Sinclair

Production details: Producing theatre housing Dundee Repertory Ensemble – Scotland's only permanent acting company. Stages 6 shows each year in the main house. Home also to Rep Engage, Scotland's largest permanent Creative Learning Department (contact Jess Thorpe and Tashi Gore). Recent productions include: *Much Ado About Nothing* and *Witness for the Prosecution.*

Casting procedures: Does not use freelance casting directors. Welcomes letters (with CVs and photographs) but not email submissions.

East Riding Theatre

10 Lord Roberts Road, Beverley,
East Yorkshire HU17 9BE
tel 01482 874050
email boxoffice@eastridingtheatre.co.uk
website www.eastridingtheatre.co.uk
Facebook www.facebook.com/ertheatre
Twitter @ertheatre
Artistic Director Adrian Rawlins *Creative Director* Vincent Regan

Founded in 2014, ERT is a professional producing and receiving house. It is managed by a voluntary board and run by community volunteers. ERT employs creative artists on a regular basis, building on its growing reputation as a high-quality performance venue. Minimum Equity rates apply. ERT also has a resident company: She Productions, an all female professional company who writes their own work and provides outreach work and in-house workshops. They are touring their original musical, *It's Different for Girls*, developed at ERT, to northern theatres in the autumn.

The main house, stages at least 4 productions a year and 5 or 6 small in-house events in the café bar (seats 50). Summer schools/community cast appear in some in-house productions. Recent productions include: *Goodnight Mister Tom* and *Beryl. Beryl* will be transferring to the Arcola Theatre in October and November 2019. ERT hosts the John Godber Company at least once a year.

Young People's Theatre and TIE: ERT performs 2 projects. Audience age range is 40-60. Additional skills required from actors include singing, the ability to play a musical instrument and to understake physical theatre. Actors are sometimes asked to lead workshops. Other Lives productions are an associated company bringing acccessible classics to ERT such as *Under Milkwood.*

Gate Theatre

Above Prince Albert Pub, 11 Pembridge Road, London W11 3HQ
tel 020 7229 0706

email gate@gatetheatre.co.uk
website www.gatetheatre.co.uk
Interim Artistic Director Stef O'Driscoll *Associate Director* Yasmin Hafesji

Production details: Presents new writing and undiscovered classics from around the world in original and visually imaginative productions. Stages 5-6 shows each year. Also runs a Community/Education programme.

Casting procedures: Does not accept unsolicited CVs/submissions. "Individual directors tend to cast from their own lists – contact with the director is the best way to ensure that your application is considered. The Gate Theatre Company is committed to promoting theatre as an activity for all."

Greenwich Theatre

Crooms Hill, Greenwich, London SE10 8ES
tel 020 8858 4447
email info@greenwichtheatre.org.uk
website www.greenwichtheatre.org.uk
Facebook www.facebook.com/GreenwichTheatreLondon
Twitter @Greenwichtheatr
Executive Director Simon Francis *Artistic Director* James Haddrell

Production details: Programmes a mix of in-house and visiting productions. Received programming focuses on emerging companies, children's theatre and classic drama. Produces occasional showcases and semi-staged readings at different times of the year. Recent productions include: *Bad Nights and Odd Days*, Caryl Churchill (London); *The Secret Love Life Of Ophelia*, Steven Berkoff (online premiere); *The After-Dinner Joke*, Caryl Churchill (online premiere); *Here*, Michael Frayn (London); *The Jungle Book* (London and Milton Keynes); *Under My Thumb* (London and Edinburgh Festival Fringe); *Grazing at a Distant Star* (London and Edinburgh Festival Fringe); *Octopus* (London and regional tour). Offers TMA/Equity approved contracts and subscribes to the Equity Pension Scheme.

Casting procedures: Generally uses freelance directors. "Please don't send unsolicited applications; do look at the casting section on the website, as we aim to provide advance information on our future productions, and answer standard questions."

Hampstead Theatre

Eton Avenue, London NW3 3EU
tel 020 7722 9301
email info@hampsteadtheatre.com
website www.hampsteadtheatre.com
Artistic Director Roxana Silbert

Production details: Hampstead Theatre is a new-writing producing house, featuring new, mid-career and established writers. Plays are bold, original and entertaining. Presents at least 7 productions on the Main Stage each year, and 7 in the Downstairs studio.

Recent productions include: The Olivier Award nominated *Folk* by Nell Leyshon, directed by Roxana Sibert; *The Forest* by Florian Zeller, directed by Jonathan Kent; *Wolf Club*, written and directed by Che Walker; and *Lotus Beauty* written by Satinder Chohan, directed by Pooja Ghai. They recently celebrated their 60th anniversary with a season of original Hampstead plays including *The Dumb Waiter* by Harold Pinter, *The Death of a Black Man* by Alfred Fagon, *The Two Character Play* by Tennessee Williams, *'night, Mother* by Marsha Norman and *Peggy For You* by Alan Plater.

Casting procedures: Main Stage casting director changes depending on the director of each production. Studio casting is led by the in-house producing team.

Harrogate Theatre

Oxford Street, Harrogate, North Yorks HG1 1QF
tel 01423 502116
email info@harrogatetheatre.co.uk
website www.harrogatetheatre.co.uk
Facebook www.facebook.com/harrogatetheatre
Twitter @HGtheatre
Instagram harrogatetheatre
Chief Executive David Bown

Production details: Stages award-winning pantomime production in the main house and also works in Education (key contact, Hannah Draper). Its two performance spaces allow for producing and presenting theatre, dance, music and comedy. Recent productions include: *Private Lives*, *The Emperor's New Clothes*, and *Dick Whittington*.

Casting procedures: Uses freelance casting directors and sometimes holds general auditions. Offers Equity approved contracts as negotiated through TMA, and participates in the Equity Pension Scheme. Committed to inclusive and diverse casting. Harrogate Theatre has no resident Artistic Director, and so unsolicited approaches are not welcome. Please check the website for any casting opportunities.

HOME

2 Tony Wilson Place, Manchester M15 4FN
tel 0161 228 7621
email info@homemcr.org
website www.homemcr.org
Head of Programme Kevin Jamieson *Programme Producer* Remi Adefeyisan *Associate Companies* 1927, Quarantine

Production details: HOME was formed by the merger in 2012 of the Library Theatre Company and Cornerhouse, HOME produces the best in contemporary theatre, visual art and film, learning and participation, creative industries and digital innovation. The company's venue, opened in spring 2015, comprises a 500-seat theatre, a 150-seat flexible studio space, a 500m², four metre-high gallery space, five cinema screens, education spaces, digital production and broadcast facilities, a café bar, restaurant and offices. HOME provides new opportunities for artists and audiences to create work in different ways together and serves as a social and cultural hub – in one building visitors can see original new work across the visual arts, theatre and film.

Offers TMA/Equity-approved contracts.

Casting procedures: Uses freelance casting directors; casting breakdowns are available from the website and Spotlight. Also holds a limited number of general auditions/interviews in the summer. Actors requesting inclusion in these are advised to write in March or April. HOME encourages applications from actors with disability, and promotes inclusive casting.

Hull Truck Theatre

50 Ferensway, Hull HU2 8LB
tel (01482) 224800
email admin@hulltruck.co.uk
email casting@hulltruck.co.uk
website www.hulltruck.co.uk
Executive Director Janthi Mills-Ward *Artistic Director* Mark Babych

Hull Truck Theatre is a pioneering theatre with a unique Northern voice, locally rooted and global in outlook, inspiring artists, audiences and communities to reach their greatest potential.

It produces and presents inspiring theatre that relects the diversity of a modern Britain and provides the resources, space and support to grow people and ideas. It is an ambassador for Hull, a flagship for the region and a welcoming home for local communities.

Key Theatre

Embankment Road, Peterborough, Cambridgeshire PE1 1EF
tel 01733 852992
website https://keytheatre.org.uk/
Artistic Director Dikla Katz

Production details: Mainly a receiving house with occasional in-house productions including an annual pantomime and TIE tours. Stages up to 4 shows each year with co-production opportunities.

Casting procedures: Does not use freelance casting directors. Occasional general auditions. Unsolicited communications are not advised. Casting requirements are sometimes available through the website, but usually through professional casting services, Spotlight link and *The Stage*. "Actors working in the area (and especially touring to the Key) are always encouraged to make contact with the Artistic Director and introduce themselves. Invitations to see artists working in productions are always welcome, and, wherever possible, accepted!" Offers TMA/Equity contracts and does not subscribe to the Equity Pension Scheme. Rarely (or never) has the opportunity to employ disabled actors.

Kiln Theatre (formerly Tricycle Theatre)

269 Kilburn High Road, London NW6 7JR
tel 020 7328 1000
email info@kilntheatre.com
website www.kilntheatre.com
Artistic Director Indhu Rubasingham

Kiln Theatre sits in the heart of Kilburn in Brent, a unique and culturally diverse area of London where over 140 languages are spoken. A newly refurbished, welcoming and proudly local venue, with an internationally acclaimed programme of world and UK premieres. The work presents the world through a variety of lenses, amplifying unheard/ignored voices into the mainstream, exploring and examining the threads of human connection that cross race, culture and identity.

Education details: The ambitious Creative Learning programme aims to champion the imagination, aspiration and potential of the Brent community young and old. It invests in creating meaningful relationships with young people to inspire and encourage their creativity, their confidence and self-esteem. Works with older people to create a thriving community around the theatre.

Casting details: Kiln Theatre encourages artists of all ages and backgrounds. Uses freelance casting directors for main house productions. For casting information contact the team at artistic@kilntheatre.com.

Leeds Playhouse (formerly West Yorkshire Playhouse)

Playhouse Square, Quarry Hill, Leeds LS2 7UP
tel 0113 213 7800
website www.leedsplayhouse.org.uk
Chief Executive & Artistic Director James Brining

Production details: Leeds Playhouse is a theatre that has existed in the heart of Yorkshire for 50 years. Its half century anniversary is being marked through a series of new productions tracing stories from across the decades as well as celebrating the many wonderful artists, participants and audience members who have shared this journey with the Playhouse. As a registered charity (No. 255460) the Playhouse seeks out the best companies to create work which is pioneering and relevant. Leeds Playhouse underwent a £16m transformation which includes improved access to and around the theatre, a new city-facing entrance and the addition of a new studio theatre, the Bramall Rock Void.

A dedicated collaborator, Leeds Playhouse works with distinctive, original voices from across the UK. Its Artistic Development programme, Furnace, discovers, nurtures and supports new voices, while developing work with established practitioners. It provides a creative space for writers, directors, companies and individual theatre-makers to refine their practice at all stages of their careers.

The sector-leading Creative Engagement team works with more than 12,000 people aged 4–95 every year connecting with refugee communities, young people, teachers and students, older people and people with learning disabilities, including working in specific areas of the city. The Playhouse pioneered Relaxed Performances ten years ago and more recently have developed Dementia-Friendly performances both of which are becoming the norm across the industry. Leeds Playhouse is proud to be the first ever Theatre of Sanctuary for Refugees and People Seeking Asylum.

The Playhouse relies on support from many partners to make great things happen. The organisation is especially grateful for the continued support from funders including Arts Council England, Leeds City Council, The Liz and Terry Bramall Foundation, as well as many charitable trusts, business partners and individuals.

Offers TMA/Equity contracts and does not subscribe to the Equity Pension Scheme. Casting procedures: Currently Leeds Playhouse casts through agents' submissions and works with casting directors on productions on a show-by-show basis. Casting information is available on the website. Leeds Playhouse is an equal opportunities employer in relation to casting.

Live Theatre

Broad Chare, Quayside,
Newcastle upon Tyne NE1 3DQ
tel 0191 261 2694
email info@live.org.uk
website www.live.org.uk
Artistic Director Jack McNamara

Production details: New writing theatre established in 1973. Produces 8-10 shows each year in the main house. Also runs TIE, Outreach and Community programmes.

Casting procedures: Does not use freelance casting directors. Welcomes submissions (with CVs and photographs), sent by post or email. Actors may write in at any time. Holds annual Live Theatre Open Auditions. Showreels and invitations to view individual actors' websites are also accepted. Offers ITC/Equity approved contracts. Actively encourages applications from disabled actors and promotes the use of inclusive casting.

Liverpool Everyman & Playhouse Theatres

5-11 Hope Street, Liverpool L1 9BH
tel 0151 708 3700
email info@everymanplayhouse.com
website www.everymanplayhouse.com
Creative Director Suba Das *Chief Executive* Mark Da Vanzo

Liverpool Everyman and Playhouse are two distinct theatres, which together make up a single artistic force. A varied programme of forward-thinking theatre is created and received across both venues.

The theatres' award-winning Young Everyman Playhouse scheme provides young people with practical training across all aspects of theatre.

Since the re-opening of the Everyman in 2014, the theatres have received numerous awards including the prestigious RIBA Stirling Prize for Architecture and the UK Theatre Award for promoting diversity.

Lyric Hammersmith Theatre

Lyric Square, King Street, London W6 0QL
tel 020 8741 6850
email enquiries@lyric.co.uk
website www.lyric.co.uk
Artistic Director Rachel O'Riordan

Production details: The Lyric Hammersmith Theatre produces bold world-class theatre.

"We are committed to being vital to, and representative of, our local community and to being a major force in London and UK theatre. We develop and nurture the next generation of talent, and provide opportunities for young people from all backgrounds to discover the power of creativity. Right in the heart of Hammersmith, a beautiful theatre that is here for everyone."

Casting procedures: Different directors cast their own productions, using freelance casting directors. Promotes recruitment of employees from diverse range of backgrounds.

Lyric Theatre

55 Ridgeway Street, Belfast BT9 5FB
email info@lyrictheatre.co.uk
website www.lyrictheatre.co.uk
Executive Producer Jimmy Fay *Casting Director* Clare Gault *Senior Producer* Morag Keating

Production details: Northern Ireland's leading full-time producing house for professional theatre. Presents a distinctive, challenging and entertaining programme of new writing as well as contemporary and classic plays by Irish, European and American writers. Recent productions include: *Educating Rita*, *The 39 Steps*, *Here Comes the Night* and *Smiley*.

Casting procedures: contact the Casting Director Clare Gault.

Does not normally use freelance casting directors. Welcomes submissions (Spolight or online CVs preferred), sent by email. Actors may write in at any time. Advises actors to check the website for its future programme. Offers TMA/Equity approved contracts. Will consider applications from disabled actors to play characters with disabilities.

Manor Pavilion Theatre

Manor Road, Sidmouth, Devon EX10 8RP
tel 01395 514413
email GWhitlock@eastdevon.gov.uk
website www.manorpavilion.com

Management of the summer season is by Paul Taylor Mills Ltd. Performs all aspects of entertainment, including Plays, Musicals, Comedies, Concerts, Variety Shows, Dance Shows, Professional Ballet and pantomime.

Menier Chocolate Factory

51/53 Southwark Street, London SE1 1RU
tel 020 7378 1712
email office@menierchocolatefactory.com
website www.menierchocolatefactory.com
Artistic Director David Babani

Production details: The Menier Chocolate Factory, which opened in 2004, is an award-winning 180-seat off-West End theatre which stages plays and musicals, live music and stand-up comedy. "There's nowhere quite like the Chocolate Factory anywhere ... the bubbliest kid on the block and one of London's great theatre hopes." (*Daily Telegraph*)

Mercury Theatre

Balkerne Gate, Colchester, Essex CO1 1PT
tel 01206 577006
email info@mercurytheatre.co.uk
website www.mercurytheatre.co.uk
Creative Director Ryan McBryde

Production details: The Mercury is a regional theatre based in Colchester which creates, hosts, and tours performances nationally. Staging classic and contemporary drama, musical theatre, new writing, panto, dance, and comedy, the Mercury also supports new talent and runs a Community programme (contact Thomas Freeth), connecting the diverse local communities. Recent productions include: *The Butterfly Lion*, *Dial M For Murder* and *Betty Blue Eyes*.

Casting procedures: For all casting enquiries, email **casting@mercurytheatre.co.uk**

The Mill at Sonning Theatre

Sonning Eye, Reading RG4 6TY
tel 0118 969 6039
email admin@millatsonning.com
website www.millatsonning.com
Artistic Director Sally Hughes

Production details: Popular 'dinner theatre' venue, producing a range of plays for audiences to watch while eating a meal. Recent productions include: *French Without Tears*, *Time to Kill*, and *It Runs in the Family*.

Casting procedures: Forthcoming productions are listed on the website. Actors should send their details, along with specific casting suggestions, to the Artistic Director 2 months before each show.

National Theatre

South Bank, London SE1 9PX
tel 020 7452 3336
email casting@nationaltheatre.org.uk
website www.nationaltheatre.org.uk/about-the-national-theatre/casting

Artistic Director Rufus Norris *Head of Casting* Alastair Coomer CDG *Casting Associate* Bryony Jarvis-Taylor *Senior Casting Assistant* Naomi Downham *Casting Assistant* Chloe Blake

Production details: The National Theatre's mission is to make world class theatre that's entertaining, challenging and inspiring – and to make it for everyone. It aims to reach the widest possible audience and to be as inclusive, diverse and national as possible with a broad range of productions that play in London, on tour around the UK, on Broadway and across the globe. The National Theatre's extensive UK-wide learning and participation programme supports young people's creative education through performance and writing programmes like Connections, New Views and Let's Play. Its major new initiative Public Acts creates extraordinary acts of theatre and community; the first Public Acts production was 2018's *Pericles*. The National Theatre extends its reach through digital programmes including the free streaming service National Theatre Collection, and NT Live, which broadcasts some of the best of British theatre to over 2,500 venues in 65 countries. The National Theatre invests in the future of theatre by developing talent, creating bold new work and building audiences, partnering with a range of UK theatres and theatre companies.

Casting details: Actors known to the directors and writers working for the theatre may be approached directly, but casting is predominantly carried out through audition. The NT will first approach agents to check actors' availability, then audition a shortlist. New talent is actively sought out, and the casting team sees several performances a week within London and (less frequently) outside. The NT does consider actors who are currently unrepresented by an agent and encourages those actors to invite the department to see their work onstage. It also attends drama schools' showcases and will sometimes approach other casting directors known to the NT. The Casting Department champions diversity in all forms within casting decisions and is dedicated to creating a safe and supportive audition environment where actors are empowered to do their best work.

National Theatre of Scotland (NTS)

Rockvilla, 125 Craighall Road, Glasgow G4 9TL
tel 0141 221 0970
email info@nationaltheatrescotland.com
website www.nationaltheatrescotland.com
Artistic Director Jackie Wylie *Associate Director* Debbie Hannan *Artistic Development Producer* Caroline Newall

Production details: The National Theatre of Scotland launched to the public in February 2006. It has no building, and instead takes theatre all over Scotland and beyond, working with new and existing venues and companies to create and tour theatre of the highest quality. This theatre takes place in the great buildings of Scotland, but also in site-specific locations, community halls and drill halls, car parks and forests. To date, over 130,000 people have seen or participated in its work. NTS has produced 28 pieces of work in 62 locations, from the Shetlands to Dumfries, and from Belfast to London. In 2007/8 NTS toured to the USA and Australasia.

Scottish theatre has always been for the people, led by great performances, great stories and great playwrights. The National Theatre of Scotland exists to build a new generation of theatregoers, as well as reinvigorating the existing ones; to create theatre on a national and international scale that is contemporary, confident and forward-looking; to bring together brilliant artists, designers, composers, choreographers and playwrights; and to exceed expectations of what and where theatre can be.

Offers actors in-house ITC/Equity approved contracts and does not subscribe to the Equity Pension Scheme.

Casting procedures: Each casting process is led by the director of each production, with advisory support from the NTS Artistic Team and Casting Director. When casting for specific shows, the Casting Director puts out a call to agents through *Spotlight*.

The NTS Artistic team makes every effort to see every theatrical event produced in Scotland, maximising the number of actors that NTS sees. The team also responds to individual requests to see actors' work. All actors' CVs and headshots that NTS receives are acknowledged and kept on file in the NTS office. The NTS Casting Director reviews these files at regular intervals, and Directors are encouraged to go through these files before casting their productions. In addition, NTS holds an annual 2-day casting workshop to connect with actors who have sent in CVs but whose work it has been unable to see during the year. Actively encourages applications from disabled actors and promotes the use of inclusive casting.

National Theatre Wales

30 Castle Arcade, Cardiff CF10 1BW
tel 029 2035 3070
email admin@nationaltheatrewales.org
website www.nationaltheatrewales.org
Artistic Director Lorne Campbell

Production details: National Theatre Wales has been making English-language productions in locations all over Wales, the UK, internationally and online since 2010. It operates from a small base in Cardiff's city centre, but works all over the country and beyond, using Wales' rich and diverse landscape, it's towns, cities and villages, its incredible stories and rich talent as its inspiration.

Casting procedures: Seeks to engage with performers underrepresented in the creative industries, including people of colour, working class, disabled, Deaf, neurodivergent, transgender and gender non-conforming. Individual productions are cast by the director and a freelance casting director. Casting breakdowns are made available via Spotlight and on National Theatre Wales' online Community hub which can be accessed via their website. Access requirements and any additional needs or support will be discussed before auditions, and actors required to travel more than 25 miles will be reimbursed for their expenses.

The New Wolsey Theatre

Civic Drive, Ipswich IP1 2AS
tel (01473) 295900
email info@wolseytheatre.co.uk
website www.wolseytheatre.co.uk
Facebook www.facebook.com/NewWolsey
Twitter @NewWolsey
Instagram @newwolsey
Chief Executive Douglas Rintoul

Production details: Mixed producing/receiving house, staging 3–4 productions a year in the main house, specialising in using actor-musicians. Alongside these productions, there is also a varied programme of Young Company and Youth Theatres. It also works in creative learning and community outreach; the contact for this is Tony Casement, Head of Creative Communities. NWT is also the lead producer for the Ramps on the Moon Project.

Casting procedures: Uses freelance casting directors and does not hold general auditions. Does not welcome unsolicited approaches from actors, unless in response to a casting breakdown. Offers TMA/Equity-approved contracts. Actively looking for disabled actors and actor-musicians and promotes inclusive casting.

New Vic Theatre

Etruria Road, Newcastle-under-Lyme ST5 0JG
tel 01782 717954
email admin@newvictheatre.org.uk
website www.newvictheatre.org.uk
Facebook www.facebook.com/
NewVicTheatreStaffordshire
Twitter @NewVicTheatre
Artistic Director Theresa Heskins

Production details: Purpose-built theatre-in-the-round with a full programme of in-house drama, concerts and occasional touring productions. Stages 10 shows each year in the main house. Also very active with Outreach and Education programmes (contact Sue Moffat and Jill Rezzano respectively). Recent productions include: *Coppelia - A Mystery*, *Beauty and the Beast*, and *Marvellous*.

Casting procedures: Theatre uses an associate casting director through Spotlight link. Casting breakdowns are posted in the casting section of the website. Submissions should be specific and referenced to a particular role.

Northern Stage

Barras Bridge, Newcastle upon Tyne NE1 7RH
tel 0191 230 5151
website www.northernstage.co.uk
Twitter @northernstage

Production details: Based in Newcastle, Northern Stage produces, co-produces and supports the production of great theatre for regional, national and international audiences in live and digital forms. As well as in-house productions, Northern Stage presents work from visiting companies throughout the year.

Casting procedures: Open auditions once a year, casting breakdowns through website, social channels and Spotlight. Young actors can apply to join the Young Company.

Nottingham Playhouse

Wellington Circus, Nottingham NG1 5AF
tel 0115 947 4361
email enquiry@nottinghamplayhouse.co.uk
website www.nottinghamplayhouse.co.uk
Artistic Director Adam Penford *Chief Executive* Stephanie Sirr *Amplify Producer* Craig Gilbert

Production details: Nottingham Theatre Trust was founded in 1948 and moved to its current location in 1963. Stages 10 shows each year in the main house, two own-produced shows in the studio. Also runs Participation programme. Recent productions include: *Touched, East is East, The Grapes of Wrath,* and *Sleuth*.

Casting procedures: Does not use freelance casting directors. Casting breakdowns are available from the casting director. Welcomes letters (with CVs and photographs) but not email submissions. Showreels and invitations to view individual actors' websites are also accepted.

Octagon Theatre

Howell Croft South, Bolton BL1 1SB
tel (01204) 529407
email info@octagonbolton.co.uk
website www.octagonbolton.co.uk
Facebook www.facebook.com/OctagonBolton
Twitter @octagontheatre
Instagram @octagontheatre
Artistic Director Lotte Wakeham

Production details: The Octagon's new, more accessible theatre building opened in summer 2021. Stages several shows each year in the main auditorium, plus some work in the studio. Also runs Education, Outreach and Community programmes. Recent productions include: *One Man Two Guvnors, An Adventure, Habibti Driver* and *Peter Pan*.

Casting procedures: Occasionally uses freelance casting directors. Actors should refer to the casting page of the company's website.

The Old Vic

The Cut, London SE1 8NB
tel 0344 871 7628
email casting@oldvictheatre.com
website www.oldvictheatre.com
Facebook www.facebook.com/OldVicTheatre
Twitter @oldvictheatre
Instagram @oldvictheatre
Artistic Director Matthew Warchus

Production details: The Old Vic is London's independent not-for-profit theatre, a world leader in creativity and entertainment. The Old Vic is mercurial: it can be transformed into a theatre in the round, a space for live music and comedy, has played host to opera, dance, cinema, music hall, classical dramas, variety, big spectacles and novelty acts. It was the original home of the English National Opera, the Sadler's Wells dance company and the National Theatre. It's also been a tavern, a college, a coffee house, a lecture hall and a meeting place.

All of this is now in the bones of the building and is as important a part of its open-armed, inclusive, welcoming personality as its grand historic decor and the iconic performances and famous productions it has housed.

Today, Artistic Director Matthew Warchus is building on 203 years of creative adventure, with the Old Vic recently being hailed as London's most eclectic and frequently electrifying theatre. Under his leadership, we aim to be a surprising, unpredictable, ground-breaking, rule-breaking, independent beacon of accessible, uplifting and unintimidating art.

Recent productions include *Endgame, A Christmas Carol, Lungs* and *Girl from the North Country*.

Open Air Theatre

Inner Circle, Regent's Park, London NW1 4NR
website www.openairtheatre.com
Facebook www.facebook.com/RegentsParkOpenAirTheatre
Twitter @OpenAirTheatre
Instagram @RegentsParkOAT
Artistic Director Timothy Sheader

Production details: Stages 4-6 shows each year in the main house, and a series of one-off events under the umbrella MOREoutdoor. Recent productions include: *Romeo and Juliet, Oliver Twist* re-imagined for ages 6+, *Legally Blonde, Jesus Christ Superstar, As You Like It* and *The Seagull*.

Casting procedures: Uses freelance casting directors, who send full casting breakdowns to agents as required for each production. "Unfortunately we are unable to consider unsolicited CVs."

Orange Tree Theatre

1 Clarence Street, Richmond TW9 2SA
tel 020 8940 3633
email admin@orangetreetheatre.co.uk
website www.orangetreetheatre.co.uk
Artistic Director Paul Miller

Production details: The Orange Tree produces and co-produces a mixture of new writing, re-discoveries,

Theatre

contemporary revivals in its uniquely intimate theatre in the round. Education and Participation work forms a major area of activity. Stages 8-9 shows each year.

Casting procedures: Please email **admin@orangetreetheatre.co.uk** for casting enquiries. Actively encourages applications from disabled actors and promotes the use of inclusive casting.

Park Theatre

Clifton Terrace, Finsbury Park, London N4 3JP
tel 020 3697 4190
email info@parktheatre.co.uk
email hire@parktheatre.co.uk
website www.parktheatre.co.uk
Artistic Director Jez Bond *Executive Director* Vicky Hawkins

Production details: Park Theatre programmes a balance of new writing and classics, plays and musicals across its two theatres - Park90 and Park200.

Looks for work that has a strong narrative and emotional drive and plays that can flourish within the intimacy of smaller theatres. Maintains a good gender balance of male and female roles on stage within a season as well as generally encouraging BAME stories and casting.Generally prefers productions with smaller casts and high production values. Recent productions include: *Boys in the Band* by Matt Crowley starring Mark Gatiss, *Madame Rubinstein* by John Misto starring Miriam Margolyes, and Ian McKellen in *Shakespeare, Tolkien, Others & You. Toast* by Richard Bean starring Matthew Kelly (UK tour and New York transfer), *An Audience with Jimmy Savile* by Jonathan Maitland starring Alistair McGowan (Edinburgh transfer) and *The Patriotic Traitor* by Jonathan Lynn starring Tom Conti and Laurence Fox.

Both produces and receives Equity-approved contracts and subscribes to Equity pension scheme, with UK Theatre agreement where applicable.

Casting procedures: Uses freelance casting directors, but does not hold general auditions. Casting breakdowns are periodically available via Spotlight. Due to small staff, unsolicited CVs cannot be responded to.

Perth Theatre, Horsecross Arts

Horsecross Arts Ltd, Perth Theatre & Concert Hall, Mill Street, Perth PH1 5HZ
tel 01738 472700
email info@horsecross.co.uk
website www.horsecross.co.uk
Artistic Director Lu Kemp

Production details: Perth Theatre, Horsecross Arts produces/coproduces 5–6 shows a year including a pantomime and programme work from independent touring companies and producing houses under the Artistic Directorship of Lu Kemp. Runs a broad Learning and Engagement programme, including the Youth Theatre, and are committed to providing innovative and relevant work for Scottish audiences.

The casting process aims to represent the breadth of Scotland's demographic and Perth Theatre welcomes approaches from local artists. See the casting page for further details **www.horsecross.co.uk/work-with-us/casting.**

Pitlochry Festival Theatre

Port-Na-Craig, Pitlochry PH16 5DR
tel 01796 484626
email admin@pitlochryfestivaltheatre.com
website www.pitlochryfestivaltheatre.com
Artistic Director Elizabeth Newman

Production details: Founded in 1951, Pitlochry Festival Theatre is a producing and presenting theatre located in the Perthshire Highlands. Comprises the main house (capacity 538), an extensive production facility, and *Explorers*: The Scottish Plant Hunters Garden, containing open-air performance spaces. Between May and October each year a 14-18 strong acting ensemble presents a season of 6 major productions performed in day-change repertoire. An autumn production is presented in October/November, a large scale festive production is presented in December and a spring production is presented in February/March. Visiting theatre, music, dance, opera and other activities are presented during the winter months. Also runs engagement programmes. Recent productions include: *Summer Holiday, The Crucible, Faith Healer, A Christmas Carol, Barefoot in the Park, North and South* and *Blithe Spirit.*

Offers UK Theatre Equity contracts.

Queen's Theatre Hornchurch

Billet Lane, Hornchurch, Essex RM11 1QT
tel 01708 443333
email info@queens-theatre.co.uk
website www.queens-theatre.co.uk

Production details: Has been a producing theatre since it was first established in 1953. Stages 8 shows each year in the main house, including revival plays, actor-musician musicals and new writing. Also runs TIE, Outreach and Community programmes. Recent productions include: *All My Sons, The Kitchen Sink* and *Love Letters.* Runs a talent development programme for Essex and outer East London actors and theatremakers.

Casting procedures: Holds auditions per production 3-5 months in advance of rehearsals; actors should write to **casting@queens-theatre.co.uk** with a Spotlight link.

Rose Theatre Kingston

24-26 High Street, Kingston-upon-Thames, Surrey KT1 1HL

tel 020 8546 6983
email admin@rosetheatre.org
website www.rosetheatre.org
Chief Executive Robert O'Dowd *Artistic Director* Christopher Haydon

The Rose Theatre Kingston opened its doors to the public in January 2008 with English Touring Productions' production of *Uncle Vanya*, directed by Sir Peter Hall. The design of the theatre was inspired by the Elizabethan Rose on London's Bankside; Kingston's Rose has the same horse-shoe shaped auditorium and an open lozenge stage, creating a sense of intimacy between actors and audiences. The Rose auditorium has a capacity of more than 850 across 3 tiers of seating, including a pit area where audiences can sit on cushions for just £7. In addition to the main space there is a studio, capacity 120, and a gallery, capacity 60. These spaces host a variety of talks and workshops led by theatre writers and practitioners. The theatre also has a strong connection with Kingston University, where it facilitates the University's MA in Classical Drama.

The Rose presents a combination of home-produced drama and received work. Since opening, it has produced 16 home-grown productions, including *Love's Labour's Lost* and *A Midsummer Night's Dream*, directed by Sir Peter Hall; *The Winslow Boy* and *The Lady from the Sea*, directed by Stephen Unwin; and two rep seasons.

Royal & Derngate Theatres

19-21 Guildhall Road, Northampton NN1 1DP
tel (01604) 624811
website www.royalandderngate.co.uk
Chief Executive Jo Gordon, *Artistic Director* James Dacre

Producing theatre; productions have toured the UK and transferred to the West End, Broadway, Shakespeare's Globe Theatre and the National Theatre. Visiting productions include musicals, dance, comedy and music.

A registered charity, the Get Involved programme engages the local community and foters new talent. Works with young people on site and in schools.

Royal Court Theatre

Sloane Square, London SW1W 8AS
tel 020 7565 5050
email info@royalcourttheatre.com
website www.royalcourttheatre.com
Facebook www.facebook.com/royalcourttheatre
Twitter @royalcourt
Artistic Director Vicky Featherstone *Casting Director* Amy Ball *Associate Directors* Milli Bhatia, Ola Ince, Lucy Morrison, Hamish Pirie, Sam Pritchard

Production details: Since 1956 the English Stage Company at the Royal Court has focused on developing, funding and producing new writing. Productions frequently transfer to the West End and Broadway. Stages about 14 productions a year. Also presents an extensive play development programme incorporating workshops and rehearsed readings. Recent productions include: *Shoe Lady* by E.V. Crowe; *Poet in da Corner* by Debris Stevenson (feat. Jammz), *Scenes with girls* by Miriam Battye, *A Kind of People* by Gurpreet Kaur Bhatti, *Midnight Movie* by Eve Leigh, *On Bear Ridge* by Ed Thomas, *A History of Water in the Middle East* by Sabrina Mahfouz, *Glass. Kill. Bluebeard. Imp.* by Caryl Churchill, *Total Immediate Collective Imminent Terrestrial Salvation* by Tim Crouch, *seven methods of killing kylie jenner* by Jasmine Lee-Jones, *the end of history...* by Jack Thorne. Offers SOLT/TMA/UK Theatre/Equity-approved contracts and offers the Equity Pension Scheme.

Casting procedures: Welcomes submissions (with CVs and photographs) by post or email all year round.

Royal Exchange Theatre

St Ann's Square, Manchester M2 7DH
tel 0161 833 9833
email box.office@royalexchange.co.uk
website www.royalexchange.co.uk
Joint Artistic Directors Roy Alexander Weise, Bryony Shanahan *Executive Director* Stephen Freeman *Director of Creative Learning and Engagement* Inga Hirst

Production details: Manchester's leading producing theatre company, comprising a main theatre and studio space. Presents 8-9 productions, on average, in the main theatre and 3-4 in the studio each year. The programme is a mixture of reimagined classics from the repertoire, musicals and an ambitious programme of new plays and contemporary theatre. Also runs Creative Learning and Community Engagement programmes involving schools, young people, community groups and theatre enthusiasts of all ages. Work is based around the theatre's repertoire and its unique building. Where possible, the department leads sessions in the theatre, and frequently works with other departments around the building to give participants an insight into how theatre, and particularly the Royal Exchange, work. Recent productions include: *Our Town, Happy Days, Guys and Dolls* and *Jubilee.*

Casting procedures: Head of Casting works with a freelance associate who together coordinate casting for each show. Actors are contracted for individual plays rather than for a season of work. Releases advance production information to around 200 agents on the website. Detailed casting breakdowns are only available for some shows.

Will consider attending performances at venues in the North West and London with sufficient notice. Accepts submissions (with CVs and photographs), but actors should bear in mind that the department expects to receive more than 2000 CVs and photos

Theatre

each season – and more in the summer months following graduation at the drama schools. All submissions are considered but they are not kept on file indefinitely.

Royal Lyceum Edinburgh

Grindlay Street, Edinburgh EH3 9AX
tel 0131 248 4800
email info@lyceum.org.uk
website www.lyceum.org.uk
Artistic Director David Greig

Production details: The Royal Lyceum is one of Scotland's largest producing theatre companies with a season of in-house drama productions and co-productions running from September to June. In addition, the theatre stages a Christmas show. Occasionally tours in Scotland and abroad, limited hosting of touring companies, and runs an ambitious and acclaimed Creative Learning Department. Recent productions include: *The Duchess of Malfi, Local Hero, Touching the Void,* and *Wendy and Peter Pan.*

Casting procedures: Does not offer general auditions. "Casting depends on individual directors' choices."

Royal Shakespeare Company

Royal Shakespeare Theatre, Waterside, Stratford-upon-Avon, Warwickshire, CV37 6BB
tel 020 7845 0500
London Office: 1 Earlham Street, London WC2H 9LL
website www.rsc.org.uk
Artistic Director Erica Whyman *Head of Casting* Hannah Miller *Artistic Director Emeritus* Gregory Doran

Production details: The Royal Shakespeare Company creates Shakespeare for everyone, made in Stratford-upon-Avon and shared around the world. The Company produces an inspirational artistic programme each year, setting Shakespeare in context, alongside the work of his contemporaries and today's writers. Productions begin life at the RSC's Stratford workshops and theatres, and are brought to the widest possible audience through touring, residencies, live broadcasts and online activity.

The RSC is at heart an ensemble company, with actors most often being contracted to perform in several productions in a season of work.

Casting procedures: We welcome performance notices sent 4-6 weeks in advance, and travel all over the UK. Please send correspondence including invitations and submissions for specific productions to **suggestions@rsc.org.uk**, and preferably in relation to specific productions.

Shakespeare's Globe

21 New Globe Walk, Bankside, London SE1 9DT
tel 020 7902 1400
email info@shakespearesglobe.com
website www.shakespearesglobe.com
Artistic Director Michelle Terry *Head of Casting* Becky Paris

Production details: A reconstruction of Shakespeare's Globe, the theatre has a repertoire which includes the work of Shakespeare, his contemporaries and new writing. The season runs from April to October with up to 10 productions staged each year. Opened second theatre in 2014, The Sam Wanamaker Playhouse, a reconstruction of an indoor Jacobean theatre. Recent productions include:*The Merchant of Venice, Nell Gwyn, The Taming of the Shrew* and *Imogen.*

Casting procedures: Welcomes letters (with CVs and photographs) but not email submissions: prefers invitations to see actors in performance. Actors should write to the Casting Department. Offers actors Equity-approved contracts through an in-house agreement. Actively encourages applications from disabled actors and promotes the use of inclusive casting. The website has more information about casting procedures.

Sheffield Theatres

55 Norfolk Street, Sheffield S1 1DA
tel 0114 249 5999
email customer.service@sheffieldtheatres.co.uk
website www.sheffieldtheatres.co.uk
Chief Executive Dan Bates *Artistic Director* Robert Hastie

Production details: Comprises 3 theatres: the Crucible Theatre (thrust stage, 960 capacity), the Studio Theatre (200-400 capacity) and the Lyceum Theatre (pros. arch, 1,168 capacity). Stages 5-6 shows each year in the Crucible, 3-4 in the Studio and 1-2 in the Lyceum. Also runs learning programmes. Recent productions include: *Standing at the Sky's Edge* and *Life of Pi.*

Casting procedures: Uses freelance casting directors. Welcomes letters (with CVs and photographs). Offers TMA/Equity approved contracts.

Sheringham Little Theatre

2 Station Road, Sheringham, Norfolk NR26 8RE
tel 01263 822117
email enquiries@sheringhamlittletheatre.com
website www.sheringhamlittletheatre.com
Theatre Director Debbie Thompson

Production details: A professional seaside repertory summer season which runs for 10 weeks from July to September, comprising 5 plays which are traditional comedies, farces, thrillers, musicals and classics.

Casting procedures: Holds general auditions. Actors should write between January and March, sending a CV and *recent* photograph. Email submissions not welcome. "As a small venue we are non-Equity, but we do work with Equity to pay a realistic wage; we also pay for accommodation and towards travel costs." Actively encourages applications from disabled actors and promotes the use of inclusive casting.

Sherman Theatre

Senghennydd Road, Cathays, Cardiff CF24 4YE
tel 029 2064 6901
website www.shermantheatre.co.uk
Artistic Director Joe Murphy

Production details: Stages several shows each year and specialises in work for young audiences. Theatre comprises two spaces: the Main House which stages touring drama, comedy, dance and opera; and the Studio which stages touring drama, fringe theatre and stand-up comedy.

Casting procedures: Does not use freelance casting directors. Sometimes holds general auditions.

Soho Theatre

21 Dean Street, London W1D 3NE
tel 020 7287 5060
email info@sohotheatre.com
website www.sohotheatre.com
Executive Director Mark Godfrey, *Creative Director* David Luff

Production details: Soho Theatre is a vibrant producer of new theatre, comedy and cabaret. Harnessing an artistic spirit that is based in new writing roots, the radical ethos of the fringe and the traditions of punk culture and queer performance, the Theatre champions voices that challenge from outside of the mainstream, and sometimes from within it too. The Theatre is a registered charity and social enterprise and audiences are diverse in age, background and outlook.

The Theatre is mission driven: success is measured through the prodution, presentation and facilitation of new work; the artists and creative talent that are nurtured; and the diverse audiences that are engaged.

Soho Theatre + Writers' Centre includes a flexible 144-seat theatre, a large self-contained studio space with 85-seat capacity, theatre bar, restaurant, offices, rehearsal, writing and meeting rooms. The Centre hosts workshops, showcases, meetings and events; and the company reaches an audience of 250,000 people a year in the Theatre and elsewhere including the Edinburgh Fringe. All spaces are accessible and available for hire. For bookings and general information, please visit **www.sohotheatre.com**.

In response to Covid-19 the Theatre relaunched its online platform, Soho Theatre On Demand, which hosted the phenomenally successful live recording of *Fleabag* and more recently released *Typical* and *Sunrise*. The Theatre has partnered with Amazon Prime Video for a three-series comedy deal.

Casting procedures: Casting is carried out by freelance casting directors, engaged on a production basis.

Southwark Playhouse

77-85 Newington Causeway, London SE1 6BD
tel 020 7407 0234

email admin@southwarkplayhouse.co.uk
website www.southwarkplayhouse.co.uk
Artisitic Director (CEO) Chris Smyrnios

Production details: Southwark Playhouse's central vision is that of a vibrant theatre in the heart of the London Borough of Southwark, serving the widest possible constituency within the Borough and beyond, providing a platform for emerging theatre practitioners and a programme of performance, education work and community drama.

Southwark Playhouse will be moving to a location in the London Bridge Station development. Please see the website for the latest details.

Stephen Joseph Theatre

Westborough, Scarborough YO11 1JW
tel (01723) 370540
email enquiries@sjt.uk.com
website www.sjt.uk.com
Artistic Director Paul Robinson *Associate Director* Cheryl Govan

Production details: Produces 6 in-house shows per year, including co-productions with other venues. Has two performance spaces: a main space in the round and an end-on studio theatre. Focuses on new writing. Recent productions include: *Jane Eyre* adapted by Chris Bush, *The Offing* directed by Paul Robinson and *Home I'm Darling* in co-production with Theatre by the Lake and Octagon Theatre.

Casting procedures: Holds general auditions for local actors annually. Welcomes submissions (with CVs and photographs) by email. Also accepts showreels and invitations to view individual actors' websites. Offers UK Theatre/Equity approved contracts and rates of pay. Has an inclusive casting policy.

Casting Director Sarah Hughes is not resident at the SJT but often works on individual productions.

Storyhouse

Hunter Street, Chester CH1 2AR
tel 01244 409113
email info@storyhouse.com
website www.storyhouse.com
Creative Director Suzie Henderson *Chief Executive* Andrew Bentley

Founded in 2017, Storyhouse is Chester's award-winning theatre, library, cinema and arts centre. It presents a year-round programme of theatre, comedy, dance and music events alongside a raft of creative festivals.

Storyhouse also produces the much-loved Grosvenor Park Open Air Theatre, Moonlight Flicks outdoor cinema in Chester's Roman Gadrens, the Chester Music Festival and Literature Festival.

Produces 5 productions in the main house a year. Equity approved contracts.

The Library Theatre

See the entry for HOME under *Producing theatres* on page 136.

Theatre

Theatr Clwyd

Mold, Flintshire CH7 1YA
tel (01352) 344101
email box.office@theatrclwyd.com
website www.theatrclwyd.com
Artistic Director Tamara Harvey *Producer* Liz Johnson

Production details: The major drama-producing company in Wales. Although most work is presented in English, some pieces are performed in Welsh. Stages 5-6 shows in the main house, and 5-6 in the studio each year, with some mid- large-scale productions touring Wales and England. Also runs TIE programmes.

Recent productions include: *Aristocrats, Season's Greetings, Copenhagen, Under Milk Wood* and *Arms and the Man.* Offers TMA/Equity approved contracts and subscribes to the Equity Pension Scheme.

Casting procedures: Theatr Clwyd employs freelance casting directors. For further information contact William James at the address above.

Theatre By The Lake

Lakeside, Keswick, Cumbria CA12 5DJ
tel 017687 74411
email enquiries@theatrebythelake.com
website www.theatrebythelake.com
Artistic Director Liz Stevenson *Producer* Amy Clewes

Production details: Each year, Theatre by the Lake produces a Summer Season of 6 plays in repertoire, an Easter production/Spring Season, and a Christmas production. Also promotes a touring programme of visiting professional work across all artforms, and runs Education and Outreach programmes. Recent productions include: *A Chorus of Disapproval, Blackbird, The Memory of Water,* and *A Midsummer Night's Dream.* Offers TMA/Equity-approved contracts and subscribes to the Equity Pension Scheme.

Casting procedures: Auditions are held 3 times a year. All casting is in-house; does not use freelance casting directors. Casting breakdowns can be obtained by postal application with sae. Does not accept general submissions from actors. Further information about the casting process can be found on the website.

Theatre Royal Bath

Sawclose, Bath BA1 1ET
tel 01225 448815
website www.theatreroyal.org.uk
Twitter @TheatreRBath
Director Danny Moar

One of the oldest theatres in Britain. Comprising three auditoria – the Main House, the Ustinov Studio Theatre and the Egg Theatre for children and young people – the Theatre Royal offers a varied programme of entertainment all year round.

Theatre Royal, Bury St Edmunds

Westgate Street, Bury St Edmunds, Suffolk IP33 1QR
tel (01284) 829945

email artistic@theatreroyal.org
website www.theatreroyal.org
Artistic Director & CEO Owen Calvert-Lyons

Built in 1819, the theatre is the only surviving Regency theatre in the country. Produces an annual pantomime at Christmas and 2 other shows a year – a spring drama and a summer community production which includes professional actors working alongside local children and young people. Offers non-Equity contracts.

Casting procedures: Casting breakdowns are published via Spotlight only. Actors wishing to be considered for the pantomime should write to the theatre in April. (The spring and summer shows are cast in January/February and April/May respectively.) Only welcomes letters and emails (with CVs and photographs) from actors previously unknown to the company during these casting periods. Does not welcome showreels, but is happy to receive performance notices. Rarely or never has the opportunity to cast disabled actors.

Theatre Royal Plymouth

Royal Parade, Plymouth PL1 2TR
tel 01752 668282
email literary@theatreroyal.com
website www.theatreroyal.com
Twitter @TRPlymouth

Specialises in the production of new plays. Its engagement and learning work engages young people and communities in Plymouth and beyond. The award-winning waterfront production and learning centre, TR2, offers set, costume, prop-making and rehearsal facilities.

Theatre Royal Stratford East

Gerry Raffles Square, London E15 1BN
tel 020 8534 7374
email theatreroyal@stratfordeast.com
website www.stratfordeast.com
Artistic Director Nadia Fall

Production details: Committed to new work which portrays the experiences of different social and ethnic communities, the theatre is constantly striving to present shows which resonate with its diverse local audiences. Stages 8 shows each year. Also runs Young People's, Outreach and Community programmes. Recent productions include: *Janis Joplin Full Tilt, The House of Inbetween* and *Love N Stuff.*

Casting procedures: Casting opportunities are advertised on the website. Welcomes submissions (with CVs and photographs) sent by post. Advises actors to research the theatre's work before writing, and to think carefully about their own suitability. Invitations to view individual actors' websites also accepted. Actively encourages applications from disabled actors and promotes the use of inclusive casting.

Theatre Royal Windsor

Thames Street, Windsor SL4 1PS
tel 01753 863444

Theatre

email info@theatreroyalwindsor.co.uk
website www.theatrereroyalwindsor.co.uk
Chief Executive Bill Kenwright *Co-Directors* Anne-Marie Woodley, Jon Woodley

Production details: A long-standing, non-subsidised producing theatre. Shows run for 1-2 weeks. Stages new productions each year with some going on to tour. Recent productions include: *The Best Man, How the Other Half Loves* and *This is Elvis.*

Casting procedures: Does not use freelance casting directors. Welcomes letters (with CVs and photographs) but not email submissions. Offers TMA/Equity-approved contracts. Will consider applications from disabled actors to play characters with disabilities.

Tobacco Factory Theatres

First Floor, Tobacco Factory, Raleigh Road, Southville, Bristol BS3 1TF
tel 0117 902 0345
email theatre@tobaccofactorytheatres.com
website www.tobaccofactorytheatres.com
Artistic Director Mike Tweddle

Production details: Stages 6-8 productions a year in the theatre space and touring work, and also works with the local community. Does not always offer Equity-approved contracts. Offers contracts where possible.

Casting procedures: Casts in-house and does not hold general auditions. Casting breakdowns are available from the website, and via postal application (with sae). Welcomes emails from actors previously unknown to the company, but does not welcome showreels or invitations to view individual actors' websites. Actively encourages applications from disabled actors and promotes the use of inclusive casting.

Torch Theatre

St Peter's Road, Milford Haven SA73 2BU
tel 01646 694192
email info@torchtheatre.co.uk
website www.torchtheatre.co.uk
Artistic Director Peter Doran *Executive Producer* Benjamin Lloyd

Production details: Stages 4-5 productions each year. Recent productions include: *Brief Encounter, One Flew Over the Cuckoo's Nest* and *Woman in Black.*

Casting procedures: Sometimes holds general auditions; actors should write in June requesting inclusion. Casting breakdowns are available by postal application (with sae) and Equity Job Information Service. Welcomes submissions (with CVs and photographs), sent by email. Showreels and invitations to view individual actors' websites are also accepted. Advises actors to join the mailing list so they know what is being planned 6 months in advance. Offers TMA/Equity approved contracts.

Actively encourages applications from disabled actors and promotes the use of inclusive casting.

Traverse Theatre

Cambridge Street, Edinburgh EH1 2ED
tel 0131 228 3223
email info@traverse.co.uk
website www.traverse.co.uk
Artistic Director Gareth Nicholls

Production details: Scotland's premier new work theatre, telling new stories for a new era across a range of platforms. Presents a mixed programme of in-house productions, partner company work, live music and festivals, spanning its two in person theatre spaces, Traverse 3 digital platform, off-site and touring venues. Also runs extensive Engagement and Creative Development programmes generating new work; see website for more details.

Casting procedures: Casting calls and open auditions advertised on the website and Spotlight. Show invitations are welcome via **casting@traverse.co.uk**. Particularly interested to hear from Scotland-based actors.

Tricycle Theatre

See the entry for Kiln Theatre under *Producing theatres* on page 137.

Tron Theatre

63 Trongate, Glasgow G1 5HB
tel 0141 552 3748
email casting@tron.co.uk
website www.tron.co.uk
Artistic Director Andy Arnold *Executive Director* Sam Gough

Production details: The Tron Theatre Company is currently under the leadership of Andy Arnold. The Tron presents the people of Glasgow and Scotland with outstanding professional productions of the finest new writing and contemporary adaptations of classic texts, with an emphasis on world, UK and Scottish premieres. The Tron also provides a supportive environment for emerging and established theatre talent, nurturing the future voices of Scottish Theatre. (Seating capacity: main house 230, studio 50.) 6 Tron productions are staged annually in the main house (including co-productions) and 1 production is staged annually in the studio. Other areas of work include our Education & Outreach programme. Recent productions include: World premiere stage adaptation of *Ulysses* by James Joyce; John Byrne's new adaptation of *Three Sisters*; *Dreams and Other Nightmares of Edwin Morgan* by Liz Lochhead; and in autumn 2015, contemporary adaptation of Ibsen's *Ghosts* by Megan Barker.

Casting procedures: Casting is done by liaising with show director and casting directors, and using details of actors on file. Actors can write at any time to request inclusion, as their submissions will be kept on

Theatre

file. Accepts submissions (with CVs and photographs) from actors unknown to the company. Actors are employed under Equity-approved contracts, and the theatre participates in the Equity Pension Scheme. Encourages applications from disabled actors and promotes the use of inclusive casting.

Watermill Theatre

Bagnor, Newbury RG20 8AE
tel (01635) 45834
email admin@watermill.org.uk
website www.watermill.org.uk
Facebook www.facebook.com/The Watermill Theatre
Twitter @watermillTh
Instagram @TheWatermillTheatre
Artistic Director & CEO Paul Hart *Executive Director* Claire Murray *Associate Director* Abigail Pickard Price *Casting and Producing Assistant* Kezia Buckland *Outreach Director* Heidi Bird

Production details: A producing theatre where actors live onsite. Stages 12 shows each year with runs of 6-8 weeks, 1 rural tour and 2 youth theatre shows. Recent productions have included: Shakespeare, Musical Theatre, New Writing and Classics.

Casting procedures: Regulary advertises roles using Spotlight. Occasionally uses freelance casting directors. Welcomes emails (with CVs and photographs) with reference to specific castings only. Offers UK Theatre/Subsidised Theatre Agreement/ Equity-approved contracts and subscribes to the Equity Pension Scheme. The Watermill Theatre is committed to equality of opportunity for all.

Watford Palace Theatre

20 Clarendon Road, Watford WD17 1JZ
tel 01923 235455
email enquiries@watfordpalacetheatre.co.uk
website www.watfordpalacetheatre.co.uk
Artistic Director and Chief Executive Brigid Larmour

Production details: Producing theatre built in 1908 and refurbished in 2002-2004. The theatre presents a varied programme including inventive, ambitious and inclusive drama, new plays, musicals, dance and family shows. All programme enquiries should be send to **programming@watfordpalacetheatre.co.uk**.

Casting procedures: Casts in-house and uses freelance casting directors. Enquiries should be sent to **casting@watfordpalacetheatre.co.uk**. Unable to respond to individual CVs. Will consider applications from disabled actors to play disabled characters. Offers UK heatre/Euity agreements. Also involved in Education and Community theatre, for which enquiries should be sent to **participation@watfordpalacetheatre.co.uk**.

Wiltshire Creative

Malthouse Lane, Salisbury SP2 7RA
tel 01722 320117

email info@wiltshirecreative.co.uk
website www.salisburyplayhouse.co.uk
Artistic Director Gareth Machin

Production details: Pan-arts organisation incorporating Salisbury Playhouse, Salisbury Arts Centre and Salisbury International Arts Festival. Produces a wide range of theatre and cross art work throughout the year, alongside an extensive Take Part programme and Theatre For Young People.

Casting procedures: Offers TMA/Equity-approved contracts. Most productions are cast using freelance casting directors although occasionally in-house. Submissions for specific productions by email are welcome. Promotes inclusive casting, and actively encourages applications from disabled actors.

Worcester Repertory Company

The Swan Theatre, The Moors, Worcester WR1 3ED
tel (01905) 726969
email sarah-jane@worcestertheatres.co.uk
website www.worcestertheatres.co.uk
Facebook www.facebook.com/worcstheatres
Artistic Director Sarah-Jane Morgan

Production details: Originally founded in 1968 and the breeding ground for directors such as David Wood OBE, John Doyle, Phyllida Lloyd CBE and Rufus Norris (Director of the National Theatre), the Worcester Rep. now produces between 3 and 4 productions a year at either of their theatres plus outdoor productions within the city. Alongside the main house pantomime, small-scale touring shows and new studio work is occasionally included. As with most companies, contracts are offered on a show-by-show basis but most actors work on more than one production with the company. The company is based at the Swan Theatre, Worcester.

Casting procedures: Casting is handled in-house. The comapny is happy to receive submissions from actors previously unknown to the company either by post of email. Please adess all casting submissions to Sarah-Jane Morgan.

York Theatre Royal

St Leonard's Place, York YO1 7HD
tel 01904 623568 (Box Office)
email admin@yorktheatreroyal.co.uk
website www.yorktheatreroyal.co.uk
Facebook @yorktheatreroyal
Twitter @YorkTheatre
Instagram @yorkthreateroyal

Production details: One of the oldest theatres in the country; seats 760 in the Main House and 71 in the Studio. Productions include classics, new writing and the famous York pantomime every Christmas. Also hosts touring companies, premières and has partnerships with tutti frutti, Wise Children and Pilot Theatre Company. Runs Outreach, Community programmes and Youth Theatre. Recent productions include: *Swallows and Amazons, Driving Miss Daisy, A*

View from the Bridge, Olivier-Award Winning *The Railway Children*, *The Grand Old Dame of York* and *Sleeping Beauty*.

Casting procedures: Occasionally uses freelance casting directors.

Young Vic

66 The Cut, London SE1 8LZ
tel 020 7922 2922
email info@youngvic.org
website www.youngvic.org
Artistic Director Kwame Kwei-Armah

Production details: The Young Vic presents a wide variety of classics, new plays, forgotten works and music theatre. The theatre is especially concerned with the art of directing. The Directors Programme is the most comprehensive in the UK. This fusion makes the Young Vic one of the most exciting theatres in the world. "Our audience is famously the youngest and most diverse in London. We encourage those who don't think theatre is 'for them'". Recent productions include: *Yerma*, *Fun Home*, *The Convert*, *Death of a Salesman*, *Tree*, *Blood Wedding* and *Portia Coughlin*.

Casting procedures: Uses freelance casting directors. Does not welcome direct submissions from actors. Offers TMA/Equity approved contracts. Actively encourages applications from disabled actors and promotes the use of inclusive casting.

Theatre

Inclusivity and allyship for the future of the industry

Tom Ross-Williams, theatre-maker, filmmaker, performer and activist
Interview by Polly Bennett

Tom Ross-Williams is a theatre-maker, filmmaker, performer and activist. They were the Creative Director of The Advocacy Academy, a social justice organisation for young people from south London, and have worked as an actor at the RSC, Kneehigh, Soho Theatre and Bush Theatre. A major focus of their activism is LGBTQ+ rights and tackling Toxic Masculinity. They write and talk about these issues in various settings, including as a regular contributor to the Huffington Post, *a frequent panellist at WOW Festival and on BBC Radio4's* The Moral Maze.

What's your role as an educator of inclusivity issues?

Not everyone has equal access to bring their full selves as they come into a rehearsal room, so I explore how we create equitable spaces that acknowledge that. I ask what it means for the person who isn't sat next to on the train because of how they look to walk into that room. What does it mean for the person who is never asked to speak first to contribute versus those that are? Making change is like going to the source of the river; rather than taking people out of the river who are drowning, you need to find out who's chucking people in to begin with. I often teach a tool called 'Oops, Ouch', which allows people harmed by microaggressions to voice that ('ouch'), as well as the person who has exacted it and their likely good intentions ('oops'). We explore ways to communicate a metaphorical 'ouch' when harm's been done so it gets acknowledged, lessons are learnt, and we are able to move on. It's so much effort to make the person that's been harmed name it and that's why we need processes and systems that do that without all that emotional and cognitive labour. I provide new lenses to see the world and try making invisible privileges more visible.

Do you feel like it's working?

Young people are so on board with making rehearsal rooms, auditions and film sets safer and more inclusive, so it feels very hopeful. Unfortunately, I've done work in lots of places where it feels tokenistic, but elsewhere there are some exciting things happening. Pastoral care systems are in place and people are starting to introduce themselves with their pronouns. It's small but it's having a seismic effect on making people feel maybe not fully celebrated, but at least accepted.

Intimacy coordination is something that you've begun exploring. Why is this role so important?

I'm really interested in consent practices and personal agency in performance. I don't feel like actors are encouraged to take agency very often and are too rarely asked to consider consent in the rehearsal process. I am being mentored by Ita O'Brien and her guidelines have shifted this in the industry hugely. Seeing the gay sex scenes in *Sex Education* was the first time I've seen an uncomplicated loving gay sex between two teenagers on screen. That would have been profound for me as a young person. Intimacy coordination feels like a change that is going to be lasting and that's why I want to be a part of it. It feels like activism to me.

What is preventing change from happening throughout the industry?

People just aren't giving up their positions of power, basically. It's all very performative. Often when I explain privilege, I play a game where there are three rows of people and whoever throws a ball into the bin from their place wins a prize. The front row can get the ball in easily, a few in the second and back row, maybe one. And everyone cheers for the person in the back row. And that's what society does, point to the person in the back row and say, 'Well, if they got it in, you can too'. And in doing this, nobody in the front row gives up their seat.

There's been some controversies recently over funding which has got its money from a history of slavery, so there has been an influx of acknowledging sentiments but maybe they should just give the endowment away to people. Like, 'Oh my gosh, my big theatre that represents the whole of the UK that's been this historic place of systemic racism, what do I do?' You give up your seat, move on! It's very hard for people to do as it's been aligned to cancel culture. But we won't get anywhere by just cancelling people. It individualises a problem that is systemic. Harvey Weinstein did not create *all* sexual violence, but he was part of an industry that supported it. So we need to find more ways to have co-creative practices so that people are collectively responsible with more shared leadership and co-writers. It's not fair to put somebody in a very virtue-signalling way in a huge position of power and give them no support. That needs to shift.

What do you think about the conversations happening about queer parts being played by non-queer actors?

I often think about how Rikki Beadle-Blair cast me in the first film I ever did as a gay character before I'd even come to terms fully with my sexuality. There's a wonderful power of stepping into somebody else's shoes as an actor and I would hate for us to completely lose that by not allowing people to experiment particularly as a young performer. But performing in an internal drama school situation is a very different situation than casting a big Hollywood film where another straight person is going to win an Oscar for playing gay, when no out queer actor has ever won an Oscar. If you're doing a final production for a drama school and there are out queer performers and there's a really wonderful role that is all about queer identity and we give that to one of the actors who identify as straight, then that does become difficult. But there needs to be a bit more nuance around these conversations and more strategy.

OK, so let's say I'm the financier on an independent feature film. It's an amazing queer love story that will show people a version of queer intimacy that never been seen before, but I'm only going to get this financed if I get a famous lead actor. There currently aren't many "big name" actors who are out and queer, so what do I do?

Ideally, you'd push for the few out queer 'big name' actors to be in your film. But, pragmatically, I want as many queer actors working as possible. So, if Keira Knightly said, 'I'll play this part but only if all of the supporting cast are queer, whether they're playing queer characters or not', that's interesting. The film gets financed and she gets to play an amazing

Theatre

role whilst giving lots of jobs to queer creatives, both on and off screen. After the Oscars, So White and #MeToo movements, lots of film actors signed inclusion riders to only work on shows that have an equal gender split or a certain amount of people of colour working on it. Ending the conversation by saying a straight actor should never play a gay role does a disservice to some of the strategic choices that could be made to allow more queer actors to get their first screen role. Of course I want LGBTQ+ actors to play those roles and I would never condone a cis actor playing trans, so there is nuance there.

So really it's about allyship and changing the system that upholds itself.

I think the oppression of minority groups is upheld through diverting the attention to individuals and to small organisations, rather than looking at the systemic shifts. I guess that's why I'm quite keen on things like policy and LGBTQ+ education. There are so many worrying decisions this government is taking – they have bowed out of their Stonewall training. That decision alone is then going to feed into the decisions around LGBTQ+ education in schools and will obviously have an effect on our industry. Practices that really commit to focussing on liberation and anti-oppression take a lot more time and under-standably we want quick fixes, but we need to think long term. I think a lot of these quick fixes mean diversity and inclusion policies are written, but then people aren't hired to make sure they're being enacted.

What I have been trying to do in the past few years is thinking about how I can remove the labour from people who've not been visible in the industry; give them an opportunity to really dream and to be artists and create those containers that support that creativity. This idea that we can't make work that's not about our own identity is difficult because it means that we don't have a world of allyship. I'm co-creating a show with some young Latinx activists and I'm ready for people to say that I shouldn't be the one to make that show because I'm not Latinx. I'm ready for criticism, but sometimes we need to be bold. I feel art should be able to do that: we're not reporters or journalists, we're artists.

To follow Tom's work visit **www.tomrosswiliiams.com** or follow them on social media **@tomrosswilliams**.

Effective audition speeches

Simon Dunmore

Audition speeches may be a fundamental part of the actor's 'toolkit', but a surprising number of otherwise good actors are not very good at doing them – and many make poor choices of material to use. It's true that most castings involve a reading, but sometimes audition speeches are asked for in advance, and occasionally you'll get, 'We'd just like to see something else; what can you show us?' It would be very silly to be caught out because you haven't done an audition speech since drama school.

Essentially, audition speeches should be self-contained, well chosen, well researched, well staged and well gauged for the space you are in and for whoever is watching you – just like a good production of a play. In fact an audition speech should be a 'mini-production' (of a 'mini-play') in its own right.

Essential parameters

Length

An audition piece should be no more than two or two-and-a-half minutes long (that's roughly 300 words, depending on pace). Two minutes (or less) can be very effective provided that it contains all the parameters listed elsewhere in this article.

How many?

The important thing is to have a good range of audition material so that you've got a library to choose from to suit each given circumstance. I suggest at least half a dozen.

What types?

Your collection should consist of a good variety of characters you could credibly play. They should be within your 'playing range' and appropriate to your appearance: an audition speech is not an acting exercise; it's part of your marketing portfolio.

You should also aim to find material that rarely (if ever) appears elsewhere on the audition circuit. Judging acting is a highly subjective business, so it is generally better to find 'original' material to heighten your chances of not being compared to others. I suggest that you only use material that is popular if you feel sure you can perform it (them) extremely well – on a bad day ...

Accents

If you choose to do a speech written in a regional accent, make sure you can do that accent well enough to convince a native. (It is important to have at least one in your repertoire that features your own accent if it is a strong and 'characterful' one.) Some people choose to 'translate' a speech into an accent with which they are more comfortable, and this can work. However, watch that in doing this you are not sacrificing too much of the quality of the original language.

Sources of speeches

Don't just rely on plays that you know; you should be steadily expanding your knowledge of dramatic literature. Seeing, reading, sitting in libraries and bookshops (especially secondhand ones); even picking up an audition book to find inspiration for a playwright (previously unknown to you) whom you could explore further.

Theatre

Look in novels, less well-known films, and good journalism (for instance) for material that could be made into good 'drama'. For example, Shakespeare copied (almost word-for-word) Queen Katherine's wonderful speech beginning 'Sir, I desire you do me right and justice ...' (*Henry VIII*, Act II, Scene 4) from the court record.

It's generally inadvisable to write your own speech(es). This rarely works, because very few actors are good playwrights. If you do decide to use a self-written piece, it can be a good idea to use a *nom de plume;* you're selling yourself as an actor, not as a playwright. You should also be prepared to talk about the whole play, even if you haven't written it yet.

Content

Too many people fail because they choose to do an indifferent speech. Even if they do it well, it somehow doesn't have much impact because of indifferent writing, lack of depth, and so on. Essentially you should go for pieces that have good 'journeys' – just like a good play.

It can be useful to find speeches that enable you to show your special skills (singing or juggling, for instance), but don't try to cram so much in that the sense is lost in a firework display of technical virtuosity. At the other extreme, avoid something that requires performance at one pace or on one note.

And, never set out to shock deliberately through content and/or crude language. That is not to say don't do 'shockers'; rather, don't set out with the specific idea of shocking your interviewer(s) as many people seem to intend. We've heard most of it before. I cannot describe how mind-numbingly tedious audition-days can become when peppered with such speeches.

Warning: There is now a lot of free audition material available on the Internet. Much of it is indifferently written; however, I have come across the occasional 'gem'.

Shape

Make sure that each of your pieces has a decent shape. In a sense it should be like a good play, with a beginning, middle and ending. Even if the character ends up back where he/she started, so long as he/she has travelled a 'journey' then that's fine.

Shakespeare and the classics

Traditionally you need to have at least one of these in your armoury. The fact is that most people perform them indifferently. Too many renditions seem as dead as their writers. The problem is that they are remote – in language and in content – from our direct experience, and therefore usually require much more research, thought and preparation than a modern speech.

Note: It's very tedious to see comedy Shakespeare speech done in a 'cod' West Country accent. If you can genuinely do one of the many variants of this accent, then that's fine, but his language works in every other regional accent in which I've heard it done.

'Trying on'

Try reading any speech that looks good to you (on the page) out loud, in front of someone else, before you start rehearsing it. If you do this, you'll get an even better idea of whether each speech really suits (and 'grabs') you. It's a bit like buying clothes: you see a pair of trousers (say) that look good on the hanger; sometimes you will feel completely different about them when you try them on. The opposite can also occur: you feel indifferent about a speech on the page; you read it out loud and it feels much, much better.

Rehearsing your speeches
'What are you bringing on stage?'
You must bring your character's life history (gleaned from the play and supplemented by your imagination) into your performance. [As the character (i.e. in the first person), write notes of all the bits of information (big and small) that you find, in order to build his/her life.] Most of what you 'bring' won't be obvious to your auditioner(s). However, it will be immediately obvious if that 'life history' is not present. Just as 90% of an iceberg is underwater, a similar proportion of a good performance is also hidden ... but must be there, underneath, to support that performance.

It is particularly important to be clear about what actually provokes the character to start speaking – the 'ignition' that kicks your 'engine' into life. Try running a brief 'film' in your imagination, culminating in the event (for instance, a statement or a gesture from someone else) that is your cue.

Your invisible partner(s)
If you choose a speech addressing another character, then it is vital that that other person (and how they are reacting through the speech) is clear to you. It is generally better to imagine an adaptation of someone you know rather than to 'borrow' someone you've only seen on a flat screen. There can be a huge difference in how we perceive others between two and three dimensions.

It's not just them (and how they are reacting); it's also important to be clear about your relationship. As well as imagining what your character's lover looks like (for instance), you must also know the feel of their touch, their smell, and so forth – and many more personal aspects.

It is also important that any other people, places and events mentioned in the speech are similarly 'clear' in your imagination.

Your invisible circumstances
You should also bring the setting, clothes and practical items with you – in your imagination. (NB I could have written 'set, costumes and props', but I believe that it's important to think of everything being 'real' and not items constructed for a production.) I believe that actors neglecting these is the cause of a high proportion of failed and indifferent speeches. It's not just the visual images, it is also what the other senses give you: the 'brush' of a summer breeze across your face, for instance. Plays are not performed in 'real' rooms (there will be at least one wall missing) and every play has at least one non-appearing character mentioned. These absences are filled by the actors' imaginations. Do the same with these 'absences' in the audition circumstances.

It isn't just the major features that you should think about, but also the apparently minor details – for instance, the mark on a wall that suddenly catches your character's eye. It can be a good idea to draw a map (or groundplan) so that the whole 'geography' of your 'circumstances' is clear for you. Then fill out your imaginary location with as much detail as possible.

Interpretation
As you are creating a 'mini-production' of a 'mini-play' (the 'child' of its 'parent-play'), I believe that it's legitimate to make changes to the given circumstances of the speech when

Theatre

it occurs in the play, especially if such changes enhance your audition performance. (After all, a 'child' can never lose the genetic code of its 'parents', but he/she will evolve their own personality, which will be different.) However, be prepared to justify it – and don't get defensive. There's usually no harm in honest disagreement.

That voyage of discovery

Be aware of the 'voyage of discovery' that shapes your speech. Don't anticipate the end at the beginning. This is a common fault in rehearsal, which is easily corrected – but a remarkable number of people fall into this trap when performing their audition speeches.

It can be very useful to write out a speech with each sentence (or even each phrase) on a separate line. It then appears less of a 'block' of words on the page and more a series of separate, but connected, thoughts and ideas. It is also a good idea to leave sufficient space between each line to write notes on what is the impulse to go on to say the next thing, and the next, and...

Beginnings

If you start your speech nebulously, your interviewer probably won't take in what you are doing for the first few seconds and may miss vital information that could make the rest of it a complete puzzle to them. You need to find a way of starting your speech that will grab their attention from the very beginning. This doesn't mean that the beginning has to be loud, simply that it should be positive and effective – almost as if the house lights were faded down and the curtain rising on... You!

Note: It can also be very useful to incorporate a simple movement to start a speech; a turn of the head, for instance.

Endings

It's also important to be clear as to why a character stops speaking after talking for two minutes. You need to be clear what your character's final thought is – crucially stopping his/her flow.

Finally

Ask yourself: 'Are my speech and my presentation of it a good piece of "Theatre?"'

Some practical considerations

Staging

Once you've done all the work set out in the previous paragraphs, you need to think carefully about how you stage each piece. Too many people seem inclined to put in extraneous moves either to compensate for the lack of the other character(s), or because they think the speech is boring if it doesn't contain enough movement. If you are properly 'connecting' to character and 'circumstances', the moves will follow naturally from each 'impulse'. However, much of the effect of your performance will be dissipated if your auditioners don't see enough of your face, and especially your eyes. In general (unless it is an address to the audience), they should be able to see three-quarters of your face for at least half the duration of the speech. To achieve this, orientate the other character(s) and 'circumstances' to suit the audition situation. For instance, place the imaginary person to whom you're talking at around 45 degrees to left or right in front of you. If your map (or groundplan) is clear in your mind, then it should be simple to angle it appropriately.

There is no point in placing a chair specifically to mark another character – or even the hat-stand which I once saw used as the object of some singular passions. If you do use such objects you'll usually find yourself concentrating on that object rather than your 'partner(s)'. They should be clearly lodged in your imagination so that the interviewer can 'see' them through you. Also, don't think that you have to stare at one place continually just to make it clear that he or she is there.

Chairs

A warning about chairs. There is a common variety of chair, as familiar as the bollard is to the motorway, that inhabits many popular audition venues. It can serve all kinds of functions as well as the simple one of being sat upon. However, don't rely on the well-known weight and balance of these plastic and steel functionaries for crucial elements of your well-prepared speech. You may suddenly find only chairs with arms or a room filled with wobbly ones. Be prepared to adapt to whatever form of seating is available.

Tip 1 Do a brief check on the mechanics of your audition-chair before you start your speech. For instance, you don't want to be thrown by the fact that the back is lower than that of the chair you rehearsed with...

Tip 2 If your audition-chair represents a different type of seat (a low, backless bench, for instance), sit on the chair as though you're sitting on that 'bench'.

Props

Avoid using props. As you haven't got a proper set, costume or lighting, too much of the visual emphasis goes on to the prop and consequently away from you. It is amazing how riveting even a small piece of paper produced for one of the numerous 'letter' speeches can become.

Props can be mimed: that mime doesn't need to be brilliant. And think how much easier it is to put down an imaginary glass on an imaginary table, without making a sound at the wrong moment. In using any imaginary prop, remember not just the shape as you 'hold' it in your hand but also its weight and its impact on your sense of touch.

The only exception to this can be a prop introduced briefly and then quickly discarded. Even then, make sure its impact doesn't take the focus from the rest of the speech.

Performing your speeches

Each presentation of a speech has to have the raw energy of a first performance. Unlike a first night, where the only new factor (in theory, at least) is the audience, you have to face numerous new and possibly unexpected factors when doing your audition speech. You need to be not only well rehearsed but also well prepared for how to cope with all the peripherals that are other people's responsibilities when you are actually doing a production. You are your own stage-management, wardrobe department, front-of-house manager, and so forth.

'Act in here?'

I don't think any audition-room is entirely satisfactory. They can be dirty and unkempt, too hot or too cold, too big or too small, have inconvenient echoes, have barely adequate waiting facilities and/or be hard to find down a maze of corridors. You'll be very fortunate if the whole session has only road traffic as a background noise. You have to be prepared to adjust the presentation of your speech(es) to each context – by fractionally slowing down and enhancing your diction slightly if there's an unavoidable echo, or scaling down your movement in a small room, for instance.

Theatre

It's your space

You should regard the space in which you are doing your speech as your stage with which to do whatsoever you wish – as long as you have due reverence for the fabric of the building, for your interviewers and their goods and chattels. Move the chairs if you need to, take your shoes off if that's necessary, and so on ... but don't ask if it's 'all right' to do so. It can get very tedious for an interviewer if you keep on asking permission every time you want to change something. Providing it doesn't affect your audience directly, just get on with what is necessary for your performance.

Don't ask where to stand; your actor's instinct should tell you the optimum place for what you are about to do. Especially, don't ask permission to start, even if it's only with one of those pathetic little enquiring looks – another way of undermining yourself in your interviewer's eyes. Once you've been given your cue, it's all yours and in your own time.

Natural hazards

Be aware of natural hazards in the room: for example, a low afternoon sun pouring through the windows that blinds you as soon as you happen to turn into it. Don't, on the other hand, stand in the deepest shadow; nobody wants an actor who cannot find his or her light.

Your interviewer will probably be sympathetic if the unexpected suddenly interrupts you, but it really is your responsibility to spot this kind of thing beforehand and adjust accordingly. If it is something impossible to anticipate, then aim to recover as quickly as possible and get back into your speech. After all, if something goes wrong during a performance, you don't just stop until it's put right; you continue as best you can, and 99.9% of the time nobody in the audience will notice that anything went wrong.

Explanations

Minimise explanations about your speech. Ask yourself if you need them at all. In fact the best speeches are self-contained and don't need explanation beyond the character's name and possibly the title and the writer of the play. Whatever their individual faults, most directors do know a lot of plays, the characters within them and who wrote them. Be careful not to insult directors by telling them what they already probably know. (For example, 'Hamlet from *Hamlet* by William Shakespeare.') On the other hand, make sure you know the title and writer of more obscure plays and be prepared to discuss them.

Sometimes, in the process of getting inside the character, actors forget to give these basic details. I don't think this matters (I enjoy trying to work them out for myself), but some directors have a nasty habit of interrupting actors' preparations with demands like 'What are you doing, then?' If you do forget and are so interrupted, don't be so thrown that you rush into your speech.

Your interviewer as the other character

Some people try to use their interviewer as the other character for the purposes of their speech. This is not necessarily a good idea. It can work but is fraught with pitfalls.

First of all, do you need to ask permission beforehand? Politeness dictates that you should. After all, you are asking the auditioner to do the job of being in your play. He or she may say, 'Yes, of course', but has probably been asked the same question in every other session of the day; it can get very tedious. Even if it is all right, the auditioner is probably not an actor, will become self-conscious in the process, not react in the way you anticipated, may well want to drop out of character to write notes and consequently won't be a consistent partner.

Preparation

Do give yourself a moment to position and check your chair and to check the 'geography' of your performance in this particular space.

A pause for thought

Then, also do give yourself that moment of thought before starting a speech – a moment to immerse yourself within your character and circumstances. Almost everybody understands that it can be hard to change gear from chatting to acting. Don't think that you are wasting time; it'll only be a few seconds, and your interviewer will almost certainly have something else to write down before concentrating on you again. (For most actors a 'few seconds' feels much, much longer in these stressed circumstances.)

However, don't take too long to wind up into your speech with lots of heavy breathing or pacing about or even just standing quietly in a corner. That may be what you have to do before you go on stage, but most directors, however understanding, will begin to wonder what kind of lunatic you are and are you going to take up precious rehearsal-time with these warm-ups? Your 'pause for thought' should be as brief as you can make it without showing your inner turmoil. Properly done, this can be riveting to watch.

Starting

One of the hardest aspects of doing a speech is starting it from cold. If you are onstage at the beginning of a stage-production (especially on a first night), you'll experience an immense, and for some, terrifying, feeling of excitement and power as the audience goes quiet. You should aim to recreate this feeling just before you start your speech. It'll give you tingles up your spine and put a real 'kick' into your speech. This will 'communicate' to your auditioners and make them really look at you – even if they've had their heads down scribbling in the preceding seconds.

Tip To help stimulate this process, get the smell of dust into your imagination – it's the pervading smell of any theatre.

Communication

You may well 'feel' your speech, but are you communicating it? Just because you are in a small room with only one person watching, don't mutter your speech at below conversation-level. How do I know you can fill a stage, however small, if you are not filling the room we're in? You have to make that room your stage, the interviewer(s) your audience. Think of them as being in the best seats in the stalls (the ones reserved for the critics on a first night) and aim just beyond the limits of the space. Only a lazy actor will give a smaller performance on stage just because there is a small audience.

Don't blast your interviewer out of his seat, either. Measure the acoustics: a lot of audition-rooms are part of church-hall complexes and tend to have high ceilings with the inevitable echo.

The 'need'

There is a 'need' that drives any speech; two minutes is a long time for someone to keep on talking. A long speech is a series of connected thoughts and ideas; underneath there has to be the 'need' to talk at such length. We all know people who 'go on' too much in

Theatre

everyday life – the odd person is able to sustain attention because of the energy and 'need' to communicate. The same is true on stage and in the audition.

Also, remember that your character hasn't usually planned to say so much. Essentially, the circumstances provoke the 'need' for them to add more, and more, and ...

Stopping

If you do need to stop during a piece – you've dried or it's started badly – do it positively and calmly, and do it without a grovelling apology. You may feel terrible but you have to get yourself out of the mess without becoming embarrassing. You can even capitalise on having handled it well. A brief (and positive) 'I'll start again' or whatever won't be held against you. If you dry or make a mistake significantly into a speech, just pause briefly and find your way back, just as you would in a public performance.

Bear in mind that most interviewers do not know how acting works. So if, say, your breathing starts going haywire, that's not a reason to stop unless it really is affecting the speech badly. You have left your teachers behind at drama school.

Finishing

When you finish you should keep the final thought in your mind and gently freeze for a moment, just as you would if you're left onstage at the end of a scene in a play. Then fade the imaginary stage-lighting (and close the curtains) at a suitable rate. (That 'moment' should last about a second. If you're unsure, say a multi-syllable word like 'Mississippi' in your head.) Then – without looking your interviewer(s) in the eye – relax back to your normal self, ready to move on to whatever your interviewer wants to do next. Many find the not 'looking your interviewer(s) in the eye' difficult, and a few even think that it might seem rude. However, if you do make eye contact at that crucial moment, you'll probably start to feel very vulnerable – and give out the 'vibe' that you're unconfident about your performance. Whatever you may really feel about that performance, there's nothing else that you can now do, except wait.

There may be a silence; your interviewer(s) may well want to write notes on what you've done. Just settle down and let them get on with it. Don't be thrown by that aching pause; you should quietly wait. The 'ball' is now very definitely in the interviewer's 'court' to restart the conversation.

'Thank you' (a)

There may be a vague 'Thank you' or 'Right', even 'Mmmm' from the interviewer at the end of your speech. Don't read anything in to these vague expostulations. If you do you'll start to undermine yourself. We directors are usually thinking about what we're going to write down about your efforts. That thinking process is dominant and what comes out of our mouths is merely our acknowledgement that you've finished – an attempt at politeness that doesn't come out quite right. (I hear myself doing this constantly, but have never found a way round it.)

'Thank you' (b)

Some actors opt for a 'Thank you', or 'That's it', at the end. Sometimes this sounds pathetic; on others it comes across as sheer arrogance (watch the way some actors do curtain calls). If you've got a good enough 'ending', you've given the cue. The director may not respond to it immediately, but you should have clearly established that the 'ball' is now firmly in his or her 'court'. It's much better to say nothing.

Switching off

It is respected that it can take a few seconds to come back to reality, particularly if it's a very emotional speech. But it's fundamental to acting that just as you can 'switch on', you can 'switch off' with apparent ease. I will never forget a woman who did a wonderfully passionate speech from Arnold Wesker's *Four Seasons* and ended up in buckets of tears. She had done it extremely well but when it was over she simply could not stop crying and had to be taken from the room and given time to recover. What would have happened if she'd had to get similarly emotional on stage and then immediately go on to do a comic scene, as can occur? This is an extreme example which exemplifies the need to look very carefully at how you change back to reality.

'Why don't you try that again? This time standing on your head'

Don't get so stuck into a way of doing a speech that you cannot do it in any other way put to you. Some directors like to work on speeches. You should understand the insides of each speech so well that you could do it 'standing on your head'.

Advice

Some directors give constructive advice. In general, take that as a compliment, even if they are critical. Nobody will waste time and energy giving notes if they didn't at least like some aspect of you and your work. However, one director's constructive notes can become another's criticisms. In rehearsal an actor will take a note and try it out. Sometimes it doesn't work, and the moment has to be looked at again. Maybe it was only half-right. In an audition there is usually no time to rehearse that note to see if it works for you. So, when you do try it, and it perhaps doesn't quite work, you have no recourse to its originator for further amplification. Take such notes as suggestions to be utilised or discarded as suits you and your speech. That's how rehearsals should be anyway.

Final note

Working on audition speeches can be a wonderful way of keeping your 'acting juices' flowing through periods of unemployment.

Simon Dunmore directed productions for over 30 years – nearly 20 years as a resident director in regional theatres and, latterly, working freelance. In that time there were over 200 productions (of all styles, colours, shapes and sizes) – including several Drama School Showcases, Maugham's *Home and Beauty* and new plays about sex, WB Yeats' up-and-down relationship with Maud Gonne, one set inside a pyramid and another about Bismarck. Past favourites included: *The Promise* (Alexei Arbuzov), *Antigone* (Jean Anouilh), a seven-handed version of *Antony & Cleopatra* and too many others to mention. He also taught acting and worked in many drama schools and other training establishments around the country. He wrote several books: *An Actor's Guide to Getting Work* (fifth edition, 2012), the *Alternative Shakespeare Auditions* series, and was formerly the Consultant Editor for *Actors' Yearbook*.

Theatre

Underststudying

Andrew Piper

Some Frequently Asked Questions
Why would I want to do it?

What's not to like? Reasonable money, loads of free time, very few responsibilities, and the possibility of playing a meaty role alongside some of your theatrical heroes or belting out the solo of a show-stopper in a West End or major provincial theatre.

What are the 'down sides'?

If you're looking for a fast-track to stardom or are in this job for the glamour and glory, then this is not the job for you. There is no getting away from the fact that the understudies are the B-team. Understudying can be a thankless task – no one pays you much attention unless the actor you're covering is off (which may be never), there's very little to do, and most of the time you're essentially getting paid *not* to act – rather like a tuneless busker being given a tenner to go and play *somewhere else*!

Perhaps more so than almost any other acting job, this is very much 'a job'. If you can squeeze some art or advancement out of it too then that's great (in some cases miraculous), but this is definitely not a contract to go into with starry-eyed optimism.

How should I prepare?

Learn the lines! The amount of actual rehearsal time (as opposed to just watching the principal cast) may be fairly minimal. When you do get to rehearse there will be a lot to learn in a very short space of time, so the more solid you are on lines the more productive your rehearsal time will be, and the sooner you'll feel confident about being ready to go on. Do as much of the usual homework – character, historical research, cultural background, etc. – that you would do for any other part. You'll get less opportunity to discuss this in rehearsal (more on that later), but again it means you'll enjoy yourself more in the rehearsal room.

How much rehearsal will I get?

In short, not a lot – certainly not as much as the principal actors will have – but (depending how soon you're called to go on) enough to get you through. You probably won't start rehearsals at all until the main cast have been rehearsing for a while – at the very least the blocking needs to have been decided before you arrive – so the chances are you'll just get a few days (at best) before production week.

During production week itself, expect to be pretty much ignored completely by everyone: their focus is now purely on the principal cast and the technical running of the show. The job of the understudy during this period is to make notes on changes to his or her blocking, become familiar with lighting, sound and other stage effects, keep working on lines, stay available … but generally just stay out of the way. Keep working on your part(s); you may only have had a few days' rehearsal by this point, but there have been enough instances of principal actors injuring themselves during a tech for you not to be complacent at this point!

Rehearsals are likely to be taken by the assistant director, or possibly even the company manager. If you're lucky, you'll have a little time for discussion about character and intentions (the more homework you've done before rehearsals, the more time you'll have), but an awful lot will be down to you to work out for yourself, simply by working on the script and watching the main cast at work.

Do I have to copy the principal actor's performance?

Understudy rehearsals differ from normal rehearsals in one important respect: all your moves (and many of your character choices) have already been decided and cannot be changed by you. In some ways this can be quite liberating – someone else has done all the hard work for you – but it can be challenging to take on these choices and make them your own. What you certainly don't want to do is produce a 'photocopy' of the principal actor's performance, which risks feeling like a hollow caricature; the challenge is to develop a performance which can slot in seamlessly to the main production, but which nevertheless feels like it's your creation. It can be disheartening to be so restricted in your choices, but trust that the principal actor's (and director's) instincts are good, and find a way to make it work for you.

Once the show is open, what are my responsibilities?

Most of your time will be spent either doing ensemble stuff on stage, or simply waiting in the dressing room. Apart from understudy rehearsals (one a week, perhaps, or possibly once a fortnight; if you're working for the RSC you may not have any understudy rehearsals at all once the show is up) your time is your own. If you're not needed for the curtain call, you may not be required to stay until the very end of the show. The rule of thumb is that you're free to go once the character you're covering has made his or her final entrance, but this can vary from production to production.

How often will I go on?

If you're working on a musical, the vocal demands of the piece will probably mean that principal performers will need to take occasional shows, or even just musical numbers, off to rest their voices, and so an understudy on a musical is pretty much guaranteed to be going on fairly frequently. In a straight play there is the distinct possibility that you will never go on at all, unless it's a long and demanding run. Even in the middle of a flu epidemic, the actor(s) you are covering may have a 'show must go on' mentality. They may be secretly hoping that the company manager will send them home, but will not voluntarily go off unless they are on the verge of being hospitalised.

It won't hurt to develop a good relationship with the actor you're covering, so that (a) they know that you actually want to go on (assuming you do; many understudies are quite happy not to) and (b) they may be more inclined to give you your moment in the sun when illness strikes and they're deciding whether or not they're fit enough to go on.

Incidentally, no company manager will allow a healthy principal to take a show off to give their understudy the chance to go on – that would be breach of contract – but I've heard stories of a few who may be wilfully credulous if the principal calls in sick for a matinee in the understudy's home town.

What's it like to go on?

When you get the call to go on, then just about everyone in the company – including the principal actors – will be focusing their energies on making sure that you have everything you need to give a good performance. Depending on how much notice you are given, you may have an opportunity to run through bits of business on stage with the principals, and they may well offer you notes on how to play it. Some of these notes may be helpful, others won't be; take what you need and discard the rest. For the next few hours you are 'one of them', playing for the A-team, and you have to trust that your skill as an actor and all the preparation you've done will get you through. This isn't the time to try anything new; just do what you've rehearsed and everything will be fine.

Don't get star-struck about the people you're on stage with. These are your colleagues, your fellow artists, and whatever your relationship off stage might be, right now they are your equals, so don't be afraid to give a full-blooded performance. Some nerves are completely understandable, so if you know you tend to rush or be a bit quiet, say, when you're nervous, be aware of this and make a conscious effort to slow down or speak up, as appropriate.

Once the nerves have started to subside, allow yourself to enjoy it. Stay focused and in the moment, remembering all the things you've rehearsed, but now that you're playing with the A-team, take on the energy of the other actors and allow it to lift your own performance. Producers are generally happy if you can just get the lines out in the right order and hit your mark – as far as they're concerned you're just there to stop too many people asking for their money back – and if you can do that, then you've done your job, but if you've done your homework, then there's no reason why you can't take it further than that and give a bloody good performance.

Will I get an understudy matinee?

Depending on the agreement you have with the producers, there may be an opportunity for an understudy performance, especially if not all the understudies have had the chance to go on during the run of the show. It's not guaranteed, but if it is going to happen, it will usually be one afternoon when there's no public performance in the theatre (or a theatre on the tour that's reasonably close to London).

All the understudies will play their covered role (or sometimes roles), and may ask supporting members of the principal cast to come in and play the others. They are not obliged to say yes, since it's not in their contract to give up their afternoon off, and they're not getting paid for it; but if asked nicely, most actors are generally happy to help out if they can. If one of them isn't available for some reason, there may need to be some nifty doubling, or the company manager may go on with a book.

Who should I invite to see me?

The understudy matinee is your chance to invite all your friends, family, former colleagues, potential employers, casts from nearby theatres – just about anyone! – to come and see your performance. Tickets will usually be free, but there may be a limit on the number of tickets available to keep front-of-house staff costs down.

I mention inviting potential employers: this can be tricky, even if the show is in the West End. Excuses for casting directors' non-attendance may be along the lines of "Oh, it's so hard to get away from the office [50 yards from the theatre!] during the day," but in reality, producers' frequent indifference to the actual acting talent of the understudy – or, for that matter, the malaise that can set in in the understudy after years sitting in a dressing room doing crosswords – can result in some really quite uninspiring performances during these matinees, and the casting directors know it. (I'm talking about straight plays here; it's a rather different story in musical theatre, where understudies are usually working members of the ensemble and more regularly pressed into service in principal roles.) It's worth asking, nevertheless, although only if you're confident in giving them a show they'll be impressed with. Don't however think that this is your moment to get seen by every casting director in town – it won't be.

Should I do it again?

A good, reliable understudy is highly prized by producers, and may even be offered work on a new production before the principal actors are cast. But once known as an understudy (with the exception, perhaps, of the RSC), it can be hard to get them to see you as someone they might want to cast in a principal role. That may not be a problem for you – in the West End, at least, it gives you terrific freedom to do other things, especially if you have family commitments or are developing another career as a writer or voice-over, say – but a life of waiting in the wings is not for everyone. If you're coming to the end of one understudy job, you must think carefully (and discuss with your agent) about how much and what kind of understudy work you'd like to be put up for in the future. Regular understudying is not the occupation of the ambitious actor, so think carefully about what the benefits and pitfalls of taking a particular understudy job might be.

Andrew Piper trained at Bristol Old Vic Theatre School and edited *Actors' Yearbook* for the 2007 and 2008 editions. He understudied the role of Bernard Woolley in the original West End transfer of Chichester Festival Theatre's production of *Yes, Prime Minister*. Thanks are due to the more experienced understudies who offered their comments on early drafts of this article.

Theatre

Independent managements/theatre producers

This section mostly lists commercial organisations that mount West End and touring productions to larger-scale venues – some of which originate in the subsidised sector. Most such productions will be led by well-known actors, but they will usually need supporting actors who can also understudy those leads. (In long-running West End productions, the understudies get a chance to do their own performance – a useful opportunity to 'showcase' for agents and casting directors.) Sometimes, such a production will tour in order to try it out before (hopefully) coming into the West End; at others, a management will tour to 'milk' further profits from a West End success.

On tour, apart from 'Acting ASMs' (assistant stage managers who also understudy), you shouldn't be asked to do any of the graft of get-ins and get-outs – unlike on smaller-scale touring. However, if you are also understudying, you will be expected to do an understudy rehearsal every week until the last stages of the tour. This rehearsal will probably be taken by the company manager (rarely, the director), despite this, it is very important to be as fully prepared as possible for the chance that the 'name' you are understudying will be unavoidably delayed one night. Touring is fraught with potential delays, and a reputation for being able to 'deliver the goods' at very short notice will enhance future employment prospects.

Touring is not for everyone: long periods away from home, wide variations in the quality of digs (often costing more in holiday resorts during the 'season'), and the fact that you could miss opportunities to be seen for other work are some of the potential disadvantages. On the plus side, contracts for large-scale tours are usually at least three months with a minimum of a week in each venue, and you should have time to see some of the most beautiful sights in the UK (if not Europe and further afield).

Although not as expensive as major films, such productions do cost a lot of money to mount, and productions have been known to collapse suddenly without any warning. When accepting work in this area it is important to have a proper Equity contract.

Ambassador Theatre Group (ATG)

39-41 Charing Cross Road, London WC2H 0AR
tel 0844 871 7627
website www.atg.co.uk
CEO Mark Cornell Executive *Group Content & Creative Director* Michael Lynas

Production details: ATG is the largest owner and operator of theatres in the UK, with a total of 58 venues across the world. It produces across the UK, Europe and the USA. Anywhere between 3 and 30 actors work on each production. Recent productions include: *Pretty Woman: The Musical, Cabaret at the Kit Kat Club, The Seagull, 9 to 5 the Musical* and *Caroline, or Change.* Offers Equity approved contracts and is "happy to make contributions [to the Equity Pension Scheme] on behalf of any members of the scheme that we employ".

Casting procedures: Uses freelance casting directors. Welcomes letters (with CVs and photographs), but not email submissions. Actors may write at any time, but prefers contact to be made via an agent and preferably during pre-production. Advises actors against sending expensive photos 'on spec', especially if unaccompanied by a letter. Actively encourages applications from disabled actors and promotes the use of inclusive casting.

Blue Star Productions

7-8 Shaldon Mansions, 132 Charing Cross Road, London WC2H 0LA
tel 020 7386 6220/4128
email hopkinstacey@aol.com
Director Keith Hopkins *Associate Director* Joshua Lawson

Production details: Founded in 1966. Specialises in children's musicals and songbook concerts. Stages 24 productions annually with 100 performances during the course of the year. Tours to 8 different theatres in Southern England, including the London area. In general 8 actors are involved in each production. Recent productions include: *West End to Broadway* and *Movie Memories.* Offers non-Equity contracts and does not subscribe to the Equity Pension Scheme.

Casting procedures: All casting is done in-house. Holds general auditions. Casting breakdowns are available on request. Welcomes letters (with CVs and photographs) but not email submissions. Advises actors: "Don't be grand when just starting." Actively encourages applications from disabled actors and promotes the use of inclusive casting.

Contemporary Stage Co

9 Finchley Way, London N3 1AG
email contemp.stage@hotmail.co.uk
Artistic Director David Graham-Young

Production details: Founded in 1993, The Contemporary Stage Company's focus is on presenting plays and adaptations of novels, with an emphasis on work from cultures outside the English-speaking world. Recent productions include: *The Master and Margarita* (Almeida Theatre), *Flight* (Lyric Theatre), *Potestad* (Gate, Glasgow Mayfest, BBC Radio 3), *Regressions* (Donmar Warehouse, RSC) and *The Tunnel* (Croydon Warehouse).

Casting procedures: Occasionally uses freelance casting directors and holds general auditions. Welcomes CVs and letters from actors previously unknown to the company. Also welcomes invitations to view individual actors' websites and performance notices. Rarely has the opportunity to cast disabled actors.

Robert Fox Ltd

website www.robertfoxlimited.com
Director Robert Fox

Production details: Founded in 1980. Theatre and film production company specialising in large-scale theatre productions and musicals as well as feature films. Performances are staged in the West End and on Broadway. Recent theatre productions include: *South Downs* and *The Browning Version* (West End) and *Hugh Jackman Back On Broadway* (Broadway). Also co-produced the films *Atonement* and, more recently, *Wilde Salome.*

Casting procedures: Employs casting directors for specific projects and does not welcome unsolicited submissions from actors.

Sonia Friedman Productions

5th Floor, 65 Chandos Place, London WC2N 4HG
tel 020 7854 8750
email queries@soniafriedman.com
website www.soniafriedman.com
Twitter @SFP_London

Producer Sonia Friedman *Executive Director* Diane Benjamin *Executive Producers* Pam Skinner and Ros Brooke-Taylor *General Managers* Ben Canning and Simon Woolley *Associate Producers* Charlie Bath, Max Bittleston, David Nock

Production details: Sonia Friedman Productions is one of the West End's most prolific and significant theatre producers, responsible for some of the most successful theatre productions in London and on Broadway over the past two decades. Since 1990 SFP has produced more than 180 new shows and has won 58 Olivier Awards, 34 Tony Awards and 2 BAFTAs.

Current and future productions include: the UK premiere of *The Book of Mormon* in London and on tour in the UK and Europe; *Harry Potter and the Cursed Child* in London, New York, Melbourne, San Francisco, Hamburg, Toronto and Tokyo; *Oklahoma!* at Wyndham's Theatre, London; *To Kill a Mockingbird* at the Gielgud Theatre, London; *Dreamgirls* on tour in the UK; *Funny Girl* in New York; *Leopoldstadt* in New York; *Merrily We Roll Along* in New York; *The Piano Lesson* in New York; *Mean Girls* on tour in the US; and *The Shark is Broken* at the Mirvish Theatre, Toronto.

David Graham Entertainment Ltd

3rd Floor, 14 Hanover Street, London W1S 1YH
tel 020 7175 7170
email info@davidgrahamentertainment.com
website www.davidgrahamentertainment.com
Director David Graham

Production details: Theatre producer and concert promoter. Specialises in music ranging from leading West End singers, tribute bands and musicals. Stages around 4 productions in 80 theatres and concert halls on an annual basis, with more than 300 performances per year. Countries covered include Britain, Holland, Germany, Canada, Spain, Norway and Ireland. In general, 12 performers work on each production. Recent productions include: *Rising Damp, Birds Of A Feather, The Wonderful West End* and *Hold Tight, It's 60s Night.*

Casting procedures: Does not use freelance casting directors or hold general auditions. Casting breakdowns available via Script Breakdown, CastCall and other casting publications.

Michael Grandage Productions

Fourth Floor, Wyndham's Theatre,
Charing Cross Road, London WC2H 0DA
tel 020 3582 7210
email info@michaelgrandagecompany.com
website www.michaelgrandagecompany.com
Producer Nick Frankfort *Artistic Director* Michael Grandage *Executive Director* Stella McCabe *Assistant Producer* Molly McCarthy

Production details: Following his hugely successful, 10-year reign at the Donmar Warehouse, director Michael Grandage set up at the Noel Coward Theatre

Theatre

for a 15-month run of plays 2012–13. During 2018, the company revived *Red* by John Logan and a new production of *The Lieutenant on Inishmore* by Martin McDonagh. The company produces films, stage and screen work across all media, nationally and internationally. It also has a general management service and looks after a select group of creative practitioners.

Hartshorn-Hook Productions

Arts Theatre, 6-7 Great Newport Street,
London WC2H 7JB
email louis@hartshornhook.com
website www.hartshornhook.com
Directors Louis Hartshorn, Brian Hook

Production details: Founded 2007, Hartshorn-Hook Productions is a commercial theatre company based in the West End. It provides general management services to theatre companies across the UK, whether professional productions or community projects. They have produced over 130 productions across 5 continents. Recent productions include: *Amelie* (West End, UK tour), *Rotterdam* (Arts, New York, Los Angeles), *Madagascar the Musical* (UK tour), *Urinetown* (Apollo), *American Idiot* (Arts, UK tour) and *Woody Sez* (Arts). Immersive theatre credits include: *Peaky Blinders: The Rise, Doctor Who: Time Fracture, NeverLand, A Christmas Carol, Richard II*, and the UK's longest ever running immersive production, *The Great Gatsby*.

Casting procedures: Welcomes invitations to attend productions in Greater London.

Paul Holman Associates

Morritt House, 58 Station Approach, South Ruislip,
Middlesex HA4 6SA
tel 020 8845 9408
email enquiries@paulholmanassociates.co.uk
website www.paulholmanassociates.co.uk
Founder and Managing Director Paul Holman
Associate Producer Nick George

Production details: Established in 1990. Produces pantomimes, summer shows and one-night attractions. See entry under *Pantomime producers* on page 228 for more details.

Image Musical Theatre

23 Sedgeford Road, Shepherd's Bush,
London W12 0NA
tel 0161 228 3149
email ian@imagemusicaltheatre.co.uk
website www.imagemusicaltheatre.co.uk
Artistic Director Ian McCracken *Composer/Lyricist* Robert Hyman

Production details: Founded in 1988. Stages 4 productions annually, with around 900 performances in 70 venues including arts centres, theatres, schools and other educational venues throughout the UK. In general 3-4 actors are involved in each production.

Recent productions include: *The Jungle Book, The Secret Garden, Tom's Midnight Garden, The Snow Queen, The Wind in the Willows*, and *Alice in Wonderland*.

Casting procedures: Sometimes holds general auditions. Actors should write in June, October and late January to request inclusion. Casting breakdowns are publicly available via the website, from Equity Job Information Service, and from CastNet and Castweb. Welcomes letters (with CVs and photographs) from individual actors previously unknown to the company only if sent by post. No emails and no showreels, but will accept invitations to view individual actors' websites. Rarely (or never) has the opportunity to cast disabled actors.

Colin Ingram Ltd

Suite 526, Linen Hall, 162-168 Regent Street,
London W1B 5TE
tel 020 8065 0427
email colin@coliningramltd.com
website www.coliningramltd.com
Director Colin Ingram *Production Associate* Simon Ash

Production details: Theatrical producers and general managers. The company offers Equity-approved contracts and participates in the Equity Pension Scheme. "Please see the website for details of recent productions and venues."

Casting procedures: Uses freelance casting directors. Does not welcome unsolicited approaches from individual actors previously unknown to the company.

Jendagi Productions Ltd

PO Box 5597, Glasgow G77 9DH
tel 0141 533 5856
email robert@robertckelly.co.uk
website www.robertckelly.co.uk
Managing Director Robert Kelly

Production details: The company has over 35 years' experience hosting productions across the UK, Ireland, Australia and New Zealand, with over 200 performances each year. Recent productions include: *Menopause the Musical, Mum's the Word, 51 Shades of Maggie* and *Fame the Musical*. Each year the company produces multiple pantomimes in the UK and Ireland. Offers Equity-approved contracts and subscribes to the Equity Pension Scheme.

Casting procedures: Uses freelance casting directors. Actively encourages applications from disabled actors and promotes the use of inclusive casting.

Gareth Johnson Ltd

Plas Hafren, Eglwyswrw, Crymych,
Pembrokeshire SA41 3UL
tel (01239) 891368 *mobile* 07770 225227
email gjltd@mac.com
website www.garethjohnsonltd.com

Production details: Founded in 2000, this general management company produces (for a client) up to 6 shows a year, West End, UK and overseas. Recent productions include *Man of La Mancha* (Coliseum); *Chess* (Coliseum); *42nd Street* (Drury Lane); *Carousel* (Coliseum); *Eifman Ballet* (Coliseum); *Sunset Boulevard* (Coliseum); *Beyond Bollywood* (London Palladium); *The King's Speech* (tour); *Oh What a Lovely War* (tour); Mossovet State Theatre Chekhov Season (Wyndham's Theatre); *From Here To Eternity* (Shaftesbury Theatre); *Wonderful Town* (Royal Exchange, Hallé and Lowry – tour); *Journey's End* (tour and West End); *Cowardy Custard* (tour). Offers Equity contracts.

Casting procedures: Uses freelance casting directors and does not welcome unsolicited contact of any kind from actors. Policy on disabled actors as instructed by client.

Jonathan Church Theatre Productions

55 The Strand, London WC2N 5LR
tel 020 7451 1732
email office@jctproduction.com
website www.jctproduction.com
Director Jonathan Church *Executive Producer* Becky Barber

Jonathan Church Theatre Productions is an award-winning London-based production company, producing high-quality theatre in the West End, nationally and internationally.

Current and forthcoming productions include: *South Pacific*; *Two Cigarettes in the Dark*; *East is East*; *The Lion, The Witch & The Wardrobe*; *Wendy and Peter Pan, Poirot and More, A Retrospective*; *Private Peaceful*; *A Monster Calls*; *Singin' in the Rain*; *Pressure*; *Blithe Spirit*.

Recent productions: *The Price* (Wyndham's); *The Man in the White Suit* (Wyndham's); *The Life I Lead* (UK tour, Wyndham's); *Misty* (Trafalgar Studios); *Vulcan VII* (UK tour); *Frozen* (Theatre Royal Haymarket); *Pressure* (UK tour, Ambassadors); *Fracked!* (UK tour); Sand in the Sandwiches (Theatre Royal Haymarket, UK tour); *Loves Labours Lost* and *Much Ado About Nothing* (Chichester, Manchester, Theatre Royal Haymarket); *This House* (Garrick Theatre, UK tour); *The Dresser* (UK tour, Duke of York's). General Management projects include: *The Lion, the Witch and the Wardrobe* (forthcoming UK tour); *Strictly Ballroom the Musical* (Toronto) and *North By North West* (Toronto).

Offers Equity contracts and is a UK Theatre member and SOLT member.

Andy Jordan Productions Ltd

16 Prior Street, Lincoln LN5 7SW
mobile 07775 615205
email andyjandyjordan@aol.com
Director Andy Jordan

Production details: Founded in 2000. Commercial production company, largely producing new plays of all genres. Stages 1-2 productions annually with 50-100 performances per year. Performs annually in 4-10 theatres across the UK. Also tours overseas. On average, 3-7 actors work on each production. Recent work includes: *COPS* (Southwark Playhouse, 2020) Strindberg's *Women* (Jermyn Street Theatre, 2016) and *Foreplay* (King's Head Theatre, 2014). Usually offers Equity-approved contracts (either TMA or ITC).

Casting procedures: Uses freelance casting directors. Supports diversity in casting. Casting breakdowns are published on Spotlight Link. Welcomes submissions (with CVs and photographs) sent by post and email.

Richard Jordan Productions Ltd

Mews Studios, 16 Vernon Yard, London W11 2DX
tel 01323 417745
email info@richardjordanproductions.com
Director Richard Jordan

Production details: Founded in 1998. Produces theatre in London and throughout the UK and internationally. Main area of work is new writing and revivals of plays; occasionally produces musicals. Company works as general managers and consultants for a wide range of producers and theatres in the UK and abroad. Stages around 10-20 productions annually with 300 performances during the course of the year. The company has produced and developed over 260 productions in the UK, as well as 28 other countries including 91 world premieres and 89 European, Australian or US premieres premiers by both new and established writers. Richard has been at the forefront of developing and presenting works by a diverse range of established and emerging writers and artists from around the world. He is the recipient of numerous major awards including the TONY and Olivier.

Casting procedures: Welcomes letters (with CVs and photographs) but not email submissions. Applications are particularly welcome if actors are currently in a production that the company can go and see. Advises that applicants should have an awareness of the type of work produced by the company before sending CVs.

Bill Kenwright Ltd

BKL House, 1 Venice Walk, London W2 1RR
tel 020 7446 6200
email info@kenwright.com
website www.kenwright.com
Twitter @BKL_Productions

Award-winning prolific commercial theatre and film production company, presenting revivals and new works for the West End, international and regional theatres. Productions include *Blood Brothers*, *Heathers*, and *The Sound of Music*.

Casting procedures: In-house and freelance casting directors. Enquiries (with CVs and photographs) to **info@kenwright.com**.

Limelight Productions Ltd

57 Glenesk Road, London SE9 1AH
tel 020 8853 9570
email enquiries@thelg.co.uk
website www.thelimelightgroup.co.uk
Facebook www.facebook.com/thelimelightgroup
Twitter @Limelight_Group
Artistic Director Richard Lewis

Production details: Established in 1996. Stages 2-3
productions annually, touring the UK and
internationally.

Recent productions include: *LazyTown Live,
Octonauts Live, Peppa Pig Live, Ben and Holly's Little
Kingdom Live* and *Some Mothers Do 'Ave 'Em.* Offers
Equity-approved contracts.

Cameron Mackintosh Ltd

1 Bedford Square, London WC1B 3RB
tel 020 7637 8866
website www.cameronmackintosh.com

Chairman Cameron Mackintosh *Head of Casting* Paul
Wooller *Casting Director* Felicity French

Production details: Stages musical theatre
productions worldwide. Recent productions include:
*Les Miserables, Hamilton, The Phantom of the Opera,
Miss Saigon, Mary Poppins.*

Casting procedures: In-house casting. Does not hold
general auditions. Welcomes letters (with CVs and
photographs) but not email submissions. Also accepts
showreels and invitations to view individual actors'
websites.

Johnny Mans Productions Ltd

PO Box 196, Hoddesdon, Herts. EN10 7WG
tel 01992 470907 *mobile* 07974 755997
email johnnymansagent@aol.com
Key contact Johnny Mans

Production details: Originally founded as a limited
company in 1989, activities include producing and
promoting one-night stands, celebrity concerts,
musicals and touring productions; casting for
television, pantomime and cruise ships; and artiste
and personal management for Sir Norman Wisdom's
estate, Max Bygraves' estate, Nicholas Parsons, Frank
Ifield, Nicki Gillis and the Rainmakers, Trace Dann,
Lezlie Anders, Dave Prowse, Issi Dye, Georgia
Tuohey, Jeremy Spake, Jess Conrad, Leah Bell,
Duncan Norvelle, Steve Barclay and many others.
Stages about 30 different productions annually,
totalling around 250 performances during the course
of the year. Tours concert productions to more than
300 different theatres and arts centres across the UK
and Ireland each year. Recent productions include:
*Just A Laugh A Minute, Frank Ifield Remembers,
Tapestry - The Carole King Story, Calamity Jane,
Beatlemania, The Spirit of Pavarotti, Rock'n'Roll
Paradise, A Slice of Nostalgia Pie, Jukebox & Bobbysox,
Be Bop A Lula, Silver Belles, Follow the Herd, Nights*

on Broadway (The Bee Gees Story). Johnny Mans
Productions also publish and edit *Encore Magazine,*
the popular light-entertainment magazine for the
showbusiness professional, which is a bi-monthly,
full-colour periodical. For details contact
encoremags@aol.com or telephone 0845-4670792.

Casting procedures: In the first instance, contact
johnnymansagent@aol.com by email, or write in
with photograph and CV/biography to the address
given above. Prospective future clients will then be
contacted accordingly. Johnny Mans Productions
offers Equity-approved contracts.

Middle Ground Theatre Co.

3 Gordon Terrace, Malvern Wells,
Malvern WR14 4ER
tel 01684 577231
email middleground@middlegroundtheatre.co.uk
website www.middlegroundtheatre.co.uk
Artistic Director/Producer Michael Lunney

Production details: Theatre company producing
drama to tour No. 1 UK theatre venues and arts
centres. Stages 1 or 2 productions a year with 180
performances across around 25 venues. Covers the
whole of Britain and Northern Ireland. Size of cast
varies from show to show. Offers actors non-Equity
contracts and does not participate in the Equity
Pension Scheme. Recent productions include:
*Meeting Joe Strummer, The Importance of Being
Earnest, Billy Liar, Dial M for Murder,* and *Tunes of
Glory.*

Casting procedures: Casts in-house. Casting
breakdowns are not publicly available (Spotlight
only). Welcomes submissions from actors (with CV
and photograph) if sent by post or email. Also
welcomes showreels and invitations to view
individual actors' websites. Will consider applications
from disabled actors to play disabled characters.

Mischief Theatre

c/o Kenny Wax Ltd, 3rd Floor,
62 Shaftesbury Avenue, Londond W1D 6LT
tel 020 7437 1736
email sarah@mischieftheatre.co.uk
website www.mischieftheatre.co.uk
Artistic Directors Henry Lewis, Jonathan Burke
Company Director Jonathan Sayer *Administrator*
Sarah Whiteside

Production details: Mischief Theatre is a comedy
theatre company based in London, first formed by a
group of LAMDA graduates. Mischief is dedicated to
creating engaging and exciting, improvised and
scripted comedy theatre of an excellent standard
through well-honed improvised and comedic
technique and strong theatrical ensemble work.

Recent productions: *The Play that Goes Wrong,*
Duchess Theatre; *The Comedy About a Bank Robbery,*
Criterion Theatre; *Groan Ups,* Vaudeville Theatre,
2019; *Magic Goes Wrong,* Vaudeville Theatre, 2019.
Touring: *Peter Pan Goes Wrong.*

Norwell Lapley Productions Ltd

Unit 4, Brindley Close, Tollgate Industrial,
Stafford ST16 3SU
tel 07768 996633
email cdavis@cdm-ltd.com
website www.nlp.com
Director Chris Davis, Derrick Gask

Production details: Produces theatre in the West
End and touring productions. Stages 4-5 productions
annually and gives 250 performances during the
course of the year at theatres nationwide.

Casting procedures: Uses freelance casting directors
and does not deal directly with actors.

Playful Productions

39 Charing Cross Road, London WC2H 0AR
tel 020 7811 4600
email aboutus@playfuluk.com
website www.playfuluk.com
Twitter @Playfulprods
Directors Matthew Byam Shaw, Nia Janis, Nick
Salmon

Production details: Produces plays and musicals for
the West End, Broadway and on tour in the UK and
internationally. Also provides general management
and production accountancy services to other
producers. 'The adventure of finding, nurturing, and
shaping an idea all the way through to a production
is incredibly rewarding. Ideas have sprung from
modern fiction, documentary television, music we
have listened to, conversations with our peers, and
overheard conversations on the tube. They would
remain ideas if we weren't fortunate enough to
collaborate with talented playwrights, composers,
designers, directors and actors at the top of their
game, who help us realise each project's ambition.'

Long-running productions: *Wicked* (Apollo Victoria)
and *Come From Away* (Phoenix Theatre). Touring
productions: *Kinky Boots, Dirty Dancing, Shrek the
Musical*. Current productions: *Get Up Stand Up! The
Bob Marley Musical* (Lyric Theatre), *Moulin Rouge!
The Musical* (Piccadilly Theatre), *My Fair Lady*
(London Coliseum). Recent productions: *Quiz* (Noel
Coward Theatre, 2018), *The Moderate Soprano* (Duke
of York's Theatre, 2018) and *Imperium* (Gielgud
Theatre, 2018).

PW Productions Ltd

2nd Floor, 80-81 St Martin's Lane,
London WC2N 4AA
tel 020 7395 7580
email info@pwprods.co.uk
website www.pwprods.co.uk
Twitter @PWProds
Executive Chairman and Joint Chief Executive Peter
Wilson *Managing Director and Joint Chief Executive*
Iain Gillie

Production details: The company, which Peter
Wilson founded in 1983, specialises in the

production, general management and bookkeeping/
accountancy for theatre presentations. Recent
productions include: *The Woman in Black*, Stephen
Daldry's production of *An Inspector Calls*, Sting's
musical *The Last Ship, Dirty Dancing, An Hour and a
Half Late*, Nigel Slater's *Toast* and James Graham's
Sketching.

James Quaife Productions

London
email james@jamesquaifeproductions.com
website www.jamesquaifeproductions.com
Producer James Quaife

Production details: Established in 2008, James
Quaife is an independent theatre producer and
general manager working in the West End. Works
mainly in theatre with new writing, and employs
actors in drama, comedy and musicals. Committed to
producing high-quality theatre in the UK; dedicated
to the production and staging of ambitious theatre
and, by doing so, contributing to the vibrancy and
development of the theatre industry. Recent
productions include: *Good People* starring Imelda
Staunton (Noël Coward Theatre); *Barking In Essex*
starring Lee Evans, Sheila Hancock and Keeley Hawes
(Wyndham's Theatre); *Happy Never After*
(Edinburgh Fringe Festival 2013, Pleasance
Courtyard); the world premiere of *People Like Us* and
Happy Never After (Pleasance Theatre, London); *Step
9 (of 12)* starring Blake Harrison (Trafalgar Studios);
the London premiere of *Precious Little Talent* by Ella
Hickson (Trafalgar Studios, 2011 London Theatre
Award for Best New Play); *Molière, Little Fish* and
Death Of Long Pig (Finborough Theatre).

Casting procedures: Uses freelance casting directors.
Casting breakdowns are sent to agents and available
from Spotlight.

The Really Useful Group Ltd

website www.reallyuseful.com

Production details: The Really Useful Group (RUG)
was founded in 1977 by Andrew Lloyd Webber. It is
an international entertainment company actively
involved in theatre ownership and management,
theatrical production, film, television, video and
concert productions, merchandising, records and
music publishing.

Squaredeal Productions Ltd

tel 020 2358 4496
email jenny@jennytopper.com
website www.jennytopper.com
Director Jenny Topper

Production details: Established in 2003. An
independent theatre producer staging on average 2
productions annually and performing in the West
End and 20 theatre venues across the UK. Also
Consultant Producer to Theatre Royal, Plymouth.
Recent productions include: *The Clean House* (10-

week tour); *Martha, Josie and Chinese Elvis* (12-week tour); *Duet for One* (West End); *End of the Rainbow* (West End, tour and Broadway); *Daytona*; *The Three Lions* and *The Nightingales* (with Theatre Royal Bath). As Consultant Producer to Theatre Royal Plymouth, productions have included: *Grand Guignol* by Carl Gross; *After Electra* by April de Angelis; *Monster, Raving, Loony* by James Graham.

Casting procedures: Does not hold general auditions. Will accept letters (with CVs and photographs) from actors previously unknown to the company, sent by post or by email. Offers Equity-approved contracts as negotiated through TMA.

Stanhope Productions Ltd

4th Floor, 80/81 St Martins Lane,
London WC2N 4AA
tel 020 7240 3098
email admin@stanhopeprod.com
website www.stanhopeproductions.co.uk
Chief Executive Kim Poster

Production details: Founded in 2001. Theatrical producing company. Stages 4-5 productions annually and gives 576 performances during the course of the year. Tours to 2-4 different theatres, primarily in the West End and London area. In general 18 actors are involved in each production. Recent productions include: *All My Sons, A View from the Bridge, Prick Up Your Ears, Carousel, Fiddler on the Roof, Summer and Smoke, Epitaph for George Dillon, A Woman of No Importance*, and *Brand*. Offers SOLT/Equity-approved contracts.

Casting procedures: Uses freelance casting directors. Holds general auditions. Casting breakdowns are available via Equity Job Information Service. Will consider applications from disabled actors to play disabled characters.

UK Productions

Brook House, Mint Street, Godalming,
Surrey GU7 1HE
tel 01483 423600
email mail@ukproductions.co.uk
website www.ukproductions.co.uk
Managing Director Martin Dodd

Production details: Established 1995. Produces pantomime, musicals and drama for No. 1 touring, nationally and internationally. (See entry under *Pantomime producers* on page 229.) Offers non-Equity contracts ("roughly in line with Equity") and does not subscribe to the Equity Pension Scheme. Recent productions include: *The Kite Runner, Oklahoma!, Seven Brides for Seven Brothers, 42nd Street, Disney's Beauty & The Beast, South Pacific*, plus many pantomimes.

Casting procedures: Casting is done in-house. Does not hold general auditions. Casting breakdowns are distributed via Spotlight or direct to agents. Welcomes performance notices but not any other unsolicited form of correspondence. "Unsolicited CVs are generally a waste of time." Will consider applications from disabled actors to play characters with disabilities.

Ulster Theatre Company

17 Duncrun Road, Limavady,
Co. Londonderry BT49 0JD
tel 028 7775 0240
email michaelpoynor@hotmail.com
website www.ulstertheatrecompany.com
Artistic Director Michael Poynor

Production details: Originally set up as a training company touring mid-scale musical productions in the UK and Ireland. The Company also produces original pantomimes, dramas and musicals, and tours from time to time. Co-productions are increasingly produced.

Recent productions include: *Comedy of Errors: The Musical, Jonathan Harker and DRACULA, Scrooge's Christmas* and *The Long Now*.

As a result of the pandemic the company expanded into streaming productions, filming and son et lumière production.

The Company offers Equity/ITC-approved contracts.

Casting procedures: Uses in-house casting directors and holds auditions as required. Casting breakdowns are available via email. Welcomes both CVs and letters from actors previously unknown to the Company, and unsolicited CVs and photographs. These should be sent via email. Also asks that applicants are aware that actors based locally are preferred due to inability to pay travel costs. Welcomes invitations to view individual actors' websites, but only attends invitations to productions within Ireland. Does not welcome showreels. Rarely has the opportunity to cast disabled actors due to the physical nature of most productions.

West End International

The Old Brewhouse, Chesham Road, Wigginton,
Hertfordshire HP23 6EH
tel 07710 091245
email alison@westendinternational.com
website www.westendinternational.com
Directors Martin Yates, Alison Price

Production details: Concert and theatre producers. Will accept casting enquiries and letters (with CVs and photographs) from actors previously unknown to the company, sent by post or email. Does not welcome unsolicited showreels.

Voicing kindness

Hazel Holder, dialect and voice coach
Interview by Joan Iyiola

Hazel Holder has been an actor, singer and theatre maker for over thirty years before retraining and receiving her MA in Voice Studies from the Royal Central School of Speech and Drama. Hazel has worked with pioneering companies such as Clod Ensemble, The Mono Box, Clean Break, Marginal Voices and Cast Women's Charity. She works across theatre, television and film.

How would you describe your role as a voice and dialect coach?

I think of myself as a bridge between the actor, the story and their performance. I think bridge is a helpful word because I believe the journey is just as important as the destination. I create imagery about where the actor is now, where they want to get to and how the work will enable them to reach their destination. When I started drama school at Mountview, I was dismissed after one term as the Head of Voice said I was 'untrainable as an actress' because I had a lisp. Thankfully, things have changed, and there are many actors now with speech impediments, but because my first encounter with a voice coach was incredibly negative, my own coaching comes from a place of deeper empathy. It's important that we don't demonise our differences in a creative space.

I want to touch on the fact that you were not always a voice coach. Tell us a bit about your pathway into the industry.

I started out in this industry as a precocious little child who loved to get up in front of everyone to sing and dance. I went to church and that gave me the confidence to sing in front of people. But I've also always relished the opportunity for growth, from working with Black Mime theatre company to singing in jazz bands and two acapella groups (Helen Chadwick Song Theatre and Orlando Gough's The Shout), to performing twice on Broadway with the National Theatre of Scotland and the Young Vic. It's been a really varied journey and I think, ultimately, the vibrations of all those different experiences are just living in my body. The variety of my work has kept me engaged and inquisitive because I know there are so many achievable choices out there.

So, what made you divert to coaching?

I've always been interested in using my voice as an instrument, not just as a thing of 'beauty.' I was performing in *Death and the King's Horsemen* at the National Theatre and a theme of the story was the clash of cultures between British colonialism and Yoruba traditions. This meant that I sang in Yoruba as well as a classical aria. During the run, Jeannette Nelson – Head of Voice at the National – said I think you should train to be a voice coach. I said no to her for a long time as I was scared about what that would entail. But thank goodness she persevered, and I eventually went to retrain in voice at Central. It turns out that as a mature student, my life/work experience was more valuable to the industry than my lack of a previous degree and I haven't looked back.

What are some of the best things that we can do as individuals to make sure our voice is looked after?

The first thing I would say, as we negotiate this extraordinary time, is to be joyful. To connect with the feeling of joy in your body, because when you have joy in your body, it is reflected, manifested by a sense of ease in your voice. I encourage people to put music on and dance, sing along, put music on and lip-bubble to it to work the breath. I also encourage people to go out into open spaces and feel their voice energetically, play, laugh a lot as laughter opens the throat. Take this time to enjoy your body and voice as it will keep it prepared for work. When you're booked for a job, why not ask for vocal help, whether that is dialect or voice, as soon as the contract is signed, or make a gentle regime that you can incorporate into daily life. When you're brushing your teeth, stick your tongue out and give it a good brush! Leave your tongue hanging out and count so you're releasing the tongue root. Then when you're in bed remember to 'clean' your teeth with your tongue, as again, circling releases tongue root tension; to help you to get to sleep you can do breathing exercises, which will also gently work the muscles of expiration. You can release a long 'sss' or 'shhh' three times, breathing low into your belly and noticing your ribs widening.

I've seen that you've paved the way for many, particularly other ethnically diverse voice and dialect coaches. What is the motivation behind this?

Part of my motivation for changing things is purely selfish. I've felt very alone as a Black voice coach in this industry and, simply, I don't want to feel like that anymore. Voice work in the UK has traditionally been very white and very middle class and with the work that is produced and hopefully the work that is to come, we need to have all types of people in creative spaces. The industry needs to stop resisting diversity that isn't in front of the camera or onstage. Being a voice and dialect coach normally means that you're a department of one, but it doesn't have to be like that. I really want to be part of a community, to bounce ideas off each other and to literally have a voice and enable others to feel the same.

What are your hopes for the future of voice and dialect coaches?

I'm helping producers understand that they always need a voice department. The nature of voice work is such a delicate balance of personalities, technique, creativity and ability, and productions can receive so much from the variety of people and ideas in the space. Having Caribbean heritage and working in African theatre a lot I look at parts of the working models of British theatre and ask, 'Do they really serve us well?' By that I mean a short rehearsal schedule, not enough time for actors to embody the work, let alone makers to create, and so on. Everyone is working on empty and the fumes of adrenaline. We can learn a lot from observing how other cultures place value on the creative journey. I hope voice and dialect coaches can be part of the catalyst for change, by asking to shift parts of previous models to ones that better put the performers, the makers and the journey of making at the centre of the work.

We believe that your work is both technical and holistic. It focuses on who each actor is as an individual. Can you tell us about your technique and why you've honed it in this way?

When I was acting and singing, I knew I couldn't perform unless I was connected to my body, able to free my mind and let go of the voice that's telling me I can't do it. Now, as a coach, I look at the whole person to assess what they need and being a magpie for information I have a variety of approaches. I am neurodivergent, so I listen to a lot of audio books because reading takes me ages. I watch videos, take courses, observe life, talk a lot with everyone, talk a lot with myself, have therapy, so then, when I'm in the space working, I draw from all the things I've learnt and ask myself what this person needs, rather than what they expect me to offer them. I don't believe that there is a one-size-fits-all prescription for everyone or every voice: our life journeys are too rich and varied for that.

Anything else to add?

Be kind to people and kindness will come back to you. You can give truthful feedback kindly. I've been on the receiving end of anger and frustration as both an actor and a coach and it's uncreative and paralysing. When I've been on the receiving end of kindness my work is better. I want there to be playfulness and laughter in the rehearsal space so that people feel free and confident. I am reminded of Maya Angelou's words 'People will forget what you say, they will forget what you did, but they will never forget how you made them feel'. Never a truer word said.

To follow Hazel's work visit **www.hazelholder.com** or follow her on Twitter **@HazelHolder** or **@hazel_holder** on Instagram.

Theatre

Ignition, inspiration and the imposter

Scott Graham

I have been lucky enough to have been the artistic director of Frantic Assembly, the company I co-founded, for the past 25 years (It will be 27 by the time the book is out). It frustrates and savages me from time to time, but that is all part of the relationship with a job that also sustains, educates and consistently surprises me. To be in a rehearsal room with a playwright and other fascinating humans is to engage in literary and historical analysis, sociology, philosophy, poetry, anthropology, politics, psychology, etc. Admittedly, we might not be talking as experts, but the breadth of that conversation, in pursuit of a better understanding of a character's predicament or the experience of an audience, is an invigorating privilege and often inspirational.

Having said that, my relationship with this career is complex.

Serendipity saw me being put forward for a play by a schoolteacher against my will and yet enjoying it immensely. Then I discovered a fascination for movement when I stepped in to help choreograph a physical scene between an Oberon, who did not turn up, and Titania, who was my first proper girlfriend. (It was not all good luck as Titania actually left me for Oberon!). When I plucked up the courage to join a drama society at university I was fortunate enough to meet people who would become some of my closest friends and allies, with whom we would have the audacity to form a company based on very little experience, a hell of a lot of energy and a sense of, well, why not?

Even back then, as soon as we learned something, we would try to teach it, to pass it on. I think this meant that we were always breaking processes down into their component parts to see how they really worked (my dad was a motor mechanic and this metaphor is as close I have got to following in his footsteps). As we had zero training, we did not have a short hand or vast technique to fall back on. If I was falling back on anything it was my years of playing sport. I could see the similarities. Sport and martial art gave me a good sense of my own balance and physicality and that awareness really helped, not only in making it more likely that I could achieve the movement, but also in puncturing some of the mystique around theatre and dance.

Sport has had a profound effect on how the company operates. We would do hundreds of workshops in schools and I would always attempt to make the students feel like they could be part of a games lesson or the best part of the playground. We were aiming for that euphoria of scoring a goal or winning as a team. I think I was trying to keep the people who might think this drama lark was not for them in the room in the hope that they, like me, would experience that revelation, see the similarities and apply their skills within the theatre studio.

When we created our free training programme, Ignition, it was with the purpose of attracting young men into our type of theatre. It was not created simply by feeling their absence, but by the strong belief that they were out there with all of their crossover skills, applying them elsewhere. They were never going to come to us because we were terrifying them. We had to look at the language we used and how we presented ourselves if we were to be an attractive proposition to these young men.

We trawled the country trying to get a diverse mix of young men who had little or no engagement in the arts and put them through an intense training programme where, in four days, they met for the first time and by the end had made and performed a show for a public audience. They were nurtured and supported by professionals at every step, but it was their bravery, generosity and commitment that got them through what can be a transformative week in their lives. Many graduates have gone on to work in theatre. Paapa Essiedu played Hamlet at the RSC in 2016. There might not be a more high-profile symbol of the success of this programme than this. Across the country, young men returned to their towns invigorated and empowered and I am immensely proud of that.

The success of Ignition has been extraordinary and in 2019 we launched our female version with a similar drive to bring new voices and energy into our theatre. Again, the focus is on the energy and ethics I have found in sport.

One of my most illuminating rehearsal periods was the creation of Frantic's boxing show, *Beautiful Burnout*. We had already researched the boxing world extensively and found intense, sensitive relationships at the heart of what might appear to be the coldest, loneliest and most brutal of sports. There is so much respect and care to be found inside these gyms. So much to learn and so much to be taught. There is something really beautiful to see how that boxer between rounds, sweating, gloves on, cannot drink or even pick up their bottle of water without a friend unscrewing it and holding it to their mouth.

We wanted to take some of that encouraging culture back into the rehearsal room for this show. In fact, we turned the room into a gym with weights, skipping ropes and punch bags set up. The effect on the performing company was startling. The room became so positive and energised. People would choose to train during their breaks. No one collapsed onto a sofa and bitched about agents. The focus was absolute.

All of this was born out of the intense circuit training and boxing warm ups. It had built a team and vast amounts of mutual respect. It was so successful that versions of it have been employed on most subsequent Frantic shows to build a culture of support, application and community. It builds the ensemble.

All of this validated my instinct about what sport could bring to theatre and how crossover skills were valuable. This was me bringing a world I felt comfortable with into the theatre experience.

My lack of training or what I might have considered a proper theatre background has, at times, made me feel an imposter. I felt unsure, that I had no right to be right. I questioned my authority to write the *Frantic Assembly Book of Devising Theatre*[1] and needed some convincing. When I was invited to speak to academics as part of my role as Visiting Professor at Coventry University I initially felt a paralysing sense that I was a charlatan and had nothing to say.

But I have also found a lack of training has been liberating, allowing me to be inspired by a vast range of stimuli. I embraced my limitations and developed a way of working that suited me and those that might be like me. I have seen that method empower skilled actors and dancers too. I have seen how they break free from their training and technique and are refreshed.

Knowledge creeps up on you. It can take a long time to recognise that you have something to say and the authority to say it. I have seen plenty of people make all the right noises and present a veneer of authority. I have been intimidated by it but I have ultimately

---

[1] *Frantic Assembly Book of Devising Theatre* by Scott Graham and Steven Hoggett, 2nd edition, Routledge, 2014.

seen through it. It comes from the same place as my imposter syndrome. It comes from our fear of the world looking at us and seeing that we might not know the answers. In theatre, what is so wrong about that? Just like my initial inexperience and limitations I have learnt to use this to my advantage. It is an exciting place to be.

When I was part of the creative team making *The Curious Incident of the Dog in the Night-Time*[2] I went through that initial fear of being found out, of being out of my depth, but what was so illuminating and empowering was seeing that same look on other people's faces. They were not trying to hide the fear that is an essential part of the creative process. We were all taking ourselves to places we were not sure about. We were taking risks, trying something new and encouraging each other to be brave. Seeing these respected and award-winning artists work in such an honest and relentless fashion was a formative creative experience that helped me deal with (accept rather than crush) my imposter syndrome and redefined my relationship with the rehearsal room.

It is now so clear to me that we enter a rehearsal room to find out what we don't yet know rather than enter to tell the world what we do know. I tell my MA students when they are setting up devising tasks, be the bad scientist, not the good scientist. The bad scientist mixes ingredients and blows their eyebrows off. As long as they remember that that concoction can do that then they have learnt something. They can use that again when the time is right. Don't be the good scientist who merely acts to prove their theory. They have not moved forward through the task. They have not discovered something new.

Training opportunities are the same. As we walk in through the door we should be asking, what can we take with us as we leave? Too often we enter with a mask and just pray it does not slip. I know I have.

This is why I love working with actors. Initially many hide behind that mask, but when you can help them to get to that place of truth you see how empowering that can be. I have seen the tiniest moment of physicality become the breakthrough for an actor to base a whole character on. Not a tic or an affectation. I mean a moment that links to the tension held within and makes sense of their interaction with the world around them. It feels seismic. It also comes from an understanding of the text. There is often a perception that physical work is not cerebral. This is a damaging miscalculation. We live the majority of our lives reading the world physically, displaying and reading nuance. I consider my movement direction to be 'direction through movement' and its ambition is to open up the text. I think it is so important that performers are open to the potential the physical approach can bring. Try not to hide what you think are your deficiencies, don't think of movement as something that you can or cannot do, it is what we *all* do! We tell and read stories physically all through our waking hours. Exploring this and embracing this nuance can only empower the actor.

This is why I love my job. I learn something every day. I learn about you, I learn about characters and I learn about me. When I get asked a question at a post-show discussion, I often think that the student believes they are asking me what I know without realising that the act of asking is helping me form those thoughts. Those thoughts can surprise me. I would not know that I thought that if they had not asked me that question.

---

[2] As of July 2022, The National Theatre's Olivier and Tony Award-winning production of *The Curious Incident of the Dog in the Night-Time* (2012) has just finished its 10th Anniversary Tour across the UK and Ireland. Directed by Marianne Elliott and adapted by playwright Simon Stephens.

I think it is important to recognise that. We can crush ourselves under the expectation that we should know all the answers. This can close us off from meaningful collaboration and kill a rehearsal room or drama studio. Sometimes holding up your hands and saying, 'I don't know what to do here' is not an admission of defeat. It is the invitation to your collaborators to step up. It often takes that explicit moment of honesty.

Scott Graham is co-founder and artistic director of Frantic Assembly. Further information about Frantic Assembly and contact details can be found in their entry in our *Middle and smaller-scale companies* listings on page 190 of this *Yearbook*. The extensive Frantic Assembly website (**www.franticassembly.co.uk**) gives details and illustrations of their previous productions, and how to apply to take part in Ignition.

Theatre

Middle and smaller-scale companies

This section covers a huge range of companies, from the very prestigious, often subsidised (like Out of Joint), which usually only perform in theatres with around 500 seats (or more), to the very small, which frequently have little or no public subsidy and perform wherever they can find a paying audience. The bigger companies operate much like the commercial 'big boys' in the previous section – except they tend to have longer rehearsal periods. The smaller companies rarely use casting directors, tend to do only one or two performances in each venue, and often pay below Equity rates – and it's probable that you'll have to help with get-ins and get-outs. It's very hard work and you have to rise to the peak of performance every time, in spite of travelling in cramped vans, sharing unsatisfactory digs and rarely, if ever, being seen by anyone who could advance your career. However, some very prestigious companies have grown from such very small beginnings, and a number of now highly respected directors, playwrights and actors have started this way. It is important to assess the potential quality of the product (as well as the pay, and terms and conditions) before accepting such a job.

As such companies tend to come and go with great rapidity, the listings only contain companies that have been in existence for three years or more.

Note: Some of the companies listed are members of the Independent Theatre Council (ITC) – **www.itc-arts.org**.

20 Stories High
Toxteth TV, 37-45 Windsor Street, Liverpool L8 1XE
tel 0151 708 9728
email info@20storieshigh.org.uk
website www.20storieshigh.org.uk
Twitter @20storieshigh
Instagram @20storieshigh
Artistic Director Keith Saha *Executive Director* Leanne Jones

Production details: Established in 2006. Creates dynamic, challenging theatre which attracts new audiences, artists and participants. Produces theatre with working class and culturally diverse young people, emerging artists and world-class professionals. Arts Council NPO from April 2012. Generally stages 1 project annually, with around 40 performances in 20 theatres, schools and youth clubs in the North West and nationally. In general 2-5 actors are involved in each production. Offers Equity-approved contracts as negotiated through ITC. Recent productions include: *The Spine*, written and directed by Nathan Powell (national tour); *Big Up!* by Keith Saha and Sue Buckmaster (national tour, co-production with Theatre-Rites); *She's Leaving Home* by Keith Saha (directed by Julia Samuels – tour to living rooms in Liverpool, commissioned as part of Culture Liverpool's Sgt Pepper at 50 celebrations); *I Told My Mum I Was Going on an RE Trip...* (written and directed by Julia Samuels – co-production with Contact Theatre; TV adaptation for BBC2 broadcast and national/international film festivals); *The Broke 'n' Beat Collective* by Keith Saha (directed by Keith Saha and Sue Buckmaster – national tour co-production with Theatre Rites); *Tales from the MP3* verbatim production written and directed by Julia Samuels (national tour); *Melody Loses Her Mojo* by Keith Saha (directed by Keith Saha – co-production with Liverpool Everyman Playhouse and Curve Theatre – national tour); and *Whole* by Philip Osment (directed Julia Samuels – national tour).

Casting procedures: Holds general auditions. Casting breakdowns are available from the website and Equity Job Information Service. Welcomes letters (with CVs and photographs) from individual actors previously unknown to the company, sent by post or email, and is happy to consider invitations to view individual actors' websites. Actively encourages applications from artists of colour disabled artists and others currently under-represented in the industry.

1623 Theatre Company
QUAD Market Place, Cathedral Quarter, Derby DE1 3AS
tel (01332) 285434
email messages@1623theatre.co.uk
website www.1623theatre.co.uk
Executive Director Sam Beckett Jr (they/them)
Creative Producer Jamie Brown (he/him) *Artistic Director* Ben Spiller (they/them)

Production details: 1623 works creatively for social justice with marginalised people and Shakespeare.

Recent productions include: *Much Ado/Hero's Song* (Century Theatre), *What We Feel* (online), *Queer Lady M* (Attenborough Arts Centre and national tour), *Lear/Cordelia (Derby Theatre)*, *Hamlet Off The Wall* (Sheffield Museums), *unclepandarus.com* (World Shakespeare Festival) and *Emergency Shakespeare* (*Watch This Space* at the National Theatre).

Casting procedures: Welcomes both CVs and letters from actors previously unknown to the Company and unsolicited CVs and photographs. These should be sent via email. Also welcomes invitations to view individual actors' websites or productions. Happy to accept showreels. Actively encourages applications from artists who are deaf, disabled, emerging, female, global majority, LGBT++, neuro-diverse and working class.

Access All Areas

Bradbury Studios, 138 Kingsland Road,
London E2 8DY
tel 020 7613 6445
email hello@accessallareastheatre.org
website https://accessallareastheatre.org
Twitter @AAATheatre
Editor Artistic Director Nick Llewellyn

Access All Areas was formed in 1976 as The Rainbow Theatre Group and renamed in 2010. They are an award-winning theatre company making disruptive performances with learning disabled and autistic artists. They represent 17 learning disabled and autistic artists and have produced performances such as *MADHOUSE*, *The Misfit Analysis* and *The Interpretation*.

In 2015, Access All Areas received the Guardian University Award for Student Diversity and Widening Participation for their Performance Making Diploma in partnership with the Royal Central School of Speech and Drama. In 2017, they were awarded National Portfolio Organisation (NPO) status by Arts Council England.

For casting enquiries, please contact Sam How on **sam@simon-how.com**.

Accidental Theatre

4th Floor, Wellington Buildings,
2-4 Wellington Street, Belfast BT1 6HT
email info@accidentaltheatre.co.uk
website www.accidentaltheatre.co.uk
Artistic Director Richard Lavery

Production Details: Accidental's theatre is a collision of perspectives, art forms and unusual collaborations – curious stories told through vibrant, ambitious performances. Accidental works with playwrights, actors, filmmakers, DJs, choreographers, musicians, poets, painters, technicians and curators to craft plays for Ireland and the world stage. Every production is a fresh invention, each play's architecture defined by the artists with whom we build it. Collective risk-

taking is the inspiration that jolts our work into new theatrical territories and opens it up to new audiences. Accidental walks the tightrope between the unexpected and the impossible, exploring the intersection between British narrative and European aesthetic styles of theatre.

Recent productions include: Gordon Osràm's *Funeral* (Dave Kingham), *The Lost Martini (devised)*, *The Kitchen, the Bedroom and the Grave* (by Donal O'Hagan), *DEATH (on a shoestring)* (by Dave Kinghan) and *The Writers' Room* (by Michael Shannon).

"Collective risk-taking is the inspiration that jolts our work into new theatrical territories and opens it up to new audiences. Accidental walks the tightrope between the unexpected and the impossible, exploring the intersection between British narrative and European aesthetic styles of theatre."

Casting Procedures: Uses in-house casting directors and hold general auditions. Welcomes enquiries, CVs and letters from actors previously unknown to the theatre. Also happy to receive unsolicited CVs, letters, showreels and invitations to view individual actors websites. Casting breakdowns are available from the theatre's website, Spotlight and *The Stage*. Promotes inclusive casting, actively encourages applications from actors with disabilities to play characters with disabilities.

Actors of Dionysus (AOD)

25 St Luke's Road, Brighton BN2 9ZD
mobile 07957 471949
email info@actorsofdionysus.com
email lucy@actorsofdionysus.com
website www.actorsofdionysus.com
Facebook www.facebook.com/ActorsOfDionysus
Twitter @aodtheatre
Twitter @TamsinShasha
Instagram @actorsofdionysus
Artistic Director Tamsin Shasha *Education Officer* Mark Katz *Content* Administrator Lucy Ruddiman *Associate Director* Katherine Sturt-Scobie, Tess Agus

Production details: National and international touring company founded in 1993. Not regularly funded. **aod** productions specialise in performing new adaptations of Ancient Greek drama and new writing inspired by myth (often with an aerial dimension), through a fusion of poetry, music and movement. "Our mission statement is to make magic from myth by reframing ancient Greek theatre for the 21st century, making it relevant, accessible and transformative through high-quality theatre that sparks debate and engagement with immediate global issues." Via its outreach arm, aodEducation, it offers an established educational programme of workshops (digital and live), pre-show talks, publications, audio-CDs and DVDs and are also now exploring KS1 and KS2. Can tour througout the year; venues include national and international touring venues. In general

Theatre

1–5 actors work on each production. Current productions: *Black Voices in Myth*, *Wonder Women of the Ancient World* and *#DailyDose*. Recent productions include: *Stories in the Garden* (2022), *Savage Beauty* (2021), *Three Graces* (2021), *Lysistrata* (2018); *Antigone* (2017); *Helen* (2016), *Bacchae* (2016) and *Paris Alexandros* (2015). Recent DVDs include: *Antigone* (2017); *Helen* (2014) and *Medea* (2013). *Antigone* (2017) is available on Digital Theatre+ for educational purposes. Recent Audio CDs include *Sappho: The Sweetness of Honey* (2014). Also holds one-off high-profile events as part of **aod** events.

Casting procedures: Does not use freelance casting directors. Holds general workshop auditions; actors should write to request inclusion in early spring and summer. Casting breakdowns are available via the website and Spotlight. Does not welcome general submissions from actors but will accept invitations to view individual actors' Spotlight links and websites.

Actors Touring Company (ATC)

email atc@atctheatre.com
website www.atctheatre.com
Twitter @ActorsTouringCo
Instagram @actorstouringcompanyatc
Artistic Director Matthew Xia *Executive Director* Andrew Smaje

Production details: Established in 1979, the Actors Touring Company are passionate about giving voice to the 'outsider within' and connecting global artistic voices to local communities. They work throughout the UK and internationally, from Scarborough to Hong Kong. At least 2 productions are staged annually, employing roughly 4-6 actors per production. Offers ITC/Equity-approved contracts. Recent productions include: *Amsterdam* (2019/20), *Dear Tomorrow* (2020/21) and *Rice* (2021).

Casting procedures: Works with specified casting directors on casting productions.

APL Theatre Ltd

3rd Floor, 207 Regent Street, London W1B 3HH
email info@apltheatre.com
website apltheatre.com
Facebook www.facebook.com/apltheatreproductions
Twitter @apltheatreltd
Instagram @apltheatreltd

Nationwide and international productions. Consultancy, mentorin and general management services. UK Theatre and SOLT member. Mental health advocates.

ARC Theatre Ensemble

Kingsley Hall, Parsloes Avenue, Dagenham RM9 5NB
email info@arctheatre.com
website www.arctheatre.com

Production details: Founded in 1984, Arc has built a strong core Management and Associate team bringing together an exceptional range of creative skills, educational experience and business and social expertise. The company is governed by an equally diverse and committed Board of Management. "We also benefit from a first-class pool of highly skilled, trained actors, storytellers, facilitators, workshop leaders, production managers and designers who are individually hand-picked to suit each programme or bespoke project." See the website for more details of its work.

Casting procedures: "To register your interest in working with Arc, please submit your details via **info@arctheatre.com**. We will keep your details on record and contact you when a suitable opportunity arises. Alternatively you can email your details to our General Manager, Nita Bocking: **nita@arctheatre.com**."

Attic Theatre Company

Mitcham Library, 157 London Road, Mitcham CR24 2YR
tel 020 8640 6800
email info@attictheatrecompany.com
website www.attictheatrecompany.com
Executive Director Victoria Hibbs *Artistic Director* Jonathan Humphreys

Production details: Attic makes theatre for both traditional and non-traditional theatre spaces and audiences, and ccommissions new work as well as classic adaptations. Many of Attic's productions are staged within Merton in libraries and community spaces. Attic also runs an extensive community programme of work with older people and young people facing disadvantage, particularly refugees, asylum seekers and EAL students. For recent and forthcoming poductions see (**www.attictheatrecompany.com**).

Casting procedures: Uses freelance casting directors. Does not hold general auditions and does not accept casting enquiries or submissions from actors.

Badapple Theatre Company

PO Box 57, York YO26 8WQ
tel 01423 331304
website www.badappletheatre.com
Director Kate Bramley

Production details: Founded in 1998. Specialises in new comedy. Stages productions at a local rural touring level, national arts centre and small- to mid-scale theatre level.

Casting procedures: Uses direct mail castings to agencies. Actors with an interest in the company are free to contact the office at any time. Directors prefer to see actors in performance prior to castings, so welcomes updates of performances in the Yorkshire region that company directors would be able to attend.

Big Telly Theatre Company

c/o Flowerfield Arts Centre, 185 Coleraine Road, Portstewart, Co. L'Derry BT55 7HU

tel 028 7083 2588
email info@big-telly.com
website www.big-telly.com
Twitter @BigTellyNI
Artistic Director Zoë Seaton

Production details: Big Telly Theatre Company is Northern Ireland's longest established professional, not-for-profit theatre company, formed in 1987 and based in Portstewart on the North Coast. The company produces theatre, interactive workshop programmes and community creativity projects, which tour throughout Great Britain, Ireland and internationally. It concentrates on the visual potential of theatre through fusion with other art forms such as dance, music, circus, magic and film to create a unique sense of spectacle. "Big Telly's work is driven by a determination to offer audiences entertainment that surprises, stimulates and ignites the imagination."

Casting procedures: Does not use freelance casting directors. Casting breakdowns are available through Spotlight, Equity and other job-information services, and are also released to agents. Welcomes submissions (with CVs and photographs) from actors previously unknown to the company sent by post or email. Invitations to view individual actors' websites are also accepted. Offers ITC/Equity contracts, and endeavours to employ disabled actors when casting for disabled characters.

Border Crossings

13 Bankside, Enfield EN2 8BN
tel 020 8366 5239
email info@bordercrossings.org.uk
website www.bordercrossings.org.uk
Director Michael Walling

Production details: Established in 1995. International company, working in theatre and combined arts, that creates dynamic performances by fusing many forms of world theatre, dance and music. Stages 1 or 2 productions per year touring to up to 15 venues including arts centres and theatres. Roughly 3-9 actors are used in each production. Recent credits include: *The Great Experiment* (2020); *This Flesh in Mine* (2014); *Consumed* (UK tour 2013); *Re-Orientations* (Soho Theatre 2010); *The Dilemma of a Ghost* (2007); *Bullie's House* (Riverside Studios); *Orientations* (Oval House); *Dis-Orientations* (Riverside Studios); and *Double Tongue* (UK tour). "We don't offer Equity contracts, although our own contracts are modelled on the ITC/Equity contract, and we usually pay above the minimum." Does not subscribe to the Equity Pension Scheme.

Casting procedures: Welcomes letters (with CVs and photographs) from actors previously unknown to the company. Invitations to view individual actors' websites and showreels are accepted. Actively encourages applications from disabled actors and promotes the use of inclusive casting.

Borderline Theatre Co.

Gaiety Theatre, Carrick Street, Ayr KA7 1NU
email enquiries@borderlinetheatre.co.uk
website www.borderlinetheatre.co.uk

Production details: Founded in 1974, the company is the longest running touring theatre in Scotland. It currently stages one touring production each year, with around 25 performances at 15-20 different venues. Venues include small to mid-scale arts centres, theatres and village halls across Scotland. In general 3-4 actors work on each production. Recent productions include: *Uncanny Valley*, *The Straw Chair* and *A Slow Air*.

Casting procedures: Does not use freelance casting directors. Currently releases casting breakdowns to agents, but may publish these on the website in future. Welcomes submissions (with CVs, Spotlight links, showreels and photographs) from actors previously unknown to the company sent by post or email.

Boundless Theatre

Units B2-B4, Galleywall Road London SE16 3PB
tel 020 7928 2811
email hello@boundlesstheatre.org.uk
website www.boundlesstheatre.org.uk
Artistic Director Rob Drummer

Production details: Established in 2001 (as Company of Angels). New and experimental work for young audiences. Offers Equity approved contracts as negotiated through ITC. Recent productions include: *Natives* (Southwark Playhouse); *World Factory* (Young Vic and New Wolsey Theatre) and Theatre Cafe Festival (venues include The Tramshed and York Theatre Royal).

Casting procedures: Actors may write at any time to request inclusion on the database for future reference. Performers previously unknown to the company should contact Boundless Theatre with their CV by email only. Boundless Theatre is an equal opportunities employer and actively encourages applications from BME and disabled actors in line with their policy on inclusive casting.

Bruiser Theatre Company

BEAT Carnival Centre 11-47 Boyd Street, Belfast BT13 2GU
tel 028 9024 3731 mobile 07540 477055
email info@bruisertheatrecompany.com
website www.bruisertheatrecompany.com
Artistic Director Lisa May

Production details: Founded in 1997, Bruiser focus on producing exciting and innovative theatre, presenting existing texts using physical theatre techniques. Recent productions include: *The Importance of Being Earnest*, *Cabaret*, *Sweet Charity* and *The 25th Annual Putnam County Spelling Bee* (in association with The MAC, Belfast); *The Complete*

Theatre

Works of William Shakespeare (Abridged), *Mojo Mickybo* and *Playhouse Creatures*. Each production consists of 2-14 actors and musicians and, on average, the company present 2 productions per year. This equates to a tour of around 45 performances at 16 venues.

Casting procedures: Uses in-house casting directors; casting breakdowns are available on the website. Welcomes both CVs and letters from actors previously unknown to the Company and unsolicited CVs and photographs throughout the year. These should be sent via email. Also welcomes performance notices, invitations to view individual actors' websites and showreels.

Cahoots Theatre Company

St Martin's Theatre, West Street,
London WC2H 9NZ
website www.cahootstheatrecompany.com
Artistic Director Denise Silvey

Production details: Founded in 1999. Produces theatre, cabaret and CD recordings, as well as acting as a general management and press agent. Stages 3-4 productions a year, with 100 performances over 15 venues (arts centres, theatres and cabaret venues) in London, Edinburgh and New York. Productions may involve from 1 to 17 performers. Offers Equity approved and non-Equity contracts. Recent credits include: *Dead Sheep* and *An Audience with Jimmy Savile* at Park Theatre, and *The Man Called Monkhouse* on tour.

Casting procedures: Casting in in-house. Also publishes casting breakdowns on the Equity JIS. Welcomes emails (but not letters) with CVs and photographs from individuals previously unknown to the company. Does not welcome showreels, but is happy to receive invitations to view actors' websites. Will consider applications from disabled actors to play characters with disabilities.

Cambridge Shakespeare Festival

11 Crossways House, Anstey Way, Trumpington,
Cambridge CB2 9JZ
mobile 07955 218824
email mail@cambridgeshakespeare.com
website www.cambridgeshakespeare.com
Artistic Director Dr David Crilly *Associate Directors* Simon Bell, David Rowan

Production details: The Festival Company was established in Oxford in 1988 by Artistic Director Dr David Crilly. The main focus for the Company is the annual Cambridge Shakespeare Festival, which runs throughout July and August. Situated in the gardens of the Colleges of Cambridge University, its pastoral setting is one of the loveliest in the world.

Cardboard Citizens

77A Greenfield Road, London E1 1EJ
tel 020 7377 8948

email mail@cardboardcitizens.org.uk
website www.cardboardcitizens.org.uk
Artistic Director Chris Sonnex

Production details: The UK's only homeless people's professional theatre company. Specialises in making forum theatre, but has broadened its scope to the provision of a range of performance-based cultural actions with, for and by homeless and previously homeless people. Productions include: *Cathy Come Home, Benefit Meta, Glasshouse, A Few Man Fridays, Mincemeat, Woyzeck* – national tour; *Timon of Athens* – national tour with RSC; *Visible* – national tour, 'down and out' community production.

Casting procedures: Uses in-house casting directors. Holds general auditions; actors may write at any time requesting inclusion. Welcomes letters, CVs and photographs from individual actors previously unknown to the company, sent via post or email. Also welcomes showreels and invitations to view individual actors' websites. Offers Equity-approved contracts. Actively encourages applications from actors with experience of homelessness, disabled people and promotes the use of inclusive casting.

The Castle Players

c/o Tilly Bailey & Irvine, 8 Newgate, Barnard Castle,
County Durham DL12 8NG
mobile 07813 001427
email info@castleplayers.co.uk
website www.castleplayers.co.uk
Chair Christine Gibson-Bell

Production details: An amateur community theatre company limited by guarantee. Established in 1987. Undertakes major open-air summer productions in a specially constructed tiered-seat theatre. Also stages minimum of one touring production annually. Recent productions include: *The Complete Works of Shakespeare (abridged), Pygmalion, Alan Bennett Office Suite, Alice in Wonderland, Macbeth, Henry V, Old Curiosity Shop, Hedda Gabler, When We Are Married, Flarepath* and a virtual production of *Life, Love and Covid*. Was also a participating company in the 2016 RSC *A Midsummer Night's Dream – A Play for the Nation*.

Casting procedures: Productions are cast from the local community at open auditions. Subscribe to the newsletter via the company website for regular updates. Uses in-house casting directors and holds general auditions; actors should write in January to request inclusion.

Chain Reaction Theatre Company

Millers House, Three Mill Lane, London E3 3DU
tel 020 8981 9527
email admin@chainreactiontheatre.co.uk
website www.chainreactiontheatre.co.uk
Facebook www.facebook.com/ChainReactionTC
Artistic Director Sarah Smit

Production details: Chain Reaction is an award-winning London-based charity that has been using theatre and media to ignite personal and social change since 1994. Chain Reaction works in partnership with schools, local councils and corporate organisations to produce high-quality, emotionally engaging projects that transform the way people relate to themselves, their community and to wider society. Works across both the public and private sector, ensuring that their work with vulnerable young people is at the heart of what they do. They currently have 12 educational shows in their repertoire, each designed for a specific age range from 5 to 16 years. Performances tackle sensitive and controversial topics including drug-awareness, sexual health, bullying, healthy eating and exercise, and emotional wellbeing. Using the power of creativity Chain Reaction engages, educates and empowers people to reach their full potential in life. Whether delivering professional theatre performances or running youth theatres, creative media workshops, social action groups or interactive training programmes, their work increases people's skills, knowledge and understanding, whilst building resilience, self-esteem and confidence.

Casting procedures: General auditions when required. Casting in-house.

Cheek by Jowl

Stage Door, Barbican Theatre, Silk Street, London EC2Y 8DS
tel 020 7382 2391
email info@cheekbyjowl.com
website www.cheekbyjowl.com
Facebook www.facebook.com/cheekbyjowl
Twitter @CbyJ
Instagram @wearecheelbyjowl
Artistic Directors Declan Donnellan, Nick Ormerod

Production details: The company was founded in 1981 by Declan Donnellan and Nick Ormerod. The name conveys an intimacy between the actors, the audience and the text; the phrase 'cheek by jowl' is quoted from *A Midsummer Night's Dream* ("Follow! Nay, I'll go with thee cheek by jowl" (Act III Sc II)) Recent productions include: *The Revenger's Tragedy* (in Italian), *The Knight of the Burning Pestle* (in Russian), *Périclès, Prince de Tyr* (in French), *Measure for Measure* (in Russian) and *A Winter's Tale* (in English).

Casting procedures: "Like the vast majority of other British theatre companies, our actors are on fixed-term contracts. However, many actors come back regularly to work with us. For each new Cheek by Jowl UK production, a Casting Director is appointed. Please do not send unsolicited CVs as we are unable to accept them."

Chickenshed Theatre

290 Chase Side, Southgate, London N14 4PE
tel 020 8292 9222
email info@chickenshed.org.uk
website www.chickenshed.org.uk

Managing Director Louise Perry; *Director of Education and Training* Paul Morrall

Founded in 1974, Chickenshed brings together people of all ages and from all backgrounds and produces theatre that entertains, inspires, challenges and educates both audiences and participants alike.

Using the power of performing arts Chickenshed helps people reach their full potential and feel accepted; and creates an inclusive environment where people don't stigmatise, label or disregard, but accept and welcome difference. Chickenshed's vision is a society that celebrates diversity and enables every individual to flourish.

Most shows run from 3–6 weeks while the Christmas show runs for 7. Chickenshed has four performance spaces which are used during the Christmas show run but at other times performance spaces are available. The Rayne Theatre is an attractive and modern theatre space seating 300. The seating can be retracted to the rear wall creating a large, flat open space for performance or workshops. The Studio Theatre is 12m x 12m and is extremely versatile with seating for up to 140. Premises are accessible to disabled performers.

Recent productions include: *Snow White, Waiting for the Ship to Sail, Mr Stink* and *Monolog.*

Casting procedures: Chickenshed generally produces in-house shows. Occasionally holds general auditions and uses website breaksown services. Please submit CVs throughout the year. Welcomes letters from individual actors previously unknown to the company and welcomes invitations to view individual actors' website and to visit other productions.

Actively promotes inclusive casting and believes that all of their actors should have access to all parts that are required. Usually casts from their own pool of actors but if there is a specific artistic casting requirement open calls may be considered.

Clean Break

2 Patshull Road, London NW5 2LB
tel 020 7482 8600
email general@cleanbreak.org.uk
website www.cleanbreak.org.uk
Facebook www.facebook.com/cleanbreak
Twitter @CleanBrk
Instagram @cleanbrk
Executive Director Erin Gavaghan *Joint Artistic Directors* Anna Herrmann, Róisin McBrinn *Producers* Maya Ellis, Nadezhda Zhelyazkova

Production details: Clean Break was founded in 1979 by 2 women serving sentences at HMP Askham Grange. The company's artistic mission is to create bold new plays by the best women playwrights, telling the stories about women and crime that are not being told elsewhere, and taking this work into prisons and onto stages across London and the UK and the world. The company generally stages 3 productions per year

Theatre

ranging from work with its Members Programme to London venues and touring productions. The average cast size is 3-4. Recent productions include: *Typical Girls* (Sheffield Crucible)*; Blis-ta* (audio drama); *[BLANK]* (Donmar Warehouse); *Sweatbox* (UK tour and folm adaptation); *Inside Bitch* (Royal Court), *Thick as Thieves* (Theatr Clwyd and UK tour); *House/Amongst the Reeds* (Edinburgh Festival Fringe); *Joanne* (RSC) and *Dream Pill* (Edinburgh Festival Fringe). Offers ITC/Equity-approved contracts and subscribes to the Equity Pension Scheme.

Casting procedures: Uses freelance casting directors. Does not issue breakdowns. Auditions are organised via actors' agents and personal management. Unable to accept unsolicited CVs or showreels from actors. "Clean Break employ only women to deliver our services in accordance with our exemption under the Equality Act 2010, Part 1 Schedule 9. We also actively seek to work with artists who have lived experience of the criminal justice system." Clean Break casts a minimum of 2 actors per production from its Members Programme – a threatre making programme for women with experience of the criminal justice system. Actively encourages applications from disabled actors and promotes the use of inclusive casting.

Clod Ensemble

Studio 1, The Rose Lipman Building,
43 De Beauvoir Road, London, N1 5SQ
tel 020 7749 0555
email admin@clodensemble.com
website www.clodensemble.com
Artistic Directors Suzy Willson, Paul Clark

Production details: A small- to mid-scale company established in 1996. Creates theatre, music and performance events, workshops and courses in London, the UK and internationally. Stages on average 1 production each year in the main house; also works in Outreach and Community. Recent productions include: *On The High Road*; *The Black Saint and The Sinner Lady*: *Listening Party*; *Hackney Rooms*; *This is My Room*; *Placebo*; *Under Glass*; *Silver Swan*; *Red Ladies*; *Zero*; *Snow*; *Must*; *An Anatomie in Four Quarters* and *The Red Chair*.

Casting procedures: Producer does the casting. Sometimes holds general auditions and actors should write to request inclusion. Welcomes unsolicited CVs and photographs if sent by email. Also accepts invitations to view individual actors' websites. Offers Equity-approved contracts as negotiated through ITC. Actively encourages applications from disabled actors and promotes the use of inclusive casting.

Cloud Nine Theatre Productions

5 Marden Terrace, Cullercoats,
North Shields NE30 4PD
tel 0191 253 1901
email cloudninetheatre@xlnmail.com
website www.cloudninetheatre.co.uk

Artistic Director Peter Mortimer *Associate Director* Colette Stroud

Production details: Established in 1997. Dedicated to commissioning and producing new work from Northern playwrights. Has produced plays by more than 24 Northern dramatists, in leading North-East venues. On average stages 2-3 productions each year. Recent productions include: *Death at Dawn - A Soldier's Tale from the Great War* (2014), *A Parcel for Mr Smith* (2015) and *The End of the Pier* (2016).

Casting procedures: Uses in-house casting directors. Depends on production; our small-scale productions tend to use members of our ensemble, but we audition for larger scale productions. Enquire first. As a North East-based company, we tend to cast with actors from this region, and generally would not encourage other actors to apply unless specifically requested.

The Common Players

72 West End Road, Exeter EX5 4QS
website www.common-players.org.uk
Artistic Director Anthony Richards

Production details: Founded in 1989, The Common Players focus on presenting both original productions and the classic texts for, and in partnership with, the communities of the West Country. Recent productions include: *Jerusalem* (by Jez Butterworth), *Educating Rita* (Willy Russell) and *Smuggler's Gold* (an educational programme). Each production consists of 2-16 actors and, on average, the company present 2-3 productions per year. This equates to 30-40 performances at 30 venues across the south west, ranging from small theatres, to arts centres, community spaces, schools and outdoor venues.

Casting procedures: Uses in-house casting directors, but does not hold general auditions. A casting breakdown is available on the website.

Communicado Productions

The Old Schoolhouse Newlandrig,
Midlothian EH23 4NS
mobile 07525 181183
website www.communicadotheatre.co.uk
Artistic Director Gerry Mulgrew

Production details: Founded in 1983, Communicado is a theatre company that has presented the classics and new stories, live music and visual and physical theatre for over 20 years. It also holds teaching workshops and does exploratory theatre work. Its productions include: *Tam O Shanter* (with Assembly Productions), *The Government Inspector* (with Aberystwyth Arts Centre) and *Calum's Road* (with National Theatre of Scotland).

Each production consists of around 10 actors and, on average, the Company present 2 productions per year. This equates to around 60 performances across Scotland, mainly arts centres, theatres and community spaces. Communicado also take their work to the Edinburgh Fringe Festival. Offers Equity/ITC approved contracts.

Casting procedures: Welcomes invitations to view individual actors' websites and to attend performances. Actively encourages applications from disabled actors and promotes the use of inclusive casting.

Complicité
14 Anglers Lane, Kentish Town, London NW5 3DG
tel 020 7485 7700
email email@complicite.org
website www.complicite.org
Facebook www.facebook.com/TheatredeComplicite
Twitter @complicite
Instagram @complicitetheatre
Artistic Director Simon McBurney

Production details: Award-winning theatre company founded in 1983. Constantly evolving its ensemble of performers and collaborators. Work ranges from entirely devised pieces to theatrical adaptations and revivals of classic texts. Recent productions include: *A Pacifist's Guide to the War on Cancer, Lionboy, everything that rises must dance, The Encounter, Beware of Pity, The Master and Margarita, A Dog's Heart, Shun-kin, A Disappearing Number, Endgame, The Elephant Vanishes* and *Measure for Measure.* Contracts vary.

Casting procedures: Invites performers to casting auditions through agents or Spotlight. Welcomes invitations to see work (accompanied by a CV and photograph), but unable to respond to everyone. "We are always more inclined to meet actors previously unknown to us if they are familiar with our work (i.e. if they have seen a Complicité show or participated in an Open Workshop). Complicité's Creative Engagement Department programmes up to 2 Open Workshop seasons for actors each year."

Concordance
Finborough Theatre, 118 Finborough Road, London SW10 9ED
tel 020 7244 7439
email admin@finboroughtheatre.co.uk
website www.concordance.org.uk

Production details: A theatrical production company, founded by Neil McPherson in 1981, at the Finborough Theatre, London – see entry under *Fringe theatres* on page 242. The company presents new writing, revivals of neglected work and music theatre.

Creation Theatre Company
3rd Floor, Cherwell House, 1-5 London Place, Oxford OX4 1BD
tel 01865 766266
email boxoffice@creationtheatre.co.uk
website www.creationtheatre.co.uk

Founder David Parrish *Associate Director* Charlotte Conquest

Production details: Produces site-specific Shakespeare. Stages 2-5 productions annually in unusual, non-traditional theatre venues (e.g. open air shows in parks, factory spaces, and a spiegeltent) with approximately 150 performances per year, mostly in Oxford. 8 actors work on each production. Recent productions include *The Snow Queen* and *King Lear.*

Casting procedures: Does not use freelance casting directors or hold general auditions. Casting breakdowns are available by email application and via Castcall. Welcomes emails (with CVs and photographs) from actors previously unknown to the company at any time of year.

Curious Monkey
Studio 47, B Box Studios, Stoddart Street, Newcastle upon Tyne NE2 1AN
email admin@curiousmonkeytheatre.com
website https://curiousmonkeytheatre.com/
Twitter @curiousmonkey_
Artistic Director Amy Golding

Production details: Curious Money's artistic programme gives a voice to under-represented people and raises awareness of the issues they face. Audiences are often young and new to the theatre. Curious Monkey makes people welcome and speaks in a clear and open language that reflects principles of inclusivity and diversity.

Casting procedures: See the "Work With Us" section of the website for opportunities, or send an email with CV attached to register interest.

Dark Horse
Lawrence Batley Theatre, Queen's Street, Huddersfield HD1 2SP
tel 01484 484441
email info@darkhorsetheatre.co.uk
website www.darkhorsetheatre.co.uk
Artistic Lead Amy Cunningham

Production details: Established in 2000. Production company exploring a range of projects that include actors with learning disabilities and promote inclusive working practices. Approximately 1 production per year touring to 10-15 venues, including arts centres and theatres in Yorkshire, the North West and internationally. Roughly 5-8 actors are used in each production.

Casting procedures: Occasionally uses freelance casting directors. Does not welcome unsolicited CVs. Actively encourages applications from disabled actors and promotes the use of inclusive casting. Offers Equity-approved contracts.

Dead Earnest Theatre
Studio 9, Replicast Studios, 5 East Bank Road, Sheffield, S2 3PT

Theatre

mobile 07855 866292
email info@deadearnest.co.uk
website www.deadearnest.co.uk
Facebook www.facebook.com/deadearnesttheatre
Twitter @deadearnest
Creative Director Charlie Barnes *Project Manager* Blue Merrick *Associate Team* Gareth Bennet-Ryan, Penny Capper, Liam Gerrard, Rachel Newman, Nick Nuttgens, Fiona Paul, Sarah Sayeed, Kitty Randle, Stacey Sampson

Production details: Dead Earnest is an Applied Theatre company based in Sheffield. Since forming in 1993, the company has delivered touring shows, commissioned performances and creative projects in South Yorkshire and across the UK. The company uses a variety of theatre techniques to explore social issues, with a particular focus on Forum Theatre.

Dead Earnest Theatre's work broadly fits into three categories: health and well-being (forum theatre for health professionals and service users); creative learning (working with universities, colleges and schools), and community theatre (working with community organisations and groups exploring issues around inequality and diversity). Has strong links with both Sheffield Hallam University, where the original Artistic Director, Ashley Barnes, is now Head of Stage and Screen, and the University of Sheffield, creating original plays based on academic research.

Stages around 20 productions each year (mainly forum theatre), which all rehearse in Sheffield but are shown throughout the country. Dead Earnest is a member of ITC and supplies Equity-approved contracts but does not subscribe to the Equity pension scheme.

Casting procedures: Uses pool of northern actors. Sometimes holds general auditions. Welcomes email submissions (with CVs and photographs) from actors previously unknown to the company. Actively encourages applications from under-represented groups (including disabled and BAME performers).

Dirty Market Theatre Company

email info@dirtymarket.co.uk
website www.dirtymarket.co.uk
Co-directors Georgina Sowerby, Jon Lee

Production details: A collective of theatre makers with classical training; aims to integrate classical backgrounds with contemporary practice to create imaginative and exciting live performance. Applies for funding on a project-to-project basis, and is a member of ITC.

Casting procedures: Uses freelance casting directors. Casts from open workshops, and actors are advised to participate in these to get to know the company's work. Advertises via the website, Mandy, agents, SPF, etc. Welcomes approaches by actors by post and by email, but prefers to receive showreels by website link. Actively encourages applications from disabled actors.

Eastern Angles Theatre Company

The Eastern Angles Centre, Gatacre Road, Ipswich IP1 2LQ
tel 01473 218202
email admin@easternangles.co.uk
website www.easternangles.co.uk
Artistic Director Ivan Cutting

Production details: Founded in 1982, the company tours theatre productions around East Anglia. New writing and a flavour of the region colour all of its original work. Stages 4-5 pieces each year, with an average annual total of 220 performances at 80 different venues. These include arts centres and theatres, educational and community venues, and site-specific locations. Tours mainly to East England but also nationally on occasion. In general, 6 actors work on each production. Offers ITC/Equity contracts; does not subscribe to the Equity Pension Scheme.

Casting procedures: Does not use freelance casting directors or hold general auditions. Casting breakdowns are not publicly available but may occasionally be posted on the website. Welcomes letters (with CVs and photographs, but not saes); email attachments will not be opened. Advises applicants to consult the website to get an idea of the sort of work the company produces. Applicants should only write once and should specify in their letter if they are local or native to the region. Will consider applications from disabled actors to play characters with disabilities.

The Edge Theatre

Manchester Road, Chorlton, Manchester M21 9JG
tel 0161 2829 776
email info@edgetheatre.co.uk
website www.edgetheatre.co.uk
Facebook www.facebook.com/theedgetheatre
Twitter @theedgemcr
Editor Instagram edgemanchester
Artistic Director Janine Waters

Production details: The Edge is Manchester's award-winning theatre for participation and is a receiving and a producing house. They are members of Paines Plough Small Scale Touring Network and have a particular interest in participatory theatre, musical theatre, new writing and theatre for children. Recent productions include: *Love Shift* (Royal Exchange Theatre 2010), *Spinach* (Royal Exchange Theatre, 2011 and Kings Head, 2012) and *Dreaming Under a Different Moon* (Edge Theatre, 2012). Edge stage 1 in-house production every 2 years. Edge offer Equity/ITC-approved contracts.

Casting procedures: Uses in-house casting directors, but does not hold general auditions. Welcomes unsolicited CVs and photographs and showreels from actors who are strong singers only. Also happy to receive invitations to view productions in the north-west. Actively encourages applications from disabled actors and promotes the use of inclusive casting.

ETT (English Touring Theatre)
25 Short Street, London SE1 8LJ
tel 020 7450 1990
email admin@ett.org.uk
website www.ett.org.uk
Artistic Director Richard Twyman

Production details: ETT are a UK based international touring company. Creating theatre which is ambitious, imaginative, responsive and alive, ETT interrogates and celebrates contemporary England and reflects the diversity of the nation. It tours to mid-large scale venues nationwide, staging a balance of new and classic work, sparking dialogue and fostering connectivity. Each yeat ETT works with around 10 venue partners, touring to 25 towns and cities and reaching an average audience of 75,000 people.

Offers UK Theatre/Equity contracts and subscribes to the Equity Pension Scheme.

Casting procedures: Uses freelance casting directors and does not encourage unsolicited submissions from actors.

The Faction
17 Vanbrugh Park, London SE3 7AF
email info@thefaction.org.uk
website www.thefaction.org.uk
Artistic Director Mark Leipacher *Co-Artistic Director* Rachel Valentine Smith

Production details: Founded in 2008, an independent theatre company dedicated to innovative revivals of classical texts. Aims to generate and sustain an ensemble of actors who share and develop skills, and who can explore a 21st-century solution to the extinct repertory system. "We question what constitutes a 'classical text', and work to determine which authors' works complement and enhance our understanding and enjoyment of Shakespeare and his contemporaries and thus should be a permanent part of the repertoire."

Stages 3+ productions annually, with around 120 performances at 4 venues (arts centres/theatres/ outdoor/educational). In general 8-20 actors are involved in each production. Recent productions include: Highsmith's *The Talented Mr Ripley* (Greenwich Theatre); Shakespeare's *Romeo and Juliet* (Greenwich Theatre); Schiller's *Joan of Arc* (New Diorama Theatre); Lorca's *Blood Wedding* (New Diorama Theatre); Schiller's *Mary Stuart* (New Diorama Theatre/UK tour/Qatar).

Casting procedures: Casts in-house. Casting breakdowns are available from the website, mailing list, email and Mandy. Welcomes letters (with CVs and photographs) from individual actors previously unknown to the company, sent by email. Also accepts showreels and invitations to view actors' websites and visit other productions. Encourages applications from disabled actors and promotes the use of inclusive casting.

Fluellen Theatre Company
14 Devon Place, Swansea SA3 4DR
tel (01792) 368269
email fluellentheatre@aol.com
website www.fluellentheatre.co.uk
Artistic Director Peter Richards *Associate Director* Claire Novelli

Production details: Fluellen is a small-scale classical theatre company producing work from Greek drama to Harold Pinter via Shakespeare. Recently included new drama into programming. All productions premiere at the Grand Theatre Swansea. Recent productions include: *The Merry Wives of Windsor* (Shakespeare), *Antigone* (Sophocles) and *The Late Marilyn Monroe* (a new play by Francis Hardy). Each production consists of a variable number of cast members and, on average, the company present 4 main productions per year, alongside 9 shorter 'Lunchtime Theatre' productions. This equates to around 60 performances at 10 venues in Wales, including arts centres, theatres and outdoor community spaces.

Casting procedures: Uses in-house casting director. General auditions are held several times throughout the year. Welcomes both CVs and letters from actors previously unknown to the Company and unsolicited CVs and photographs. These should be sent via email. Also welcomes invitations to view individual actors' websites and showreels. Happy to consider applications from disabled actors and will consider inclusive casting.

Forced Entertainment
The Workstation, 15 Paternoster Row, Sheffield S1 2BX
tel 0114 279 8977
email fe@forcedentertainment.com
website www.forcedentertainment.com
Key personnel Tim Etchells (*Artistic Director*), Robin Arthur, Richard Lowden, Claire Marshall, Cathy Naden, Terry O'Connor

Production details: Since forming the company in 1984, the 6 core members of the group have sustained a unique artistic partnership, confirming their position as "trailblazers in contemporary theatre". The company's substantial canon of work reflects an interest in the mechanics of performance, the role of the audience, and the machinations of contemporary urban life. Its work, framed and focused by Artistic Director Tim Etchells, is distinctive and provocative, delighting in disrupting the conventions of theatre and the expectations of audiences. Forced Entertainment's trademark collaborative process – devising work as a group through improvisation, experimentation and debate – has made them pioneers of British avant-garde theatre, and touring all over the world has earned them an unparalleled international reputation. Visit the website for a full archive of work.

Forest Forge Theatre Co.

The Theatre Centre, Endeavour Park,
Crow Arch Lane, Ringwood, Hants BH24 1SF
tel 01425 470188
email hello@forestforgetheatre.co.uk
website www.forestforgetheatre.co.uk
Creative Producer Sharon Lawless

Production details: Tours 3 productions a year into
studios, village halls and arts centres, and has a large
Creative Learning programme. The company is
particularly interested in commissioning new work
with rural or regional themes, and second
productions. Recent commissions include: *Free Folk*
by Gary Owen, and *For the Record* by Joyce Branagh.

Frantic Assembly

Brixton House Theatre, 385 Coldharbour Lane,
London SW9 8GL
tel 020 3161 4031
email admin@franticassembly.co.uk
website www.franticassembly.co.uk
Facebook www.facebook.com/franticassembly
Twitter @franticassembly
Artistic Director Scott Graham *Executive Director*
Kerry Whelan

Production details: Award-winning theatre company
Frantic Assembly's method of devising theatre has
been impacting theatrical practice and unlocking the
creative potential of future theatre-makers for over 25
years. Frantic Assembly has toured extensively across
Great Britian, and has worked in 40 countries
internationally collaborating with some of today's
most inspiring artists. Frantic Assembly are currently
studied as leading contemporary theatre practitioners
on five British and international academic syllabuses
and introduce over 15,000 workshop participants to
the company's process of creating theatre annually.
With a history of commissioning writers such as
Simon Stephens, Mark Ravenhill, Abi Morgan and
Bryony Lavery, the company has been accclaimed for
its collaborative approach.

Casting procedures: Does not hold open auditions.
Does not accept unsolicited CVs. External casting
directors are used to cast for productions.

Frantic Theatre Company

32 Wood Lane, Falmouth TR11 4RF
tel 0870 165 7350
email bookings@frantictheatre.com
website www.frantictheatre.com

Production details: Founded in 1990. Stages 2
productions annually with around 900 performances
in venues throughout the UK and Ireland every year.
Venues include arts centres, village halls, theatres,
outdoor venues, educational and community venues,
private homes and hospitals. On average 2 actors
work on each production. Recent productions
include: *You Hum It, I'll Play It.*

Casting procedures: Holds general auditions. Actors
should write in May and November to request

inclusion. Casting breakdowns are available at Call
Pro. Actors are advised not to telephone and to send
their details only when they have researched the
company's very specific work and are able to explain
their suitability.

Freedom Studios

Bradford Design Exchange, 34 Peckover Street,
Little Germany, Bradford BD1 5BD
tel 01274 730077
email hello@freedomstudios.co.uk
website www.freedomstudios.co.uk
Associate Artistic Director Dermot Daly

Production details: Established in 2007. A national
touring, devising theatre company. Stages theatrical
events and experiences at arts centres, theatres and
outdoor venues across the UK. In general 2-4 actors
are involved in each production. Offers Equity-
approved contracts as negotiated through ITC.
Recent productions include *Street Voices 2*. Also holds
the Asian Theatre School for a 15-week period each
year, for aspiring Yorkshire British Asian, Black and
ethnic minority artists; and Unit 4, "a twice-yearly
platform event for some of the most exciting voices
in the UK contemporary arts scene".

Casting procedures: Sometimes holds general
auditions. Welcomes letters (with CVs and
photographs) from individual actors previously
unknown to the company, sent by post or email; also
accepts showreels and invitations to view individual
actors' websites. Will consider applications from
disabled characters to play characters with disabilities.

Galleon Theatre Company Ltd

50 Openshaw Road, London SE2 0TE
tel 020 8310 7276
email boxoffice@galleontheatre.co.uk
website www.galleontheatre.co.uk
Artistic Director Alice de Sousa *Theatre Director* Bruce
Jamieson

Production details: For recent productions, please
see the website. Also has a film company, Galleon
Films Ltd, which is developing a slate of 4 feature
films.

Casting procedures: Uses an in-house casting
director. Holds general auditions; actors should write
to request inclusion when the company is casting for
a specific project. Casting breakdowns are available
through CastNet and advertisements in *The Stage*.
Welcomes letters (with CVs and photographs) but
not email submissions. Showreels and invitations to
view individual actors' websites are also accepted.

Goat and Monkey

email info@goatandmonkey.co.uk
website www.goatandmonkey.co.uk
Director Joel Scott *Producer* Sally Scott

Production details: Founded in 2004, Goat and
Monkey create immersive and site-specific theatre

that is highly visual, detailed and ambitious. Their work pushes the boundaries of audience interaction and theatrical form and looks to provide a unique experience for audiences in a variety of different environments. Recent productions include: *The Devil Speaks True* (tour), *The Moonlight Club*, *The Perils of Poisonous Plants* (Kew Gardens) and *The Seed* (live performances, online story and real-world treasure hunt. Each production can include 1-45 actors and, on average, the company present 1 production and several smaller research-based projects per year. Performances take place in theatres, found sites and outdoor venues across London and the south-east. Offers ITC-based contracts.

Casting procedures: Uses freelance casting directors and only holds production specific auditions. Welcomes both CVs and letters from actors previously unknown to the company if sent by email. Also welcomes invitations to view individual actors' websites, but does not welcome showreels. Casting breakdowns are available through the website and Spotlight. Would welcome the chance to cast disabled actors.

Gomito Productions

email sam@gomito.co.uk
website wwww.gomito.co.uk
Producer Sam Worboys

Production details: Founded in 2001, Gomito is a collaboration of artists making new visual theatre. The company is an ever-changing family of performers, designers, directors, musicians and writers who want to share stories in a certain way; with creativity, entertainment, humour, emotion and homespun roughness; with theatricality at its simplest. Recent productions include: *The Achemystorium*, *Woodland* and *Chester Tuffnut*. Each production consists of 3-6 actors and, on average, the company present 1-3 productions per year. This equates to over 50 performances at over 25 venues, including art centres, theatres and educational establishments. Productions also tour nationally.

Casting procedures: Gomito primarily uses its open workshops for casting at various times throughout the year. Email or join the mailing list on the website for details. Welcomes both CVs and letters from actors previously unknown to the company and unsolicited CVs and photographs. Also welcomes invitations to view individual actors' websites and showreels.

Graeae Theatre Company

Bradbury Studios, 138 Kingsland Road,
London E2 8DY
tel 020 7613 6900
email info@graeae.org
website www.graeae.org
Artistic Director Jenny Sealey

Production details: Founded in 1980 and artistically led by Jenny Sealey, Graeae boldly places D/deaf and disabled actors centre stage.

Graeae's signature aesthetic is the compelling creative integration of sign language, captioning and audio description, which engages with both disabled and non-disabled audiences. Championing accessibility and providing a platform for new generations of artists, Graeae leads the way in pioneering, trail-blazing theatre. Graeae also run an extensive programme of creative learning opportunities throughout the year, training and developing the next generation of D/deaf and disabled artists. These programmes include Write to Play and Ensemble.

Recent productions and co-productions include: *Reasons to be Cheerful*, *Cosmic Scallies*, *The House of Bernarda Alba*, *The Solid Life of Sugar Water*, *Blood Wedding*, *The Threepenny Opera*, *Belonging*, *Blasted* and *Bent*. Spectacular outdoor productions include *This is Not for You*, *The Limbless Knight*, *Prometheus Awakes* and *The Iron Man*.

Graeae are strategic partners on the Ramps on the Moon consortium and are a National Portfolio Organisation (NPO) of Arts Council England.

Green Ginger

Unit 18, Albion Dockside Estate, Hanover Place,
Bristol BS1 6UT
mobile 07977 465850
email mail@greenginger.net
website www.greenginger.net
Facebook www.facebook.com/greengingertheatre
Twitter @greenginger
Artistic Director Chris Pirie *Patron* Terry Gilliam

Production details: Founded in 1978, Green Ginger creates and tours original theatre with complementary educational activities for all ages and all abilities. Green Ginger collaborates with major arts organisations, including Welsh National Opera and Aardman Animations. Its members teach at University of Bristol, École Supérieure Nationale de la Marionette (France) and the Royal Welsh College of Music and Drama. Recent productions include: *Outpost* (2014), *Intronauts* (2018) and *RATLab* (2021).

Each production consists of 3-4 actors and, on average, the company presents 2 productions a year. The company tours extensively, having performed around the world for 40 years. Touring productions can be adapted to a variety of venues including schools, theatres, community spaces and outdoor and non-traditional theatre spaces. Offers Equity/ITC approved contracts at above minimum rates.

Casting procedures: Uses freelance casting directors and occasionally holds general auditions. Casting breakdowns are available online and on social media. Welcomes both CVs and letters from performers previously unknown to the company and unsolicited CVs and photographs. Also welcomes invitations to view individual actors' websites and showreels. The company welcomes the opportunity to cast performers with protected or under-represented characteristics.

Theatre

Grid Iron Theatre Company

Suite 4/1, 2 Commercial Street, Edinburgh EH6 6JA
tel 0131 555 5455
email admin@gridiron.org.uk
website www.gridiron.org.uk
Co-Artistic Directors Judith Doherty, Ben Harrison

Production details: Founded in 1995. Produces new writing and site-specific theatre. Stages 1-3 productions annually and gives 20-50 performances every year. Performs in theatres, outdoor and site-specific venues in Scotland, England and Northern and the Republic of Ireland. Recent productions include: *Huxley's Lab, Barflies, Once Upon a Dragon* and *Roam.*

Casting procedures: Sometimes holds general auditions. Actors may write requesting inclusion at any time throughout the year. Welcomes submissions (with CVs and photographs) sent by post and email. Showreels and invitations to view individual actors' websites are also accepted.

Headlong Theatre

Third Floor, 207 Waterloo Road, London DE1 8XD
tel 020 7633 2090
email info@headlongtheatre.co.uk
website www.headlong.co.uk
Artistic Director Holly Race Roughan

Production details: National touring theatre company dedicated to creating exhilarating contemporary theatre through a provocative mix of innovative new writing, reimagined classics and influential 20th century new plays. Tours nationally and internationally. Recent productions include: *Jitney* (Leeds Playhouse, Old Vic, UK tour); *Corrina, Corrina* (Liverpool Everyman, Playhouse); *Best of Enemies* (Young Vic); and *After Life* (National Theatre).

Casting procedures: Offers TMA/Equity approved contracts. Casting not dealt with in-house. Independent casting directors used on a show-by-show basis. Show invitations can be sent via email.

Hidden Talent Productions Ltd

50ᴅ Wickham Road, Brockley, London SE4 1NZ
mobile 07905 175934
email info@hiddentalent.org.uk
website www.hiddentalent.org.uk
Artistic Director Adam Linsson *Casting Director* Andrew Miller

Production details: Established in 2006 as a not-for-profit, small-scale theatre producing company. Stages primarily new musicals and cabarets. Aims to raise the profile of musical theatre in the community by producing new works. Tours to small venues across the UK. Offers closed workshop performances and readings through to fully staged musical productions in larger theatres. Stages on average 1 production in the main house and 2 in the studio each year. Recent productions include: *Heaven Sent, A New Musical Comedy* (World Premiere – New Wimbledon Studio); *Manhattan Melodies in the West End* (Dominion Theatre Studio) and numerous cabarets.

Casting procedures: Uses in-house casting directors. Sometimes holds general auditions; actors may write in at any time, but preferably when the company is casting specific projects. Casting breakdowns are available via the website or on postal application with an sae. Welcomes letters (with CVs and photographs) from individual actors previously unknown to the company sent by post or email. Accepts showreels and invitations to view individual actors' websites. Will consider applications from disabled actors to play characters with disabilities.

Highly Sprung Performance Company

Daimler Powerhouse, Sandy Lane Business Park, Sandy Lane, Coventry, CV1 4DQ
tel 07810 263355
email team@highlysprungperformance.co.uk
website www.highlysprungperformance.co.uk
Artistic Director Mark Worth *Executive Director* Sarah Worth

Production details: Founded in 1999. Aims to create original and innovative performances exploring the relationship between dance, text and physical theatre. Also runs community and educational activities alongside productions. Stages 1 production annually with 25 performances every year. Tours 10-15 venues annually: these include arts centres, theatres, outdoor and educational venues in the West Midlands, London, Manchester and Edinburgh. On average 2-8 actors work on each production. Recent productions include: *Pretend I'm Not Here* and *More Than Kisses.*

Casting procedures: Holds general auditions. Actors should send CVs and photographs by post or email. These will be kept on file for future auditions. Casting breakdowns are available on the website, by postal application and via Equity Job information Service and advertisements in *The Stage.* Showreels and invitations to view individual actors' websites are also accepted.

Hijinx

Wales Millennium Centre, Bute Place, Cardiff CF10 5AL
tel 029 2030 0331
email info@hijinx.org.uk
website www.hijinx.org.uk
Facebook www.facebook.com/HijinxTheatre
Twitter @HijinxTheatre
Instagram @HijinxTheatre
Artistic Director Ben Pettitt-Wade

Production details: An award-winning not-for-profit professional theatre company. Hijinx always casts actors with learning disabilities and/or Autism in their shows which tour the world.

Offers ITC/Equity-approved contracts and does not subscribe to the Equity Pension Scheme.

Casting procedures: Shows are cast by the Artistic Director. Welcomes letters, CVs and photographs from actors previously unknown to the company. Welcomes applications from disabled and non-disabled actors.

Historia Theatre Company
8 Cloudesley Square, London N1 0HT
tel 020 7837 8008
email historiatheatre@yahoo.co.uk
website https://historia25.wixsite.com/historicatheatre
Facebook @theatrecompanyhistoria
Artistic Director Catherine Price

Production details: Established in 1997, now a registered charity. "Historia presents plays that have their source or inspiration in history." 1 production annually, with 20-30 performances. Plays in small theatres in London mainly for short runs; touring productions visit theatres, arts venues, National Trust houses, museums, churches, schools and village halls both nationally and in London. Roughly 6-8 actors are used in each production. Recent productions include: *Mayflower: They Knew They Were Pilgrims* (2020–22); *Dear Chocolate Soldier* (2018–19); *Fire and Phoenix* (2016); *Magna Carta* (2015); *Queen Anne* (2014); and schools tour of *The Sound of Breaking Glass* by Sally Sheringham (2012–2013). Offers ITC/Equity rates where possible.

Casting procedures: Does not use freelance casting directors or hold general auditions. Breakdowns are published via Equity's Job Information Service and Spotlight link. Unsolicited approaches from actors are discouraged. Will consider applications from disabled actors when casting for characters with disabilities.

Horse + Bamboo
679 Bacup Road, Waterfoot, Rossendale, Lancashire BB4 7HQ
tel (01706) 220241
email info@horseandbamboo.org
website www.horseandbamboo.org
Facebook www.facebook.com/horseandbamboo
Twitter @horseandbamboo
Instagram @horseandbamboo
Creative Development Director Esther Ferry-Kennington *Executive Producer* Jenn Camilleri

Production details: Established in 1978. A puppetry, mask and processional theatre. Houses a 90 seat theatre and bar, and a Creative Centre offering a rehearsal room and fully equipped making workshop for artists to collaborate, create and share their work. Also includes a unique archive of 4 decades of visual theatre, national and international touring, processional arts, puppetry, music and mask. Producers of Waterfoot Wakes annual summer festival. Offers Equity contracts. Members of ITC.

Casting procedures: Welcomes communication from touring theatre companies and socially engaged artists.

Icarus Theatre Collective
5 Elephant Lane, London SE16 4JD
tel 020 7998 1562
website www.icarustheatre.co.uk
Facebook www.facebook.com/icarustheatre
Twitter @icarustheatre
Instagram @icarustheatre
COO Georgina Evans *Artistic Director* Max Lewendel

Production details: Icarus creates theatre that is kinetic, intellectual, and visceral: theatre that moves. We choose to relish what others shy away from, destroy boundaries when others would create rules. We explore harsh, brutal themes with a modern exploration of Theatre of the Absurd in classic and contemporary storytelling. We are changing our focus this year to tackle the increasingly dangerous nativist, misogynist, and racist rhetoric. We will:

• Put female, EU, and BAME artists in staff positions and the central role of new productions
• Ensure disability and demographic are no barrier to making art
• Defy the stigmas surrounding mental health, proving it is a prevalent issue in our society and one that all our central characters live with.

Also work in Education, Outreach & Community, for which the key contact is **edu@icarustheatre.co.uk**. Recent productions include: *How to Be a Bad Girl* by Sabrina Chap; *Macbeth* and *Hamlet* by William Shakespeare; *The Trials of Galileo* by Nic Young; *H.P. Lovecraft's At the Mountains of Madness* adapted by Max Lewendel; *The Lesson* by Eugène Ionesco; *Journey's End* by R.C. Sherriff; and *Vincent in Brixton* by Nicholas Wright.

Casting procedures: Uses in-house casting directors. Holds general auditions; actors should write in when advised to do so by the company's newsletter. Casting breakdowns are available from the website and are advertised in Spotlight. Welcomes letters (with CVs and photographs) sent by post or email but no attachments via email. Accepts showreels or invitations to view individual actors' websites or performances.

Jam Theatre Company
45A West Street, Marlow, Buckinghamshire SL7 2LS
tel 01628 483808
email office@jamtheatre.co.uk
website www.jamtheatre.co.uk
Artistic Director Jo Carter *Company Director* Mark Hartley

Production details: Founded in 2006, Jam Theatre Company is a professional theatre company writing and producing original productions for their own studio theatre and for transfer to commercial theatres. Shows are available for co-productions and licensing in the UK and America with Samuel French, London or via the Jam Theatre website. Jam also offer full-time and e-learning programmes in theatre and performing arts. Jam pays above Equity minimums, but doesn't offer approved contracts. Recent productions include: *Cinderella and the 7 Dwarfs*, *Santa's Secret Escape* and *Spots and Stripes*.

Casting procedures: Casting breakdowns are available through the website, Spotlight and Castweb. Welcomes CVs and letters from actors previously unknown to the company via email and online links to showreels. Also happy to receive production notices and invitations to view individual actors' websites. Will consider applications from disabled actors to play characters with disabilities.

Jasperian Theatre Company

Milsrof, Eglos Road, Ludgvan Churchtown, Penzance TR208HG
tel 01736 740907 *mobile* 07941 616177
email tony.jasper@btinternet.com
website www.jasperian.org
Artistic Director Tony Jasper *Production Directors* Kenneth Pickering, Peter Moreton, Harry Gostelow, Clare Davidson

Production details: Founded in 1992, JTC specialises in plays and revues that have a religious underpinning and/or deal with the human condition. The company casts all shows on artistic ability – not on any religious affiliation. Normally stages 3-5 productions each year with possibly a total of around 100 performances. Tours to a variety of different venues including theatres, churches and private houses across the UK. In general 3-7 actors work on each production. Recent productions include: *Charles Wesley 1707* (100 venues), *Stories of Grace, It Happened One Friday* and *God's Trombones*.

Casting procedures: Uses freelance casting directors. Actors may write requesting inclusion in the next round of auditions at any time, but the beginning of February, June and September are normally good times. Casting breakdowns are available through casting agencies. Prefers actors to send in their details by post but will accept the occasional email. Showreels are also accepted. Advises actors to read audition notices carefully and only come if suitable and available over the time period specified. Offers non-Equity contracts; however, "Apart from usually £250-£350 I also offer all accommodation and meals paid, and in some instances this is better than a basic Equity contract. I attempt to cast only Equity members. In 18 years, no-one has been owed money [by me]." Encourages applications from disabled actors and promotes the use of inclusive casting.

Kabosh

Imperial Buildings, 72 High Street, Belfast BT1 2BE
tel 028 9024 3343
email artisticdirector@kabosh.net
website www.kabosh.net
Artistic Director Paula McFetridge

Production details: Founded in 1994. Produces innovative physical and visual theatre for local,

national and international touring and site-specific work. Stages 2-4 productions annually with 56 performances during the course of the year. Tours to around 30 venues annually, including arts centres and theatres, and site-specific locations. In general 2-6 actors are involved in each production. Countries covered include Northern Ireland, Republic of Ireland, England (including London), Scotland, Wales, parts of Europe and North America. Recent productions include: *Rhinoceros* and *Todd*.

Casting procedures: Auditions are by invitation only. Actors should write requesting inclusion in July (for autumn productions) and November (for spring productions). Welcomes applications (with CVs and photographs) sent by post and email. Also accepts invitations to view individual actors' websites. Any actor known to the company is welcome to send a CV and headshot (which will be kept on file) and to notify the director of performances where their work may be seen. The director will endeavour to see new actors. Any unseen actor who has sent a CV will be notified of open auditions, should they arise.

Kali Theatre Company

The Albany, Douglas Way, Deptford, London SE8 4AG
tel 020 8694 6033
email info@kalitheatre.co.uk
website www.kalitheatre.co.uk
Artistic Director Helen Bell

Production details: Founded in 1991 to develop and promote new writing by women of South Asian descent. One touring production each year, playing to national audiences. Nurtures emerging playwrights through a two level Writer Development Programme alongside commissioning mid-career playwrights for production. Script development work culminates in annual public readings of new plays. Has worked with writers such as Tanika Gupta, Rukhsana Ahmad, Nessah Muthy, Naylah Ahmed and Shelley Silas among others. Recent productions include: *Homing Birds, Sundowning, The Dishonoured, Mustapha* and *My Big Fat Cowpat Wedding*. See website for further details.

Casting procedures: Welcomes letters (with CV and photograph) from South Asian actors previously unknown to the company by email. Does not accept showreels or invitations to view individual actors' websites. Rarely (or never) has the opportunity to cast disabled actors. "Phone to find out what we are casting before sending CVs and photos".

LipService

Z-Arts, 335 Stretford Road, Manchester M15 5ZA
tel 0161 232 6093/4
email info@lip-service.net
website www.lipservicetheatre.co.uk
Joint Artistic Directors Sue Ryding, Maggie Fox

Production details: Over the past 20 years, LipService has established itself as one of the leading comedy touring companies, producing shows for the theatre which have a strong base in popular culture. These include: *The Picture of Doreen Gray*; *Inspector Norse* (a self-assembly Swedish crime thriller); *Desperate to be Doris*; *Jane Bond* (blonde and dangerous; a spoof of all things Bond); *Very Little Women* (a comic version of Louisa May Alcott's *Little Women*); *Hector's House* (an epic tale of togas and taramasalata); *The Importance of Being Earnest* (a trivial comedy for serious people); *Women on the Verger* (a hilarious look at romantic women's fiction); *Move Over Moriarty* (an impenetrable case for Sherlock Holmes and Doctor Watson); and *Withering Looks* (a slice of life with the Brontë Sisters).

LipService attracts audiences from a wide social mix and age range. Based in Manchester, the company has built up a solid touring circuit in the North of England and throughout the rest of Britain. Challenges its audience by setting up a recognisable form and subverting it. This is partly achieved by two women playing all the characters, but also by ingenious theatrical surprises. "Along with the National Theatre of Brent, LipService is one of our great 2-person ensembles." (*Guardian*)

Casting procedures: Uses casting directors of co-producing venue. Does not hold general auditions. Actors should write requesting inclusion when extra performers are needed for a new production. Casting breakdowns are available direct from the co-producing theatre; details of co-producers are available via the website. Welcomes invitations from actors to view their work and from actors familiar with the company's work. Offers TMA/Equity-approved contracts.

London Bubble Theatre Co.

3-5 Elephant Lane, London SE16 4JD
tel 020 7237 4434
email admin@londonbubble.org.uk
website www.londonbubble.org.uk
Artistic Director Marie Vickers

Production details: The company's mission is "to attract and involve a wide range of audiences and participants, particularly those experiencing theatre for the first time, to inventive and unpredictable events that reflect the diversity of our city and its people".

To this end, the company has the following aims:

• To work particularly with and for people who do not normally have access to theatre for geographical, financial or cultural reasons
• To encourage and enable people to develop their own theatre and related skills
• To work to create a popular theatre form which is open, exciting and accessible
• To produce events which demonstrate and celebrate the creative abilities of all those taking part
• To examine issues of common concern to all those involved through the choice of material for workshops, projects and professional performances

• To challenge prejudice and bigotry through the company's organisation, working processes and final product
• To achieve a diversity of influence that is discernible throughout the company's work and consciousness

Recent productions include: the We Need to Act On Showcase, *Primary*, *Tales from the Arabian Nights*, *After Hiroshima*, *Hopelessly De-Voted*, and *From Docks to Desktops*.

Lurking Truth

Gwynfryn, Newtown Road, Machynlleth, Powys SY20 8EY
tel (01654) 702200
email davidianrabey@gmail.com
website www.theatre-wales.co.uk/companies/company_details.asp?ID=21
Artistic Director & Secretary David Ian Rabey

Production details: Founded in 1986, Lurking Truth present contemporary work and premieres by dramatists such as Howard Barker, David Ian Rabey, David Rudkin and Arnold Wesker. This is sometimes done in association with Aberystwyth University Department of Theatre, Film and Television Studies, and several alumni of the department have gone on to work with the company.

Casting procedures: Uses in-house casting directors. Welcomes unsolicited CVs (with photographs) sent by email. Also welcomes invitations to view individual actors' websites, but does not welcome showreels.

Magnetic North Theatre Productions

Summerhall, Summerhall Place, Ediburgh EH9 1PL
email mail@magneticnorth.org.uk
website www.magneticnorth.org.uk
Director Nicholas Bone *Producer* Darrell Williams
Marketing James Coutts

Production details: Founded in 1999. Commissions and produces new plays, music-theatre, installations, online events and films. Also runs a cross art form Artist Development programme for early- and mid-career artists. Stages 1-2 productions annually and gives 20-40 performances during the course of a year. Tours on average to 12 venues annually. About 5 actors are involved in each production. Recent productions include: *Our Fathers*, *A Walk at the Edge of the World*, *Sex and God*, *Pass the Spoon* and *Walden*.

Casting procedures: Sometimes holds general auditions. Actors should write to request inclusion when productions are announced on the website. Casting breakdowns are publicly available through the website. Welcomes submissions (with CVs and photographs) sent by post or email. Also accepts invitations to view individual actors' websites. Advises that the company has a low turnover of productions and a small staff, and finds it difficult to respond to general enquiries about available work.

Theatre

MANACTCO (formerly Manchester Actors Company)

31 Leslie Street, Manchester M14 7NE
tel 0161 445 8477
email admin@manactco.org.uk
website www.manactco.org.uk
Artistic Director Stephen Boyes

Production details: Established in 1980 and now the North West's leading provider of theatre in schools. "We are emphatically *not* a TIE company." Reaches well over 60,000 young people each year with around 3-4 touring productions. Recent productions include: *The Tempest, Of Mice and Men, The Pirate Queen, Much Ado About Nothing,* and *Poetry in Motion.*

Casting procedures: Uses in-house casting directors and sometimes holds general auditions. Actors may write in June/July requesting inclusion. Casting breakdowns are available via Equity Job Information Service and specific casting websites, for example Mandy. Welcomes letters (with CVs and photographs) from individual actors previously unknown to the company, sent by post or email; also welcomes showreels and invitations to view individual actors' websites. Actively encourages applications from disabled actors and promotes the use of inclusive casting. "We give priority to formally trained actors who have completed recognised courses at drama school. We like actors who can face the rigours of touring with good humour!"

Guy Masterson Productions

email guy@guymasterson.com
Artistic Director Guy Masterson

Production details: Olivier Award-winning producer of small- to mid-scale touring theatre work. Stages 4-6 productions annually with up to 400 touring performances a year. Touring access to 500 different national and international venues, including arts centres, theatres, arts festivals and outdoor, educational and community venues. Recent productions include: *The Shark is Broken, The Marilyn Conspiracy, A Christmas Carol, Morecambe* (Olivier Award for Best Entertainment), *Shylock* and *The Odd Couple.*

Casting procedures: Rarely holds auditions. Mainly works with actors seen previously or by invitation.

Meeting Ground Theatre Co.

4 Shirley Road, Nottingham NG3 5DA
tel 07730 384000
website www.meetinggroundtheatrecompany.co.uk
Artistic directors Tanya Myers and Stephen Lowe

Production details: Since 1985 Meeting Ground has been celebrating the meeting of artists from different disciplines and cultures. Administered from its Nottingham base, the company draws together writers, actors, musicians, directors, puppeteers, designers and digital artists, and encourages community participation. Work is based on the belief that by taking artistic work across barriers, whether they be national, psychological, intellectual, cultural, spiritual or disciplinary, new sources of energy and creativity can be engendered. At the heart of the company's artistic policy and vision is the theatrical exploration of what we call the 'politics of the imagination; issues and questions that control the imagination and shape all our destinies. We actively seek to listen and give voice to the unheard.'

Casting procedures: Offers ITC/Equity contracts and does not subscribe to the Equity Pension Scheme. Actively encourages applications from disabled actors and promotes the use of inclusive casting.

Middle Child

67 William St, Hull HU1 2SP
tel 01482 221857
website www.middlechildtheatre.co.uk
Twitter @MiddleChildHull
Artistic Director Paul Smith

Production details: A Hull-based company creating gig theatre that brings people together for a good night out with big ideas. Tells untold stories which capture the electrifying moment when the beat drops, mixing original live music with bold new writing. Recent shows include *Us Against Whatever, Canary and the Crow* and *The Little Mermaid.*

Casting procedures: Usually runs open auditions for productions and will share all details of these opportunities on the website, social media and artist development mailing list. Sign up to mailing list on the website to hear about opportunities. Occasionally casts directly, especially if there are specific requirements for a particular show. For further information, see relevant email contacts on website.

Midland Actors Theatre (MAT)

25 Merrishaw Road, Northfield,
Birmingham B31 3SL
tel 0121 608 7144 *mobile* 07946 006511
email david@midlandactorstheatre.com
website www.midlandactorstheatre.com
Facebook www.facebook.com/midlandactors
Twitter @midlandactors
Instagram @midlandactors
Director David Allen *Associate Director* Gillian Adamson

Production details: Founded in 1999. Produces classics and new work. Specialises in theatre tours, community productions and schools-based projects. Stages 1-2 productions annually with 30-40 performances during the course of the year. Tours on average to 25 different theatres, schools and other venues in the West Midlands, East Midlands and nationally each year. Around 2-5 actors are involved in each production. Recent productions include: *Descent, Macbeth, Prospero's Island, The Children, The Mothers, The Good Person of Sezuan* and *The White*

Shining Land. Offers ITC/Equity-approved contracts and does not subscribe to the Equity Pension Scheme.

Casting procedures: Sometimes holds general auditions. Actors should write requesting inclusion when auditions are advertised; general casting enquiries are most welcome in January and June. Casting breakdowns are publicly available via the Equity Job Information Service. Advises that the company is primarily interested in actors who are Midlands based. Actively encourages applications from disabled actors and promotes the use of inclusive casting.

Mikron Theatre Company

Marsden Mechanics, Peel Street, Marsden, Huddersfield HD7 6BW
tel 01484 843701
email admin@mikron.org.uk
website www.mikron.org.uk
Twitter @mikrontheatre
Artistic Director Marianne McNamara

Production details: Theatre anywhere for everyone, by canal, river and road. Has been touring for 50 years: "Mighty little Mikron" (*Guardian*). Only works with actor musicians. Tours on Tyseley, the company's historic narrowboat, on the inland waterways of Britain in the summer, and by road in the autumn months.

Casting procedures: Does not hold general auditions. Actors are advised to keep an eye on the website. Casting breakdowns are publicly available from the website, via Spotlight. Welcomes letters and emails (with CVs and photographs) from actor musicians only. Does not accept showreels. Asks actors to "please bear in mind that this is a hard tour: boating all day and shows and get-ins every night. Do consult the website before applying".

Mimbre

Unit 4, Energy Centre, Bowling Green Walk, London N1 6AL
tel 020 7613 1068
email info@mimbre.co.uk
website www.mimbre.co.uk
Artistic Directors Lina Johnansson, Silvia Fratelli

Production details: A local and international circus and street theatre company, using circus skills and dance to produce innovative work and promote a strong, positive image of women. Works in unconventional settings, creating moments of the unexpected and reclaiming some beauty in the urban environment. Mimbre's performances and participation programme are designed to reach beyond social, financial and cultural boundaries and find fresh ways to engage, encourage and inspire audiences, both nationally and internationally. Stages 1-2 main shows and works in collaboration with 50-60 performances in 15-20 arts centres, outdoor and festival venues, and theatres across the UK and Europe. In general 3-6 performers are involved in each production. Latest productions: *Look Mum, No Hands!* (co-production with Daryl Beeton Productions, premiered April 2022), *The Sofa Dance* (first broadcast July 2020) and *Lifted* (premiered June 2019).

Casting procedures: Uses in-house casting directors; holds general auditions only when producing a new show. Welcomes letters (with CVs and photographs) from individual performers previously unknown to the company, sent by email. Accepts showreels, performance notices and invitations to view performers' websites. Actively encourages applications from disabled actors and promotes the use of inclusive casting.

New Earth Theatre

The Albany, Douglas Way, Deptford, London SE8 4AG
tel 020 8694 6631
email hello@newearththeatre.org.uk
website www.newearththeatre.org.uk
Artistic Director Kumiko Mendl

Production details: New Earth Theatre presents and develops work with British East and South East Asian (BESEA) artists that asks key questions of identity, of the world we live in and our place in that world. It produces touring plays and readings across the year, nurtures BESEA talent through their Academy acting and writing courses and Professional Writers' Programme, as well as bringing artists to communities, museums and schools. New Earth Theatre was established in 1995 and is a member of ITC.

Casting procedures: Casts in-house. Sometimes holds general auditions. Welcomes emails with CVs and photographs from actors with East and South East Asian heritage only. Promotes the use of inclusive casting.

East and South East Asian includes: Brunei, Burma, Cambodia, China, East Timor, Hong Kong, Indonesia, Japan, Laos, Malaysia, Mongolia, North Korea, Philippines, Singapore, South Korea, Taiwan, Thailand, Vietnam and their diasporas.

New Perspectives Theatre Co.

8 Park Lane Business Centre, Park Lane, Nottingham NG6 0DW
tel 0115 927 2334
email info@newperspectives.co.uk
website www.newperspectives.co.uk
Artistic Director Angharad Jones

Production details: Founded in 1973. A leading East Midlands touring theatre company; also tours nationally. On average stages 2-3 productions each year, touring all over the county including theatres, arts centres and rural venues. Equity-approved contracts as negotiated through ITC. Recent productions include: *The Fishermen* (HOME, Edinburgh, national tour and West End run); *A Fortunate Man* (Edinburgh, national tour, Singnapore Fringe, Cologne); *The Wolf, The Duck and The Mouse* (Unicorn Theatre co-production); national tours of *Crossings* (co-production with Pentabus); *The Man Without A Past*; and *trade*.

Casting procedures: Promotes the use of inclusive casting. Casting breakdowns are available through Spotlight Link and from the website.

New Shoes Theatre

email admin@newshoestheatre.org.uk
website www.newshoestheatre.org.uk
Facebook www.facebook.com/NewShoesTheatre
Twitter @newshoestheatre
Artistic Director Nicolette Kay

Production details: The company stages 1 or 2 productions annually. Recent productions include: *Hurried Steps* by award-winning writer Dacia Mariani, which is performed to raise awareness of violence against women and girls, in arts centres, theatres, educational and community venues; and *Jeannie* by Aimée Stuart produced in association with Neil McPherson for the Finborough Theatre. Up to 8 actors can be involved in each production.

Casting procedures: Uses in-house casting directors. Casting breakdowns can be found on sites such as their website, *The Stage*, Spotlight, Mandy and Arts Jobs, and social media such as Twitter and Facebook.

No Limits Theatre

Arts Centre Washington, Biddick Lane, Washington NE38 8AB
tel 0191 4154966
email info@nolimitstheatre.org.uk
website www.nolimitstheatre.org.uk
Artistic Director/Chief Executive Janet Nettleton
Associate Director Alan Parker

Production details: Founded in 1995, No Limits is a touring theatre company that works with adults with and without learning disabilities. Aims to produce high-quality, devised work that challenges traditional perceptions of theatre and disability, staging 1 production in 20 different venues across the UK each year. It also has a strong commitment to outreach and development work. In general 5-8 actors work on each production. Recent productions include: *Attic*, *The Winged State* and *Cuckoo Jack*.

Casting procedures: Welcomes letters, CVs and photographs from actors previously unknown to the company, but does not accept emails or unsolicited showreels. Advises that the company already has a core acting team but often takes on new actors in workshop training sessions.

Northern Broadsides Theatre Company

Fletchers Mill, Dean Clough, Halifax HX3 5AX
tel 01422 369704
website www.northern-broadsides.co.uk
Facebook www.facebook.com/NorthernBroadsides
Twitter @NBroadsides
Instagram @northern_broadsides
Artistic Director Laurie Sansom

Production details: Formed in 1992 by Barrie Rutter, Northern Broadsides is a multi-award winning touring company based in Halifax. The company has built up a formidable reputation performing Shakespeare and classical texts with an innovative, popular and regional style. The company tours extensively in the UK, and has delighted audiences across the world, touring to India, Brazil, the USA, Greece, Cyprus, the Czech Republic, Poland, Germany, Austria and Denmark.

Makes bold, radical and accessible productions of classic and new plays that both reflect the diversity and multiplicity of voices in the north, and act as a catalyst for change throughout the region.

Northern Broadsides' work is characterised by its vitality, humour and passion.

NTC Touring Theatre Company

The Dovecote Centre, Amble, Northumberland NE65 0DX
tel 01665 713655
email admin@northumberlandtheatre.co.uk
website www.northumberlandtheatre.co.uk
Artistic Director Louis Roberts

Production details: Founded in 1978 as Northumberland Theatre Company. Small-scale touring theatre company performing at village halls, small theatres and community venues in predominantly rural areas. Main areas of work are new writing and physical theatre pieces. Stages 2+ productions annually with more than 90 performances during the course of the year. Up to 5 actors are involved in each production.

Casting procedures: Holds audition workshops for locally based actors, usually in the spring. Casting breakdowns are available on the website, Facebook via Equity and Arts Jobs. Welcomes submissions (with CVs and photographs) by email. Also accepts invitations to view individual actors' performances and will always reply to individual actors. Particularly interested in locally based actors or actors with local origins, and will keep details on file for future reference unless requested to do otherwise. Actively promotes the use of inclusive casting.

Open Clasp Theatre Company

The Stephenson Building, 173 Elswick Road, Newcastle-upon-Tyne NE4 6SQ
tel 0191 272 4063
email info@openclasp.org.uk
website www.openclasp.org.uk
Facebook www.facebook.com/OpenClaspTheatreco
Twitter @OpenClasp
Artistic Director Catrina McHugh MBE

Production details: Open Clasp makes truthful, risk-taking and award-winning theatre informed by the lived experiences of working-class women, women disenfranchised in the theatre and society, those from minority communities and women affected by the criminal justice system. They take a special interest in women and young women from the North, shining a light on their experiences through our work. Open Clasp make space for debate, encouraging audiences to walk in the shoes of the most disempowered women in society. Their work is performed in theatres, prisons, village halls, schools, conferences and community centres and most recently, the Edinburgh Fringe and off-Broadway to national and international acclaim. It resonates deep into the communities where it is created and outside ensures the under-respresented are seen in a new light by women, men and those with the power to make a difference.

On average stages 1 touring production per year, usually in Oct-Nov, first stage developments in March and one-off project commissions. Tours/previews include approx. 30 performances in 20+ arts centres, theatres and educational and community venues in the North East, South East, Yorkshire and London. Recent productions include: *Rattle Snake, Key Change, Sugar* (preview tour), *The Space Between Us, Swags & Tails, BlueGiro,* and *Rattle & Roll.*

Casting procedures: Sometimes holds general auditions; actors requesting inclusion should write in January. Casting breakdowns are available from the website, by postal application with sae, and from online casting services. Welcomes letters (with CVs and photographs) from individual actors previously unknown to the company, sent by post or email, but does not accept showreels. Will consider invitations to view individual actors' websites if accompanied by a full CV. Encourages applications from disabled actors. "It is paramount that our actors share the ethos of the company. Open Clasp ensures that casting is representative of the diverse groups we work with, the issues explored, and the characters they have created."

Original Theatre

Dovedon Hall Office, Chedburgh Road, Whepstead, Bury St Edmunds, Suffolk IP29 4UB
tel 0870 803 0158
email info@originaltheatre.com
website www.originaltheatre.com
Artistic Director Alastair Whatley

Production details: Operating and touring since 2004, the Original Theatre company has toured extensively all over the UK and in 2020 launched Original Theatre online. Recent online productions include *Birdsong, Apollo 13: The Dark Side of the Moon, The Haunting of Alice Bowles, Barnses' People* and *A Splinter of Ice*; *Being Mr Wickham, A Cold Supper Behind Harrods* and *The System* were streamed

online. Recent stage productions include *The Hound of the Baskervilles, A Splinter of Ice, The Croft,* Sarah Waters' *The Night Watch,* Stephen Jeffreys' *Valued Friends* (co-produced with Rose Theatre Kingston), Torben Betts' *Caroline's Kitchen* (originally *Monogamy*), Alan Bennett's *The Habit of Art,* Oscar Wilde's *The Importance of Being Earnest,* Frederick Knott's *Wait Until Dark,* Torben Betts' *Invincible,* Evelyn Williams' *Night Must Fall,* Terence Rattigan's *Flare Path* and the award-winning tours of Sebastian Faulk's *Birdsong* adapted by Rachel Wagstaff.

Casting procedures: Casting breakdowns are available from the website and from Spotlight. Welcomes letters (with CVs and photographs) from individual actors previously unknown to the company, sent by post only. Also welcomes showreels and invitations to view individual actors' websites. Actively encourages applications from disabled actors and promotes the use of inclusive casting.

Ovation

Upstairs at the Gatehouse, Highgate, London N6 4BD
tel 020 8340 4256
email events@ovationproductions.com
website www.upstairsatthegatehouse.com
Artistic Directors John and Katie Plews

Production details: Established in 1997, Upstairs at the Gatehouse offers a varied programme of drama, musicals and fringe theatre productions.

The main theatre has flexible seating configurations: thrust has seating for 122, L-shaped has seating for 108, cabaret has seating for 140 and traverse (for in-house productions only) has seating for 116. The usual duration of a run for a show can be between one night and six weeks. Subbsidised rates are not available. Hire rates are available on application.

Casting procedures: Produces three in-house shows a year. Castings are announced on the website. General auditions are not held. Casting breakdowns are available on the website and Spotlight. Letters (with CVs and photographs) from invidivual actors not previously known to the company are only welcome when casting. Unsolicited CVs and photographs sent by email are only welcome when casting. Showreels are not welcome.

Ovation Productions

Upstairs at The Gatehouse, Highgate, London N6 4BD
tel 020 8340 4256
website www.ovationtheatres.com
Directors John Plews, Katie Plews

Production details: Founded in 1985. Owns and operates Upstairs at the Gatehouse, a fringe theatre in North London (see entry under *Fringe theatres* on page 246). Recent productions include: *Anything Goes, Return to the Forbidden Planet, Top Hat, Flat Out* and *Nice Work If You can Get It.*

Casting details: Casting breakdowns are always posted on **www.upstairsatthegatehouse.com** and on

Theatre

Spotlight. Welcomes email submissions. Offers non-Equity contracts. Will consider applications from disabled actors to play characters with disabilities.

The Oxford Shakespeare Company

98 Galloway Road, London W12 0PJ
mobile 07581 751198
email info@osctheatre.org.uk
website www.oxfordshakespeare.co
Directors Nicholas Green, Emma Randle, Charlotte Windmill

Production details: Founded in 2001. Stage Shakespeare and other classic plays. The OSC are celebrated for their open air, site-specific performances both at their summer residency at Wadham College and across the Historic Royal Palaces sites of Hampton Court, Kensington Palace, Tow of London and the Banqueting House, Whitehall. Stages 3 productions with up to 100 performances during the course of the year. Acting company of up to 12 including actor/musicians. Recent productions include: *Much Ado About Nothing*, *Love's Labour Lost*, and *Twelfth Night* (Nicholas Green and Nick Lloyd Webber), *As You Like It* (Michael Oakley and Nick Lloyd Webber); *A Midsummer Night's Dream* (Gemma Fairlie) and *The Tempest* (Mick Gordon and Nick Lloyd Webber).

Casting procedures: Casting breakdowns are released to agents and are available via Spotlight. For further information, see Contact form at bottom of web page.

Paines Plough

2nd Floor, 10 Leake Street, London SE1 7NN
tel 020 7240 4533
email office@painesplough.com
website www.painesplough.com
Co-Artistic Directors Charlotte Bennett, Katie Posner

Production details: Founded in 1974, the company is dedicated to producing and touring new writing. Recent work includes: Vinay Patel's *Stick and Stones*; Simon Longman's *Island Town* and George Christous' *How To Spot An Alien* (all part of the Roundabout season); Anna Jordan's *Pop Music* and Simon Stephens' *Sea Wall*.

Casting procedures: Casts all productions in-house. Does not accept unsolicited CVs or photographs, but holds open auditions throughout the year to meet new actors.

Pendle Productions

Bridge Farm, 249 Hawes Side Lane, Blackpool, Lancashire FY4 4AA
tel (01253) 839375
email admin@pendleproductions.co.uk
website www.pendleproductions.co.uk
Director TS Lince

Production details: Touring professional theatre company. Stages between 10 and 15 productions each year, with 600 performances nationally in 300 venues of all types. Recent productions include: *Cinderella*, *Sinbad* and *Treasure Island*.

Casting procedures: Sometimes holds general auditions; actors should write in April-June requesting inclusion. Casting breakdowns are publicly available via the usual channels. Welcomes letters (with CVs and photographs) from individual actors previously unknown to the company sent by post or email. Accepts showreels but prefers not to receive invitations to view individual actors' websites. Actively encourages applications from disabled actors, and promotes the use of inclusive casting.

Pentabus Theatre Company

The Old School, Bromfield SY8 2JU
tel (01584) 856564
email info@pentabus.co.uk
website www.pentabus.co.uk
Artistic Director Elle While

Production details: Pentabus is the nation's rural theatre company and the only professional theatre company in the UK whose vision is singularly rural. Tours new plays about the contemporary rural world to new audiences in village halls, fields, festivals and theatres, telling stories with local relevance, plus national and international impact. Believes that every person living in an isolated rural community has a right to exceptional theatre. Pentabus is based in a Victorian school in rural Shropshire, and to date all of their work has been made there. It then tours village halls and theatres locally and nationally. Over four and a half decades they've produced 174 new plays, reached over 500,000 audience members, won a prestigious South Bank Show award, a Fringe First and were the first to live stream from a village hall.

The Company has hosted a writer in residence since 2014 and they have gone on to be commissioned by the Birmingham Repertory, the Bush Theatre, HighTide, Nottingham Playhouse, the National Theatre, Royal Court and Royal Welsh College.

Casting procedures: Occasionally uses freelance casting directors. Casting breakdowns are available via Spotlight. No CVs or email enquiries. Will attend shows by invitation.

The People's Theatre Co

69 Manor Way, Guildford, Surrey GU2 7RR
tel 0843 515 8543
email ptc@ptc.org.uk
website www.ptc.org.uk
Facebook www.facebook.com/people.theatre.company
Twitter @the_ptc
Instagram @ptcuk
Director Steven Lee

Production details: Established in 2003. The company has built an international reputation for its unique brand of sophisticated original pop musicals. Stages 120+ performances per year, touring across theUK and abroad to Receiving Houses and number 1/number 2 venues. 2-7 actors are generally involved in each production. Recent productions include: *How The Koala Learnt To Hug*, *There Was An Old Lady Who Swallowed A Fly*, *Don't Dribble on tghe Dragon* and the award-winning Bink trilogy of full-scale family musicals.

Casting procedures: Casting is done in-house. Holds general auditions. Actors should only write requesting inclusion in response to casting calls. Actors can also follow the company on social media for first alerts to castings. Casting breakdowns are obtainable via the usual array of sources including Spotlight and Mandy.com. Accepts submissions (with CVs and photographs) from individual actors previously unknown to the the company; submissions sent by email are also accepted. Applications from disabled actors are considered to play disabled characters. "We want a well-presented CV with personal information, training, experience and detailed skills – particularly singing, as most of our work is musicals. New actors and recent graduates welcome."

People Show
Pophub, 41 Whitcomb Road, London WC2H 7DT
tel 07916 027682
email people@peopleshow.co.uk
website www.peopleshow.co.uk
Facebook www.facebook.com/peopleshowltd
Twitter @peopleshow
Instagram @peopleshowltd
Company Gareth Brierley, Sadie Cook, Fiona Creese, George Khan, Mark Long, Jessica Worrall

Production details: The longest-running experimental theatre company in the UK, touring nationally and internationally since 1966, creating devised work for arts centres, theatres, and outdoor and site-specific venues. Anything from 3 to 65 actors are involved in each production. Offers Equity-approved contracts as negotiated through ITC. Recent works includes: *People Show 137: God Knows How Many*; award-winning short film, *138: LAST DAY*; and *Anything Could Happen Next: A Celebration of the People Show at The British Library*.

Casting procedures: People Show is an ensemble company with a core group of 6 artists, and an extended network of 45 plus associate artists. Does not use freelance casting directors or hold general auditions. Welcomes approaches from performers previously unknown to the company.

Pilot Theatre
York Theatre Royal, St Leonards Place, York YO1 7HD
tel 01904 635755
email info@pilot-theatre.com
website www.pilot-theatre.com
Artistic Director Esther Richardson

Production details: Pilot Theatre is an international touring theatre company based in York, UK. They devise and develop projects with particular focus on working for and with young audiences. They also work across platforms to produce and distribute work digitally, run training conferences, livestream events and performances, provide a wide range of online educational resources.

A wide range of work over the last few years includes the six-camera livestream of the York Myserty Plays for The Space and a range of specially commissioned plays including: *Loneliness of the Long Distance Runner*, *Running on the Cracks*, *Blood + Chocolate* and more recently the new adaptation of *Antigone* by Ry Williams.

"We work with established artists, leading practitioners and diverse teams alongside nurturing young and emergent talent to develop our practice across all platforms of delivery. The audiences and communities we aim to reach are reflected by the diverse teams who make and deliver our work."

Casting procedures: The company regularly posts casting information online. "Please try and avoid sending surface mail for casting, as we are trying to minimise wastage and energy usage." Please email your details to: **casting@pilot-theatre.com**.

Prime Cut Productions
Unit 5, 8 Maxwell Street, Belfast BT12 5FB
tel 07879 557341
email info@primecutproductions.co.uk
website www.primecutproductions.co.uk
Artistic Director Emma Jordan

Production details: Established in 1992, Prime Cut Productions is an independent theatre producing organisation based in Belfast. We are committed to producing excellent contemporary theatre that is accessible and entertaining for as wide an audience as possible, forge artistic links locally and internationally, and continue to nurture the development of theatre practice and artists in Northern Ireland. We have produced 60 highly acclaimed Irish premieres of the best of international theatre as well showcasing the work of Northern Irish theatre artists across the Island of Ireland and beyond.

Since 2014 Prime Cut have been the recipients of the BBC Performing Arts Fellowship, three Weston Jerwood Creative Fellowships, the Allianz Arts & Business Member of the Year Award (2015), Artistic Director Emma Jordan received the Paul Hamlyn Foundation Breakthrough Award and the 2015 Spirit of Festival Award at Belfast International Arts Festival. Our production of *Scorch* has played to overwhelming critical acclaim at the Adelaide Fringe, Edinburgh Fringe, across Ireland, UK, Sweden and Germany winning seven international awards including an Irish Times Theatre Award, an Irish Writers' Guild Award the Holden St Award, a Fringe

Theatre

First, an Adelaide Fringe Best Theatre Award and an Adelaide Critics' Choice Award. Our 2017 production of *Red* was the recipient of four awards at the recent Irish Times Irish Theatre Awards including Best Production, Best Director for Emma Jordan, Best Actor for Patrick O Kane and Best Set Design for Ciaran Bagnall. The 2019 production of Fionnuala Kennedy's *Removed* was selected as the only one of two show from the island of Ireland for IPAY2020 and is the recipient of the Irish Writers Guild Award for Best Theatre Script.

Prime Cut delivers under three main strands: CREATE, INNOVATE and PARTICIPATE.

• CREATE: an artistic programme of two professional productions annually of the best of international drama featuring casts and creative teams of the highest quality.

• INNOVATE: our Annual Artistic Development Programme. It drives forward the development of Northern Irish professional theatre through the provision of the finest international training and professional development opportunities for Northern Irish artists.

• PARTICIPATE: our Community Engagement Programme providing year-round opportunities for arts access and participation for young people, older people, disadvantaged people and people from minority groupings, through a range of arts including theatre, dance, movement, film, music and visual art.

Proteus Theatre Company

Proteus Creation Space, Council Road, Basingstoke, Hants RG21 3DH
tel 01256 354541
email info@proteustheatre.com
website www.proteustheatre.com
Facebook www.facebook.com/proteustheatrecompany
Twitter @proteustheatre
Artistic Director Mary Swan

Production details: Established in 1981. Touring theatre company operating nationally. Stages 2-3 productions annually touring to 80 venues including arts centres, theatres, outdoor venues, educational and community venues. Recent credits include: *Becoming Hattie*, *Macbeth* and *The Bloody Chamber*.

Casting procedures: Casting breakdowns available via the website and Equity Job Information Service. Does not welcome unsolicited CVs. Actively encourages applications from disabled actors and promotes the use of inclusive casting. Offers ITC/Equity-approved contracts.

Punchdrunk

Canon Factory, Ashley Road, London N17 9LH
tel 020 8191 0100
email info@punchdrunk.com
website www.punchdrunk.com
Facebook www.facebook.com/punchdrunkuk
Twitter @PunchdrunkUK
Artistic Director Felix Barratt

Since 2000, Punchdrunk has pioneered a game-changing form of theatre in which roaming audiences experience epic story-telling inside sensory theatrical worlds. Blending classic texts, physical performance, award-winning design installation and unexpected sites, the company's format rejects the passive obedience ususally expected of audiences. Much of the work has a strong and choreographic focus.

Punchdrunk has developed a reputation for transformative productions that focus as much on the audience and the performance space as on the performers and narrative. Inspired designers occupy deserted buildings and apply a cinematic level of detail to immerse the audience in the world of the show.

This is a unique theatrical experience where the lines between space, performer and spectator are constantly shifting. Audiences are invited to rediscover the childlike excitement and anticipation of exploring the unknown and experience a real sense of adventure. Free to encounter the installed environment in an individual imaginative journey, the choice of what to watch and where to go is theirs alone.

Offers Equity-approved contracts through ITC; does not subscribe to the Equity Pension Scheme.

Punchdrunk Enrichment works with schools, colleges, community groups and partner organisations. Recent productions include: *Lost Lending Library* (2013–current); *Against Captain's Orders* (2015), *The Drowned Man* (2013–2014).

Casting procedures: Apply for auditions when advertised, following the instructions. Advertises on website, social media, arts job- and dance-specific websites. Unable to view productions for casting purposes but encourages aplpications from all.

Pursued by a Bear Productions

Trestle Arts Base, Russet Drive, St Albans, Herts, AL4 0JQ
website www.pursuedbyabear.co.uk
Artistic Director Rosamunde Hutt

Production details: Theatre and digital film company specialising in new writing commissions. PBAB produces and tours 1 new (Arts Council funded) theatre production annually and creates large-scale community and educational film (most recently funded by Heritage Lottery). Recent theatre tours include: *Kalashnikov: In the Woods by the Lake* by Fraser Grace (Theatre 503 & South East Tour); *Footprints in the Sand* by Oladipo Agboluaje and Rukhsana Ahmad (Oval House & South East tour). Forthcoming theatre production: *Kabaddi-Kabaddi-Kabaddi* by Satinder Chohan (National UK Touring 2012/13). Forthcoming Film: *On Hungry Hill* (Screening November 2012).

Casting procedures: Welcomes submissions (with CVs and photographs) sent by post or email. For more information see Contact page on website.

Red Ladder Theatre Company
3 St Peter's Buildings, York Street, Leeds LS9 8AJ
tel 0113 245 5311
email info@redladder.co.uk
website www.redladder.co.uk
Twitter @RedLadderTC
Artistic Director Rod Dixon

Production details: Red Ladder's mission is to create theatre based around, and influenced by, human struggle. They aim to create galvanising and life-affirming productions that redefine and reclaim notions of the popular, the political and the radical in a theatre context. The company, founded in 1968 in London, has a colourful history. It spans 50 years, from the radical socialist theatre movement in Britain known as agitprop, to its current position.

The company moved to Leeds in the 70s and is still based in the city. During the 80s it re-defined itself, changing its co-operative structure to a hierarchy. Acknowledged today as one of Britain's leading national touring companies producing high-quality new plays.

Recent productions include: *The Damned United* (Anders Lustgarten from the David Peace novel, co-production with the Leeds Playhouse) and *Glory* by Nick Ahad (co-produced with The Dukes Theatre, Lancaster).

Red Rose Chain
Gippeswyk Hall, Gippeswyk Avenue, Ipswich, Suffolk IP2 9AF
tel 01473 603388
email info@redrosechain.com
website www.redrosechain.com
Directors Joanna Carrick *Producer* David Newborn

Production details: A film and theatre company which spends every summer outdoors with its theatre-in-the-forest event. Runs workshops and develops new writing. "Our diverse work all serves to underpin Red Rose Chain's aim: to use theatre and film to challenge thinking and make connections with those who are normally ignored or avoided by mainstream arts." Stages 4 productions annually, with 50 performances in 20 venues including arts centres, theatres, and outdoor, educational and community venues in East Anglia. In general 3-12 actors are involved in each production. Recent productions include: *A Winter's Tale* (Rendlesham Forest); *Slide Down the Rainbow* (Nowton Park); and *I love Kitkats* (Red Rose Chain).

Casting procedures: Sometimes holds general auditions; casting breakdowns are available via the website. Welcomes letters (with CVs and photographs) from individual actors previously unknown to the company, sent by post or email. Also

welcomes showreels and invitations to view individual actors' websites. Actively encourages applications from disabled actors and promotes the use of inclusive casting.

Reveal Theatre Company
The Creative Village,
Staffordshire University Business Village,
72 Leek Road, Stoke on Trent ST4 2AR
email enquiries@revealtheatre.co.uk
website www.revealtheatre.co.uk
Director Julia Barton

Production details: Established in 1999. A professional small- to middle-scale producing company for touring and residency. Also has a strong outreach department. Stages on average 3 productions each year. Recent productions include: *Beauty and the Beast* (directed by Alex Shepley) and Stephen Sondheim's *Into The Woods* (directed by Robert Marsden).

Casting procedures: Uses in-house casting directors; casting breakdowns are available via the website. Actors may write at any time requesting inclusion. Welcomes submissions (with CVs and photographs) sent by post, but not by email. Also welcomes showreels, and invitations to view individual actors' websites. Offers Equity-approved contracts as negotiated through ITC. Will consider applications from disabled actors to play characters with disabilities.

Riding Lights Theatre Company
Friargate Theatre, Lower Friargate, York YO1 9SL
tel 01904 655317
email email info@rltc.org
website www.ridinglights.org
Facebook www.facebook.com/ridinglights
Artistic Director Paul Burbridge *Artistic Associates* Sean Cavanagh, Bridget Foreman

Production details: Initially a community theatre project founded in York in 1977, today Riding Lights tours at least 4 diverse productions a year throughout the UK. The company is recognised both as a pioneer in reinstating the value of theatre in Christian communication and for significant original and artistic achievement. Recent productions include: *Maryland* (co-production with York Theatre Royal) and *My Place* (in partnership with Home for Good).

Rifco Theatre Company
Watford Palace Theatre, 20 Clarendon Road, Watford WD17 1JZ
tel 01923 810305
website www.rifcotheatre.com
Artistic Director Pravesh Kumar

Production details: Rifo Theatre Company develops, produces and tours vibrant, accessible and high-quality theatre locally from its base in Watford. The company develops both new plays and musicals of scale and spectacle, and works alongside a wide range of artistic collaborators. The work is developed to encourage and engage new and diverse audiences, reflecting and celebrating contemporary British Asian experiences, culture and society.

Offers UK Theatre/Equity-approved contracts. Recent productions include: *Laila The Musical*, *The Masala Queens* and *Dishoom*.

Casting procedures: via casting directors and professional agents. Welcomes letters (with relevant links) from individual actors previously unknown to the company, via email **casting@rifotheatre.com**.

Rocket Theatre

17 Groveland Road, Wallasey, Merseyside CH45 8JX
tel 0151 637 1481 *mobile* 07788 723570
email martin@rockettheatre.co.uk
website www.rockettheatre.co.uk
Director Martin Harris

Production details: Rocket Theatre was set up in 1995. It has produced work and toured throughout the UK with completely new work and regional premieres of work originally staged by some of London's new-writing venues (particularly the Royal Court, the Bush and the National). The company has won several awards. Previous productions include: Oscar Wilde's *Lord Arthur Savile's Crime*, *I Licked a Slag's Deodorant* by Jim Cartwright; *Howie the Rookie* by Mark O'Rowe; *A Skull in Connemara* by Martin McDonagh and *Dealer's Choice* by Patrick Marber, as well as several new plays by Jim Burke. The company is currently working on a production of Spoonface Steinberg By Lee Halland a brand new musical based on the life of Fred Dibnah – see the website for details. Rocket Theatre is keen to hear about any interesting collaboration opportunities with other companies or individuals.

Casting procedures: Casting breakdowns are available on the Rocket website and through various industry casting resources. Does not welcome applications from actors unless casting is called for specific parts.

Scene Three Creative

Hampton, London TW12
mobile 07899 825152
email info@scenethreecreative.co.uk
website www.scenethreecreative.co.uk
Directors Philip Dart, Claudia Leaf

Production details: A creative production company making work for many different venues and communities.

Casting procedures: "We regret that we are unable to hold general auditions or see actors outside of designated casting periods. Agents' information services such as Spotlight are normally supplied with casting breakdowns."

Shared Experience

c/o We Are Team Ltd, 26 South Road,
Kirkby Stephen CA17 4SN

tel 01768 371885
email conrad.lynch@sharedexperience.org.uk
website www.sharedexperience.org.uk
Producer Conrad Lynch

Production details: An award-winning theatre company founded during the 1970s, Shared Experience stages 2-3 productions annually and tours to different arts centres and theatres in the UK and abroad. In general 6-10 actors are involved in each production. Recent productions include: *Mermaid*, *Mary Shelley*, *The Caucasian Chalk Circle*, *A Passage to India*, *Jane Eyre*, *Kindertransport* and *War and Peace*.

Casting procedures: Uses freelance casting directors. Advises that actors should contact the office by phone to enquire about the current casting director. "Please do not send unsolicited mail." Offers TMA/Equity-approved contracts. Actively encourages applications from disabled actors and promotes the use of inclusive casting.

Simple8 Theatre Company

Heath House, Lyneham Road,
Milton-under-Wychwood, OX7 6LW
mobile 07710 174717
email chris@simple8.co.uk
website www.simple8.co.uk
Twitter @simple8theatre
Directors Chris Doyle, Sebastian Armesto, Emily Pennant-Rea, Dudley Hinton, Hannah Emanuel, Mat Wandless

Production details: Simple8 is a critically-acclaimed and award-winning ensemble based theatre company who specialise in creating innovative, bold new plays using large casts – all performed on a shoestring. Their approach is rooted in 'poor theatre', which focuses on the story and revolves around the ensemble, who create the atmosphere and setting without relying on extravagant lighting, scenery, props or sound. Simple8 have produced 8 productions to date, at Arcola Theatre and Park Theatre. Simple8 is an associate company of Shoreditch Town Hall. Winners of the Peter Brook Award for Best Ensemble 2013 and 2015.

Casting procedures: Uses freelance casting directors, but does not hold general auditions. Instead Simple8 recommend actors submit their details for consideration once they have seen a Simple8 production, attended a workshop, or introduced themselves in person. Welcomes both CVs and letters from actors previously unknown to the company and unsolicited CVs and photographs. These should be sent via email. Also welcomes invitations to view individual actors' websites and attend productions, but does not welcome showreels. Happy to consider disabled actors, though this is dependent on each individual project.

Sky Blue Theatre Company

1 Kelling Gardens, Croydon CR0 2RP
mobile 07941 012293

email info@skybluetheatre.com
website www.skybluetheatre.com
Twitter @SkyBlueTheatre
Directors Frances Brownlie, John Mitton

Production details: Founded in 2007. A Cambridge-based company touring schools, theatres and community venues with new plays, Shakespeare productions and workshops. Founded the British Theatre Challenge, an international playwriting competition. Works with young people through its own theatre school and with colleges developing skills in performing arts. Stages 6 productions for young people's theatre and TIE annually, giving around 100 performances in 40 venues nationally. In general, 4 actors ago on tour, playing to audiences aged 7 to 18. Actors are sometimes expected to lead workshops. Recent productions include: *Much Ado About Nothing*, *Real Love – A New Musical*, and *Romeo and Juliet* workshops.

Casting procedures: Holds general auditions, for which breakdowns are available via Mandy and the website. Welcomes letters (with CVs and photographs) from individual actors previously unknown to the company, sent by post or email. Does accept showreels and will consider invitations to view actors' websites and performances. Will consider applications from disabled actors for any role.

Slung Low

The Holbeck, Jenkinson Lawn, Holbeck,
Leeds LS11 9QX
email info@slunglow.org
website www.slunglow.org
Twitter @SlungLow
Artistic Director Alan Lane

Production details: Founded in 2000, Slung Low is an award-winning theatre company specialising in making epic productions in non-theatre spaces, often with large community performance companies at their heart.

Casting procedures: Slung Low's casting depends on the nature of the project. Send your CV to alan@slunglow.org. Also offers producing and production internships. These are opportunities that offer travel expenses only, email to enquire.

Small World Theatre

Theatr Byd Bychan, Bath House Road, Cardigan,
Ceredigion SA43 1JY
tel (01239) 615952
email info@smallworld.org.uk
website www.smallworld.org.uk
Facebook www.facebook.com/SmallWorldTheatre
Director Ann Shrosbree *Artistic Director* Bill Hamblett
Administrator Helene Cheung

Production details: Small World Theatre is an arts sustainability organisation housed in a near zero carbon venue with a variety of areas of work: production house (making original performances and touring theatre); presenting house; project work including theatre for development, theatre forum; education and training; outdoor street spectaculars and giant lantern parades. Incorporating Syrcas Byd Bychan Ariel circus and training.

Casting procedures: Uses in-house casting directors, issues rare casting calls. Will consider submissions (letters, CVs and photographs) from actors previously unknown to the company, sent by post or email. No unsolicited showreels. Casts actors with disabilities in inclusive roles, and to play differently able roles.

Sole Purpose Productions

The Playhouse, Artillery Street, Derry BT48 6RG
tel 0044 (0) 28 7127 9918
email solepurpose@mac.com
website www.solepurpose.org
Facebook www.facebook.com/
solepurposeproductions
Twitter @SolePurpose_
Artistic Director Patricia Byrne

Production details: Sole Purpose Productions is a multi-award winning theatre company founded in 1997. It creates new dynamic theatre on social and public issues. The company has toured extensively throughout Ireland, the UK and the USA. Recent productions include: *Mothers Out Front* by Edie Shillue (a tragicomedy on climate change) and *Blinkered* by Patricia Byrne (a play on mental health and suicide) which won the Special Jury Prize at Origin Theatre's 1st Irish Festival in New York 2019 and received four nominations.

Each production consists of 3-5 actors and, on average, the company presents 1-2 productions per year, touring to theatres and community venues nationally and internationally.

Casting procedures: Holds general auditions at various times throughout the year and a casting breakdown is available via the Sole Purpose website when a production is coming up. Welcomes both CVs and letters from actors previously unknown to the Company and unsolicited CVs and photographs. Also welcomes invitations to view individual actor's websites and showreels. Sole Purpose promotes inclusive casting and welcomes applications from ethnic minorities, LGBTQ and disabled actors.

Spanner in the Works

95 Old Woolwich Road, London SE10 9PP
tel 020 7193 7995
email info@spannerintheworks.org.uk
website www.spannerintheworks.org.uk
Artistic Director Darren Rapier

Production details: Spanner in the Works produce plays and films, as well as running workshops in all media disciplines for a variety of clientele. The company produces films and books in partnership with Tualen Pictures and Tualen Press. Primarily,

Theatre

Spanner in the Works concentrate on stage productions and workshops. They have produced musicals, plays, short films and audio drama, as well as community theatre pieces. Recent productions include: *Riverscross* (online soap), *Blind Man's Bluff* (short film) and *Worlds Apart* (theatre).

Casting procedures: Uses in-house and freelance casting directors. Casting breakdowns are available, although this is dependent on the project. Will happily consider applications from disabled actors, but their inclusion is dependent on the nature of each individual project.

Sphinx Theatre Company

78 Lyford Road, London SW18 3JW
tel 020 3669 8210
email info@sphinxtheatre.co.uk
website www.sphinxtheatre.co.uk
Artistic Director Sue Parrish

Production details: Established 30 years ago, the company specialises in writing, directing and developing roles for women. Recent work includes: the Sphinx 30 playwright development programme, What Share of the Cake? Research project, and Women Centre Stage.

Casting procedures: Casting breakdowns are available via email (with CVs and photographs)

Ed Stephenson Productions

7 Hawthorn Road, Little Sutton, Cheshire CH66 1PR
tel 0151 339 6145
email roger@edstephensonproductions.co.uk
website www.edstephensonproductions.co.uk
Company Administrator Diane Barker

Production details: Founded in 2004. Film, stage and podcast company. Stages on average 1 production every 1-2 years. Recent productions include: *Burning Grief* (2017, film), *The Quarry Clock* (2018, stage show, Liverpool Everyman) and *Vronny and Arwen* podcast series (2020).

Casting procedures: Uses in-house casting directors. Sometimes holds auditions. Uses casting agencies for auditioning. Welcomes letters (with CVs and photographs) from individual actors previously unknown to the company, sent by post or email. Accepts showreels and invitations to view individual actors' websites. Will consider applications from disabled actors where appropriate for the role. "Our contracts are heavily based on ITC/Equity contracts."

TABS Productions

151 Birches Lane, South Wingfield, Derbyshire DE55 7LZ
email admin@tabsproductions.co.uk
website www.tabsproductions.co.uk
Director Karen Henson

Production details: Founded in 1989, the company stages approximately 6 productions each year totalling around 300 performances. It has produced No. 1 and middle-scale tours and has co-produced with repertory theatre companies. Generally tours to about 45 different arts centres, theatres and outdoor venues across the UK annually. The average cast size is 4-8 actors.

Casting procedures: Welcomes letters, CVs and photographs from actors previously unknown to the company, but does not accept emails or showreels. Actors should only write when a job has been advertised to agents.

Taking Flight Theatre Company

Chapter Arts Centre, Cardiff CF5 1QE
email admin@takingflighttheatre.co.uk
website www.takingflighttheatre.org.uk
Director Elise Davison

Production details: Established in 2007. Accessible, professional productions with integrated casts/ support teams. Stages 1-2 productions annually. In general 6-10 actors are involved in each production. Recent productions include: *peeling*, *You've Got Dragons*, *The First Three Drops* and *The Curious Case of Aberlliw*.

Casting procedures: Sometimes holds general auditions and actors may write at any time to request inclusion. Casting breakdowns are publicly available via the website, Equity Job Information Service and Mandy, as well as from the Disability Arts Cymru site. Welcomes letters (with CVs and photographs) from individual actors previously unknown to the company sent by post or email, as well as showreels and invitations to view individual actors' websites. Actively encourages applications from Deaf and disabled actors. "We are very eager to hear from Deaf, disabled and/or sensory impaired actors."

Talawa Theatre Company

Fairfield Halls, Park Lane, Croydon Surrey CR9 1DG
tel 020 7251 6644
email contact@talawa.com
website www.talawa.com
Artistic Director Michael Buffong

Production details: Founded in 1986, Talawa is the UK's outstanding Black British Theatre company, whose purpose is to champion Black excellence in theatre; to nurture talent in emerging and established artists of African or Caribbean heritage and to tell inspirational and passionate stories, reflecting Black experiences through art.

Offers ITC/Equity contracts and has Ethical Management Status.

Casting procedures: Often co-produces work, but when available casting details can be found on the website.

Tamasha Theatre Company

RichMix, 35-47 Bethnal Green Road, London E1 6LA
tel 020 7749 0090

email admin@tamasha.org.uk
website www.tamasha.org.uk

Production details: Founded in 1989. Produces 'untold stories' in mainstream theatre venues. Stages 1-3 productions annually and gives approximately 60 performances during the course of the year. Tours annually to small- and mid-scale theatre venues in London and regionally In general 2-15 actors are involved in each production. Recent productions include: *The Arrival, Snookered, Wuthering Heights, The Trouble with Asian Men* and *Strictly Dandia.*

Casting procedures: Only holds auditions when casting for a specific production. Uses Spotlight and own files when inviting people to audition plus casting director on specific projects. Welcomes CVs and headshots by post at any time; these will be kept on file and looked at afresh during each casting process. Also runs professional artist development scheme: Tamasha Developing Artists – see website for details. Offers ITC/Equity-approved contracts.

Tara Theatre

356 Garratt Lane, London SW18 4ES
tel 020 8333 4457
email info@taratheatre.com
website www.tara-arts.com
Artistic Director Abdul Shayek

Production details: Founded in 1977, the company's range of in-house and touring work spans European and Asian classics through to new plays. Recent productions include: *Macbeth, The Miser, Bollywood Jack, Paradise of the Assassins, Chigger Foot Boys* and *Combustion.* The new Tara Theatre, opened in September 2016 by the Mayor of London, Sadiq Khan, is Britain's first multi-cultural theatre. Its cross-culture architecture is echoed by a diverse programme of classic and new plays produced by Tara and visiting companies, connecting worlds of imagination.

Theatr Genedlaethol Cymru

Y Llwyfan, College Road, Carmarthen SA31 3EQ
tel 01267 233 882
email thgc@theatr.com
website www.theatr.com
Artistic Director Steffan Donnelly

Production details: Founded in 2003, Theatr Genedlaethol Cymru is the Welsh-language national theatre of Wales. Its work includes national tours, community projects and site-specific work. Recent productions include *Y Bont, Blodeuwedd, Y Negesydd* (*The Messenger*) and *Chwalfa.* Each production consists of 6 or more actors and, on average, the company present 5-7 productions per year. This equates to over 70 performances across the UK hosted at various venues, including arts centres, theatres and community spaces. Offers Equity-approved contracts negotiated through UK Theatre.

Casting procedures: Uses in-house casting directors, but does not hold general auditions. Welcomes both

CVs and letters from actors previously unknown to the company and unsolicited CVs and photographs only when casting. These should be sent via email. Also welcomes invitations to view individual actors' websites, productions and showreels. Actively encourages applications from disabled actors.

Theatre-Rites

Unit 3, Energy Centre, Bowling Green Walk, London N1 6AL
tel 020 7164 6196
email info@theatre-rites.co.uk
website www.theatre-rites.co.uk
Facebook www.facebook.com/TheatreRites
Twitter @TheatreRites
Instagram @theatrerites
Artistic Director Sue Buckmaster

Production details: Committed to creating challenging productions which push the boundaries of theatrical form by experimenting to combine different artistic disciplines. Highly imaginative visual experiences for families to share together. Stages two productions annually, with around 45 performances in 12 arts centre and theatres across all English regions, in Scotland and internationally. In general 4-8 actors go on tour, playing to audiences of various ages, often 5+.Actors are sometimes expected to lead workshops; singing, musical instrument, dance physical theatre and puppetry skills, depending on the project. Recent productions include: Big Up!; Siyanda: *The Welcoming Party, Beasty Baby, The Broke 'n' Beat Collective* and *Rubbish.*

Casting procedures: Casting breadowns are available via the website and artsjobs. Welcomes letters (with CVs and photographs) from actors previously unknown to the company. Also welcomes showreels and invitations to view individual actors' websites. Offers Equity-approved contracts as negotiated through ITC. Promotes the use of inclusive casting. Multi-disciplined performers are always very welcome.

Theatre Absolute

Shop Front Theatre, 38 City Arcade, Coventry
tel 07799 292957
email info@theatreabsolute.co.uk
website www.theatreabsolute.co.uk
Artistic Director/Writer Chris O'Connell
Producer Julia Negus

Production details: Founded in 1992, the company commissions, develops and produces new work for theatre. In 2009, Theatre Absolute founded the UK's first professional Shop Front Theatre in Coventry, West Midlands. Work includes performances, script readings, writing workshops, and mentor support for actors, writers, producers and emerging theatre makers.

Casting procedures: Actors should consult the website for details of the next project. 'If you are a local actor, do come to a show/event or drop in and introduce yourself in the first instance'.

Theatre Alibi

Emmanuel Hall, Emmanuel Road, Exeter EX4 1EJ
tel 01392 217315
email info@theatrealibi.co.uk
website www.theatrealibi.co.uk
Facebook www.facebook.com/TheatreAlibiUK
Twitter @TheatreAlibi
Artistic Director Nikki Sved

Production details: Founded in 1982, the company creates new work for all ages that is physically and visually inventive and often enriched by other art forms including music, animation, film, puppetry, dance and photography. Stages 2 productions a year, with a total of around 130 performances. Tours theatres and arts centres as well as schools and community venues, the nature of the venue depending on the individual show. The company offers ITC/Equity-approved contracts and is an ITC Ethical Manager.

Recent productions include: *Falling* (small-scale national tour of theatres and arts centres for adult audiences) and *Table Mates* (tour of primary schools, community venues and theatres for 5-11-year-olds, mainly in the South West).

Casting procedures: Casts in house as well as welcoming new performers. Runs occasional general auditions and for some productions publishes casting breakdowns and is instigating open auditions. Welcomes letters and emails with CVs and photographs at any time of year. Also welcomes links to showreels and individual websites.

Theatre Broad

Easter Ballat, Balfron Station, Nr Glasgow G63 0SQ
tel 01360 440480
email info@theatrebroad.co.uk
email actors@theatrebroad.co.uk
website www.theatrebroad.co.uk
Artistic Director Carol Metcalf

Production details: An innovative theatre company dedicated to providing regular, affordable, quality theatre to people in the Stirling area, then touring throughout the country. Aims to provide audiences with the opportunity to see the best available plays, from a broad range of styles, writers and cultures.

In addition to its mainstream productions, the company's award-winning Community Roots programme is in association with Forth Valley College, Stirling, Falkirk and Clackmannan. Disabled adult students appear in specially devised productions where they are supported in the rehearsal room and in performance by professional actors and practitioners.

Tours 2-4 projects annually, with around 20-40 performances at 6-12 venues in Stirling, Central Scotland, Dumfries and Aberdeenshire. Venues include mid-scale theatres, arts centres, village halls and art galleries. In general 2-15 actors go on tour, depending on the production. Recent productions include: *An Afternoon Delight* by Ross Mather and Gordon Reid (Stirling's Studio Theatre); *Ludus – PlayfulLlove*, devised and directed by Carol Metcalf (Scottish and Cumbria tour); *Bruce's Quest – The Musical* by Gareth Candy; *Our World* (a community productions on global warming) by Carol Metcalf; *Brush Up Your Shakespeare* (celebrating Shakespeare's 400th anniversary) devised by Carol Metcalf; *Prelude and Fugue* by Clifford Bax; *SuperNatural* by Gareth Candy. A Scottish and Cumbria tour of Ira Levin's *Deathtrap*; *3 Stars and a Quest: Tron Labyrinth* (by Gareth Candy and Carol Metcalf); a Scottish tour of *J. M. Barrie: Peter Pan Man* (by Anne Stenhouse and J.M. Barrie); *When Santa Got Lost In Space* (a pantomime by Carol Metcalf).

Casting procedures: Casting is done in-house by the Artistic and Executive Directors, and actors may write at any time to request inclusion. Casting breakdowns are available from the website, Equity Job Information Service and Mandy. No hard copy submissions, but will accept CVs and photographs sent by email, as well as showreels and invitations to view individual actors' websites/other productions. Encourages applications from disabled performers and promotes the use of inclusive casting. Theatre Broad is a member of The Federation of Scottish Theatre.

Theatre Lab Company

76 St Dunstan's Avenue, London W3 6QJ
mobile 07541 974613
email theatrelabco@gmail.com
website www.theatrelab.co.uk
Artistic Director Anastasia Revi

Production details: Established in 1997, Theatre Lab is an international company, known for visual storytelling, mesmerising imagery and physical theatre. Works on classical texts, contemporary Greek writing, new writing and devised experimental theatre. Stages 2-3 productions annually, including 2–3 week runs at theatres in London, and tours in other UK cities and abroad. The average cast size is 8. Contracts vary: some are Equity-approved as negotiated through ITC when funded; some are non-Equity. Recent productions include: *Don Juan* (2022, 2018), *A Respectable Wedding* (2022, 2018), *Emmeline* (2021), *Great Expectations* (2019), *Jamaica Inn* (2017), *Salome* (2012–17), *Dancing with the Devil* (2016) and *Medea* (2014).

Casting procedures Uses in-house casting directors. Holds production-specific auditions and actors may contact the company to request attendance. Casting breakdowns are published on Spotlight and posted on the website and social media. Welcomes applications through Spotlight, emails (with CVs and headshots) and showreels. Encourages applications from disabled actors and promotes the use of inclusive casting.

Théâtre Sans Frontières

2A Tanner's Yard, Hexham,
Northumberland NE46 3NL
tel 01434 603114
email info@tsf.org.uk
website www.tsf.org.uk
Facebook www.facebook.com/theatresansf
Twitter @theatresansf
Artistic Directors Sarah Kemp (CEO), John Cobb

Production details: Founded in 1991. Set up by former students of Philippe Gaulier and Monika Pagneux. Specialises in physical theatre and stages texts in different languages for adults and children using international performers. Stages 2-3 productions annually with 60-100 performances in venues including arts centres, schools and theatres. In general 3-6 actors are involved in each production. Recent productions include: *Lipsynch* (co-produced with Robert Lepage and Ex Machina, toured internationally); *La Chanson du Retour* (with Sage Gateshead); *Canary Gold* (collaboration with Teatro Tamaska), Le Moulin Magique. *Heaven Eyes, Lorca: Amor en el Jardin, Chernobyl@30* (with Theatre Arabesky, Ukraine), *A Frog Called Woanda* (with Theatre À L'Envers, Quebec) and UK schools' tour Ti Jean et La Chèvre (for children aged 8 to 12 years).

Casting procedures: Sometimes holds general auditions. Actors may write at any time requesting inclusion. Casting breakdowns are available on request. Welcomes submissions (with CVs and photographs) sent by post or email. Invitations to view individual actors' websites are also accepted. "We are usually looking for actors who have languages other than English (especially French, Spanish or German), and who have a clear physical theatre training (i.e. Le Coq, Gaulier, Pagneux or Complicite)."

Theatre Without Walls

Hillsborough, County Down BT26 6AS
tel 02892 82125
email hello@theatrewithoutwalls.org
website www.theatrewithoutwalls.org
Directors Jason Maher, Genevieve Swift

Production details: Established in 2002. Award-winning theatre company specialising in forum, education and new writing. Productions represent only one-fifth of its output; also produces television and corporate films. 2 productions are staged annually with 60 performances per year, touring to 20 venues including arts centres, theatres and outdoor venues. Tours cover the UK, Ireland and Europe. 3 actors are employed in each production. Actors are employed under ITC/Equity-approved contracts. Recent productions include: *Don Quixote*

(Banbury Mill); *The Hold* (Cheltenham Everyman) and *The Plant Hunters* (National Trust).

Casting procedures: "We cast mostly through agents and our own knowledge/word of mouth/recommendations. We sometimes post casting information via Equity JIS and other 'freely available resources'. We never use casting services which actors have to pay for, except for Spotlight. Any information obtained via paid-for services has simply been copied from another source. Please don't send us any information (such as photos, CVs, showreels, etc.) unless we have requested it. We regularly hold actors' labs and often cast from them." Theatre Without Walls is a member of ITC and most of its work is undertaken using Equity contracts. Those working with vulnerable adults or children must have a current enhanced Criminal Record Bureau/Police Check and hold full insurance equal or greater than that provided by Equity for its members. Considers applications from disabled actors to play disabled characters.

See also the company's entry under *Role-play companies* on page 286.

Third Party Productions Ltd

Moresk Court, Truro Vean Terrace TR1 1HA
mobile 07768 694211
email gleave@thirdparty.org.uk
website www.thirdparty.org.uk
Director Anthony Gleave *Project Theatre Director* John Wright

Production details: Established in 1992. A UK and International touring theatre company. Work based on classic plays which are deconstructed and re-imagined during the rehearsal process; live music. Interested in any collaboration which sounds fun and begins with studio scale exposure. Last production pre-covid was The Sagas of Noggin the Nog, based on the TV series created by Oliver Postgate and Peter Firmin.

Tilted Wig Productions

tel 07837 912285 / 07843 092783
email katherine@tiltedwigproductions.com
website www.tiltedwigproductions.com
Producers Matthew Parish, Katherine Senior

Production details: Tilted Wig Productions was formed in 2017. Has 12 years' experience producing and touring plays throughout the UK both as Tilted Wig and Creative Cow – a Devon-based theatre company we co-founded in 2007. An ensemble of actors, crew and creatives has taken over 20 productions on the road, touring in the depths of the British countryside, setting up shows in pubs and skittle alleys. Shows now tour to some of the biggest theatres in the UK yet that same ethos is still the driving force behind the company.

Recent productions: *Lady Chatterley's Lover*, 2020; *The Legend of Sleepy Hollow*, 2021.

Theatre

Casting procedures: Does not hold general auditions; the company works with a pool of performers, but is always interested in meeting new actors – either by personal recommendation or by seeing their work. Casts for some roles via agents through Spotlight. Encourages applications from disabled actors and promotes the use of inclusive casting.

Tin Shed Theatre Company

46 Lennard Street, Newport NP19 0EJ
mobile 07921 366038 / 07511 139773
email connect@tinshedtheatrecompany.com
website www.tinshedtheatrecompany.com
Creative Producer/Co-Director Georgina Harris
Company Manager Naomi Underwood

Production details: Established in 2008. Specialises in devised theatre which lends itself to performance in unusual spaces. High-energy, high-impact work that focuses on many different genres. Also has an educational programme with an emphasis on the English curriculum.

Stages 1 production each year in the main house and 3 in the studio. Recent productions include: Brighton Fringe 2012, Edinburgh Fringe 2013 and national tour of *Dr Frankenstein's Travelling Freakshow*; *The Ritual*; *An Immersive* and Halloween Experience 2013.

Casting procedures: Uses freelance directors; actors may write at any time to request inclusion. Casting breakdowns are available from the website. Welcomes unsolicited approaches by post and email, and accepts showreels and invitations to view individual actors' websites/visit other productions. Encourages applications from disabled actors and promotes the use of inclusive casting.

Tinderbox Theatre Company

Crescent Arts Centre, 2-4 University Road, Belfast BT7 1NH
tel 028 9043 9313
email info@tinderbox.org.uk
website www.tinderbox.org.uk
Artistic Director Patrick J. O'Reilly *Company Manager* Alice Malseed

Production details: Founded in 1988. Produces, develops and stages new work and provides professional theatre training. Stages 2-3 productions and tours annually, including arts centres, theatres and site-specific locations in the UK and Ireland. Recent productions include: *The Man Who Fell To Pieces*, *Ubu the King* and *Hubert and the Yes Sock*.

Casting procedures:Holds open calls for auditions. Welcomes letters (with CVs and photographs) and email submissions. Invitations to view individual actors' websites are also accepted. Offers Equity-approved contracts. Encourages applications from disabled actors and promotes the use of inclusive casting.

Told by an Idiot

c/o Unicorn Theatre, 147 Tooley Street, LondonSE1 2HZ

tel 020 7407 4123
email info@toldbyanidiot.org
website www.toldbyanidiot.org
Artistic Director Paul Hunter

Production details: Founded in 1993, the company tours to theatres nationally and internationally.

Casting procedures:Casting is either in-house or with a freelance casting director, depending on the project. Offers ITC/Equity contracts.

Trestle Theatre Company

Trestle Arts Base, Russet Drive, St Albans AL4 0JQ
tel 01727 850950
email admin@trestle.org.uk
website www.trestle.org.uk
Twitter @TrestleTheatre
Executive Director Clare Winter *Creative Director* Helen Barnett

Production details: Founded in 1981 as a touring theatre company, now also with a home venue (Trestle Arts Base), national and international workshop programme and a global business making and selling handcrafted theatre masks. Performers/facilitators used across all areas of the company. All projects concentrate on new, devised or commissioned work, incorporating mask, text, physical theatre, dance and other movement forms, storytelling, puppetry, music and song. Currently 2 shows touring schools with high quality performances, workshops and resources – national and international tours. In general 2-5 performers are involved in each project. Offers ITC/Equity contracts.

Casting procedures: Rarely holds general auditions. Does not welcome on-spec CVs. Will consider invitations to see actors in shows if the performance style is relevant to the way in which Trestle works. If looking for suggestions, casting breakdowns will be posted on the website. Usually casts actors with strong physical/visual theatre acting training or experience. Actively encourages applications from disabled actors and promotes the use of inclusive casting.

Two's Company

244 Upland Road, London SE22 0DN
tel 020 8299 3714
email graham@2scompanytheatre.co.uk
website www.2scompanytheatre.co.uk
Facebook www.facebook.com/2sComp
Twitter @2sComp
Artistic Director Tricia Thorns *Producer* Graham Cowley

Production details: Founded in 1999, Two's Company occasionally produces new plays, but mainly focuses on presenting 'new plays of the past', forgotten plays from earlier times which depict events or people contemporary to them. For example, produced a series of plays about the First World War, originally written at the time. Recent productions include: *Staircase* by Charles Dyer, *Bodies* by James Saunders, *A Day by the Sea* by N.C. Hunter, *The Fifth Column* by Ernest Hemingway, *The Cutting of the Cloth* by Michael Hastings, *What The Women Did* (Southwark Playhouse) and *Go Bang Your Tambourine* by Philip King. Each production consists of 6-10 actors and usually the company presents 1 production per year, occassionally 2. This usually equates to around 28 performances at 1 London venue, mainly small London theatres. Occasionally, a tour will go out to small theatres and arts centres.

Casting procedures: Hardly ever uses freelance casting directors, and does not hold general auditions. Welcomes both CVs and letters from actors previously unknown to the company and unsolicited CVs and photographs but only when casting. These should be sent via email. Also welcomes invitations to view individual actors' websites, especially if they include showreels. Rarely has the opportunity to cast disabled actors.

TYPE (The Yellowchair Performance Experience)

89 Birchanger Lane, Birchanger, Bishop Stortford, Herts CM23 5QF
email contactTYPE@gmail.com
Key contact Hugh Allison

Production details: Aims to give new talent their first break on the UK Fringe (not limited to actors). Recent productions include: *Your Sacrament Divine, As You Like It, A Midsummer Night's Dream.*

Casting procedures: Does not use freelance casting directors or hold general auditions. Actors may write in at any time. Casting breakdowns are usually available at **mandy.com**. Welcomes letters (with CVs and photographs) from individual actors previously unknown to the company, sent by post. May cast disabled actors, depending on the role.

UK Arts International

6 Fort Crescent, Margate CT9 1HN
tel 07778 168805
email janryan@ukarts.com
website www.ukarts.com

Production details: Mainly presents productions from overseas and tours them throughout the UK.

Casting procedures: Does not hold general auditions and does not welcome submissions from actors previously unknown to the company.

Unlimited Theatre

c/o Yorkshire Dance, St Peter's Buildings, 3 St Peter's Square, Leeds LS9 8AH
tel 01138 805682
website www.unlimited.earth
Twitter @untheatre
Executive Producer Alice Massey *Core Artists* Jon Spooner, Tyrrell Jones, Ali Pidsley, Lauren Nicole

Production details: Founded in 1997. Creates work intended to "explore how personal experience can illuminate political debate, and which puts marginalised voices centre-stage". Stages 1-2 productions annually with 50-100 performances. Tours to 10-20 different venues each year, including arts centres and theatres throughout the UK (including Glasgow, Edinburgh and Belfast) and overseas. In general 4-6 actors are involved in each production. Recent productions include: *Money the Gameshow, Play Dough, Am I Dead Yet?, The Astro Science Challenge* and *How I Hacked My Way Into Space.*

Casting procedures: Sometimes holds general auditions. Welcomes responses to casting calls but not email submissions. Follow on Twitter or sign up to newsletter for info on casting calls. "We are a small- to middle-scale organisation and only occasionally employ freelance actors. We are always interested in hearing from potential new collaborators." Offers ITC/Equity-approved contracts. Actively encourages applications from disabled actors and promotes the use of inclusive casting.

Unrestricted View

109 St Paul's Road, Islington, London N1 2NA
tel 020 7704 2001
email felicity@henandchickens.com
website www.unrestrictedview.co.uk
Artistic Directors Felicity Wren, James Wren *Theatre Manager* Mark Lyminster

Production details: Unrestricted View produce new writing and comedy. Run by actors for actors, the company offer a safe, supportive space for creative people to work in. The theatre is also a cinema space. The theatre hosted 3 productions in 2014 and offers financial and professional support to 3 resident acting companies. Theatre productions are hosted on 3-week runs and comedy shows are hosted on an individual basis, with the theatre in use as a performance space 355 days per year. Recent productions include: *Get It Seen* (a month of feature films and shorts from independent producers – affliated with the BFI) and *A May's Plays* (a 15-year celebration of the theatre with 10 new 15-minute plays supplied by the company's sister theatre in New York City – The WorkShop Theater).

The main theatre space has 54 seats, which can be arranged in a number of different configurations. Hire-rates are as follows: £1,200 per week, or on a day-by-day basis of £120 (until 7.30pm) or £150 (until 9.30pm).

Casting Procedures: Uses in-house casting directors. A casting breakdown is available on Mandy and the website, with details of upcoming productions on Twitter and Facebook. Happy to consider applications from disabled actors.

Vanguard Productions

30 Coombe Rise, Findon Valley, Worthing, West Sussex BN14 0ED

Theatre

tel 07718 345167
email vanguardproductions573@gmail.com
website www.vanguardproductions.co.uk
Artistic Directors Nelson. E.Ward, Amaryllis Crooke,
Rachel Ward

Production details: Founded in 1996, Vanguard
takes theatre and entertainment to areas of the
community that are socially excluded. This includes
residential and nursing homes, day centres, museums
and village halls as well as small-scale theatre venues.
An outreach programme also exists for schools and
colleges. Recent productions include: *Maxie: The Life
of Max Miller* (Edinbrugh Festival), *What A Swell
Party* (village halls) and the Neil Simon play *I Ought
to be in Pictures* (Tristan Bates Theatre, London).
Village hall productions usually employ 3-4 actors
and Vanguard presents 4 productions per year. This
equates to about 30 performances annually at venues
across the south of England.

Casting procedures: Uses an in-house casting system
and only holds general auditions periodically. Casting
breakdowns are put on Mandy, Spotlight and Equity
job information service. Welcomes both CVs and
letters from actors previously unknown to the
Company and unsolicited CVs and photographs.
These should be sent via email.

Volcano Theatre Company

27-29 High Street, Swansea SA1 1LG
tel 01792 464790
website www.volcanotheatre.wales
Facebook www.facebook.com/volcanotheatrecompany
Twitter @volcanouk
Instagram volcanotheatreuk
Artistic Director Paul Davies

Production details: Original theatrical productions
and site-specific events. Small-scale national and
international touring company based in Wales.
Devised and collaborative work, physical theatre, new
writing, adaptations/deconstructions of classics.
Stages 2-4 productions and gives 50-80 performances
each year. Venues include arts centres and theatres in
the UK, Europe and worldwide. Usually 2-8
performers per production. Recent productions
include: *Hamletmachine, The Populars, Seagulls* and
Hispaniola.

Casting procedures: There are no casting
breakdowns. Performers are selected through
workshops and invited auditions. Unsolicited
admissions are read but not held on record.

Walk the Plank

Cobden Works, 37–41 Cobden Street,
Salford M6 6WF
tel 0161 736 8964
email info@walktheplank.co.uk
website www.walktheplank.co.uk

Production details: Walk the Plank is one of the
UK's leading outdoor arts organisations, creating
innovative productions and performances which
engage artists and communities in a wide range of
outdoor settings. Based in Salford, the company
works regionally, nationally and internationally.

Has a track record of making work that engages
citizens in public celebration founded on ambitious
creativity that connects with ordinary people. From
Capital of Culture opening ceremonies to fire gardens
and site-responsive installations to parades and
podcasts, the company showcases talent from a range
of performing artforms.

Starting your own theatre company

Pilar Ortí

The first question you should ask yourself before starting a theatre company is – do you really need to set up a company, or do you just want to put on a show? In order to put on a show you don't need to go through all the hassle of setting up a company. If you *do* want to set up a company – why? In some cases this might be as difficult a question to answer as, "Why do you want to act?", but it's worth having an idea of why you want to invest so much time and energy in setting up and running an organisation rather than looking for acting work. Whatever your answer, be honest with yourself. And the clearer you can be, the better, as your answers will affect the kind of organisation you end up creating.

Of course, many companies emerge after a group of actors produce a show together: at some point, someone decides that, as a company of people, you are worth keeping together. If this is the case, then you are ready to run a company of your own. But there are many ways of making theatre, as you well know, and the range of theatre produced is also vast. What kind of work do you want to do? At this point it is worth bearing in mind your 'artistic policy', and coming up with a couple of sentences that describe the work you do. I know that 'policy' sounds dry, but if you end up constituting yourself as a non-commercial organisation and applying to public funds (or trusts and foundations), you will need to learn a whole new vocabulary which seems to have little to do with your art. You should never lose sight of your artistic dreams and ambitions – but you may need to talk about them in terms of policy, objectives, qualitative evaluation, benefits, management structure, cultural diversity, contingency ... the list goes on and on. This article is meant to inspire you, not send you off to sleep, so don't despair: learn the language and then use it in a creative way that makes sense to you.

Allow yourself to dream

Long-term plans are necessary – so learn to dream. (Okay, give it a try in the first instance by putting on a show. Then, if you enjoy it, carry on!) Plans, of course, can change along the way: I suggest that you have an absolutely ambitious dream plan and a let's-try-and-see-what's-possible-now plan. Opportunities arise when you least expect them, and if you know where you are heading, you can grab them without letting them throw you off-course.

I view running a theatre company rather like directing a show: the more theatre you watch, the stronger the idea you will have of what *you* want the show to be, what is unique about it, and what you can realistically achieve. So if you, like me, trained as an actor or actress and suddenly find yourself running a company, seek advice and look at how others operate. If you consider how other people do things, you will be able to adapt the bits you like and which make sense to you. In a sector such as ours, it is not difficult to find those who are pleased to help – and the freshness of people just starting out reminds us all of how much can be achieved when we don't know our limitations.

Seek help

There is an awful lot of free/cheap advice out there. During the year in which we focused on building the administrative foundations for our company, my colleague and I talked

Theatre

to as many consultants, local authority officers, venue managers, etc. as we could. Some of these conversations came about through informal meetings; others, by taking part in official programmes. We found out what funders were really looking for, and what other companies were doing in our area; we learnt to draw up business plans with budgets covering three and five years; and we discovered what our strengths and weaknesses were, and what threats and opportunities exist 'out there'.

A word of warning: take *all* advice (including that which I am giving you now) with a pinch of salt, especially from those who hardly know you and your work. Follow your gut instinct. When we were in pre-production for *Antigone*, a business consultant suggested that we invite Funeral Services to advertise in our programme, "seeing as how they all die in the end". Mmm.

The best consultancies are those which have been carefully structured so that the consultant spends time with you, getting to know you and your plans, and then helps you find your own answers by providing their expertise.

Making it 'proper'

Once you have decided on the work you want to do and how you want to go about producing it, you will need to find a legal structure for your company. This shows outsiders that you are serious, and it also makes monetary transactions easier.

Forbidden's first show was produced in Edinburgh: the only 'proper' thing the company had was a bank account (and a name!). We then registered the name and became a limited company, and after our first London show, became a registered charity. This was a good idea as our income mainly comes from trusts and foundations (most of which require you to be a charity in order to receive their grants, for tax purposes); it also allows us to claim Gift Aid when we receive donations from individuals. (Gift Aid is great: the donor claims their donation as tax-deductible, and you receive an extra 23 per cent from the Inland Revenue.)

Setting up a charity still allows you to pursue your own artistic programme: making theatre for the public is considered to 'advance education', which is a charitable objective. So you can still run your company as a business, drawing salaries, etc. and making sure that any annual profits stay within the company.

Just like a limited company, a registered charity is governed by a Board. The main difference between the two set-ups is that those who sit on a charity's Board (the Trustees) do so on a voluntary basis. It therefore would make no sense for *you* to be part of the Board (although there is talk of a possible change in the law to allow Trustees to be remunerated for their work). This means that, in theory at least, you are putting the fate of your company in the hands of other people. So choose your Trustees very carefully, and try to include people who have some knowledge of legal matters and accountancy.

This set-up has worked for Forbidden, as we have been extremely lucky: we have managed to find experienced individuals with integrity and a passion for what we do. You might prefer a different kind of set-up which gives you more legal control: banks and Business Links offer free advice on the different options. If you want some focused advice and have a bit of cash to spare, you might attend the Independent Theatre Council's (ITC) seminar on 'Starting a Theatre Company'. And when you have a bit more cash, you might want to join the ITC – membership is bound to come in handy when questions on legal matters arise. (Have a look at the website, **www.itc-arts.org**.)

Learn as you go along

Know your strengths and weaknesses. Setting up a theatre company will involve doing ten thousand things you might never have done before; however, a lot of it can be learnt along the way, and much of it is common sense. It won't take you long to discover those things you are useless at, and those that you absolutely hate. You then have two choices: do them anyway, or find someone else to do them for you/with you.

If there are more than two of you running the company, decide who will be in charge of what. Certain things, like fundraising, might be too daunting for one person to do on their own, but you can break it down into more manageable pieces. Someone might have a clearer head for numbers and can prepare the budget, and someone else can write the description of the show and why it will make a huge contribution to theatre in this country.

Let's talk about money

And seeing that I've come to fundraising, I shall dwell on it. You can't escape it. No matter how much your company grows, no matter how successful you are, no matter how large your staff is – if you are in charge, you will worry about it, so learn to enjoy it. I know that this sounds perverse, but fundraising applications are your chance to enthuse someone else about what you do. To tell them about your plans – about what you want to do and why you want to do it. Tell them how you want to make a difference; about *why* you think it's different; about how it will help you, and others, grow. And yes, you will need to learn some new vocabulary, and be able to distinguish between qualitative and quantitative evaluation, but it helps if you see this as a game with which you have to keep up. (At the last ITC annual general meeting, I found out that 'well-being' is a new way of convincing funders that theatre is necessary to people's lives!) What's really important is to convince funders that you really want to do the work, and that you want to do it well. (When I talk about funders, I am referring to anyone who might want to donate to or invest in your company. I have no experience of commercial deals, but I imagine that these work in a similar way: you find out what it is that people want in return for their money, and then convince them that you can provide it – as well as putting on a really good show.)

This is also where having long-term plans comes in handy: funding applications usually take between six weeks and three months to be assessed. Sometimes, even more: our first successful application for an Education Officer took more than one year from the date on which I sent it to the day the letter of acceptance came through. While I'm on the subject of those who will give you money – *nurture your relationships with them*. We have found that those trusts, foundations and individuals who are willing to help us out once, are likely to do so again.

I have also discovered that funding applications help you plan in detail how you are going to realise a production or a project. Good funding applications might come in useful even if you don't get the money – they will probably provide a good description of your plans, which you can then show others interested in your work. (For books and directories on fundraising, check out the Directory of Social Change's website, **www.dsc.org.uk**.)

Final words

I have left the most important thing until last. *Treat those working with you well, especially your actors.* Make working with you an enjoyable experience. If you hold auditions, make them worthwhile for those attending. When you are able to pay your personnel, pay them

Theatre

on time. Treat them like the professionals that they are. And when things go wrong, as they inevitably will, take responsibility for your company and make up for the hassle with a gesture, however small – custard creams work for me!

When I first started running Forbidden, I kept hearing that I should treat it like running a business. What I have discovered is that it is an exercise in people management. Forbidden exists because people have believed in our work and are willing to invest their time and money in what we do. Different organisations work in different ways: I hope these words have helped you find one that will work for you.

After running Forbidden Theatre Company as Artistic Director for seven years, Pilar now uses her people management skills to facilitate learning in leaders and in teams. She is director of Unusual Connections, a company which uses theatre-based training to deliver Leadership Programmes and Strategic Team-Away days. She also freelances as workshop leader and voice-over artist, and can be contated via **info@unusualconnections.co.uk**

Finding funding for projects

Sinead Mac Manus

Finding funding for projects is an essential part of the subsidised theatre scene. Unless you are working in the commercial sector, most theatre productions do not generate enough income to cover their costs. Fundraising provides the shortfall. The funding landscape in the UK is wide and varied, and can seem to the beginner to be an impossible terrain to navigate. However, as with most things, there are tricks of the trade that you can learn, and the process *does* get easier with practice.

Starting points

There are two good starting publications that I would recommend for fledging arts fundraisers: the first entitled 'Guide to Arts Funding in England', is an excellent overview of arts funding available to download for free from the Department for Culture, Media and Sport (DCMS) website (**www.culture.gov.uk**). Also recommended is Susan Forrester's and David Lloyd's *The Arts Funding Guide* published by the Directory of Social Change in 2002 (**www.dsc.org.uk**), which may be available in your local library. These guides take the user through the areas where you can find funding for projects, such as Government grants including Arts Council funding, Lottery funding, funding from your Local Authority, grants from charitable trusts and foundations, and bursaries.

Research, research, research

Successful fundraising is all about research, and matching available funds to your projects. If you approach fundraising creatively you should be able to adapt projects to available funds while still retaining your artistic integrity. So how do you discover what is out there? Get on the arts mailing lists to find out about new rounds of funds. Research the funding bodies and their criteria. Talk to your local Council about what funds they can offer you and your project. Find out what venues support new work with bursaries, or support in kind such as free space. Find out what trusts and foundations there are and who they give money to. Look up fundraising directories in your local library or one of the resource centres at organisations such as CIDA in east London and the Directory of Social Change (**www.dsc.org.uk**).

The Funder Finder website (**www.omacl.co.uk**) features downloadable resources including a handy budget tool and grant application tool. They also have a free comprehensive advice pack on their website which has downloadable leaflets on areas such as budgeting, planning a funding strategy and tips for successful applications. The website also has a comprehensive A–Z list of trusts and foundations that have available funds.

It is important to research the funder that you are applying to, in order to find the 'essence' of the funder. This is essential so that you can match your projects to the relevant funder. For example, a Lottery Funding scheme such as the Community Fund (**www.tnlcommunityfund.org.uk**) distributes public money for the benefit of local communities. Therefore any application to them must be for a project that demonstrates clear benefit to an identified community or body of people.

Similarly, the Arts Councils of England, Wales, Scotland and Northern Ireland all distribute public funds and have to be very open and transparent about how their funds are distributed.

Theatre

Arts Council England (ACE) is the development and funding agency for the arts in England. You can apply to ACE as an individual for funding between £200 to £30,000. Organisations can receive up to £100,000. You can apply any time and there are no deadlines. A decision will be forthcoming within six weeks for grants under £5,000 and twelve weeks for grants over £5,000. ACE set aims every three years which form the basis of their grant-making policy, so it is important for applicants to think about how their project will fit into these aims. As with any funding body, building a relationship is paramount. Even before you approach ACE for funding, you should be inviting them to your productions and telling them about your projects. Full details of how to apply, including guidance notes, are on the website (**www.artscouncil.org.uk**).

The Arts Council of Wales (**www.artswales.wales**) has a similar funding system and structure to England, but there are regular funding deadlines throughout the year. Creative Scotland (formerly The Scottish Arts Council; **www.creativescotland.com**) has a slightly more complicated funding system with deadlines for different funding streams. The Arts Council of Northern Ireland (**www.artscouncil-ni.org**) has different funding schemes for individuals and organisations, and different closing dates for individual schemes.

In contrast to the Arts Councils in the UK, many charitable trusts and foundations only distribute funds to limited companies, and, in some cases, registered charities. Some can fund individuals, but they are not many. When applying to trusts and foundations, it is important to remember they were usually set up to address an issue or problem. You will need to identify what this is and ensure that your project addresses this.

Find out what you can about the funding body that you are applying to and what their funding priorities are. Make sure you fit into their guidelines and that you are eligible to apply. Remember that all funders have agendas – they do not give money away for nothing. For example, many Local Authority arts funding schemes usually look for local projects that impact on the community and have public benefit. View researching and applying for funding as you would looking for a job. You would not apply to a company if you did not think you were qualified. Similarly, you are wasting your time and theirs if you apply for funding that you are not eligible to get, e.g. your theatre company is not a registered charity, or they only fund work with older people and you work with children.

The proposal

An easy to read guide on writing funding proposals is Tim Cook's *Avoiding the Wastepaper Basket – A practical guide to applying to Grant Making Trusts* (LVSC, 1998). The book is written from the perspective of the funding body, and looks at examples of good and bad funding proposals.

If there is no application form, write a clear and concise (2 x A4 page) proposal. Write in plain English and do not use jargon. Find what the 'grain' of the funding body is. Do their work for them. Show in your funding application exactly how you meet their criteria and fit into their funding policy. Again to use the analogy of applying for a job, use the exact wording of the guidelines in your application when you are talking about your project, much in the way you would use the wording in the Person Specification when you are applying for a job. You can even highlight their criteria in bold or italics to make it stand out.

Follow the guidelines of the fund to the letter – supply all the information that they require but do not add in additional information if it is not requested. If you have something that you think may be of interest to them, mention in your application that this is available on request. Convey your enthusiasm and passion for your project and your belief in yourself and/or your company. Show how the project will be successful. Funders like to back winners.

When you are finished, show your finished application to a non-arts person and ask them to read it for clarity. If you do get a grant, remember to say thank you! Start to build a relationship with the funder and keep them updated on progress with the project. If you are not successful, ask for feedback from the funder on why.

Business sponsorship

Business sponsorship can be a useful way of raising funds for projects if you are not eligible to apply for grant project funding. Business sponsorship is where a company gives your organisation or project cash, or support in kind, in exchange for publicity for their product or service. It is important to remember that businesses will not give you money or support for nothing – they will require something in return. Sponsorship is essentially a commercial deal between yourself and the business, and therefore there should be a clear exchange of benefits, e.g. advertising benefit for the company and monetary benefit for the arts organisation, and there should be a value to the benefit given or received.

Income generation

An important part of finding funding for projects is generating your own income. Income can be earned or generated from a number of different sources: venues can pay you a fee or share the box office receipts of a production. They can also commission or co-produce a work. You can sell merchandise such as programmes, t-shirts or postcards at your events. You can generate income through education work including fees for workshops and residencies. Individuals can give you money for your projects (angels) or they can invest in your work and expect (or not!) a return. You can also raise funds through events ranging from theatre related events such as benefit performances and cabarets to 'fun' events such as sponsored walks to parachute jumps.

Creative thinking

When you are starting out, it can be difficult to see where you can obtain the money for projects. The Arts Council do prefer to fund artists or organisations with a track record, and therefore you may have to find alternative funding initially for your productions or projects. Trusts and foundations tend to only fund limited companies or registered charities, and so again this may not be an area of funding that you can tap into immediately.

Therefore it is important to think of ways of funding your work outside the traditional funding system. In many cases, this may mean that you have to fund your work yourself and hope that you can get a return on it, or at least break even. This is how the majority of companies fund their Edinburgh Festival Fringe run – by investing the money upfront in the hire of the venue, the accommodation and travel and the cost of the production and hoping that the take at the box office will cover these costs and give everyone involved in the production some wages. If you are using your own money to mount a production, you need to be able to assess what level of risk you are willing to accept and think of ways of lessening this risk. Examine your budget and see where you can reduce or cut costs. You could try to get free rehearsal space from a local school in exchange for workshops or use a local printer for your flyers in exchange for advertising in your programme. Consider

Theatre

sharing your venue with another company for a double bill (check that this is acceptable to the venue in advance) to halve the costs of the hire. Book a venue in your local area that you know so that you can at least invite friends and family to have a guaranteed audience. Ask friends and family to invest small amounts of money in your production. This can be done as a gift or on an investment and return basis e.g. an individual invests £100 and is guaranteed a return of £75 or an amount above £100, depending on how well the show does. Offer credits for purchase in the production as gifts – purchasers get credit in the publicity material, and an invitation to a performance.

There are many examples of artists and companies that have used creative ways to get their projects up and running. One company sold performances in the customer's sitting room on eBay for cash. Another company raised the money for a string of rural performances by doing a sponsored walk from venue to venue. Another company raised the money for a production by offering to do up a local community centre – they got free rehearsal space and a venue as part of the deal.

Remember that you are a creative individual! Use some of that creativity to think outside the box when it comes to finding money for projects.

Sinead Mac Manus has worked for a wide range of arts organisations, including Frantic Assembly, Tall Stories and Mimbre. She is currently a freelance creative business consultant and trainer, and has many years of experience working with and training creative entrepreneurs. She is the author of *eVolve Graduate Handbook: a practical guide to producing performance*. Her activity in developing new business models around the idea of e-learning for creative entrepreneurs using web 2.0 tools and social media led her to be chosen this year as one of the Courvoisier: Future 500 to watch.

Get Seen as an Actor/Comedy Writer Performer

Chris Head

As an actor, you are often waiting on others. Waiting for someone to write a script, stage a play, produce a movie. You can't show your brilliance until you're given the opportunity to. Until then you have to wait. A well established creative way around this bind is to devise and produce your own theatre work, and there are many examples of actors who have broken through by devising in this way.

Then there is comedy. Stand-up is brilliantly simple to get started at and there are more collaborative paths too like sketch comedy and short film. Writing comedy for yourself makes you proactive, generating your own projects, and it gives you a way to showcase yourself which is not dependent on waiting for others. Then when you do audition you will be a more attractive, match fit proposition; and making your own work can get you that audition in the first place. Here I explore a range of ways that as an actor you can get into comedy.

Stand-up

When Aisling Bea left drama school she found work as a serious actor hard to come by. So she started doing stand-up. Fast forward to 2012 and she wins the So You Think You're Funny stand-up competition at the Edinburgh Fringe and follows that up with an award nomination for her 2013 solo stand-up show *C'est La Bea*. Her comedy career properly launched, Bea went on to write and star in the acclaimed Channel 4 comedy *This Way Up...* and is now an in demand actor.

Of course not everyone will have the stellar trajectory of Aisling Bea, but if you're an actor waiting around for an audition, you could do a lot worse than start doing stand-up. You might shudder at the thought of stand up, but it's the quickest and most direct way to get yourself in front of audiences and with luck and persistence there's a clear progression to paid gigs.

Stand-up courses (ahem, like my own in London) can help ease you into it, and there are many supportive and friendly new act nights especially in cities. Why as an actor might you do stand-up? It shows gumption and bravery, and it means you are getting regular stage time in front of audiences. All far more attractive than "resting" between jobs. It also opens up other avenues such as presenting and compering. And you never know, maybe you will follow in Aisling Bea's footsteps.

The default in stand-up is to appear as a heightened version of yourself. In this case, *you* become a character; you're playing a version of yourself. As part of your act you can also deliver act-outs and dialogue as other characters thereby showcasing your acting and vocal talents. For example, I directed the Hollywood actor and producer Hopwood DePree in a touring festival show *The Manc is a Yank* where he both created a persona for himself and played a range of characters.

Why the title? Researching his ancestry online he discovered that via the long lost British branch of the family he is heir to a crumbling stately home outside Rochdale! Putting his acting on hold he relocated to the UK to pursue this passion project of restoring Hopwood Hall. ("Hopwood" being the original family name.) He didn't want to totally neglect his performing whilst in the UK but at the same time had to juggle the restoration project. So the simple and direct form of stand-up was the perfect vehicle and when he approached me for help it was a no-brainer to develop a festival show with him telling his amazing true story.

In the show, he creates a stand-up version of himself that was a fish-out-of-water, clownish figure (as he says exaggerating the truth just a bit!) and he also gets to play the northern hall caretaker Bob, the local historian Geoff, a bemused hotelier and a shopkeeper and a range of other characters as he tells his stories. In Hopwood's case, an unexpected side effect of telling his story onstage in an hour long show was that it eventually became a book, *Downton Shabby*.

Character comedy

If you don't like the idea of being yourself on stage however, you can also perform as a fictional character in stand-up contexts. I have worked for a number of years with comedic actor-writer-film maker Steve Whiteley. On the live stage he has found success performing in character as the spoken word artist Wisebowm. Initially performing short sets in comedy clubs in character, he progressed with me as director to doing full-length festival shows. To make the leap to this broader canvas, we fleshed out the wider world of characters around Wisebowm treating the one-man show in effect like a sitcom. This then made the next step to a BBC Radio 4 sitcom pilot (that I script-edited) a natural one.

Someone else I have worked with as director and coach over a number of years is Katia Kvinge. This Scottish-Norwegian comedian-writer-actor began doing stand-up as herself but felt more at home performing characters. This eventually developed into full-length festival shows where she interacts with the audience as herself *and* showcases a range of character performances. For her this is the best of both worlds. The audience can meet her and hear her story and she gets to perform a range of character pieces too.

This is true too of actor-writer Helen Wood who I have directed in autobiographical one-woman shows on her idiosyncratic passions. Her breakthrough show *The OS Map Fan Club* was seen at Edinburgh, on a national tour and at Ordnance Survey HQ! When she'd previously performed in acting roles she had to hide her glee at playing a role but in these shows her joy at taking on a character is all part of the charm of the piece.

Sketch comedy

A perhaps more sociable way to showcase a range of characters of your own devising is in sketch comedy. Stand-up Janine Harouni also writes and performs with the sketch group Muriel alongside Meg Salter and Sally O'Leary; all three of whom I have intensively coached in sitcom writing. The discipline of creating characters and sketches is a great grounding for the longer form of sitcom narrative and there are many examples of sitcoms that had their beginnings in sketch work. And what a great opportunity sketch shows present to you, the actor, to show your versatility and range and to try out characters and situations in short form.

Muriel perform live sketch comedy and also make sketches for social media and online consumption, racking up millions of views. This combination, live and online, I feel is the optimum approach giving you invaluable immediate feedback from live audiences alongside a potentially vast online audience. And once you have established an online presence, there are the conventional broadcasters who are commissioning material for their social media channels. The Muriel team have produced sketches for BBC3 as has Katia Kvinge who has also made online shorts for Comedy Central and Channel 4.

Short film

Another way to showcase your talents is through the short film. The aforementioned Steve Whiteley took that route with his comedy short *Swiped*, that helped develop and script-edited. It became an official selection at the Palm Springs International Shorts Festival. As well as getting him interest from TV producers as a writer-performer, going over to the festival lead to Steve landing a part as an actor in a sitcom pilot – an acting job he certainly wouldn't have got if he were just waiting for the phone to ring.

I asked Steve if he had any thoughts for someone looking to branching out into the world of comedy writing and performing and I think his insights are the perfect way to end this piece: "Be courageous. Don't be afraid to experiment and try new things. Dying on stage is a rite of passage and every time you die, you are reborn (deep) with a new found knowledge on what you can do differently next time. Be persistent. It takes a long time to develop your act and material, the likelihood of overnight success is slim, but if you have a passion for it and you're half decent then stick with it and good things will eventually happen. Collaborate. The more you workshop your ideas with others the more likely it is that you'll develop your act-material-content quicker and have some thing more rounded. Don't be precious about getting feedback. Finally enjoy it! Otherwise what's the point. You may as well be handsomely paid (or not) and be miserable at a real job."

Chris Head is a comedy director, coach and consultant. He is the author of *A Director's Guide to the Art of Stand-up* and *Creating Comedy Narratives for Stage & Screen*, both published by Methuen. He teaches comedy writing at BBC Writers Room, the British Library and at Bath Spa University and stand-up independently in London, alongside directing live shows. www.chrishead.com.

Theatre

Routes to stand-up comedy

Geoff Whiting, stand-up comedian and founder of leading comedy bookers, Mirth Control
Interview by Rob Ostlere

Geoff Whiting has over twenty years' experience as a stand-up comedian and is a successful comedy booker with his company Mirth Control, the UK's largest independent comedy bookers. Geoff is also a manager for new acts and has worked on building the careers of some of the biggest names in the industry. In this interview he explains the pathways into stand-up and what it takes to make it as a comedian.

You've worked with hundreds of comedians, Geoff, but I'd like first to hear about your path into the industry?

I started off in Bath in 1997 as an open-mic spot; in other words, doing five, occasionally ten minutes for various venues. But in 1998 I reached the final of a competition called The Daily Telegraph Open Mic Award at the Edinburgh Festival. That was what launched me to a different level. I turned pro within two years and was earning a living within about two-and-a-half from just stand-up.

And this was at the same time as working as a booker and managing other comedians' careers?

That was something I hadn't actually planned. I answered an advertisement in *The Stage* newspaper from a new club in Plymouth. I did fifteen minutes, it went well and after the show the guy said, "Can you come next week?" I explained to him I'm a new comic and that's all I had but I could bring another comedian with me, warm up the audience myself and then introduce them. And that's how I became a booker. In those early years we had lots of notable people: Jason Manford, Jimmy Carr, Russell Howard, John Robins, Jon Richardson. All of them played as an opening act and came back to be the closing act. After that, my career as a booker just snowballed really. At the same time, I was booking for 100 clubs, I was still working four to five nights a week as a comedian. I then eventually opened up a management arm, taking comedians from unknown acts through the levels you go to be a professional.

What are those levels?

The principles haven't changed since I began. You start by doing five minutes for nothing. If that's good then you'll be asked to come and do ten minutes for nothing. If that's good, we'll talk about paying you for ten minutes, then twenty. It could be a few weeks later that you're asked back, it could be a few months; it depends on the club and the demand. After that, you work your way up towards closing a show. That's another hurdle completely because you need to have either a very solid twenty or thirty, or forty minutes for some arts centres. To get to the next level you need forty-five minutes. Then after that you'd get two forty-five minutes together for a tour show.

How long does that take?

It depends but in general, for a brilliant comedian, maybe three to four years. A decent, hard-working comic I'd say we do that journey in five to six years. And a not-inspirational-but-determined comic might make that journey in eight to ten years.

So beyond playing as many gigs as possible, what other routes are there? Comedy courses are becoming more popular aren't they?

I do Q&As on a course in Bath about everything we're talking about; how you go from being an unpaid act to a professional. The actual courses are over several weeks and at the end you'll get in front of an audience of eighty to a hundred people. That's the first time ever for most people on the course and it's crucial; can you get up and do your six or seven minutes without forgetting it, avoiding the pitfalls and without losing the plot. And if somebody has a great show, then they've got a video of it they can promote themselves with.

New act competitions are another way in?

New act competitions are great. They're open access so anybody can enter. The ones like I did with the *Daily Telegraph*, for example the BBC Introducing Radio 4 Comedy Award or So You Think You're Funny, tend to have their finals up in Edinburgh. They're massive platforms with TV, YouTube or radio coverage.

What about Edinburgh more generally?

What's great about Edinburgh is you can do shows that are two, three, or four-handers. You might be an act who's been going for a short while, you've only got fifteen minutes, but it's stuff you've road-tested and you're confident is working. You then find two or three other comedians in the same position. You put together a package and there's four of you to do the marketing, the flyer-ing and the social media for it. Or you do Free Fringe, which has really exploded in the last maybe ten years. Imran Yusuf getting nominated as best new comedian on a Free Fringe show was a breakthrough because suddenly people realised it doesn't mean you're marginalised. All you need to do is pay for the technician, set the room up and make your own flyers and posters. If you get sixty people in and you have a great show they'll put money in the bucket. Four amateurs can get together and, if they're good at promoting it, can breakeven and they've done an Edinburgh run.

How do agents fit into all this?

Some people make it through sheer hard work and go fully from being a new act to a professional without an agent. For others, the breakthrough is getting signed. It depends entirely on your path. I can think of comics who worked for years doing another job at the same time as working their way up. And then there's someone like Joe Lycett, who won the Bath New Act Competition. One of the judges was a TV commissioner, who immediately called a very big agent and told them someone's just stormed it.

It sounds like part of working your way up is trying lots of different things, getting yourself out there?

I learned very early on that a certain percentage is talent and the rest is application. I literally gigged twenty-eight nights out of thirty most months. My contemporaries were doing it as well. Daniel Kitson was famous for only having six nights off an entire year. Russel Howard, when he started, gigged almost every night. It's no coincidence that most of the people who I see on TV now worked night-in night-out all the time as new acts.

That's a lot of dedication!

I appreciate some people might read this interview and say that's all very well but I've got a day job, I work long hours, or I haven't got a car so I can't do gigs all over the place. I

Theatre

guess it depends on your mindset and how much you want to do it. In my case, once I realised I had the potential – I'd done my first fifteen gigs or so and comics were saying to me you've got something – I had a sort of plan and determination as a comedian. I went into debt to do it and it was three-and-a-half years before I got back to square one. If you're absolutely and utterly determined and focused you can find a way.

What other qualities do you think new comedians need?

You have to be tenacious and prepared to do anything when you start. Jimmy Carr's first ever paid gig was for me. He said to me, "Geoff, anything you got, anywhere, I'll do it, no problem". And I said, "Well, when you say 'anywhere', I've got a gig in Devon on Tuesday. You'll have to drive there and it might only be £80". His answer was, "Fine, I'll be there".

You told me you started out by writing letters to get your fist gigs. Nowadays, of course, that's very different

There is way more access to networking, to knowing who books shows and how to reach them, with Facebook groups for the south-east, the south-west and so on, and Edinburgh, new act competitions and more. You can network with other comics and promoters, and posts do go up: "I need some acts tomorrow or next month … are you free?" Get yourself a Facebook page as a comic, not just your own personal one. Load content on: a decent video, decent pictures and a basic CV with a few bullet points about you. And then go on the forums. You'll get opportunities to do stage-time and you can build from there.

From the thousands of gigs you've done, Geoff, is there one final piece of advice you'd give to someone building their act?

Yes, the audience should be your editor. Record your shows on a phone when you're starting out, even just the audio. Listen to what the audience are laughing at. We all have a favourite joke that doesn't work but you've got to listen to where the audience is laughing and take note of that.

To find out more about Geoff's stand-up, go to **www.geoffwhiting.co.uk**. Geoff's booking and management company can be found at **www.mirthcontrolcomedy.com**

Pantomime

This section lists some of the major pantomime producers and some of the theatres and arts centres that produce their own pantomimes. These latter (often subsidised by a local authority) largely present touring and (sometimes) amateur productions. However, a number do mount their own professional pantomimes and it can be useful to look through the Theatres & Provincial/Touring section of *Contacts* to check which.

Another way of finding out is to check through the listings and reviews in *The Stage* every Christmas. (Also look at **www.its-behind-you.com** which lists forthcoming pantomimes.)

Some of these theatres occasionally produce their own shows throughout the year, especially as part of the work of their Education departments. Where possible we have included this information in each entry, but it is also worth visiting the theatre's website for further details.

PANTOMIME PRODUCERS

Chaplins Entertainment Ltd
Chaplins House, The Acorn Centre, Roebuck Road, Hainault, Essex IG6 3TU
tel 020 8501 2121
email fun@chaplinspantos.co.uk
website www.chaplinspantos.co.uk
Directors Mr J Holmes *Productions Manager* Jessica Djemil

Production details: A touring pantomime and theatre-in-education company which also works in film and television production. Stages 26 productions annually, performing in small theatres, schools, social clubs and community centres.

Casting procedures: Uses freelance casting directors and holds general auditions; actors requesting inclusion are asked to write from July until the end of October only. Casting breakdowns are publicly available from the website, by postal application (with sae), in *The Stage* and via Mandy. During the period specified, the company welcomes letters (with CVs and photographs) from individual actors previously unknown to them, sent by post or email, and will accept showreels and invitations to view individual actors' websites. Rarely or never has the opportunity to cast disabled actors.

Crossroads Pantomimes Ltd
1st Floor, 6 Kean Street, London WC2B 4AS
tel 020 7836 6544
email info@xroadspantomimes.com
website www.pantomime.com
Casting Director/Producer Jonathan Kiley *Producer/Chief Executive* Michael Harrison

Production details: The largest of the commercial pantomime producers with 24 pantomimes across the UK: His Majesty's, Aberdeen; Grand Opera House, Belfast; Hippodrome Theatre, Birmingham; The Alhambra, Bradford; The Bristol Hippodrome; The Churchill Bromley; New Theatre, Cardiff; Hippodrome, Darlington; The Orchard, Dartford; Kings Theatre, Edinburgh; Hull New Theatre; The London Palladium; The Opera House, Manchester; Milton Keynes Theatre; Theatre Royal, Newcastle upon Tyne; Theatre Royal, Nottingham; Theatre Royal, Plymouth; The Richmond Theatre; Cliffs Pavilion, Southend; Mayflower Theatre, Southampton; The Regent Theatre, Stoke; Grand Theatre, Swansea; The New Wimbledon Theatre and New Victoria Theatre, Woking.

Casting procedures: Actors should send CVs and photographs by email to Jonathan Kiley from March (star-casting only in February). Welcomes performance notices by email or by post.

Evolution Productions
Little Statenborough House, Sandwich Road, Eastry, Kent CT13 0DH
tel 01304 615333
email info@evolution-productions.co.uk
website www.evolution-productions.co.uk
Facebook www.facebook.com/evolution.pantomimes
Twitter @pantomimes
Producer Emily Wood *Producer/Director* Paul Hendy

Production details: Founded in 2005 and run by husband-and-wife team, Emily Wood and Paul Hendy. Produces pantomimes and Large-scale productions (recently produced *Mister Maker!* and *The Shapes Live!* (UK tour), *Morcambe* (UK tour), *Dear Santa* (UK and Singapore tour) and *Oliver!* at The Central Theatre, Chatham. Stages 8 pantomimes a year: The Marlowe Theatre, Canterbury; The Hawth Theatre, Crawley; The Grove Theatre, Dunstable; Lichfield Garrick, Lichfield; Lyceum

Theatre

Theatre, Sheffield; Theatre Severn Shrewsbury; Alban Areana, St Albans and the Octogan Theatre, Yeovil. Offers non-Equity, in-house contracts ("Equity equivalent") and does not subscribe to the Equity Pension Scheme.

Casting procedures: Casts in-house – all casting enquiries should be addressed to Kate Roddy (**casting@evolution-productions.co.uk**). Holds general auditions; the best time to write to request inclusion is March/May. Casting breakdowns are published via Spotlight and through agents. Welcomes letters (with CVs and photographs) and performance notices from actors previously unknown to the company, sent by post or email. Happy to receive appropriate showreels and invitations to view individual actors' websites. Will consider applications from disabled actors to play disabled characters.

Extravaganza Productions

Old Ferry House, 4 London Road, Boston, Lincs PE21 8AA
tel 01642 815181
website www.extravaganza-productions.co.uk
Directors David Vickers, Richard Chandler

Production details: Established in 1995. Presenting Pantomimes for The Plaza, Stockport and Middlesborough Theatre. Number of productions staged annually varies.

Casting procedures: Casting is carried out in house; actors can write at any time to request inclusion. Submissions (with CVs and photographs) should be addressed to Richard Chandler, Casting Director. Also accepts invitations to view individual actors' websites, and showreels. Applications from disabled actors are considered to play disabled characters.

Paul Holman Associates

Morritt House, 58 Station Approach, South Ruislip, Middlesex HA4 6SA
tel 020 8845 9408
email enquiries@paulholmanassociates.co.uk
website www.paulholmanassociates.co.uk
Managing *Director* Paul Holman

Production details: Produces Pantomimes, Summer Seasons, Tours and other commercial projects. Stages between 10-15 productions annually. Venues where productions are staged include: Bridlington, Aylesbury (Civic), Catford (Broadway), Derby (Assembly Rooms), Leeds (Carriageworks), Newark (Palace), Redditch (Palace), Weston-super-mare (Playhouse). Summer Seasons: The Pier Theatre (Bournemouth), Princess Theatre (Hunstanton). Offers non-Equity (Variety) contracts and does not subscribe to the Equity Pension Scheme.

Casting procedures: Casting is done by in-house casting director. Occasionally hold general auditions; spring is the best time to write requesting auditions. Casting breakdowns are available on Castweb. Accepts submissions (with CVs and photographs)

from individual actors, sent by post or email. Invitations to view showreels and to attend other productions are also accepted. Will consider applications from disabled actors to play disabled characters, but in practice rarely has the opportunity to cast them.

Imagine Theatre Ltd

2 Brandon House, Woodhams Road, Middlemarch Business Park, Coventry CV3 4FX
tel 024 7630 7001
email casting@imaginetheatre.co.uk
website www.imaginetheatre.co.uk
Artistic Director Eric Potts *Managing Director* Stephen Boden *Business Director* Sarah Boden

Production details: Imagine Theatre (since 2009; formerly Wish Theatre) produces pantomimes and children's theatre for No. 1 tours, including *The Tweenies* and *Fun Song Factory*. Venues for pantomime include: Eden Court, Inverness; Beacon Arts Centre, Greenock; Adam Smith, Kirkcaldy; Palace Theatre, Kilmarnock; Southport Theatre; Victoria Theatre, Halifax; Grimsby Auditorium; Palace Theatre, Newark; DeMontfort Hall, Leicester; Belgrade Theatre, Coventry; Spa Centre, Leamington Spa; Hexagon, Reading; Grand Pavilion, Porthcawl and Queen's Theatre, Barnstaple. Also tours Santa Shows. Offers in-house contracts ("enhanced Equity") and does not subscribe to the Equity Pension Scheme.

Casting procedures: Casts mainly in house. Holds general auditions; actors should email the company in March-May to request inclusion. Casting breakdowns are not published except on Spotlight. Welcomes CVs and photgraphs from actors previously unknown to the company; prefers these to be emailed rather than posted. Will consider applications from disabled actors to play disabled characters. "Panto isn't a cop-out: it's a serious business. We use actors who can engage with the audience and have fun. It is really useful if actors can indicate their location/home town, which helps with accents and knowing if an individual is local to one of our pantomime venues. Please do not send showreels or invitations to view websites."

New Pantomime Productions

27 Shooters Road, Enfield, Middlesex EN2 8RJ
tel 020 8363 9920
email newpantomime@aol.com
Facebook www.facebook.com/newpantomimepro/
Directors Simon Barry, Paul Graham

Production details: Produces pantomimes at 7 venues: Theatr Colwyn, Colwyn Bay; Brindley Arts Centre, Runcorn; Southport Theatre; Kings Theatre, Southsea; Princess Theatre, Torquay; Grand Opera House, York. Offers non-Equity contracts and does not subscribe to the Equity Pension Scheme.

Casting procedures: Casts in house. Holds general auditions; actors should write in July to request inclusion. Casting breakdowns are not publicly available. Welcomes emails only (with CVs and photographs) from actors previously unknown to the company. Does not welcome showreels or invitations to view individual actors' websites. "Make sure you're suitable for the job you're applying for. We have employed disabled actors – and not just to play disabled characters. So long as the actor is good, that's all that matters."

Pantoni Pantomimes

205 Bexhill Road, St Leonards on Sea,
East Sussex TN38 8BG
tel 01424 443400
email david@pantoni.com
website www.pantoni.com
Facebook www.facebook.com/newpantomimepro/
Directors David Lee, Rita Proctor

Produces pantomimes for the Doncaster Civic Theatre; Empire Theatre, Consett; New Floral Pavilion, New Brighton; The Leatherhead Theatre; Library Theatre, Luton; and Octagon Theatre, Yeovil.

Spillers Pantomimes

The Old Post Office, Honey Tye, Leavenheath,
Suffolk CO6 4NX
tel 07785 327006
email info@spillers-pantomimes.co.uk
website www.spillers-pantomimes.co.uk
Production Director (Mr) Bev Berridge

Production details: Established 1989. Produces pantomimes for Alexandra Theatre, Bognor Regis; Epsom Playhouse; Woodville Hall Theatre, Gravesend; Motherwell Theatre; Majestic Theatre, Retford; Civic Theatre, Rotherham; The Music Hall, Shrewsbury; Pavilion Theatre, Weymouth. Offers actors non-Equity contracts and does not contribute to the Equity Pension Scheme.

Casting procedures: Casting is done in house. Holds general auditions. Best time for actors to write (with CV and photograph) to request inclusion is March/April. Casting breakdowns are published in *The Stage*. Welcomes CVs and photographs from actors previously unknown to the company, sent by post or email. Will consider applications from disabled actors to play disabled characters.

UK Productions

Brook House, Mint Street, Godalming,
Surrey GU7 1HE
tel 01483 423600
email mail@ukproductions.co.uk
website www.ukproductions.co.uk
Managing Director Martin Dodd

Production details: Established 1995. Produces pantomimes, musicals and plays for No. 1 national and international touring and West End. Also set, costume and production hire. (See entry under *Independent managements/theatre producers* on page 172.) Offers non-Equity contracts.

Casting procedures: Casting is done in house. Does not hold open auditions. Casting breakdowns are distributed via Spotlight. Welcomes performance notices but not any other unsolicited form of correspondence. Will consider applications from disabled actors to play characters with disabilities.

IN-HOUSE PANTOMIMES

Buxton Opera House

Water Street, Buxton, Derbyshire SK17 6XN
tel 01298 72190
email admin@boh.org.uk
website www.buxtonoperahouse.org.uk
Chief Executive Officer Paul Kerryson *Theatre Secretary* Pat Russell

Production details: A receiving theatre presenting around 450 performances each year including dance, comedy, children's shows, drama, musical concerts, pantomime and opera as well as Fringe Theatre and Community and Education Programme. Edwardian theatre designed by Frank Matcham, restored in 2001.

Casting procedures: Commissions Channel Theatre Company to produce its annual pantomimes. Philip Dart, Artistic Director of Channel Theatre, is responsible for casting.

Cambridge Arts Theatre

Programming & Production Department,
6 St Edwards Passage, Cambridge CB2 3PJ
tel 01223 578904
email info@cambridgeartstheatre.com
website www.cambridgeartstheatre.com
Director Dafydd Rogers

Production details: Seating capacity 665. A receiving theatre which presents a wide range of work, including children's theatre, music, dance and drama. Produces in-house panto annually.

Casting procedures: Engages a freelance director who, together with the producer and choreographer, is responsible for casting the panto. Actors should contact the theatre to request an audition for the pantomime in March/April. These submissions will be forwarded to the director, and marked for the attention of Sue Lowe. Actors are employed under Equity-approved contracts. Invitations to see actors in other productions are only welcomed from actors in whom the director has already shown interest. Will consider applications from disabled actors to play disabled characters.

The Capitol

North Street, Horsham, West Sussex
tel 01403 750220
email contact@thecapitolhorsham.com
website www.thecapitolhorsham.com
General Manager Matthew Effemey

Theatre

Production details: Multi-arts community venue, comprised of a 410 seat Theatre, 2 cinema screens, studio theatre and gallery space. Produces a professional pantomime each year. Offers TMA/Equity-approved contracts.

Casting procedures: Uses in-house casting director. Optimum time to write requesting an audition is in spring/summer. Casting breakdowns are publicly available on the website, or by postal application (with sae). Accepts letters (with CVs and photographs) from individual actors previously unknown to the company, sent by post or email. Also welcomes invitations to view showreels and to attend other productions. Will consider applications from disabled actors to play disabled characters.

The Theatre, Chipping Norton

2 Spring Street, Chipping Norton, Oxfordshire OX7 5NL
tel 01608 642349
email administration@chippingnortontheatre.com
website www.chippingnortontheatre.com
Director John Terry

Production details: The Theatre is a pivotal part of the artistic life of the area, and takes care to programme as diverse a range of performances – theatre, film, dance, comedy and opera – as possible. Its Community & Education programme takes film and opera out to village halls.

An intimate space, it seats 217 (including 4 wheelchair spaces) in either proscenium (end-on) or in-the-round configurations. While predominantly a receiving house, The Theatre produces an annual pantomime which runs for around 80 performances over the Christmas period, as well as occasional smaller ventures. Recent productions include: *Mother Goose* and *Puss in Boots*, new pantomimes by Simon Brett; and *Taste*, a new play which toured Normandy. The Theatre offers TMA/Equity-approved contracts and subscribes to the Equity Pension Scheme.

Casting procedures: Does not use casting directors. Welcomes unsolicited CVs and photographs from actors unknown to the company, as well as invitations to view actors' websites. Casting breakdowns for the pantomime are available March and September via Spotlight; this is the best time to write to request inclusion. Actively encourages applications from disabled actors, and promotes the use of inclusive casting.

City Varieties Music Hall

Swan Street, Leeds LS1 6LW
email a.wadsworth@leedsheritagetheatres.com
website www.leedsheritagetheatres.com
General Manager Ian Sime

Production details: Seating capacity 467. Grade II* listed building, built in 1865. World-famous as the home of BBC TV's *Good Old Days*. Produces a professional pantomime each year, running from the end of November to mid-January. Also continues to produce *Good Old Days* music hall entertainment.

Actors are employed under UK theatre/Equity-approved contracts and the theatre subscribes to the Equity Pension Scheme.

Casting procedures: Optimum time to write requesting an audition for the pantomime is between January and June. Accepts submissions (with CVs and photographs) from individual actors previously unknown to the company.

Connaught Theatre

Union Place BN11 1LG
tel 01903 206206
email boxoffice@wtm.uk
website www.wtam.uk
CEO & Creative Director Amanda O'Reilly

Production details: Part of Wothing Theatres and Museum. Operates as a theatre and cinema. Seating capacity 512 with 6 wheelchair spaces.

The Courtyard

The Courtyard Centre for the Arts, Edgar Street, Hereford HR4 9JR
tel 01432 346555
email ian.archer@courtyard.org.uk
website www.courtyard.org.uk
Chief Executive & Artictic Director Ian Archer

Production details: Seating capacity 436. The Courtyard opened in September 1998 and was the first Lottery-funded theatre to be built in England. It provides "an eclectic programme of work, from produced to received, and offers something for the whole community". Produces a professional pantomime each year, from the end of November to mid-January. Provides actors with Equity-approved contracts as negotiated through UK Theatre.

Casting procedures: Uses in-house casting directors; actors may write in June to request an audition. Casting breakdowns are available from the website, or via CastNet and Castweb. Welcomes letters (with CVs and photographs) from individual actors previously unknown to the company, sent by post or email. Also accepts showreels and invitations to visit other productions. Actively encourages applications from disabled actors and promotes the use of inclusive casting.

Cumbernauld Theatre

Kildrum, Cumbernauld, Glasgow G67 2BN
tel 01236 732887
email info@cumbernauldtheatre.co.uk
website www.cumbernauldtheatre.co.uk
CEO Sarah Price *Operations Director* Amanda Young

Production details: Established in 1978. A year-round producing theatre with a broad range of artist development and creative learning programmes. Produces a professional pantomime each year, together with other in-house plays, musicals and 'seasons'. Recent productions include: *The Wasp Factory* by Iain Banks.

Casting procedures: Casting is done by the Artistic Director. Auditions are held all year round; actors should obtain casting breakdowns from the website only. Welcomes letters (with CVs and photographs) from individual actors previously unknown to the company, sent by post or email. Will consider invitations to visit other productions, but requests that no showreels be submitted. Actively encourages applications from disabled actors and promotes the use of inclusive casting.

The Customs House Trust Ltd

Mill Dam, South Shields, Tyne & Wear NE33 1ES
tel 0191 454 1234
email mail@customshouse.co.uk
website www.customshouse.co.uk
Executive Director Ray Spencer

Production details: Seating capacity 439. Established in 1994 as an arts centre, gallery, cinema and theatre. Produces approximately 3 in-house shows each year, and is a member of the North East Theatre Consortium. Stages a professional pantomime in early December which runs through to the first week in January, as well as new writing and occasional new musicals. Provides actors with Equity-approved contracts.

Casting procedures: Uses both in-house and freelance casting directors. The pantomime is cast in June, and CVs are received all year. Welcomes letters (with CVs and photographs) from individual actors previously unknown to the company, sent by post or email. Also accepts invitations to visit other productions. Advises actors to "find out about the venue via our website. Mention our work; it makes us feel important and makes you look as if you care!".

The Everyman Theatre

Regent Street, Cheltenham,
Gloucestershire GL50 1HQ
tel (01242) 572573
email admin@everymantheatre.org.uk
website www.everymantheatre.org.uk
Creative Director Paul Milton *Chief Executive* Mark Goucher

Production details: Seating capacity: main house 668, studio 60. Built in 1891. A receiving theatre which presents a wide range of work, from stand-up comedy to children's theatre and including live music, dance and drama. Also works with many emerging and established theatre companies from Gloucestershire and beyond, creating partnerships and productions that are performed at the Everyman and on tour across the county. Produces in-house plays and pantomime as well as promoting new writing.

Casting procedures: A freelance director is engaged to direct the panto. This director is responsible for the casting process and will choose how and where the casting breakdowns are made available. Actors should write in February to request auditions for the panto, as auditions are held in March and April. Submissions (photos and CVs) are welcomed from actors previously unknown to the company for both

panto and new writing projects; these should be marked for the attention of Millie Krstic-Howe (Theatre Secretary). The Everyman also runs an Actor's Lab, providing professional training and opportunities to meet and work with established directors. The Everyman Theatre is an equal opportunities employer and gives due consideration to applications from all sectors of the community.

Hackney Empire

291 Mare Street, London E8 1EJ
tel 020 8510 4500
email info@hackneyempire.co.uk
website www.hackneyempire.co.uk
Executive Director Jo Hemmant
Artistic Director Yamin Choudury

Production details: Grade II listed Frank Matcham theatre built in 1901. Recently renovated and refurbished. Provides a wide range of productions for the local community and London as a whole. Seating capacity is up to 1,280. Produces an immensely popular and critically acclaimed traditional pantomime, eschewing 'celebrities' in favour of the core elements of traditional pantomime: a well-conceived narrative line, spectacular sets and costumes, magical spectacle, music, dance and slapstick comedy. Offers TMA/Equity-approved contracts.

Casting procedures: Casting breakdowns are not publically available, but actors wishing to audition for the pantomime should contact Susie Mckenna, by post or email, in August/September. Happy to receive appropriate showreels and invitations to view individual actors' websites. Actively encourages applications from disabled actors and promotes the use of inclusive casting.

macrobert

University of Stirling, Stirling FK9 4LA
tel 01786 466666
email info@macrobert.org
website www.macrobert.org
Artistic Director Julie Ellen

Production details: A busy multi-venue arts centre seating 472, with particular emphasis on work with and for young people. Produces several professional shows per year, in November and December. Offers Equity-approved contracts as negotiated through TMA. Subscribes to the Equity Pension Scheme.

Casting procedures: Uses freelance and in-house casting directors; actors may write in April and May to request inclusion. Welcomes letters (with CVs and photographs) from individual actors previously unknown to the company, sent by post or by email. Accepts showreels and invitations to visit other productions. Rarely (or never) has the opportunity to cast disabled actors.

Millfield Theatre

Silver Street, Edmonton, London N18 1PJ
tel 020 8807 6680
website www.millfieldtheatre.co.uk

Production details: Produces panto in house and hosts a year-round programme of theatre, comedy, music, dance and variety shows. Home of Platinum Performing Arts Schools.

Casting procedures: Casting is done by liaising with show director and in-house producer. Breakdowns for the panto are sent out to agents via Spotlight Link. Contracts offered are negotiated directly with actors or their agents.

Stafford Gatehouse Theatre

Eastgate Street, Stafford ST16 2LT
tel 01785 619080
email gatehouse@freedom-leisure.co.uk
website www.staffordgatehousetheatre.co.uk
Production Manager Richard Goodman

Production details: Celebrated its 40th anniversary in 2022. A receiving theatre which presents a wide range of work, from stand-up comedy to children's theatre, and including live music, dance and drama. Usually produces its own in-house panto, with the occasional co-production. The Gatehouse also produces the annual Stafford Shakespeare production every Summer in the grounds of Stafford Castle.

Includes two performance spaces: the main auditorium seats 545 and the MET Studio seats 140.

Casting procedures: Casting is done by freelance casting directors. Breakdowns are available via Spotlight to agents only. Will consider applications from disabled actors to play disabled characters.

Theatre Royal, Bury St Edmunds

Westgate Street, Bury St Edmunds, Suffolk IP33 1QR
tel (01284) 829945
email artistic@theatreroyal.org
website www.theatreroyal.org
Artistic Director & CEO Owen Calvert-Lyons

Built in 1819, the theatre is the only surviving Regency theatre in the country. Produces an annual pantomime at Christmas and 2 other shows a year – a spring drama and a summer community production which includes professional actors working alongside local children and young people. Offers non-Equity contracts.

Casting procedures: Casting breakdowns are published via Spotlight only. Actors wishing to be considered for the pantomime should write to the theatre in April. (The spring and summer shows are cast in January/February and April/May respectively.) Only welcomes letters and emails (with CVs and photographs) from actors previously unknown to the company during these casting periods. Does not welcome showreels, but is happy to receive performance notices. Rarely or never has the opportunity to cast disabled actors.

Theatre Royal, Margate

Addington Street, Margate, Kent CT9 1PW
tel 0333 660 661

email admin.wintergardens@yourleisure.uk.com
website www.margate-live.com

Production details: Seating capacity 465. A grade 2 star listed Georgian Theatre in the heart of Margate town presenting a year-round programme of mixed incoming professional and locally produced community work. Thriving youth theatre and strong relationships with local arts organisations and associate companies. Owned by Thanet District Council, managed by Your Leisure.

Theatre Royal, Norwich

Theatre Street, Norwich NR2 1RL
tel 01603 598500
email janewalsh@norwichtheatre.org
website www.norwichtheatre.org
Programming Director & Executive ProducerManager Jane Walsh

Seating capacity 1300. Produces an annual pantomime and is a receiving house for the rest of the year, so very little scope on casting. Actors wishing to audition for the pantomime should contact Jane Walsh **janewalsh@norwichtheatre.org** from March/April. Welcomes emails (with CVs and photographs) from actors not previously known to the company. Does not welcome showreels or performance notices. Will consider applications from disabled actors on the same basis as for non-disabled actors.

Theatre Royal, Nottingham

Theatre Square, Nottingham NG1 5ND
tel 0115 989 5500
email Director@nottinghamcity.gov.uk
website www.trch.co.uk
Managing Director Peter Ireson

Production details: Seating capacity 1186. Pantomimes are produced by Crossroads Pantomimes; those produced in house are by its education-based Royal Company, which includes members of the community. Offers actors Equity-approved contracts but does not subscribe to the Equity Pension Scheme.

Casting procedures: Actors wishing to request an audition should contact Crossroads Live.

Theatre Royal, Winchester

Jewry Street, Winchester, Hampshire SO23 8SB
tel 01962 840440
email info@playtothecrowd.co.uk
website www.theatreroyalwinchester.co.uk
Director James Barry

Production details: Seating capacity 400. A receiving theatre which presents a wide range of work, from stand-up comedy to children's theatre and including music, dance and classic plays. Produces panto in house.

Casting procedures: Casting is done by the director of the show.

English-language European theatre companies

This small section seems to be populated by companies set up by enthusiasts who have kept on going with very little subsidy – and sometimes with none at all. Although living away from home and isolated from auditions, it can be fun working for such companies. It is important to note that the work often involves educational projects and/or touring.

Dear Conjunction Theatre Company

6 Rue Arthur Rozier, 75019 Paris
website www.dearconjunction-paris-theatre.com
Artistic Directors Leslie Clack, Patricia Kessler

Production details: Founded in 1991, this bilingual company is composed of professional actors, directors and writers who are resident in Paris and who present productions in both French and English. Past productions include: Pinter's *Ashes to Ashes* and *The Hothouse*; and *Someone Who'll Watch Over Me* by Frank McGuinness.

Casting procedures: Welcomes letters and emails (with CVs and photographs) from actors previously unknown to the company. Contact Leslie Clack for more information.

English Theatre Frankfurt

Kaiserstrasse 34, D-60329 Frankfurt
tel +49 692 423 1615
email mail@english-theatre.de
website www.english-theatre.de
Artistic & Executive Director Daniel John Nicolai

Production details: Founded in 1979. Presents contemporary plays, musicals and classics. 5 productions performed in the main house each year, totalling 260 performances.

Casting procedures: Uses London-based freelance casting directors. Does not hold general auditions. Actors should write in April to request inclusion. Casting breakdowns are only available via Spotlight.

The English Theatre of Hamburg

Lerchenfeld 14, 22081 Hamburg
tel +49 40 227 7089
email ethamburg@onlinehome.de
website www.englishtheatre.de
Contacts Robert Rumpf, Clifford Dean, Paul Glaser

Production details: Founded in 1976 by 2 Americans, Robert Rumpf and Clifford Dean, who originally trained and worked professionally in the USA. Together they published a 336 page book entitled The English Theatre of Hamburg 1976-2021. Along with Paul Glaser, they share general management responsibilities, plan the artistic programme and direct most of the productions. Since 1981 the theatre has occupied its present premises at Mundsburg, 22081 Hamburg. Performs 8 times per week from September to June. A typical season at the English Theatre includes a classic American or British drama, a comedy and thriller or modern classic. Recent productions include: *Fat Pig*, *The Whipping Man*, *Orphans*, *Othello* and *April in Paris*. Also produces educational material.

London Toast Theatre

Kochsvej 18, DK 1812 Frederiksberg C. Denmark
tel +45 3322 8686
email mail@londontoast.dk
website www.londontoast.dk
Facebook www.facebook.com/LondonToast
Twitter @LondonToast
Instagram @londontoasttheatre
Managing Director Søren Hall *Artistic Director* Vivienne McKee

Production details: Founded in 1982, London Toast Theatre is the largest English-speaking theatre company in Northern Europe. Presents theatre productions and provides corporate entertainment, stand-up comedy and Murder Mystery shows in Scandinavia and abroad. The company's voice-over bureau, 'Speaker's Corner', provides English and American voices for films and commercials. Recent productions include: *Shakespeare's Ghost*, *Hamlet* at Kronborg Castle, *Planet Rump - The Farce Awakens*, *Fogg's Off*, *Oh Baby – It's Cole!*, *The Three Brexiteers* and *Shirley Valentine*.

Prague Shakespeare Festival

Divadlo Kolowrat, Kolowratsky palac, Ovocny trh 579/6, Prague 1, 110 00
email info@pragueshakespeare.org
website www.pragueshakespeare.org
Artistic Director Guy Roberts

Production details: Founded in 2008. The Festival presents professional theatre productions, workshops, classes, lectures and other theatrical events, of the highest quality, conducted primarily in English by a multinational ensemble of professional theatre artists, with an emphasis on the plays of William

Theatre

Shakespeare. Stages 12-18 productions annually, and holds workshops and classes on an ongoing basis. Recent productions include: *Amadeus*, *The Winter's Tale*, *Macbeth*, *Richard III* in association with the National Theatre at the Estates Theater and Venus in Fur, *Macbeth*, *Much Ado About Nothing* on international tours to the United States and Egypt.

Casting procedures: Casts in-house; check the website for annual casting and breakdowns. Welcomes approaches (with CVs and photographs) from actors by post and by email, and accepts showreels and invitations to view individual actors' websites. Actively encourages applications from disabled actors to play characters with disabilities, and promotes the use of inclusive casting.

Simply Theatre

Centre Choiseul, Avenue de Choiseul 23A,
1290 Versoix, Switzerland
tel +41 22 860 0518
email academy@simplytheatre.com
website www.simplytheatre.com

Company details: Founded in 2005. Offers English theatre and courses for young people and families featuring professional actors, and an English-speaking Drama Academy for students. A professional English theatre for Switzerland and Continental Europe; and an English-speaking Drama Academy. Predominantly stages family-orientated theatre and shows for children.

Casting procedures: Casting breakdowns are available from Spotlight and Mandy.

Vienna's English Theatre

UK address: VM Theatre Productions Ltd,
c/o Hutchinson Rowntree Ltd,
The Deptford Mission, 1 Creek Road,
London SE8 3BT
tel 020 3355 8567
email office@englishtheatre.at
Theatre address: Josefsgasse 12, A-1080 Vienna
tel (0043) 1402 12 60-0

website www.englishtheatre.at

Production details: Founded in 1963; the oldest English-language theatre in continental Europe. Stages 5 shows each year in the main house and sends 5 Theatre-in-Education tours around the schools of Austria. The season runs from September to July each year.

Casting procedures: Casting breakdowns are occasionally posted on the website and actors may email the UK address above with their CV and photograph at anytime. Showreels are not accepted. "Contracts are especially written for us by Equity."

White Horse Theatre

Boerdenstrasse 17, 59494 Soest, Germany
tel +49 2921 339339
email theatre@white-horse-theatre.eu
website www.white-horse-theatre.eu
Artistic Director Michael Dray

Production details: Founded in 1978. Tours schools, theatres and art centres in Germany with occasional visits to neighbouring countries and to Japan and China. Contracts are for 10-11 months. 9 companies of 4 actors each perform 3 plays. Recent productions include: *The Glass Menagerie*, *Oliver Twist*, *Hamlet*, *Twelfth Night* and numerous plays for 14-16 year-olds, for 10-13 year-olds, and for primary school pupils.

Casting procedures: Does not use freelance casting directors. Holds general auditions; actors should write in April requesting inclusion. Casting breakdowns are available through the website, email application, Equity Job Information Service and Mandy. Welcomes postal and email enquiries from actors previously unknown to the company. Invitations to view individual actors' websites are also accepted. Contracts are approved by GDBA (the German equivalent of Equity). Rarely has the opportunity to cast disabled actors since "all our actors must take part in 3 different plays, and they must also cope with the rigours of touring".

A touring actor's survival guide

Maev Alexander

Touring is more tiring, harder work, more all-consuming and more relentless than playing in one house. In order to give your best to it and get the best from it, you need to be thoroughly organised and disciplined. The main differences are, of course, the travelling and the accommodation. If you arrange these well in advance, you're on your way to having a happy and rewarding experience and saving yourself angst and money.

Getting there

At the beginning of rehearsals, or even before, you'll be given a schedule of dates and venues and a sheaf of digs lists. Work out as early as you can how you will travel and where you will stay.

If you have your own transport you can plan your journeys on a week-by-week basis, pulling maps and route finders and estimated journey times off the Internet – if you have access – both to digs and to theatres. A good company manager will supply maps of town centres with the venue clearly marked. A satnav can be reassuring, but don't rely on it in big town centres – we had to hold the curtain for a leading lady in Sheffield when her instructions were impossible to follow in a new road layout, so it's a good idea to keep your map-reading skills honed. It's amazing how they improve when you *have* to find digs and theatres within a tight timeframe.

If you don't have your own transport, ask around the company and find out if anyone lives close enough to you, and is willing, to give you lifts. Make it clear that you will contribute to petrol costs, be punctual and not bring too much luggage. If you are using public transport, book as far in advance as you can: Apex (or the equivalent) on trains and low-budget airlines will save you huge amounts of money. The touring company will expect you to do this, and will calculate the amount they give you in fares as economically as possible. Be aware that fares are worked out from venue to venue, and not to your home and out again. Remember also that you may get stuck on a Saturday night if your show comes down after the last train, which is more likely than not; this may add to your accommodation expenses. It also eats into your only day off; most No. 1 tours play Monday to Saturday, running for a week in each venue.

The rule for fares and touring allowance is: outwith 15 miles of your permanent base to qualify for fares only, and 25 miles to qualify for touring allowance. This is calculated from postcode to postcode – not by the most convenient or quickest route. Equity has negotiated sharp rises in the level of touring allowance over the last few years, and this is now reasonable. It's meant to cover accommodation and living expenses – and if you're frugal and careful, it can. You have to balance the level of comfort and convenience with which you need to live happily with the budget on which you have to do it.

Finding the right digs

Digs lists cover hotels, guesthouses, self-contained flats, houses for sharing, B&Bs and rooms in private houses. They normally tell you the price (per night or per week), the type of accommodation, the facilities, the prohibitions (i.e. no smoking, no pets), the extras (TV, kettle in room) and the distance from the theatre. The headliners can probably afford

Theatre

to stay in hotels (and many hotels do deals for touring actors), but other ranks will have to juggle their priorities. If you can feel comfortable in a room in a private house, sharing a bathroom and having access to a kitchen, you can do so remarkably cheaply. If you can't do without an en suite or need to be self-contained, this will obviously be more expensive, and so on up the scale; but read the list carefully and you will find something that will tick most of your boxes without too much compromise. The people who do the letting are generally friends of the theatre in some way, and the standard of accommodation is usually pretty high. I have heard horror stories of rooms booked in hotels on last-minute websites – all-night disco music and overpowering 'room fragrancers'.

Start ringing the most promising-sounding digs as soon as possible, before everyone else does. Good options are places within a 15-minute walk (obviating cabs or long, lonely walks or parking problems), or a house or cottage that is further out, possibly in country-side, to share with fellow company members, both in terms of rent and transport. Beware of landlady-speak for 'a 15- to 20-minute walk' – some landladies clearly have seven-league boots! The level of rates varies from place to place: locations like Bath and Malvern tend to be more expensive across the board than, say, Southampton and Coventry. In big centres like Glasgow, Manchester, Birmingham and Leeds you will probably have to travel to the outskirts unless you can afford hotels.

When you've agreed terms with a landlord/lady, write to confirm the booking and the dates, and arrange to ring a couple of days in advance of the stay to negotiate a mutually convenient time to arrive (leave half an hour's leeway so you don't panic about getting lost). It's wise to at least drop off your luggage before the show so that you know you know where the place is, have keys and don't disturb anyone at a late hour – especially on the first night when there are likely to be drinks front-of-house afterwards. Sorting out digs gets easier the more you tour and the more contacts you acquire. If you're new to it, do ask experienced tourers – most actors are very generous about sharing the secrets of top digs. For future reference, keep records of where you've stayed and what it was like. Pay up front, and remember to leave keys when you leave; get a receipt and behave well enough for the landlord/lady to wish to stay on the digs list. You represent future tourers.

What to take

It's important to pack well. Travel as light as you can, and have as much of your luggage on wheels as possible. You need enough clothes for a week, or longer if you need to go straight to the next venue; keep it simple, remembering to have something warm and something cool (because this is Britain) and something smart for the first-night drinks often provided by the host management or friends of the theatre. A towelling robe doubles as a dressing gown and post-shower gear. Take comfortable, reasonably weatherproof shoes, since you'll spend a lot of time walking. Remember your phone charger (it's worth having a spare for touring), and a toothbrush charger and adapter in case there are no shaving points. It's also worth having an emergency kit containing plasters and painkillers and cold remedies. In most places towels are provided, but pack a hand towel just in case. Travel with a hottie in winter: the only miserable digs I've had were very smart but *freezing*. I complained – do complain; you're not paying to freeze. A pocket torch is useful for unfamiliar, unlit keyholes. Don't forget comforts like books or a radio or iPod.

If you have to be away from your base for extended periods, negotiate doing your laundry with the wardrobe department. If you're home on Sunday, it saves time and hassle if you've put what needs washing into a separate bag in your case so that repacking is straightforward and quick. I was told early in my career that no proper actor has less than three weeks' worth of underwear!

You can generally transport your make-up and other dressing-room necessities, comforts and amusements in a bag or box on the truck transporting the set and props, etc. This is not an automatic right, though, so check with your company manager. Some reasonably rigid receptacle is optimal to avoid breakage; label it clearly with the name of the production and your own name, and do not expect anyone else to lug it to or from your dressing room week by week. Pack it as soon as you can on Saturday night, and check where you can leave it so it's not in the way of the get-out.

Eating and drinking

It's easy to be lazy about eating sensibly on tour – financially and nutritionally. Even if there are cooking facilities in your digs, it's not always convenient to be there and it's tempting to eat out all the time or grab burgers. You're going to need all your energy, so make a point of eating healthily.

In most theatres you'll have access to a microwave and possibly a fridge: ring the stage door and check. They're often in the crew room, so ask if you may use them and be considerate about clearing up after yourself. Making an interesting dressing-room picnic is a worthy challenge even if everything has to be cold. Supermarkets do better and better ranges of salads and sushi. Invest in a mini kettle for your touring box and pack a plate, a mug and cutlery. Set yourself a daily budget for food and then you'll know if you can splash out on a restaurant meal.

It's also tempting to do a great deal more after-show drinking when you're away from home: it can feel as if you're living in a bubble, out of the real world. Ask yourself if you're getting jaded/broke, and limit alcohol to within sensible limits. (The same sense of not being quite in the real world can lead also to the most unlikely affairs: be discreet, whether it involves other people or yourself.)

Bonding and recreation

After-show company meals, weekly or fortnightly, are good bonding exercises providing you all get on. Remember that it's not only part of your job to get on, but also in your best interests. It's even more important in the living-in-each-others'-pockets world of touring to be a good company member; leave your troubles firmly at the stage door and don't moan or gossip. If there's someone you find tricky, keep out of their way. In my experience, touring companies bond well and form even more of a parallel family than usual.

That said, getting away by yourself for a time is restoring. Find the local Tourist Information Office and find out about places of interest and specialist shopping. There's bound to be something that appeals to you, even if you're not a galleries/museums/castles/cathedrals person (the ABC of touring is famously, "another bloody cathedral"). I am lucky – and not alone – in regarding touring as being paid to go sightseeing. Stage door, or your company manager, can tell you of gym and leisure facilities and often arrange temporary membership; they can also point you in the direction of the nearest supermarkets and best-value restaurants.

Sussing out the theatre

One of the interesting and rewarding things about touring is playing the same show in lots of different theatres – from 900-seaters to 2000-seaters; from raked stages to flat ones;

Theatre

from Victorian to modern; from those with acres (seemingly) of orchestra pit to those where the front row is looking up your nose. You'll be called early in the first day of each new venue, generally at about 5 or 6pm, to walk the stage, get to know the backstage layout and take note of significant differences. The presence or lack of a rake may mean more or fewer steps on a staircase, for instance; furniture may be closer together or further apart; wing space may be tight; prop tables may be in different places; dressing rooms will be varying distances away and you may be sharing in one venue and by yourself in another. Take time to absorb these differences, test the acoustic and plan how you're going to accommodate any changes you personally will have to make. Discuss these changes too with anyone else they may affect. Bear in mind that the audiences are always different, as well: it's amazing that what makes people laugh or weep in Cardiff is not the same as what makes people laugh or weep in Hull.

Find out when stage door opens; most theatres allow you access to your dressing room from quite early in the day, which is useful for dumping shopping or 'nesting' when it's tipping with rain. A few don't open until much later, though, which is a great bore and makes it good to have digs close by.

Money matters

On a business level, keep a work diary and note down all your expenses (and mileages if you're driving). Have an envelope or plastic wallet in which to file all your receipts and payslips: it's easy to lose track of these when you're away from home.

Tax offices vary in what they will allow you to claim on tour. Travel and accommodation expenses above your allowances are OK, but some accept claims for all eating expenses (again over and above), some for restaurant/cafe receipts only, and some – including my own – clearly expect you not to eat at all.

Research a mobile phone tariff that will let you keep in touch with family and friends, and your agent, as cheaply as possible.

Finally ...

More and more of the available work involves touring at some level. You might just as well maximise your chances of having a good time and making a decent profit. Regard it as an adventure.

Maev Alexander trained at the Royal Scottish Academy of Music and Drama and has been working in theatre, television and radio for 40 years. She has performed in Rep all over the country, playing everything from Cleopatra to a French poodle, been a member of the RSC, and holds the record as the longest-serving Mollie in *The Mousetrap*. She has starred in two TV series and guested in many others, presented the Newsdesk on *That's Life*, and played in dozens of radio dramas. After completing her 7th No. 1 tour in as many years, and transferring the last but one – *A Man for All Seasons* – to the Theatre Royal Haymarket in 2006, she has filmed *Death Defying Acts* with Catherine Zeta Jones and Guy Pearce, and recorded the second series of *The Eliza Stories* for BBC Radio 4.

Theatre

Fringe theatres

Essentially, the idea of 'fringe theatre' began at the Edinburgh Festival more than half a century ago. It really started taking off (especially in London) in the late 1960s as an arena for 'alternative' and 'experimental' theatre. The 1990s saw a huge expansion in the number of venues being used, and a downturn in the exploration of theatre forms: the 'fringe' became more commercial and much more competitive – and not just in London and Edinburgh. Today, the terms 'alternative' and 'experimental' are far less frequently used, and the Fringe is now largely seen as a way for actors, directors and writers to showcase their work.

Casting for Fringe productions is usually advertised by one or more of the casting information services, and agents and casting directors do scout for new talent in them. However, it's highly unlikely that you will make any money from participating in such a production – you might end up with a net loss after deducting your expenses. Also agents and casting directors get blitzed with so many invitations that the chances of getting one of them to see you are not high. The only reasons for being in a Fringe production are (a) you might be 'seen'; (b) you fundamentally believe in the production's potential; and (c) it could help keep your acting-juices flowing. But you might find classes less time-consuming and possibly more beneficial.

The Edinburgh Festival Fringe

There is a real sense that every actor should try this 'Carnival of theatre' experience – 'the biggest theatrical lottery in the world' – at least once. You'll meet lots of new people, make contacts and it's a great few weeks, even if your own production doesn't hit the heights.

Good advice on mounting a production on the Edinburgh Festival Fringe is available from the Festival Office (details below).

The listings that follow are restricted to the more 'established' venues, with performance spaces for hire. Some Fringe theatres only programme in work known to them.

Note: If you are thinking of mounting a Fringe production and/or starting your own theatre company, start researching and planning well in advance. It is well worth consulting the Independent Theatre Council (ITC) – **www.itc-arts.org**.

UMBRELLA ORGANISATIONS

Edinburgh Festival Fringe

The Fringe Office, 180 High Street, Edinburgh EH1 1QS
tel 0131 226 0026
email admin@edfringe.com
website www.edfringe.com

The Edinburgh Fringe Festival started in 1947 and the Fringe Society was formed in 1959 to coordinate publicity and ticket sales, and offer a comprehensive information service both to performers and to audiences. It compiles information about venues, press and suppliers, and produces a series of publications designed to answer frequently asked questions. Its brochure contains details for Fringe venues and shows in Edinburgh. The office is open all year round and the staff are available to help by phone, email or personal appointment.

OffWestEnd

email info@offwestend.com
website www.offwestend.com; www.offies.london
Twitter @OffWestEndCom
Instagram @OffWestEndcom

OffWestEnd supports, promotes and celebrates the exciting and innovative work performed in the 100+ independent, alternative and fringe theatres outside London's West End, and organises a range of awards, including the Offies, OffComm, OffFest and OnComm. Tickets are sold directly from these Off West End theatres.

Theatre

Society of Independent Theatres (SIT)

mobile 07973 502189
email john@ovationproductions.com
website www.sitgb.org

The Society of Independent Theatres (SIT) is an alliance of small independent theatres (under 300 seats) in the UK. Venue owners, venue managers and artistic directors of independent theatres. Objectives are as follows:

• To raise the profile of small/independent/fringe/pub style venues within the theatre industry and with the general public.
• To encourage the development of the performing arts within independent venues.
• To exchange information on theatre companies and suppliers.
• To exchange ideas and proposals for marketing, promotion and audience development.
• To provide a better understanding of employment laws relevant to our sector of the industry.
• To liaise with Equity and other organisations over issues affecting our industry.

LONDON FRINGE VENUES

The Albany

Douglas Way, Deptford, London SE8 4AG
tel 020 8692 4446
email reception@thealbany.org.uk
website www.thealbany.org.uk
Chief Executive/Artistic Director Gavin Barlow

Production details: A multi-use arts centre programming music, spoken word, dance, comedy and family shows. The Albany is an artistic and community resource with a fully equipped theatre space, studio theatre, café and rehearsal and meeting rooms for hire. Has a strong commitment to working collaboratively with the diverse communities of London and encouraging participation, especially by young people and isolated older people and those least likely to engage in the arts. As well as programming performances, the Albany programme and manage two external venues in Lewisham and Southwark. The centre is home to 25+ resident organisations and the national Fun Palaces and Family Arts Campaign movements. It is a social hub and facilitator for partnership working. The Albany co-chairs Future Arts Centres with ARC, Stockon, runs a major partnership with Social Housing providor Lewisham Homes and recebtly launched a campaign to provide free theatre tickets to every 5-year-old child in Lewisham.

Seats 300 (500 standing); 2 secondary spaces seat 60 or 70. Performances also take place in the café – capacity 80. All spaces have fully configurable seating; there is also seating on the balcony. Shows usually run from 1 night to 2 weeks. Hire rates may be subsidised depending on community or charity status

– see website for rates of different spaces. There is disabled access. Recent productions developed in partnership with the Albany include Tiata Fahodzi's *Good Dog*; Belarus Free Theatre's *Tomorrow I Was Always a Lion*; Teatro Vivo's *The Residents* and *Muhammad Ali and Me* from Majisola Adebayo, plus seven regular platforms for neew work. *Lipsticks and Lollipops* by Deafinitely Theatre; *A Warwickshire Testimony* by April de Angelis (Mountview Theatre School); and transfer from the Royal Court of *Gone Too Far!* by Olivier Award-winner Bola Agbaje.

Casting procedures: Does not produce in-house shows.

artsdepot

5 Nether Street, North Finchley, London N12 0GA
tel 020 8369 5454
email info@artsdepot.co.uk
website www.artsdepot.co.uk
Chief Executive Monique Deletant

The only professional arts venue in the London Borough of Barnet. Committed to providing a diverse range of high-quality visual and performance arts for everyone. artsdepot has brand new, state-of-the-art facilities in the form of the large Pentland Theatre, smaller Studio Theatre and Education Spaces, for the provision of drama, dance and visual arts, and a gallery, as well as an excellent café and bars.

Barons Court Theatre

The Curtain's Up, 28ᴀ Comeragh Rd, West Kensington, London W14 9HR
mobile 07833 913760
email info@baronscourttheatre.com
website www.baronscourttheatre.com
Facebook www.facebook.com/BaronsCourtTheatre
Twitter @BaronsCourt_W14
Artistic Director Sharon Willems

Founded 1991. The Barons Court Theatre is a 62-seat theatre in the heart of of West London, between Hammersmith and Chelsea. Situated in the basement of the Curtains Up Pub, close to Queen's Club. Offers a variety of new writing, classical work and magic show.

Battersea Arts Centre

Lavender Hill, London SW11 5TN
tel 020 7223 2223
email programmingenquiries@bac.org.uk
website www.bac.org.uk
Artistic Director Tarek Iskander

Battersea Arts Centre's (BAC) mission is to inspire people to take creative risks to shape the future. Each year the organisation works with over 400 artists to develop new forms of theatre and connect with audiences and participants. The emphasis is on devised rather than script-based work. BAC is the original home and foremost pioneer of Scratch, a model that has transformed the way in which people make and experience theatre. Scratch is a shared space in which ideas are exchanged between artists and audiences as a way to develop the work. Finished shows are then performed throughout the centre's old town hall building and often go on to more unusual spaces across London, the UK and the world.

Work is rarely programmed on the strength of a proposal alone, and unsolicited scripts are not accepted. Instead they prefer to build up a relationship with artists over time. Typically, one of the producers might see a show or workshop by a company at another venue and then start a conversation. A significant exception to this is Freshly Scratched – once or twice a year, BAC programme a week of short 10-minute Scratches by artists who have never presented their work at BAC before, purely on the basis of paper applications.

Blue Elephant Theatre

59A Bethwin Road, Camberwell, London SE5 0XT
tel 020 7701 0100
email info@blueelephanttheatre.co.uk
website www.blueelephanttheatre.co.uk
Facebook www.facebook.com/blueelephanttheatre
Twitter @BETCamberwell
Artistic Director Niamh de Valera

The only theatre in Camberwell. A vibrant arts venue aiming to nurture new and emerging artists across the performing arts. Promotes cross-artform work and all types of theatre, from physical and dance to new writing and classics.

Co-produces all shows and is particularly interested in supporting new and emerging London-based artists across the perfoming arts with work that complements the black-box performance space. Those interested in bringing a project to the Blue Elephant should submit a written proposal with suggested dates and a full background to the Director.

The Bridewell Theatre

Bride Lane, Fleet Street, London EC4Y 8EQ
tel 020 7353 3331
website www.sbf.org.uk

The Bridewell Theatre is a versatile space, which provides both an atmospheric entertainment venue and a unique conference facility in the heart of the City. In addition to a 12x8m performance space, there is a modular tiered seating system that in standard configuration can accommodate a raked audience of 134 people. The theatre also offers dressing rooms with en suite amenities, as well as a box-office/reception area and a fully equipped bar. All areas of the theatre are accessible to disabled users via a lift.

The Broadway Studio Theatre

Broadway Theatre, Catford SE6 4RU
tel 07787 977794
email carmel@broadwaytheatre.org.uk
website www.broadwaytheatre.org.uk
Theatre Manager Carmel O'Connor

Originally opened in 1932, the venue is Grade II listed by English Heritage as a beautiful example of 1930s art deco architecture. There are 2 venues: the Main Theatre seats 800, and the Studio Theatre seats 100. "The Broadway Studio Theatre has extremely limited availability."

Camden People's Theatre

58-60 Hampstead Road, London NW1 2PY
tel 020 7419 4841
email foh@cptheatre.co.uk
website www.cptheatre.co.uk
Twitter @camdenPT

A central London space dedicated year round to supporting early-career artists making unconventional theatre. In particular, those whose work explores issues that matter to people now.

Canal Café Theatre

Delamere Terrace, Little Venice, London W2 6ND
tel 020 7289 6056 (Box Office) / 020 7289 6054
email mail@canalcafetheatre.com
website www.canalcafetheatre.com
Artistic Director Emma Taylor

A cabaret, comedy and new writing 60-seat theatre situated above the Bridge House pub in Little Venice. Home to NewsRevue.

Charing Cross Theatre (formerly New Players Theatre)

The Arches, Villiers Street, London WC2N 6NG
tel 020 7930 5868
email info@charingcrosstheatre.co.uk
website www.charingcrosstheatre.co.uk
Facebook www.facebook.com/charingcrossthr
Twitter @charingcrossthr
Instagram @charingcrossthr

Since 1864 there has been a theatre under the arches at Charing Cross Station. Known by many names over the years, the theatre was rechristened the Charing Cross Theatre in 2011. The venue offers an eclectic mix of drama, musicals, comedy, cabaret and late-night shows, plus periodic Sunday performances of traditional Victorian Music Hall. It is also a distinctive setting for screenings, conferences and corporate hires, complete with on-site bar and kitchen.

Chelsea Theatre

World's End Place, King's Road, London SW10 0DR
tel 020 7352 1967
email admin@chelseatheatre.org.uk
website www.chelseatheatre.org.uk

A 110-seat theatre which can be booked up to 6 months in advance. Particularly welcomes new writing.

Chiswick Playhouse

2 Bath Road, Turnham Green, London W4 1LW
tel 020 8995 6035
email info@chiswickplayhouse.co.uk
website www.chiswickplayhouse.co.uk
Executive Director Mark Perry

Situated within the Tabard building with own independent entrance, close to Turnham Green tube. Offers 3-4 week runs which are programmed 4-5 months ahead.

The Cockpit

Gateforth Street, London NW8 8EH
tel 020 7258 2925
email reception@thecockpit.org.uk
website www.thecockpit.org.uk
Theatre Director Dave Wybrow

Theatre seats 240 (60 seats on 4 sides) or 180 (60 seats on 3 sides) and should be booked 6 months in advance. Welcomes classics, foreign-language theatre and other niche market work. Also creates own in-house productions.

The Courtyard Theatre

Bowling Green Walk, 40 Pitfield Street,
London N1 6EU
tel 020 7739 6868
email info@thecourtyard.org.uk
website www.thecourtyard.org.uk

The Courtyard Theatre is housed within the Grade II listed, former public library in Pitfield Street, Hoxton. It has a 150-seat main house theatre, 80-seat studio theatre, 220 capacity music venue, bar and multiple rehearsal spaces.

Etcetera Theatre

Above the Oxford Arms, 265 Camden High Street,
London NW1 7BU
tel 020 7482 4857
email admin@etceteratheatre.com
website www.etceteratheatre.com
Facebook www.facebook.com/
etcetera_theatre_camden
Twitter @etcetera_theatre_camden
Instagram @etcetera_theatre_camden

A black-box studio space with 42 raked seats, this intimate theatre is perfect for everything from new writing to comedy and cabaret all the way through to acoustic music. Open 7 days a week with an early and late slot. Available for one-off bookings as well as week runs and any number of shows in between. The Etcetera is also available during the day for rehearsals, auditions and workshops with rates starting from just £15 an hour.

Finborough Theatre

118 Finborough Road, London SW10 9ED
tel 020 7244 7439
email admin@finboroughtheatre.co.uk
website www.finboroughtheatre.co.uk
Artistic Director Neil McPherson

Production details: Founded in 1980, the multi-award-winning Finborough Theatre presents plays and musical theatre, concentrated exclusively on vibrant new writing and unique rediscoveries from the 19th and 20th centuries. The programme is unique — never presenting work that has been seen anywhere in London during the last 25 years.

The main theatre space has flexible seating for 50 in a variety of formats. The normal run of a show is 4 weeks.

Hire rates: Box office profits are split 50/50. The theatre's share is capped at £6,000.

Many productions transfer to New York and the West End.

Casting procedures: Produces in-house shows but does not hold general auditions. Casting breakdowns are available through the Spotlight Link casting service. Letters (with CVs and photographs) from previously unknown actors are not welcomed, neither are unsolicited CVs or showreels sent by email. Invitations to other productions are welcome. Welcomes applications from disabled performers but there is no wheelchair access to the theatre.

Hackney Empire Studio Theatre

291 Mare Street, London E8 1EJ
tel 020 8510 4500
email info@hackneyempire.co.uk
website www.hackneyempire.co.uk
Artistic Director Yasmin Choudury

80-seat studio attached to the historic, Grade II listed, Matcham-designed Hackney Empire. Contact Frank Sweeney for booking details.

Hen & Chickens Theatre

Above Hen & Chickens Theatre Bar,
109 St Paul's Road, Islington, London N1 2NA
website www.unrestrictedview.co.uk
Twitter @TheHenChickens

A 54-seat theatre welcoming new writing. Directly opposite Highbury and Islington station. Offers 1-3 week runs for theatre and specific slots on Sundays and Mondays for comedy.

The Hope Theatre

Hope & Anchor Pub, 207 Upper Street, Islington,
London N11 1RL
email info@thehopetheatre.com
Artistic Director Phil Bartlett

Production details: The multi-award-winning Hope Theatre is a 50-seat pub theatre in the heart of Islington. It nurtures and develops new producing models, working with both emerging and established companies to tell stories that are dramatic, surprising and have something to say about the world we live in. Although The Hope Theatre receives no regular public subsidy, it was the first Off West End venue to open with a house agreement with Equity, to ensure a legal wage for all actors and stage managers staff working at the theatre.

Casting procedures: All in-house productions are cast via Spotlight and Mandy. Please do not send unsolicited CVs. Invitations to see actors perform at other London venues should be sent via email.

The Jack Studio Theatre

410 Brockley Road, London SE4 2DH
email admin@brockleyjack.co.uk
website www.brockleyjack.co.uk
Facebook www.facebook.com/BrocJackTheatre
Twitter @BrocJackTheatre
Artistic Director Kate Bannister *Theatre Producer* Karl Swinyard

Production details: A vibrant award winning performance space situated in South East London, offering a diverse theatre programme throughout the year. Home also to Scratch nights, workshops and screenings. Comfortable cinema-style raked seating for 50; can be configured end-on or on 3 sides or in the round. The performing space is step-free and wheelchair accessible but the rehearsal room is not. Winner of Most Welcoming and Best Programming Policy in Off West End Public Awards 2022.

Casting procedures: Produces in-house shows; uses both in-house and freelance casting directors. Casting is generally by invitation. Does not welcome unsolicited submissions from actors, but will accept invitations to view individual actors' websites and to visit other productions. Actively encourages applications from disabled actors and promotes the use of inclusive casting.

Jacksons Lane Arts Centre

269A Archway Road, London N6 5AA
tel 020 8430 5226
email admin@jacksonslane.org.uk
website www.jacksonslane.org.uk
Artistic Director Adrian Berry

A wide range of rooms are available for hire on a daily or hourly basis for private functions, rehearsals, filmshoots, meetings and performances. The largest space holds up to 120, with other studios having ample space for 25–40 people. The theatre has an audience size of up to 170.

Jermyn Street Theatre

16B Jermyn Street, London SW1Y 6ST
tel 020 7434 1443 (Executive Director: Penny Horner) and 020 7287 2875 (Box Office)
email info@jermynstreettheatre.co.uk
website www.jermynstreettheatre.co.uk
Artistic Director Tom Littler

Hire rates: Theatre seats 70, 5 rows facing, 2 rows on side. Stage space is 8 metres long x 4 metres deep x 3.5 metres high (to grid), 2 dressing rooms with fridges, sofas, microwaves, kettles, iron + ironing board. The theatre is air conditioned.

• Main Shows – The theatre is now a fully programmed producing house. However, some weeks can be rented as a receiving house. Weekly rent is £3,000 (this includes get-in, fit-up time, technician operating/rigging, also operates sound as well as lights). A 30% non-refundable deposit is required when the contract is signed.
• Showcases/Rehearsed Readings/Seminars – £90 per hour. Theatre is available on Tuesdays/Wednesdays/Thursdays between 10am and 4pm (includes technician).
• Sunday Nights (Cabaret Evenings) – £395 for the evening, available from 6.30pm on the night for 8pm show, includes rehearsal Friday before (includes technician).

Lion & Unicorn Theatre

42-44 Gaisford Street, Kentish Town,
London NW5 2ED
lionandunicorn@proforca.co.uk
website www.thelionandunicorntheatre.com
Artistic Director David Brady

A 60-seat black box studio theatre based above the Lion & Unicorn pub at in Kentish Town. The venue will provides a home for fringe theatre talent and supports new writing, as well as provide opportunities for associate artists and companies who form part of our diverse artistic programme.

New Diorama Theatre

15-16 Triton Street, Regent's Place,
London NW1 3BF
tel 020 7916 5467
email hello@newdiorama.com
website www.newdiorama.com
Artistic and Executive Director David Byrne

New Diorama is an 80-seat theatre located in central London. "We host and support theatre companies, both emerging and established, presenting a variety of productions ranging from comedy to drama. We want to find and support the next generation of Complicites, Kneehighs, Headlongs whilst also offering a space to established companies wanting to work in intimate spaces."

Old Red Lion

418 St John Street, Islington, London EC1V 4NJ
tel 020 7833 3053
email info@oldredliontheatre.co.uk
website www.oldredliontheatre.co.uk
Executive Director Damien Devine

Founded in 1979, the Old Red Lion Theatre is a 60-seater Fringe theatre primarily dedicated to new writing. Companies wishing to hire the venue should post a script, some company information and a production proposal to the Executive Director. Normally programmes 3 months ahead.

Omnibus Theatre

1 Clapham Common Northside
tel 020 7622 4105

email enquiries@omnibus-clapham.org
website www.omnibus-clapham.org
Artistic Director Marie McCarthy

The heart of Omnibus Theatre's ambitious programme, inspired by their building's literary heritage, lies in both classics re-imagined and contemporary storytelling. Provides a platform for new writing and interdisciplinary work, aiming to give voice to the underrepresented and challenge perceptions. 'We believe in affordable tickets and theatre for all.'

Since opening in 2013 notable in-house productions include: *Woyzeck* (2013); *Macbeth* (2014); *Colour* (2015); *Mule* (2016); *Spring Offensive* (2017); *Zeraffa Giraffa* (2017); *To Have To Shoot Irishmen* (2018); *Perfect* (2018) and *The Little Prince* (2019). Registered charity and receives no core funding.

Our venue is home to the 90–110 seat Theatre and the Studio Upstairs (80 seats), a café/bar and two more performance and rehearsal spaces.

Pentameters

28 Heath Street, Hampstead NW3 6TE
tel 020 7435 3648
email theatre@pentameters.co.uk
website www.pentameters.co.uk
Founder and Producer Léonie Scott-Matthews

Located in the heart of Hampstead village, among an abundance of cafés, restaurants, bars, pubs and shops and just a minute's walk from Hampstead tube. Aside from the choice of venues to have pre- or post-theatre drinks or dinner, Hampstead is also well-known for its artistic character, offering a supportive, interactive and thriving local community, making it an ideal spot to promote live theatre and creative arts events. To discuss requirements, please telephone Léonie Scott-Matthews directly on the above number: "Please leave a message, and we will respond."

The Playground Theatre

Latimer Road, London W10 6RQ
tel 020 8960 0110
email info@theplaygroundtheatre.london
website www.theplaygroundtheatre.london
Co-Artistic Directors Peter Tate, Anthony Biggs

The Playground Theatre, formerly a bus depot, was set up as a creative space for innovative theatre artists of all disciplines to come and 'play' with their imaginative ideas. One such project, 'Terrific Electric' won the Samuel Beckett Award for Innovative Theatre and was part of the Bite season at the Barbican Theatre. The decision to become a public theatre was born from the desire to bring the exceptional artists work, who 'played' with the company, to full production. Continues to work with both established and emerging artists from the UK and internationally. The ethos is one of cross-fertilisation between different forms and different cultures in search of a universal language that speaks

to all. Many international artists were invited to experiment with the Playground Theatre including Poland's Henryk Baranowski, winner of Poland and Russia's top award as best director, Salius Varnus from Lithuania, and Hideki Noda, currently head of Japan's National Theatre. From the UK, the company has worked closely with Marcello Magni, co-founder of Theatre De Complicité, along with his colleague Linda Kerr Scott. Programme includes international plays, classical concerts, dance, and film. The Playground Theatre is located within a very diverse community and its work will reflect this.

Pleasance Theatre Trust

Carpenters Mews, North Road, London N7 9EF
tel 020 7619 6868
email info@pleasance.co.uk
website www.pleasance.co.uk
Facebook www.facebook.com/ThePleasance
Twitter @ThePleasance
Director Anthony Alderson

Founded in 1984, the Pleasance has 3 versatile spaces: the Mainhouse, seats between 200–250; and the StageSpace, created to nurture the best in new theatre writing and emerging comedy talent, seats 54.

The standard configurationof the Main House and StageSPace are end on but the seating is completely flexible in both spaces. Shows are programmed for various lengths of run from 1 night to 6 weeks. There is no programme of shows in London during August, during which the Pleasance operates 3 sites at the Edinburgh Festival Fringe. The Mainhouse and Downstairs are fully accessible, however, unfortunately the StageSpace is not wheelchair accessible. Please visit the Pleasance website for hire rates and more information.

RADA Studios

16 Chenies Street, London WC1E 7EX
tel 020 7307 5060
email venuehire@rada.ac.uk
website www.rada.ac.uk/about-us/venue-hire/
Events and Hires Manager Michelle Snyder *Venues and Events Coordinator* Ben Jones

RADA Studios is a receiving theatre located in Chenies Street at the heart of the West End. The Studio Theatre is a hugely versatile space, and we currently host a large variety of work, including theatre, musicals, dance, opera, radio recordings and screenings.

We also have several studio spaces within the RADA Studios building, perfect for castings, read-throughs, rehearsals or fittings in a vibrant and creative atmosphere that continues to inspire future generations of actors, writers, directors and technicians.

Rich Mix

35-47 Bethnal Green Road, London E1 6LA
tel 020 7613 7490

email info@richmix.org.uk
website www.richmix.org.uk
Chief Executive Judith Kilvington

A 132,000 square foot flagship arts and cultural centre, boasting "the best in art, performance, fashion, design, music, dance, film, theatre and comedy – 5 floors of vibrant creativity and excellence".

Rosemary Branch Theatre

2 Shepperton Road, London N1 3DT
tel 020 7704 2730
email info@rosemarybranchtheatre.co.uk
website www.rosemarybranch.co.uk

The theatre holds about 61 seats including a "royal box". Presents a diverse programme including opera, classics, new writing, puppetry and just about any genre you care to mention. Affordable rehearsal space available in the Pink Room as well as the theatre during the day. The theatre offers all visiting companies lots of support and goodwill. One-offs, part week and full week rentals all considered.

The Space

269 Westferry Road, London E14 3RS
tel 020 7515 7799
email info@space.org.uk
website www.space.org.uk
Artistic Director Adam Hemming *Theatre Manager* Keri Mason

The Space was founded in 1996 and is managed by the registered charity, St Paul's Arts Trust. In a converted church hall, The Space provides an atmopheric yet flexible Off West End setting. Certainly not a typical 'black box' theatre, a number if staging options are achievable including end-on, in the round, traverse and thrust.

The Space programmes three seasons a year: in spring (Jan-April), summer (May- Aug), adn autumn/ wonter (Sept-Dec). In each season they aim to schedule a minimum of 2 three-week runs alongside shorter runs. The Space offers a range of theatre events within each season, including a mixture of classics, new writing, revivals, puppetry, physical theatre, immersive theatre and musicals. It programmes drama and comedy and works with new, emerging and established companies.

The in-house company Space Productions produces 1-3 shows a year and has received six Off West End nominations to date. Also runs a community theatre company, SpaceWorks, which engages with childen and adults in the local area.

In 2015, a new performance space, Crossrail Place Roof Garden, was inaugurated and operates in the summer only. Performances at this new outdoor amphitheatre ideally run for an hour. Tickets at the Roof Garden must be free so a commission is paid to companies (between £600-£1,000).

The main theatre space seats between 45 and 90 depending on configuration. End on: between 60 (large playing space) and 90 seats (small stage area only, suitable for recitals and solo performances). The end-on configuration can also be reversed, with audience seating on stage. This configuration tends to seat 65 audience members; traverse: between 40-60 seats; thrust: 50-60 seats; in the round: 50-60 seats.

Viewing and speaking with one of their team is recommended before applying.

The normal duration of a show is between 1 and 3 weeks on a box office split basis. Runs shorter than a week will usually be programmed ona straight hire basis, although this is occasionally negotiable.

The main space is used all year round and open submissions are three times a year, announced on the wensbite. Roof Gadren Perforamcne Space is sed in the summer only.

Discounts are offered on block bookings for rehearsals.

Hire rates: rehearsals (10am–6pm) £15/hr + VAT, £12/hr + VAT (when 10+ hrs are booked in one go); workshops (10am–6pm) £20/hr + VAT; performances £150 + VAT per performance (inclusive of inclusion of all of The Space's marketing, full use of lighting/sound equipment and a full box office service). Application for shows on a 50/50 box office split three times a year.

Premises are accessible to disabled performers.

Recent productions include: *The Lighthouse* by Rachel Claye; *The Collector*, an adaptation of John Fowles's novel performed by the visiting company Blink and the One Festival — a celebration of solo performers now in its fourth year.

The Space also produced in-house productions. General auditions are advertised on a project-by-project basis, actors can amial Isabel Dixon (isabel@space.org.uk) to be added to the mailing list for casting opportunities. Jobs are also posted on Spotlight and Mandy. Welcomes letter (with CVs and photos) from individual actors previously unknown to the company. Also welcomes showreels, unsolicited CVs and photos sent by email and invitations to view individual actors' websites and to visit productions. Actively encourages applications from disabled actors and promotes the use of inclusive casting.

Theatre503

The Latchmere, 503 Battersea Park Road, London SW11 3BW
tel 020 7978 7040
email info@theatre503.com
website www.theatre503.com
Artistic Director Lisa Spirling

Situated above a public house, Theatre503 aims to provide a venue for new playwrights, comedians and directors to develop their shows. It has a working relationship with television commissioners and producers, literary managers of established theatres and literary agents, and tries to offer a stepping-stone from Fringe to 'big' theatres.

Theatro Technis

26 Crowndale Road, London NW1 1TT
tel 020 7387 6617 *mobile* 07535 801399
email info@theatrotechnis.com
website www.theatrotechnis.com

Theatro Technis is a 120-seat theatre on three sides with a high ceiling, and a licensed front of house/bar. There are also two rehearsal rooms: Studio 1 is 5 x 5m in size and Studio 2 is 4 x 4m.

The theatre's productions maintain a balance between the classics and contemporary work that serve to embrace a variety of diverse art forms, ranging from theatre, dance, art, music and film. It produces and presents a variety of work with a whole range of companies committed to serving London in all its diversity.

Toynbee Studios

28 Commercial Street, London E1 6AB
tel 020 7247 5102
email admin@artsadmin.co.uk
website www.artsadmin.co.uk/toynbee-studios
Artistic Director Roise Goan

Toynbee Studios is run by Artsadmin for the development and presentation of new work. Toynbee Studios comprises a 280-seat theatre, rehearsal spaces, technical facilities, and the Arts Bar & Café, hosting rehearsals, meetings, performances and events throughout the year. Office facilities are also provided for a range of arts organisations.

Toynbee Studios has 6 spaces for hire ranging from the intimate to larger high-spec dance and theatre studios. Requests for public events will be reviewed alongside Artsadmin's artistic policy. Spaces are usually hired daily/weekly Monday-Friday 10am-6pm. Occasional evening and weekend hires are available on request.

Artsadmin was founded in 1979 and has been based at Toynbee Studios since 1995. Artsadmin is a company of creative people working with artists to develop and make performance projects for local, national and international audiences. They offer a range of support for artists and rehearsal studios, workspaces and a programme of public events.

Tristan Bates Theatre

See Seven Dials Playhouse on page 44.

Union Theatre

204 Union Street, Southwark, London SE1 0LX
tel 020 7261 9876
email info@uniontheatre.biz
website www.uniontheatre.biz

Primarily a new writing venue, the theatre aims to present a diverse programme featuring the best new talent. Guest performances are supplemented by regular in-house productions. Normally offers 3-week runs.

Upstairs at the Gatehouse

The Gatehouse Pub, North Road, London N6 4BD
tel 020 8340 3488
email events@ovationproductions.com
website www.upstairsatthegatehouse.com
Directors John Plews, Katie Plews

Seats 122 (140 in cabaret style). See also the entry for Ovation Productions under *Middle and smaller-scale companies* on page 199.

White Bear Theatre

138 Kennington Park Road, London SE11 4DJ
mobile 07496 442747
email info@whitebeartheatre.co.uk
website www.whitebeartheatre.co.uk
Artistic Director Michael Kingsbury

Aims to foster new talent and create a space for creative risk-taking. The studio space has seating for up to 50. Generally prefers new writing but occasionally accepts revivals.

Wimbledon Studio Theatre

In Wimbledon Theatre, 93 The Broadway, London SW19 1QG
tel 020 8545 7900 (Admin)
website www.atgtickets.com/venues/studio-at-new-wimbledon-theatre

A black box studio theatre with flexible seating for up to 66. Normally offers 1-2 week runs which are programmed 6 months ahead. The auditorium is wheelchair-accessible.

EDINBURGH FESTIVAL FRINGE VENUES

Many of these venues are only available for hire during the Edinburgh Festival Fringe in August. For a full list of venues, see **www.edfringe.com/venues**.

Assembly Rooms

Assembly Theatre, 250 George Street, Edinburgh EH2 2LE
tel 0232 220 4348
email enquiries@assemblyroomsedinburgh.co.uk
website www.assemblyroomsedinburgh.co.uk

The Assembly Rooms have presented more than 1,000 productions featuring most of the major names in British comedy – as well as a huge array of theatre, dance and music events which have been seen by more than 1.5 million people over the last 20 years of the Edinburgh Festival Fringe. The daily programme runs from 11am to 3.30am with exhibitions, a café, 2 public bars and a club bar. Aims to programme a balance of theatre, comedy and new work.

Augustine's

Augustine United Church, 41 George IV Bridge, Edinburgh EH1 1EL
tel 0131 220 1677

Part of Augustine United Church. During the Festival it is adapted by Paradise Green to house 2 performance spaces: The Sanctuary seats 110; The Studio seats approximately 107. Programmes theatre, musicals, dance and children's theatre from the UK and elsewhere.

Bedlam Theatre

11b Bristo Place, Edinburgh EH1 1EZ
tel 0131 225 9873
email info@bedlamtheatre.co.uk
website www.bedlamtheatre.co.uk

A 90-seat black-box theatre in central Edinburgh housed in a neo-gothic church. The theatre is available for hire when not in use by the Edinburgh University Theatre Company.

C venues

Edinburgh Festival Fringe
tel 0131 581 5500
email info@cvenues.com
website www.cvenues.com

C venues programmes and hosts over 200 productions and events at the Edinburgh Fringe each August at multiple venue locations in central Edinburgh. Buildings include original Fringe venues from the first days of the Fringe and some of the newest venues on the Fringe. Alongside a broad theatre-based programme incorporating drama, new writing, physical theatre, musical theatre and children's theatre, C has developed a speciality programming immersive, interactive and site-specific theatre, and in hosting cabaret, circus theatre, performance art and cross-genre work. C's productions have come from and toured around the world, and have won Fringe First, Total Theatre and other awards. C venues is a founder member of Edinburgh's Associated Independent Venue Producers.

Greyfriars Kirk

Greyfriars Kirk, Greyfriars Place, Edinburgh EH1 2QQ

Two performance spaces, one of which is wheelchair accessible. As well as poetry recitals and performances, the acoustics make the space perfect for orchestral and choral concerts and organ recitals.

The Pleasance

The Pleasance Courtyard: 60 The Pleasance, Edinburgh EH8 9TJ; *The Pleasance Dome*: 1 Bristo Square, Edinburgh EH8 9AL; *The Pleasance Administration Office*: Carpenters Mews, North Road, London N7 9EF
tel 020 7619 6868
email info@pleasance.co.uk
website www.pleasance.co.uk
Facebook www.facebook.com/ThePleasance
Twitter @ThePleasance

The Pleasance presents more than 220 shows across 3 sites and 33 venues during the 4 weeks of the Festival Fringe. With more than 500,000 visitors every year, it remains one of the most popular venues of the Fringe, offering a diverse mix of comedy, theatre, dance, music and everything in-between.

Traverse Theatre

10 Cambridge Street, Edinburgh EH1 2ED
tel 0131 228 1404
email info@traverse.co.uk
website www.traverse.co.uk
Executive Producer Linda Crooks

Centre for new plays in Scotland. All-year-round venue in underground purpose-built theatre with 2 auditoria and off-site rehearsal facilities. Has staged many premieres, including work by Stef Smith, Rob Drummond, Gary McNair, David Greig, David Harrower, Rona Munro, Zinnie Harris and Gregory Burke.

The Underbelly

Edinburgh Permanent Office: 26 Frederick Street, Edinburgh EH2 2JR
tel 0131 5102270
email enquiries@underbelly.co.uk
website www.underbelly.co.uk
Underbelly Directors Ed Bartlam, Charlie Wood

Comprises 23 Fringe spaces over 5 sites with multiple bars. Venues cater for audiences of 60-900 with different seating configurations available. Programmes new writing, theatre, dance, circus and comedy.

OTHER FRINGE LOCATIONS

Komedia

44-47 Gardner Street, Brighton BN1 1UN
tel 01273 647100
email info@komedia.co.uk
website www.komedia.co.uk

Komedia host around 700 performances of comedy, music, cabaret and kids shows and club nights.

All taking place under one roof, Komedia incorporates two unique performance spaces with flexible set-ups and a kitchen serving freshly prepared food at most seated shows.

Komedia's programme features the international and national performers and includes a unique range of

Theatre

Komedia-grown resident shows such as the *Krater Comedy Club*, *Comic Boom* and *Bent Double*.

Sevenoaks Stag Theatre

London Road, Sevenoaks, Kent TN13 1ZZ
tel 01732 450175
email enquiries@stagsevenoaks.co.uk
website https://stagsevenoaks.co.uk/

The theatre can seat up to 453 and has provision for wheelchair-users. Companies should book the space up to 6 months in advance. Programmes a wide range of theatre and dance events.

Watermans Arts Centre

40 High Street, Brentford, Middlesex TW8 0DS
tel 020 8232 1010
email info@watermans.org.uk
website www.watermans.org.uk

West London's leading arts centre comprising a 236-seat theatre (plus 2 wheelchairs), 121-seat cinema (plus 3 wheelchairs), a gallery and 2 studios, used for rehearsals, workshops and small-scale performances. There is also a restaurant and bar with river views of the Thames. The programmes covers a range of different artforms including cinema, theatre, cabaret, dance, new media arts and participative arts.

Theatre

The direction of collaboration
Ned Bennett, theatre director and teacher
Interview by Polly Bennett

Ned Bennett is a freelance theatre director and teacher. He makes theatre with young people and in prisons, as well as directing professional projects. Most recently he directed Unprecedented *for Headlong and BBC Arts,* Dick Whittington *at the National Theatre,* Equus *for Theatre Royal Stratford East, the English Touring Theatre and Trafalgar Studios and* Baddies *with Synergy Theatre. He trained at Manchester University, LAMDA and the Royal Court Theatre.*

What common misconceptions do you think there are about what a theatre director does?

I think a common misconception is the term 'director' itself. It implies a top-of-the-pyramid overly hierarchical approach to making work. This may be the case sometimes, but needn't be necessarily. A common misconception is that the director tells everyone what to do, but a large part of the job is facilitating the space for people to find what to do themselves.

Is that something that you're conscious of in your practice?

I'd like to think I am. I'm quite interested in playing and seeing what can come from the room as late as possible, and then going through an editing process. I think it's interesting to drill down into how the 'director tells people what to do' hierarchical approach is dictated by the inherent time and financial structures that force you into a corner. It's specific to an almost one-size-fits-all British theatre way of putting on plays that I imagine has its roots in the rep system.

By which you mean, 'Here's a play. Let's employ a director to do it, director reads it, says "yes please", gets a designer, keeps going through the creative team, lights, sound, maybe movement, maybe dialect if it needs it'. Would you say that's how British theatre is being made?

I think it often is that. Our theatres have to plan so far in advance that productions are fitted into a matrix. I think what I'm trying to do more is work out what the production needs first, before it's gone too far in one direction determined by parameters informed predominantly by previous shows rather than what this particular play and group of people making it require.

And I guess who does this particular play require.

Exactly.

Are you trying to change the system we've become used to then? How do you mitigate this conversation with a theatre?

I think it is starting to happen. It's been expedited by the last year, with the recognition that artists need to be more embedded in buildings and more involved in decision making. A recurring point of view from freelancers at the beginning of the pandemic was the desire to make less work more slowly.

Theatre

What might this look like?

It might be about what creatives are in Associate positions or even how planning and programming is made more transparent and collaborative with people who are actually going to be making the shows. But also it could be theatres having a conversation with a potential creative team when looking at what shows to do so that their involvement starts from the get-go.

I'd find that really empowering. That's actually genuinely never happened to me.

Empowering yes. It's a way of preventing anyone being treated as a hired hand and recognising that directing as a job is relatively new in the grand scheme of things, which makes other creative team positions even newer. Which means that the behemoth that is the industry is having to keep up. Sometimes making theatre can feel like you're on a runaway train and the enforced slowing down of things during this period has meant there's been some really constructive, clearer conversations about what people need and how it can be achieved. It feels like organisations are open to re-thinking things from a holistic perspective, considering when is a creative team engaged, what's their input and how early can that be, down to the nuts and bolts of design deadlines and how they relate to a timeline in relation to the building and money stuff.

You used the word 'artists' earlier, which I think lots of people shy away from using in theatre because of the overriding habit to define ourselves by the job role. If you're treating everyone as equal artists, everybody has the capacity to have a voice in the experience more, right?

Yeah, and actually maybe there's something liberating about defining ourselves as artists because perhaps it's the categorisation that is a big part of an inbuilt imposter syndrome. Categorisation implies a definite concrete angle on what your job is, as opposed to how your own sense of creative self can be channelled.

You just made a gesture – like a scooping action from your belly – which perhaps summarises the 'full-bellied', 'on-the-table' way you put on a play and what you want from the people you work with. What does collaboration mean to you?

Ultimately the communal aspect of it, of making a mini-community in a space. I do feel like the more you attempt to bring what you and your team, everyone in the room, are all genuinely actually interested in – whether it's something particular you've seen in a music video or a style of comedy that you've become fixated with on TV, or a political ideology. If you're able to try and bring that into the room, then that's what makes the journey so satisfying and nourishing. There's an unhelpful misnomer about collaboration that it's driven exclusively by a mystical, magical alchemy. Alchemy is certainly a thing, but I also think that collaboration is underpinned by a conscious awareness of how to build a culture between a group of people. I think the freelancing, visiting nature of working somewhere, can sometimes feel like stuff is slightly blocking that. Whether it's an insecurity driven by a lack of experience or whatever it may be, or not knowing where the loo is, not knowing the boundaries of something ...

Not feeling welcome in the space ...

Not feeling welcome ...

Not feeling as able to participate if you are there as ...

...As a visiting guest. And sort of how that affects everything really. So, I think it then becomes a question of how you ringfence time for a creative team to actually hear each other. The Russo Brothers who made *The Avengers* films and the TV show *Community* described the two of them working together not as being double the ideas, but as being an exponential growth of ideas, which I think is such a useful way of looking at collaboration. Which is to say that the more a team can bounce off each other, the more they can go deeper down the rabbit hole in trying to understand what something is and what something can be and where it can go. That's the theory, but in practice, where it gets complicated is the fact that creative teams often feel like their time is crushed by needing to do ten other jobs at once to earn enough money to live, and it sometimes feels impossible to get together in one room for more than half a day before rehearsals.

With these reflections on your own personal practice and how it's developing and changing, what would you say to a theatre director – or artist – coming into the industry?

I am often reminded of Anne Bogart's concept of Learn One, Do One, Teach One. I think she was quoting brain surgeons and how they structure their learning to develop their practice. At first, I was going between different spaces working with community groups, young people and professionals instinctively, I think because I thought I was going to become a teacher. Then a few years ago, I became more consciously aware that *doing* that was actually really vital to my practice. The different spaces become symbiotic to what you learn – you develop how you understand something yourself and you can selfishly experiment with process when there isn't necessarily a result. Doing plays is stressful so it makes for a more manageable, mentally healthy use of time. A director I wrote to a long time ago said to me passion isn't limitless and I'm increasingly understanding what he means by that. I think that you find your passion through working with other people and through not having to constantly deliver something. Work becomes more about creativity and collaboration and relationships.

And in terms of the work?

The seeming insularity of the industry can sometimes mean that we end up second-guessing what we think, what should be made or should be said and all of that. I appreciate this is easier said than done but attempt to make what you actually want to see on stage.

To follow Ned's work visit **www.nedbennett.co.uk**

Theatre

Edinburgh or bust: is it worth it?

Shane Dempsey

The Edinburgh Festival Fringe was established in 1947 and has grown into one of the world's most renowned and diverse arts festivals. From its humble beginnings as an alternative to the Edinburgh International Festival, the Fringe has continued to increase and multiply, and, despite the growing costs to companies and performers alike, it still remains high on the agenda of many. The Fringe can be incredibly daunting and at times even crippling. My aim is not to shatter you, but to ensure that you are armed with as much knowledge as possible before you decide if it's worth it.

In 2009 there were 2098 shows performed in Edinburgh and an estimated 18,901 performers in 265 venues. These figures give you an idea of the level of competition for audiences during the three weeks of August. This is an aggressive and over-saturated market. In the Fringe environment, the efforts of many go unrewarded and often even unnoticed. So, can you break through with your production?

Evaluate your work honestly and realistically

The first thing to do is evaluate the production itself. Ask yourself, "What is the appeal of my particular production? What is it about my show that will make it stand out from the crowd? Do I have permission from the author or their estate to perform the piece? If so, what percentage of my overall income will this take, and what are the possibilities of extending this performance licence post-Edinburgh?"

If the piece is new writing or devised then there are fewer issues with performance rights, but it is crucial to discuss billing and authorship, as these can potentially cause problems later. Circumstances change, so with new work it is essential to secure written agreement over the intellectual copyright of the piece – and this also extends to directorial concepts and vision. Get it down on paper so you always know where you stand and can avoid or deal with any issues that may arise.

As well as fledgling companies taking new work to Edinburgh, the festival is also a testing ground for many established, heavyweight companies and producers. They have years of experience, and they have the economic power to invest large sums in PR and marketing. So ask yourself what will bring an audience to your venue, and why. The reality is that you are in direct competition with these established companies as well as with the other thousands who are newer to the game.

Choose the right venue

There are many venues associated with the Fringe. You need to be clear about the kind of work they are interested in programming; some are very specific as to their requirements, while others have a broader remit. Consider not only the price, but also the reputation and the location of a venue, as they vary considerably.

Your time slot is another point of negotiation: late evenings tend to be dominated by comedy, and a great deal of theatre now plays during the day and late afternoon. A general rule is that the more established venues have the best reputations and tend to charge significantly more for their services than smaller, up-and-coming venues. All venues will require you to sign a contract, and you need to be aware of the small print, as it has been known for companies to skim over this only to discover that they were not aware of all the terms and conditions.

Consider venue costs and other expenses

Many venues offer either a box-office split or ask for a flat fee. Almost all will require a deposit in advance. The average cost of mounting a production in Edinburgh is £8,0-00–10,000, and deposits will often be required months in advance – so unless you have access to sufficient funds, consider seriously if there is a more cost-effective way of getting your work out there.

And there are other expenses, including music performance rights, public liability insurance and VAT. Accommodation costs soar during the festival, and local landlords take advantage of the influx of artists and tourists, but if you're organised it is possible to secure a deal by booking early. Many companies choose to stay in Glasgow, which is an hour-long commute, but the time and energy required to do this needs to be weighed up against the convenience and cost of staying in Edinburgh.

What do you want from the experience?

Ask yourself early on what you want to achieve out of the experience. Too often this is not given enough thought, so that it is difficult, if not impossible, to achieve any significant outcomes. Remember that Edinburgh is a massive arts market, and that within any market you need to be specific about your audience – be it the general public or producers who can potentially remount your work post-Edinburgh.

If you want a London transfer, regional tour or international tour, target your promotions pack specifically to relevant individuals and always research their programming tastes. Invite them to the show, ensure that they are given complimentary tickets and try to set up a meeting after they have seen your work. Many international producers are seeking work that would be programmed two to three years after the festival, so you have to have a long-term plan for the production and ensure that it has the necessary factors that will support its longevity.

Network!

Many deals in Edinburgh are set up over late-night drinks and midnight meetings, often to fit in with the schedules of producers who are seeing work all day long. They can be fairly informal, but keeping your professional hat on is essential to any success. There are incredible opportunities to meet new people in Edinburgh, and there are numerous events specifically aimed towards networking, including the Producers' Breakfast.

In addition you can take part in a range of informal activities in which you can make connections that may lead to future work and collaborations. This is often triggered by seeing a company's work: the research trip I made recently to Russia to investigate ensemble practice has been greatly aided by contacts I met in Edinburgh. The key to any networking is to find the common links between you and the other practitioner, and then to develop them into a cohesive relationship. Be honest about what you do and why you do it, and people will usually respond positively.

Press officers have essential contacts with the media and could be a valuable asset to your production. They can not guarantee that your work will be reviewed, but having a person working on your behalf can give you a major advantage over the competition. If, like many companies, you are bringing the show to Edinburgh on a very tight budget,

Theatre

allocate one member of the company to be the designated press officer as this makes life a lot easier for all parties. Again, reputation means a lot in the world of the press and some papers will hold more influence than others. Target the ones that you believe will be interested in your work and be sure to read the reviews every day to get a flavour of what the festival has to offer.

Design, marketing, and word-of-mouth

In a market such as the Fringe, the role of good graphic design and web design is often overlooked, but it is essential to ensure that your work is seen – and seen at its best. Ensure that your production pack has strong imagery. The old cliché of a picture painting a thousand words still rings true, especially to overtired editors at the busiest time of their year. The array of flyers that are seen on the streets of Edinburgh is mind-boggling, but eye-catching design can really aid your marketing campaign.

Over and above marketing, however, is word-of-mouth – one of the key influences in persuading people to see your show. Such recommendations are difficult to achieve, and are dependent on your getting healthy, happy audiences early in your run. The majority of companies spend their days marketing their work, sending emails, chasing the press and leafleting: this is the Fringe, and if you're not prepared to do this to the point of exhaustion, stay at home!

For inclusion in the much-coveted Fringe Brochure you will be asked to submit 50 words of copy to describe your production. Keep it simple and clear, and remember that you are going to have to live with this for the life of your show in Edinburgh, so make sure it really sums your work up. It can be useful to have a quote in there from previous work – after all, everybody wants to see a show from a five-star company – but if it's not true, don't claim it to be so! Fabrication rarely, if ever, helps. The Fringe website provides comprehensive guidelines on producing work in Edinburgh: see **www.edfringe.com/take-part**. The information is there if you look for it, so take the time to investigate. It could save you much stress and money.

Dreams can come true ...

The likelihood of your company or show being picked up for a transfer or tour is extremely slim. The financial burden on companies is very high, and you have to weigh this up against the potential exposure and the possibility of gaining other work after the festival. There has been a recent rise in smaller fringe festivals happening outside of the main Fringe, partially in response to its overtly commercial nature. Notably, the Free Fringe and the Big Red Door are proving to be hugely popular and offer far better deals to the artists. Fragments' production of *The Bay* by Hannah Burke was performed at the Big Red Door, Te-Pooka; we also managed to be seen by representatives of the Traverse, Manchester International Festival, and were transferred into London's prestigious Theatre 503. So yes, dreams can come true ... but only after a serious amount of hard graft, and no little luck too.

Shane Dempsey trained as a director at E15 Acting School and runs Fragments, an international ensemble of theatre and video artists (fragments.ie). His work has been staged in Ireland, London, Scotland and Belgium. In 2008 he filmed the groundbreaking documentary *Mothers of Modern Ireland*. His production of *The Bay* toured extensively in 2009, and he is currently preparing to stage a new adaptation by Hannah Burke of Mikhail Bulgakov's *The Master & Margarita*. He has strong Russian connections, and was invited to observe rehearsals by Lev Dodin of the Maly Theatre of St Petersburg in Paris, November 2009 as well as observing acting workshops at GITIS and Vakhtangov Institute, Moscow 2010.

Open Book: fairer finances for fringe theatre

Piers Beckley

What is 'Open Book Theatre'?

Most fringe theatre productions don't make a profit. And as a large number of fringe productions offer only a profit-share as financial recompense for the actors performing in them, this can be a big problem.

Something that can be especially galling for an actor is to perform in front of a house filled with people, and still not receive any money at the end of the run because the production hasn't made a profit. But if half of those tickets are paper to fill the house in early shows in order to help word of mouth, then the number of people that you see in the audience may not give an accurate measure of how much money is actually coming in.

If the tickets were priced too low, or the producer failed to get a good deal on the advertising, or any number of other things, it's very easy for a production to make a loss. And without financial transparency throughout the process, there can always be the niggling suspicion that something, somewhere, has gone horribly wrong that need not have.

By its nature, fringe theatre will never have as much money to spend on props, print, advertising, design, or on actors as a fully professional production. But if a company can't provide the cold hard cash which we all desire, the very least that they can provide is transparency in recording what money goes in and comes out, so that everything is fair and above board, and is seen to be so.

Open Book Theatre is a new way of running the financial books for a fringe production, so that every member of the cast and crew can see the business of putting on a show. In an Open Book production, the budget is viewable by anyone involved – from first draft through to final income statements. This means that as well as knowing that they've been treated fairly throughout the entire process, everyone will be able to see how the production is doing – and, if all goes well, exactly how much of the profit-share pot they'll receive when the money comes in from the theatre.

Open Book Management is a set of techniques that have been used by companies across the world over the last 40 years. It's all about giving the people involved a stake in the outcome, and then giving them the tools to affect what that outcome is. In a business environment, the stake is most often shares in the company, while in Open Book Theatre (at least at the fringe level) it usually consists of a portion of the profit from the show.

What does Open Book Management involve?

Free access and exchange

There are three main points at the heart of an Open Book production:
- Free access to all financial information
- Regular updates on changes
- Listening to suggestions and implementing them

Theatre

So how would you go about bringing this to life?

One of the easiest ways of sharing information is to use budget spreadsheets showing estimated outgoings and income, which are later updated as the real figures come in. These spreadsheets can be placed on a password-protected website, or emailed to the cast and crew every week to show exactly how much money has come in and gone out.

Because the budgets are available for all to see, as well as knowing exactly where the money has gone on advertising, design, print – all of the things that are necessary to a production, but which generally don't cross an actor's desk – then everyone involved can help suggest improvements.

Perhaps someone has a photographer friend who'll be able to take publicity shots in exchange for a credit or a lower fee. Or perhaps they will know a way to get the fabric needed by a costume designer more cheaply. If everyone knows the cost of the things that make up a production, and how those will affect the profits, then they can suggest ways to make things better for all.

As the financial spreadsheets are regularly updated throughout the show, then everyone involved can see the clock ticking towards breakeven – that magical moment when income from sales and advertising rises above what's been spent on the production, and everyone knows that they're going to be taking some money home with them. It's also nice to be able to celebrate when your production reaches a milestone – for example, when half-way to breaking even.

As well as making the budget documents visible to all, an Open Book production will ensure that all of the documents that are legally required are on display: the insurance schedule, health and safety policy, venue contract, and risk assessment documents. Seeing this information proves that you're dealing with a professional company and a professional production – not just one person's vanity project.

Fair profit-share: the 'tronc system'

In a fringe production, the final part of the Open Book story comes with the division of the profit-share pot. After all costs have been paid (and everyone will know what they are, because they can look at the income and expenditure of the show at any point throughout the production), then any gross profits can be divided between those who brought the show to life.

One way of doing this fairly and equitably is to use what's known as a tronc system, based on the tips system used in many bars and restaurants. In a tronc, everyone involved in the production is allocated a certain number of points depending upon their involvement. So the director and writer might have two points each, while each member of the ensemble cast has one point. It's important to be up front about how any profits will be divided – for example, if the star of the show is to receive more points than the other actors.

After the gross profit has been worked out, the value of each point can be derived by simply dividing the profit by the total number of points – and then everyone is paid that amount for each point that they have.

Control and visibility for everyone involved

Taken all together, these practices mean that everyone involved in a show can see exactly where the money flows from and to, and can be assured of the honesty and integrity of everybody involved in the process.

While some producers have been known to say that their books are open if the financial information for the production is published at the end of the show – or even the end of the year – that's not going to help the members of the production get involved. As well as the honesty of the system, Open Book Theatre relies on helping everyone to see the implications of creative decisions, and that means they need to be able to see what's going on throughout the course of production – not just take a look at a spreadsheet at the end.

The Open Book model, especially at the level of fringe theatre, shouldn't be seen as an attempt in any way to replace an Equity contract, which we would always recommend using. What Open Book Theatre should do, though, is provide some protection for actors working in those profit-share productions which currently are not in a position to use Equity contracts.

Running your productions on the Open Book model means more control and visibility for everyone involved, ensuring that you can be confident that things are under control – or, at least, as under control as they get.

Hopefully within ten years the question won't be, 'What is Open Book Theatre?', but rather, 'Why did we ever do things differently?'

Piers Beckley is a writer and producer. He's been a production manager, stage manager, project manager, line manager, extra, actor, web producer, copywriter, interviewer, sub-editor, video editor, and director. Writing credits include *The Treason Show, NewsRevue, Week Ending, Splendid, Spooks Interactive*, and acclaimed productions of *A Christmas Carol* and *Oliver Twist* for the Lion and Unicorn Theatre. He produced *The Just So Stories* and *Hans Christian Andersen's Fairy Tales* for Red Table at the Pleasance Theatre. You can generally find out what he's up to at his website **fatpigeons.com** or on Twitter as **@piersb**.

Theatre

Children's, young people's and theatre in education

Paul Harman

Work in this very large sector of employment for actors in the UK varies greatly – both in the style of theatre created and presented, and in the wages and conditions offered by employers. Anyone taking work in the field should always be clear about the aims and status of their prospective employer.

Most producing theatres offer plays for young audiences as part of a season, and Christmas shows and pantomimes are mounted by a large number of receiving theatres and commercial touring companies. Some 200 independent touring companies regularly present original theatre productions, usually in schools, reaching a total audience of at least five million annually. Smaller touring companies may operate for profit, or as profit-share partnerships. Companies which are members of ITC (Independent Theatre Council) offer pay and conditions agreed with the performers' trade union, Equity.

Reality check

There is no official agency that collects reliable statistics or regulates the quality of what is offered. Your work may never be publicly reviewed – and it can be hard and demanding. Casts are often small, and living conditions on the road are sometimes difficult. The work may involve a lot of driving (if you are over 25 and insurable) as well as humping sets in and out of vans. However, the rewards for good-quality work conscientiously presented lie in the warmth of welcome from audiences and bookers alike, and a directness and openness of audience response which is often less evident at more formal, adult-orientated theatre events. In schools, you will perform in daylight, very close to children – so it helps if you like them. They can see every blemish on you, and you can see every reaction on a hundred faces.

You will need physical stamina; the ability to play many parts convincingly; and the facility to hit a peak of performance two or more times in a day, six days a week. You may need skill in playing a musical instrument. In addition, other aptitudes may be called upon. A play may be preceded or followed by workshop activity with young people – from 'hot-seating' in character to involving children in a performance. An understanding of drama education techniques is therefore an advantage, and experience of Youth Theatre useful.

What shows?

For good economic and marketing reasons, most theatre for children presented in larger houses is based on well-known stories by established authors, or on characters from TV shows. Companies may receive financial support from official agencies to present plays on health and social issues. Plays related to the National Curriculum, such as science topics, are in great demand from schools.

Theatre in Education (TIE) is a term commonly used to mean many kinds of theatre in schools. In the strict sense, TIE implies an extended theatre event, combining performance and participatory elements and designed to engage pupils in exploring their own knowledge, feelings and attitudes. This is quite a different process from explaining how magnets work, or presenting an account of an historical event. Very few companies nowadays can afford the time and staffing needed to support real TIE, but there are many opportunities to create and present challenging educational plays on a wide variety of subjects.

Independent touring companies receiving public subsidy from Arts Councils in England, Wales, Scotland and Northern Ireland generally aim to present original, commissioned drama. A small group of writers specialises in this field, addressing personal and social topics, from fear of the dark or the break-up of families to genetics and migration. This group of companies – whose aims are primarily artistic, rather than just to entertain or deliver educational messages – find like-minded companies in 70 countries through ASSITEJ (International Association of Theatre for Children and Young People). Overseas tours and international collaborations are increasing.

Above all, don't look upon this field as an easy step towards something else. Your first experiences may well be tough, but an apprenticeship served with a supportive company will open an area of work that you can return to with growing enjoyment and professional satisfaction.

Paul Harman has worked as an actor and director in professional theatre since 1963. He joined Belgrade Theatre in Education team in 1966, headed Education work at Liverpool Everyman from 1970, and founded Merseyside Young People's Theatre Company in 1978. In 1994 he became Artistic Director of CTC Theatre, Darlington and is now the Chair of TYA (Theatre for Young Audiences) – the UK Centre of ASSITEJ.

Theatre

Children's, young people's and theatre-in-education companies

Notes:

• Some of the companies listed are members of the Independent Theatre Council (ITC) – **www.itc-arts.org**.
• The Criminal Records Bureau (CRB) is now called the Disclosure and Barring Service (DBS); CRB checks are now termed DBS checks.

Action Transport Theatre

Whitby Hall, Stanney Lane, Ellesmere Port,
Cheshire CH65 9AE
tel 0151 357 2120
email info@actiontransporttheatre.org
website www.actiontransporttheatre.org
Artistic Director Nina Hajiyianni

Production details: "A new writing company creating brave, collaborative theatre for, by and with young people." Stages 3 projects annually, with around 60 performances in 10 venues including schools, arts centres, theatres and community venues across the UK. In general 4-5 actors go on tour, playing to family (5+) and adult audiences. Incoming actors should have singing, musical instrument and physical theatre skills, and may be expected to lead workshops. Recent productions include: *My Mother Told Me Not to Stare, 10 Tiny Plays* and *Four for the Port.*

Casting procedures: Holds general auditions and actors may write at any time to request inclusion. Casting breakdowns are available from the website, by postal application (with sae), through Equity Job Information Service and Mandy, and in *The Stage.* Welcomes letters (with CVs and photographs) from individual actors previously unknown to the company, sent by post or email. Will consider invitations to view individual actors' websites. Offers Equity-approved contracts as negotiated through ITC. Actively encourages applications from disabled actors, and promotes the use of inclusive casting.

Actionwork Creative Arts

Ground Floor, 6 The Centre, Weston-super-Mare,
North Somerset BS23 1US
mobile 01934 815163
email admin@actionwork.com
website www.actionwork.com

Production details: Actionwork is a theatre and film company that seeks to promote empowerment and reduce bullying and violence in schools. They are committed to producing work through a number of different mediums in order to promote understanding of youth conflict and violence. 3 recent productions include: *Million a Week* (2013), *Out of the Box* (2013) *Cyber Tears* (2014), *Power For Good* (2015), *Silent Scream* (2016) and *CYBER* (2017). Winner of the Anti-Bullying Flame Award.

Each production consists of 3 actors and, on average, the company present 6-10 productions per year to audiences aged between 4 and 17. This equates to over 300 performances at over 150 venues across the UK, ranging from schools to community spaces, art centres and churches. Cast members are sometimes expected to lead workshops and activity sessions and it is advantageous for them to have a driving licence and some singing and dancing ability.

Casting procedures: Uses in-house casting directors and holds general auditions during September. Casting breakdowns are available through PCR and Bristol Online. Welcomes both CVs and letters from actors previously unknown to the company and unsolicited CVs and photographs. These should be sent via email. Also welcomes invitations to view individual actors' websites, but does not welcome showreels. Actively encourages applications from disabled actors.

Aesop's Touring Theatre Company

The Arches, 38 The Riding, Woking,
Surrey GU21 5TA
tel 01483 724633 *mobile* 07836 731872
email info@aesopstheatre.co.uk
website www.aesopstheatre.co.uk
Facebook www.facebook.com/aesoptheatre
Twitter @aesoptheatre
Instagram @aesoptheatre
Director Karen Brooks

Production details: Established in 1999, a professional Theatre in Education company specialising in National Curriculum based plays for the nursery and primary age range. Tours extensively on a daily basis performing interactive plays and both associated and bespoke drama workshops. Plays are mostly performed in schools but also embrace theatres, community centres, village halls, arts centres and party venues. On average stages 300 performances each year, in 225 venues across London, in the Home Counties and further afield. 2 actors usually go on tour, plus occasionally a driver or stage manager. Applicants should be fit, versatile, all-round actors and must have their own transport to easily reach bases in Weybridge or Woking, Surrey for very early morning starts. Applicants will be expected to drive the company estate car. A current DBS is essential.

Casting procedures: Auditions are held in May and actors may write in at any time: 'We reply to all enquiries'.

Arty-Fact Theatre Co.

27 Mount Drive, Nantwich CW5 6JG
tel (01270) 627990
email yvonne@arty-fact.co.uk
website www.arty-fact.co.uk
Artistic Director Yvonne Peacock *Co-director* Brian Twiddy

Production details: Has been performing in schools since 1993, running history workshops, original plays and classics. Performs 6-7 projects annually, with an average annual total of 500-600 performances in 200-300 schools across England. In general 2-4 actors go on tour and perform to audiences aged 7-18. Physical theatre skills and a driving licence are required. Actors may be expected to lead workshops. Recent productions include: *The Time Capsule 1914*, *A Christmas Box* and *Let's Eat Grandma*.

Casting procedures: Holds general auditions twice a year; actors are advised to write in April and July to request inclusion. Casting breakdowns are available via the website, Equity Job Information Service and Castcall. Welcomes letters (with CVs and photographs) from individual actors previously unknown to the company sent by post or email.

Big Wheel Theatre in Education

80A Gaisford Street, London NW5 2EH
mobile 07802 235514
email info@bigwheel.org.uk
website www.bigwheel.org.uk
Facebook www.facebook.com/BigWheelTheatre
Twitter @BigWheelTheatre
Instagram @bigwheeltheatre
Artistic Directors Roland Allen, Jeni Williams

Production details: Specialises in developing interactive theatre workshops for use in education and training. Works in primary and secondary schools, libraries, museums and other heritage settings. An extensive programme of workshops covers subjects ranging from English language and literature and French literature to road safety, sustainability and climate change. Works in pairs and tours in teams of 4-6 for up to 6 weeks at a time.

Casting procedures: Holds general auditions every few years; prosepctive facilitators may write at any time requesting inclusion. Check website for details.

Recruits facilitators from both acting and teaching backgrounds. Looks for good communicators, team players who can be flexible, and people who enjoy working with young people and being silly. Particularly interested in performers with fluent French for French language workshops in the UK. Facilitators must hold a UK driving license; the company applys for work permits where necessary.

Box Clever Theatre Company

c/o The Riverhead Theatre Company
tel 020 7793 0040
email admin@boxclevertheatre.com
website www.boxclevertheatre.com
Artistic Director Michael Wicherek

Production details: Founded in 1996, the company produces contemporary theatre for young people: new plays, contemporary adaptations of classic texts, and issue-based and educational work. 6 major national tours are staged each year with an average annual total of approximately 600 performances in 500 different venues. The company performs to more than 60,000 young people every year. Venues include arts centres, theatres, and educational and community venues nationwide.

Casting procedures: Welcomes submissions (with CVs and photographs) from actors previously unknown to the company if sent by post and if in response to casting breakdowns only.

C&T

University College Worcester, Henwick Grove, Worcester WR2 6AJ
tel 01905 855436
email info@candt.org
website www.candt.org
Artistic Director Paul Sutton

Production details: Founded in 1988. A theatre company incorporating performance, learning and digital media. Works in schools, colleges and universities in the UK and across Europe. Normally tours 2-3 projects each year with an average annual total of 50-100 performances at 50-100 different venues. In general 2-3 actors go on tour and play to audiences aged 5-65. Dance/physical theatre skills, proficiency with computers and digital media, and a driving licence are required. Actors are also expected to lead workshops. Recent productions include: *Living Newspaper.com*, a docu-drama project online for schools.

Casting procedures: Sometimes holds general auditions; actors should write in September requesting inclusion. Accepts submissions (with CVs and photographs) from actors previously unknown to the company sent by post or email. Will also accept showreels and invitations to view individual actors' websites.

Cahoots NI

Cityside Retail & Leisure Park, 100-150 York Street, Belfast BT15 1WA

Theatre

email info@cahootsni.com
website www.cahootsni.com
Facebook www.facebook.com/CahootsNI
Twitter @CahootsNI
Instagram @cahoots_ni
Artistic Director Paul Bosco McEneaney

Production details: Creates theatrical magic for young audiences. Aims to expand the imagination of children, and to stimulate their artistic creativity through the visual potential of theatre and the age-old popularity of music, magic and illusion. Tours productions to arts centres and theatres both nationally and internationally, as well as schools and healthcare settings. Actors should have singing, musical instrument, physical theatre, circus and magic skills, and are sometimes required to lead workshops. Recent projects include: *The Grimm Hotel, The University of Wonder and Imagination, Secrets of Space, Under the Hawthorn Tree, Milo's Hat Trick, Penguins, Shh! We Have a Plan, Nivelli's War, Egg, Danny Carmo's Mathematical Mysteries, The Incredible Book Eating Boy, Duck, Death and the Tulip* and *The Snail and the Whale.*

Casting procedures: Sometimes holds general auditions; actors may write at any time to request inclusion. Welcomes letters (with CVs and photographs) from actors previously unknown to the company sent by post or email, and is happy to receive showreels. Does not welcome invitations to view individual actors' websites. Actively promotes the use of inclusive casting.

Cwmni Theatr Arad Goch

Stryd Y Baddon, Aberystwyth, Ceredigion SY23 2NN
tel (01970) 617998
email post@aradgoch.org
website www.aradgoch.cymru
Facebook www.facebook.com/aradgoch
Twitter @AradGoch
Artistic Director Jeremy Turner

Production details: Founded in 1989. Main focus of work is theatre. Normally tours 6 projects each year with an average annual total of 200 performances and more than 100 different venues. Venues include schools, theatres and community venues across Wales and occasionally abroad. In general 3-6 actors go on tour and play to audiences of all ages. Singing ability, proficiency with a musical instrument, fluency in Welsh and a driving licence are required. Actors may also be expected to lead workshops. Recent productions include: *SXTO,* a performance for secondary school pupils written by Bethan Gwanas; *Cysgu'n Brysur,* an ambitious, large-scale musical drama; *Diwrnod Hyfryd Sali Mani,* a Welsh-language stage play for 3-7-year-olds and families based on Mary Vaughan Jones's classic, timeless characters; *Hola!,* the story of Welsh emigration to Patagonia 150 years ago; *King Hit,* the story of two boys at a party – where a bit of fun escaltaes into a fight with serious

consequences. The company also performed works from their repertoire at various venues in Europe. Offers ITC/Equity-approved contracts and does not subscribe to the Equity Pension Scheme.

Casting procedures: Holds general auditions every year; actors requesting inclusion should send submissions (CVs and photographs) to the company by post or email. Will also accept showreels and invitations to view individual actors' websites. Will consider applications from disabled actors to play disabled characters.

Fevered Sleep

15ᴀ Old Ford Road, London E2 9PJ
tel 020 3815 6430
email info@feveredsleep.co.uk
website www.feveredsleep.co.uk
Artistic Directors David Harradine, Samantha Butler

Production details: Established in 1996. Creates original performances, installations, films, books and digital art for adults and for children. Fearless about experimentation and passionate about research, develops projects that challenge people to rethink their relationships with each other and with the world. Work appears in very diverse places across the UK and beyond, from thatres, galleries and cinemas, to parks, beaches and schools, and the spaces of everyday life; in people's homes, on phones, online. "Whatever we make and wherever it's experienced we're driven by an ambition to present otstanding and transformative art."

Tours 3 projects annually, in around 10 venues (theatres, arts centres, galleries, and site-specific) in the UK, internationally and in London. In general, 3-5 performers go on tour, playing to audiences of all ages. Incoming artists may be expected to lead workshops, and may require dance, physical theatre and/or musical instrument skills, depending on the project. Recent productions include: *Men & Girls, Dusk* and *Stilled.*

Casting procedures: Sometimes holds general auditions, artists may write at any time. Welcomes CVs by email only from individual performers previously unknown to the company, sent by post or email, as well as invitations to view individual artists' websites – but prefers not to receive showreels. Offers Equity-approved contracts as negotiated through ITC. Will consider applications from disabled actors "in line with our equal opportunities policy".

Freshwater Theatre Company

St Margaret's House, 21 Old Ford Road, Bethnal Green, London E2 9PL
tel 020 8983 3601
email info@freshwatertheatre.co.uk
website www.freshwatertheatre.co.uk
Directors Helen Wood, Carol Tagg

Production details: Established in 1996 with the aim of offering high-quality, affordable, innovative drama opportunites to primary school children and teachers and MFL workshops for secondary schools. Runs workshops and storytelling sessions addressing a range of curriculum areas including history, geography, Shakespeare, citizenship, multicultural studies, maths, science, cross-curricular and modern foreign languages and the needs of early years pupils. Also runs drama CPD courses for teachers. Does not tour, but provides over 200 difference sessions all year round at nurseries, schools, libraries and community venues in Greater London, South West, Essex, the West Midlands conurbation and Greater Manchester. Around 60 freelance facilitators work with audiences aged 3 to 12. Relevant experience is required, and actors are expected to lead workshops. Recent workshops include: *Mary Seacole*, *The Three Musketeers*, and *Great Fire of London*.

Casting procedures: Holds general auditions once a year; actors may write in at any time. Welcomes letters (with CVs and photographs) sent by post or email, but only from experienced workshop facilitators. Does not accept showreels or invitations to view individual actors' websites. "We only engage dedicated, experienced workshop leaders to undertake our drama sessions, and will only consider those who can provide regular and ongoing availability within the areas we cover."

Gazebo Theatre in Education Company

2nd Floor, Chancel Court, 2 Wellington Road, Bilston, Wolverhampton WV14 6AA
tel 01902 296199
email info@gazebotheatre.com
Twitter @gazebotheatre
Strategic Director Pamela Cole-Hudson

Production details: Founded in 1979. Normally tours 3-5 projects each year plus workshops, with an average annual total of 300 performances and 250 different venues; these are mainly schools and community venues in the West Midlands and South Shropshire. In general between 1 and 3 actors go on tour and play to audiences aged 4-25. Musical ability and movement skills are sometimes required, as is a driving licence. Actors may also be expected to lead workshops. Recent productions include: *Billy No Mates!* (Special Needs); *If you see a crocodile* (Nursery & Reception); *Presents from the Past* (KS2); *Doing our Bit* (KS3).

Casting procedures: Casting breakdowns are sometimes available by postal application (with sae) or through Equity Job Information Service. The company website will also show details of auditions and artists opportunities. Accepts submissions (with CVs and photographs) from actors previously unknown to the company if sent by post. Open auditions take place over the summer months. Will accept invitations to view individual actors' websites. Does not welcome unsolicited emails. Offers non-Equity contracts. Actively encourages applications

from disabled actors and promotes the use of inclusive casting.

Gibber Theatre Ltd

2ᴀ Woodleigh Road, Whitley Bay, Tyne & Wear NE25 8ET
tel 0191 252 2039
email hello@wearegibber.com
website www.wearegibber.com
Twitter @wearegibber
Directors Victoria Blackburn, Tim Watt

Production details: Founded in 1999. An educational theatre company specialising in innovative multimedia performances for young people of all ages. The company has built a reputation for making a difference in education, by delivering high-quality, hard-hitting interactive performances that effect positive changes in attitudes and behaviours. On average performs 10 projects each year, with approximately 400 performances in schools across the UK and Australia. In general, 3 actors go on tour, playing to audiences aged 5 to 16. Actors may be required to lead workshops, and should have singing and physical theatre skills as well as a driving licence.

Recent productions include environmental education tours: *Super Splash Heroes* (primary) and *The Waste Watchers* (secondary), *Smashed*, an alcohol education awareness tour of Australian high schools, and several careers education tours in both the UK and Australia.

Casting procedures: Sometimes holds general auditions; actors may write at any time. Any specific breakdowns are posted on the company website and social media. Welcomes letters (with CVs and photographs) from actors previously unknown to the company, sent byemail. Accepts showreels and invitations to view individual actors' websites. Will consider applications from disabled actors to play characters with disabilities.

Gostory (UK) Ltd

95 Selkirk Road, London SW17 0EW
email info@gostory.co.uk
website www.gostory.co.uk
Artistic Director Adam Bampton-Smith

Production details: Aims to present high-quality theatre to younger audiences across the UK and to represent the best of British theatre craft abroad. Strives both to entertain and to inform young people, drawing from different cultures and traditions. On average 3 actors tour 3 projects annually, with 400 performances at around 80 venues including arts centres and theatres in the UK, US, Canada and the Far East. Audiences range from 2 to 8 years. Recent productions include *Monstersaurus!*, *Aliens Love Underpants*, *STUCK*, *The Way Back Home*, and *Don't Let the Pigeon Drive the Bus!*

Casting procedures: Casting breakdowns are available from Spotlight, Castnet and Castcall. Welcomes approaches from actors previously unknown to the company, sent by email only.

Theatre

Greenwich & Lewisham Young People's Theatre (GLYPT)

The Tramshed, 51–53 Woolwich New Road,
Woolwich, SE18 6ET
tel 020 8854 1316
email info@glypt.co.uk
website www.glypt.co.uk
Artistic Director Jeremy James

Production details: GLYPT creates theatre for, with
and by young people. It runs Youth Theatre
workshops for 8-21 year-olds, and specialist
programmes for young people with learning
difficulties. The company also runs a comprehensive
programme of workshops for young refugees and
new arrivals. Tours 2 productions a year to young
audiences across South East London and beyond;
these visit schools as Theatre in Education
programmes, and also play at community and arts
centres and at theatres. The work explores current
and provoking issues that affect the lives of young
audiences, and offers a platform for aesthetic and
educational debate. Recent productions have
included: *The Inquiry, Mud City, SK8 Angel* and
Master Juba.

Casting procedures: Operates the ITC/Equity
contract and works with actors committed to the
young people's theatre sector. "We actively encourage
applications from disabled actors and promote the
use of inclusive casting." Welcomes letters and emails
(with CVs) from actors and skilled workshop
facilitators.

Half Moon Theatre

43 White Horse Road, London E1 0ND
tel 020 7265 8138
email admin@halfmoon.org.uk
website www.halfmoon.org.uk
Facebook www.facebook.com/halfmoontheatre
Twitter @halfmoontheatre
Instagram @halfmoon_theatre
Director Chris Elwell

Production details: Established in 1990, Half Moon
is a local organisation with a national remit, based in
Tower Hamlets, East London. The company gives
young people from birth to 18 (25 for disabled young
people) an opportunity to experience the best in
young people's theatre, both as a participant and as
an audience member. Half Moon tours its own
productions nationally, as well as a portfolio of work
through its producing arm Half Moon Presents to
venues including theatres, libraries, schools,
community spaces and festivals. The portfolio covers
a range of work from artists and companies drawn
from all the genres of theatre, spoken word, new
writing and dance, reflecting the UK's contemporary,
diverse communities. Half Moon has ethical status
with ITC and offers ITC/Equity-approved contracts.

Casting procedures: Casting breakdowns are
available through the company's website, circulated

to agents and through Spotlight. Actively encourages
applications from disabled actors and promotes the
use of inclusive casting.

Hopscotch Theatre Company

2nd Floor, 7 Water Row, Glasgow G51 3UW
tel 0141 440 2025
email info@hopscotchtheatre.com
website www.hopscotchtheatre.com
Producer and Co-Manager Thomas McCulloch

Production details: Founded in 1988. A Theatre in
Education company touring to primary schools,
theatre and community venues across Scotland.

Casting procedures: Accepts CVs, photographs and
covering letter from actors previously unknown to
the company sent by post or email. Will also accept
showreels.

Jack Drum Arts

St Cuthberts Centre, Church Hill, Crook,
County Durham DL15 9DN
tel 01388 765002
email info@jackdrum.co.uk
website www.jackdrum.co.uk
Managing Director Helen Ward

Production details: Founded in 1986. Delivers a
strong programme of participatory arts for all sectors
of the community, often linked to the production of
touring theatre. Historically, toured 2 theatre projects
annually with an average annual total of 40
performances at up to 40 different venues, including
schools, arts centres, theatres, outdoor venues and
community venues across the UK and abroad, with a
focus on rural touring and schools. In general,
productions involve 3-4 actors, playing to audiences
of pre-school age and upwards. Singing ability,
proficiency with a musical instrument and a driving
licence are required for some shows. Actors may also
be expected to lead workshops.

Recent productions include: 3 new shows for young
audiences created as part of Children & the Arts
START scheme, and a co-production with Mad Alice
Theatre Company of a play for family audiences
inspired by the Lindisfarne Gospels and the stories of
the Northern Saints. Other projects include large-
scale community play productions, which are created
with local communities working in tandem with
professional practitioners and film/media projects.
For the First World War commemoration the
company is looking to retour its adult production *Set
in Stone* by David Napthine, which was originally
created in 1999 to coincide with the Millennium
Pardon Campaign and is mentioned in Hansard.

Casting procedures: Accepts submissions (with CVs
and photographs) from actors with a North East
connection. "We like to know who is around in the
North East, especially if based in County Durham.
Can help access local networks and professional
development." Offers Equity and non-Equity

contracts. Rarely (or never) has the opportunity to cast disabled actors, but would be interested in developing projects which can make this possible. Particularly interested in actors who have BSL skills.

Krazy Kat Theatre Company

173 Hartington Road, Brighton BN2 3PA
tel 01273 692552
email krazykattheatre@ntlworld.com
website www.krazykattheatre.co.uk
Artistic Director Kinny Gardner

Production details: A children's theatre company founded in 1982, specialising in highly visual forms of theatre that are accessible to Deaf children. Normally tours 2 projects each year with an average annual total of 50 performances and 35 venues. Venues include schools, arts centres, theatres, outdoor venues and community venues throughout UK. In general 2 actors and a technician go on tour and play to audiences aged 3-7. Singing ability, physical theatre skills, British sign language and a driving licence are required. Actors may also be expected to lead workshops. Recent productions include: *A (Midsummer Night's) Dream*, *Petrushka*, *The Pied Piper*, a Victorian *Mikado* and *The Very Magic Flute*.

Casting procedures: Sometimes holds general auditions; actors can write at any time requesting inclusion. Accepts submissions (with CVs and photographs) from actors previously unknown to the company if sent by post. Does not welcome unsolicited emails. Will also accept invitations to view individual actors' websites. Offers non-Equity contracts but at Equity and ITC rates. Actively encourages applications from disabled actors and promotes the use of inclusive casting.

The London Bus Theatre Company

37 Chestnut Close, Hockley, Essex SS5 5EQ
tel 01208 814514
email kathy@londonbustheatre.co.uk
website www.londonbustheatre.co.uk
Principal Chris Turner

Production details: The London Bus Theatre Company increases young people's confidence, self-esteem, employability and life skills through a range of drama and filmmaking activities.

It provides councils, NHS Trusts, Essex Police, youth organisations and schools and colleges with drama workshops and DVDs on issues such as bullying, drugs, alcohol and antisocial behaviour and job interview techniques. Approximately 16,000 young people benefit from the workshops in schools every year. In recent years the Company has focused on a long-term filming project Angels vs Bullies funded by The National Lottery Community Fund, The Arts Council and Esmee Fairbairn Foundation.

The London Bus Theatre Company has received sponsorship from BP, Tesco, Umbro and KeyMed. The award-winning anti-bullying play Nutter has

been filmed by the BBC and is sold by the National Theatre. The Kick It DVDs used in Citizenship programmes produced from 2002–2017 have outsold the BBC and Channel 4 equivalents. Their young actors regularly gain places at RADA, LAMDA, The Bristol Old Vic and The Poor School as well as the National Youth Theatre.

Casting procedures: Holds general auditions and actors may write in at any time. Welcomes letters (with CVs and photographs) from individual actors previously unknown to the company, sent by post or email. Accepts showreels and will consider invitiations to view individual actors' websites. Considers applications from disabled actors to play characters with disabilities.

Loudmouth Education & Training

374 Moseley Road, Birmingham B12 9AT
tel 0121 446 4880
email info@loudmouth.co.uk
website www.loudmouth.co.uk
Facebook www.facebook.com/loudmoutheducationandtraining
Twitter @LoudmouthUK
Instagram @loudmouthuk
Company Directors Chris Cowan, Eleanor Vale

Production details: Founded in 1994. Supplies interactive education and training programmes for young people on personal, social and health education issues, and accessible training for adults to aid personal and professional development. On average we work in around 800 UK venues each year; venues include schools, colleges, community venues and youth centres. Actors are expected to lead workshops and must have a full driving licence. Recent productions include: *Working for Marcus* – an interactive theatre programme focusing on child sexual exploitation and grooming.

Casting procedures: Holds general auditions. Welcomes letters with CVs and photographs from individual actors previously unknown to the company. Will accept unsolicited CVs and photographs sent by email. Does not welcome showreels or invitations to view individual actors' websites. Rarely or never has the opportunity to cast disabled actors.

M6 Theatre Company

Studio Theatre, Hamer County Primary School, Albert Royds Street, Rochdale OL16 2SU
tel 01706 355898
website www.m6theatre.co.uk
Artistic Director Gilly Baskeyfield

Production details: M6 Theatre Company specalises in producing and touring high-quality, accessible and emotionally engaging theatre for young audiences. Founded in 1977, the company tours 3-5 productions each year, through approximately 300 performances/workshops. Touring venues include theatres, schools, festivals, prisons and early years settings across the North West and nationally. Cast sizes are generally 2-4; actors may be expected to participate in workshops accompanying productions. Recent productions have included: *One Little Word* (a sensitive and moving production for children aged 3+ exploring friendship and conflict resolution, underscored with original music and with only 1 spoken word); *Sunflowers and Sheds* (a heart-warming tale of friendship, family and fun on the allotment, for ages 5+ and anyone who's ever made a friend); *Mavis Sparkle* – touring Spring 2013 (this delightful new production mixes illusion, animation and laughter to discover the magic and wonder in the universe, each other and ourselves – ages 5+). M6 also creates and delivers an exciting participatory programme of creative, free time; theatre-arts based workshops and sharing events – ACT NOW! A diverse range of young people from Rochdale (8-18s) participate in and lead activities at M6's purpose-built Studio Theatre and at a range of outreach community settings in Rochdale. ACT NOW! is an ambitious extension of M6's participatory workshop programme, building on proven successful experience, practice and partnerships. Participants' involvement and achievements will be shared with the local community regularly throughout the 3-year project (Big Lottery Reaching Communities funded) and will culminate in a high-profile showcase event/Youth Theatre Festival in 2014.

Casting procedures: Accepts submissions (with CVs and photographs) from actors previously unknown to the company. Unfortunately the company is unable to return photos. Actor contracts are ITC/Equity-approved.

Magic Carpet Theatre

18 Church Street, Sutton on Hull,
East Yorkshire HU7 4TS
tel 01482 709939
email jon@magiccarpettheatre.com
website www.magiccarpettheatre.com
Facebook www.facebook.com/magiccarpettheatre
Artistic Director Jon Marshall

Production details: Professional touring children's theatre company presenting shows and workshops in the UK and abroad. Tours 3-4 productions annually, with around 250 performances in 250 venues including schools, arts and community venues, and festivals. In general 3 actors go on tour, playing to audiences aged 5-11. Actors may be expected to lead workshops. Recent productions include: *Mr Albert's Big Finish*; *The Wizard of Castle Magic* and *Magic Circus*.

Casting procedures: Does not hold general auditions; actors may write in the autumn to request inclusion. Advises actors to "ring us rather than sending CVs, etc., to see when we are casting".

Nimble Fish

30 Wilton Square, London N1 3DW
mobile 07930 394158
email getnimble@nimble-fish.co.uk
website www.nimble-fish.co.uk
Directors Samantha Holdsworth, Greg Klerkx

Production details: Since 2006, award-winning Nimble Fish have been developing and producing projects that explore important social issues as well as engaging audiences that feel the arts have little or nothing to do with them. Recent productions include national tours of *Lost in Blue* by Debs Newbold (2016) and *My Father and Other Superheroes* by Nick Makoha (2015). *You, Me and Everyone in Portsmouth* (2013) became the UK's biggest-ever collaborative storytelling project. In 2007, their production of *The Container* by Clare Bayley won an Amnesty International Freedom Award and an Edinburgh Fringe First.

Casting procedures: Sometimes holds general auditions. Does not welcome unsolicited approaches from individuals not previously known to the company. Offers Equity-approved contracts via ITC. Actively encourages applications from disabled actors and promotes the use of inclusive casting.

Nottingham Playhouse Participation

Nottingham Playhouse, Wellington Circus,
Nottingham NG1 5AF
tel 0115 947 4361
email enquiry@nottinghamplayhouse.co.uk
website www.nottinghamplayhouse.co.uk
Artistic Director Adam Penford

Production details: Participation creates 1-2 small-scale productions per year. These are performed mostly in East Midlands schools, with some performances in small theatre venues – including own studio at Nottingham Playhouse. Employs 3-6 actors each year, on contracts usually lasting from 6 to 12 weeks. Actors are usually multi-skilled. Singing and physical theatre are essential for many of the productions, and actors often have workshop skills and/or play a musical instrument as well. A driving licence is helpful. The company has a specialism in creating theatre for young people with profound learning difficulties and autism, and Makaton signing skills are very welcome for these productions.

Casting procedures: Casting, which is inclusive in every sense, is carried out by the director of the production, usually in collaboration with the Playhouse's Casting Director, Sooki McShane. Welcomes CVs by email or permanent web link, marked for the attention of the Associate Director. Offers ITC/Equity contracts.

Oily Cart Company

Smallwood School Annexe, Smallwood Road,
London SW17 0TW
tel 020 8672 6329
email oilies@oilycart.org.uk
website www.oilycart.org.uk
Artistic Director Ellie Griffiths

Production details: One of the leading theatre companies in the UK creating highly interactive multi-sensory performances for and with the very young (6 months to 6 years) and young people (aged 3–19) with complex needs and/or who are on the autistic spectrum. Tours national and international venues like theatres and arts centres with early years shows, and takes its special-needs work to special schools around the UK.Recent productions include: *In A Pickle* (sheep's-eye view of Shakespeare's *The Winter's Tale* for under 5s); *Hippity Hop*; *Kubla Khan* and *Splish Splash* – an interactive show performed in hydrotherapy pools

Casting procedures: Casting breakdowns are available on the website **www.oilycart.org.uk** and the Arts Jobs website **www.artsjobs.org.uk**. Offers ITC/Equity-approved contracts. Actively encourages applications from D/deaf or disabled actors and promotes the use of inclusive casting.

Onatti Productions Ltd

8 Greville House, Warwick, CV34 4UJ
tel 07377 410053
email info@onatti.co.uk
website www.onatti.co.uk

Production details: Produces foreign-language productions performed at Primary and Secondary schools throughout the UK, France and Spain. Plays are produced in French, German, Spanish and English; all are written by the company and used as an exciting way of promoting and enhancing languages in schools. Onatti produces around 8 tours each year. Employs native foreign actors for contracts from 3 to 10 months. Actors are sourced from the UK and Europe.

Pied Piper Theatre Company

1 Lilian Place, Coxcombe Lane,
Chiddingfold GU8 4QA
tel 01428 684022
email info@piedpipertheatre.co.uk
website www.piedpipertheatre.co.uk
Patron Dame Julie Walters *Artistic Director* Tina Williams *Associate Director* Nicola Sangster

Production details: Founded in 1984, Pied Piper creates exciting, high quality magical plays for children, babies and toddlers. Tours to schools, theatres, libraries and arts centres in the UK, Europe and Asia, specialising in new writing or new adaptations of favourite stories or books. Funded by Arts Council South East. ITC/Equity contracts. Ethical Member.

Pilot Theatre

York Theatre Royal, St Leonard's Place,
York YO1 7HD
tel 01904 635755
email info@pilot-theatre.com
website www.pilot-theatre.com
Artistic Director Esther Richardson

Production details: A national mid-scale touring company producing a programme of education resources for young people. Stages on average 3-6 projects annually, with 150 performances in 20 arts centres and theatres across the UK. In general 6-10 actors go on tour, playing to audiences aged 11-25. Actors are sometimes expected to lead workshops.

Casting procedures: Actors may write in May and August to request inclusion. Casting breakdowns are available on the website or via Spotlight. Welcomes unsolicited CVs and photographs if submitted by email. Also accepts showreels and will consider invitations to view individual actors' websites. Offers Equity-approved contracts as negotiated through TMA/ITC. Actively encourages applications by disabled actors and promotes the use of inclusive casting.

The Play House

c/o Birmingham Repertory Theatre,
Centenary Square, Broad Street, Birmingham B1 2EP
tel 0121 265 4425
email info@theplayhouse.org.uk
website www.theplayhouse.org.uk
Artistic Director Jo Sadler-Lovett

Production details: Established in 1986. An educational theatre charity that uses uses participatory theatre and drama to stimulate and support the language and learning of children and young people. Best known for its *Language Alive!* theatre-in-education tours, which bring the curriculum to life for 3-11 year olds and a range of issue-based projects as well as INSET and CPD for teachers. Tours an average of 10-15 projects annually, with around 1,000 performances in 60-70 schools, outdoor and other venues in the West Midlands. In general 2-3 actors go on tour, performing to young audiences aged 3-18. Skills required vary according to the project and a clean driving licence is required. Actors may be expected to lead workshops.

Casting procedures: Sometimes holds general auditions; actors should write in when these are advertised. Rarely or never has the opportunity to cast disabled actors.

Playbox Theatre (Generator)

The Dream Factory, Stratford Road,
Warwick CV34 6LE
tel 01926 419555
email stewart@playboxtheatre.com
website www.playboxtheatre.com
Artistic Director Emily Quash, *Directors* Stewart McGill, Mary King, Juliet Vankay

Production details: Established in 1986, Generator is the professional acting company of Playbox Theatre, reworking classic drama for young, contemporary audiences. 2 productions staged annually, touring nationally to arts centres, theatres, outdoor venues and educational venues. Based in Warwick. Up to 12

Theatre

actors used in each production. Offers Equity approved contracts. Recent productions include: *A Doll's House* and *Henry VI – The Wars of the Roses*.

Casting procedures: Accepts submissions (with CVs and photographs) from actors previously unknown to the company sent by post or by email. Actively encourages applications from disabled actors and promotes the use of inclusive casting.

Playtime Theatre Company
18 Bennell's Avenue, Whitstable, Kent CT5 2HP
tel (01227) 26648
email Playtime@dircon.co.uk
website www.playtimetheatre.co.uk
Artistic Director Nickolas Champion

Production details: Established in 1983 with the aim of bringing imaginative and innovative professional theatre and workshops to children and young people. Has grown to become "one of the leading children's theatre companies in the South East", and tours both nationally and internationally. Normally tours 2-4 projects each year with an average annual total of 200 performances and 190 venues. Venues include schools, arts centres, theatres, community venues and festivals. Tours have covered the South East, Yorkshire and various countries in Europe and the Middle East. In general 2-4 actors go on tour and play to targeted audiences of 5-7, 4-11, 7-11, 9-13 and 14+. Actors are expected to offer 1-2 additional skills, e.g. singing, proficiency with a musical instrument, physical theatre, puppetry or mime skills. A full driving licence is useful. Actors may also be expected to lead workshops. Recent productions include: *A Midsummer Night's Dream*; *The Dark Castle*, an interactive medieval adventure story; *TUI*, a road and cycle safety play; and *A Silent Song*, a WW1 play looking at pacifism. We also run an extensive Drama Workshop programme. These can be an adjunct to a performance or bespoke.

Casting procedures: Holds general auditions; actors should write in August requesting inclusion. Casting breakdowns are available through the website and Mandy. Applications can be submitted via email or post (with sae), Equity Job Information Service and *The Stage*. Welcomes submissions (with CVs and photographs) from actors previously unknown to the company sent by post or email. Also accepts showreels and invitations to view individual actors' websites (if actor is shown performing). Advises actors to: "Be truthful. Tell us about the things that make you stand out. Tell us briefly why you want to work in children's theatre and why you like touring. Seriously consider the implications of living away from your base for months on end!" Offers non-Equity contracts. Will consider applications from disabled actors to play characters with disabilities. All actors need proof of DBS and covid vaccination status.

Polka Theatre
240 The Broadway, Wimbledon, London SW19 1SB
tel 020 8545 8320
email stephen@polkatheatre.com
website www.polkatheatre.com
Artistic Director Peter Glanville

Production details: Established in 1979. A theatre for children aged 0-12. 6 productions staged annually with 700-800 performances per year. The following skills are required from actors: singing, musical instruments, dance, puppetry and physical theatre. Offers TMA/Equity contracts.

Casting procedures: Casting breakdowns sometimes available. Actors are invited for specific shows. Links to showreels and invitations to view individual actors' websites are accepted. Actively encourages applications from disabled actors and is committed to inclusive casting. "Find out in advance what we're doing, come and visit Polka and see the work."

Q20 Events
Q20 Creative Arts Hub, Dockfield Road, Shipley, West Yorks BD17 7AD
tel (01274) 221360
email info@q20theatre.co.uk
website www.q20events.co.uk
Facebook www.facebook.com/q20eventsuk
Co-Creative Directors Scott Vipond-Clarke, Charlotte Vipond-Clarke

Production details: Tours in excess of 10 projects each year with an average annual total of 350+ performances. Venues include outdoor venues, corporate workspaces and shopping centres throughout the UK. In general 2 or more actors go on tour and play to audiences of all ages. Singing ability and dance/physical theatre skills are required. Recent productions include: *HiveMind* for Saltaire Festival; *Duelling Wizards* for Alnwick Castle; 'Snail Sex' Show for Natural History Museum; *Get Thinking About Your Drinking* for NHS Kirklees; *Superheroes* at Metrocentre; *Beatrix Potter* for Bradford Litertaure Festival; *Pirate Pandemonium* at Geronimo Festival; Percy Veer's *Rockets and Robots* for Glowworm Festival; and *Tales from the Hoard* for Potteries Museum and Arts Council England.

Casting procedures: Does not hold general auditions – auditions are for specific productions only. Will accept submissions (with CVs and photographs) from actors previously unknown to the company, preferably by email. Will also accept invitations to view individual actors' websites.

Quantum Theatre
The Old Button Factory, 1-11 Bannockburn Road, Plumstead SE18 1ET
tel 020 8317 9000
email office@quantumtheatre.co.uk
website www.quantumtheatre.co.uk
Artistic Directors Michael Whitmore, Jessica Selous

Established in 1993. 15 productions performed annually. National touring productions visit schools, arts centres, theatres and outdoor venues. Casting breakdowns available. Holds general auditions. Accepts submissions (with CVs and photographs) from actors previously unknown to the company – email idea. Showreels, voicereels and invitations to view individual actors' websites are also accepted. Operates own contracts based on TMA Equity terms and conditions.

Replay Theatre Company

East Belfast Network Centre,
55 Templemore Avenue, Belfast BT5 4FP
tel 028 9045 4562
email info@replaytheatreco.org
website www.replaytheatreco.org
Artistic Director Janice Kernoghan-Reid

Production details: In 2018, Replay turned 30. Started from a spare bedroom in 1988, Replay has grown up to become one of the leading theatre companies in Northern Ireland. Makes innovative, quality work for everyone under the age of 19: from the tiniest babies to the oldest teenagers, for disabled children and young people, for school groups, for families, for festivals. Tours locally, nationally and internationally - from Belfast to Broadway and lots of places in between.

Seeks to ignite imaginations through leading-edge theatre adventures created especially for our audiences. Each show is shaped through creative consultation with their audience.

"We believe that theatre for young audiences has all sorts of benefits – it's fun, it asks questions and starts conversations, it encourages empathy, it creates a climate of aspiration, it speaks to children about their concerns, and it promotes imagination. And we believe that every child has the right to imagine."

Casting procedures: Replay holds open auditions on a bi-annual basis. From these auditions a list of potential actors will be registered and contacted when appropriate work becomes available. All auditioning opportunities are announced on the website and social media.

S4K International Ltd

Oxted Production Office, PO Box 287, Oxted,
Surrey RH8 8BX
tel 01883 723444
email carolyn@s4kinternational.com
website www.shakespeare4kidz.com/
Producer and Director Julian Chenery *Producer*
Carolyn Chenery

Production details: S4K International produces 4 musical theatre productions, including Shakespeare 4 Kidz shows, each year. Performances are now touring mainly to the Middle East and play to 200,000+ students and children each year. The Touring Company consists of between 8 and 20 actors, technicians and musicians, and plays to audiences from 5 years old upwards. S4K now uses mainly actor/musicians with strong singing ability and

dance/physical theatre skills. Recent productions include: *Dr Dolittle, Three Billy Goats Gruff, Narnia, Goldilocks and the Three Bears, The Snow Queen, The Wonderful World of Oz, Snow White, Peter Pan, Beauty and the Beast, Jungle Book, The Snow Queen, Aladdin* and *Pinocchio.*

Casting procedures: Holds general auditions throughout the year. Casting breakdowns are available through the website and Spotlight. Accepts submissions (with CVs and photographs) from actors previously unknown to the company sent by post or email. Will also accept showreels and invitations to view individual actors' websites.

Scene Productions

54 Weybridge Mead, Yateley, Hampshire GU46 7UX
mobile 07946 005844
email kelly@sceneproductions.co.uk
website www.sceneproductions.co.uk
Artistic Directors Kelly Taylor-Smith

Production details: Founded in 2004 by Kelly Taylor-Smith and Katharine Hurst, Scene Productions is a physical theatre company which creates vibrant, fast-paced and immersive adaptations of classical texts as well as their own devised work. Their unique style combines mask, puppetry, movement, sound, text and tightly-choreographed movement sequences.

The company became the associate company of Redbridge Drama Centre in 2010 and the associate company of South Hill Park in 2013. They have worked extensively in over 400 schools, arts centres and theatres throughout the UK, Ireland and Belgium, and their style and approach to theatre is studied in schools nationwide.

In 2009 they performed a 3-week run of *The Other Side*, a devised physical theatre piece based on true stories from the Israeli/Palestinian conflict, during the Edinurgh Fringe. In 2013 they were commissioned by South Hill Park to co-produce and direct the centenary production of *Oh! What a Lovely War!* in association with Bracknell Forest Council. With their love of promenade-style theatre, they have just finished their promenade production of *Alice in Wonderland* in the grounds of South Hill Park.

Their work includes a strong focus on learning, and the company lead a variety of workshops offering students and adults the chance to re-discover theatre in fresh, bold and imaginative ways. The company also offers work experience to students, and collaborative and participate in workshops with other theatre companies.

Casting procedures: Sometimes holds general auditions and actors may write in May to request inclusion. Welcomes letters (with CVs and photographs) from actors previously unknown to the company, sent by post or email. Does not accept showreels, but will consider invitations to view individual actors' websites. Rarely (or never) has the opportunity to cast disabled actors.

Theatre

Sky Blue Theatre Company

1 Kelling Gardens, Croydon CR0 2RP
mobile 07941 012293
email info@skybluetheatre.com
website www.skybluetheatre.com
Twitter @SkyBlueTheatre
Directors Frances Brownlie, John Mitton

Production details: Founded in 2007. A company touring new plays, Shakespeare productions and workshops. Founded the British Theatre Challenge, an international playwriting competition. Works with young people through its own theatre school and with colleges developing skills in performing arts. Stages productions for young people's theatre and TIE annually, giving around 130 performances in 60 venues nationally. In general, 4 actors go on tour, playing to audiences aged 7 to 18. Actors are sometimes expected to lead workshops. Recent productions include: *Much Ado About Nothing*, *Real Love – A New Musical*, and *Romeo and Juliet* workshops.

Casting procedures: All casting is done in house. Holds general auditions, for which breakdowns are available via Mandy Network and the website. Welcomes letters (with CVs and photographs) from individual actors previously unknown to the company, sent by email. Accepts showreels and considers invitations to view actors' websites and performances. Will also consider applications from disabled actors for any role.

Small World Theatre

Bath House Road, Cardigan, Ceredigion SA43 1JY
tel 01239 615952
email info@smallworld.org.uk
website www.smallworld.org.uk
Facebook www.facebook.com/SmallWorldTheatre
Instagram @smallworldtheatre
Directors Ann Shrosbree and Bill Hamblett *Marketing Manager* Sam Vicary

Production details: Small World Theatre creates unique, flexible puppet theatre performance that tours to small/mid-scale venues across Wales, the UK and internationally. These include schools, arts centres, theatres, outdoor spaces, community venues, and festivals. It makes giants for large-scale outdoor and site specific performances. The work is environmentally sensitive and socially engaging.

In general 3-4 actors go on tour, playing to audiences of all ages. Actors are generally expected to be skilled in areas such as puppetry, mime, singing and physical theatre. They must perform in Welsh and English and be able to facilitate creative/drama workshops.

Small World Theatre also manages a near zero carbon venue in Cardigan, West Wales. The venue and its creative programme of events and classes are a reflection of Small World Theatre's values and provides an accessible, welcoming, sustainable example for other groups working towards a zero carbon future. Most recent production is *The Lightning Path/Y Llwybr Mellt*, supported by Arts Council Wales.

Casting procedures: Uses in-house casting directors. May hold general auditions and advertise casting breakdowns. Will consider submissions (letters, CVs and photographs) from actors and invitations to view indiividuals' details online. No unsolicited showreels. Small World Theatre casts actors with disabilities in inclusive roles.

Solomon Theatre Company

5 Doolittle Yard, Froghall Road, Ampthill, Bedfordshire MK45 2NW
tel 01722 786845
email office@solomontheatre.co.uk
website www.solomontheatre.co.uk

Production details: Founded in 2003. Specialises in communicating messages that result in crime reduction, improved community safety and the promotion of healthy schools and healthy lifestyles. Has performed award-winning plays to tens of thousands of people in schools and community locations across the country, as well as producing films and support material for national programmes. Performs around 7 tours annually in more than 300 venues, including schools, theatres and community venues in the South West, South East, Midlands, Wales and Northern Ireland. On average 12 actors go on tour, performing to audiences aged 12-16. Likes to hear from actors with a driving licence, this would be great be not essential and may be required to lead workshops. Recent projects include: *Last Orders* (alcohol education); *Trickster* (burglary education); *Gemma's Wardrobe* (drugs education) and *Power of Love* (domestic violence education) and *Skin Deep* (knife education).

Casting procedures: Holds general auditions; actors may write in July, November and April to request inclusion. Welcomes letters (with CVs and photographs) from actors previously unknown to the company sent by post or email. Also welcomes showreels and invitations to view individual actors' websites. Does not offer Equity-approved contracts but does offer Equity rates. Will consider applications from disabled actors to play characters with disabilities.

Spare Tyre Theatre Company

The Albany, Douglas Way, Deptford, London SE8 4AG
tel 020 8692 4446 (ext 273)
email info@sparetyre.org
website www.sparetyre.org
Instagram @sparetyretheatre
Artistic Director Rebecca Manson Jones

Production details:

• Work with older people aged 60+, outreach workshops for older people, and interactive storytelling for people with dementia. Work with carers.
• Work with people with learning disabilities.
• Work with women who have experienced violence.
• Work with people with long Covid and other long-term health conditions.

London and nationwide. Skills required from actors include workshop-leading and facilitation skills, experience of working with community groups and a sensitivity to, and understanding of, relevant issues.

Casting procedures: Casting breakdowns are published and on the website. Unsolicited approaches at other times – including CVs, showreels and invitations to view individuals' websites – are discouraged. Offers ITC/Equity-approved contracts. Actively encourages applications from disabled actors and promotes the use of inclusive casting.

Splendid Productions

The Dairy, 5 Marischal Road, London SE13 5LE
tel 020 8318 6469
email info@splendidproductions.co.uk
website www.splendidproductions.co.uk
Artistic Director Kerry Frampton

Production details: Founded in 2003. Splendid Productions are theatre makers with nearly 20 years' experience of touring high-impact theatre. They tour creative adaptations of classic texts to schools, colleges and theatres across the UK, and this regular audience of over 15,000 per year has given them a base for establishing a strong theatrical identity creating work that appeals far beyond the education sector. Splendid also provide a range of practical drama-based workshops and teaching resources that are sold across the world. Splendid are also now cited as influential practitioners by WJEC/Eduqas, EdExcel and OCR exam boards at both GCSE and A level. Students across the UK and throughout the world are studying the company, performing its adaptations and creating their own work in the Splendid style.

The company has performed in schools and colleges in the UK and internationally and has performed at the Edinburgh Festival Fringe, the National Theatre's "Watch This Space" Festival, and are programmed at numerous theatres including The Pleasance London and The Lowry in Salford.

Actors require strong physicality, some musical skills, an understanding of clown, must be politically engaged and ideally hold a driving licence. Recent productions include: *UBU, The Oresteia, Meamorphosis, Macbeth, The Odyssey, Medea, Everyman, The Trial, Dr Faustus* and *Woyzeck*.

Casting procedures: Does not hold general auditions. Actors may write during April/June to request inclusion. Welcomes letters (with CVs and photographs) from actors previously unknown to the company, sent by post or email. Does not accept showreels but is happy to receive links to individual actors' websites. Will consider applications from disabled actors to play characters with disabilities. "We work hard and are very passionate about working with young people. You need to be flexible, approachable and keen to create good theatre in education. Look at our website to see what we do before getting in touch."

The Take Away Theatre Company

10 Millbank Street, Dalrymple, Ayrshire KA6 6FE
tel 0800 158 3840
email admin@takeawaytheatre.co.uk
website www.takeawaytheatre.co.uk
Producer Lee O'Driscoll

Production details: Founded in 2007. A theatre-in-education company delivering "high-impact and dynamic drama projects in schools and other venues throughout the UK". Tours 9 projects annually with 270 performances at schools, arts centres, theatres and community venues. In general 4 actors go on tour, playing to audiences aged 1 to 101. Actors may be expected to lead workshops and should hold a current driving licence; singing, musical instrument, dance and physical theatre skills are an advantage. Recent productions include: *The Jungle Book, Scotland (an' a' that), The Wind in the Willows* and *Hansel and Gretel*.

Casting procedures: Sometimes holds general auditions; actors may write at any time to request inclusion. Casting breakdowns are available via the website, by postal application (with sae), and from Mandy and CastNet. Welcomes letters (with CVs and photographs) from individual actors previously unknown to the company, sent by post or email. Also accepts showreels and invitations to view individual actors' websites. Will consider applications from disabled actors to play characters with disabilities.

Tall Stories Theatre Company

Tall Stories Studio, 68 Holloway Road, London N7 8JL
tel 020 8348 0080
email info@tallstories.org.uk
website www.tallstories.org.uk
Artistic Directors Olivia Jacobs, Toby Mitchell *Executive Producer* Lucy Wood *General Manager* Harriet Billington *Marketing Manager* Clare Lewis *Creative Coordinator* Robyn Wilson *Finance Manager* Sheila McClenaghan *Production Assistant* Eman Ansari

Production details: Tall Stories brings great stories to life for audiences of all ages. Founded in 1997, Tall Stories is a registered charity which is internationally recognised for its exciting blend of storytelling theatre, original music and comedy. Recent productions include: *The Gruffalo* (UK tour), Room on the Broom (UK tour, West End), The Smeds and the Smoos (UK tour, Edinburgh Fringe) and The Canterville Ghost (UK tour, Southwark Playhouse). Performers are expected to have good singing and devising abilities, and experience of physical theatre, and the ability to play an instrument is useful. Performers may occasionally be expected to lead workshops, with training given. Each production consists of 3-4 actors and, on average, the company undertakes 3 UK and 5-6 international tours per year. This equates to over 1,500 performances at around 650 venues, ranging from schools and arts centres to West End theatres.

Casting procedures: Tall Stories holds 3-4 workshop auditions a year for up to 75 actors. Actors can send in a CV and covering letter at any point during the year for consideration. Casting breakdowns are either posted on Spotlight, or the company invites actors that have written to them directly or via agent recommendations. Offers contracts based on ITC, UK Theatre or SOLT guidelines. Welcomes applications from disabled actors and promotes inclusive casting.

Theatr Iolo

Chapter Arts Centre, Market Road, Cardiff CF5 1QE
tel 029 2061 3782
email hello@theatriolo.com
website www.theatriolo.com
Artistic Director Lee Lyford

Production details: "Formed in 1987, Theatr Iolo aims to produce and programme the best of live theatre, making it widely accessible to children and young people in Cardiff and the Vale of Glamorgan to stir the imagination, inspire the heart and challenge the mind. Theatr Iolo works alongside teachers and advisers to enhance teaching and learning across the curriculum." Normally tours 5 projects each year with an average annual total of 150 performances across 120 venues. Venues include schools, arts centres and theatres in Wales and occasionally England, and international festivals. Cast sizes vary, playing to audiences aged 3-18. Singing ability, proficiency with a musical instrument, dance/physical theatre skills and a driving licence are frequently required. Actors may also be expected to lead workshops. Recent productions include: *Grimm Tales* by Carol Ann Dufy; *Lenny* by Francis Monty (trans. Paul Harman) and *Under the Carpet* by Sarah Argent.

Casting procedures: Sometimes holds general auditions; actors should write in June requesting inclusion. Casting breakdowns are available through Equity Job Information Service. Accepts submissions (with CVs and photographs) from actors previously unknown to the company if sent by post. Emails are also welcome, as long as the file is not too big. Offers ITC/Equity-approved contracts. Actively encourages applications from disabled actors and promotes the use of inclusive casting.

Theatr na nÓg

Unit 3, Milland Road Industrial Estate,
Neath SA11 1NJ
tel (01639) 641771

email drama@theatr-nanog.co.uk
website www.theatr-nanog.co.uk
Facebook www.facebook.com/theatrnanog
Artistic Director Geinor Styles

Production details: Theatr na nÓg was established in 1984 to produce theatre for a wide spectrum of audiences throughout Wales in a variety of venues and locations, in both languages. "The literal translation of Theatr na nÓg is theatre of eternal youth and this encasplutates the ethos of the company by creating theatre that has the power to excite and engage audiences of all ages." The company is a regular provider of main stage work throughout the country and continues to expand its portfolio of venues. Theatr na nÓg continues to evolve from being a company that solely produces work for schools to being recognised by the Arts Council of Wales as one of their producing theatre companies that will be encouraged to produce work to a variety of audiences throughout Wales and beyond.

Casting procedures: Although most casting goes through Spotlight and casting agents, Theatr na nÓg also holds general auditions (depending on the project); actors may write at any time requesting inclusion. Acceps submissions (with CVs and photographs) from actors previously unknown to the company sent by post or email. Will also accept invitations to view individual actors' websites.

Theatre-Rites

Unit 3, Energy Centre, Bowling Green Walk,
London N1 6AL
tel 020 7164 6196
email info@theatre-rites.co.uk
website www.theatre-rites.co.uk
Facebook www.facebook.com/TheatreRites
Twitter @TheatreRites
Artistic Director Sue Buckmaster

Production details: Committed to creating challenging productions which push the boundaries of theatrical form by experimenting to combine different artistic disciplines. Highly imaginative visual experiences for families to share together. Stages 2 productions annually, with around 45 performances in 12 arts centres and theatres across all English regions, in Scotland and internationally. In general 5-8 actors go on tour, playing to audiences of various ages, often 5+. Actors are sometimes expected to lead workshops; singing, musical instrument, dance, physical theatre and puppetry skills may all be advantageous, depending on the project. Recent productions include: *Beasty Baby The Broke'n'Beat Collective, Recycled Rubbish, Bank On It, Mischief* and *Hang On.*

Casting procedures: Sometimes holds general auditions; actors may write at any time to request inclusion. Casting breakdowns are available via the website and Spotlight. Welcomes letters (with CVs and photographs) from individual actors previously unknown to the company, sent by post or email. Also welcomes showreels and invitations to view individual actors' websites. Offers Equity-approved contracts as negotiated through ITC. Actively encourages applications from disabled actors, and promotes the use of inclusive casting. "The work is devised and often physical, so we frequently look for performers with previous experience of this kind."

Theatre Centre

The Albany, Douglas Way, London SE8 4AG
tel 020 7729 3066
email admin@theatre-centre.co.uk
website www.theatre-centre.co.uk
Facebook www.facebook.com/Theatre_Centre
Twitter @TCLive
Instagram @theatrecentre
Artistic Director Rob Watt

Production details: Theatre Centre brings world-class theatre straight into the heart of schools. Productions present big ideas and difficult questions that can help young audiences make sense of a complex and changing world. Uses the power of stories, writing and performance to support students and teachers in their learning across a range of subjects to build confidence and aspirations.

"Our vision is that children and young people are empowered in their activism and leadership through theatre, using their voices and ideas to make change in themselves and the world around them."

Offers ITC/Equity and ITC/WGBB contracts. Subscribes to the Equity Pension Scheme.

Casting procedures: Casting breakdowns are available through the website, Spotlight and agents.

Theatre Company Blah Blah Blah!

Interplay Theatre, Armley Road, Leeds LS12 3LE
tel 0113 426 1394
email admin@blahs.co.uk
website www.blahs.co.uk
Facebook www.facebook.com/theatreblahs
Twitter @theatreblahs
Artistic Director Deborah Pakkar-Hull *Executive Creative Director* Iain Bloomfield

Production details: A Leeds-based theatre company, founded in 1985, which specialises in participatory theatre for children and young people, performing in schools, community settings and theatres. The company usually tours 1 performance each year, regionally and nationally, accompanied by associated project activity. Offers Equity minimum contracts; does not subscribe to the Equity Pension Scheme.

Casting/recruitment procedures: Opportunities are advertised through the company's website, social media and through industry outlets.

Theatre Hullabaloo

The Hullabaloo, Borough Road, Darlington DL1 1SG
tel (01325) 405680
email info@theatrehullabaloo.org.uk
website www.theatrehullabaloo.org.uk
Artistic Producer Miranda Thain

Production details: Founded in 1979. A specialist producer of theatre for young audiences based in specialist venues for children and families. Tours regionally, nationally and internationally for audiences aged 0 to 16 years, with an emphasis on theatre for early years. Recent productions include: *Baba Yaga* (7+).

Casting procedures: General auditions are sometimes held and casting opportunities are advertised mainly through social media. Welcomes letters (with CVs and photographs) from individual actors previously unknown to the company but who have a demonstrable track record in TYA, sent by post or email. Also accepts showreels and invitations to view individual actors' websites. Offers Equity-approved contracts as negotiated through ITC.

Tin Shed Theatre Company

46 Lennard Street, Newport NP19 0EJ
mobile 07921 366038/07511 139773
email connect@tinshedtheatrecompany.com
website www.tinshedtheatrecompany.com
Artistic Director Georgina Harris *Company Manager* Naomi Underwood

Production details: Established in 2008. Specialises in devised theatre which lends itself to performance in unusual spaces. High-energy, high-impact work that focuses on many different genres.

Tours 1 project annually, with around 30 performances in 20 venues, including schools, arts centres and theatres. In general 7 actors go on tour, performing to audiences aged 11 to 16. Actors are required to lead workshops. Recent productions include *Of Mice and Men* by John Steinbeck.

Casting procedures: Uses freelance directors, actors may write at any time to request inclusion. Casting breakdowns are available from the website. Welcomes unsolicited approaches by post and email, and accepts showreels and invitations to view individual actors' websites/visit other productions. Encourages applications from disabled actors and promotes the use of inclusive casting.

Travelling Light Theatre Company

Wellspring Settlement, 43 Ducie Road, Barton Hill, Bristol BS5 0AX
tel 0117 377 3166
email info@travellinglighttheatre.org.uk
website www.travellinglighttheatre.org.uk
Twitter @tl_theatre
Instagram @tl_theatre
Artistic Director Heidi Vaughan *Executive Director* Dienka Hines

Production details: Since 1984 the company has produced innovative and inspiring work for young audiences using live music, visual and physical performance in its work. Produces on average one tour each year and at least one Christmas show with an extended run. Venues include theatres, arts centres, community venues, local schools and

Theatre

festivals across the UK, as well as touring internationally in China and the US. Target audiences vary from 0-adult. Casts are usually 1-5 actors.

Singing ability, proficiency with a musical instrument and physical theatre skills are often required; most plays are devised with the cast. Recent touring productions include: *Boing* (age 2–5); *I Wish I was a Mountain* (age 7+) and *Igloo* (age 0–3).

Casting procedures: Castings are listed on the company website, Arts Jobs and Disability Arts Online. Speculative CVs are not accepted.

Unicorn Theatre

147 Tooley Street, London SE1 2HZ
tel 020 7645 0500
email stagedoor@unicorntheatre.com
website www.unicorntheatre.com

Production details: The Unicorn Theatre was founded by Caryl Jenner as a touring company in 1947, with a commitment to giving children a valuable and often first-ever experience of quality theatre, and a philosophy that "the best of theatre for children should be judged on the same high standards of writing, directing, acting and design as the best of adult theatre".

Today, the Unicorn is the national home of theatre for children and young people. Its purpose-built premises at London Bridge contains 2 theatres, 4 floors of public spaces and 2 rehearsal studios dedicated to producing and presenting work for and about audiences aged up to 13. It is an Arts Council National Portfolio Organisation. Offers TMA and ITC/Equity-approved contracts and subscribes to the Equity Pension Scheme.

Casting procedures: Generally by invitation via agent, but will read CVs and photographs from actors previously unknown to the company if sent by email.

Wizard Theatre Ltd

Blenheim Villa, Burr Street, Harwell, Oxfordshire OX11 0DT
tel 0800 583 2373
email info@wizardtheatre.co.uk
website www.wizardtheatre.co.uk
Facebook @WizardTheatre
Twitter @WizardTheatre
Artistic Director Leon Hamilton *Associate Producer* Oliver Gray *Production Manager* Richard Tall

Production details: Established in 2002. Performs in schools, theatres and conferences across the country. Message-based shows and workshops are commissioned annually. Working with various organisations, from the Met Police to the DSM

Foundation, and delivering ongoing drama therapy classes in schools with their Power of Drama and Power of Reading programmes. Their winter show tours in theatres: 2022's production is *Robin Hood*.

Stages 10+ projects annually, with more than 800 performances in 400 venues across London, the Home counties and beyond. In general 2-4 actors go on tour, playing to audiences aged 4-18. Actors may be required to lead workshops. Good singing, musical instrument, driving and stage combat skills are useful. Recent productions include: *I Love You Mum I Promise I Won't Die* by Mark Wheeller, *The Adventures of Dr Dolittle, Choices* and *On the Right Road*. We are always looking for excellent facilitators and drama teachers. The Power of Drama Project also always requires goood actor/teachers to join the team.

Casting procedures: Sometimes holds general auditions; actors are welcome to write in at any time. Casting breakdowns are available via Spotlight, Mandy and on the Equity Job Information Service. Welcomes unsolicited approaches by actors/facilitators/teachers by post or email. Also accepts showreels and will consider invitations to view individual actors' websites. Does not offer Equity-approved contracts: "Usually we pay well above Equity rates." Rarely or never has the opportunity to cast disabled actors.

Young Shakespeare Company

213 Fox Lane, Southgate, London N13 4BB
tel 020 8368 4828
email youngshakespeare@mac.com
website www.youngshakespeare.org.uk
Artistic Directors Christopher Geelan, Sarah Gordon

Production details: One of the longest-established and most respected educational theatre companies in the UK. Currently performs Shakespeare to more than 100,000 young people each year, working in schools and theatres to provide a year-round programme of performances and workshops. On average stages 10 productions each year, with around 1,000 performances in theatres and schools throughout England. In general, 5 actors per show perform to audiences aged 6-16. Actors may be expected to lead workshops. Recent productions include: *Twelfth Night, Romeo and Juliet, Macbeth, The Tempest, Hamlet* and *A Midsummer Night's Dream*.

Casting procedures: Holds auditions every June for autumn season and every November for spring season. Casting breakdowns are available via Spotlight link. Also welcomes emails from individual actors previously unknown to the company.

Shakespeare changes prisoners' lives

Bruce Wall

'Correction and instruction must both work 'ere the rude beast will profit.'
William Shakespeare, *Measure for Measure*, III ii

If prisons really worked there would be fewer of them. Certainly, there were would be fewer people than the 86,000 plus currently locked in British cells. Whereas UK criminal justice regimes have historically failed institutionally, success has been captured by peeking through the keyhole of individual arts successes. They serve as role models. They deserve to be cherished.

The Prison Reform Trust in 2017 reported that the overall number of staff in UK prisons has fallen from 45,000 in 2010 to just under 31,000 in 2016. Over 7,000 UK prison officers have been cut in but five years. Training programmes have been shredded to an unrealistic minimum.

Over the past quarter century, the UK prison environment has become ever more challenging; ever more violent; ever more drug infested; ever larger and ever more dangerous. It is – as even the Prison Service itself acknowledges – unsustainable. Still the arts work inside endures. Somehow.

Historically, there have been many charities running valuable arts programmes in UK prisons. The oldest – groups like the Koestler Trust, Clean Break (itself founded by two female ex-offenders); Fine Cell Work; Dance United and Music in Prisons – have continued to make inroads. Notwithstanding it has become progressively difficult for arts groups to survive, let alone thrive.

The London Shakespeare Workout (LSW) is a charity I had the privilege to co-found opposite the legendary Dame Dorothy Tutin in 1997. It seeks 'to employ the works of Shakespeare and other major dramatic writers/thinkers as a tool towards effective interaction to (a) create new work and (b) promote confidence through the will to dream for all.' Notice that prison does not feature in its title. Terminology is key. To the men and women, we are privileged to work with that is important. They are serving time for the past. LSW trades in futures.

The word 'drama' in ancient Greek means 'conflict'. It might be argued that the world's greatest dramatic/musical art has itself been created in and around adversity. Assuming that to be correct the climate described above is ripe in its artistic potential to both educate and entertain. The arts can step in where more conventional educational programmes have failed. Over the past two decades, LSW has been privileged to engage with more than 9,000 offenders of every race, gender, orientation, colour and creed. Currently, over 82,000 UK prison inmates are adult males, while women account for fewer than 3,200 places. LSW's production of Lorca's *The House of Bernarda Alba* – originally mounted in one women's prison, HMP Send, in an original version translated by a woman serving a life sentence in another – marked the first time in this country that prisoners had been allowed out to perform in London's West End. In this instance at the Criterion Theatre. This production – as almost all LSW's have been – involved a mix of prisoners and professional actors.

Indeed, we've been honoured to work alongside more than 12,000 professional actors or those in training. These sessions/workshops/productions have taken place in venues

Theatre

ranging from 100 different prisons in England alone to Broadway; from the House of Lords to the United Nations; from Yorkshire's Stephen Joseph Theatre to the Royal Opera House; from the RSC's Swan Theatre to the celebrated Stratford Festival in Ontario, Canada.

One example: in a round with a mix of juvenile offenders and professional actors in a correctional estate in fashionable Henley-upon-Thames, a lad – no more than fifteen years old – haphazardly pulls a Shakespearean line from a manila envelope. Visibly shocked at what he sees his chin begins to quiver. Bravely he summons up sufficient courage to haltingly read: 'Thought is free'. At the day's end, he asks me – the person leading the session – if he might keep that slip of paper. I knew full well it was against regulations. He could potentially use that wafer-thin slice to self-harm. Still, I didn't have the heart to take it from him. 'It's yours,' I said. He beamed with pride. Minutes later I stood and watched as an officer undertaking a search remove it from him at the gate outside. For a moment, he looked crestfallen. Then he turned back and looked at me through the hut's window. He grinned. I did the same. He put his thumb up. He knew – in the most real sense – he now owned IT.

A second example: we'd done a number of sessions at HMP The Mount in Hertford-shire. On this day, there were forty in the room; fourteen actors and twenty-six inmates. At one point, we launched into a 'Shakespeare interspersal'. In this exercise, an actor uses the Shakespeare in his head to intersperse with an inmate who responds to the language he/she hears in approximate length of line while addressing a scenario selected by their peers. These lads decided it should be set in a 'church in Brixton'. The actor would be the 'father confessor' and the inmate was 'coming in to confess a murder'. I asked for volunteers. One young black lad (many of the inmates in Southern UK prisons are BAME) put up his hand. (He'd been to other sessions we'd run before but never done any individual work.) 'You,' I said: 'You have a go.' Dutifully, Benson (for that's what the guys called him) entered the circle. 'The tempter or the tempted ... who sins most?' the knelling actor, Alasdair Craig, a War Horse veteran, began. Benson responded well. As Angelo questioned his own conscience in that speech, Benson got the brilliant idea that he'd been duped. It had been the father confessor who'd been the perpetrator of the crime. Masterfully he turned the tables ... but that's not the point of this story.

We went on to do many other activities that day and at the end I noticed a prison officer at the door. She'd obviously been crying. Concerned, I went over to her and said I hoped that she had not taken any offence as I was sure none had been intended. She grabbed me. 'You don't understand,' she pointedly said, 'that boy [gesticulating at Benson] has been in this prison for three years and he has never, ever, made a sound.'

Still, why *this* language? 'Why Shakespeare?' I'm asked that question more than any other. One, then twenty-three-year-old, London inmate gives the best answer I've ever heard. In but fifteen minutes, he pens a sonnet in answer to the query. It begins: 'It's addictive. First time's never enough/You wanna taste it again and again.' His final couplet – in perfect scansion – sings out:

> Do you wanna taste this drug? Go on 'ere
> Don't worry. It's harmless. It's just Shakespeare.

He's enrolled in LSW's year-long (2005/6) – precedent setting – drama school lodged in HMP Brixton, the first within a UK prison walls. (For an entire year previously I was entitled to travel to male prisons throughout the country doing workshops and moving men to Brixton who showed aptitude and commitment.) These inmates will study voice with Cicely Berry and text with the likes of Olivier, BAFTA, Tony and Oscar-winning Mark Rylance and Dame Janet Suzman. The lads call it the 'Dream Factory' For many that's what it is.

Today, Dream Factory graduates have worked for, among others, the RSC and the Globe. One leads a film unit in Berlin and another one of the UK's leading youth arts programmes. Of those who were released during the programme's tenure none has reoffended. Throughout the Dream Factory's history, lads take part in countless Shakespeare Workouts with actors from 'the outside'. For the prisoners, these become the equivalent of a ballet dancer's morning class. They instil discipline into their studied craft. Many guests will be recent drama school graduates. Many will later note that this theatrical interaction remains 'profound' in terms of their professional work. Still more will say this experience was 'life changing'.

LSW has worked in a similar light not just in the UK but throughout the world aside a vast array of international talent. The positive response remains universal in locales ranging from Chile to China; from India to Afghanistan. Now LSW dreams of a prison interaction for every UK drama student being aware – as we are – that this is a vital part of their training as future communicators. For the past eighteen years, LSW has been privileged to share prison interactions with graduating students from the Royal Academy of Dramatic Art (RADA). In 2017, we were particularly honoured when this outreach work was embedded as part of every RADA student's core BA curriculum. Indeed, in the 2017 RADA graduating class there is an ex-offender who once defined himself as 'a career criminal'. Today he is a talented actor.

Twenty years of forging history in this arena has taught us that for a performing artist – any performing artist – there are very few things one can do where you immediately know that what you do is vitally important; is socially critical. This incentive offers just such an opportunity. It holds, as t'were, a mirror up to many and contrasting natures; your own as much as anyone else's. To this end, LSW and HMP Pentonville have created the 'Linked Up Initiative' or LUP for short. We've coined a new word much as the Bard often did. It is an ACTIVE verb: 'To LUP' means 'to bring disparate bodies together in hope'. Linked up thinking – or 'lupping' – is not something often celebrated inside prisons but Shakespeare always celebrates community. It is his magnet that melds: It lups.

Yesterday, one eighteen-year-old young offender currently housed within HMP Pentonville, an adult prison, told me that he 'now' knew 'why' he'd been sent to prison. 'It was to do this.' I, myself, know full well we learn from each other.

As usual Shakespeare unifies in whole: 'We are such stuff as dreams are made on'.

Having toiled from childhood onwards as an actor and later a director in the theatre and other media in London, New York and elsewhere, **Bruce Wall** additionally plied his talents as a Director of the Harkness House for Ballet Arts, for the Metropolitan Opera and in 1983 – as the youngest Artistic Director of a LORT (League of Regional Theaters) theatre in the USA – created the first international exchange on a fully fair contractual basis between an American and British actor. Happily, that precedent continues to this day. Dr Wall co-founded the London Shakespeare Workout and remains its Executive Director. Perhaps most aptly the NY Times christened him 'a theatrical missionary'.

Theatre

Festivals

These are populated by all kinds of companies listed in previous sections. Some are hired-in by a festival's organisers; others 'hire' space in order to participate – the latter predominate at the most famous festival of all, in Edinburgh. Participation in a festival can be enormous fun, and a great opportunity to meet other actors and see other productions. However, the chances of such a production transferring, let alone making money, are limited.

UMBRELLA ORGANISATIONS

British Arts Festivals Association (BAFA)
mobile 07756 309844
email bafa@artsfestivals.co.uk
website www.artsfestivals.co.uk
Facebook www.facebook.com/BritArtsFests
Twitter @BritArtsFests

Provides information and a professional network for the festivals movement in the UK, working to promote the profile and status of arts festivals. As well as providing a festival directory on the website, BAFA produces an advance festivals press pack each January and May and is the British hub for the prestigious European Festivals Association. Members have the opportunity to attend BAFA conferences, access to partnership deals and discounts and vital festival resources. Membership is open to all arts festivals in the UK and associate membership to other arts organisations, universities, students and agents.

The European Festivals Association
Sainctelettesquare 17, 1000 Brussels, Belgium
tel +32 2 644 48 00
email info@efa-aef.eu
website www.efa-aef.eu

The European Festivals Association is the umbrella organisation for festivals across Europe and beyond. The oldest cultural network in Europe, it was founded in Geneva, Switzerland, in 1952 as a joint initiative of the eminent conductor Igor Markevitch and the great philosopher Denis de Rougemeont. Since its foundation, the Association has grown from 15 festivals into a dynamic network representing more than 100 music, dance, theatre and multidisciplinary festivals, national festival associations and cultural organisations from 40 countries.

UK ARTS FESTIVALS

Arundel Festival
tel 01903 883474
email secretary@arundelfestival.co.uk
website www.arundelfestival.co.uk

For 10 days each August, the market town of Arundel is host to a multi-arts festival which began in 1977. Street theatre and a festival Fringe are regular features, as are concerts, exhibitions, fireworks and jazz. The festival culminates in an open-air production of a Shakespeare play in the grounds of Arundel Castle. Each production is led by a cast of experienced professional actors, and extended with members of the local community, who work with the professionals throughout the 6-week rehearsal period.

Barbican
Barbican Centre, Silk Street, London EC2Y 8DS
tel 020 7638 4141
email theatre@barbican.org.uk
website www.barbican.org.uk
Facebook www.facebook.com/BarbicanCentre
Twitter @BarbicanCentre
Instagram @BarbicanCentre

The Barbican showcases international theatre, dance and performance by leading companies, auteurs and emerging artists that challenge the idea of what theatre can be. It invests in the artists of today and tomorrow through the commissioning of new work, showcasing emerging talent and collaborating with their Artistic Associates - Boy Blue, Cheek by Jowl, Michael Clark (choreographer) and Deborah Warner.

Brighton Festival
tel 01273 700747
email info@brightonfestival.org
website www.brightonfestival.org

Founded in 1967. For 3 weeks in May, there are more than 300,000 attendances at 800 separate arts events taking place in venues across Brighton and Hove. Artists from a number of different countries are represented in theatre, dance, music, opera, books, events and outdoor spectaculars.

Running alongside Brighton Festival, Brighton Festival Fringe (previously called 'the Open') has been in existence for 37 years, and is the biggest in England, showcasing a variety of artforms and activities. Applicants for the Fringe should first read the 'How to be in Brighton Festival Fringe' document available on the website, and then register online.

Canterbury Festival

8 Orange Street, Canterbury, Kent CT1 2JA
tel 01227 452853
email info@canterburyfestival.co.uk
website www.canterburyfestival.co.uk

One of the UKs longest established arts festivals, the Canterbury Festival takes place over 2 weeks in late October/early November. Classical concerts in Canterbury Cathedral, world music of all kinds plus circus and cabaret in the beautiful Spiegeltent, the programme also includes theatre, dance, science, talks, walks and exhibitions. Spanning school half-term, there is a wide range of events for families and young people. With over 200 events in the fortnight, the Festival is the highlight of Canterbury's cultural calendar – and a marvellous time to visit the historic city. Festival guests in the past have included Van Morrison, Sir Bryn Terfel and the Tallis Scholars, while the year-round public engagement programme works with more than 2,000 young people annually.

Dumfries and Galloway Arts Festival

Gracefield Arts Centre, 28 Edinburgh Road, Dumfries DG1 1JQ
tel 01387 259627
email info@dgartsfestival.org.uk
website www.dgartsfestival.org.uk

Established in 1979. Scotland's largest perfoming Arts Festival – runs for 10 days at the end of May. The festival programme includes a diverse programme of world class events covering music, contemporary dance, theatre, comedy and spoken word. Events take place in a wide range of venues throughout the region including arts centres, pubs, theatres and village halls.

Also runs Dumfries and Galloway Arts Live, established in 2016. A network of venues, promoters and performing artists set up to bring quality live events to venues throughout Dumfries and Galloway year-round. Organised by the Dumfries and Galloway Arts Festival team.

Edinburgh Festival Fringe Society

180 High Street, Edinburgh EH1 1QS
tel 0131 226 0026
email admin@edfringe.com
website www.edfringe.com

The Fringe began in 1947, when 8 theatre companies decided to perform uninvited alongside the first Edinburgh International Festival. It is now the largest arts festival on the planet, with over 45,000 performances of over 2,800 shows in more than 250 venues across Edinburgh each August. The Fringe is still entirely open-access and anyone who wants to bring a show can do so.

The Fringe Society was formed in 1959 to provide a comprehensive information service both to performers and to audiences. You can contact the Society year round with general questions and advice on how to take part.

Edinburgh International Festival

The Hub, Castlehill, Edinburgh EH1 2NE
tel 0131 473 2000
email performing@eif.co.uk
website www.eif.co.uk
Executive Director Francesca Hegyi

Founded in 1947, the Edinburgh International Festival is an annual event held over 3 weeks in August, using venues across the city. With music, opera, classical music and dance, the festival is recognised as one of the world's most important celebrations of the performing arts. Also offers a programme of year-round education and outreach activities. Performance at the Edinburgh International Festival is by invitation only, issued by the Festival Director.

Fierce Festival

Albert House, 12-26 Albert Street, Birmingham B4 7UD
email contact@wearefierce.org
website www.wearefierce.org

Biennual festival of live art in theatres, bars, clubs, galleries and public spaces across Birmingham and the West Midlands. The festival takes place in October with smaller events and artist development opportnuities throughout the year.

Grassington Festival

The Festival Office, Grassington Festival, Grassington, North Yorkshire BD23 5AT
tel 0330 088 6933
email admin@grassington-festival.org.uk
website www.grassington-festival.org.uk
Festival Director Penny Hart-Woods

An annual multi-disciplinary festival featuring contemporary and classical music, theatre, dance, comedy, talks, workshops, walks, visual arts and creative challenges taking place in the last 2 weeks of June.

Greenwich and Docklands International Festival (GDIF)

Pepys Building, 2 Cutty Sark Gardens, London SE10 9LW
tel 020 8305 1818
email admin@festival.org
website www.festival.org
Artistic Director Bradley Hemmings

The Greenwich and Docklands International Festival programmes multi-disciplinary arts events around East London each summer. As well as programming large-scale, visually impressive work, the festival places emphasis on educational projects and participatory arts.

HighTide

24A St John Street, London EC1M 4AY
tel 020 7566 9765

Theatre

email info@hightide.org.uk
website www.hightide.org.uk
Artistic Director Clare Slater

HighTide Theatre develops productions and programmes that engage diverse communities with new theatre writing in the East of England and beyond. It is renowned for identifying and developing talented new playwrights, showcasing the future of British theatre.

Hotbed: Cambridge New Writing Theatre Festival

Cambridge Junction, Clifton Way, Cambridge CB1 7GX
tel 01223 403361
email patrick@menagerie.uk.com
website www.menagerietheatre.co.uk
Twitter @menagerie_

Menagerie Theatre Company (**www.menagerietheatre.co.uk**) and Cambridge Junction (**www.junction.co.uk**) join forces to present Hotbed, the Cambridge New Writing Theatre Festival. Events include new full-length plays, short commissions from the Young Writers' Workshop, guest productions and a selection of workshops, talks, masterclasses and seminars also included in the programme.

All opportunities are advertised on the Menagerie website (**www.menageriestheatre.co.uk**). For further information about the next Hotbed and how to get involved contact Paul Bourne at **paul@menagerie.uk.com**.

Lichfield Festival

Donegal House, Lichfield, Staffordshire WS13 6NE
tel 01543 306271
email info@lichfieldfestival.org
website www.lichfieldfestival.org
Facebook @lichfieldfestival
Twitter @lichfieldfest
Instagram @lichfieldfest
Festival Director Damian Thantray

Annual 10-day multi-arts festival in July, Literature Festival in March, plus occasional seasonal events.

London International Festival of Theatre (LIFT)

Toynbee Studios, 28 Commercial Street, London E1 6AB
tel 020 7968 6800
email info@liftfestival.com
website www.liftfestival.com
Facebook www.facebook.com/theLIFTfestival
Twitter @LIFTfestival
Editor Instagram @liftfestival
Artistic Director/CEO Kris Nelson

Started in 1981, LIFT is a biennial summer festival introducing some of the world's most exciting artists and theatre-makers to London. LIFT events have been staged in more than 50 London venues as well as in a number of site-specific venues such as cemeteries, car park roofs, disused buildings, the river, parks and open spaces.

LIFT also runs developmental and educational programmes exploring the nature of exchange and creativity for a range of audiences including schoolchildren and industry leaders.

London International Mime Festival

email direction@mimelondon.com
website www.mimelondon.com
Directors Joseph Seelig, Helen Lannaghan

Founded in 1977 by Joseph Seelig and Nola Rae, the London International Mime Festival presents contemporary visual theatre. Events are non-text based and can include circus theatre, puppetry, mask, mime, clown and live art. Most work will be either a UK or a London premiere.

The festival takes place each January with the deadline for submissions is 1st June. Participation is by invitation only. To be considered, email Helen Lannaghan and Joseph Seelig at the email address above.

Manchester International Festival (MIF)

Blackfriars House, Parsonage, Manchester M3 2JA
tel 0333 322 8679
email info@mif.co.uk
website www.mif.co.uk
Facebook www.facebook.com/mcrintfestival
Twitter @MIFestival
Instagram @mifestival

Manchester International Festival (MIF) is a biennial festival of original, new work, created by a wide range of major international artists. The first festival took place in June–July 2007; the next edition will take place in July 2023. Strengthening Manchester's reputation as a leading cultural city, the Festival features work reflecting the spectrum of performing arts, visual arts and popular culture. MIF supports a year-round Creative Engagement programme, bringing opportunities for people from all backgrounds, ages and from all corners of the city. MIF will also run The Factory, the new world-class cultural space currently being built in the heart of Manchester which will commission, present and produce a year-round programme, featuring new work from the world's greatest artists and offering a space to make, explore and experiment.

The Mayor's Thames Festival

website www.thamesfestival.org
Director Adrian Evans

The Mayor's Thames Festival is a free annual event that takes place on and around the River Thames between Westminster and Southwark Bridges. Using the river as a powerful unifying symbol for the whole of London, one of the festival's main aims is to enable more collaborations between artists and community groups. Over 1 weekend in September it programmes events such as night carnivals, fireworks spectaculars, mass choirs, music stages, a range of participatory activities, and both artist-led and river-orientated events.

The Minack Theatre

Porthcurno, Penzance, Cornwall TR19 6JU
tel 01736 810181
email info@minack.com
website www.minack.com

The Minack Theatre stages a full programme of live performances from Easter to October, including music, drama, musicals and opera. The Minack supports Cornish artists but also welcomes national and regional touring companies.

National Student Drama Festival (NSDF)

NSDF, 2nd Floor, 10 Leake Street, London SE1 7NN
mobile 07539 768087
email info@nsdf.org.uk
website www.nsdf.org.uk
Facebook www.facebook.com/nsdfest
Twitter @nsdfest
Director Nathan Powell *General Manager* Lizzie Melbourne

For over 60 years, NSDF has been at the heart of the British Theatre. NSDF selects and presents work created by young people and empowers and inspires young talent – providing masterclasses, workshops and year-round practical advice from experienced professionals including a core team of selectors.

The NSDF has a remarkable alumni including Olivia Vinall, Ruth Wilson, Alex Jennings, Lucy Prebble, Simon Russell Beale, Meera Syal, Kate Mellor, Steve Pemberton and many, many more.

For all information, please visit the website. NSDF is an Arts Council England National Portfolio Organisation.

Theatre

Role-play companies

Actors have long used their craft in promotional areas like selling products and services over the phone and in department stores; work opportunities in these fields are advertised in *The Stage*. More recently, the idea of using theatre skills deeper inside the world of business (and the service professions, like medicine) has grown considerably. Essentially, the high level of co-operation ('interactivity') and the excitement, creativity and inspirational power of good theatre is being grasped by hierarchies 'outside the proscenium arch'. Role-play practitioners today are using techniques evolved by the Theatre in Education movement in the 1960s and 70s – but with far better-paying 'customers'.

The established companies – mostly created by actors – have built up a great deal of expertise in this new world, and do not take on new 'role-players' lightly. It is therefore especially important to research each individual company's *modus operandi* before spending time and money in contacting them. However, this is a world well worth exploring as an exciting and lucrative alternative area of work.

aardvark productions ltd

Withywinds, Mill Hill, Edenbridge TN8 5DQ
tel 0800 3285 766
email info@aardvarkproductions.biz
website www.aardvarkproductions.biz
Facebook www.facebook.com/aardvarkproductions1
Twitter @aardvarkprods
Directors Daniel Kerry, Angela Youngs

Company's work: Formed in 1991, aardvark creates themed events for corporate and private clients. They also supply historical characters to museums, country houses and schools for education and entertainment as well as performing murder mysteries for any kind of event.

Recruitment procedures: Uses in-house casting directors, but only holds auditions as and when people apply. Welcomes both CVs and letters from actors previously unknown to the company and unsolicited CVs and photographs. Also welcomes invitations to view individual actor's websites and showreels. Happy to consider disabled actors for all roles. However, a lot of their roles would be difficult to manage for those with disabilities. Currently, there are 4 actors with differing disabilities working for aardvark.

Activation

The Old Coach House, 83 Dennis Road,
East Molesey, KT8 9EE
tel 020 8783 9494
email info@activation.co.uk
website www.activation.co.uk
Director Paul Gilmore

Company's work: A leading provider of bespoke interactive training. Services include forum theatre, role-play, scriptwriting and performance and the design and delivery of training programmes. Incoming actors are trained by the company, according to the requirements of the project. Strong acting and listening skills are required of all the actors. Recent clients include: Diageo, Barclays and Lloyds TSB.

Recruitment procedures: Periodically extends its actor-base, often by word-of-mouth but also using the Internet. Welcomes letters (with CVs and photographs) from actors previously unknown to the company if sent by post, but not by email. Does not welcome showreels, but is happy to receive invitations to view individuals' websites. Will consider applications from disabled actors to play characters with disabilities.

Actors in Industry Ltd (Aii Training)

30 Dover Road, London E12 5EA
mobile 07841 018968
email enquiries@actorsinindustry.com
website www.actorsinindustry.com
Directors Carry Clubb

Company's work: Established in 1992. "We are the foremost interactive training company in the UK, using role-play, facilitation and interactive training and coaching to create meaningful skills improvement and behavioural change for individuals and organisations." Requires incoming recruits to possess a good knowledge of business, giving feedback, and the ability to understand the perspective of delegates on training programmes. Provides training for associates in the form of an induction, group workshops and one-to-one sessions. Recent clients include: PWC, Amey, Linklaters, Astellas, Barclays, Lilly, Kraft, Johnson & Johnson, RBS, IBM, Jones Lang Lasalle, Mercer and Ernst & Young.

Recruitment procedures: Interviews twice yearly, and recruits via emailed CVs (business and role playing) and covering letter. Advises recruits to be honest about experience; over-elaboration will be discovered very quickly. When submitting files with an application, please make sure that all file names contain the name of the applicant, e.g. NOT roleplay CV but John Smith roleplay CV.

Adhoc Actors

Lordhoill House, Mill Street, Whitchurch, Shropshire SY13 1SE
tel 0161 2360 618
email info@adhocactors.co.uk
website www.adhocactors.co.uk
Artistic Director Guy Hepworth

Company's work: Founded in 2005, Adhoc Actors have worked mainly in the public and private sector business for the last 14 years. They have provided training, writing, drama, entertainment and educational workshops to a number of different organisations. The company requires its actors and performers to have excellent feedback skills and experience of working in corporate role-play, as well as being skilled at improvisation, and comfortable with interactive/immersive performance. However, there is a thorough briefing before any job is undertaken. Clients include: Merseyside Police, Penguin Random House, Macmillan Cancer Support, Next and Arrow Global (Breathe POD).

Recruitment procedures: Uses in-house casting directors but does not hold general auditions. Casting breakdowns can be available from the Equity JIS and Mandy websites. Welcomes letters (with CVs and photographs) from individual actors previously unknown to the company and unsolicited CVs with photographs, sent by email. Will consider invitations to view individual actors' websites and performance notices. Also welcomes showreels. Will consider applications from disabled actors to play characters with disabilities.

AKT Productions

Registered Office: 7 Savoy Court, London WC2R 0EX
tel 020 7620 0843
website www.aktproductions.co.uk
Director Marc Bolton

Company's work: Established in 1996. Provider of theatre-based learning resources, developing quality learning and development programmes. Incoming actors are expected to have some experience of corporate role-play. Actor-base is extended every 8-12 months via recommendations and applications.

Recruitment procedures: Accepts submissions (with CVs and photographs) from actors previously unknown to the company. Prefers CVs and photographs sent via email. Invitations to view individual actors' websites are also accepted. Applications from disabled actors are considered.

Apropos Productions Ltd

53 Greek Street, London W1D 3DR
tel 020 7062 9198
email info@aproposltd.com
website www.aproposltd.net
Director Paul DuBois

Company's work: Established in 2004. First feature film completes post-production August 2015, *Dark Signal* (executive producer Neil Marshall). Short films: *The Juror*, *X-Why* and *Cocktail*. Web series: award-winning web series: *A Quick Fortune* and *Le Method* (2016). Script events include *My German Roots are Showing* at the Arcola Theatre, London, starring Miriam Margolyes.

Provides training for local, national and international clients. Key focus is on Organisational Behaviour. Training is provided for incoming actors. Corporate experience is useful but not essential. Actor-base is extended annually through agents, the website and Equity Job Information Service. Clients include: SKANKSA, Sony Computer Entertainment, House of Commons, UBM and the Discovery Network.

Recruitment procedures: Accepts submissions (with CVs and photographs) from actors previously unknown to the company. Disabled actors regularly form part of its teams and are actively encouraged to apply.

Michael Browne Associates Ltd (MBA Roleplay)

The Cloisters, 168c Station Road, Lower Stondon, Beds SG16 6JQ
tel 01462 812482
email hello@mba-roleplay.co.uk
website www.mba-roleplay.co.uk
Directors Michael Browne, Angie Smith

Company's work: Established in 1997. Holds an extensive database of more than 750 professional, corporate actors. Works closely with clients to cast, devise, manage and interpret events and assessments to inform, challenge, develop, assess and train. Will provide training for incoming actors on particular clients' material as and when required. Actors should have professional drama training and experience in the corporate world using role-play for assessment, training and development. Clients include IOPC, Met Police, the MoD, KPMG, Nationwide, the NHS, CBRE, Local Government, Barclays, HSBC and the Open University.

Recruitment procedures: Periodically extends its actor-base when required "via interview/workshop after personal application and recommendation". Welcomes letters (with CVs and photographs) from actors previously unknown to the company, sent by email. Accepts showreels and invitations to view individual actors' websites. Will consider applications from disabled actors for specific projects.

CentreStage Partnership

South Hill Park, Ringmead, Bracknell, Berkshire RG12 7PA

Theatre

tel 01344 304305
email info@cstage.co.uk
website www.cstage.co.uk
Contact Pippa Shepherd, Julian Hirst

Company's work: A leading development consultancy specialising in the use of drama to enhance learning.

Recruitment procedures: In the first instance, actors should send a CV outlining their acting and business experience, along with a recent photograph and covering letter, to Pippa Shepherd via **info@cstage.co.uk**.

Characters

12 Stillness Road, Honor Oak Park,
London SE23 1NG
tel 020 8856 4005 *mobile* 07710 493483
email cathhamilton@characters.uk.com
website www.characters.uk.com
Contact Catherine Hamilton

Company's work: A well-established role-play company with 14 years' experience. Owned by Catherine Hamilton, whose background combines a professional acting career with community health experience. The company focuses on working with police forces, prison services, social care, the NHS and it has now expanded into the private sector.

Dramanon

email info@dramanon.co.uk
website www.dramanon.co.uk
Directors Melanie Nicholson, Steven Brough

Company's work: With over 25 years of experience, Dramanon is a leading provider of live training using actors in creative scenarios and storytelling. Works in the training room, conference space and for larger immersive programmes of work. Stories are bespoke and written for each buisness area, opeation or the requirements of the message being shared.

Dramanon uses a blend of forum theatre and role-play bespoke to each client to enable the most productive training experience. Works with mainly blue chip business clients and on high profile projects but also supports smaller enterprises and charities and have a broad range of clients across the UK, Europe and beyond.

Dramanon also designs and produces white-board animatied film, audio podcasts and film for drama, documentary, re-contsruction and marketing purposes.

Based at TW1, Twickenham Film Studios soon to be Twickenham Media Village in London, with offices, production facilities and rehearsal space. A commercial production branch was launched in 2022 with their first project due to shoot in 2023.

Instant Wit

6 Worrall Place, Worrall Road, Clifton,
Bristol BS8 2WP

mobile 07808 960826
email info@instantwit.co.uk
website www.instantwit.co.uk
Facebook www.facebook.com/groups/49979367942/
Twitter @InstantWit
Instagram @instantwitimprov
Directors Chris Grimes, Stephanie Weston

Company's work: "A quick-fire comedy improvisation show packed full of sketches, gags, songs, surreal situations, flying packets of 'Instant Whip' and prizes! The show is completely improvised and shaped around audience suggestions. Because of this, each show is unique and takes the form that you – the audience – want it to take."

Interact

138 Southwark Bridge Road, London SE1 0DG
tel 020 7793 7744
email operations@interact.eu.com
website www.interact.eu.com

Company's work: Through the skill of expert consultants, behavioural specialists and linguistic analysts, Interact creates immersive practice-based training for the corporate world. Real-to-life scenarios coupled with the latest thought leadership provides participants with an exponential level of development. Practice, when delivered hand-in-hand with evidence-based forensic feedback gives participants the opportunity to develop new perspectives, develop skill, and take ownership for their own learning.

Role-play assessments for medical colleges, for example the Royal College of General Practitioners and the College of Optometrists constitutes about 20% of our work. Associates delivering these assessments are trained specifically for these exams. Our bespoke programmes for corporate clients, have included workshops for Allianz, Sainsbury's and Transport for London. These deliveries require actors to go through Interacts Accreditation Programme to become an Interact Certified Professional.

Periodically Interact will interview and recruit new actors that have contacted us directly, responded to an advertisement or have been recommended. For all prospective associates fluency, confidence, strong acting and improvisation skills are required. Business and forum theatre experience is also an advantage.

An email including a cover letter, CV and current headshot is preferred. Those with previous experience are most likely to be invited to interview.

Maynard Leigh Associates (MLA)

International House, 24 Holborn Viaduct, London,
EC1A 2BN
tel 020 7033 2370
email info@maynardleigh.co.uk
website www.maynardleigh.co.uk

Company's work: MLA is essentially a community of about 25 people who share common values, are committed to their own and other people's personal growth, and are passionate about their work affecting an increasing number of individuals and organisations. Associates are required to be expert workshop leaders with an interest in the psychological aspects of human potential development. Clients include: Aviva, DHL, Hewlett Packard, Ernst & Young, BBC TV, Barclays and Visa.

Recruitment procedures: All new consultants and leaders go through a rigorous and lengthy process, regardless of their professional experience. It can take up to 18 months of participation in Maynard Leigh activities before being allowed to represent the consultancy with clients. There are regular personal development sessions. As Maynard Leigh invests heavily in its existing associates, its pace of growth is limited. Professional actors with a good working knowledge of business and corporate life should submit their details by email.

Pearlcatchers Ltd

Office B, Windsor Trade Centre, Dedworth Road, Windsor SL4 4LE
tel (01753) 670187
email hello@pearlcatchers.co.uk
website www.pearlcatchers.co.uk
Director Sharon M Young *Customer Relationships Manager* Karen Hanley *Business Operations Manager* Lucy Foster

Company's work: A training consultancy empowering people, teams and organisations to change, learn and grow. They offer a fresh approach to learning, developing successful and emotionally intelligent people, relationships, organisations and leaders through bespoke, blended, accelerated learning.

Provides actors with opportunities for role play, forum theatre, hot seating, thought bubble and business scenarios.

Requires business skills/knowledge and prior experience in corporate role play and forum theatre. Clients include: UK Emergency Services, BP, Tesco, London Underground, local councils, BUPA and the RAF.

Recruitment procedures: Extends its actor base every 2 years, recruiting via *The Stage*. Welcomes letters (with CVs and photographs) from individual actors previously unknown to the company, sent by post or email. Also accepts showreels and invitations to view individual actors' websites. Considers applications from all actors, no exclusions.

The Performance Business

78 Oatlands Drive, Weybridge, Surrey KT13 9HT
tel 01932 888885
email info@theperformance.biz
website www.theperformance.biz
Directors Michael McNulty, Lucy Windsor

Company's work: Provides incoming actors with personal assessments and one-to-one coaching.

Requires excellent feedback skills and experience of working in business. Clients include: organisations in the financial, pharmaceutical, engineering, and manufacturing & public sectors.

Recruitment procedures: Periodically extends its actor-base, recruiting via the website and CastNet. Welcomes letters (with CVs and photographs) from individual actors previously unknown to the company, sent by post or email. Will consider invitations to view individual actors' websites. Actively encourages applications from disabled actors and promotes the use of inclusive casting.

Role-Players NGA Ltd

mobile 07984 471512
email info@role-players.co.uk
website www.role-players.co.uk
Proprietor Nick Gasson

Company's work: Established in 2003. Provider of professional actors as corporate role-players to the industry, in both the private and public sector. Incoming actors are expected to have experience of corporate role-play. Clients include accountancy and law firms, property development companies and management consultancies.

Recruitment procedures: Applications are accepted throughout the year, but mostly through personal recommendation from the company's existing actor list, and through potential actors applying having seen their website. Prefers CVs and photographs sent via email and does accept unsolicitied CVs and photographs via the same method. Invitations to view individual actors' websites are also accepted.

Roleplay UK

4th Floor, Rex House, 4-12 Regent Street, London SW1 Y4R
tel 0333 121 3003
email actors@roleplayuk.com
website www.roleplayuk.com
Managing Director James Larter *Director* Felicity Hall

Company's work: Established in 1994. Drama-led communications and training. Provides training for incoming actors in the form of workshops.

Recruitment procedures: Periodically extends its actor-base every 6 months or every year, depending on demand. Recruits via Equity Job Information Service. Does not welcome unsolicited approaches by individuals unknown to the company, but actively encourages applications from disabled actors and promotes the use of inclusive training.

Simpatico UK Ltd

8 Manor Park, Histon, Cambridge, CB24 9JT
tel 01638 602491
email alan@simpaticoagency.co.uk
website www.simpaticoagency.co.uk
Chief Executive Director Alan Orme

Company's work: Founded in 2003. Focuses on medical and veterinary role-play. Specialising in communication skills.

Theatre

Theatre Without Walls

Hillsborough, County Down BT26 6AS
tel 02892 82125
email hello@theatrewithoutwalls.org
website www.theatrewithoutwalls.org
Directors Genevieve Swift, Jason Parkes

Company's work: Established in 2002. Award-winning producing theatre company with an active training/corporate wing, working in the public and private sector. Also produces television and corporate films. Clients include: National Trust, Gloucestershire Local Authority, Apollo, BBC and The Prince's Trust. Training is provided for incoming actors in the form of workshops and rehearsals in forum, role-play and interactive drama. Incoming actors require good improvisational skills.

Recruitment procedures: Actors are recruited through agents and Equity Job Information Service. Disabled actors regularly form part of the team and are actively encouraged to apply. See also the company's entry under *Middle and smaller-scale companies* on page 209.

Trainerpool Ltd

Avonview Farm, The Star, Holt, Trowbridge, Wiltshire BA14 6QB
mobile 07802 530468
email info@trainerpool.co.uk
website www.trainerpool.co.uk
Director Andy Collett

Company's work: Provides corporate training, workshops, coaching, facilitation, roleplay, events and speakers and presenters for corporate events. Requires actors to have prior knowledge and experience of corporate roleplay work. Clients include: BMW, Hill Group and LEVC.

Recruitment procedures: Extends its actor-base on a quarterly basis, recruiting via direct approach and word-of-mouth. Welcomes letters (with CV and photograph) from individual actors previously unknown to the company, sent by email. Also welcomes showreels. Happy to receive unsolicited CVs and photographs via the same method. Will consider performance notices and invitations to view individual actors' websites. Does not generally recruit disabled actors unless this is specifically required for a role by a client.

In 1882, the great actor manager Sir Henry Irving founded the **Actors' Benevolent Fund** with a promise to help actors, actresses and stage managers experiencing hardship due to accident, illness or old age.

Over a century later, the Fund remains true to that promise.

If you are in need of support please visit our website, or call us to find out about how the Fund might be able to help you. All enquiries are treated in the strictest confidence.

020 7836 6378
actorsbenevolentfund.co.uk

Registered charity number 206524

THEATRE RECORD

Chronicling the British Stage since 1981

www.theatrerecord.com

Theatre Record collates theatre critics' reviews for major productions in London and across Britain all in one place, together with production details and cast lists. We also provide listings of current and future productions.

WITH THEATRE RECORD YOU CAN:

> Read the latest theatre reviews for major productions

> Explore and search the full archive of back issues with reviews from more than 52,000 productions spanning over four decades

> Check what's on, where and when, both now and in the future

Log on for a free preview or to subscribe
WWW.THEATRERECORD.COM

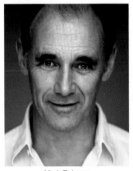

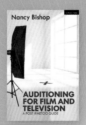

FIND YOUR NEXT AUDITION PIECE

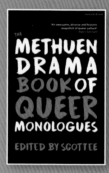

bloomsbury.com/drama

methuen | drama

Media
Introduction

The last few decades have seen incredibly rapid advancements in recording technology, computers, digital media and the Internet. There has also been an enormous growth in the principal broadcasting companies contracting-out much of their output; this in turn has led to an increase in the number of independent companies employing actors. (There are also companies whose output does not include drama – these have not been included in the listings.)

Most film and television companies use casting directors (usually freelance), and it's usually a waste of time and money writing to anyone else unless you have a personal contact. It is worth remembering that many companies do work for businesses – training and promotional films, for instance.

Student films may be a somewhat poor relation to Hollywood blockbusters, in terms of pay (if any) and exposure, but they can provide useful experiences, be a good addition to your CV, and have the potential to lead onto something that is properly paid and much more prestigious. Extracts from such a film could also be useful for your showreel.

Casting for radio is much more akin to that for theatre, although often without the use of a casting director.

Television companies

These almost always use casting directors who, in turn, will circulate casting breakdowns to agents they trust. However, a carefully timed (and crafted) submission from an individual can occasionally excite interest.

BBC NETWORK TELEVISION

BBC Northern Ireland

BBC Broadcasting House, Ormeau Avenue, Belfast BT2 8HQ
tel 028 9033 8000
website www.bbc.co.uk/ni
Head of Content Commissioning Eddie Doyle

BBC Northern Ireland produces a broad spectrum of radio and TV programmes, both for the BBC's networks and for its home audience. Output includes news and current affairs, documentaries, entertainment, comedy, music and events.

In addition to making network radio programmes, broadcasting on BBC Radio 1, 2, 3, 4, and 5 Live and BBC World Service, BBC Northern Ireland also makes programmes for its local radio listeners.

BBC Scotland

40 Pacific Quay, Glasgow G51 1DA
tel 0141 422 6000
website www.bbc.co.uk/scotland
Head of Commissioning Louise Thornton

BBC Scotland is the BBC's most varied production centre outside London, producing drama, comedy, entertainment, children's, leisure, documentaries, religion, education, arts, music, special events news, current affairs and political coverage.

Services span BBC Scotland, BBC One Scotland, BBC Alba, BBC News Scotland, BBC Sport Scotland and BBC Radio Scotland.

BBC Studios

London office: 1 Television Centre, 101 Wood Lane, London W12 7FA
tel 020 8433 2000
Elstree Studios: BBC Elstree Centre, Eldon Avenue, Borehamwood WD6 1NL
website www.bbcstudios.com
Casting Directors Rowland Beckley, John Cannon, Gemma Hancock, Stephen Moore, Laura McSwan, Rachelle Williams-Parker *Casting Executive* Julia Crampsie *Casting Associate* Wayne Linge

Casting information: Casting Directors will accept letters from actors (including CVs, headshots, showreels and performance notices). These should be addressed to the individual Casting Director or one letter addressed to "The Casting Team" and will be seen by the whole department. These should be sent to the BBC Elstree address. However, actors are advised that the casting department is extremely busy and may not be able to reply. See the Casting directors section on page 100 for more information.

BBC Wales Cymru

3 Central Square, Cardiff CF10 1FT
tel 029 2032 2000
email commissioningwales@bbc.co.uk
website www.bbc.co.uk/wales
Head of Commissioning Nick Andrews

BBC Wales provides a range of services in both English and Welsh, on radio, television and online.

The Drama department produces programmes for local and network BBC television channels and local and network radio stations. BBC Wales spans BBC ONE Wales, BBC TWO Wales, BBC Radio Wales and BBC Radio Cymru.

INDEPENDENT TELEVISION

ITV (**www.itv.com**) is the biggest commercial television network in the UK. It is made up of a network of 15 different regional licences, each with its own set of obligations and conditions designed to reflect the particular character of their region and the interests of their viewers. Eleven of the licences in England and Wales are owned by ITV Plc (**www.itvplc.com**), formed in 2004 following the merger of Carlton and Granada. SMG owns the two Scottish licences, Scottish Television and Grampian; UTV and Channel Television own the licences for Northern Ireland and the Channel Islands respectively.

Note: Many companies commission from independents, so do not have casting departments.

ITV Yorkshire (Calendar)

The Television Centre, Leeds LS3 1JS
tel 0113 222 7555

email calendar@itv.com
website www.itv.com/news/calendar

Providing news updates throughout the day for Yorkshire, Lincolnshire, North Nottinghamshire and North Derbyshire.

ITV Tyne Tees & ITV Border

Television House, The Watermark, Gateshead, Tyne and Wear NE11 9SZ
tel 0844 881 5153
email ttvnews@itv.com
email btvnews@itv.com
website www.itv.com/tynetees; www.itv.com/border

Broadcasts to the North of England 7 days a week, 24 hours a day.

ITV Wales & ITV West

Cardiff office: ITV Wales, 3 Assembly Square, Britannia Quay, Cardiff CF10 4PL
tel 0844 881 0100
email news@itvwales.com
Bristol office: ITV West, Television Centre, Bath Road, Bristol BS4 3HG
email westcountry@itv.com
website www.itv.com/wales; www.itv.com/west

Provides programmes for Wales and the West of England during the whole week. Produces programmes for home and international sales.

ITV Central

Gas Street, Birmingham B1 2JT
tel 0844 881 4122
website www.itv.com/central

Provides ITV programmes for the East, West and South Midlands.

ITV Anglia

Anglia House, Norwich NR1 3JG
email anglianews@itv.com
website www.itv.com/anglia

Provides news for the East of England.

ITV London

2 Waterhouse Square, 138-142 Holborn, London EC1N 2AE
website www.itv.com/london

The ITV franchise-holder for London.

ITV Granada

Orange Tower, MediaCity UK, Salford M50 2NT
tel 0161 952 1000
email casting@itv.com
website www.itv.com/granada

The ITV franchise-holder for the North West of England. Produces programmes across a broad range for both its region and the ITV network.

Welcomes submissions (with CVs and photographs) from actors previously unknown to the company sent by post or email. As the Casting Department is extremely busy, it cannot guarantee to respond to all submissions. Advises actors to call to find out what projects are being cast, and to send in their details as and when appropriate.

ITV Channel Television

Le Capelain House, Castle Quay, St. Helier, Jersey JE2 3EH
email channelnews@itv.com
website www.channelonline.tv
Facebook www.facebook.com/ITVChannelTV
Twitter @ITVChannelTV
Instagram @itvchanneltv

Provides programmes for the Channel Islands during the whole week, relating mainly to Channel Islands news, events and current affairs. Does not produce any in-house drama.

ITV Meridian

Fusion 3, 1200 Parkway, Whiteley, Hampshire PO15 7AD
tel 08448 812000
email itvnewsmeridian@itv.com
website www.itv.com/meridian

Provides news for the South and South East coast of England.

SKY UK Ltd

tel 0333 100 0333
email skypress@sky.com
website www.skygroup.sky/corporate/home

Casting procedures: Sky UK Ltd does not have its own casting department, production companies hire freelance casting directors.

STV Studios

Glasgow office: STV Studios, Pacific Quay, Glasgow G51 1PQ
tel 0141 300 3000
London office: STV Studios, 9 Savoy Street, London WC2E 7EG
tel 020 3931 0445
website www.stvstudios.com
Managing Director David Mortimer Creative Director Drama Sarah Brown

STV studios is one of the UK's leading content businesses and is Scotland's biggest production company. The company has an impressive track record of success across drama, entertainment and factual, with commissions spanning BBC1 and 2, ITV, Channel 4, Channel 5, BBC Scotland, Discovery, VH1/MTV and Sky One.

Credits include the TV film Elizabeth is Missing for BBC1 which aired in December 2019, receiving numerous five-star reviews and earning its star, Glenda Jackson, the BAFTA for Best Actress in a Leading Role and an International Emmy in 2020.

STV Studios also produced critically-acclaimed thriller *The Victim* for BBC1 in April 2019, which saw leading actress, Kelly Macdonald, win a BAFTA Scotland award later that year.

STV Studios generally uses independent casting directors on a programme-by-programme basis.

UTV

tel 028 9032 8122
email info@u.tv
website www.itv.com/utv

Provides programmes for Northern Ireland. Part of ITV.

Casting for television

Janie Frazer

Media

There are now many casting directors working in television, and each will have their own way of working. This is my own viewpoint and may not be shared by others, but I hope it may be helpful.

I came into casting by way of the theatre. When I was a schoolgirl I fell in love with the theatre and, being good at English, thought perhaps I could become a drama critic. However, some wise person suggested that before writing about the theatre I should work within it, and so I managed to get a job – at first unpaid, sweeping the stage and as a dresser, and subsequently as an ASM and then handling publicity for the Citizens Theatre Glasgow. I had also been involved in the big auditions held at the start of each season for the Citizens, and had come to realise that the actors were the thing that interested me most about the theatre. Subsequently I moved to London and incessantly badgered LWT for a job as a casting assistant, which finally transpired. I have worked there, through several mergers which have resulted in the company currently known as ITV, for many years. I have cast for all types of television productions; mainly drama, comedy drama and situation comedy, but also sketch comedy, factual drama, hidden camera, animation (voice-over), and various others programmes which defy definition.

Each production has its own specificity, but there are basic requirements that apply to all of them.

The script

This is the first principle and the foundation for everything else, even though the script may change beyond recognition during the process of getting the production to the screen. The script contains the characters, their descriptions, and the dialogue; from this, in consultation with the director and producer, I will put together a list of suggested actors for the roles.

Casting for television carries with it certain commercial considerations. The casting of the main characters is often crucial to a programme getting commissioned in the first place, since in commercial television the advertisers need to be assured of getting a specific audience for the programmes around and within which they buy advertising space. This is the reason for the often-heard grumble that the same well-known faces crop up again and again, and the reason for it is that they have good form – i.e., the programmes they appear in produce good viewing figures, which is what both ITV and the BBC are striving to maintain.

Beyond the 'name' casting, the casting for other roles involves interpreting the director's vision, style, ideas and the tone of the piece, to come up with suggestions that will best express the way in which the director wants to portray the material. Therefore, the same script may elicit different suggestions from me, according to the individual director.

Suggestions for actors

How do I arrive at these? I have many lists, and many files, sorted in an idiosyncratic fashion over the years and added to constantly after seeing actors' work on stage and screen. Also there is Spotlight, which is the casting director's invaluable and indispensable tool. If there was only one piece of advice I could offer to an actor, it would be to appear in *Spotlight*, and to keep one's entry accurate and up to date. I now use *Spotlight* almost exclusively via the Internet, as the information contained on the website is wonderfully comprehensive and well organised, and allows me to do cross-reference searching (e.g. for a 30-year-old Punjabi speaker with a Manchester accent) which is extremely swift and useful. The information contained on the site does however rely entirely on the input of the actors who subscribe to *Spotlight*, and it is therefore very important that they keep their credits and personal details current.

Also and most importantly, their photographs. To state the crashingly obvious, television is a visual medium. It's vital that an actor's photograph is up to date and actually looks like them. Vanity should not be the issue, as television requires all types and ages to be portrayed; moreover, an inaccurate photograph can be misleading and time-wasting. Spotlight's website has now progressed to offer audio and video clips of each actor, and I have found that these can be really useful to play to a director when discussing casting. Therefore, I would strongly recommend that actors make full use of all the opportunities offered by *Spotlight* to show their wares.

Via the Spotlight Link I am also able to send out a breakdown of characters to the agents, who then relay back their suggestions, which I can order, prioritise and follow up. I will discuss with the director and producer the various suggestions we have made between us, and those that have come from agents; I will then arrange casting sessions for the various roles.

Getting in touch

I would love to be able to say that receiving letters with photos and CVs, or emails with all those attachments, is always a boon – but I'm afraid it's not usually the case. More useful is to be notified of actors' forthcoming performances: even if it's not always possible to cover these, it's good to know what work you are doing, and one may ask other casting directors if they have seen you in the piece.

Showreels can be useful to view as examples of an actor's work, but tend not to be so significant if they arrive unsolicited – there are simply not enough hours in the day to watch everything that is sent in. I find I am most likely to watch them if they are directly relevant to a current project (for instance, if I am looking for young Northern actors, or working on a sketch comedy show, I will select to watch those that might fall into the relevant categories).

When you are called for audition

Almost invariably now, casting sessions for television dramas and comedy are video-taped. This allows for greater scrutiny of the actor, and assessment of their presence on screen away from the social context of the audition. It does not mean that the actor has had to produce a flawless reading, but many things emerge from watching an actor on screen which may have been missed during the live reading. The camera is sensitive to minute changes in thought-processes and expression as the actor is being filmed in close-up; this is something the actor needs to bear in mind during a television casting audition – that the performance will be watched at close hand, and therefore a loud voice and large expressions will convey considerable impact and may need to be scaled down.

Whatever an actor's looks, the most important feature on screen is the eyes. The people casting the programme need to see yours. Therefore, it will help enormously if you are able to absorb, familiarise yourself with, or, best of all, learn the scene so that you are able to raise your eyes from the script. Almost all 'sides' or scenes for reading will have been emailed to your agent or yourself prior to audition. Make sure you have an email address. Acquaint yourself with script formats such as Final Draft (at the time of writing, a free download for viewing scripts in Final Draft format is available from the website **www.finaldraft.com**). If you wear glasses, print the scene in a large font so that you can still read it if at the casting they would prefer to see you without glasses.

Other basic things to bear in mind are to arrive on time; make sure you know the specific whereabouts of the casting venue, and how long it is likely to take you to get there. You may be unavoidably kept waiting, in which case make sure you let the casting director know if you have another appointment you need to attend. If you can, do some prior research, both about the project, and also about the producer and director of the programme. You can find out about their previous work via the IMDb website, **www.imdb.com** – and since they will after all be looking at your CV, they may be impressed and flattered if you also know something about theirs.

Spend some time thinking about the material you've seen, so you have something to say about it. Many actors would be surprised at how much their observations have contributed to the final version of the script. In television as in film, time is money. Pre-production periods have been reduced to the minimum, which means that there is often very little time for rehearsal once shooting begins. Directors often therefore use the casting process to try out ways in which they would like to scenes to play – this can be rewarding for the actor, and useful even if they do not finally land the part; often directors keep their interview lists, and bear actors in mind whom they've liked but who haven't been quite right for the part in question.

If you look good, I look good

Sometimes actors view casting interviews as an exam, or as some sort of test they have to pass. However, there is at least one person in the room who is completely on your side – the casting director. The casting director's reputation relies on the calibre of the actors invited for interview, and if the actors aren't up to it then the casting director is the one who's on the line. Therefore, by getting you in for audition, the casting director is demonstrating faith in your ability and rightness for the part.

Know your value

Everyone has their own USP – their unique selling point. Even if you are Mr/s Ordinary, then that's it. It's valuable. Get to know what it is that is most intriguing about you, and play to your strengths. Ask your colleagues for constructive criticism and listen to it. Emphasise your strengths and don't pretend to be what you are not. Whereas the theatre can thrive on disguise and artifice, the camera takes no hostages and is ruthless in its exposure.

Did you get it?

If you got the part, then congratulations! But an actor is often confused as well as disappointed about not getting a part. They will ask: should I have done it like this, dressed like that, what did I do wrong? It's hard to explain to an actor that the choice is not dependent on something they did or didn't do, but often is the result of someone else being more right for the part than they are. This is a nebulous assessment which I can appreciate is very unsatisfactory to hear, but it is nevertheless the truth. Those actors who have ever been on the other side of the casting process often remark how they now understand what this means, but it doesn't help much with the feeling of frustration. One can only suggest that, by the law of averages, eventually the part will come up for which you are the most right; that you've done pretty well to get the interview in the first place; that the director may well have clocked you for the future – and that the whole experience stands you in good stead.

For most of her professional life **Janie Frazer** worked as a casting director for ITV Productions, the programme-making division of ITV. She is now working freelance. Janie's career in casting has covered all the genres of single drama, drama series, continuing drama, factual drama, comedy drama, situation comedy, single comedy and sketch comedy. Amongst the many productions she has cast are *Spaced*, the cult comedy series with Simon Pegg; *Coronation Street*, Britain's longest-running soap; and *Blue Murder*, the detective series starring Caroline Quentin.

Auditioning for camera
Nancy Bishop

'The camera is your friend' is the first lesson I teach in my courses on auditioning for camera. The ironic truth is that many theatre actors who feel perfectly comfortable performing in front of thousands of people become timid in front of a small piece of electrical equipment. The antidote to camera fear is to practise on screen as often as possible. Own a camera, use it, grow comfortable with the lens, love it – and it will love you back.

Media

What's the difference between auditioning for film and auditioning for theatre?

In theatre, you are often asked perform a prepared monologue, while in film, you read from 'sides' (short scenes from the actual screenplay.) In theatre, you can find yourself reading with another actor, while in film you might end up reading with a talentless casting director.

Actors are deluded in thinking that if they were actually on location, with all of the props and sets, it would be easier than acting in an empty casting studio. ("If I had the actual laser gun then I could act it so much better.") But acting in a dull audition room or in front of a green screen in a film studio is not so different from acting during Shakespeare's time. The Globe didn't have elaborate sets, which is why characters say obvious lines such as, "Well, this is the Forest of Arden." There was no forest on stage … just a wooden O. So the actors had to use their imagination.

It's the same now. When you're doing a horror film, the oozy monster doesn't perform with you. He's created by a computer geek later on. *Actors must use their imagination.* This includes imagining that you have a brilliant scene partner to play off, even when you only have a casting assistant in a bad sweater.

What can I expect at an on-camera audition?

Slating and introduction

Your first audition is likely to be a screening process, or 'pre-read'. Often the director will not be there, so the casting director will need to 'slate' – which means slipping a name card in front of camera and asking you to turn both profiles. Yes, it feels like a prison shot, and every casting director has heard that joke before.

Next the casting director may ask you to introduce yourself, for the benefit of the absent director. For some reason, this trips up a lot of actors. They feel perfectly comfortable playing some one *else*, but when they have to be *themselves* for a few minutes they stumble around. The introduction, however, may be the most interesting part for the casters. We want to see who you *really* are, your personality. It's the alchemy between the actor's unique energy and the screenwriter's written word that creates the character.

It's best to have some kind of pithy introduction semi-rehearsed so that you don't corpse for camera when the casting director asks you to introduce yourself. Remember that it's all about spin. This is your opportunity to sell yourself for the role. Be enthusiastic and be yourself. Here are a few examples of good and poor introductions.

If you already have professional credits:

• Poor spin: "I had a tiny role on *Inglorious Bastards*. I waited on set forever and I think my line didn't make it to the final cut."

• Good spin: "I had a great time working with Quentin Tarantino on my last project."
  If you are new to the business:
• Poor spin: "I haven't really played any big roles before. I'm just out of drama school."
• Good spin: "I'm just out of drama school and can't wait to land my first job. I really like this project. I've always wanted to work on a World War II film."

These are the kind of personal details you might include in an introduction (such things humanise you; it's interesting to us if you're a mother, if you like to travel, etc.):

• "I just celebrated my daughter's third birthday;"
• "I just got back from a fascinating trip to India;"
• "I work part time in a homeless shelter."

It's better not to include such comments as "I'm working as a temp in an office right now and I hate it." This tells us that you're not really a professional. True, you might have to work a day job to support yourself, but you don't have to emphasise it.

How do I best play to camera?

You should ask the camera operator about frame size. It's a perfectly professional question. What does the camera see? Is it wide, medium or close? If it's a close-up, you're wasting your energy with hand gestures. Be careful not to pop out of frame, and calibrate the performance in your face, where the camera will detect inner monologue.

Calibrating a performance to frame size can be one of the trickiest parts of screen acting. Often the actor's fear is that the camera will amplify their performance so that they will appear to be over-acting. In my screen-acting courses, actors sometimes become discouraged when they watch the play-back and realise that they haven't hit the right level; they see themselves either popping out of the screen, or plagued by the opposite problem which I call *dead face* – when a performance is boring and dead. Nice house but nobody is home.

Theatre actors often fall prey to dead face because great screen actors create the illusion, to the unstudied eye, that they are 'doing nothing'. It's a great misnomer. In a close-up, the actor becomes a talking head, and the only thing that matters is the information communicated by the face. Therefore the performance may have to be even intensified in the eyes and face. The antidote to dead face is an active and ever-changing inner monologue. The camera photographs thought and it loves to watch a character thinking.

This is true of acting in any medium, but in screen acting, listening and reacting become more than half of the performance. One of the most common mistakes in an audition is when an actor reads along with his or her scene partner's lines rather than truly listening and reacting in the moment.

Where do I look? Directly into camera?

The answer is no. Unless specifically asked, you only look directly into camera when you are introducing yourself. There are exceptions, like in the mock-documentary genre. In the US TV series *Modern Family*, for example, the characters speak directly into camera as if questioned by an imaginary interviewer. It's the modern form of Shakespeare's soliloquy; the character speaks his/her thoughts out loud to the audience. That is the exception, not the rule. Most film and TV genres still assume the removal of the fourth-wall type of realism, wherein the characters go about their lives, not knowing that they are being observed.

The best place to focus is somewhere near the lens. This will give the viewer a three-quarter view of your face. You want to be as generous as possible about playing towards the camera. We won't cast you if we can't see you. Placing an off-screen reference on the floor will only bring your eyes down. Hopefully the casting director will help you with this by placing the reader directly next to the lens. But if not, you can focus on a fixed point, rather than on the reader. Know your best side for photography and play accordingly.

How can I prepare for a project when I only have a few pages of text?

You can ask for information. The casting director should provide a summary, but if they don't, then ask for information or ask to read the script. Sometimes it's available and sometimes not, but a question never hurts. If you can't get the script, then you need to make decisions about the pages according to the information you have. If the script wasn't available to you, then it wasn't available to other actors either, and you have an even playing field. Start with the basic Stanislavski questions:

• *Who am I?*
• *Where am I?*
• *Who am I talking to?*
• *What do I want?*

I also encourage actors to add:

• *What are the stakes?* Make the stakes as high as possible, and this will drive the dynamics of the performance.

Answering these questions is one of the basic tenets of acting, yet many actors (even experienced ones) forget to do this for an audition, and they find themselves floating in a sea of too many possibilities. Anchor yourself in the 'W' questions; this will guide your performance.

In order for actors to develop their onscreen skills and comfort level, they must practise. Screen acting is like driving a car. No one gets in a car the first time and just drives. You have to learn how to give the car gas and ease up on the clutch so that the car doesn't jerk. This is why I encourage actors to own a camera, practise with it and take on-camera courses. Modern smart phones with cameras are equally useful for practice and self-filmed auditions, which are increasingly prevalent.

Last of all, I always advise actors to have fun and enjoy the process. If you're enjoying yourself, then so will we, the casters. Love the camera – it will love you back.

"Good actors are good because of the things they can tell us without talking." Cedric Hardwicke

Nancy Bishop is an Emmy-award nominated CSA casting director who casts from Prague. She has cast large-scale studio pictures such as *Mission Impossible IV* and *Prince Caspian*. She also coaches actors and teaches master classes on audition technique throughout Europe and the US. She is the author of Methuen Drama's *Auditioning for Film and Television*.

Media

Self-taping auditions

Ros Hubbard

Time is the enemy! When we set up Hubbard Casting in London in 1976, we had much more time and money (!) available to us. Now with film budgets under far more pressure there are more and more time constrictions. We have been forced to come up with a solution to actors being considered all over the world for parts: self-taping. The positive development that has influenced the simultaneous growth in numbers of actors to be considered for any one role is that there is much more of an international focus. Films have been enhanced by the growth of international audiences and their taste for more broadly based stories with multinational casts, so there is a greater chance of more actors being considered. The facility of self-taping cuts out so much delay caused by booking a live audition, when wanting to take a first look at an actor.

Once I have accepted your agent's recommendation that you be considered for a role, self-tapes allow me to see your acting even if you are working in a different country or elsewhere in the UK, on a theatre job, another film shoot, or even on holiday. Several well-known actors self-taped behind their agent's backs for *The Lord of the Rings* and *The Hobbit*. It is worth chancing your luck by submitting unsolicited self-tapes. I do look at these, but make sure you are brilliant, if you want to catch and hold my attention. However you cannot ring to see if they have arrived, as casting directors do not have the time to respond to such requests. Similarly, if you have been rejected from an arranged submission, you just have to accept it. Do not attempt to open a dialogue about it. You may be called to a live meeting from self-tapes but actors are rarely cast directly from them. Sam Underwood is one of the exceptions we have just cast at the time of writing (summer, 2014).

Now, I may actually physically meet only three to five actors per character, but I like to be inundated by possibilities, and will publicise my search anywhere I think I may discover a new talent. But this itself can demand a big investment of hours, weeks, months. For a film with ten speaking characters, I can watch up to 600 actors on tape. Recently, I was thrilled to be asked to cast John Carney's (director of *Once*) *Sing Street*. With two Irish mid-teens at the centre of the film, my nets would have needed to be cast wide and deep for one of my favourite challenges: hunting the unknown. Regrettably, calculating existing commitments, I knew I could not afford to employ my usual tactics and had to decline the offer, because it would have involved a huge amount of internet searches and self-tapes.

Much of what I have to say about making self-tapes may seem plain common sense, but each piece of advice I give here is based on scores of bad examples seen in the thousands of self-tapes sent to Hubbards in the very few years in which self-taping has become the most prevalent form of first-level audition.

1. The simplest way of self-taping is on an iPhone – it is also very effective. Laptops' sound reproduction is not so good. You can enhance the quality of the filming by using a camera placed on a tripod, but a friend filming you on an iPhone should really be quite sufficient. You should use a closed room, not the corner of a hall or passageway, which is more likely to pick up extraneous noise. If shooting for an American show, try to hire a room at Spotlight. They will put the video on a link for you.

2. Be off-book! No paper should be in view. Margie Haber in LA says you do not need to be off-book in the US, but you would have to be amazing not to be. She runs workshops in on-book auditions, but US auditions can be as many as up to seven a day, so it is impossible to learn that many for one day. You should allow at least one night to prepare. Form a group of actor friends to read in during preparation and filming, so you can support each other and know that at least one of them will always be available to work with you.

3. Remember to have the phone/camera mic as close to you as possible: a foot between your legs is ideal. We embarrass ourselves and the actors ramming the camera and mic close up, but it is the difference between being heard and not being heard. Casting offices are as noisy as chip shops. All four members of the Hubbard family have at least their associate caster working with them at any one time. In the summer of 2014 Amy Hubbard was casting the fourth series of *Homeland* and had just finished *24*, so had a team of ten assistants whirling around the office. The actor on the tape needs to be heard above all that racket. It does not matter if your recording level sounds unnaturally loud – it can always be lowered.

4. Shoot from an angle that shows more of you, with your head and chest occupying the centre of the image – keep it close. It's your soul they are after. A director may later call for an actor to reshoot the scene as full length. Try to shoot in daylight, but *don't sit in front of windows or all we will see is your silhouette*. Filming on camcorders in electronic light is much less effective. Keep your eyes level with the camera. Looking down on the floor or the script will kill the opportunity. Do not look directly at the camera. You should look at your just-off-camera scene partner. If the scene demands physical contact, then you can use a certain amount of movement. Some part of the partner can be visible, but just indicate the action, do not try to be sensational. American casters never use any actors to read in – so your partner can sound very flat and you have to really energise yourself. Do not use any props apart from a cup or a cigarette. There should be no people in the background, or any children or pets anywhere in the field of vision. Do not use too much make-up. Electronic signals are hard and make-up makes you look hard and older.

5. If your tape has been solicited and sides have been sent to you to record, you will be handicapped in doing thorough character preparation, if you are not sent the script or given any other guidance. It never harms to ask for a synopsis of the whole story. You don't have to shoot the whole scene. It will be clearly said to your agent or you how much dialogue is required. I am likely to edit tapes before forwarding them to the director. Don't use showreel material in place of a self-tape, but they are a useful addition. Your showreels should only consist of clips from your films and TV productions. Do not use personally manufactured scenes. Look at other actors' showreels before choosing your own selection. There should not be too many other actors in the clips, especially actors, who look like you – very confusing for us old dears!

6. Do not try charming the casting director by using moody talk or blathering on about what you are doing at the moment. Never bring your fears into an audition, live or re-corded. Leave them on a coat hook before you enter the room or screen. Your spoken introduction on tape should simply give your full name, height, your agent's details or whether you are representing yourself, the title of the scene and your availability for a live

meeting and the shoot dates. If an accent is required for the scene, use it for your intro-duction as well, even if it is less than technically perfect because the effort made will impact positively on your performance. Do not read out the stage directions. Do not underscore the tape with music.

7. You must discipline yourself to closely examine the tape. In the first place you may have forgotten something essential. Ask a friend or friends to give their honest opinion of how well your tape serves the scene, and trust it. This will help you avoid subjective judgements such as choosing the tape most flattering of your general appearance, as opposed to what suits the character best. You can send two versions, especially if the scene is short. Do not announce differences between the two takes. Be subtle in your introductory explanation for sending two. In live auditions, I will always listen to an actor, who feels they have not done themselves justice, and would like to rerun their audition. But it is not always possible to get you back and there have been many occasions when an actor has thought that they read badly and got the part – you are your own worst critic!

8. Use a watermark app on your phone to protect the copyright of your self-tape. You may be the next big thing within two to three years, but in any case do not put your self-tapes on YouTube: that would be even more silly. Also, the script is not your property or the public's. You are in a position of trust. The producers can decide against you no matter how good you are for indiscreet behaviour with scripts. I have seen uploads on YouTube before I can get it out to the director and that is where it ends for you.

9. Do not use an ordinary attachment to email your tapes because their downloading time clogs up our inboxes and slows up the casting process even more. Use web transfer services, e.g. Hightail, WeTransfer or Vimeo. Label your file with your name and the character you are playing.

Good luck with your careers!

Ros Hubbard was born in Dublin and ran a model agency there in the late 1960s. She moved to London and became 'Queen of the Commercials', at which point her husband, John, joined her as a casting director. They went on to cast a myriad of films and TV dramas. The company expanded to include both their daughter Amy and son Dan. Ros and John now live in London but they call their real home Dingle, in Co. Kerry, Ireland.

Are you ready for Pilot Season?

Brendan Thomas

It has been suggested that the exodus of British actors, especially young British actors, to Los Angeles each spring is somewhat akin to the 1840/50s Californian Gold Rush. They come to participate in the casting frenzy of Pilot Season. The surge is understandable as the quantity and quality of UK actors in leading roles in American features and TV series appears to be on an ever-rising tide. Despite this increasing visibility of UK actors on American screens, I would advise others against hoping for great outcomes from purely speculative trips to the US before their careers have gained any momentum. However, if such visits are thought of as largely gaining knowledge for the future combined with aspects of a vacation, there is much to be learned if you come with as much information about the American industry as possible. An initial trip could be very useful in determining how difficult your personal negotiation of the increasingly fierce border regulations would be, as well as giving you the opportunity of discovering how compatible you are with life in Los Angeles.

The internet has transformed pilot season in numerous ways. One of those ways is self-taping for auditions. This is used if an actor cannot make an audition, or is out of town etc. A casting director will review the tapes and, if there is interest, pass it along to producers/ studio/ network. If there is further interest, you may be asked to fly out to test for the role, or in some cases, they will use your original self-tape. You can participate in American pilot season virtually anywhere in the world. For initial contact with a US manager, I would recommend a discussion over Skype. Most managers are very amenable to these.

There are a number of different temporary visas that could cover your investigative trip/ participation in Pilot Season. Obviously you would not be receiving a fee for auditioning, but the nature of Pilot Season is such that you could be filming within weeks. The audition process could range from three auditions a day to radio silence for a week, you really never know how busy you will be. There are also circumstances where you could be under consideration for several pilots. If you are one of the lucky ones to do so you can only continue as a series regular in one. Most roles are already made as offers to known actors so the wider auditioning process is one for insurance/ back-up in case offered roles are not accepted. This may seem dispiriting but there is a chance that the offered actor's deal may not work out for all sorts of different reasons, leaving room for the newcomer.

The commitment to screen test is really a very heavy one as effectively you will have agreed in advance to film the full series, if you are accepted to test for the pilot. A series can continue for up to seven years, so you have to know that you are legally available, which means having more than a temporary visa. While it is possible to audition for most series regular roles without the appropriate visa (productions will often sponsor if they like the actor enough) there is not time, normally, to sort your paperwork out between accepting a role and filming. This may feel like Catch 22 territory. You will require a O-1B visa petition (as an individual with an extraordinary ability in the arts or extraordinary achievement in the motion picture or television industry) to be filed at least 60 days before you wish to enter the US to avoid delays in the visa processing. This will permit you to accept most roles: star, regular, recurring or guest star, but certain networks in some cases can demand Green Card (permanent residency) status. It is important to note that any entertainer or artist cannot file for a visa on her/his own behalf – your visa application must be lodged by your sponsor or petitioner. The O-1B filing entity must be an employer (the actual production company/ network/ studio that is offering you work), or a US agent or Management company located in the US – meaning they must be an organization or entity that has an American address and an IRS (Internal Revenue Service) Employer tax number. A blanket 0-1B visa, which lasts for three years, costs on average about $5,000. A Green Card can cost up to twice that amount.

Beware of companies that offer to act as a 'middle man' to help secure visas. They say the folk who made the most money in the Gold Rush were the ones selling the shovels. These 'middle men' are charging an unnecessary fee to help secure a visa which is easily done by contacting an American lawyer, and his/her paralegal. Some of these legal services are advertised on the web, but if you are operating without ready access to an American agent or manager, it would probably be safer to take a recommendation from an actor friend who has been through the process.

Pilot Season has served not only as the core mechanism for the American television networks' collective market research for programming their subsequent year's drama productions, but as a huge actor job-seeking convention. It has incorporated the advent of the cable channels joining the process and, so far, the explosion of online streaming companies such as Hulu, Amazon and Netflix's expansion into production of original drama television: Netflix's *House of Cards* being the most prominent example so far, while in June 2015 Netflix announced it would be making its first feature film, *War Machine*, starring Brad Pitt. An increasing number of pilots are being made outside the January–March box with many going year round. Aside from stand-alone pilots, there are many shows that are straight to series, meaning there will be ten episodes set to air as opposed to shooting a one-episode pilot and seeing how that rates.

It is already common practice for shows to engage casting directors in other countries, alongside their lead home casting director, especially as more and more drama is shot abroad or elsewhere in the US. There can be a casting director in Los Angeles, New York, Ireland, London and Canada (Vancouver/Toronto) all for the same series. The magnetism of American television has grown over the last decade, attracting top writers, directors and actors. There is no longer a stigma for marquee actors to do television. Everything is material driven as opposed to where it will be shown or viewed.

For the lone UK actor venturing into Pilot Season without the direct support of a single representative, or even one audition in place, there is a lot of casting information to be gleaned free of charge on the web from the sites of the trade journals such as *Variety*. American agents and managers (and some UK agents) have access to each network's comprehensive grid of the pilots they are seeking to cast, so it is possible to align all the grids and gain an overview of all the roles available. These grids contain far more detail than the related articles that appear in the trade journals. They are used and reorganized differently at each agency, however, they all contain the vital information about projects throughout all stages of development. They show all the elements to each show: network; studio; producers; length of the episode; shoot dates being aimed for; location; number of episodes; logline; the writer, director, actors attached; executives at network/ studio; roles: type, description status; and are updated at each stage of the process.

Having identified a number of roles you think match your casting profile, it is possible to submit your profile to the casting directors through *Breakdown Express*'s Actors Access, part of *Breakdown Services*: a near equivalent to the interactive casting services of the UK's *Spotlight*, but without its link to a comprehensive actor directory. Individual agencies and personal managements can organize all data relating to their clients' acting credits, diaries (including upcoming auditions, rehearsal calls and filming schedules) and vital statistics, on *Breakdown Services* but they cannot access files of *any* other agencies/managements or those of *any* individual actors, who are not their own clients.

Breakdown Services introduced Actors Access via its website to stem illegal trading of *Breakdown Express*'s casting information between represented and unrepresented actors. The latter are able to receive the same breakdowns that agencies/ managements do. However, casting offices have the option to have *Breakdown Services* release their breakdowns strictly to agents/ managers only. The option to release breakdowns to Actors Access is not made clear, so most if not all of the big project breakdowns go straight to agents/ managers and bypass the actors. Nevertheless you should be able to obtain enough information from sources in the public realm (e.g. deducing there would be a role to match your profile from a plot summary), you can research the casting director's address and make a submission via postal services. You may not receive any response to your submitted CV/ resume and/or tape, or you may be asked to go back on tape incorporating the casting director's notes. A manager would monitor your tapes for you, weeding out ineffective material. This reflects the distinction between the roles of the American agents and managers. While both categories submit their joint clients for castings, the agents deal with booking of meetings and contracts, while the manager works more closely with her/his clients, shaping careers and strategies, forming the basis of decision making for accepting roles. As with any American casting, if your tape is successful you will be asked over for a film test, if you are not already in situ for Pilot Season. Your flight will be paid for and you will receive a $60 per diem. The flights used to be booked "business" class until the recent SAG (Screen Actors Guild) agreement rolled the status back to "coach", though this is subject to variation from case to case.

Signing up to a seven-year deal may appear to be the key to Hollywood from where you stand at the moment, but could become a dreary, unfulfilling commitment, which entraps you from taking much more creatively fulfilling and perhaps more lucrative opportunities over those years. On the other hand, you might not be filming continuously. It is possible to combine filming different series on both sides of the Atlantic, for example O.T. Fabengle shot the first series of *Looking* (San Francisco) alongside (but not clashing specific shoot dates) *The Interceptor* (UK) hopping back and forth across the Atlantic in two incredibly diverse roles. However the chances are your best opportunities elsewhere would arise exactly across your annual commitment to an American series.

From the point of view of general experience, auditioning in America is likely to up your game. It is very, very tough over here. There is a massive amount of competition for roles. Preparation is vital but you often don't get a lot of time to prepare your sides, nevertheless the expectation to be entirely off book is universal here, while not always the case in the UK. Your American accent needs to be 100 per cent in place. Expect blunt criticism if it is not right. Some casting directors have advised, if you are meeting producers etc. in the casting, that you should come into the room speaking in an American accent,

Media

otherwise, if you come in speaking in your own accent, and then switch, their attention is focused on what's not right with the accent rather than focusing on the work. Ultimately the choice is yours, but you may need to decide what lessens the odds against you getting the job. See a reputable dialect coach. There are many – generally actors trying to supplement their income – who are not suitably qualified. On the positive side you may sometimes have up to three castings a day in different parts of LA which often entails a lot of driving across often busy freeways. A full driving licence is essential.

Having digested all this information you may feel more secure about striking out alone for next year's Pilot Season, but here is one final warning: the overall chance factor will be against you, but is higher in some years and unpredictable. Which way will the dice fall for you?

Brendan Thomas is one of a number of managers at **Untitled Entertainment** which is led by two partners and has offices on both coasts repping actors, writers and directors. Brendan comes to the UK three or four times a year combining seeing his UK clients in theatre performances or on film/ TV sets and locations, including elsewhere in Europe, while maintaining face-to-face contact with their UK agents.

Independent film, video and TV production companies

Media

Companies in this field start up and close down all the time, and it is very important to have a proper contract if offered work with an independent. If in doubt, check with Equity.

Absolutely Productions

Unit 19, 15 Ingestre Place, London W1F 0JH
email info@absolutely-uk.com
website www.absolutely.biz
Twitter @absolutelyprod1
Instagram @absolutelyprod
Managing Director Gordon Kennedy

Founded in 1988. Produces scripted drama and comedy for radio, TV and film including: *Absolutely*, *Trigger Happy TV* and *The Jack Docherty Show*.

ALL3 Media

Berkshire House, 168-173 High Holborn, London WC1V 7AA
tel 020 7845 4377
email info@all3media.com
website www.all3media.com/companies.php

The group comprises over 40 production companies. Specialises in high-quality film and television, including BAFTA award-winning *Gogglebox* and *Call the Midwife*, and Oscar award-winning *1917*.

Big Red Button Ltd

PO Box 75733, London E17 0TY
email hello@bigredbutton.tv
website www.bigredbutton.tv
Key personnel John Burns, Pier Van Tijn, Sagar Shah

Production details: Established in 2002. Specialises in short films and music videos. Works in live action, puppetry and animation. Also employs actors in drama, comedy and commercials.

Casting procedures: Holds general auditions and actors can write to request inclusion at anytime. Casting breakdowns are available on the website. Does not offer Equity-approved contracts. Rarely has the opportunity to cast disabled actors.

Big Talk Productions

26 Nassau Street, London W1W 7QA
tel 020 7255 1131
email info@bigtalkproductions.com
website www.bigtalkproductions.com
Facebook www.facebook.com/bigtalk
Twitter @bigtalk
Instagram @bigtalk
Managing Director Matthew Justice *CEO (Executive)* Kenton Allen *Development Editor (Comedy)* Lara Singer *Drama Producer* Luke Alkin

Production details: Big Talk Productions Ltd is a British film and television production company founded by Nira Park in 1994. Big Talk was acquired by ITV Studios in 2013.

Recent films: *The Brothers Grimsby*; *Baby Driver*; and *The Kid Who Would Be King*. Recent TV: *Raised by Wolves*; *Houdini and Doyle*; *Mum*; *Cold Feet*; *Defending the Guilty*; *The Imitation Game* 2018.

Work experience: As an ITV company, offers work experience placements at Big Talk to enable people to experience what it is like to work in a production company and to learn more about the film and television industry in general. Most placements take place at the office on Nassau Street where participants get involved with development tasks, shadow runners and assist them with their varied task load. Provides the opportunity to learn how things operate, meet people in the industry and work on a variety of projects.

Submissions policy: Does not accept unsolicited material. For administrative reasons, does not respond to individual submissions. **Anything sent to Big Talk Productions will not be read and will be destroyed.**

Blakeway Productions

17 Dominion Street, Finsbury, London EC2M 2EF
tel 020 7428 3100
email hello@zincmedia.com
website www.blakeway.co.uk

Established in 1994. In 2004 the company was bought by Ten Alps PLC and in 2007 it merged with 3BM Television and Ten Alps TV, bringing together strong track records of successful production across the genres of documentaries, docu-dramas, current affairs and factual entertainment formats.

Has produced more than 200 hours of prestigious programming for the BBC, Channel 4, ITV and Five in the UK, and for leading US broadcasters including PBS, National Geographic, HBO, The History Channel and Discovery. Recent hits include: the Emmy-nominated docu-drama *9/11: The Twin Towers*, a co-production with Dangerous Films for BBC1 and Discovery; *The Clinton Years* for Radio 4 and the BAFTA-winning docu-drama *Nuremberg: Goering's Last Stand* for Channel 4 and The History Channel.

Blueprint Pictures

32-36 Great Portland Street, London W1W 8QX
tel 020 7580 6915
email info@blueprintpictures.com
website www.blueprintpictures.com
Chairmen Graham Broadbent, Peter Czernin
Managing Director Diarmuid McKeown *Head of Production* Emma Mager *Head of Film* Ben Knight

Production details: Founded in 2005 by producers Graham Broadbent and Pete Czernin, Blueprint Pictures develops and produces film and television drama for international audiences.

Submissions: Does not read unsolicited screenplays unless submitted via a recognised agent.

Known for the film: *In Bruges* (2008). Recent films: *The Riot Club* (2014), *The Second Best Exotic Marigold Hotel* (2015) *Three Billboards Outside Ebbing, Missouri* (2017), *The Guernsey Literary and Potato Peel Pie Society* (2018), *The Mercy* (2018), *Emma* (2020), *The Last Letter From Your Lover* (2021) and *A Boy Called Christmas* (2021). Recent TV: *The Outcast* (2015), *The Last Dragonslayer* (2016), *A Very English Scandal* (2018) and *A Very British Scandal* (2021).

Cactus TV

1 St Luke's Avenue, London SW4 7LG
tel 020 7091 4900
email jobs@cactustv.co.uk
website www.cactustv.co.uk
Joint Managing Directors Amanda Ross, Simon Ross

Specalises in broad-based entertainment, features and chat shows. Since its inception in 1994 Cactus has produced more than 40 distinct titles in the UK, for 10 different channels.

Calamity Films

16 Carlisle Street, London W1D 3BT
email info@calamityfilms.com
website www.calamityfilms.co.uk
Twitter @calamityfilmsuk
Producer David Livingstone *Development Executive* Emily Bray

Production details: Calamity Films develops and produces feature films and television. David Livingstone was President of Worldwide Marketing and Distribution at both Universal Pictures International and Working Title Films. Emily Bray joined Calamity Films after four years at Independent Talent Group in the agency's Literary Department. She started out in the industry freelancing in development and production and worked on various music videos, short films and features. Does not accept unsolicited submissions.

Films and TV include: *Pride*, 2014; *Last Christmas*, 2019 *Judy*, 2019; *Brassic*, 2019-22.

Carnival Film & Television Limited

6 Agar Street, London WC2N 4HN
tel 020 3618 6600

email info@carnivalfilms.co.uk
website www.carnivalfilms.co.uk
Executive Chairman Gareth Neame *Managing Director* Nigel Marchant

Production details: Founded in 1978. Part of Universal International Studios, a division of Universal Studio Group. Works mainly in TV production, creating drama with a popular and international feel and employs actors for drama. Commissioned by UK broadcasters including BBC, ITV, Sky One and Netflix. Has received various prestigious awards/nominations, including Oscars, BAFTAs, Golden Globes and Emmys. Recent credits include: *Belgravia, The Last Kingdom, Jamestown, Stan Lee's Lucky Man* and *Downton Abbey*.

Casting procedures: Uses freelance casting directors, does not deal directly with actors. Offers PACT/Equity contracts. Will consider casting disabled actors to play disabled characters.

Celtic Entertainment Ltd

9 Orme Court, London W2 4R
tel 020 3490 3730
email stuart@celticfilms.co.uk
website www.celticfilms.co.uk

Production details: Established in 1986, Celtic Films has acted as a co-producer for a variety of award-winning films and TV shows. Also produces commercials. Recent productions include: *The Man Who Fell to Earth* (2022); *Kandahar* (2022); *Killing Eve*, Season 3 and 4 (2020-22); *The Good Fight*, Season 5 (2021); *Top Boy*, Season 4 (2021); and *Champions* (2021).

Casting procedures: Accepts submissions (with CVs and photographs) from actors previously unknown to the company if sent by email. Showreels, voicereels and invitations to view individual actors' websites are also accepted. Offers Equity-approved contracts. Will consider applications from disabled actors to play characters with disabilities.

Coastal Productions

c/o 16 The Plantations, Wynyard Woods, Wynyard, Teesside TS22 5SN
tel 01740 644032
email coastalproductions@msn.com

Created in 1997 by Sandra Jobling and Robson Green with the aim of making feature films and TV dramas in the North East of England – and supporting local young people wanting to get into the industry. The company's many production and co-production credits include: *Take Me, Blind Ambition, The Last Musketeer, Touching Evil, Close and True, Grafters 1 & 2, Rhinoceros, Hereafter, Unconditional Love, Rocketman, Wire in the Blood* and *Place of Execution*.

The Comedy Unit

Unit D, Glasgow North Trading Estate, 24 Craigmont Street, Glasgow G20 9BT

tel 0141 305 6666
email info@comedyunit.co.uk
website www.comedyunit.co.uk
Managing Director Rab Christie

Produces some of Scotland's best-loved television and radio shows, as well as a range of programmes for transmission across network and satellite channels. Formed in 1996, became part of the RDF Media Group in 2006 and part of the Zodiak Media Group in 2010. Does not accept unsolicited scripts.

Company Pictures

3-7 Ray Street, Farringdon, London EC1R 3DR
tel 020 7380 3900
email enquiries@companypictures.co.uk
website www.companypictures.co.uk
Managing Director Michele Buck

Does not accept unsolicited submissions. Proposals should be submitted through agents.

Cowboy Films

48 Russell Square, London WC1B 4JP
tel 020 3962 4421
email info@cowboyfilms.co.uk
website www.cowboyfilms.co.uk
Managing Director Charles Steel

Until recently, Cowboy Films represented a range of top-quality commercial and music video directors, and also worked on feature films such as The Hole and Goodbye Charlie Bright. Sister company Crossroads Films in the US has taken over the roster of music video and commercial projects, while Cowboy continues to work on features. Kevin Macdonald's The Last King of Scotland is the company's most recent project.

Don Productions (London) Ltd

Studio 116, Netil House, 1 Westgate Street, London E8 3RL
tel 020 3095 9425
email london@donproductions.com
website www.donproductions.com

Japanese/English bilingual TV and media production company based in London. Produces corporate films and TV documentary programmes. Clients include: Japan Broadcasting Corporation, Nippon Television and Channel 4.

Ecosse Films Ltd

Brigade House, 8 Parsons Green, London SW6 4TN
tel 020 7371 0290
email info@ecossefilms.com
website www.ecossefilms.com
Director Douglas Rae Head of Drama Robert Bernstein

Founded in 1988. Works mainly in TV and feature film production and employs actors in dramas and comedies. Recent credits include: Mrs Brown, Nowhere Boy and Wuthering Heights. Uses freelance casting directors. Welcomes CVs but is unable to respond to every submission due to the high volume. Does not accept unsolicited scripts.

Extra Digit Ltd

website www.extradigit.com
Twitter @extradigit

Production details: Founded in 2002. Works in film and television and employs actors in drama, comedy and documentary. Recent credits include: Somewhere, starring Hugh Cornwell, and Life is a Circus, starring Steve Ryland.

Casting procedures: Occasionally uses freelance casting directors. Welcomes approaches by actors by post only (please see website for postal contact details), with CVs and photographs. Will accept showreels if these do not require a response. Has no equal opportunities policy: "If you can do the part better than anyone else, you get the job – regardless." Please do NOT contact by phone or email, use current contact details from the 'Recruitment' section on the website.

Eye Film

17-19 St George's Street, Norwich NR3 1AB
tel (01603) 441174
email info@eyefilm.co.uk
website www.eyefilmandtv.co.uk
Managing Director Charlie Gauvain

Independent producers of film and TV drama and documentaries. Also produces corporate, commercial, education and training material. Clients include: BBC, ITV1/Anglia, Channel 4, Five and First Take Films. Recent credits include: The Quest for His Majesty's Silk and Life on the High Wire.

Focus Productions Ltd

4 Leopold Road, Bristol BS6 5BS
tel 0117 230 9726
email info@focusproductions.co.uk
website www.focusproductions.co.uk
Directors Ralph Maddern, Martin Weitz

Production details: Established 1993. Specialises in TV features and documentaries. Employs actors in TV, radio and film; also for presentation and voiceovers. Recent credits include: The Real Rain Man, Painting the Mind, The Piano Player and Vivaldi's Fantasia.

Casting procedures: Holds general auditions. Actors are advised to apply requesting inclusion at any time. Casting breakdowns are available by telephone. Welcomes letters (with CVs and photograph) from actors previously unknown to the company if sent by post, but not by email. Also accepts invitations to view individual actors' websites. Offers Equity-approved contracts. Rarely has the opportunity to cast disabled actors. Proposals for new formats and ideas should be sent to **info@focusproductions.co.uk.**

Media

Fremantle

1 Stephen Street, London W1T 1AL
tel 020 7691 6000
website www.fremantle.com
Facebook www.facebook.com/FremantleHQ
Twitter @FremantleHQ
Instagram @fremantle

Fremantle is one of the largest creators, producers and distributors of scripted and unscripted content in the world. From *Got Talent* to *My Brilliant Friend*, *Family Feud* to *The Young Pope*, *Idols* to *American Gods* and *The Price is Right* to *Neighbours*. Fremantle has an international network of production teams, companies and labels in over 30 countries including UFA (Germany), Wildside (Italy), Abot Hameiri (Israel), Miso Film (Denmark, Sweden and Norway), Blue Circle (Netherlands), Original Productions (USA) and Easy Tiger (Australia).

Fremantle produces in excess of 12,000 hours of original programming, rolls out more than 70 formats and airs 400 programmes a year worldwide. Also distributes over 30,000 hours of content in more than 180 territories.

Fremantle is a world leader in digital and branded entertainment, has more than 470 million subscribers across 1,600 social channels and over 40 billion views across all platforms.

Galleon Films Ltd

50 Openshaw Road, London SE2 0TE
tel 020 8310 7276
website www.galleontheatre.co.uk/galleon_films.html
Chief Executive Alice De Sousa

Production details: An independent film and drama production company.

Casting procedures: Uses freelance casting directors and sometimes holds general auditions. Casting breakdowns are publicly available via all actor-accessible publications and the website. Does not welcome unsolicited letters and CVs or showreels, but will consider invitations to view individual actors' websites. Actors are employed under Equity-approved contracts.

Handstand Productions

13 Hope Street, Liverpool L1 9BQ
tel 0151 708 7441
website www.handstand-uk.eu
Creative Director & Producer Han Duijvendak
Producer Nicholas Stanley

Produces documentary TV series, promotional and informational films, and training films. Also creates film-making programmes for schools and youth centres. Rarely requires actors, so please do not submit anything unless a specific casting requirement has been made available on the website.

Hat Trick Productions Ltd

33 Oval Road, London NW1 7EA
tel 020 7184 7777

email reception@hattrick.com
website www.hattrick.co.uk
Twitter @HatTrickProd
Instagram @HatTrickProd
Managing Director Jimmy Mulville

Founded in 1986, Hat Trick Productions is one of the UK's most successful independent production companies working in situation and drama comedy series and light entertainment shows. Recent credits include: *The Kumars at No. 42*, *Worst Week of my Life*, *Have I Got News for You* and *Room 101*.

Heavy Entertainment Ltd

111 Wardour Street, London W1F 0UH
tel 020 7494 1000
email info@heavy-entertainment.com
website www.heavy-entertainment.com
Director David Roper

Production details: Established in 1992. Audio, video and web producers. Areas of work include drama, corporate, commercials, audiobooks and actor showreels (audio and video). Offers Equity-approved contracts.

Casting procedures: Welcomes showreels and voicereels (via agents only), and invitations to view individual actors' websites.

Hurricane Films Ltd

13 Hope Street, Liverpool L1 9BQ
tel 0151 707 9700
website www.hurricanefilms.net
Facebook www.facebook.com/HurricaneFilms
Twitter @hurricanefilms

Founded in 2000, Hurricane Films develop feature films, feature documentaries and TV series. Credits include: *Of Time and the City* (dir. Terence Davies); *Sunset Song* (dir. Terence Davies); *A Quiet Passion* (dir. Terence Davies); *Unsung Hero: The Jack Jones Story* (dir. Solon Papadopoulos); *A Prayer Before Dawn* (dir. Jean Stephane Sauvaire) and *My Letter to the World* (dir. Solon Papadopoulos). BAFTA-nominated twice; awarded six Royal Television Awards.

Jason Impey Films

90 Hainault Avenue, Giffard Park, Milton Keynes, Bucks. MK14 5PE
mobile 07732 476409
email jasonimpey@live.com
website www.jasonimpey.co.uk
Facebook www.facebook.com/jason666films
Twitter @jasonimpey
Instagram @jason666films
Director Jason Impey

Production details: Works mainly in film, making feature horror films. Also employs actors in the fields of drama, comedy and documentary. Recent credits include: *Fluid Boy*; *Grim Places*; *VIPCO The Untold Story*; *Twink*; *More Sex, Lies and Depravity*; *Boys*

Behind Bars; Lustful Desires and *Sex, Lies and Depravity* (all feature films).

Casting procedures: Uses freelance casting directors and holds general auditions; actors may write in at any time requesting inclusion. Casting breakdowns available via postal application with sae. Welcomes letters (with CVs and photographs) from individual actors previously unknown to the company, sent by post or email. Also accepts showreels and invitations to view individual actors' websites. Actively encourages applications from disabled actors and promotes the use of inclusive casting. "Always on the lookout for new talent."

John Walsh Filmmaker

email john@walshbros.co.uk
website www.johnwalshfilmmaker.com
Facebook www.facebook.com/JohnWalshFilmMaker
Twitter @walshbros
Instagram @johnwalsh_filmmaker

Double BAFTA- and Grierson-nominated film company. Productions range from television series and dramas to feature films. Recent productions include: *Sofa Surfers*(BBC), *Headhunting the Homeless* (BBC), *Don't Make Me Angry* (Channel 4), *Monarch* and *Toryboy: The Movie*.

Left Bank Pictures

7th Floor, The Place, 175 High Holborn,
London WC1V 7AA
tel 020 7759 4600
email info@leftbankpictures.co.uk
website www.leftbankpictures.co.uk
Chief Executive Andy Harries

An independent television and film production company founded in July 2007 by Andy Harries and Marigo Kehoe, and named "Best Independent Production Company" at the Broadcast Awards in 2011. "We continue to work with the UK's leading writing, directing and onscreen talent to produce bold, innovative feature films, television dramas and cutting-edge comedy. We also pride ourselves on nurturing and championing exciting new talent set to create the hits of tomorrow."

MARV Films

71 Queen Victoria Street, London EC4V 4BE
email info@marvfilms.com
website www.marv.com
Instagram @marv_films
Executive Matthew Vaughn

Production details: Matthew Vaughn is best known for starting his career working as a producer for the Guy Ritchie films: *Lock, Stock and Two Smoking Barrels, Snatch and Swept Away*. Recent films include: *Kingsmen: The Secret Service*, 2014; *Fantastic Four*, 2015; *Eddie the Eagle*, 2015; *Kingsmen: the Golden Circle*, 2017; *Rocketman*, 2019.

Casting procedures: Accepts handwritten enquiries only to 11 Portland Mews, London W1F 8JL.

Maya Vision International Ltd

tel 020 7796 4842
email info@mayavisionint.com
website www.mayavisionint.com
Facebook www.facebook.com/mayavisionint
Twitter @mayavision
Founder & Managing Director Rebecca *Company Director & Producer* Sally Thomas Dobbs
Writer Michael Wood

Maya Vision International is an independent film and television production company, founded in 1983. Since then it has won many awards, and become renowned for making work of the highest quality.

Specialising in producing "original, landmark documentaries, features and drama for film and television", Maya Vision has developed a unique style, making some of history's great stories accessible to a wider public.

Working alongside many broadcasters and funders, including the BBC, ITV, Channel 4, Five, PBS, UK Film Council, BFI and Arts Council England. Maya Vision's acclaimed catalogue has been screened in more than 140 territories worldwide.

Met Film Production

Ealing Studios, Ealing Green, London W5 5EP
tel 020 8280 9127
email assistant@metfilm.co.uk
website www.metfilmproduction.co.uk
Facebook www.facebook.com/MetFilmProductions
Twitter @metfilmprod
Managing Director Jonny Persey *Directors* Jerry Rothwell *Producers* Stewart le Maréchal, Al Morrow

Enterprise dedicated to the development and production of feature films for national and international audiences. Also produces short films. The company has a number of feature films in development.

Recent credits include: *Deep Water, Wondrous Oblivion* and *Soloman & Gaenor, Heavy Load* and *The Pied Piper of Hutzovina*.

Neal Street Productions

26-28 Neal Street, London WC2H 9QQ
tel 020 7240 8890
email post@nealstreetproductions.com
Co-Directors Sam Mendes, Pippa Harris, Nicolas Brown *Executive* Julie Pastor *Head of Development* Lola Oliyide *Production Executive* Caroline Reynolds

Production details: Neal Street Productions is one of the UK's most respected production companies, producing film, television and theatre. Set up in 2003 by Sam Mendes, Pippa Harris and Caro Newling, Nicolas Brown was appointed to the Board of Directors in 2013. In 2015, Neal Street moved under the umbrella of parent company, All3Media, which is owned jointly by Discovery Communication and Liberty Global. Neal Street Productions makes distinctive, popular, award winning projects on both sides of the Atlantic.

Known for the film *1917*, 2019.

Recent TV includes: *Penny Dreadful*, 2016–20; *Britannia*, 2017–21; *Informer*, 2018; Call the Midwife, 2012–21.

Submissions: Does not accept unsolicited material.

NFD Productions Ltd
21 Low Street, South Milford, Leeds LS25 5AR
tel (01997) 681949
email alyson@nfdproductions.com
website www.nfdproductions.com
Director Alyson Connew

Production details: Production company producing feature films specialising in 3D, children and teenage programmes specialising in 3D, and commercials.

Casting procedures: Please send CVs to **alyson@northernfilmanddrrama.com**. Requires a minimum of 4 featured/named roles in either a film or TV series.

Number 9 Films
8-9 Stephen Mews, London W1T 1AF
tel 020 7323 4060
email info@number9films.co.uk
website www.number9films.co.uk
Twitter @number9films
Producers Stephen Woolley, Elizabeth Karlsen *Head of Development* Kate Lawrence

Production details: Number 9 Films is a British independent film production company co-founded in 2002 by producers Elizabeth Karlsen and Stephen Woolley, after a long collaboration at both Palace Pictures and Scala Productions. They are best known for *The Crying Game*, 1992; *Interview with the Vampire*, 1994; *Michael Collins*, 1996; *Made in Dagenham*, 2010. In 2005, the company was awarded one of the much sought-after Slate Development Funding schemes by the UK Film Council. The company has gone on to establish itself as one of the UK's leading independent production companies, forging relationships with a wide range of talent in the UK, across Europe and in the States. The company aims to produce between 2 and 3 films a year.

Recent films: *Carol*, 2015; *Youth*, 2015; *The Limehouse Golem*, 2016; *Their Finest*, 2016; *On Chesil Beach*, 2017; *Colette*, 2018; *Mothering Sunday*, 2021.

OVC Media Ltd
88 Berkeley Court, Baker Street, London NW1 5ND
tel 020 7402 9111
email eliot@ovcmedia.com
website www.ovcmedia.com
Director Joanne Cohen

Production details: Established in 1982. Areas of work include TV, film, video and documentary

production. Recent credits include: *History of the World Cup*, *African Odyssey* and *My Matisse*.

Casting procedures: Accepts submissions (with CVs and photographs) from actors previously unknown to the company if sent by post or email. Showreels, voicereels and invitations to view individual actors' websites are also accepted. Offers Equity approved contracts and does not subscribe to the Equity Pension Scheme. Will consider submissions from disabled actors to play disabled characters.

The company also owns a vast production library, and in some cases will finance the soundtrack for TV and films. The company also owns Red Bus Recording and TV Studios.

Park Village Ltd
1 Park Village East, Regents Park, London NW1 7PX
tel 020 7387 8077
email hello@parkvillage.co.uk
website www.parkvillage.co.uk
Executive Producer Adam Booth

Established in 1972. Film and photography production company working mainly in commercials, music videos and marketing content. Casting is done by freelance casting directors. Recent credits include commercials for Woolmark, Moneybox, Wise, Cazoo; photography for Channel 4; and music videos for Joel Corry. Actors are employed under Equity-approved contracts. Applications from disabled actors to play disabled characters, and diversity of all kinds, encouraged.

Picture Palace Films Ltd
13 Egbert Street, London NW1 8LJ
tel 020 7586 8763
email info@picturepalace.com
website www.picturepalace.com

Founded in 1972. Works mainly in feature films and TV drama production. Recent credits include: *Sharpe's Peril*, *Sharpe's Challenge*, *Frances Tuesday* and *Extremely Dangerous* (all ITV); *Rebel Heart* (BBC) and *A Life for a Life* (*The True Story of Stefan Kizko*).

Pinball London Ltd
tel 0845 273 3893
email smash@pinballonline.co.uk
website www.pinballonline.co.uk
Facebook www.facebook.com/pinballonline
Twitter @pinballonline
Director Paula Vaccaro

Production details: Founded in 2009. Independent film production company assembled by creative and business entertainment industry professionals with a common goal of producing independent auteur-oriented films. Film is main area of work, but may do music promos, TV and Internet content. Recent credits include: *A Day in Two Lives* (short); *Margo & Max* (long feature); and *Perempay & Dee* feat. Shola Ama (DJPLAY music video).

Casting procedures: Uses freelance casting directors. Sometimes holds general auditions; actors may write at any time to request inclusion. Only accepts postal submissions, which *must* include CV, professional actor's reel on DVD, and headshot photos. Does not accept unsolicited scripts or ideas.

Replay Film & New Media

25 Museum Street, London WC1 1JT
tel 020 7637 0473
email webenquiries@replayfilms.co.uk
website www.replayfilms.co.uk
Directors Dave Young, Stuart Slade

Production details: Established in 1990. Activities include: drama, documentary, corporate, e-learning, training, consultancy. Involved in all aspects of film and new media, working mainly in TV, video and computer media production.

Casting procedures: Casting breakdowns are available publicly on the website and Castweb. Invitations to view individual actors' websites are accepted.

Sightline

Surrey Technology Centre, 40 Occam Way, Guildford GU2 7YG
tel 01483 813311 *mobile* 07554 019436
email keith@sightline.co.uk
website www.sightline.co.uk
Twitter @SightlineVideo
Senior Producer and Director Keith Thomas

Production details: A Black Ox Media and Events company. Fully resourced, long-established video and interactive content production company specialising in corporate and training videos, media for the Web, animation and 360 video. Employs actors in corporate work.

Casting procedures: Welcomes emails (with CVs and photographs) from actors previously unknown to the company. Invitations to view individual actors' websites are welcome.

Sixteen Films

email jack@sixteenfilms.co.uk
website www.sixteenfilms.co.uk
Twitter @KenLoachSixteen
Director Ken Loach *Producer* Rebecca O'Brien

Film production company. Welcomes CVs from actors, asking them to be directed to casting director Kahleen Crawford.

Speakeasy Productions Ltd

1A Shandon Crescent, Edinburgh EH11 1QE
tel 0131 376 7210
email info@speak.co.uk
28 St Johns Square, London EC1M 4DN
tel 020 7336 6066
website www.speak.co.uk
Facebook www.facebook.com/SpeakeasyProductions Ltd

Twitter @speakeasyuk
Company Directors Jonathan Young, Shona Johnstone, Jeremy Hewitt

Production details: Corporate media production company and event management company based in London and Edinburgh. Works mainly in video production, employing actors in documentary, corporate and commercials. Occasionally holds general auditions. Recent clients include: Lloyds Banking Group, Food Standards Scotland, Student Loans Council, Scottish Enterprise and the Scottish Government.

Casting procedures: Accepts submissions (with CVs and photographs) from actors previously unknown to the company. Will also accept CVs and photographs sent via email. Invitations to view showreels and individual actors' websites are also accepted. Promotes inclusive casting and applications from disabled actors are considered.

Stagescreen Productions

website www.stagescreenproductions.com
Director Jeffrey Taylor *Development Executive* John Segal

Founded in 1986, Stagescreen is a film and TV production company with offices in London and Los Angeles. Credits include: *What's Cooking*, directed by Gurinder Chadha (Lionsgate); *Young Alexander the Great* directed by Jalal Merhi (ProSeiben) and *Jekyll*, directed by Douglas Mackinnon and Matt Lipsey (BBC).

Offers PACT/Equity-approved contracts and does not subscribe to the Equity Pension Scheme. Will consider applications from disabled actors to play disabled characters.

Tiger Aspect Productions

4th Floor, Shepherds Building Central, London W14 0EE
tel 020 7434 6700
email general@tigeraspect.co.uk
website www.tigeraspect.co.uk
Facebook www.facebook.com/TigerAspectProductions
Twitter @TigerAspectUK
Co-managing Directors Ben Cavey, Will Gould

Founded in 1993. Produces TV comedy and drama with the aim of "investing in and working with the leading writers, performers and programme-makers to produce original, creative and successful programming". Credits include: *Ripper Street* (BBC1), *Teachers* (Channel 4), *Good Karma Hospital* (ITV), *Peaky Blinders* (BBC2), *Bad Education* (BBC3), *Benidorm* (ITV) and *Mount Pleasant* (Sky).

Twenty Twenty Productions Ltd

Level 2, 2 College Square, Bristol BS1 5UE
tel 020 7284 2020
email enquiries@twentytwenty.tv
website www.twentytwenty.tv

Twenty Twenty Television is one of the UK's leading independent television production companies, making award-winning documentaries, hard-hitting current affairs, popular drama, attention-grabbing living history series and engaging children's shows.

Twenty Twenty remains truly independent and is still run by creative and enthusiastic programme-makers. Its work has been broadcast by networks around the world including the BBC, CBBC, ITV, Channels 4 and Five in the UK, and ABC, The Discovery Channel, Turner Original Productions, Sundance Channel, CNN, The Arts and Entertainment Channel and WGBH in the USA.

Video Enterprises

12 Barbers Wood Road, High Wycombe,
Bucks HP12 4EP
tel (01494) 534144 *mobile* 07831 875216
email videoenterprises@outlook.com
website www.videoenterprises.co.uk
Director Maurice R. Fleisher

Video Enterprises is a UK-based video production company specialising in broadcast, corporate, industrial, theatrical and social events programme-making.

Wilder Films

1 Fernsbury Street, London WC1X 0HZ
tel 020 7631 3417
email jobs@wilderfilms.co.uk
website www.wilderfilms.co.uk
Managing Director Richard Batty

Production details: Established in 2003. Works mainly in film and video production, especially corporate, brand short films and commercials.

Casting procedures: Uses in-house and freelance casting directors and holds general auditions, but "will look for people if needed". Does not welcome unsolicited approaches but may accept invitations to view individual actors' websites.

Working Title Films

26 Aybrook Street, London W1U 4AN
tel 020 7307 3000
website www.workingtitlefilms.com
Facebook www.facebook.com/WorkingTitleFilms
Twitter @working_title
Instagram @workingtitlefilms
Chairmen Tim Bevan, Eric Fellner *President* Liza Chasin *President UK Production* Debra Hayward

World Productions Ltd

5th Floor National House, 60–66 Wardour Street, London W1F 0TA
tel 020 7156 6990
email info@world-productions.com
website www.world-productions.com
Facebook www.facebook.com/worldproductionsltd
Twitter @worldprods

Produces TV drama features, series and serials. Recent credits include: *Line of Duty* (BBC2), *The Bletchley Circle* (ITV), *The Great Train Robbery* (BBC1) and *The Fear* (Channel 4).

Film schools

Although the work is minimally paid (if at all), it is well worth contacting film schools for casting consideration. Despite mostly working with incipient talents, the potential of the experience is possibly greater than that of participating in a Fringe theatre production – and the end result could contain material worthy of use in a showreel. Some schools keep files of actors' CVs and photographs for students to refer to when casting.

Castings for many low- or non-paid films are advertised on Shooting People (**www.shootingpeople.org**) – see entry on page 420.

Arts University Bournemouth
Wallisdown, Poole, Dorset BG12 5HH
website www.aub.ac.uk
Facebook www.facebook.com/inspiredAUB
Twitter @inspiredAUB
Instagram @inspiredAUB
Key contact David Munns

Students do not only consider local actors for their short films. Actors are either paid Equity minimum (both MA and BA Film Production Films) or are offered their expenses and a DVD copy. Also needs actors for exercises and workshops. Welcomes enquiries (containing CV, photograph and covering letter) from new actors; actors' details are kept on file.

London College of Communication
Elephant and Castle, London SE1 6SB
website www.arts.ac.uk/colleges/london-college-of-communication
Facebook www.facebook.com/londoncollegeofcommunication
Twitter @lcclondon
Instagram @lcclondon

A long-established film and television course with both BA and FdA programmes. Students work on 16mm, video and HD, and cast for projects throughout the year. Letters and CVs are welcome. Expenses only are offered, but a copy of finished work is supplied for showreels.

London Film Academy
The Old Church, 52A Walham Grove, Fulham, London SW6 1QR
tel 07493 890182
email info@londonfilmacademy.com
website www.londonfilmacademy.com
Facebook www.facebook.com/londonfilmacademy
Twitter @LDNfilmacademy
Instagram @London_film_academy
Joint Principals & Founders Daisy Gili, Anna MacDonald

Specialises in professional, practical full-time training and short, specialised courses across all areas of filmmaking. Students make a series of short graduation films and commercials using both professional and non-professional actors.

"Students use agents, casting directors and various Internet websites and paper casting publications to recruit actors". Accepts submissions (with CVs and photographs) from actors previously unknown to them. Actors' details are kept on file for student reference and actors are contacted directly. Payment to actors depends on the individual project budgets. Expenses will usually be paid and the actor will be provided with rushes for their showreel.

The London Film School
24 Shelton Street, London WC2H 9UB
tel 020 7836 9642
email info@lfs.org.uk
website www.lfs.org.uk

London Film School offers a 2-year MA course in the art and technique of filmmaking, with approximately 120-130 student short films being made each year. Students generally recruit actors through Spotlight, Star Now, and Talent Circle. Expenses and a DVD copy of the film are normally offered to actors cast in student films. "The school welcomes enquiries from actors (with CVs and photographs), but asks that students use websites such as Spotlight and CastingCall Pro to recruit their actors".

National Film and Television School
Beaconsfield Studios, Station Road, Beaconsfield HP9 1LG
tel (01494) 671234
email info@nfts.co.uk
website www.nfts.co.uk
Facebook www.facebook.com/NFTSFilmTV
Twitter @nftsfilmtv
Instagram @nftsfilmtv

Offers 2-year MA courses in Cinematography; Composing for Film and Television; Creative Business for Entrepreneurs and Executives; Digital Effects; Directing Animation; Directing Documentary; Directing Fiction; Directing and Producing Science and Natural History; Directing and Producing Television Entertainment; Editing;

Media

Film Studies Programming and Curation; Games Design; Marketing, Distribution, Assistant Camera (Focus Pulling and Loading); Assistant Directing and Floor Managing; Cameras, Sound and Vision Mixing for Television Production; Creative Producing for Digital Platforms; Directing Commercials; Factual Development and Production; Graphics and Titles for Television and Film; Model Making for Animation; Production Accounting for Film and Television; Production Management for Film and Television; Sound Development; Sports Production; Writing and Producing Comedy.

Students generally recruit actors through casting directors and Spotlight. Has a formal agreement with Equity. Welcomes enquiries (with CVs and photographs) from new actors. Actors are often used throughout the year for workshops and CVs/ photographs are kept for this purpose. Graduation projects are cast by external casting directors.

Screen and Film School

84-86 London Road, Brighton, East Sussex BN1 4JF
tel (01273) 602070
email info@screenfilmschool.ac.uk
website www.screenfilmschool.ac.uk

Film-industry-recognised. Provides training in all aspects of motion-picture production: screenwriting, directing, cinematography, editing and production management. More than 30 student short films are made each year; students generally recruit actors through their sister college, the Institute for Contemporary Theatre (ICT) and Shooting People (**www.shootingpeople.org**). There is no formal agreement with Equity. Students do not only consider local actors. Actors are generally offered their expenses and a digital copy. Welcomes enquiries (containing photograph and 1-page CV) from new actors if sent by post.

University of the Creative Arts

Farnham campus: Falkner Road, Farnham GU9 7DS
tel (01252) 722441

email enquiries@uca.ac.uk
website www.uca.ac.uk

BA (Hons) Film Production at Farnham is accredited by the BKKSTS, the International Moving Image Society and CILECT. The course offers students the opportunity to work on 16mm film and HD formats on both fiction and documentary. Students can specialise from the second year in directing, producing, screenwriting, cinematography, editing, sound and production design. Over 100 short films are produced every year.

BA (Hons) Acting based in Farnham, integrates acting for the screen and stage from day one. The course is taught at the university and at our partners Farnham Maltings.

The **BA (Hons) Television Production** course is CILECT accredited. Based at Maidstone Studios, it offers students the opportunity to study in a live working studio environment. Actors are recruited through online casting sites such as Mandy and Stage Castings.

The **BA (Hons) Acting** course is based at UCA Rochester, integrates performance and technology and offers collaborative opportunities with Tevelvision Production and Design for Film, Theatre and Performance students.

University of Westminster

University of Westminster, Watford Road, Northwick Park, Harrow, Middlesex HA1 3TP
tel 020 7911 5000
website www.westminster.ac.uk/film-and-television-courses

Westminster Film School: Makes around 40 short films per year, from 3 minutes to 20 minutes in length, on 16mm film and digital. Films regularly win prizes at international and UK film festivals. Expenses are reimbursed and a DVD copy of the film is supplied to actors. Welcomes letters (including CV and photograph) from actors previously unknown to the school.

Actors and video games

Mark Estdale

As the game industry continues to grow, the demand for actors grow. With over 1,900 games in development in the UK and over 6,000 in the US the opportunities are myriad.

Games have changed the way we are entertained. As a medium they bring together two strands of human leisure; the active nature of playing and interacting, and the passive engagement of being an audience. The essence of the video game experience is choice and consequence.

Games today embrace every genre. And it's no exaggeration to say games are also transforming the way we inform and live our lives. They're in the classroom and they're in your phone, your watch, your car's computer and your workplace. Games are never far away when you go online and they are at the frontiers of Virtual Reality and Augmented Reality. They are everywhere, they are here to stay, and they are brimming with performances. They require actors of all ages, accents and nationalities.

So how does an actor get started in acting for games?

Games currently present actors with two avenues down which work can be found: performance capture and voice acting.

Performance capture

The UK boasts some of the world's most well-known performance capture studios working with games.

Since the technique was first truly brought to public attention with Andy Serkis's definitive performance as Gollum in Peter Jackson's *Lord of the Rings*, performance capture has grown into a global industry serving hundreds of games and films every year. And as performance capture technology advances, it becomes more accessible cost-wise and more commonplace. The trend is not going to slow down.

Training resources like The Mocap Vaults (Twitter: **@themocapvaults**) are the perfect place to start a journey into the rapidly expanding world of performance capture. Actors should also look up studios like Audiomotion, Centroid and Andy Serkis's Imaginarium to find out more. The film *Avatar* and the acclaimed *Uncharted* series are great examples of this type of work.

Voice acting

For voice acting, the story is a similar one. Ultimately the demand is high and growing, yet recording for games does have its challenges.

A game script is unlike any other. The mapping needed to create player choice and consequence can make a script huge and complex. A game with hundreds of characters and 30,000 lines of dialogue isn't unusual. Imagine any play, TV or film script as a piece of string with a beginning and an end. Pull the ends and you have a straight line. A game script, by comparison can be a huge knot, like a mussed-up, detailed map of London with no street names.

Now add the fact that your performance is in a virtual environment. There's no set, and no audience, and potentially no other actors around to perform against. The skill for the actor is in being true to the moment, however it is presented to you.

Casting

To be cast for a game, the first obvious thing is to be open to taking part in casting and letting your acting and voice agent know you are available and keen to work with games. Some agents still remain blissfully unaware of this $91 billion industry. Spotlight and online services like voicespro.com are worth trawling for opportunities.

Second, it is helpful to have a pertinent showreel. The ideal reel is a dramatic character one with real characters and perfect accents. If you approach the reel as if it were a film casting which is to be shot in close up, you'll be in the right space: real and intimate.

Have no other voice on your reel than yours, and don't use music or sound effects. You may be required to keep in character consistently for weeks in the studio, so don't include performances you cannot sustain. The most common submission error is to think of games as 'games' then produce a reel that is cartoony and heightened.

When casting for a game I think like an intelligence officer selecting an agent to work undercover. If the candidate can be who I want them to be, in an alien environment, and not attract suspicion, they have potential. I look for decisive character choice and flexibility. Good game actors are instinctive. Being true to character whatever is thrown at them is core. Spycraft is a powerful perspective as agents working undercover have no script and there's no scene rehearsal. It is character first.

For an audition you will usually get a short character brief, hopefully with an image and a few lines of text to perform. Make firm decisions and flesh out the character with what you have. After a first run through expect to be asked to interpret the character differently and to be given something to cold read as well. Sight reading is an essential skill as it is rare that you will get a script in advance once hired.

Valuable acting skills that are beneficial to voice acting in most games are strong sight reading, radio drama, ADR and experience. Performance capture that combines movement with voice recording is staged theatrically. It requires precise physical performances where screen, theatre and acrobatic skills come into play.

Pay

An actor adding their voice to a game character is paid well. They normally get more for a few hours in session than they would for a week on the West End. However, being paid well is not quite as simple as it could be as there are no industry pay standards for voice work in video games. It is a buyer's market and as such voice actors are being exploited.

I know of actors being offered credits on IMDb as 'payment' for working on a game. I have also heard of actors being used as pawns in bidding wars between production companies; undercutting their competition by offering to pay significantly less to the cast.

Currently there are no pay guidelines for video games, so below I've created a table based on what I've gathered from the grapevine. I've matched it with corresponding production budgets to give a better overview. At the 'micro', cash-strapped and, to my mind, most interesting and innovative end of the scale you can find openness to the idea of profit sharing in return for services.

Production Budget Type	Production Budget £	1st hour	2nd
Triple A	>1m	£750	£250
Medium Budget	>400k <1m	£450	£200
Low Budget	>100k <400k	£350	£150
Very Low Budget	>30k <100k	£250	£100
Micro Budget	<30k	£100	£50
Average professional rate	NA	£400	£200

The industry is varied like the film industry; it goes from zero budget productions to those with budgets greater than £100m. So if you have to negotiate a fee, a good starting point is to base it on the production budget.

The weighting for the first hour comes from the practice of paying a royalty buyout for the work. However, this is being challenged. The UK stands alone as the most expensive place in the world to hire actors because of it; the UK loses a lot of work as a result. The thinking is towards having a flat hourly rate that is on par with US rates.

There is another pay debate focused on the idea of paying actors by word or line, based on average recording speeds of lines/words per hour. Fundamentally, why should an efficient and fast actor be paid less than someone who is slow? As inexperienced actors are generally slow, when pay is time based there is a disincentive to hiring them. Paying by word or line with a minimum start fee does have its attractions.

If you want to find out more about rates talk to the voice agents, lobby Equity or plug into Facebook, Twitter, LinkedIn and the voice-acting community via groups like The VoiceOver Network (Twitter: **@NetworkVO**). They may all disagree with the table but the goal here is to stop actors being exploited by having better transparency. A heated debate is better than silence.

If you're still unsure what the games industry can offer you, here are a few statistics. The UK has the largest games-development community in Europe, with the most recent study indicating over 1,900 games-development companies are based here, employing almost 10,000 creative staff. Data from the UCAS web portal for undergraduates demonstrates that there are now 315 specialist video games degree courses in the UK.

And the audience may surprise you. There are more gamers today older than 50 than there are those aged under 18. The average player is in their 30s, and 49 per cent of players are women. Violent crime rates have gone down as game sales have increased. That may or may not be related, but games today are too diverse and established to be the stimulant for aggression that some headlines might have you believe.

According to figures fromNESTA, the games industry is growing at an extraordinary rate. Almost nine out of ten game companies began operations in the 2000s or the 2010s. And between 2011 and 2013, the number of games companies grew at 22 per cent per year, while current estimates indicate the global industry will pass $100 billion in value soon. In 2014 alone, games contributed £1.7 billion to the UK games industry.

To embrace the opportunity in games the willing actor jumps in. Games need actors.

Originally an actor, **Mark Estdale** founded **Outsource Media Ltd** (**OMUK**) in 1996. It is the UK's largest independent production company providing voice casting and recording of video games. Mark also coaches actors for working with games. OMUK has produced audio content for over 600 titles including titles nominated for 18 BAFTA Game Awards since 2004.

Radio and audio book companies

Unlike in the visual media, many radio directors have their roots in theatre and will go to stage productions to inform their future casting. And, unlike their visual media counterparts, they have a far greater understanding of actors and acting, and are far more open to casting against obvious physical type.

The BBC has by far and away the biggest radio drama output, and also uses actors to read poetry, narrations and stories. Some of this 'output' is made in-house; a good proportion is contracted out to independent companies. This is one area of work that doesn't very often use casting directors. It is a good idea to listen to radio drama in order to become aware of its ways – you won't hear much swearing, for instance. Also see 'Voice-over agents' (page 96) and 'Showreel, voicereel and website services' (page 380); some of the latter have excellent advice on making a voice demo on their websites.

INDEPENDENT RADIO COMPANIES

Art and Adventure Ltd

website www.artandadventure.org
Twitter @arbenture
Creative Director Roger James Elsgood

Production details: A production company specialising in making high production-value, location-recorded long-form drama for BBC Radio 3, 4 and the World Service with international casts and directors. Recent work includes: *The Two Gentlemen of Valasna* and *The Mrichhakatikaa* for Radio 3, both recorded entirely on location in India; *To the Wedding* for Radio 3 – a collaboration with Complicite; *Shooting Stars* for Radio 3 (directed by Mike Hodges and starring Michael Gambon, Michael Sheen and Clive Owen); *King Trash*, the second play in Mike Hodges' radio trilogy, *Inferno* with Corin Redgrave, Alex Jennings and Laurie Anderson, and *Miss Julie* with Sofie Gråbøl, Lars Mikkelsen and Marie Bach Hansen.

Casting procedures: The company is always happy to receive submissions and voice demos from actors, and auditions as necessary. It sometimes offers Equity contracts. Actively encourages applications from disabled actors and promotes the use of inclusive casting. Art and Adventure Ltd is actively working with actors with south Asian and Middle Eastern heritage and welcomes creative relationships accordingly.

The Comedy Unit

Unit D, Glasgow North Trading Estate,
24 Craigmont Street, Glasgow G20 9BT
tel 0141 305 6666
email info@comedyunit.co.uk
website www.comedyunit.co.uk
Managing Director Rab Christie

Production details: Founded in 1996. Works in TV and radio productions. Areas of work include drama, sitcoms, comedy and other light entertainment.

Casting procedures: Sometimes holds general auditions. Actors can write at any time requesting inclusion. Submissions from actors previously unknown to the company are accepted, sent by post or email. Voice demos and invitations to view individual actors' websites are also accepted.

Culture Wise

website www.culturewise.org
Facebook www.facebook.com/CultureWiseProductions
Twitter @CultureWiseUK

Production details: Founded in 1988. Areas of work include TV and radio documentaries.

Casting procedures: Does not hold general auditions. Invitations to view individual actors' websites are accepted. The company rarely employs actors, as the primary focus is on factual output: actors are generally used for short readings only, within a feature programme.

Curtains for Radio

58 St Helen's Gardens, London W10 6LH
tel 020 8964 0111
email contactus@curtainsforradio.co.uk
website www.curtainsforradio.co.uk
Facebook www.facebook.com/CurtainsforRadio
Producers & Directors Andrew McGibbon, Jonathan Ruffle, Nick Romero, Louise Morris, David Quantick

Production details: Established in 2001. Specialises in comedy, comedy drama, drama, factual, music and arts in film, television and audio. The ability to perform in foreign languages, regional dialects and singing are among the skills required by actors. Records/films 1 production play annually. Recent

Media

titles include: *With Nobbs On* (2012); *The Pickerskill Reports* – 4 series (2005-2013); *I Was ...* (2005-2017); *A Waste of Space* (2016); *A Call to Art* (2016-2019); *From the Outside In* (2016); *Street City Goodbyes* (2018); *Drawing on Water* (2018); *In Stitches* (2017); and *Looking for Oil Drum Lane* (2018).

Casting procedures: Casting is carried out by freelance casting director Rachel Freck and others. Accepts submissions from actors previously unknown to the company. Voice demos and invitations to view individual actors' websites are also accepted. Voice demos can only be accepted on MP3/wav files. Online links to audio, music or film are accepted. Voice-over artists are employed under Equity-approved contracts. Actively encourages applications from disabled actors and BAME actors, and are committed to diversity both on and off air.

Fiction Factory Productions Ltd
mobile 07837 982771
email fictionfactoryproduction@gmail.com
website www.fictionfactory.co.uk
Key personnel John Taylor

Production details: Founded in 1993. Makes radio drama and features for the BBC. Areas of work include drama, documentaries, light entertainment and voice-overs. Recent drama credits include: *Macbeth* for BBC Eduction; Kafka's *The Castle* and Michael Butt's *Chronicles of Ait: Stay With Me* both for BBC Radio 4.

Casting procedures: Does not hold general auditions. Submissions from actors previously unknown to the company are accepted if sent by post. Voice demos are also accepted. Does not welcome email submissions or invitations to view individual actors' websites. "It is helpful if showreels contain material appropriate to the kind of work sought; for example, corporate voice-overs or radio advertisements don't necessarily show off ensemble acting skills."

Heavy Entertainment Ltd
111 Wardour Street, London W1F 0UH
tel 020 7494 1000
email info@heavy-entertainment.com
website www.heavy-entertainment.com
Director David Roper

Production details: Established in 1992. Audio, video and web producers. Areas of work include drama, corporate, commercials, audiobooks and actor showreels (audio and video). Offers Equity-approved contracts.

Casting procedures: Welcomes showreels and voicereels (via agents only), and invitations to view individual actors' websites.

Loftus Media Ltd
2A Aldine Street, London W12 8AN
tel 020 8740 4666
email office@loftusmedia.co.uk
website www.loftusmedia.co.uk
Twitter @loftusmedia
Instagram @loftusmedia
Directors Joanne Rowntree, Richard Berry *Associate Director* Kirsten Lass

Production details: Award-winning content production company (podcasts, radio, visuals) which produces features, documentaries and readings. Requires plain narration and poetry from actors. Titles include *Black Roots* and Book of the Week for Radio 4, *Private Passions* for Radio 3, *The Secrets in Us* for Audible, *A Thorough Examination* with Drs Chris and Xand for BBC Sounds and the Sound Unbound series for the Barbican.

Casting procedures: Accepts submissions from individual actors previously unknown to the company. Will also accept submissions sent via email. Straight narration is preferred on voice demos and should be sent as an MP3. Actors are employed under Equity-approved contracts. Applications from disabled actors are welcomed.

Pier Productions
8 St George's Place, Brighton BN1 4GB
tel (01273) 691401
email broadcastassistant@pierproductionsltd.co.uk
website www.pierproductionsltd.co.uk
Facebook www.facebook.com/pierproductionsltd
Twitter @PierProdLtd
Managing Director Peter Hoare

Production details: Founded in 1993, an award-winning Brighton-based company and a significant supplier of factual and drama productions to BBC Radio 4. The company employs actors for drama productions and is keen to work with talent located in Brighton and the surrounding area.

Casting procedures: Does not hold general auditions. Not currently accepting unsolicited submissions. It must be emphasised that opportunities in radio drama are limited and that the company does not use the services of voice-over artists.

Lou Stein Associates Ltd
email info@loustein.co.uk
website www.lousteinassociates.com
Producer & Director Lou Stein

Production details: Lou Stein founded the Gate Theatre, Notting Hill, and was Artistic Director of the Palace Theatre, Watford 1986-95. Lou Stein Associates was formed in 2002 to continue Lou's interest in new work, adaptations, music theatre and media. Employs actors for drama programmes. Currently Artistic Director, Chickenshed Theatre Company. Recent drama credits include: *Blowin' in the Wind* (Chickenshed); *Trumpets and Raspberries* (Chickenshed); *Kindertransport* (Chickenshed); *Adventure to Oz* (Chickenshed); *The Midnight Gang*

Media

(Chickenshed, world premier); *Mr Stink* (nominated for an Offie Award for Best Production Children 8+); *My Month with Carmen* (starring Miriam Colon and Julian Glover); *Embers* (adapted by Lou Stein from the novel by Sandor Marai and starring Patrick Stewart); *The Possessed* (written and directed by Lou Stein from the Dostoevsky novel, starring Paul McGann); *Performances* by Brian Friel (Wilton's Music Hall, starring Henry Goodman and Rosamund Pike) and *Crossing the Sea* (an opera by Deirdre Gribbin).

Casting procedures: Voice demos and invitations to view individual actors' websites are accepted, but actors are requested to email in first instance. Please note that no reply will be given unless the actor is suitable for immediate casting. Names will be retained on file. Offers Equity-approved contracts. Actively promotes inclusive casting.

Whistledown Productions

8A Ayres Street, London SE1 1ES
tel 020 7407 8001
email info@whistledown.net
website www.whistledown.net

Production details: Founded in 1998. One of the largest independent suppliers to BBC Radio, with a background in features and landmark documentaries, as well as programme strands such as Radio 4's *The Reunion*. Also podcast and online audio producers. Custom-built studio available for commercial hire.

The Wireless Theatre Company

email casting@wirelesstheatre.co.uk
website www.wirelesstheatre.co.uk
Facebook www.facebook.com/wirelesstheatre
Twitter @wirelesstheatre
Artistic Director Mariele Runacre Temple *Executive Producers* Cherry Cookson, David Beck

Production details: Multi-award winning London-based audio production company at the forefront of modern, online audio drama. Provides original audio plays, comedy, stories, sketches and more to be downloaded from the website and produces long form multi-cast audio content for external clients such as BBC Radio 4 and Audible.

The company is very keen to hear from versatile actors with a large range of accents and vocal styles. Experience is not essential, but does prefer some sort of audio sample from actors when applying. Records a minimum of 1 new play each month, as well as several live recordings in theatres per year. Recent titles include: *The Hound of the Baskervilles*, *The Jane Austen Collection*, *Little Women*, *Black Beauty*, *Les Liason Dangereuses*, *Ram Runner Sue*, *Lance Manley* and *Bog Girl*.

Casting procedures: Casting done in-house. Advertises casting through CCP, but once an actor has worked for WTC they become part of the company and are used frequently. Also casts through

Facebook and Twitter. Welcomes submissions by email at **info@wirelesstheatrecompany.co.uk**, and all details are kept on file. Prefers applications with voicereels: simple, definitely without long musical introductions (rarely will listen to more than 2 minutes of any voicereel) and with 1 example of natural accent and some other, shorter samples of accents or voices. Welcomes invitations to view individual actors' websites. Roles are paid.

AUDIO BOOKS

Barefoot Audio Books Ltd

23 Bradford Street, 2nd Floor, Concord, MA 01742
email help@barefootbooks.com
website www.barefootbooks.com
CEO & Co-founder Nancy Traversy *Editorial Director* Emma Parkin

Production details: Produces books with audio for children.

Casting procedures: Does not use freelance casting directors. Accepts submissions from actors previously unknown to the company if sent by post, but does not welcome email enquiries. Voice demos and invitations to view individual actors' websites are also accepted. Singing ability is required from actors.

HarperAudio

HarperCollins Publishers, 1 London Bridge Street, London SE1 9GP
tel 020 8741 7070
email audiobooks@harpercollins.co.uk
website www.harpercollins.co.uk
Group Audio Director Jo Forshaw *Senior Audio Editor & Producer* Abigail Fenton *Senior Audio Editor & Producer* Tanya Brennand-Roper *Audio Assistant* Jack Chalmers

Production details: Has produced more than 2,000 titles for both children and adults. Work spans all genres including crime, comedy, literary fiction, mass market fiction, non-fiction and classics. Foreign languages and regional dialect skills are required from actors.

Casting procedures: Does not use freelance casting directors. Advises actors to make contact through an agent or studio.

Isis Audio (a division of Ulverscroft Ltd)

Unit 14, Kings Meadow, Ferry Hinksey Road, Oxford OX2 0DP
email studio@ulverscroft.co.uk
Facebook www.facebook.com/Isis.Soundings
Twitter @isisaudio
Instagram @isisaudio
Audio Production Manager Catherine Thompson

Production details: Founded in 1975. Records titles for Ulverscroft Ltd, as well as Boldwood, Choc Lit, Orneda and Verve.

Casting procedures: Does not use freelance casting directors. Accepts submissions from actors with proven audiobook experience if sent by post or email, but does not welcome telephone enquiries. Actors should have a range of voices and good sight-reading ability. Offers non-Equity contracts and does not subscribe to the Equity Pension Scheme. Actively encourages applications from disabled actors and promotes the use of inclusive casting.

Macmillan Audio Books

20 New Wharf Road, London N1 9RR
website www.panmacmillan.com

Casting procedures: Casts in-house. Does not accept unsolicited demos.

Naxos AudioBooks

5 Wyllyotts Place, Potters Bar, Herts EN6 2JD
tel (01707) 653326
email info@naxosaudiobooks.com
website www.naxosaudiobooks.com
Producer/Director Anthony Anderson

Production details: Founded in 1994. Produces classic fiction, modern fiction, non-fiction, drama, poetry and children's classics for CD and download. Titles include: *The Decline and Fall of the Roman Empire*, *Remembrance of Things Past*, *Middlemarch* and *Julius Caesar*. Regional dialect skills are required from actors. Accepts voice demos from agents.

Orion Audio Books

Orion Publishing Group, Carmelite House,
50 Victoria Embankment, London EC4Y 0DZ
tel 020 3122 6876

email audio@orionbooks.co.uk
website www.orionbooks.co.uk
Audio Publisher Paul Stark

Production details: Established in 1996, Orion Audio draws mainly on the Orion Group imprints to create their audio list, with notable authors such as Ian Rankin, Candice Carty-Williams, Michael Palin, Michael Connelly, Ben Aaronovitch, Sarah Millican, Adam Rutherford, Joe Abercrombie and Patrick Rothfuss. Orion is now firmly established in the digital download market and produces over 250 unabridged audiobooks a year, across all genres.

Casting procedures: Casts in-house. Useful skills include regional dialects and occasionally singing ability. Welcomes submissions and voice demos from actors previously unknown to the company. Happy to receive submissions from actors from all backgrounds with the right skills for the job.

Penguin Random House Audio

20 Vauxhall Bridge Road, London SW1V 2SA
tel 020 7840 8400
email audio@penguinrandomhouse.com
website www.penguinrandomhouse.com/books/audiobooks

Production details: Created in 1991, the Audio Books division of Random House publishes writers such as James Patterson, Andy McNab, Lee Child, Ian McEwan and Kathy Reichs.

Casting procedures: Uses freelance casting directors. Accepts submissions from actors previously unknown to the company, sent by post. Voice demos and invitations to view individual actors' websites are also accepted.

Media

Acting for radio

Gordon House

I remember once, in a burst of evangelical enthusiasm at having decided never to touch a cigarette again, upbraiding a distinguished member of the Radio Drama Company for her constant disappearances to the Green Room to light up. (Nowadays, of course, all BBC Green rooms are smoke-free, and your poor cigarette-smoking actor has to shiver in the car park.) "My dear man," she wheezed grandly. "The only reason you employ me on the wireless is because of my nicotine-nourished, port-soaked larynx. Living badly has made me the radio actress I am today!"

Well – it's a point of view. Just as the camera relishes certain skin textures, so the microphone may embellish the actor or actress who has lived a little – resulting in, shall we say, an idiosyncratic oesophagus. But as a way of getting a radio part, it's not a course of action I'd recommend. Radio simply doesn't pay enough to sustain a life of alcoholic debauchery.

So how do you get into radio? "It's a closed shop," moaned one actor to me the other day. "You hear the same names, time and again – and there's no way of breaking into this magic circle." I personally have worked with well over 800 actors, so it can't be that much of a closed shop ... although it's true that given the ruthless time constraints of the medium (a 60-minute play will be rehearsed and recorded in two days), there's a natural tendency for producers to work with those actors whom they know can 'deliver' quickly. There's no joy to be had in the seventh take of a difficult scene when your nervous newcomer is finally coming to grips with the ambiguities of his or her character, as well as the technical demands of this strange new medium, while everyone else's performances have long-since peaked and are now beginning to sound tired and lacklustre.

But that said, new writers and new actors are the lifeblood of the medium. And what do you need to be a good actor on radio? It's simple. You need to be a good actor. If you're successful in the theatre, in film, on TV – then of course you can be successful on radio. A good actor is a good actor. It obviously helps if your voice doesn't sound like a creaking door (given that creaking doors are a staple diet of many a radio play), and the medium has no place for prima donnas. With every producer sparingly counting his or her loose change, there's no such happy luxury as a radio 'extra'; so if you're cast as Hamlet, you can also expect to do your fair share of off-mic mumbling in Claudius' court. And if that doesn't appeal, don't do radio.

You also have to be prepared to work fast and make almost instant decisions. Over the years I've worked with a few actors whom I admire hugely; whom I've seen – in other media – give performances of rare charm and intelligence; but who in radio have simply been unable to 'come off the page' – make the character they're playing sound truthful and real. Of course this may simply be attributed to the crass inadequacy of the director. But for some actors the sheer speed at which they have to make decisions about character, motivation, sub-text and so forth is incredibly daunting. And then there's the physical absurdity of much of what they have to do: "How the xxx do you expect me to be 'truthful' when I'm carrying a xxxing great script in my left hand, a glass of water, masquerading as gin, in my right, and you want me to walk through a carpet of scrunched-up audio tape and pretend it's a meadow," shrieked one despairing actor to me a couple of years ago.

And yet that's exactly what we expect – truth. There's no medium as unforgiving for exposing over-acting or over-emoting (or worse – simple 'reading'). A radio play – and particularly a contemporary, naturalistic play – should make listeners feel that they are eavesdropping on real conversation. It's a medium that may owe much to theatre for providing it with great writing and acting talent (though the reverse is equally true), but the technique of radio acting is far closer to that of film than of theatre. "Less is more! Less is more!" as my erstwhile colleague, Martin Jenkins, one of Radio Drama's finest practitioners, used to impress on his casts. (It was Martin, incidentally, who uttered the memorable phrase: "Good Luck – Please!" before the umpteenth take of one particularly stressful scene.)

How do you bring yourself to the attention of radio producers? Well – there's no denying the fact that a lovingly crafted CD arriving on your desk just as you're in the process of casting your next play, and can't for the life of you think who you can get to play the embittered Glaswegian ex-shipbuilder who's contemplating a sex change, can make all the difference. But choose the pieces you record with care – and keep them short. If varied accents are not a speciality, there's no point in doing all sorts of varied accents. Obviously, it's a great asset to be master – or mistress – of many different voices, this being a medium where 'doubling' and 'trebling' is done with impunity. But a CD where the truthfulness of most of your extracts is undone by your game, but doomed, attempt to do a passable Geordie, won't help anyone. Many years ago I remember auditioning Jeremy Sinden for a part. "What accents do you do?" I asked him. "I do two actually," he said. "I do posh. And I do very posh." Well a mere two accents didn't stop Jeremy getting a load of work in every medium – including radio – in his all-too-brief, but exhilarating, career.

Having recorded your tape or (preferably) CD, you can, of course, circulate it to every producer who's ever made a radio play. But my advice would be to be a little more discerning. Listen to some radio plays (a great way of determining for yourself what works and what doesn't) and note the names of the producers whose productions particularly appeal to you. You can then write a personal note to them – you know the kind: "I must say, Mr House, I really enjoyed your fascinating and unusual interpretation of *Hedda Gabler* on Radio 3 last night, and incidentally Hedda is a part I've always yearned to play myself,"(etc.). I'm not saying it will get you a part, but producers are as vain as the next person (I should know) and it may well make them more inclined to slip your CD into the CD player, on the basis that anyone with such discerning judgement as yours must be worth hearing.

Radio is a fantastic and hugely under-rated medium, and actors, by and large, love working for it. It can also be the stepping-stone to fame and fortune. For many years we've been running our own radio bursary scheme for accredited drama schools – the Carleton Hobbs Competition (named after one of the great 20th century radio actors) – and the role-call of actors who have been winners, from Richard Griffiths to Stephen Tompkinson, from Nerys Hughes to Emma Fielding, is hugely impressive. Our new bursary scheme, the Norman Beaton Fellowship, for actors who didn't go to an accredited drama school, is also providing us with some excellent new talent. Details of both these schemes can be found on the BBC website.

And of course we producers don't simply wait to receive your CDs, but are constantly on the lookout for new and exciting talent from wherever we can find it. You may not need to approach us – we may approach you! As World Service Drama producers, Hilary Norrish and myself gave a young actor called Ewan MacGregor his first two professional jobs, having seen him in a drama school showcase. And Ewan – if you ever get to read this – where are the invitations to those glamorous film previews you promised you'd send us when you were famous? Remember – it was radio that gave you your first break!

Gordon House is the former Head of the BBC Radio Drama Department. He joined the BBC as a studio manager in 1972, working in Children's Television and Radio Sport before becoming a drama director. For 14 years he headed the small BBC World Service Drama team, during which time the Unit won more than 30 national and international awards. In 1998 Gordon won the Writers' Guild Special Prize for services for his work with new writers, and has twice won the Sony Drama Award. He is a founder member of The Worldplay Group, a radio association of drama directors from broadcasting stations around the world, which initiates a yearly season of international radios dramas broadcast on BBC World Service, ABC, CBC, RTE, Radio New Zealand and Radio Television Hong Kong.

Media festivals

These are geared towards showcasing directors, rather than actors. However, they can be useful places to network, learn and (if your film is short-listed) to gain extra exposure.

Belfast Film Festival

The Exchange Place, 23 Donegal Street,
Belfast BT1 2FF
tel 028 9032 5913
email info@belfastfilmfestival.org
website www.belfastfilmfestival.org
Twitter @BelfastFilmFes1

Normally held in March/April each year, the Belfast Film Festival brings the best of independent, world, local and classic cinema to screens across Belfast. In addition there are panel discussions, workshops, music events and a series of related club events in venues across the city.

Candidates may submit features, shorts, animation and documentaries for inclusion in the festival. The deadline for submissions is normally early December. While all categories will be considered for screening, the only competitive category is the Irish short film. To be eligible for the £1,000 Kodak Short Film Prize, films must have been shot in Ireland during the previous year and last no longer than 20 minutes.

BFI London Film Festival

21 Stephen Street, London W1T 1LN
tel 020 7 255 1444
website www.bfi.org.uk/lff

The BFI London Film Festival is Europe's largest public film event taking place in October each year. Leading figures in the film industry present their work at the festival, and the programme is supported by a number of interviews, industry and public forums, lectures, education events, Gala films and special screenings promoting the best in cinema across the world.

Cambridge Film Festival

Arts Picture House, 38-39 St Andrew's Street,
Cambridge CB2 3AR
email info@cambridgefilmfestival.org.uk
website www.cambridgefilmfestival.org.uk
Facebook www.facebook.com/CambridgeFilmFestival
Twitter @camfilmfest
Instagram @camfilmfest

Established in 1977, the festival is a celebration of film – past, present and future. It's a chance to relive and enjoy past glories, but also to see what's happening in film right now, and reveal new talents who will shape the future of cinema. Screens films from around the world, many of which may not be available elsewhere. The Cambridge Film Festival attracts big names but is nonetheless intimate and approachable.

Celtic Media Festival

Celtic Media Festival, 5th Floor, Trongate 103,
Glasgow G1 5HD
tel 0141 553 5408
email info@celticmediafestival.co.uk
website www.celticmediafestival.co.uk

The Celtic Media Festival celebrates the cultures and languages of Cornwall, Brittany, Ireland, Scotland and Wales in film and in television broadcasting. Awards include: Short Drama Award, Drama Feature Award and Drama Series Award. The festival is attended by producers, directors, commissioning editors, film executives, media students, distributors and schedulers.

Chichester International Film Festival

Chichester Cinema at New Park, New Park Road,
Chichester PO19 7XY
tel 01243 786650
email info@chichestercinema.org
website www.chichesterfilmfestival.co.uk
Facebook www.facebook.com/ChichesterCinema
Twitter @newparkcinema
Instagram @newparkcinema
Director Roger Gibson

An 18-day festival in August/September presenting more than 70 feature films, Q&As with visiting directors and related talks. More than half the films shown are previews and premieres; the remainder form retrospectives on important contributors to the film world.

Encounters (Short Film and Animation Festival)

The Station, Silver Street, Bristol BS1 2AG
email hello@encounters.film
website www.encounters.film
Facebook www.facebook.com/EncountersSFF
Twitter @EncountersSFF
Instagram @EncountersSFF

Encounters is an international short film and animation festival which runs in Bristol for 1 week in September. It discovers, supports and develops new talent in filmmaking, providing a platform for emerging and established filmmakers from around the world, and a unique meeting place for the industry. Connecting industry and audiences, the festival celebrates the creativity, diversity and impact of short film. It enjoys excellent links with the prestigious BAFTAs, Cartoon D'Or and European Film Awards. It is a qualifying festival for the Academy Awards. With screenings of diverse new shorts from around the world, alongside special guests and events, parties, awards, seminars, masterclasses and focus sessions, the festival offers insights and advice from industry professionals about every aspect of film. For advice about submitting your work, visit the website.

BFI Flare

c/o BFI Southbank, Belvedere Road, South Bank, London SE1 8XT
tel 020 7928 3232 (Box Office)
website https://whatson.bfi.org.uk/flare

The London LGBTQIA+ Film Festival presents the best of British and international Queer Cinema in all its forms, from the mainstream to the avant garde. Features and shorts are complemented discussions, interviews, retrospectives and musical performances.

Foyle Film Festival

7-8 Magazine Street, Derry~Londonderry BT48 6HJ
tel 028 7126 0562
email info@nervecentre.org
website www.foylefilmfestival.org
Facebook www.facebook.com/FoyleFilmFest
Twitter @foylefilm
Festival Director Ms Bernie McLaughlin

Established in 1987, the annual Foyle Film Festival is the flagship project of the multi-media Nerve Centre. For 10 days in November, the Foyle Film Festival capitalises on all the technical expertise of the Nerve Centre to produce a unique programme of film, music, digital technologies and education. The festival delivers a programme of art house cinema: international and local premieres, foreign language, documentaries, classic film, industry workshops, presentations, outreach events, as well as a stand-alone education programme which is curriculum focused, and targets all local primary and secondary schools, colleges and universities.

The festival competition has received Oscar and BAFTA recognition for its Light In Motion (LIM) Film Awards. Foyle Film Festival is renowned for attracting top industry professionals to the city, with past guests including high-profile names such as: Brendan Gleeson, Ray Winstone, Richard E. Grant, Jim Sheridan, Danny Boyle, Andrea Arnold, Julie Christie, Neil Jordan, Wim Wenders, Kenneth Branagh, Jenny Agutter, Julien Temple, Christiane Kubrick, Andrew Eaton, Brenda Blethyn, Roddy Doyle, Irvine Welsh, Stephen Frears, Ronan Bennett, Jimmy McGovern, Rob Coleman, Sam Taylor-Wood, Kate Adie, Jonathan Rhys Meyers, Cillian Murphy, Ardal O'Hanlon and Dervla Kirwan.

Leeds International Film Festival

Leeds Town Hall, The Headrow, Leeds LS1 3AD
tel 0113 378 5999
email filmfestival@leeds.gov.uk
website www.leedsfilm.com
Director Chris Fell

Leeds International Film Festival (LIFF) has been presenting extensive programmes of new and unseen cinema from around the world since 1987, supported by a number of events and workshops for those wanting to get into film and TV. The main areas of LIFF include: Official Selection, for new narrative feature films with a focus on emerging filmmaking talent; Cinema Versa, for new documentary features and short films; Fanomenon, for genre filmmaking including comedy, action, horror and science fiction; and Leeds Short Film Awards, which include the Academy Award-qualifying Leeds International Short Film Competition and World Animation Competition, and the British Short Film Competition.

LIFF also has two sister film festivals: Leeds Young Film Festival for children and families each Easter and the INDIs Film Festival for 16-25 year olds every February.

London Independent Film Festival (LIFF)

website www.liff.org
Facebook www.facebook.com/LondonIFF
Twitter @londoniff
Festival Director Erich Schultz

The London Independent Film Festival is the premier event for micro-budget and no-budget films in the UK. LIFF offers a fantastic opportunity for indie filmmakers to showcase their achievements, with spaces reserved for first- and second-time filmmakers and for films that have been overlooked by other events. LIFF presents the best of low-budget filmmaking from around the world and mixes it with relevant industry discussions and targeted social networking events. LIFF's audience is London's sizeable independent filmmaking community; it's an indie film festival for indie filmmakers.

Manchester International Short Film Festival

website www.kinofilm.org.uk

British New Wave and an International Panorama of film provide the main focus to the festival, with a regional showcase, 'Made up North', aimed at promoting films from local and regional filmmakers. Education and Professional Development events are also hosted by the festival and are presented by external curators and organisations.

The festival is open for film submissions each year from January to June, with shortlisted entries being screened at the festival itself in October. Short films on any theme, subject or category and made on any format are eligible, as long as they run no longer than 20 minutes and have been made within the 18 months prior to the festival. The Kinofilm Awards acknowledge outstanding achievements in short film, with awards in many categories. Rules, regulations and application forms are available on the website.

Raindance Film Festival Ltd

10 Craven Street, London WC2N 5PE
tel 020 7930 3412
email info@raindance.co.uk
website www.raindance.org
Producer David Martinez

Running for 2 weeks at the end of September and early October, Raindance is the UK's largest independent film festival and is committed to screening the boldest, most innovative and challenging films from the UK and from around the world. Weighted heavily towards new talent, the festival offers more than 100 features (many of which are directorial debuts), 20 shorts programmes and a wide range of events, workshops and parties.

UK Jewish Film Festival

5.09 Clerkenwell Workshops,
27-31 Clerkenwell Close, London EC1R 0AT
tel 020 3176 0048
email info@ukjewishfilm.org
website www.ukjewishfilm.org
Facebook www.facebook.com/ukjewishfilm
Twitter @ukjewishfilm
Instagram @ukjewishfilm

Established in 1997, the festival is committed to showing a wide variety of films which celebrate the diversity of Jewish cultures and identity, and which reach both Jewish and wider audiences. In addition to film screenings there are education projects and talks with directors. The UK Jewish Film Festival Short Film Fund offers two grant for the production of a short film or video (drama, animation or factual) of a Jewish theme and with a significance both to Jewish and to general public audiences. The UK Jewish Film Short Doc Fund offers 5 filmmakers a budget of £1,000 to make a short documentary about modern British Jewish life, which is then screened at the festival. For application details, consult the website.

Disabled actors
Introduction

This section brings together companies and organisations dedicated to the work of disabled actors and practitioners.

Note: The UK Government recognised BSL as an official language in March 2003, and the Editor acknowledges that many deaf people consider themselves to be members of a linguistic and cultural minority – Deaf with a capital 'D' – rather than disabled people. For the sake of simplicity, however, this book uses a broad definition of disability to encompass Deaf people (although an individual entry will retain the distinction if present in the material provided to us by that company).

With thanks to Silvie Fisch (of The National Disability Arts Forum) and the staff of Graeae Theatre Company for their help in compiling this section.

TRAINING

Apart from the training offered by drama schools, a number of theatre companies and organisations operate training schemes or courses for disabled actors. Many of these schemes are relatively short – a few days or weeks – but Lawnmower's Liberdade, Chickenshed's BTEC National Diploma and Mind the Gap's Staging Change operate over a longer term. Shorter courses are run by (among others) Birds of Paradise, Candoco, and Oily Cart. (Details for all the theatre companies listed here can be found in the *Sources of work* section below.)

SOURCES OF WORK

About Face Theatre Company

15A Church Street, Leominster, Heresfordshite HR6 8NE
tel 01568 616301
email admin@aboutfacetheatre.org.uk
website www.aboutfacetheatre.co.uk
Facebook www.facebook.com/aboutfacetheatreuk

Established in 1995. Work with actors with learning disabilities by offering four different experiences: the performance company, Drama for All (drama without working towards performance), Theatre Skills and Stage Craft. Participants are placed according to interests, abilities and availablity.

Access All Areas Theatre

Bradbury Studios, 138 Kingsland Road, London E2 8DY
tel 020 7613 6445
email hello@accessallareastheatre.org
website https://accessallareastheatre.co.uk

Offer a range of opportunities for creatives with learning disabilities, including a Performance Making Diploma, in collaboration with the Royal Central School of Speech and Drama. Their 'Take Part' programme works intensively with learning disabled adults in East London and beyond to improve well-being and mental health foster inclusion and give voice to a marginalised part of the arts community. Also provides a range of consultancy to help create accessible audiences and authentic representation.

Amici Dance Theatre Company

Turtle Key Arts, Lyric Hammersmith, Lyric Square, King Street, London W6 0QL
tel 020 8964 5060
email amici@turtlekeyarts.org.uk
website www.amicidance.org
Artistic Director Wolfgang Stange

Dance theatre company integrating disabled and non-disabled artists and performers.

Anjali Dance Company

tel (01295) 251909
email info@anjali.co.uk
website www.anjali.co.uk
Facebook www.facebook.com/anjalidance
Twitter @AnjaliDance
Artistic Director Nicole Thomson

Production details: A professional contemporary dance company. All Anjali's dancers have a learning disability. The company produces and tours performances, and undertakes Educational and Outreach work; it is one of the first of its kind in the world. It aims to show that disability is no barrier to creativity. Stages 1-2 productions a year with up to 10 performances over 6-8 venues around the country, such as the Mill Arts Centre (Banbury), Stratford Circus (London) and the Pegasus Theatre (Oxford).

Casting procedures: Casts in-house, does not issue casting breakdowns, and welcomes letters (but not emails) from individuals previously unknown to the company. Welcomes invitations to view individuals' websites, but not showreels.

Apropos Productions Ltd

53 Greek Street, London W1D 3DR
tel 020 7062 9198
email info@aproposltd.com
website www.aproposltd.net
Director Paul DuBois

Company's work: Established in 2004. First feature film completes post-production August 2015, *Dark Signal* (executive producer Neil Marshall). Short films: *The Juror*, *X-Why* and *Cocktail*. Web series: award-winning web series: *A Quick Fortune* and *Le Method* (2016). Script events include *My German Roots are Showing* at the Arcola Theatre, London, starring Miriam Margolyes.

Provides training for local, national and international clients. Key focus is on Organisational Behaviour. Training is provided for incoming actors. Corporate experience is useful but not essential. Actor-base is extended annually through agents, the website and Equity Job Information Service. Clients include: SKANKSA, Sony Computer Entertainment, House of Commons, UBM and the Discovery Network.

Recruitment procedures: Accepts submissions (with CVs and photographs) from actors previously unknown to the company. Disabled actors regularly form part of its teams and are actively encouraged to apply.

Bedazzle Arts

tel 020 4511 4500
email officeadmin@bedazzlearts.org
website www.bedazzlearts.org/bedazzle-inclusive-theatre
Facebook www.facebook.com/Bedazzleprojects/
Instagram @bedazzle_communitytheatre

Theatre company that aims to forefront disabled and Autistic performers. Offers performers with diverse lived experience the opportunity to create ground-breaking theatre.

Birds of Paradise Theatre Company

Old Sheriff Court, Brunswick Street, Glasgow G1 1TF
tel 0141 552 1725
email all@boptheatre.co.uk
website www.boptheatre.co.uk
Artistic Directors Robert Softley Gale

Birds of Paradise is a force for change in Scottish theatre, creating world class projects and performances that place disabled artists centre stage. BOP's artistic vision is of a culture where disabled artists are recognised for the excellence of their work, celebrated for the stories they bring to the stage and are a vital part of the artistic landscape of Scotland.

BOP is the only professional, disability-led theatre company in Scotland and they exist to:

• make world class, innovative and accessible work using Creative Access approaches that are made by disabled and non-disabled artists, writers and theatre-makers drawn from diverse cultures to reach a wide demographic nationally and internationally;
• play a key strategic role in Scotland's theatre ecology, and wider art scene, by supporting the sector to nurture the next generation of disabled artists, performers and audiences through addresing barriers to opportunities and involving disabled people in the processes.

Previous productions include: *Role Shift* by Lesley Hart; *Purposeless Movements* by Robert Softley Gales; *Crazy Jane* by Nicola McCartney; *Wendy Hoose* by Johnny McKnight; *The Farce of Circumstance* by Tom Lannon; *The Resistible Rise of Arturo Ui* by Bertolt Brecht; *Tongues* by Sam Shephard and Joseph Chaikin; *Working Legs* by Alistair Gray; *Playing for Keeps* by Archie Hind; *Merman* by Susan McClymont and Dave Buchanan; *Twelve Black Candles* by Des Dillon; *The Irish Giant* by Garry Robson; *Brazil 12 Scotland 0* by Ian Stephen; and *Mouth of Silence* by Gerry Loose.

Candoco Dance Company

c/o Mountview, 120 Peckham Hill Street, London SE15 5JT
tel 020 7704 6845
email info@candoco.co.uk
website www.candoco.co.uk
Artistic Director Charlotte Darbyshire

Candoco is a world-leading contemporary dance company. Bridging the mainstream and the experimental, Candoco's bold approach and powerful collaborations create distinctive performances and far-reaching learning experiences. The company celebrates different ways of seeing, of being and of making art, putting it at the forefront of conversations around dance and disability. Candoco regularly commissions artists and choreographers to create dance works that tour nationally and internationally. It also runs a variety of training courses, residencies and workshops, and Cando2 – Candoco's Youth Dance Company.

Chickenshed Theatre

Chase Side, Southgate, London N14 4PE
tel 020 8292 9222 (181001 020 8292 9222 Typetalk)
email susanj@chickenshed.org.uk
website www.chickenshed.org.uk
Facebook www.facebook.com/chickenshed

Twitter @CHICKENSHED_UK
Instagram @chickenshed_uk
Managing Director Louise Perry *Director of Education and Training* Paul Morrall *Senior Creative Producers* Dave Carey, Jonny Morton

Chickenshed makes beautiful and inspirational theatre, where imagination translates into empowerment. By bringing together people of all ages and from all backgrounds we produce outstanding theatre that entertains, inspires, challenges and educates both audiences and participants alike.

Using the power of performing arts Chickenshed helps people reach their full potential and feel accepted. We create a truly inclusive environment where people don't stigmatise, label or disregard, but accept and welcome difference.

Chickenshed's vision is a society that celebrates diversity and enables every individual to flourish.

For more company information see the Chickenshed Theatre entry in the *Middle and Smaller-scale companies'* section, page 185.

In addition the company runs:

• An inclusive theatre education workshop programme for more than 800 members from the ages of 5 upwards
• 3 nationally accredited education courses
• Community Outreach projects in the UK and internationally
• A growing number of satellite 'sheds' nationally and internationally
• Training in inclusive practice through workshops and seminars for a range of professionals from a range of fields including education, social services and health,

Cutting Edge Theatre
6 Albion Terrace, Edinburgh EH7 5QX
tel 0131 652 0968
email info@cuttingedgetheatre.co.uk
website http://cuttingedgetheatre.co.uk

Established in 1995. Creative organisation working with and for those who share one or more protected characteristics defined by the Equality Act 2010. This includes projects and productions across Scotland and abroad, and the Inspire programme.

Dark Horse
Lawrence Batley Theatre, Queen's Street, Huddersfield HD1 2SP
tel 01484 484441
email info@darkhorsetheatre.co.uk
website www.darkhorsetheatre.co.uk
Artistic Lead Amy Cunningham

Production details: Established in 2000. Production company exploring a range of projects that include actors with learning disabilities and promote inclusive working practices. Approximately 1 production per year touring to 10-15 venues, including arts centres and theatres in Yorkshire, the North West and internationally. Roughly 5-8 actors are used in each production.

Casting procedures: Occasionally uses freelance casting directors. Does not welcome unsolicited CVs. Actively encourages applications from disabled actors and promotes the use of inclusive casting. Offers Equity-approved contracts.

Deafinitely Theatre
PO Box 1160, Wembley HA9 1LQ
tel 020 7387 3586
email info@deafinitelytheatre.co.uk
website www.deafinitelytheatre.co.uk
Facebook www.facebook.com/deafinitelytheatre
Twitter @DeafinitelyT
Instagram @deafinitelytheatre

Artistic Director Paula Garfield

Established in 2002 to create theatre for deaf and hearing audiences, the company continues to be deaf-led with a bilingual focus - in British Sign Language and spoken English - which means the work remains accessible to both deaf and hearing people. Deafinitely Theatre also runs an extensive education and training programme, which includes a youth theatre, CPD for emerging and established artists and an innovative Hub programme. It has produced over 40 shows across the UK in the past seventeen years. Recent productions include: Everyday (New Diorama Theatre, Birmingham Rep, York Theatre Royal and Northern Stage, 2022); *4.48 Pyschosis* (New Diorama Theatre and Derby Playhouse, 2018 and 2019), winner of Broadway World UK Award for Best Direction of a New Production of a Play; *Contractions* (ND2, 2017), winner of the Off West End Award for Best Production.

DIY Theatre Company
The Angel Centre, 1 St Philips Place, Chapel Street, Salford, Lancs. M3 6FA
email diytheatre@gmail.com
website www.diytheatre.org.uk
Facebook www.facebook.com/DIYTheatreco
Twitter @diytheatreco
Instagram @diytheatreco

Established in 1994. A theatre company creating accessible theatre and educational projects for performers with learning disabilities.

Extant
86-90 Paul Street, London EC2A 4NE
tel 020 7820 3737
email info@extant.org.uk
website https://extant.org.uk
Facebook www.facebook.com/pages/extant/358300895909
Twitter @extantltd
Instagram @extantltd

Disabled actors

Founded in 1997. A theatre company for visually impaired performers, practitioners and audiences. As well as creating productions, Extant leds art community seminars and research in access and technology. Email to register interest about participating in future projects.

Face Front

52 Market Square, Edmonton Green,
London N9 0TZ
tel 020 8350 3461
email info@facefront.org
website www.facefront.org
Instagram @facefronttheatre

Founded in 1998. Inclusive and accessible theatre for schools and the public with disabled and non-disabled performers. Working across London and touring nationally.

Fingersmiths

website www.fingersmiths.org.uk
Twitter @fingersmiths1
Instagram @fingersmiths_theatre

Touring theatre company with Deaf and hearing actors. Uses phyiscal theatre with British Sign Language and spoken English to bring to life 20th Century plays.

formidAbility

tel 07968 436588
email info@formidability.org
website www.formidability.org
Facebook www.facebook.com/AbilityFormid
Twitter @AbilityFormid
Instagram @FormidAbility
Artistic Director Joanne Roughton-Arnold

Opera company that puts accessibility at the centre of their process, working for inclusion on stage and off.

Graeae Theatre Company

Bradbury Studios, 138 Kingsland Road,
London E2 8DY
tel 020 7613 6900
email info@graeae.org
website www.graeae.org
Artistic Director Jenny Sealey

Production details: Founded in 1980 and artistically led by Jenny Sealey, Graeae boldly places D/deaf and disabled actors centre stage.

Graeae's signature aesthetic is the compelling creative integration of sign language, captioning and audio description, which engages with both disabled and non-disabled audiences. Championing accessibility and providing a platform for new generations of artists, Graeae leads the way in pioneering, trail-blazing theatre. Graeae also run an extensive programme of creative learning opportunities throughout the year, training and developing the next generation of D/deaf and disabled artists. These programmes include Write to Play and Ensemble.

Recent productions and co-productions include: *Reasons to be Cheerful, Cosmic Scallies, The House of Bernarda Alba, The Solid Life of Sugar Water, Blood Wedding, The Threepenny Opera, Belonging, Blasted* and *Bent*. Spectacular outdoor productions include *This is Not for You, The Limbless Knight, Prometheus Awakes* and *The Iron Man*.

Graeae are strategic partners on the Ramps on the Moon consortium and are a National Portfolio Organisation (NPO) of Arts Council England.

Hijinx

Wales Millennium Centre, Bute Place,
Cardiff CF10 5AL
tel 029 2030 0331
email info@hijinx.org.uk
website www.hijinx.org.uk
Facebook www.facebook.com/HijinxTheatre
Twitter @HijinxTheatre
Instagram @HijinxTheatre
Artistic Director Ben Pettitt-Wade

Production details: An award-winning not-for-profit professional theatre company. Hijinx always casts actors with learning disabilities and/or Autism in their shows which tour the world.

Offers ITC/Equity-approved contracts and does not subscribe to the Equity Pension Scheme.

Casting procedures: Shows are cast by the Artistic Director. Welcomes letters, CVs and photographs from actors previously unknown to the company. Welcomes applications from disabled and non-disabled actors.

IMPACT Theatre

IMPACT Community Arts Centre,
Ealing Central Sports Ground,
Horsenden Lane South, Perivale UB6 8GP
tel 020 8997 8979
email info@impacttheatre.co
website www.impacttheatre.co
Facebook www.facebook.com/impacttheatreuk
Artistic Director Kim Mughan FRSA

IMPACT (IMagine, Perform And Create Together) Theatre was founded in 1999. It was set up by and for adults with learning disabilities. While not a professional company, IMPACT helps to develop skills of performance and self-expression for its actors, musicians and dancers. Some of our artists are undertaking professional work. IMPACT Theatre stages original productions featuring up to 60 performers with learning disabilities. In addition to the disability arts that IMPACT has become known for in West London, it is now embarking on innovative inclusive arts work.

Krazy Kat Theatre Company

173 Hartington Road, Brighton BN2 3PA
tel 01273 692552
email krazykattheatre@ntlworld.com
website www.krazykattheatre.co.uk
Artistic Director Kinny Gardner

Production details: A children's theatre company founded in 1982, specialising in highly visual forms of theatre that are accessible to Deaf children. Normally tours 2 projects each year with an average annual total of 50 performances and 35 venues. Venues include schools, arts centres, theatres, outdoor venues and community centres throughout UK. In general 2 actors and a technician go on tour and play to audiences aged 3-7. Singing ability, physical theatre skills, British sign language and a driving licence are required. Actors may also be expected to lead workshops. Recent productions include: *A (Midsummer Night's) Dream*, *Petrushka*, *The Pied Piper*, a Victorian *Mikado* and *The Very Magic Flute*.

Casting procedures: Sometimes holds general auditions; actors can write at any time requesting inclusion. Accepts submissions (with CVs and photographs) from actors previously unknown to the company if sent by post. Does not welcome unsolicited emails. Will also accept invitations to view individual actors' websites. Offers non-Equity contracts but at Equity and ITC rates. Actively encourages applications from disabled actors and promotes the use of inclusive casting.

Lawnmowers Independent Theatre Company

Shields Road, Pelaw, Gateshead NE10 0QD
tel 0191 478 9200
email hello@lawnmowerstheatre.com
website www.lawnmowerstheatre.com
Facebook ww.facebook.com/LawnmowersITC
Twitter @LawnmowersITC

Theatre company addressing issues of concern for people with learning difficulties, often with an international dimension. Uses theatre and drama as a means for people with learning difficulties to explore and develop ideas, and help plan and take control of their futures.

Lung Ha

30ʙ Grindlay Street, Edinburgh Eh3 9AX
tel 0131 221 9568
email info@lungha.com
website http://lungha.com
Facebook www.facebook.com/lunghas
Twitter @LungHasTheatre

Scottish theatre company for people with learning disabilities. Auditions for new company members are held annually in the Spring.

Magpie Dance

The Churchill Theatre, High Street,
Bromley BR1 1HA
tel 07942 319815
email admin@magpiedance.org.uk
website www.magpiedance.org.uk
Facebook www.facebook.com/MagpieDance
Twitter @MagpieDance
Instagram @MagpieDance

Magpie Dance is a company for people with learning disabilities. Based in Bromley, Magpie can also deliver workshops to any region in the UK. With an emphasis on ability rather than disability, the company has a national reputation for its exciting approach to inclusive dance.

Mind the Gap

Mind the Gap Studios Bradford, Silk Warehouse, Patent Street, Bradford BD9 4SA
tel (01274) 487390
email arts@mind-the-gap.org.uk
website www.mind-the-gap.org.uk
Executive Director Julia Skelton

Production details: Founded in 1988, Mind the Gap is one of Europe's leading learning disability led companies. It believes in equality and inclusion, and its mission is to dismantle barriers to artistic excellence so that learning-disabled and non-learning-disabled performers can collaborate, and more learning-disabled performers are seen on our stages and screens. The company has 3 main areas of activity:

• Performance and touring: Since 2014, Mind the Gap has created and toured contemporary new work, and developed these into major projects involving multiple activities. The live performance at the centre of *CONTAINED* (2014–17) explored the real-life experiences of nine learning-disabled performers. In 2018–20 the company collaborated with Gecko physical theatre company to create and tour *A Little Space*. Between 2015–20 the company delivered the *Daughters of Fortune* project, including the large-scale outdoor production *ZARA* – a co-production with Walk the Plank.
• Academy: The company's thriving training and professional development supports learning-disabled artists to gain core skills in theatre, music and dance. It supports around 65 aspiring artists through its main programmes each year, and many more through short courses and workshops.
• MTG Studios: Its premises in Bradford offer exemplary access in three spaces equipped for excellence in performing arts. The company occasionally hosts work by visiting companies, and provides support for local artists and organisations through the Open Space programmes.

Casting procedures: Casts in-house and open recruitment. When seeking to recruit an actor from outside the core company, the company contacts agents, and advertises in specialist arts media. Welcomes letters (with CVs and photographs) as well as showreels and invitations to view individuals' websites. Welcomes approaches from people from diverse backgrounds, particularly those who are currently under-represented in the arts. Our contracts comply with Equity standards.

Oily Cart Company

Smallwood School Annexe, Smallwood Road,
London SW17 0TW
tel 020 8672 6329
email oilies@oilycart.org.uk
website www.oilycart.org.uk
Artistic Director Ellie Griffiths

Production details: One of the leading theatre
companies in the UK creating highly interactive
multi-sensory performances for and with the very
young (6 months to 6 years) and young people (aged
3–19) with complex needs and/or who are on the
autistic spectrum. Tours national and international
venues like theatres and arts centres with early years
shows, and takes its special-needs work to special
schools around the UK.Recent productions include:
In A Pickle (sheep's-eye view of Shakespeare's *The
Winter's Tale* for under 5s); *Hippity Hop*; *Kubla Khan*
and *Splish Splash* – an interactive show performed in
hydrotherapy pools

Casting procedures: Casting breakdowns are
available on the website **www.oilycart.org.uk** and the
Arts Jobs website **www.artsjobs.org.uk**. Offers ITC/
Equity-approved contracts. Actively encourages
applications from D/deaf or disabled actors and
promotes the use of inclusive casting.

Ramps on the Moon

www.rampsonthemoon.co.uk

Collaborative partnership, led by New Wosley
Theatre, of six theatres (Birmingham Repertory,
Theatre Royal Stratford East, Nottingham Playhouse,
Leeds Playhouse and Sheffield Theatres) and two
assocaite partners (Wiltshire Creative and RTYDS).
The partnership produces an annual, large-scale
touring production, led by one of the partnership
theatres that aims to normalise the presence of D/
deaf and disabled people on and off stage.

Salamanda Tandem

52 Albert Road, Nottingham NG2 5GS
tel 0845 293 2989
email info@salamanda-tandem.org
website www.salamanda-tandem.org
Artistic Director Isabel Jones

Producer of contemporary art works, creative
environments and sensory performances, where
people can choose to observe or become part of the
artwork itself. Works with a wide spectrum of people,
and in particular people with disabilities. Strong
advocate for ethical practice in arts and health.
Publishes articles and conducts training and
professional education.

Solar Bear

The Old Sheriff Court, c/o Scottish Youth Theatre,
105 Brunswick Street, Glasgow G1 1TF
email angela@solarbear.org.uk
website https://solar.org.uk
Facebook www.facebook.com/solar.bear

Twitter @TheSolarBear
Creative Director Jonathan Lloyd *General Manager*
Angela Coates

Established in 2002. Theatre company working with
deaf and hearing actors, theatremakers, artists and
young people. Their work includes establishing the
BA Performance in BSL and Enlgish at Royal
Conservatoire of Scotland; setting up deaf theatre
clubs and awareness training, producing theatre and
showcasing work of deaf and hearing professionals.

Spare Tyre Theatre Company

The Albany, Douglas Way, Deptford,
London SE8 4AG
tel 020 8692 4446 (ext 273)
email info@sparetyre.org
website www.sparetyre.org
Instagram @sparetyretheatre
Artistic Director Rebecca Manson Jones

Production details:

• Work with older people aged 60+, outreach
workshops for older people, and interactive
storytelling for people with dementia. Work with
carers.
• Work with people with learning disabilities.
• Work with women who have experienced violence.
• Work with people with long Covid and other long-
term health conditions.

London and nationwide. Skills required from actors
include workshop-leading and facilitation skills,
experience of working with community groups and a
sensitivity to, and understanding of, relevant issues.

Casting procedures: Casting breakdowns are
published and on the website. Unsolicited approaches
at other times – including CVs, showreels and
invitations to view individuals' websites – are
discouraged. Offers ITC/Equity-approved contracts.
Actively encourages applications from disabled actors
and promotes the use of inclusive casting.

StopGAP Dance Company

Farnham Maltings, Bridge Square, Farnham,
Surrey GU9 7QR
tel 01252 745443
website www.stopgapdance.com
Artistic Director Lucy Bennett

A vibrant integrated dance company that includes
disabled and non-disabled dancers. It challenges
traditional notions about dance by using each
dancer's physical and intellectual potential as a
starting point for creating new work. "We work from
a philosophy of physical, psychological and social
integration. In so doing, we recognise and celebrate
individuality and the differences between people,
while continually seeking artistic and technical
excellence in all that we do."

Taking Flight Theatre

Chapter Arts Centre, Market Road, Canton,
Cardiff CF5 1QZ

tel 029 2023 0020
website www.takingflighttheatre.org.uk
Facebook www.facebook.com/TakingFlightco
Twitter @takingflightco
Instagram @takingflighttheatre
Artistic Director Elise Davison *Executive Director*
Louise Ralph

Founded in 2008. Produces theatre productions for
Deaf, disabled and non-disabled performers. Runs
inclusive professional training courses and mentoring
schemes for deaf and disabled artists.

Theatre Without Walls
Hillsborough, County Down BT26 6AS
tel 02892 82125
email hello@theatrewithoutwalls.org
website www.theatrewithoutwalls.org
Directors Genevieve Swift, Jason Parkes

Company's work: Established in 2002. Award-
winning producing theatre company with an active
training/corporate wing, working in the public and
private sector. Also produces television and corporate
films. Clients include: National Trust, Gloucestershire
Local Authority, Apollo, BBC and The Prince's Trust.
Training is provided for incoming actors in the form
of workshops and rehearsals in forum, role-play and
interactive drama. Incoming actors require good
improvisational skills.

Recruitment procedures: Actors are recruited
through agents and Equity Job Information Service.
Disabled actors regularly form part of the team and
are actively encouraged to apply. See also the
company's entry under *Middle and smaller-scale
companies* on page 209.

Touchdown Dance
Waterside Arts Centre, Sale M33 7ZF
tel 0161 912 5760
email info@touchdowndance.co.uk
website www.touchdowndance.co.uk
Facebook www.facebook.com/touchdowndance
Twitter @touchdowndance
Director Katy Dymoke

Touchdown Dance provides workshops based on
contact improvisation for visually impaired people.
They tour worldwide as a dance company, working
with both disability rights organisations and
mainstream dance theatre groups.

VisABLE People Ltd
93 High Street, Evesham WR11 4DU
tel 020 3488 1998 *mobile* 07729 738317
email office@visablepeople.com
website www.visablepeople.com
Facebook www.facebook.com/visablepeople
Twitter @visablepeople
Instagram @visablepeople
Agents Louise Dyson MBE

Founded in 1994, VisABLE is the world's first agency
representing only disabled people for professional

engagements. It represents artistes with a wide range
of impairments and in every age group, including
children. 2 agents represent around 150 artistes in all
areas of acting, including presenting.

Does not welcome performance notices. Happy to
receive applications from disabled actors via VisABLE
website only. Showreels should always be via a link
sent by email. Also happy to receive invitations to
view individual actors' websites. Recommends the
London photographer Richard Bailey. *Commission*:
10%-17.5% (commercials: 20% agency fee).

Wolf + Water Arts Company
The Plough Arts Centre, 9/11 Fore Street,
Torrington, Devon EX38 8HQ
mobile 07846 935 949
email office@wolfandwater.org
website www.wolfandwater.org

Wolf + Water Arts Company has brought its creative
and therapeutic approaches to a wide variety of
groups locally, nationally and internationally. These
groups have included people with learning
difficulties; people with mental health issues; people
in conflict situations; offenders; communities; young
people at risk; children with life-threatening illnesses
and their families; and staff groups working with all
the above. The company produces original topical
performances for conferences and for tour, and
provides a wide range of training courses for those
wishing to use drama and arts techniques in special-
needs situations. Work has taken the company
throughout the UK, the Republic of Ireland,
Scandinavia, the Middle East and the Balkans.

ARTS ORGANISATIONS

Ableize Arts
website www.ableize.com/disabled-arts

A selection of disabled arts sites, from theatre and
dance to visual arts. The Ableize site also features a
wide varity of links, from accommodation and travel
to support groups and employment and benefits.
Posts are both new and archived.

Arcadea
Kelburn House, 7-19 Mosley Street,
Newcastle NE1 1YE
tel 0191 222 0708
email info@arcadea.org
website www.arcadea.org
Facebook www.facebook.com/ArcadeaArts

Arcadea was founded by disabled people in 1991 to
address the inequality of disabled people in the arts.

Artlink Central
Stirling Old Town Jail, Saint John's Street, FK8 1EA
tel 01786 450971
email info@artlinkcentral.org
website www.artlinkcentral.org
Facebook www.facebook.com/artlinkcentral

Twitter @ArtlinkCentral
Instagram @ArtlinkCentral

Established in February 1988, Artlink Central is a registered charity founded in the belief that involvement in the arts is life-enhancing and should be available to all. It enables a wide range of disabled and/or marginalised people to work with experienced professional artists on high-quality arts projects in the Stirling, Falkirk and Clackmannanshire areas of Central Scotland.

Artlink Edinburgh

13A Spittal Street, Edinburgh
tel 0131 229 3555
website www.artlinkedinburgh.co.uk

Artlink's Edinburgh branch.

Carousel

Community Base, 113 Queens Road,
Brighton BN1 3XG
tel 01273 234734
email enquiries@carousel.org.uk
website www.carousel.org.uk
Director Liz Hall

Carousel helps learning disabled artists develop and manage their creative lives, true to their voice and vision, challenging expectations of what great art is and who can create it.

Carousel believes that learning disabled artists make a vital contribution to the world we live in. It is an organisation that puts learning disabled people in control of their art, in film, music, performance and production. Carousel's work is planned, managed and delivered by learning disabled teams and 50% of the board members have a learning disability.

DaDaFest

The Bluecoat, School Lane, Liverpool L1 3BX
tel 0151 707 1733
email info@dadafest.co.uk
website www.dadafest.co.uk
Facebook @DaDaFest
Twitter @DaDaFest
Artistic Director Ruth Gould

DaDa-Disability is an innovative and cutting edge disability and Deaf arts organisation based in Liverpool, established in 1984. Its vision is to inspire, develop and celebrate talent and excellence in disability and Deaf arts. The organisation's work covers the whole of the North West of the UK, as well as operating on an international scale. DaDaFest is an integral part of the campaign for greater equality and access for disabled, Deaf and neurodivergent people in the arts.

Disability Arts Cymru

Sbectrwm, Bwlch Road, Fairwater, Cardiff CF5 3EF
tel 07726 112784
email post@dacymru.co.uk
website www.disabilityarts.cymru
Facebook www.facebook.com/disabilityartscymru

Twitter @DACymru
Instagram @DACymru
Director Ruth Fabby

Disability Arts Cymru is the lead disability arts organisation in Wales, and the only organisation in Wales providing Disability Equality Training (DET) specifically for arts providers. DAC works with the arts sector to create career progression routes for emerging/professional disabled artists across all arts forms and to build a future where there is equality of access and opportunity for disabled people. A number of documents are available from the website, which offer advice on a range of subjects including access issues for touring companies.

Disability Arts Online (DAO)

c/o Lighthouse, 28 Kensington Street,
Brighton BN1 4AJ
mobile 07751 175389
email admin@disabilityarts.online
website www.disabilityarts.online
Facebook www.facebook.com/disabilityarts.online
Twitter @disabilityarts
Instagram @disabilityarts

Disability Arts Online offers a platform for the wider arts sector to engage with disabled artists, writers and performers by sharing opportunities on their listings pages, reading about artists' work on blogs and editorial and with partnerships and training facilitated by DAO's consultancy services.

Diverse City

3 Manwell Drive, Swanage, Dorset BH19 2RB
info@diversecity.org.uk
website www.DiverseCity.org.uk
Facebook www.facebook.com/DiverseCity1
Twitter @diversecity1
Instagram @diverse_city

Advocates for and delivers diversity and equality of opportunity in culture and learning.

Prism Arts

Central Methodist Hall, 5 Market Street,
Carlisle CA3 8QJ
tel (01228) 587691
email office@prismarts.org.uk
website www.prismarts.org.uk
Director Catherine Coulthard

Promotes art without barriers through diverse access to creative arts activities in Cumbria. Runs Studio Theatre for learning-disabled performers.

Shape

Floor 2 Peckham Library, 122 Peckham Hill Street,
Peckham, London SE15 5JR
tel 020 7424 7330
email info@shapearts.org.uk
website www.shapearts.org.uk
Facebook www.facebook.com/shapearts

Twitter @shapearts
Instagram @shapearts

Shape's mission is to provide skills, opportunities and support for disabled artists, individuals and cultural organisations and to help build a more inclusive cultural sector.

Think Bigger
tel 07538 194422
email enquiries@thinkbigger.org.uk
website www.thinkbigger.uk.com
Facebook www.facebook.com/thinkbigger.uk
Twitter @thinkBIGGER!
Instagram @thinkBigger!

Training and consultancy designed to build equality in screen industries.

University of Atypical
109-113 Royal Avenue, Belfast BT1 1FF
tel 028 9023 9450
email administration@universityofatypical.org
website www.universityofatypical.org
Chief Executive Officer Damien Coyle

University of Atypical is a disabled-led arts charity, taking an empowerment-based approach towards supporting disabled and D/deaf people's involvement in the arts. The organisation specialises in developing and promoting the work of disabled and D/deaf artists and in reaching disabled and D/deaf audiences.

RIGHTS, ADVICE AND SUPPORT

Access All
website www.bbc.co.uk/programmes/p02r6yqw

The BBC's collection of stories shared by people with disabilities about their experiences. Includes videos, a podcast and links to resources and support.

Creative Diversity Network
35-47 Bethnal Green, London E1 6LA
email enquiries@creativediversitynetwork.com
website https://creativediversitynetwork.com/
Twitter @tweetCDN

Executive Director Deborah Williams

Enables UK broadcasting industry to increase diversity and inspire inclusion. Incentives include Doubling Disability and Diamond, a system used by the BBC, ITV, Channel 4, Paramont, UKTV and Sky to obtain diversity data on their programme commissioning.

Directgov
website www.direct.gov.uk/disability

The government's Public Services portal, with links to information and advice on employment, home and housing options, financial support, health, education and training, rights and obligations, transport, travel and caring for someone.

PACT Diversity
3rd Floor Fitzrovia House, 153-157 Cleveland Street, London W1T 6QW
tel 020 7380 8230
email info@pact.co.uk
website https://diversity.pact.co.uk
Twitter @PactUK
Chief Executive John McVay

PACT is the UK trade association (see page 426) that represents and promotes the commercial interests of independent feature film, television, animation and interactive media companies. PACT Diversity hosts a range of information and resources to promote diversity in screen industries.

Skill: National Bureau for Students with Disabilities
Skill closed on April 4th 2011. Following a period of financial difficulty, Skill's Board of Trustees decided it was no longer viable to keep the charity open. Some parts of the Skill website (**www.skill.org.uk**) are still available as a free information archive to disabled people, parents and key advisers.

Disabled actors

Opportunities for disabled actors

Jamie Beddard

The plethora of journeys and experiences of disabled performers over the past 30 years has ranged from the lonely, demoralising, and depressing to the downright bizarre. The barriers encountered far outreach the regular obstacles preventing non-disabled actors from learning, and plying their trade. Performance attributes of technique, voice, improvisation and movement seem distant concepts when you cannot get through the doors of drama school, producers baulk at the idea of employing disabled performers, and most training and employment opportunities are based around strict notions of 'the classical actor'. This is altogether surprising in the creative industries, which should surely celebrate uniqueness, individuality and diversity. However, where once black actors were denied access to stage and screen, so those with different bodies have fought similar battles for opportunity, acknowledgement and representation. This, against a backdrop in which esteemed, non-disabled actors regularly pick up Oscars for their touching portrayal of characters with disability: Daniel Day Lewis in *My Left Foot*; Jamie Foxx in *Ray*; John Voight in *Coming Home*; Tom Hanks in *Forrest Gump* – there's a long list, and they are one-dimensional replications of impediments, far outweighing any considerations around full and meaningful characterisations. Authenticity has been a label seldom attached to the portrayal of disability in the mainstream.

Personal anecdotes are perhaps best served by exploring the issues faced by disabled performers, as, until recently, there have been no formal routes of progression into the industry. Those few who have made the periphery have tended to have random and short-lived paths, based around such indeterminates as maverick directors, word of mouth or, as in my particular case, luck. The groundbreaking film *Skalligrigg* – a road movie in which a rag tag of disabled characters take to the road on a mythical quest – threw my staid career path into chaos, and levered a window (previously boarded up!) into performance. In the absence of disabled actors, many first-timers with no experience were suddenly thrust onto a film set; I thought the sound-boom was a cheap prop! 'Rough diamonds' probably most accurately described those of us fortunate enough to get such a break, and, for me, the film opened up a completely new, and exciting, world. A mixture of bluff, wide-eyed enthusiasm and no little begging had to suffice in the absence of any formal training.

This 'new and exciting world' was also populated by baffling and disheartening prejudices, and initial enthusiasm soon became tinged with disappointment and anger. A casting director for *Eastenders* once informed me that a disabled character – played by a disabled actor, heaven forbid! – would place the programme in the realm of freak show. So much for diverse communities and gritty realism! This attitude is unfortunately still painfully prevalent, and theatre directors are worried that their audiences will be put off by seeing a disabled person on stage.

I contacted Graeae Theatre Company – a company that had been going since the early 1980s, and was run by, and for, actors with sensory and physical disabilities. Graeae had become accustomed to (and was hardened by) irksome battles against prevalent prejudices and barriers. I found a group of like-minded individuals who were challenging these ridiculous, outdated and offensive attitudes, and were determined to pursue careers considered impractical and unrealistic. They were developing, writing and performing theatre as does any small-scale company; sometimes very good, and sometimes not so good. However, the normal critical faculties brought to bear on other companies seemed strangely absent from assessment of Graeae's work, with emphasis on the 'oh so strange impairments' rather than art. The *Independent*, when reviewing Graeae's 2002 production – *Peeling* – came up with such helpful insights as, "Beaty is four feet tall; Coral has tiny limbs and a torso about the same size as her head." Apart from gross inaccuracies, the obvious offence to the individual actors involved and the banality of such revelations, what relevance has this to the art? Hopefully, the paying public didn't recoil in shock at this assembled collection of bizarre physical specimens!

I always yearned for a bad – rather than ignorant, ill informed and avoiding – review, because this would suggest a considered judgement based on the same criteria as any other performer. Undoubtedly, I have been involved in a few 'turkeys', and they should be recognised as such! However, fascination with individual impediment always seems the central tenet of any assessment of performance. Perhaps it would be interesting to apply such criteria to the wider acting fraternity – solely judging Woody Allen on his glasses, Tom Hanks on his stature, or Kenneth Williams on his nasal inflection.

Over the years, the profile of Graeae, and of disabled performers in general, has grown, and there has been a gradual acceptance that it is no longer acceptable to marginalise their talents, aspirations and contributions. In many ways the Arts have lagged behind society in taking the first steps towards embracing and committing to diversity. Although, there has, in many quarters, been a genuine will to broaden participation, the stick of the Disability Discrimination Act has been instrumental in initiating fundamental appraisal and change. The possibility of legal challenges has shaken many organisations, venues and makers from their comfy inertia. Even tokenism is preferable to apartheid!

Drama schools, in particular, have found the concept of students with disability difficult to grasp, but the introduction of the Dance & Drama Awards (DaDAs) has started the process of drama schools thinking not only about the physical access to their buildings, but also about the attitudinal access, and ways to promote inclusive teaching. This is very exciting, and will no doubt pave the way for young disabled people to go through mainstream training rather than be reliant on Graeae.

While the process of change will take time (especially the attitudinal aspect), Graeae has had to respond to the obvious demand by setting up the training course in conjunction with London Metropolitan University. This course offers all the elements found in drama schools, and provides the skills, disciplines and training that were denied people of my age. Lack of sufficiently trained and experienced disabled actors has long been an excuse for the 'cripping up' of non-disabled actors, while training providers continually stress the unlikelihood of disabled graduates sustaining careers in the industry. A classic chicken-and-egg situation, in which aspirant disabled performers are denied entrance at all levels. However, the percentage of those who have graduated through Missing Piece, and have gone into the industry, compares favourably with other drama schools, and Graeae is frequently approached by casting directors looking for disabled talent. So, young people with disabilities do share the same aspirations as any others; there is an increasing demand for such actors; and the institutions are failing to shoulder responsibility.

Missing Piece is fulfilling this vacuum, and has now been running since 2000. The nine-month (September to May) intensive training allows disabled students to work with a wide range of theatre practitioners – both specialist and mainstream. The course can act as a foundation course to further education or drama school – access and will permitting! – or, as is often the case, a direct gateway into the industry. Academic and practical elements of performance are covered, and opportunities for showcasing and touring afforded. Recent years have culminated in professional touring productions of *Mother Courage* and *George Dandin*, and many relationships have been brokered between Graeae's performers and directors, producers and casting directors. There is a crossover with the Performing Arts degree at London Metropolitan, with disabled performers working alongside, and in collaboration with, tutors and students at the University. As well as the main Missing Piece course, Graeae run a series of taster workshops throughout the year for prospective actors.

So strides are being made by Graeae, and by other companies; the excuses and barriers preventing inclusion are slowly being dismantled. There are viable careers for those with the talent, determination and thick skin when necessary.

BBC has set up a talent fund for disabled actors to try and address dated attitudes, and to encourage writers to write storylines which are not always hospital-based or about the whole 'disability thing'!

However the failure of mainstream films such as *Inside I'm Dancing*, which continue to propagate stereotypes and exclusion – with all the main disabled characters played by non-disabled actors – will hopefully mark a sea-change in attitudes and imaginations among creators. The existing, and perspective, body of talent out there no longer allows for petty excuses or wilful misrepresentation. Disabled people, like any others, can make good, bad or indifferent performers, and should be judged as such. However, we have a right to expect the same opportunities, treatments and prospects as all. Banging the door down has become boring – just let us in. It's not rocket science!

Jamie Beddard is an actor, writer and director. Involved with Graeae since 1991, he was Associate Director of the company for some years. He is currently working as a freelance director and co-editor of *DAIL* magazine. Graeae productions 2006/7 include *Blasted* by Sarah Kane, touring March to May; *Once Beyond These Walls, A Girl* by Richard Cameron, touring October to November; and *Whiter Than Snow* by Mike Kenny – a co-production with Birmingham Rep, touring February to April 2007. For full details, visit the website **www.graeae.org.**

Resources
Introduction

This section covers practical items (and sources of more detailed help and advice) that are an absolute necessity to an actor. Some may be irrelevant to you – for instance, you may feel as though you could never have the organisational skills to set up your own company. Others are essential to all actors: good photographs, for example. Whatever your needs, time taken to formulate clearly your requirements before approaching any of the contacts listed below will be time well spent.

Equity

Equity is the only trade union to represent performers and people working creatively across the entire spectrum of arts and entertainment, both live and recorded. The main function of Equity is to negotiate minimum terms and conditions of employment throughout the whole world of entertainment, and to ensure that these take account of social and economic changes. They look to the future as well, negotiating agreements to embrace the new and emerging technologies which affect performers as well as at national level by lobbying government and other bodies on issues of paramount importance to the membership. In addition we operate at an international level through the Federation of International Artists which Equity helped to establish, the International Committee for Artistic Freedom, and through agreements with sister unions overseas.

As well as these core activities, Equity strives to provide a wide range of services for members so that they are eligible for a whole host of benefits which are continually being revised and developed. These include helplines, job information, insurance cover, members' pension scheme, charities and others. (For more information, visit the Equity website **www.equity.org.uk**. For details of Equity's Job Information Service, see entry under Spotlight, casting directories and information services.)

Equity
Head Office, Guild House, Upper St Martins Lane, London WC2H 9EG
tel 020 7379 6000
email info@equity.org.uk
website www.equity.org.uk

A trade union of more than 47,000 performers and creative practitioners united in the fight for fair terms and conditions in the workplace. Provides assistance with work, pay and contracts. There are regional offices in Manchester, Cardiff, Glasgow and Belfast. The tax and welfare rights helpline can be contacted on **020 7670 0223** and **helpline@equity.org.uk**.

North West and Isle of Man
Express Networks, 1 George Leigh Street, Manchester M4 5DL
tel 0161-244 5995
email northwestengland@equity.org.uk

Scotland and Northern Ireland
114 Union Street, Glasgow G1 3QQ
tel 0141-248 2472 *fax* 0141-248 2473
email scotland@equity.org.uk
email northernireland@equity.org.uk

Wales and South West England
Transport House, 1 Cathedral Road, Cardiff CF1 9SD
tel 029-2039 7971
email wales@equity.org.uk
email southwestengland@equity.org.uk

Act For Change

Kobna Holdbrook-Smith

Why?

Actors' faces and voices ultimately represent the months or sometimes years that go into making a production. In January 2014, a UK broadcaster released a trailer for its coming season. Each room in a warm, bustling house showed scenes or characters from forthcoming dramas. Out of eleven people, none was deaf, disabled or of colour; only three were women, none of whom spoke any words and one was weeping. What made that trailer possible? It had been conceived, collated, approved and aired without anyone noticing the exclusions. Again.

Ideas about art are ideas about society and erasing people from our imaginings and artworks, deliberately or not, is harmful on two levels. Clearly it excludes people from careers or involvement in the arts industries, and there are not many good reasons to carry on with that. The second, deeper level of harm is that this unpeopling of imagined worlds reflects a dark desire for the same thing to happen in real life. That is well worth opposing. The Act For Change Project started when the actor Danny Lee Wynter saw that trailer and felt compelled to gather like-minded people from the industry.

What?

The Act For Change Project works to enhance diversity and inclusion in Britain's live and recorded arts. This includes all the people and characteristics missed from the trailer mentioned above as well as LGBT+ people, those above a certain age and those from varying economic backgrounds and more.

We don't yet have staff, just a board of trustees and our committee. The success of the Act For Change Project, in terms of awareness and visibility, is the direct result of actors, whose faces and voices are loved by many people, donating their time to it. We have been based at the National Theatre (NT) in London since 2015. We were invited there after our Diversity in Theatre event because the NT wanted to commit actively to diversity. The NT fully supported Charlotte Bevan transferring from its casting department to act as lead on inclusion and difference. She has been superb, driven and detailed in the execution of her new role. She set up regular internal talk sessions focusing on a different group or diversity issue each week. They were well attended, well supported and seem to be having a lasting positive effect. Morale appears to be higher as people have found friends and colleagues they might not otherwise have encountered. Charlotte has also sought out disabled actors previously unknown to the NT, calling them in to meet her casting department colleagues, and recording auditions onto a proper database. Look out for our podcast interview with Charlotte so you can hear more about what informs, influences and inspires her to do this work.

How does Act For Change work?

Campaigning keeps supporters and the public informed. We campaign by producing videos of testimonies, interviews and discussions; by publishing our newsletters; by using social media to highlight issues, discuss news and share information; and we work with print and online publications to make more formal comment. One of our early hashtags was #KeepTheConversationGoing because conversation is key, rather than each of us in our lonely silos being scared to get things wrong.

Advocacy is behind-the-scenes work, demonstrating and sharing better ways of thinking and working. Because many of us are actors, we have been able to access a wide range of links to different people and groups. It has also meant direct and meaningful contact with TV commissioners, theatres and producers, strong partnership with Equity, and alliances with organisations like Tonic, and Equal Representation For Actresses. These consultations happen on an organisation-by-organisation basis and can be one morning, one day or one month, casual or formal. Some of our activity is published in the Act For Change newsletter along with that of our allies and co-campaigners.

Policy shifts organisational thinking and overlaps with advocacy. Despite many schemes, pledges and initiatives, things only seem to move forward slowly, or they slip back. When we had Jenny Sealey, Artistic Director of Graeae Theatre, on our 2015 event panel she said she had sat on thirty-seven different panels over eighteen years. It shouldn't take that amount of dedication to combat the culture of exclusion. Only policies can really prevent that. They find out how and where to make positive changes, create conditions that support those changes, build them into the running and operations of an organisation.

Monitoring refers to gathering data to inform policy. It shows which groups, people or characteristics are being under- or over-used. It is vital that people fill in equality monitoring forms as ignoring them really bruises the effort. No data, no difference. According to figures released by creative skillset and amplified by Lenny Henry's fine speeches at BAFTA, 2014, and updated at the Houses of Parliament 2017, the British, Asian and minority ethnic (BAME) workforce in the UK TV industry has declined rather than increased, going from 6.7 per cent (2009) to 5.4 per cent (2014) and this is despite 13 per cent of the total UK population being BAME.

Figures for deaf and disabled professionals, whether on or off screen, backstage or on stage, have never been provided. The deaf and disabled workforce is continually marginalised or, even worse, forgotten entirely. In most cases the data, if it's even been recorded, is just not made readily available. And without evidence to show whether numbers have risen or fallen, the reality is avoided. The Creative Diversity Network has a project called Diamond (Diversity Analysis Monitoring Data) that gathers equality and diversity data sets from the BBC, ITV, Channel 4 and Sky. At the time of writing, their results remain unpublished but the characteristics they will focus on are gender, gender identity, age, ethnicity, sexual orientation and disability. Monitoring requires a lot of resources to become effective evidence. We conducted some ourselves, looking at TV, West End plays and later diversity in training for the arts. See the article by Giovanni Benne in our Spring 2017 newsletter where he explains our monitoring project methodology, where we struggled and why we need more.

Events bring campaigning, policy and advocacy together. Each year we hold a discussion event focusing on a diversity-related theme or subject. In 2014, our first event, it was diversity in television, 2015 was diversity in theatre, and 2016 was diversity in training for the industry. We think of provocations or questions that will stimulate debate, choose a relevant panel, ideally from varying perspectives, and fill the venues with as many supporters and change-makers as possible. Events introduce us to partner organisations, invigorate our support base and, most importantly, encourage people to take diversity seriously. What makes us especially proud is the conversations they amplify and the issues which, broached by us, can be discussed when individuals alone might be scared to raise them. We try to unpack complicated issues then disseminate the best thoughts about how, why and when to make changes.

Who?

You. People ask how they can get involved with the charity. We need so much volunteer support. People can be researchers for our monitoring work, they can help to produce, shoot or subtitle our videos, we need podcast help, we need help at our events, social media support, fundraising, development and marketing help. Email us and tell us what you can do.

Do

The best and most powerful things actors do are listen and talk. In that order. It is similar for this. Talk to and involve others, especially those that don't know what you know. The more you share ideas the wider the context becomes. Ask complex questions, especially of people with power; hold your own discussion events, notice difference and look for positive progress. Connecting to culture and events that are new to you is another way of doing. Support work and artists you haven't heard of, just to see. People do it with music all the time – try it with ideas and ways of thinking. These are all simple things you can make happen that, in small ways, fortify diversity and inclusion.

Commit

Passion can wane but commitment (like policy) will outlast that. It all starts with thinking, but you cannot dragoon people into adopting ideas, they can only join willingly. A constant readiness to respond is part of making art, that's how artists can respond but like physical exercise or learning we must listen and ask questions regularly. To become effective let your support become part of you.

Visit **www.act-for-change.com** for podcasts, newsletter and much more.

Kobna Holdbrook-Smith is a stage, screen and voice actor, vice chair of the Act For Change Project, Gate Theatre board member, a National Theatre Associate and chair of trustees at the arts education charity Dramatic Need. Films include *The Commuter*, *Dr Strange* and *The Double*. Theatre includes *Hamlet* (Barbican), *Edward II* (NT). TV includes *Dark Heart* (ITV), *The Split* (BBC/AMC).

Resources

Beyond #metoo

Kelly Burke

#metoo

In October 2017, the *The New York Times* published an article accusing Hollywood film mogul Harvey Weinstein of decades of sexual harassment and assault. The entertainment industry's apparent astonishment caused actress Alyssa Milano to tweet, 'If all the women who have been sexually harassed or assaulted wrote "Me too" as a status, we might give people a sense of the magnitude of the problem.'

Within twenty-four hours, 4.7 million people had engaged with #metoo on Facebook alone.[1] Over eighty women came forward with accusations against Weinstein, and a raft of allegations began to surface against other high-profile figures. It became clear that the magnitude of the problem was great indeed.

Since October 2017, conversations have spread through rehearsal rooms and drama schools, agencies, film sets and board rooms, asking the twin questions: How did we get here? and What can we do about it? In the UK, new safeguarding policies have been implemented industry-wide, starting with rigorous guidelines from Equity, the BFI and the Royal Court, geared towards creating safe workplaces, preventing harassment and holding perpetrators accountable. 'Intimacy direction' (in which sex scenes are choreographed by an outside professional, much like stage fights) and ideas around active consent have been gaining traction in creative spaces. Performers are seeking ways to set boundaries and say 'no' without being regarded as difficult or un-creative.

With thousands of people participating in the conversation, there has inevitably been disagreement about where the line between 'harmless' and 'harassment' is drawn, how much banter is too much banter, and how much safeguarding is too much safeguarding. There is anxiety in some corners of the industry that new regulations will compromise artistic freedom, that allegations will turn into witch hunts, and that the logical conclusion of #metoo (in the arts, at least) will be that we're afraid to touch each other, frisson will disappear from our stages and screens, and our work will be condemned to sexless, frightened monotony.

But this puts us in danger of ignoring two important – if subtle – factors:

1. The implementation of codes of conduct, safeguarding, consent negotiations, etc., is not a call for sex to be eliminated from our industry. Instead, it is an insistence that, where sex *does* come into our work, it is negotiated professionally and openly, with input from all involved. Because, of course:

2. The sexual harassment crisis isn't really about sex. It's about power. It's about work.

Power and parity

After all, the women speaking out against Harvey Weinstein weren't sexually assaulted on dates, or by strangers on the street (which would be bad enough). They were assaulted as a condition of their work, in order to get or sustain employment.

To understand why this is so critical, consider:

• Men outnumber women 2:1 on screen — and 3:1 in children's programming
• Crowd scenes in film use about 17% women[2]

[1] www.theguardian.com/world/2017/oct/20/women-worldwide-use-hashtag-metoo-against-sexual-harassment
[2] https://seejane.org/research-informs-empowers

• Women make up just 7% of film directors[3] and 23% of crews[4]
• 16% of working film writers in the UK are female (this statistic *has remained unchanged for the past 10 years*)[5]
• Only 1 in 5 artistic directors funded by Arts Council England is female; women control just 13% of the ACE theatre funding budget[6]

What does this mean?

Well, to start with it means that women at the beginning of their careers are less likely to work than their male colleagues. This means that a disproportionate number of female film- and theatre-makers are confined to self-producing work on the fringe, often at their own expense. It means that most female performers, writers, directors, stage managers, DoPs, etc., will at some point find themselves working for little – or no – pay. And this is before we consider the repercussions of having children (or being over 40) on a woman's career – or the dire impact of intersectionality, which puts BAME women, d/Deaf and disabled women, and queer women at an exponential disadvantage.

Less work overall means a less impressive CV, which leads, again, to less work. It also leads to less opportunity to refine one's craft, so skills start to stagnate and confidence deteriorates. This leads to – less work. In this way, many women's careers can become so precarious that they simply cannot afford to 'speak up', whether to advocate for better pay or to reject unwanted advances.

Even for those women who manage sustainable careers, the work itself can be problematic. Acting jobs overwhelmingly push women into sexually objectified and stereotyped roles, where they are often the victims of violence – and rarely have professional status. (For example, the BFI reports that, although women make up 52% of GPs in the UK, only 15% of on-screen doctors are women. On the other hand, women make up 94% of on-screen prostitutes.[7])

This gives our young people a skewed perception of what to expect from the world, and reinforces the fact that a woman's sexuality ultimately determines her (box office) value. It teaches our aspiring film- and theatre-makers that the stories worth telling are men's stories, which results in more work for men – and the cycle repeats itself.

Encouragingly, there are more and more exceptions to this kind of programming, and every day companies are making commitments towards shifting the paradigm. Indeed, if we truly want to eliminate sexual harassment *as a condition of work*, then the content of our work – and the content-makers – will have to change.

Navigating the grey area

In the meantime, we are suspended between the old industry and a hopeful but as-yet-unrealised one. So, what can we do?

Get involved. Campaigns like ERA 50:50, Time's Up UK, and Act for Change are all doing exciting, proactive work to change the landscape of the industry.

Be proud and professional. We can often feel so relieved to be employed that we put up with things which are deeply unprofessional. It can be frightening to say 'no', whether

[3]https://seejane.org/symposiums-on-gender-in-media/gender-bias-without-borders
[4]https://stephenfollows.com/gender-of-film-crews
[5]https://writersguild.org.uk/women-shut-out-of-top-screenwriting-jobs-for-over-10-years
[6]www.thestage.co.uk/opinion/2018/sphinx-theatres-sue-parrish-we-must-break-down-barriers-to-gender-parity
[7]www.bfi.org.uk/news-opinion/news-bfi/announcements/bfi-filmography-complete-story-uk-film

in the context of turning down underpaid work or unwelcome advances. But we must remember that we are professionals and expect to be treated professionally, with respect and dignity. This means:

Don't work for free. Unless there's a really good reason (i.e. we've written a solo show for ourselves or are doing our best friend a favour), we should insist on being paid for our work – like professionals in any other industry. It is *illegal* to employ people for less than the minimum wage: we are likely to be much more vulnerable in projects which have already engaged us on dubious terms.

Know your rights. It is essential to understand our contracts so that we know what we are agreeing to – in everything from working hours to nudity. We should also know what can and *cannot* be required of us in an audition.[8] If we have questions about a contract, we can call Equity to talk us through it.

Talk about it. Having a conversation with our colleagues to set down expectations and parameters before starting intimate work can be enormously freeing and reassuring. It allows us to navigate sensitive work by making conscious choices, rather than resorting to unexamined, automatic ones.

Be clear about boundaries. In our industry, where the line between fiction and reality sometimes blurs, there will be inevitable moments of ambiguity, even discomfort. It is important to recognise within ourselves when we are uncomfortable versus when we are *unsafe*, when we are willing to push our boundaries and what consists of a violation of those boundaries.

Know where to go for help. If something untoward does happen, contact Equity immediately (main switchboard: 020-7379 6000, harassment/bullying helpline: 020-7670 0268) or, if needed, the police. Anyone you work for has a duty of care, but if you don't feel able to talk to someone in the company, remember that your venue is also responsible for your well-being and approach someone in the building. There are more avenues for support and intervention than we might think.

Don't be a bystander. If you see something inappropriate happening, report it.

Remember, it's up to all of us. Men are also subjected to sexual harassment and assault, and are as straight-jacketed as women by gender stereotypes. Our industry leaves almost no place for our trans and non-binary colleagues. The work towards gender equality is everyone's work, and benefits everyone. But we must be sensitive to each other's experiences along the way, and be compassionate with each other when we fail.

Join Equity. The performing arts union, Equity, is our professional safety net. Not only can they provide support in situations of harassment or bullying (including legal support), they can answer contract questions, protect us on vulnerable jobs, and make sure we're paid correctly. Equity also negotiates the terms of our contracts with the industry's biggest employers and campaigns for equal and diverse representation across the performing arts. The more of us are part of the union, the stronger it is and the better supported we are. It is our industry family.

Lastly:

Let's make the work we want to see. We can start changing the industry *by changing the industry*. Write new stories, work with people who excite you, find ways to be nourished by the work you do.

---

[8]For example, the Equality Act states that one should not be asked about age, gender, ethnicity, disability, pregnancy, health or other 'protected characteristics'. Nor should you be asked to undress to any extent without warning and without a mutually agreed third party present. For more information, visit **www.equity.org.uk/getting-involved/campaigns/manifesto-for-casting** or call **0207 379 6000**.

There's no going back from #metoo now. If we insist on parity and respect – and if we make a commitment to looking after one another – we have the chance to turn our industry into something infinitely richer than the one we've inherited.

See you out there.

Kelly Burke is an actor, singer and writer. She trained at RADA and is Chair of Equity's Women's Committee, an Equity councillor, and part of the team that drafted the union's Agenda for Change. **www.kellyburke.com**

Resources

Spotlight, casting directories and information services

Spotlight is slowly becoming a fundamental part of the fabric of the acting profession, although lower-cost alternatives are becoming more and more common. Once again it is important to research thoroughly the value to you of investing in one of these. As well as trying to assess whether such an investment will really enhance your visibility to employers, an essential part of that research is to read the 'small print' properly.

With some exceptions (major musicals, for instance), many employers do not openly advertise the properly paid acting work they have to offer. It's simpler to contact agents whom they know and trust for casting suggestions. This limits the number of submissions, largely prevents time-wasting via unsuitable applicants, and goes some way towards ensuring that those suggested for consideration are really suitable for the parts available. It can take a day's work to go through a thousand submissions to select whom to interview; it can take another day's work to interview just 30 of these.

Casting information services – often allied to casting directories – glean their information from all kinds of sources. The important thing to remember is that some of the information about 'properly paid acting work' is of a second-hand nature – that is, it was not sent directly to them in the first instance. Consequently, it is important to research reputations for accuracy (and 'up-to-dateness') before committing your funds to such companies. However, many Fringe production and student film opportunities are directly advertised in such publications and such opportunities might lead on to 'properly paid acting work'.

ArtsJobs
website www.artsjobs.org.uk

Details of casting information services: Freely advertises a range of opportunities within the arts sector, including positions that require specialist knowledge and skills, unskilled positions at arts organisations and internships.

Casting Networks
website www.castingnetworks.co.uk

Details of casting information services: Casting Networks offers casting professionals a means to distribute breakdowns and receive submissions, with the purpose of streamlining, simplifying and facilitating the subsequent casting process. Includes a range of features such as straightforward actor check-in; integration of audition video-recording into online casting tools; and software for handling the scheduling and arranging of auditions.

Actors can upload their photos, reel and CV, search through thousands of projects, and submit their profile for consideration.

"Casting Networks continuously improves the casting process through the application of innovative solutions, cutting-edge technologies, and superior customer support, making a career in the entertainment and advertising industries more efficient, accessible, and fun for everyone involved."

Castweb
7 St Luke's Avenue, London SW4 7LG
tel 020 7720 9002
email info@castweb.co.uk
website www.castweb.co.uk
Key contact Rodney Watney

Details of casting information services: Established in 1999. A daily information service is available online, with casting breakdowns circulated to subscribers throughout the day. Castweb has circulated casting opportunities for over 4,000 production companies and casting directors. It is now received by more than 1,000 agents across Europe.

Dramanic
email info@dramanic.com
website www.dramanic.com/uk
Facebook www.facebook.com/Dramanic
Twitter @Dramanic
Instagram @dramanic.actor

Details of casting information services: Dramanic, developed in 2009, is an online resource for professional actors only, helping them find work opportunities at theatre companies around the UK. "Anyone new to the business will find that keeping tabs on different theatre companies is challenging and time-consuming, and marrying that with your normal lives leaves you no time to effectively find acting work. Dramanic takes all the hassle out of that by alerting you when opportunities arise at the hundreds of theatre companies in our system."

Features include:

• Casting calendar – know what theatre companies are casting well in advance
• Theatre company research profiles, giving you up-to-date information about company personnel and actor-relevant news
• Contact details of agents, personal managers and casting directors
• Swap plays/books with other Dramanic users
• Look for casual employment between acting jobs

IMDb Pro (Internet Movie Database)
website www.imdb.com

Details of casting information services: This is not just a comprehensive database of film and television around the world, but also an opportunity for actors to post their photos and CVs ('resumés') for a fee, currently starting at $12.50 per month. Also creates an opportunity to network by providing access to a huge international contact database of people and companies, and the facility to track film and television projects from development to post-production.

The Mandy Network
tel 020 7288 7404
email emails@mandy.com
website www.mandy.com

Details of casting information services: Formerly Casting Call Pro and established in 2004, The Mandy Network is one of the world's leading casting directories, designed with the actor in mind. Featuring over 2.8 million professionals all over the world, the site is updated daily with a wide range of casting breakdowns including film roles, theatre tours, corporate work and commercials. Mandy also provides a wealth of resources for actors, including a directory of photographers, agents and guides. Additional services include a lively forum, news service and free surgeries with top casting directors. All members have an entirely free profile in the online directory, which is used by thousands of employers and casting directors. Additionally, Mandy offers a Premium Service with a wider range of features. The Mandy Network also includes services for dancers, singers, musicians and voice over artists. To discover more about the benefits of using Mandy as well as current subscription rates and latest updates to the service, please visit the website.

Seven Dials Playhouse
1ᴀ Tower Street, London WC2H 9NP
tel 020 3841 6600
email boxoffice@sevendialsplayhouse.co.uk
website www.sevendialsplayhouse.co.uk
Facebook www.facebook.com/SevenDialsPlayhouse
Twitter @7DialsPlayhouse
Instagram @7dialsplayhouse
General Manager Amanda Davey

Details of casting information services: Founded in 1978, formerly the Actors Centre. Seven Dials Playhouse runs workshops and courses from its venue in the heart of the West End. The Centre boasts five studios, a Green Room Cafe and Bar, and incorporates the Tristan Bates Theatre. With established links within the industry, it offers opportunities to network with other actors and industry professionals. Also runs workshops and courses for non-members, programmed throughout the year and on a bespoke basis. Please see website for more information.

Shooting People
email contact@shootingpeople.org
website www.shootingpeople.org
Co-founders Cath LeCouteur, Jess Search

Details of casting information services: Shooting People allows thousands of people working in independent film to exchange information via a range of daily email bulletins, including a daily UK Casting Bulletin. This allows actors to discuss their craft and receive casting calls from directors, producers and casting directors. Shooting People's overall membership is currently more than 38,000. Actors can create a public casting profile as well as get significant discounts off key film products and services.

Full membership costs £39.95 per year or £9.95 per month and entitles users to a range of other services. See entry under *Publications, libraries, references and booksellers* on page 420 for further details.

Spotlight
Head Office, 7 Leicester Place, London WC2H 7RJ
tel 020 7437 7631
email performers@spotlight.com
website www.spotlight.com

Details of casting information services: Spotlight was founded in 1927 and has since become a world-famous casting platform, with over 65,000 performers. As the industry's leading casting resource, Spotlight is used by TV, film, radio and theatrical companies throughout the UK, and many worldwide. Spotlight connects performers with casting professionals and roles; the industry recognises that the performers are guaranteed to have professional skills and experience. As well as access to exciting acting opportunities, performers benefit from discounts and continued development as a Spotlight member.

Performers can upload showreels, voice-clips and additional photos to enhance their online CVs, which is a far quicker and more cost-effective way of promoting themselves than sending out endless copies to casting directors and agents in the post. Artists are also issued with a pair of unique PIN numbers which allow them to access their CV whenever they wish – keeping credits and skills up-to-date – and to email a link to their Spotlight CV to others. Spotlight is used on a daily basis by production professionals sending out casting briefs to agents, with 99% of UK television work being cast through the Spotlight platform.

To join Spotlight, visit the website **www.spotlight.com**. Entry is strictly limited to professionally trained and/or professionally experienced performers, and applications are always vetted.

'Point me in the right direction': navigating the casting services

Isabelle Farah

The hardest battle for an actor has and will always be 'where do I find my next job?' Different services will suit different actors. Some gear themselves more to certain media and some cover all areas with varying degrees of success. My advice, seven years into a career, is to work out what you want from your subscription – is it to make your living exclusively from performing if that includes corporate work, children's parties, etc., or are you looking to expand/improve your show-reel? Do you only want to work in theatre? I hope that this can provide you with some insight as to which might be best for you.

There's no denying that Spotlight is the market leader and has been forever. It's expensive and can feel (particularly if you don't have an agent) like a lot of money with little (or no) payback, but I believe that you cannot be an actor without it. In the US, there is no one market leader and actors are required to pay for several similar services, so while this situation is not ideal, it's definitely not the worst!

It is important to remember that this is your profession, the craft by which you want to make your living. While you may have to accept you have to make money doing something else in between acting jobs and are not going to be employed by Stephen Spielberg straight after graduating from drama school, if you are paying for a casting service, you should expect to get work from it. Ideally paid in cold, hard cash, rather than lukewarm exposure.

The best bit of advice about the services is to be astute about them. Keep an eye on what you're spending (particularly in direct debits) and which services are working for you. Is the cost of the service with the time spent going through it as productive as, say, making your own work, writing a carefully considered letter to a casting director or director you wish to work with or doing a workshop once a month? I believe connections made in person are much stronger than any application via a casting service.

It's worth noting that many will advertise that they have had high-profile work cast through them, but these, with some exceptions, will be the ones that require more niche skills (languages, musical skills, etc.) and will likely be on Spotlight as well.

Many of these services have other features included in the cost, but I have looked solely at their capacity as a casting resource.

Backstage

Cost: £14.95/month

An import from the US, Backstage has been around for a long time and the website is easy to use and navigate. At the time of writing it is offering six months free to new members (don't forget to cancel though if you're not going to continue). There's currently not a lot going through here that isn't elsewhere, but that may change.

Casting Networks

Cost: Registration fee: £10, £5/month for 'Pro Subscription' thereafter

Casting Networks is another import from the US which arrived with a lot of hype a few years ago. Some breakdowns appear here from certain casting directors, commercials and short films most often, though generally not exclusive to Casting Networks. The only advantage to a Pro Subscription appears to be the extra media storage.

Dramanic

Cost: 1 month £11.99; 3 months £34.99 (+1 month); 6 months £54.99 (+2 months); 12 months £99.99 (+3 months)

Rather than advertising jobs as and when casting directors list them, Dramanic gives you as many details as they have about upcoming theatre projects soon after they have been announced. Dramanic takes out a lot of the research hassle involved in writing letters but, as a letter will almost always be needed, is no quick fix solution to getting a job. Most of the work is in theatre, including some regional touring with small but well-known companies as well as the mainstream West End/Off-West End stuff. All jobs I saw had some payment and many looked like they were offering Equity/ITC rates. If your focus is theatre and you don't have an agent, then this comes highly recommended.

Equity

Cost: included in your Equity subscription

Equity's hook here is that all work is paid and in theory you pay your subscription for more than just the jobs board. The work tends to be teaching rather than performing so worth checking if that's what you're after to see you through a month.

IMDb

Costs: $179/year

There are breakdowns here, but not many and usually low/no pay; on the flip side, they tend to be very high quality (the film makers are required to be members themselves, and I don't think you'd bother until you're quite serious). It's not one I'd pay for simply for the breakdowns, but if you reach a point where you think it's useful (when I was in a co-op we'd use it for general research and I found it invaluable as an agent) then it can be worth looking through what's available there.

Mandy

Cost: £20.40/month or £156/year if you want access to paid jobs

Now an amalgamation of the old Mandy and Casting Call Pro, Mandy.com is a stalwart service. The site displays numerous castings. There are some good paid jobs and plenty of unpaid opportunities, including interesting small-scale tours, commercial work, short films and voiceovers. The jobs here are not going to make you a household name, but you can make money from lower-profile jobs and build your CV without an agent using it. Some of the more 'niche' roles in big productions are regularly advertised on here. The premium service includes workshop opportunities, agent and employer directories, and you can upload several photos and reels.

Shooting People

Cost: £9.95/month, £39.95/year

Shooting People is great for independent film work. The site itself is user-friendly and clean with social network type tagging features. Most of the work advertised is still low/no pay films, but the advantage is that these jobs tend to only be listed here and the yearly subscription rate is good value (there are also often discounts floating around the internet).

Spotlight
Cost: £154/year
Spotlight is where the breakdowns are. I don't think any other service gets as many or from as wide a pool of good casting directors through their sites, let alone exclusive to their sites. Many features (search functions on the Link board, etc.) are not available to actors. Agents see significantly more than you but don't be fooled into thinking there is nothing there. With some pushing, Spotlight will change things that need to be changed. If you want to be in something, it's probably cast here, and your chance of making your money back is far higher here than anywhere else. Make sure your profile is up to date with your skills as casting directors search on here first.

The Stage
Cost: £9/month or £84/year for The Stage Castings; £11/month or £99/year for The Stage Castings and a newspaper subscription
At the time of writing, The Stage is nearly ready to relaunch the casting section of their website. It looks like it will be very easy to use and offer both paid and unpaid jobs. It will also act as a directory for performers, though you will have to link to media hosted on other websites rather than what is uploaded here. Pricing is competitive. They say their target market is actors looking to build their CVs and show-reels at the beginning of their careers or branch into new media.

To Be Seen
Cost: £5.99/month billed £35.94 every 6 months; £6.99/month billed £20.97 every 3 months; £9.99/month billed £9.99 monthly
There are things here, generally corporate or low/no budget films, which aren't available elsewhere.

Work in Europe
Currently, London is where many commercials for Europe are cast and also where many European actors choose to base themselves. There's no denying that it's the industry hub of Europe. This may change over the next year or two, particularly if it is made more difficult for EU nationals to work here or for those with British passports to work in the EU. These two may be useful for anyone who can, does or wants to work in other markets.

enCAST
Cost: £8.40/4 weeks; £20.40/12 weeks; £32.50/6 months
This is relatively new to the market. It covers castings across Europe in all languages so it could well be worth using if you speak another language/s to a high-enough standard. There is a high volume of work advertised but it is spread across all of Europe. France, Belgium, Germany and Italy seem to be the largest players. The jobs are often paid, but it's worth bearing in mind that you are applying as a local, so are unlikely to get travel or accommodation expenses. There is some work in the UK advertised here, but it's likely to be more useful to those who have contacts, bases or interest in building their networks in other countries. You can look at the breakdowns and apply for unpaid work without paying, but must pay to apply for any paid work.

e-TALENTA

Cost: 89€/year

e-TALENTA is another for Europe-based work. The site looks very shiny and is easy to use, but it does not have a huge volume of work coming through their boards. Its main function is as a platform for CVs with show-reels, photos, voice-reels, etc.

Isabelle Farah is an actor, writer, and comedian. She trained as a serious actor at Drama Studio London and after some pratfalls and upstaging, branched into stand up and character comedy. You can find out more about her work by following her @irresponsabelle but preferably not in real life ...

Be prepared for publicity

Jayne Trotman

Congratulations! You get a great job, meet the director, producer, cast members, start work and then someone asks whether you will you do some publicity for the project. What does that really mean and do you have to do it? If you have been asked, then the answer is most probably yes. Publicity plays a vital role in the marketing process of many film, television and theatre projects. Here are some useful tools to help you navigate the publicity process.

What is publicity?

I have worked with many actors and film makers during publicity for film campaigns – some seasoned household names and others entirely new to publicity. Whilst publicity is an exciting, vital part of the job, and can mean travelling around the globe for weeks (sometimes longer) on end to promote a film, it is hard work. It's essential that you are well prepared and take good care of yourself.

I am sure many of you will have seen an actor sitting next to a mounted film poster, answering questions about what it was like working with their co-star on a soon-to-be-released blockbuster film. Or you will have watched that co-star on a chat-show sofa recounting tales of pranks that said actor played on set before a clip from the film is shown and the audience applaud. To get back to basics, that is all part of the publicity campaign and another skill that actors should appreciate, practise and perfect.

Granted your first job may not be a Hollywood blockbuster; it may well be a touring show or fringe theatre production where local newspaper coverage, radio interviews and podcasts will be the key. Whatever the job is, you should be publicity-ready as you may well be newsworthy, and you'll make many a producer very happy if you are already well prepared.

How can I prepare?

When you play a role you will have researched and honed that character well. This is no different. It's you on your best day with stories aplenty, open and interested to be meeting new people for a good chat. If there are any things you are uncomfortable talking about, think about them in advance and have answers to those questions prepared.

It's definitely worth seeking out those you admire when they are on the publicity trail. Watch them on TV shows (both here and in the US, if you can), read interviews with them and listen to what they have to say if you hear them on the radio. Sometimes interviews don't go quite so well. Those pieces are worth watching and reading as much as the successful ones. Think what *you* might have done in that situation.

Being interviewed is a skill that needs to be worked on – it's hard work at times and some people are just better at it than others. But if you spend time preparing and practising, you will become more adept. I urge you to do your research as much as you can in advance.

It's also important to think about how you look. You may be able to roll out of bed for an early film or television call, know you will have time to get ready and might even have people to help you – but that's not always the case on the press side. Make sure that you look your best and always ask in advance what the set-up will be and what you are expected to be wearing etc. In my years working for major film studios, we have had actors turn up

Resources

for press days in old crumpled t-shirts (albeit their favourite one), having to call flatmates to go through wardrobes for extra clothes to be sent across. Or, on one occasion, the person arrived for their first major press conference and photo-call with the world's media in a tracksuit and top. On that occasion we kept thinking they would get changed any minute but they didn't. Luckily, we had a budget, an experienced team on hand to help and just enough time to dash to a shop for an outfit change. They looked great in the end and were quite brilliant, but it did not help their nerves (or ours!) in the run-up.

Your publicity moments should and can be enjoyable. I promise it will help if you have done the work in advance.

What am I publicising?

Essentially, the play, TV show, film, event you are in or have created. Make sure you ask for and come armed with all the key facts about the project. If you have not been directly asked to do press, it is always good to check (usually with the producer, director or creator) that it's OK for you to be talking publicly about the piece and that all the key people involved in the project are aware.

You are also publicising brand 'you'. You are a business, so – as we touched on above – please make sure you are bringing the best version of you to work that day. You should also take a moment to consider what people can find out about you if they were doing their research. You are probably on social media. If so, and even if you have not been active for a while, what would people think about you if they looked at your posts online? Brand 'you' and a career path as an actor or performer may not have been on the cards when you first posted on social media. As you are coming into the public eye, you need to start thinking what you are communicating on each channel. You may well have decided to spend time and money creating a stylish new website to help you get work and to promote you as an actor and performer. This will be useful and you can control and curate everything on there. You now need to be mindful of everything you post on social media, may have posted in the past and what friends and family post about you. Your website may be great, but you don't necessarily want a journalist to see everything that happened on that fun night in Ibiza from a social media post. Always think before you post.

Can anyone help me?

Yes, always ask questions and seek out help and advice. If you are working on a project and have been asked to do publicity, your company manager, director or producer should be happy to advise. If you have one, then ask your agent. It's likely they will have other clients well-versed in the publicity circuit. You can also speak to one of your tutors from drama school as they may well be able to help and advise you. Fellow cast members can be very useful too and often more than happy to share their experiences. There will always be someone who can help. Don't be afraid to talk to people: you will be amazed what you can find out when you open up and start asking questions.

Publicists

A high-profile element of the publicity campaign is what is known as a 'press junket'. This is a series of print and broadcast interviews with the cast and film makers, often in a hotel (watch that scene with Hugh Grant posing as a journalist from *Horse and Hound* in the film *Notting Hill*). Many actors are often accompanied by a publicist – someone hired by the actor or film maker to help them navigate publicity requests, promote the film and their role as well as other elements of their careers). You may not need a publicist when you are starting out, unless your first role is on a major high-profile project and, in that case, you may be assigned a publicist to help and advise you. My role as part of a studio's publicity team is to work with the publicist and sometimes directly with the actors, to help and advise them during the publicity campaign. You may well be helped through the process by someone like me if you get cast in a high-profile title.

There are so many additional aspects to the role of being an actor or performer and publicity is often one of the unexpected elements. Please enjoy it, don't be afraid to ask questions, do your research and be prepared. We look forward to seeing the results.

A bit about me: I originally trained as an actor and worked across theatre and television for several years. A colleague I had worked with in a touring theatre company called out of the blue one day and asked if I could help in their London office when their whole team were away covering a film festival. I ended up doing this for many years and, from that and through meeting other people in the industry (and often in between acting jobs), worked for many of the studios before joining Warner Bros as a temp in 1997. I joined the team full time as a publicist, was promoted to Director of Publicity and stepped down as Executive Director of Publicity for Warner Bros UK, having successfully overseen the launch of over 400 films almost 20 years later. I now run my own film and entertainment consultancy.

Photographers and repro companies

Good photographs (and quality reproductions) are an essential part of an actor's professional armoury and there is absolutely no point in trying to scrimp on them. ('A picture is worth a thousand words.')

Your photograph is a silent, static, two-dimensional representation of vocal, mobile, three-dimensional you. It should be of your head down to your shoulders, reasonably stylish and well-produced without necessarily being too glamorous. It should look natural and have life, energy and personality – especially in the eyes, the most important part of your face.

Crucial to the final result is finding a good photographer (a) who understands the world that the end result is intended for and (b) with whom you can work well. In the listings that follow, you'll find a wide range of prices and deals. It is important to research as many of these as possible, without making cost your prime consideration. Ask friends, teachers and your agent (if you have one) for recommendations, and check through *Spotlight* and websites to see samples of work. Read the details under each listing to get a 'feel' for who might produce the 'goods' for you. Once you have a shortlist of possibilities, phone or message each with appropriate questions (what to wear, studio or natural light, and so forth) in order to get a sense of how well you might be able to work with them. Only *after* you've done all this research should cost be a consideration. Even then, a cheap deal could mean that the photographer will spend much less time, and take fewer photographs, than a more expensive one. You might be lucky with the former, but you'll enhance your chances of getting really good results with the latter.

Note: Bear in mind that as the deadline for *Spotlight* gets nearer, photographers become increasingly busy and it becomes more difficult to book a session.

APHP following a photographer's name denotes membership of the Association of Professional Headshot Photographers, a non-profit group of the UK's leading casting photographers. Founded in 2016 on principles of education, expertise and excellence, it establishes new, neutral standards of headshot professionalism, offers a path to qualification for photographers, and promotes the highest standards in casting portraiture.

Copyright

Under the Copyright, Designs & Patents Act 1988, the photographer owns the copyright on any new photograph, even though you've already paid for the original. That means that you have to obtain his/her permission to have new photographs reproduced in *Spotlight* or anywhere else. Your photographer may be happy to approve such reproduction, but may not be so happy about any cropping or other alterations: you must get permission if you intend to do this. The other important new legal requirement is that your photographer must be credited on any reproduction of the original. Some of the repro companies are now doing this as a matter of course.

Abacus Photography

12 Ashwood Road, Corsham SN13 0LF
mobile 07966 551909
email nick@abacus-photography.co.uk
website www.abacus-photography.co.uk

Services & rates: Established in 1992. Prices start
from £75 in a fully equipped studio. Images supplied
on disc so you can make your own prints
economically, or email them to casting agents.
Discounts available for group bookings.

Vincent Abbey

6 Lynton Road, Chorlton, Manchester M21 9NQ
mobile 07960 038057
email vabbey@yahoo.com
website www.vincentabbey.co.uk

Services & rates: Established in 1995. Charges £90 for
a photoshoot, which includes approximately 100
shots and 3 touched up. Additional images are £8
each. Shoots take place at home studio. Has taken
publicity photos for over 2,000 actors.

Simon Annand

mobile 07884 446776
email simonannand@blueyonder.co.uk
website www.simonannand.com

Services and rates: Charges £350 for a photo shoot,
which includes approximately 450 shots.
Concessionary rate of £310 available for full time
students and the unemployed. The whole session is
taken away on the day; after the actor chooses 6
images, these choices are fully photoshopped in
colour and b&w. Photos are usually taken at a home
studio with natural light, but can be taken outside if
preferred – will travel if necessary. Home studio is
wheelchair-accessible.

Work portfolio: With 40 years' experience, has taken
publicity shots for around 4,000 actors. Clients
include: Mark Rylance, David Morrissey, Lindsay
Lohan, James Norton, Meera Syal, John Hannah,
Eddie Redmayne, Claire Foy, Benedict Cumberbatch,
Tamla Kari, Dan Stevens, Jane Asher and Vicky
McClure. Advises actors: "There is no time-limit for
the session; I see one person a day. Please bring 6-8
different tops and previous photos to discuss."
Author of *Time to Act* and *The Half*; has worked for
Peter Brook, Sonia Friedman, Ian Rickson, the NT,
RSC and Royal Court amongst many others.

Ric Bacon

mobile 07970 970799
email ric@ricbacon.co.uk
website www.ricbacon.co.uk

Services & rates: Photo shoot includes
photographer's fee, processing of 2 b&w 36exps,
6x4in print of every shot (rather than a contact sheet)
and all negatives. Offers reduced rates to students.
Shoots in a very relaxed manner, in natural light or

studio and offers advice on all aspects including
clothing and make-up. Prints are ready to view in 1
hour and will be reviewed with the client, offering
advice on selection of images for self-promotion if
needed. Happy to look at old photographs of the
client that they particularly like or dislike. Works
with film or digital.

Work portfolio: Established in 1999. Photographs
can be viewed on the website and has a
comprehensive portfolio at Spotlight's offices. Has
taken publicity shots for around 500 actors.

david bailie photography

tel 020 7460 1105
email davidbailie@davidbailie.co.uk
website www.davidbailie.photium.com

Services & rates: Photographer since 2007. Charges
£180 (inc. VAT). Quote ACTORS HANDBOOK for
20% discount. Special discount for students. 2-hour
shoot consisting of approx. 120 shots with all contacts
saved to disc. Each shoot also includes 4 8x10in or A4
prints, with additional ones available at £15 each.
Offers this package at a special rate of £145 (inc.
VAT) to actors and £95 (inc. VAT) to students. Uses
studio in Kensington and outdoor location for
shoots. Only the outdoor location is wheelchair
accessible.

Work portfolio: Examples of work can be seen on
the website. Has taken photographs for many actors,
among them Kevin McNally, Nick Bartlett,
Mackenzie Crook, Chris Adamson, Dermot Kelly,
Katrina Vasiliev and Patricia Merrick. See also
YouTube channel, search mdebailes.

Pete Bartlett Photography APHP

61B Cornwall Crescent, London W11 1PJ
mobile 07971 653994
email info@petebartlett.com
website www.petebartlett.com

Services & rates: Photographer since 2004. Charges
£275 for photo shoot, which includes 150-200 digital
photographs. A student rate of £255 for a shoot is
also available. Shoots from amazing studio with
natural light.

Work portfolio: Examples of work can be seen on
the website. Has taken photographs for around 2,000
actors. Recent clients include: Elliot Knight (*Sinbad*),
Jeff and Matt Postlethwaite (*Peaky Blinders*), Matt
Milne (*Downton Abbey*), Jo Brand (*Getting On*), Ian
Hislop (*Have I Got News For You*) plus many of
London's top agents such as United Agents,
Independent Talent, Troika and Middleweek
Newton. "I give you 100% to get that killer set of
headshots. Please check out my website, drop me an
email and we can begin the process today."

Richard Battye

107A Telsen, 55 Thomas Street, Aston,
Birmingham B6 4TN

Resources

mobile 07860 824101
email info@riverstudio.co.uk
website www.riverstudio.co.uk
Facebook www.facebook.com/
RiverStudioBirmingham
Twitter @richardjbattye

Services & rates: Charges from £95 for a photoshoot, which includes 30-60 shots with the best 5 edited. 10x8in prints are charged at £9 each. Special packages are available, please call to discuss. Digital photography offered at commercial/advertising rates. Shoots take place at the Birmingham studio and locations around the city, most locations are wheelchair accessible.

Work portfolio: Established in 1990. Has taken publicity shots for around 180 actors. Recent clients include: Birmingham Theatre School, self-employed actors, Sharon Foster Productions and Birmingham Royal Ballet.

Jonathan Bean

mobile 07763 814587
email mail@beanphoto.co.uk
website www.beanphoto.co.uk
Facebook www.facebook.com/beanphoto
Twitter @beanphoto
Instagram @beanphotog

Services & rates: Established in 2004. Offers a digital service only and charges £125 for a photo shoot, which includes editing, online contact sheet and a choice of 3 selected hi-res files or 10x8in prints. Additional prints or files may be purchased seperately. A discounted 10% rate is available to students. All shoots are non-studio based.

Work portfolio: Examples of work can be seen on the website. Portfolio includes many actors, writers and musicians, including Blake Morrison, Andrew Michael Hurley, Carol Birch and John Hegley. "My aim is to make you comfortable and relaxed for natural-looking, great portrait photos that show you at your best."

A Beautiful Image Photography & Design (Debal Bagachi)

tel 020 8568 2122 *mobile* 07956 861698
email debal@abeautifulimage.com
website www.abeautifulimage.com

Services & rates: Photoshoot includes photographer's fee, studio and equipment costs, processing of 2 b&w 36exps, contact sheets and 2 10x8in prints (either hand- or digitally printed). Occasionally offers 10% discount for clients sharing a shoot. Digital photography is also available at the same rate; images can be supplied on CD-ROM. Also able to provide website and print publicity. Advises actors to keep make-up simple for b&w photography and wear unfussy, unpatterned tops with simple necklines.

Work portfolio: Established in 1994. Photographs can be viewed on the website and at Spotlight's

offices. Has taken publicity shots for around 50 actors.

Nev Brewer Photography

website www.nevbrewerphotography.co.uk
Instagram @nevbrewer

Services & rates: Photographer for actors and performers since 2013. Price £145.

Shoots in the studio, but if required, outdoors can be accommodated as well. Sessions typically last between 90 and 120 minutes. This usually gives sufficient time for an informal discussion, the shoot itself – including clothing changes to help develop a range of looks and a review of images both during and at the end of the shoot. "The session time is just a guide; it is important not to feel rushed and so there is no set time limit. The key aims are that you leave having enjoyed the session and happy in the knowledge that you have the images you came for."

Following the session, images (contact sheets) are sent online – usually on the day but always within 24 hours. Once a selection has been made, retouched images are sent for approval before the final files are sent through. Works to a 7-day turn around to cover busy periods this is usually done within 48 hours. Will do everything possible to meet urgent deadlines.

When booking a shoot, full details of how best to prepare and get the most out of the session will be sent.

Sheila Burnett

email sheila@sheilaburnett.com
website www.sheilaburnett-photography.com
website www.sheilaburnett-headshots.com

Services & rates: Charges between £250 and £450 for a photo shoot. Includes 100 colour proofs plus 4-6 highly finished high res images. Your chosen finished high res images are sent to you by email. Sessions take place in their home studio and locations in nearby Portsmouth Harbour. Works with up to 250 actors a year; clients have included Imelda Staunton, Catherine Tate, David Soul, Paul Freeman, Jon Culshaw, Simon Pegg, Anita Harris, Jackie Clune, Caroline Quentin, Jim Carter and Helen Lederer.

APHP approved.

"Appointments can be made either online or by phone. I always advise on what is good to bring with you on the day. Rail from Waterloo takes 90 minutes to Portsmouth Harbour; easy parking close to premises. My goal is to make sure you have vibrant natural headshots that stand out from the crowd." Visit the website for further details.

Charlie Carter APHP

mobile 07989 389493
email charlie@charliecarter.com
website www.charliecarter.com

Services & rates: Established in 1998. Digital – colour and b&w. Charges £425 for 4.5 hour sessions, tailoring images specifically to you and your casting. Allows plenty of time for many changes of clothing, shaving and reviewing images as the shoot progresses. The shoot includes a web gallery and 4 Spotlight-ready and large file jpegs. Sessions are in a home studio on the 2nd floor, so not wheelchair-accessible.

Work portfolio: Examples of work can be viewed on the website and at Spotlight's offices. Clients include: Kenneth Branagh, Simon Russell Beale, Philip Franks, Tom Hollander, Roger Allam, Emily Blunt, Isla Blair, Jemma Redgrave, Jamie Glover, Tom Mison, Cush Jumbo, Chloe Pirrie, Sarah MacRae, Eve Best, Harry Enfield, Eleanor Bron, Martin Shaw, Joanna Van der Ham, Kerry Condon, Jasmine Hyde, Paul McEwan, Serena Evans and Charlie Condou – as well as agents The Artists Partnership, The Richard Stone Partnership, Rebecca Blond Associates, Conway van Gelder Grant, Independent, United, Markham & Froggatt and many others.

"However lovely a photograph is, it has to work. It has to look like you *and* be accurate to your casting – somehow tell the casting directors who to expect will walk through their door. The way I work is totally collaborative – we talk about your casting and what your range is. We look at how you see yourself. We do it together. I suggest you prepare for it as you would for a significant interview by making sure yo do what is necessary to look and feel your best."

Andrew Chapman
198 Western Road, Sheffield S10 1LF
tel 0114 266 3579 *mobile* 07779 861921
email andrew@chapmanphotographer.eclipse.co.uk
website www.andrewsphotos.co.uk

Services & rates: Charges from £125 for a photo shoot, which includes all photography and computer labour charges, studio and equipment costs. The session includes 100+ photos, b&w and/or colour) which are transferred to the computer; you may select any or all images and these are written to a CD for you to take away for immediate use. Prints and contacts are available (e.g. a 10x8in is £15) if required, but in most cases images are emailed directly to Spotlight and for repros. Also gives clients a 'release note' so that photos can be used for PR, repros, agents, Spotlight etc.

Black and bright colours work well in b&w, and higher necklines are usually better than low: "I always advise people on an individual basis. Ideally, allow about 2 hours for the session."

Work portfolio: Has more than 3,500 actors on database as well as singers, dancers, models, martial artists and others. Clients are from agents across the country; they include: Philippa Howell, Sharron Ashcroft, Jane Hollowood, Liberty Management, David Daly, Direct Line and Act One. "Qualified member of BIPP, SWPP, BPPA with over 25 years' experience."

John Clark Photo Digital APHP
82 Heathwood Gardens, London SE7 8ER
mobile 07702 627237

email info@johnclarkphotography.com
website www.johnclarkphotography.com
Facebook www.facebook.com/john.clark.5283166
Twitter @JohnClarkPhoto

Services & rates: Sessions last for one hour and include one retouched image. Additional images can be purchased. See website for latest rates. Book via online calender.

Work portfolio: Established in 1982. Photographs and advice can be found on the website. Has taken publicity shots for around 500-600 actors. Recent clients include: actors represented by Roger Carey Associates, Collis Management, Crawfords, Rossmore and Langford Associates.

John Cooper Photography
Unit 2, Kelvin Trading Estate, Eastvale Place, Yorkhill, Glasgow
mobile 07803 929091
email studio@johncooperphotography.com
website www.johncooperphotography.com
Facebook www.facebook.com/johncooperphotography
Twitter @jcooperphoto
Instagram @jcooper_photo

Services & rates: Sessions from £175 (all photography is digital). Can offer student discount for multiple bookings. Shoots take place at own studio.

Work portfolio: Established in 2005. Has taken publicity photos for hundreds of actors. Recent clients include: Duncan Lacroix (*Outlander*), Grant O'Rourke (*Outlander*), Billy Boyd (*Lord of the Rings Trilogy*), Jordan Young (BBC *River City*), Keira Lucchesi (BBC *River City*), Scottish Opera (emerging artists), Jean-Luc Picard (Assoc. Conductor RSNO), Greg Esplin (In Your Face Theatre, *Trainspotting*), Mark Cox (BBC's *Chewin' The Fat* and *Still Game*), Katrina Bryan (*Taggart* and Children's BBC), Des Clarke (SMTV Live and Capital Radio), Pamela Byrne (BBC *River City*), Claire Knight (BBC *River City*). Advises actors: "I think a lot of actors' headshots are very intense and serious looking – because it's easy to do. I help my clients produce contemporary publicity images, with energy and personality, which really improves their casting opportunities."

Nicholas Dawkes Photography APHP
London W4
mobile 07787 111997
email studio@nicholasdawkesphotography.co.uk
website www.nicholasdawkesphotography.co.uk
Facebook www.facebook.com/nicholasdawkesphoto
Instagram @nicholasdawesphotography

Services & rates: Prices start at £305 for headshots. Includes a full consultation, 2-3 hour session in a large fully-equipped studio, shooting in both natural and studio light. Up to 200-300 pictures taken, with full review of images on a large screen. Same-day uploading of images in colour and b&w on private client area, with email links to the client and their agent. Retouching 4 images included in price.

"The aim of my shoots is to show life and character in your headshots through one-to-one direction and explore and capture your different casting brackets."

Sean Ellis
mobile 07702 381258
email sean@seanellis.co.uk
website www.seanellis.co.uk
Instagram @seano_ellis

Services & rates: Photographer since 1986. Charges £150 for a 2–3-hour photo shoot including 200 shots. All images will be supplied via email in low-res format from which 5 can be chosen to be enhanced/retouched and supplied in high-res digital format. Additional images will be charged at £25 per image. Bespoke 10x8in prints can be supplied at £25 per print. If a large print run is required, this can be arranged at a more economical price. Uses a purpose-built studio at his home.

Work portfolio: Examples of work can be seen on the website. Has taken photographs for hundreds of actors, almost all of them have been for the Buttercup Agency website and their Spotlight entries. "Bring your upbeat, positive self with a clear idea of what you want and we'll do the rest together!"

Elliott Franks Photography Services
mobile 07802 537220
email elliottfranks@gmail.com
website www.elliottfranks.com

Services & rates: Charges £175 for a location shoot in the London area.

Work portfolio: Established in 1997. Photographs can be viewed on the web gallery. Has taken publicity shots for more than 800 actors. Elliott Franks is one of the UK's leading performing arts press photographers.

Greg Goodale
mobile 07768 173503
email greg@gregveit.com
website www.gregveit.com
Facebook www.facebook.com/Greg.Veit.Photography
Twitter @veit_photo

Services & rates: Established in 2009 and has worked extensively in stage photography in the UK and abroad. Offers 3 shoot types: Budget: £220 for 1 hour session, includes 150 images and a final selection of 40 images (2 retouched); Standard: £290 for 1.5 hour session, includes 250 images and a final selection of 60 images (4 retouched); Premium: £340 for 2.5 hour session, studio and location, 300 images and a final selection of 80 images (5 retouched). Works exclusively in digital photography. Clients include the National Theatre, Finborough Theatre, Pleasance Theatre and York Shakespeare Festival. Has on-going projects with Italia Conti Academy of Theatre Arts, Dream Arts and ArtsAdmin.

Work portfolio: Greg Goodale was stage photographer of the Gdansk International Shakespeare Festival. His work has appeared in many publications including *The Guardian, The Stage, Exeunt* and *The Telegraph.*

Nick Gregan Photography
21A Cowper Road, London SW19 1AA
tel 0800 0029 087
website www.nickgregan.com
Facebook www.facebook.com/NickGreganHeadshotPhotographer
Twitter @nickgregan
Instagram @nickgregan

Services & rates: Charges £285 for a 2-hour photo shoot, which includes unlimited photos and 4 retouched images (more can be purchased for £25 each). Charges £395 for a 3-hour headshot portfolio session, which includes unlimited photos and 6 retouched images (full or 3/4 lngth). Students are offered a discount on production of a valid student card. Also offers digital photography, for which the same rates apply. Photos are taken in a studio or outdoor location and both are wheelchair-accessible. Coaching and direction are provided throughout and there is a 24-hour turnaround time for images.

Work portfolio: Established in 1992. Has taken publicity photos for over 20,000 clients, including Paul Danan, Lucinda Rhodes and Jenny Powell. "My website offers '7 secrets to a great headshot' – check it out for loads of useful information." Author of *The Headshot Bible - 50 Tips for a Perfect Headshot.*

Claire Grogan APHP
18 Calverley Grove, London N19 3LG
mobile 07932 635381
email claire@clairegrogan.co.uk
website www.clairegroganphotography.com
Facebook www.facebook.com/Claire-Grogan-Photography-105661542805602/
Twitter @ClaireGroganPix
Instagram @ClaireGroganPix

Services & rates: Actors headshots: shoot prices from £200-£380. Digital shoots outdoor and/or studio. Natural light or flash. Discounted rates for full-time drama students. Offers full advice and help with clothing and make-up. Shoot times range from 2-4 hours in a relaxed environment. Studio and private outdoor space. Time and facilities for changing clothes/hair/make-up or shaving during shoots.

Specialises in capturing shots that really reflect the actor's personality and casting potential, also special TLC for those who normally find having their headshots done difficult.

Work portfolio: Established in 1991, with past clients including Denise Welch, Raji James, Martin Freeman,

Stephen Tomkinson, Steve McFadden and Heather Peace. Photographs can be viewed on the website, Facebook, Instagram and Twitter.

HCK Photography

Based in London
tel 020 7112 8499 (Studio)
email info@hckphotography.co.uk
website www.hckphotography.co.uk
Twitter @HCKPhotography

Services & rates: Established in 2007. Specialises in headshots and publicity photography. Charges £250 for a 2-hour session which includes pre-shoot consultation and 5 retouched images. Offers student discounts. Studio based.

Work portfolio: Has taken publicity photos for many actors. Recent clients include: Shane Rangi and Kiran Shah.

Jamie Hughes Photography

website www.jamiehughesphotography.com/headshots

Services & rates: Charges £285 for a bespoke photo shoot lasting up to 2 hours in a relaxed atmosphere. Over 300 images are shot with the best supplied on CD to take away, plus retouching and processing of 3 10x8in prints and digital originals. Additional prints (including retouching) are available for £15 each. Uses a studio and outdoor location, both of which are wheelchair accessible. Please see website for examples.

Remy Hunter Photography

Flat 5, Queen's Court, London N16 5UW
email remy_hunter@hotmail.com
website www.remyhunterphotography.co.uk

Services & rates: Specialist actors headshot photographer since 2001 and member of the APHP. Offers free, no obligation headshot sessions; only pay for images: 1-3 for £30 each, 4 for £110, 5 or more for £20 each. Location: Studio (London, N16) or outdoor (Barbican, City of London). Sessions available 7 days a week. 1 hour shoot time, not including a pre-shoot discussion. Images are available to view online on the same day. High- and low-res files supplied, subtle retouching and enhancing available.

Nick James APHP

451 Wick Lane, London E3 2TB
mobile 07961 122030
email nickjamesphotography@hotmail.co.uk
website www.nickjamesphotography.co.uk
Instagram @nickjamesphotography

Services & rates: Photographer since 2005. Digital service only. Charges £420 for a photoshoot, which includes processing of 800 shots taken with 500 on contact sheets and 4 images retouched. Student and previous clients rate available at £390 a session. A 2-hour session is also available for £320, 500 shots taken and 3 images retouched. Student and previous clients rate £300 a session. Does not provide prints, but extra photographs are available for £35 each. Uses mainly studio natural light and flash.

Work portfolio: Examples of work can be seen on the website.

Matt Jamie

Gateshead, Newcastle upon Tyne
mobile 07976 890643
website www.mattjamie.co.uk/portraits

Services & rates: Established in 2000. Digital photography. Cost of photoshoot is £145, £75 student rate. Additional £30 studio fee; can also shoot at outdoor locations selected by the client, or at collages/dramaschools on request. Shoot includes 1-hour studio session and 3 final high res images. Extra studio time and images can be purchased. 100% satisfaction promise with no fee charged if you're not happy with the images.

Work portfolio: Examples of photography can be seen online. Matt also works as an actor and film maker, so understands the requirements of the shot and the pressures involved. He offers a relaxed, informal shoot. You can bring a variety of different clothes, wigs, friends or anything else you might want with you to make you feel confident on the shoot.

JK Photography

202 Fir Tree Road, Epsom, Surrey KT17 3NL
tel (01737) 362043
email james@jk-photography.net
website www.jk-photography.net

Services & rates: Established in 1997. Sessions from £250 (studio and outdoors, no time limit) which include a minimum of 300-400 images and 4 retouched images, all in high-res, b&w and colour, delivered the next day.

Work portfolio: Has photographed over 500 actors with 20 years of industry experience. "Our creative team will ensure a relaxed session amd images that are a true representation of your casting needs."

Carole Latimer

113 Ledbury Road, Notting Hill, London W11 2AQ
tel 020 7727 9371
email carole@carolelatimer.com
website www.carolelatimer.com

Services & rates: Professional photographer for over 25 years. Charge for actors' headshots is £350 inc. VAT (student rate is £300). An electronic contact sheet is provided and up to 5 chosen images are put on to a CD. Photographs are taken in a studio and occasionally outdoor locations. The studio does not have wheelchair access.

Work portfolio: Has provided publicity photos for approximately 2,000 actors, including: Kate O'Mara,

Alistair McGowan, Maureen Lipman, Zoe Lucker and clients from the following agencies: Independent, Conway Van Gelder Grant, Narrow Road. "No large patterns. If it's a b&w shoot, bring at least one black top. Always bring a selection of tops so I have a choice. I have an exceptional daylight studio with full lighting equipment. Good facilities for make-up."

Steve Lawton APHP
20 Ockham Building, 9 Arts Lane, Bermondsey, London SE16 3GB
mobile 07973 307487
email info@stevelawton.com
website www.stevelawton.com

Services & rates: Charges £290 for a photoshoot, which includes pdf contact sheets; all shots in colour and b&w; and 4 touched-up hi-res jpegs. The same package is offered to students at the reduced price of £260. Additional 10x8in jpegs are priced at £25 each. Advises clients not to bring patterned tops; fitted t-shirts and v-necks in blue, grey or black are most effective.

Work portfolio: Established in 2001. Has taken photographs for more than 3,000 actors and is recommended by Curtis Brown, Independent Talent Group, United Agents, Lou Coulson, Jorg Betts, Shane Collins, International Artists and Bronia Buchanan, amongst others. A full portfolio and price information is available on the website.

LB Photography
website www.lisabowerman.com

Services & rates: Working actress and photographer for 30 years. Charges £225 for a photo shoot (student rate available). No VAT chargeable. Includes 7 high-res, re-touched images in colour and b&w. Based near Redhill Surrey (30 mins on the train from Victoria and the client can be picked up at the station). If the weather is bad the shoot can be rearranged for a different day. For portfolio and more details, visit website.

Pete Le May
mobile 07703 649246
email pete@petelemay.co.uk
website www.petelemay.co.uk/headshots

Services & rates: Based in London and established in 2002. Typically charges £250 (£200 for students) for a relaxed photography session lasting 2-3 hours, a download link of all the photographs in both colour and black-and-white – allowing you to make as many prints as you want – and retouching of your favourite 6 images. Photos are made in natural light, both indoors and outdoors. Visit the website for full details and examples of recent work.

Leejay Photography
100 Woodside Road, London N22 5HT
mobile 07590 463428

email leejay@leejayphotography.com
website www.leejayphotography.com
Facebook www.facebook.com/leejayphotography
Twitter @leejayphoto

Services & rates: Charges £180 (student rate £130) for a 2-3 hour session which includes 2 retouched photos (colour and b&w). Additional retouched photos can be purchased for £15 each, or 100 high res. unedited shots for £20. Shoots take place at own studio as well as outdoors.

Work portfolio: Established in 2011. Has taken publicity shots for around 150 actors. Recent clients include: Nick Julian (Independent Talent Group), Lisa Kerr (Conway Van Gelder Grant), Kim Ensor (K Talent), Annabel Lloyd (International Theatre Collective). Advises actors: "I trained as an actor and feel in most cases it takes an actor to take a great actors' headshot."

MAD Photography APHP
17 Starling Lane, Cuffley EN6 4JX
tel 01707 708553 *mobile* 07949 581909
email mad.photo123@gmail.com
email info@mad-photography.co.uk
website www.mad-photography.co.uk

Services & rates: Charges £350 (£300 for returning clients) for actors' photoshoot which includes photographer's fee, studio and location shoot, 200 proofs contact sheets emailed same day and 4 high-res images on disc. Offers a discounted rate of £275 to students (includes as above, but with 3 images on disc); also offers student shared shoots at £175 each (includes as above, but with 75 proofs contact sheets and 2 images on disc). Extra 10x8in prints are priced at £30 each and images on disc are £25. "Hair and make-up should be natural. Bring 4 tops in any colours: one v-neck, one collar, one t-shirt and one jacket. No white!"

Work portfolio: Established in 1997. Photographs can be viewed on the website and in *Contacts* and on Mandy. Has taken publicity shots for over 6,000 actors and student actors. Clients include: Shane Richie, Michelle Ryan, Susan Penhaligon, Michael Knowles, Jessica Wallace, John Partridge, Tom Law, Belinda Owusu, Janie Dee and Phoebe Thomas.

Raymondo Marcus
9 Hazel Close, Marlow SL7 3PW
mobile 07505 827071
email rm.224555@gmail.com
website www.raymondmarks.co.uk

Services & rates: Photographer since 2009. Minimum charge £250 (no VAT), full usage licence included. Headshots: Images guaranteed suitable for Spotlight and to meet agreed brief. Performances and events: Can cover performances and has had images featrued in *The Stage*. Testimonials from show business subjects provided on request.

Work portfolio: Examples of work can be seen on his website. Has taken photographs for a number of different actors and actresses, among them Suzanne Kendall, Laura Waddell, Shirley Anne Field, Jo Brand, Emma Thompson, Valerie Leon, Henry Jameson, Claudia Schiffer and Daniel Craig. "I have a good understanding that to generate casting calls is to present you as well as possible but so that there should be no surprises for casting directors i.e. quality images with no reliance on airbrushing."

Kirsten McTernan Photography & Design

Cardiff
mobile 07791 524551
email kirsten@kirstenmcternan.co.uk
website www.kirstenmcternan.co.uk

Services & rates: A professional and comfortable, relaxed headshot session in the studio overlooking Chapter Arts Centre in Cardiff. "We can discuss what you need from your headshot and work towards tailoring it to your needs but most importantly looking like you." The session normally lasts around an hour and as part of the fee two final images (in digital format) are included. Clients can purchase other photographs (or the entire session) for an additional cost.

Work portfolio: Established in 2005. Professional theatre and portrait photographer working exclusively within the performing arts community. Has taken publicity photos for over 400 actors. Recent clients include major casting agents such as: The Artists Partnership, Regan and Rimmer, Emptage Hallett, Boom Talent and David Chance, etc.

John Need

Studio 147, 1 Summerhall, Edinburgh EH9 1QE
mobile 07756 178947
email hello@johnneed.co.uk
website www.johnneed.co.uk

Services & rates: Photoshoot includes 200-250 shots. Prints are optional and charged individually. Only shoots digital. Shoots take place at own studio which is wheelchair accessible.

Work portfolio: Established in 2008. Has taken publicity shots for around 400 actors, a collection of which can be viewed on the website. Advises actors: "I know that getting photos right for media is a high priority for any performer. Whether you're in the biz or trying to get into it, get in touch, as I've shot hundreds of actors, presenters and DJs. First impressions count, so give casting directors what they're after – you!"

Claire Newman-Williams

The Studio, Elfin Cottage, 86 Chittoe, Chippenham SN15 2EL
mobile 07963 967444
email claire@clairenewmanwilliams.com
website www.clairenewmanwilliamsheadshots.com
Twitter @CNWHeadshots

Services & rates: Claire is a fine art and portrait photographer who has worked with actors in both the US and the UK, beginning in 1999. 3-hour+ photoshoots. All photographs are digital and each session includes unlimited shots edited down to 150 pictures on contact sheets. 2 10x8in retouched digital images are included as part of the session and further copies are available. Student rate is also available. Full details about headshot sessions can be seen on the website. Uses a studio for each photo shoot, though this is not wheelchair accessible.

Work portfolio: Has taken photographs for around 2,500 actors, among them Stephen Fry, Tom Hiddleston, Joanna Page, Ben Barnes, Richard Armitage and Kerry Ellis.

North London Headshot Photography

The Studio, 9A Sylvester Road, London N2 8HN
tel 020 8349 3632
email lynnherrick@gmail.com
website www.headshotslondon.co.uk
Twitter @herrickphoto
Instagram @createdbylynn

Services & rates: Charges £150–200 for a photoshoot, which includes 25+ images sent as digital files. Retouching is included in packages. Work takes place in the studio and attached garden. Has taken publicity photos for around 900 actors.

Michael Pollard Photographer APHP

21 Edenhurst Road, Mile End, Stockport, Greater Manchester SK2 6BT
tel 0161 456 7470 *mobile* 07800 989457
email info@michaelpollard.co.uk
website www.michaelpollard.co.uk
Facebook www.facebook.com/michaelpollardphotographer
Twitter @MichaelActors
Instagram @michaelpollardphotography

Services & rates: Charges £145 for a 2 hour shoot, includes at least 150 shots on the contact sheets and 5 edited images of your choice. Additional images are charged at £10 each. The shoot is unhurried and relaxed and can be both outdoors in natural light and in a studio environment to give the widest variety of images possible. Colour contact sheets are then emailed to the actor and can be sent to their agent also.

"Actors can bring a number of tops ranging from lighter to darker tones. Tops should be simple and comfortable with generally a round- or V-neck, though more character-based shots are now also taken which may involve a wider variety of clothing and styling. Hair generally needs to be tidy but avoid going to the hairdresser the day before to have it cut or styled. For women, make-up should be simple and sparing, avoiding lip liner or lipstick that is too dark or too red. For men, they can arrive with a beard or stubble and shave part way through. The key is to keep things simple and natural and to be positive and be prepared. Think how you want to look and how you don't want to look. Enjoy it and be yourself!"

Work portfolio: Established in 1993. Photographs can be viewed on the website and social media.

David Price Photography
Hackney, London
mobile 07950 542494
email info@davidpricephotography.co.uk
website www.davidpricephotography.co.uk

Services & rates: Established since 2003. Currently divides his time between Los Angeles and London. Please email for availability.

Work portfolio: See website for full details.

Ben Rector
mobile 07770 467791
email ben@benrector.com
website www.benrector.com

Please view my updated portfolio on website.

Robin Savage Photography APHP
North London
mobile 07901 927597
email contact@robinsavage.co.uk
website www.robinsavage.co.uk
Facebook www.facebook.com/people/Robin-Savage-Photography/
Twitter @robinsavagepics
Instagram @robin_savage_headshots

Services & rates: A London-based actors' headshot photographer. Has been in business for over 15 years. Has worked with actors who have appeared in the West End, the National Theatre, the RSC and theatres all around the world who have worked in feature films, major TV dramas, soaps, sitcoms, sketch shows and commercials. Sessions are £295 (£280 for students). Visit the website for more information and to get in touch.

Howard Sayer Photography
mobile 07860 559891
email howard@howardsayer.com
website www.howardsayer.com

Services & rates: Casting headshots and portraiture photos, please email for current rates. Fast turnaround and option to shoot on location.

Karen Scott Photography
London SW19
mobile 07958 975950
email info@karenscottphotography.com
website www.karenscottphotography.com
Facebook www.facebook.com/karenscottphoto
Twitter @karenscottphoto
Instagram @karenscottphoto

Services & rates: Charges £225 for Actors Headshot Shoot. Unlimited images are taken during a relaxed

and unhurried shoot (with outfit changes as necessary) and edited to approximately 150 proofs. All proofs are b&w and colour and cropped to 10x8in. High quality contact sheets of the proofs are then emailed to you, after which your chosen 4 images are fully finished including contrast and tonal adjustments and retouching. The 4 finished images in colour and b/w are then uploaded to a private folder, these are high resolution downloadable and printable files. 4-7 day turnaround. Outdoor or indoor locations used using natural light. Student rates are available; a 'half-shoot' can be booked at the discounted rate of £125 for actors transitioning back into work after lockdown.

Work portfolio: Portfolio of images can be viewed on the website, please check for details of contemporary shoots for models, dancers, musicians, etc. Production, publicity and live shoots are also possible – check website for details.

Catherine Shakespeare Lane
The Monsell Stores, 43 Monsell Road, London N4 2EF
tel 020 7226 7694
email catherineshakespeare.lane@gmail.com
website www.csl-art.co.uk

Services & rates: Photoshoot includes photographer's fee, studio and equipment costs, processing of 2 b&w 36exps, contact sheets and 4 10x8in prints. Offers a student package (1 roll of 36 and 2 10x8in prints). Uses natural light inside and favours a natural look. "My aim is to show my clients at their most interesting."

Work portfolio: Established in 1975. Photographs can be viewed at Spotlight's offices and in *Contacts*. Has taken publicity shots for more than 2,000 actors.

Michael Shelford
Parkhall Business Centre, Dulwich
email shelford.michael@gmail.com
website www.shelfordheadshots.com
Instagram @michaelshelford

Services & rates: Charges £330 for a standard photoshoot; student discount of rate £300. A portfolio shoot is £450.

Work portfolio: Has taken publicity photos for 900-plus actors. Recent clients include: David Adjala (Independent Talent Group), James Norton (Artist Partnership), Alexandra Roach (Gordon and French), Nick Hendrix (Ken McReddie), Daniel Ings (The Rights House), James Rastall (Rebecca Blond), Antonia Thomas (Curtis Brown), Theo James (Markham & Froggatt) and Shazid Latif (Lou Coulson).

Alan Sill Photography
43 Surtees Road, Peterlee, County Durham SR8 5HA
tel 0191 518 1677 *mobile* 07977 141809
email alansillphotography@gmail.com
website www.alansillphotography.co.uk
Facebook www.facebook.com/alansillphoto

Services & rates: Established in 1990. Photoshoot includes as many shots as it takes to complete the assignment. Prints are charged individually. Discount for students with a valid student union card. Works on location, at the client's home or at a home studio, which is wheelchair accessible. Member of the National Union of Journalists.

Faye Thomas Photography

London
mobile 07813 449229
email booking@fayethomas.co.uk
website www.fayethomas.co.uk
Facebook www.facebook.com/
fayethomasphotography
Twitter @FayeThomasPhoto
Instagram @fayethomasphoto

Services & rates: Charges £380 for standard headshots which includes a 2-3 hour shoot, 3 retouched, hi res. images and next day delivery. Student rate is available. Charges £520 for deluxe headshots which includes 8 retouched, hi res. images with full edit service and 14 day delivery. Shoots take place in an outdoor location or studio – neither is wheelchair accessible.

Work portfolio: Established in 2005. Recommended by top London agencies including Hamilton Hodell, Troika, Conway Van Gelder Grant, Curtis Brown, United Agents, 42, Independent Talent Group, The Artists' Partnership, Markham Froggatt & Irwin and many more. High profile clients include: Hayley Atwell, Phoebe Waller-Bridge, Jodie Comer, Emma Corrin, Michelle Dockery, Sam Heughan, Jodie Whittaker, Maisie Williams, Bradley James, Joseph Morgan, Victoria Hamilton, Evanna Lynch, Emily Beecham, Matt Ryan, Charity Wakefield, Tuppence Middleton, Tom Riley, Lauren Cohan, Marc Warren, Kieran Bew, Lucy Griffiths, Lisa Dwan, Ramin Karimloo, Hannah New, John Light, Michelle Fairley, Shaun Evans, Samuel Barnett, Cara Theobold, Jemima Rooper, Elliot Cowan, Alex Hassell, Sam Spiro, Dervla Kirwan, Freddie Highmore and Cressida Bonas. See portfolio on website.

TM Photography & Design

Unit 41, The Maltings Business Centre,
Roydon Road, Stanstead Abbotts,
Hertfordshire SG12 8HG
tel (01920) 318040
email studio@tmphotography.co.uk
website www.tmphotography.co.uk

Services & rates: Established in 1995. All photography is digital. Cost of a 1 hour photoshoot is £75. The cost includes 1 b&w or colour, retouched image. Images can be viewed by the client as they are taken. Images are loaded on to a private webpage to be viewed. Orders can be placed online. Student photoshoot is discounted at £40. Photos taken in studio or outdoor locations or client's home. Studio is wheelchair accessible.

Work portfolio: Has photographed approximately 3,000 actors, walk-ons and background artists. Has photographed many of the clients of Allsorts Agency, Ray Knight, G2 and Guys & Dolls. Actors photographed include: Fraser Hines and Antonia Okonma. Photoshoots can be booked at short notice. Also offers repro service and promotional products such as websites, model cards and CV creation.

Tony Blake Photography

68 Watergate Street, Chester CH1 2LA
mobile 07974 8044403
email tony@tonyblakephoto.co.uk
website www.tonyblakephoto.co.uk
Twitter @tonyblakephoto
Director Tony Blake

Services & rates: Established in 2001. Based in the north west of England and shoots natural light headshots in a relaxed studio environment. Offers standard and bespoke packages for actors.

Prices start from £150 depending on shoot length which is normally between one-and-a-half and two hours. Check the website for full details. Clients receive contact sheets of all edited-down images to select their favourites for re-touching and processing. Digital files only. Photographs are taken in natural light studio. Studio is not wheelchair accessible.

Work portfolio: A portfolio of images can be viewed on the website.

Steve Ullathorne

London
tel 07961 380969
email steve@steveullathorne.com
website www.steveullathorne.com
Facebook www.facebook.com/
SteveUllathornePhotography
Twitter @steveullathorne
Instagram @ullathorne

Services & rates: Charges £250 for a digital photo shoot; this covers all fees, studio costs and contact sheet. Will offer a discount to students, negotiable at the time of booking. All clients receive an online contact sheet with a web address that they can pass on to their agent. Prior to the shoot, clothing and locations will be discussed with the client on the telephone. All photos are retouched in Photoshop to remove any blemishes plus any other light retouching required by the actor. Email proofs are sent of each chosen image. Rather than specifying a number of images, prices are dictated by duration of the shoot, which is 2 hours. Actors usually end up with more than 100 shots to choose from.

Work portfolio: Please see website for samples.

Vanessa Valentine Photography

mobile 07904 059541
email valentine.photography@hotmail.com
website www.vanessavalentinephotography.com

Services & rates: Headshots. Based in London. Please see the website for more details.

Greg Veit Photography

mobile 07768 173503
email greg@gregveit.com
website www.gregveit.com
Facebook www.facebook.com/greg.veit.photography
Twitter @veit_photo

Services & rates: Prices start from £180 for 2 shots. Works exclusively in digital photography. Photographs taken in studio or on location. Studio has wheelchair access.

Work portfolio: Established in 2009. Studio in central London, closest Tube Tottenham Court Road. An experienced headshot and stage photographer; has photographed 500 actors. Recent clients include Jane Paul Gets, Sandra Meunier, Tristram Kimborough, James Arama and Giorgio Borghes.

Ana Verastegui Photography

tel +34 628 000 814
email anaphotography@me.com

Services & rates: Photo shoot includes approximately 150 shots and 3 10x8in prints. Student rate is available. Also offers digital photography at the same rates. Shoots take place mainly outdoors in wheelchair accessible locations.

Work portfolio: Established in 2008. Has taken publicity photos for over 100 actors. Clients include: Cordelia Bugeja, Polly Maberly and Hannah Melbourn.

Vincenzo Photography

tel 020 8372 0428 *mobile* 07962 338289
email info@vincenzophotography.com
website www.vincenzophotography.com

Services & rates: Photographer since 2000. Charges £230 for a 2-hour photoshoot, which includes 8 high-res. digital files, 4 each in b&w and colour. Offers a student rate of £200 per session. Uses a studio with garden for external shots or is happy to arrange another location of a client's choosing.

Work portfolio: Examples of work can be seen on the website. Has taken photographs for many actors, among them Ken Stott, Hayley Atwell and Paul Nicholas.

Philip Wade

88 Englefield Road, London N1 3LG
tel 020 7226 3088 *mobile* 07956 599691
email pix@philipwade.com
website www.philipwade.com
Facebook www.facebook.com/
PhilipWadeHeadshotPhotography
Twitter @philipwadepix

Services & rates: Provides a variety of packages. Charges £350 for a headshot package which includes pre-shoot consultation, 4 retouched images and 12 images available in high res. colour and b&w. £225 pro-headshot package includes 6 images. £150 headshot session includes 3 images. £50 Spotlight headshot offer includes 1 image. Sessions are in the studio and outside with a wide variety of backgrounds. Clients given acces to a personal online gallery to view images.

Work portfolio: Has taken publicity shots for hundreds of actors. Recent clients include: PHM, Abacus, Imperium, Shepherd Management and Sandra Boyce.

Michael Wharley Photography APHP

Waterloo, London, Zone 1
mobile 07961 068759
email michaelwharley@michaelwharley.com
website www.michaelwharley.com

Services & rates: Established in 2006. Shoots in digital, featuring studio-lit and outdoor, colour and b&w shooting as standard. Two-hour 'Pro' shoot suitable for all actors. Between 150 and 400 photos taken. Photos supplied in industry-standard web- and print-optimised formats. See website for full details of packages and approach.

Work portfolio: Has taken hundreds of photos for each edition of *Spotlight* – 'Top Theatre Photographer' (*The Stage*). Works for actors and agencies across the spectrum of the industry. Recent clients have been represented by agencies such as United, Angel & Francis, Curtis Brown and Felix de Wolfe, studied at drama schools like RADA and Central, and worked on high-profile film, theatre and TV projects. Also writes regularly on headshot and digital trends in the acting industry (see **www.wharleywords.co.uk**).

Alex Winn Photography

Studio P, Container City II, Trinity Buoy Wharf, 64 Orchard Place, London E14 0JW
tel 020 3432 4408 *mobile* 07816 317038
website www.alexwinn.com
Twitter @alexwinn

Services & rates: Photographer since 2006. Offers 3 packages priced between £200-£325 for sessions starting at 2hrs up to 4hrs. Depending on package selected, they include either 2, 4 or 6 professionally retouched images delivered via digital download. Contact sheets are made available online 24 hours after each session in both b&w and colour. All sessions are shot and delivered digitally. Studio and outdoor location (both wheelchair-accessible).

Work portfolio: Examples of work can be seen on the website. Has taken photographs for several hundred actors, among them Elizabeth Carling (Curtis Brown), Rafe Spall (Troika), Preeya Kalidas

(Cole Kitchenn), Richie Campbell (AHA Talent), Claire Hope-Ashitey (United Agents), Arnold Oceng (Troika), Martin Jenson (Simon & How), James Farrar (Cole Kitchenn), Olly Yellop (A&J Management), Michael Rivers (Marcus & McCrimmon) and Wil Johnson (CAM). "I operate in a relaxed but professional way to ensure that everyone can feel as comfortable as possible in front of the camera. I think good headshots are the result of a collaboration between myself and the actors I work with so each session is tailored accordingly."

Robert Workman

Studio 32, West Kensington Mansions, Beaumont Crescent, London W14 9PF
mobile 07814 126260
email bob@robertworkman.co.uk
website www.robertworkman.co.uk
Facebook www.facebook.com/robert.workman.10420
Twitter @BobWorkman
Instagram @ro_bert4940

Services & rates: Casting portrait session includes portraits taken both in the studio and outside in a nearby park, a web gallery of the results, the client's choice of 5 retouched 10x8in prints, and jpegs ready for digital submissions to casting directors and Spotlight online.

Work portfolio: Photographs can be viewed on the website or in a portfolio kept in Spotlight's offices. Has been taking publicity shots for actors every year for nearly 30 years.

REPRO COMPANIES

Image Photographic

6 Stonehouse Street, Plymouth PL1 3PE
tel (01752) 202929
email spectrum91@yahoo.co.uk
website www.imagephotographic.com

Image Photographic is now part of Spectrum Photo Labs Ltd.

Various print sizes available from 6x4 to 10x8 in b&w or colour. File upload facility and online ordering with secure payment facility available. Same day dispatch if ordered by 10am. Please email or phone with any queries.

Visualeyes Repro Ltd

tel 020 8875 8811
email imaging@visualeyes.co.uk
website www.visualeyes.co.uk
Facebook www.facebook.com/pages/Visualeyes-Repro/32217334051
Twitter @visphoto

Dedicated reproduction of performers' photographic headshots. Free postage on orders over 10 prints. Print sizes: 6x4in, 7x5in, 8x6in, 10x8in. Other services include: retouching, captioning, online ordering. Standard or 5-day economy service. Multi-run print discount and individual student or group discounts available. See website for details.

Getting the most from your photographs

Angus Deuchar

When searching for actors, most casting directors or directors start with a pile of photographs. Their time is limited, so they really only want to see the people who stand a chance of being right for a part – and the picture will be a vital part of their decision-making process. It's important therefore, to ensure that the photographs you use are as good as they can possibly be.

Have a flick through *Spotlight*. As well as being compulsive entertainment for any actor, it can be a great way to decide what works and what doesn't. If *you* were the casting director, who would (and wouldn't) you see? Try it for different types of production: a musical, a Shakespeare play, a TV drama. You may be surprised at the assumptions you make based on the photographs.

I'm going to look at what makes a good actor's photograph; help you think through how to choose a photographer; and discuss how you can get the best results from a photo session. Here is a list of, in my opinion, some important qualities to look for in a good headshot. It should be:

• **Honest.** This to me is the key to a good actor's photograph. Decisions at interviews are often largely made in the first few seconds, so it's important that the person who walks through the door is the person they saw in the photograph. If an actor looks different in some way, the interviewer's first reaction may well be disappointment. Which can't be a good start!

• **Well lit.** The face and hair should be well lit. If there are excessively bright areas or shadows on the face, the photo is probably not doing the actor any favours.

• **In focus.**

• **A good connection with the eyes.** These are possibly the most important feature, as these are what we generally look at first. We make a connection with the eyes. They should be well lit, in focus, looking *at* the camera and not squinting. They should also be 'alive' and not glazed over.

• **Well framed.** Ideally just head and shoulders. Not too close up, as it can look a bit overbearing. Likewise, not too far away as the face becomes too small.

• **Nothing 'tricksy'.** No fake hand-gestures, and certainly no props!

Can't I just get my friend to take some pictures in the back garden? Well, you could (in fact, some do). But what kind of image of yourself would that portray? You can always see such pictures in *Spotlight* – the actor looking awkward, squinting into the sunlight or the picture out of focus. Again, if you were the casting director, would you consider that actor to be serious? There's no point in cutting costs here. Decent photographs can more than pay for themselves.

Finding a photographer

Assuming you've decided to employ a photographer, how do you find the right one? Professional photographers are not all alike. Some who may be fantastic at, say, press or fashion, may not be good at actors' portraits. It's important that the photographer knows the business of Acting. There are countless listings of specialist actors' photographers – in publications like this one; as adverts in *Contacts*; or on posters in The Actors Centre; but the style of photographs, and the ability of the photographers, are as varied as the prices and packages. It is therefore essential to check out their work for yourself. Have a look at their website if they have one, or at least try to see several different examples of their work.

Don't make a choice based solely on price. The amount a photographer charges is not necessarily an indication of how good (or bad) they are. Wherever possible, make your decision about a photographer based mostly on the *work* they produce, rather than how much they charge. It's important ultimately that you get the best possible photographs.

Find out the following:

• **Studio or natural light?** Studio light is easier to standardise and can be used at any time of the day or night and during any weather. It can be made to flatter someone, but won't necessarily show what they will look like in 'real life'. I prefer natural light, as I believe it to be generally more honest. Good natural light can still show someone at their best, but it won't deceive. It can also be more relaxing for the subject to be outside for the session. Casting directors often prefer natural light as it gives a better indication of who is actually going to walk through the door.

• **Film or digital?** Digital technology has moved on to such an extent that the quality of either format is comparable. Digital tends to produce a cleaner, less grainy image *and* you can check the results as you go along. It is essential however, that whoever is preparing the final photograph knows how to convert the image into a good-quality black and white print, with decent contrast and without loss of detail. This takes a reasonable amount of skill and know-how.

• **How much do they charge?** Does that include VAT? If relevant, you may want to ask about concessions for students.

• **How many photos do I get?** Find out how many photos will actually be taken at the session and how many different, finished 8x10 prints you can choose.

• **How will I view my proofs?** Some photographers will put your proofs onto a website enabling you to view them blown up on the screen. You may prefer a paper contact sheet, which, although much smaller to view, is more portable. If you want both, you may need to pay extra – so ask.

• **How long until I see my proofs?** Websites can often be published the same day as the session, while a paper contact will usually need to be produced and posted, so will take a few days. Some photographers will show you pictures on a computer straight away. This can be useful as a guide, but you probably shouldn't try to make final decisions without a bit of time to think.

• **How long will it take until I get my finished prints?** Try to get an indication of how long you should expect to wait after placing your final order. Hopefully, no more than a few days.

• **Do I get a CD?** As well as the prints, a few electronic versions of the final photos are extremely useful. They can be used on a website, to send a submission via email, to send to Spotlight, to print out yourself, or to act as the master-copy for your 'repros'. Find out if the photographer will provide you with a few different versions on a CD, and if it's included in the price.

Resources

The session itself

Here are some important things to prepare before – or think about during – your photo session.

• **Your 'look'.** Do you want to appear neutral or as a particular 'type'? For instance, earrings (on men especially) or other piercings, may limit you to modern or even 'alternative' characters. A formal jacket might suggest a business person or MP. Any of these looks may be fine, as they can make you 'ideal' for a particular type of role – but it's likely that that's all you'll ever be seen for while using that photograph! You decide – it really depends upon how you are marketing yourself.

• **Make-up and hair.** Preferably little or no make-up, but certainly no more than you would wear normally, day to day. Some photographers provide a 'hair and make-up' service but I would strongly discourage actors from using this. Don't confuse actors' portraits with having a glamorous photo to stick on top of the piano! If someone else prepares you, you're unlikely to look like the 'normal' you and it may be difficult to recreate that look in the future. Likewise, if you're planning to get a new hairstyle before your session, do so several days in advance to give you a chance to get used to it.

• **What to wear.** Concentrate on the neckline. Wear something you feel comfortable in, but avoid distracting patterns or logos. Most colours are fine, and black often works well. Bright white can affect the exposure so is less helpful. A jacket of some sort for some of the photos can often work well. Jewellery can be distracting so is usually best avoided.

• **Facial expression.** A big smile is often great for musicals or front-of-house pictures, but for other casting purposes it can seem a little over the top. Any kind of 'emoting' can seem over-earnest or, worse, corny. I tend to favour a good neutral expression with 'spark' behind the eyes. A kind of a relaxed, open look with the smallest hint of a smile.

Ultimately, photographs play an important part in helping you get a foot in the door. But once you've been called for the interview, it's over to you.

Angus Deuchar trained as an actor, during which time he subsidised his grant by taking photographs of his fellow students. When he left drama school in 1987 he soon realised that this was an ideal way to make a living between jobs! He pursued both careers for the first seven years, but has continued with just the photography since then.

The changing face of voiceovers

Simon Cryer & Marina Caldarone

So, you have a voice, but do you really know how to place it in the voice industry? It is increasingly common for people to call our voice agency and say:

"*I've always dreamt of being a voiceover, will you sign me?*" or
"*My friends keep telling me I should be a voice actor, can I be on your books?*"
"*I've been told I've got a really good voice, can I get into voiceover*" or even
"*How much does it cost for you to represent me?*"

Cue the alarm bells ... they clearly know little about the industry that they want to be a part of. So, is a call to an agent the appropriate first stage of the process? It isn't.

We always suggest that the potential voice actor should start by getting some training before they step anywhere near a recording studio or indeed before they speak to any other voice agents. Not 'off-the-shelf' online video training that is not tailored to their requirements, but bespoke training to help them focus their personal skillset, to teach them about how the voice works, how to identify delivery styles within the script and for themselves, how to ensure fullest range and connection, how to take direction, how to communicate with the microphone ... all conducted, ideally, with a professionalvoice coach who works in audio. Professional singers go through years of training to ensure that when they open their mouth, the right sound is produced immediately, not after the third attempt, but instantly – upon demand. The same expectation is at play in the audio industry. Time is money. You'll be re-booked if you work efficiently and creatively within the time constraints. Training supports that.

Think of the voiceover like the score to a movie – it should effortlessly, or seemingly effortlessly, guide us to the end result rather than pull focus and fight the content around it. It's an art. You might need professional guidance to get there.

This core skill set is covered for the most part in the standard conventional drama school training.

You would then book an expert to record a voice-reel for you to showcase your skill as a voiceover artist. This enables agents and prospective clients to listen to the fullest range within your natural voice, in order to consider you for representation or bookings. So, making the right choice choosing a production company is really important.

There is a cost to making a reel, you are paying for a certain level of expertise, for an industry standard quality This all helps to ensure that you enter the industry fully 'tooled up'.

How has the industry changed post pandemic?

The voiceover industry has gone through an overhaul during the last few years. This industry moved online during the pandemic and kept going. There are long-standing experts in their fields still thriving (voice agencies), and then there are countless 'pretend' agencies popping up (and closing down) trying to sell 'talent' (industry standard term for 'voice artists') for less than would be their minimum rate.

Home studios (however crudely set up) are the 'New Norm' and this is largely a progressive and positive thing in certain circumstances, however, by taking away the sound engineer and/or director, one loses that extra pair of ears that often helps ensure the client gets a kick ar$e performance rather than a weak or 'safe' performance. Learn to self-scrutinise. Record yourself on your phone, your computer, play back and listen and give yourself notes to improve performance.

There is also an unprecedented volume of unrepresented talent in the market who have completed a 4-week online training course and who then define themselves as 'professional'. Consequently, we sometimes spend time in the studio with clients (the industry standard term for the person/organisation buying the 'product,' or the 'voice') who have tried to cut corners and then find themselves having to re-cast the talent in order to bring their project to life.

The following is a Quick Guide to some of the terminology of the voiceover world

A voice-reel

This averages 6-10 tracks in length, each track lasting anything from a 20-second commercial to a 90-second piece of documentary or narration. It should be professionally edited to include music and effects where appropriate; it should not be a series of dry recordings of you reading, but rather should play to your strengths. It should not include 'everything' you think should go on – the reel itself needs to be about **diversity within your natural range,** not about you showing every accent you can do. Focus on the different colours and weights and drives within your natural voice. You need not include a Drama track/monologue. Voice-Over agents won't sell your voice to the audio drama market, but your acting agent might. If In doubt, include one.

The reel needs to include some factual material/documentary commercials and maybe fiction/audio book. This should be delivered to you post-recording as MP3 files and WAV files. You must also insist on the Voice Only files too (the final performance minus the music and effects).

You should also ask for a Megamix. This is a 'best of' compilation of excerpts of your full voice-reel. Megamixes are (usually) 2 x 1-minute in length (one clip being all commercial excerpts, and the other covering everything else), or 1 x 2-minute maximum compilation of the whole reel.

Voice-Over agent as opposed to Acting Agent

A Voice Over Agent focuses on the unseen performer, and anything that does not require any kind of physical performance. This means they will represent you for all audio only content (you are promoted for work in the Radio Drama generally by your *acting* agent) Many actors have two separate agents, as the work lies in two very sperate spheres.

A **Voiceover Rate Card** specifies what each voiceover artist charges for the work they provide. There is a minimum rate set by Equity; however, the rates aren't always adhered to. And some voiceover agents, in an attempt to get their client the job, will undercut that rate. It's not difficult to see where this leads to – fees spiralling lower for all.

The **Basic Studio Fee** (BSF) is what each voiceover agent will set for their clients. Most rates start at around £275 per hour, sometimes a little less for low-budget games, often much more for larger advertising campaigns.

The **Usage Fee** is a variable based on many other criteria, such as distribution, whether there is web usage, global coverage, amount of airtime, size of the potential audience, passive or paid media, socials, cinema, radio, broadcast TV, VOD – the list goes on. Asking the right questions is crucial before you agree to anything.

When it comes to usage fee, the client will often dictate what they want to pay and try and avoid giving you detailed information on how the content will be used. This should cause concern and clearly they are not versed in industry rates or are trying to save on budget by not paying you the proper rate. Everything placed in the public domain requires a license to do so. This is the usage rights fee and ALL jobs require some level of usage. If you're unsure, ask a friendly Voice Agent before committing to anything.

Lastly, never sign a contract before you have it checked and NEVER sign away 'All Rights' without having the contract checked by an expert.

The most commonly asked questions – answered

If I make a Voicereel, will I get work?

Without a voicereel it is unlikely that you will ever get paid work – potential clients need to hear what you sound like in order to cast you. If you have an agent, they will source work for you, but if you don't, you can join the Pay to Play Websites in order to source work. Be careful though, those websites often pay you much less than they should. Know your worth.

So how do I select a company to make my Voicereel?

Do your research, check out their credentials and their website. Listen to examples of their work, which should be online. Do they provide a Producer/Director, or just an engineer, and what is the quality of their edit? Who are their previous clients? Look at testimonials. All companies will recycle, to some extent, the same scripts, but to what extent? They should be able to tell you. If it looks too good to be true, it generally is. Aim for mid-market prices and stay clear of the £99 voice-reel – with my agent head on, this will not be suitable. We need content directed by practitioners who are well versed in getting a great performance from you and who are tapped into current market trends in order for the agent to pitch you to clients. Also we need to hear full versions of each track. The £99 package sometimes is *just* the mega mix. If you're paying for a service where they just record, edit, deliver and offer little direction, then most agents, if they're interested in you, will ask you to start the process again of making a reel – so shop wisely and choose a specialist rather than a popup service.

How do different companies make the voicereels?

Each Voice-over production company will have a house style, of sorts, but the first voice we hear on your reel should be the one that is closest to your natural voice; that is undisputed. Some companies, at very little cost, will provide a basic reel, that does not truly tap into nuances of your natural sound, or indeed explore your voice beyond where you naturally use it. This is often not good enough for an agent to source work for you as mentioned earlier. Others will invite you on to their website for you to select your own choice of material from their online archive, adjusting that choice on the recording day if it isn't quite right for you. Some will have a chat with you on the phone, get the measure of your voice and email you relevant material; others will see you for a one-on-one consultation before the recording day, go through scripts and make a selection for you to take away and prep along with direction notes. The latter is by far the most satisfactory for all (although often this is done remotely to save clients travelling to the studio twice).

What should I expect to pay to have a voicereel made?

Anything from £99 to £1000.

Look for producers in the range of £300-£500 for a full reel and ensure the team that produce are experienced producers and practitioners in the industry and not just suppliers who churn out generic reels at volume to keep the price down.

I have an existing voicereel, but it's a bit tired and old fashioned. What should I do?

Upgrade it. But check out whether there is anything there you can recycle before getting rid of it all. Send it to the company you are making the reel with; they will listen to it and recommend whether there is anything there you could keep for the new voice-clip and in turn, advise on new material. Note, your voice changes over time, as do script trends, so you should be looking to update your reel every 5+ years.

How do I approach voiceover agents about representation?

Research who they currently have on their books. Your opening gambit, with your voice-clips and CV attached, should be that you note they don't already represent anyone like you. Do not approach anyone who has 'your voice' already. Do not chase for responses, agents are busy and if they're interested, they will be in touch. Follow the guidance on the website to the letter and address your application to a person and not 'Dear Agent'. Some of the more 'modern' agents will have a submission system and will not accept email requests – so do your homework.

I've got my first voiceover job, what does the employer expect?

For you to be efficient, precise, imaginative, and quick to take and interpret direction and turn it into a performance. To be positive, upbeat, someone who won't let their irritation show when asked to repeat the same sentence 30 times, with the only direction being, 'Can you try something different?' Someone who will be fine about running a little over time. If that really is an issue, take it up with your agent, after the booking; they will know how and whether to act on it. Studio etiquette is paramount, this can't be overstated.
A useful mantra, 'if you're on time, you're late' *always* be early early early...

Should I include a Radio Drama track?

Being a strong actor does not mean you will necessarily be a good voiceover. The skills are quite different. The pay rates are different, the representation is different, and your 'regular' agent would put you forward for it, not your voiceover agent. As mentioned earlier. So, in spite of some agents saying that there is no need for the actor to have any drama on the voicereel, this can feel like a wasted opportunity. You need to play to your natural casting, as long as it offers an alternative take on your voice. And of course it is the only track on the reel which is *transformative* – every other track is *you* but each track a different version of you.

The Animation and Gaming reel

If the voice reel is all about the fullest range within your *natural* voice, then the Animation and Gaming clip is about fullest range within the *unnatural* voice. An Animation reel needs to include at least 15 extraordinary voices. And the Gaming reel needs to play to the Gaming archetypes that exist in that world. Do your research. Then create and script your own sentences, to bypass copyright, that respond directly to those industry trends. Show what you can do. This clip would stand apart from your voice reel. It's a different market. If you want to flag an ability for this market, without making an entire animation clip, then ask whoever is making your reel to find a fantasy story which requires lots of different character voices, characters which ideally aren't 'human', but dragons, elves, giants, witches, animals, monsters …and flaunt your voice acting ability to create totally diverse characters that wow the listener.

Simon Cryer is the CEO of Crying Out Loud and Damn Good Voices and has 25+ years' experience working as a VoiceOver Director. He has been VOD for award-winning international advertising campaigns, corporate content and Documentaries. **Marina Caldarone** is a Voice Director with Crying Out Loud (www.cryingoutloud.co.uk), a company that has been making voiceover reels for actors since 1999, when they were CDs... She is a Radio Drama Producer, Theatre Director and Acting Coach and is co-author with Maggie Lloyd Williams of the bestselling *Actions – An Actors Thesaurus*. She has been a tutor in actor training since 1984. Which makes her older than she would care to admit to…

Showreel, voicereel and website services

Over the last decade, there's been an undeniable shift in how self-marketing works for actors: now, with just a mobile phone and an Internet connection, anyone can convincingly and effectively market themselves. There has also been a significant increase in the amount of (sometimes contradictory) advice offered to actors on content, length, format and so much more.

Voicereels (also known as 'voice demos' and, sometimes confusingly, 'showreels') have been around for several decades, and a good one could attract the attention of a voice agent. However, the world of voice-overs is hard to break into and so a quality-produced 'reel' is very important. Showreels (applied to videoed performances) are a more recent innovation but they've quickly become equally crucial, and a good one may just tip the balance in your favour.

Personal websites (for actors) are becoming more popular, but are still far from being essential. After all, you should already have a web presence via Spotlight's website, or a regularly updated social media page.

If you intend to put together a professionally produced voicereel or showreel, it's important to check the details (including pricing) of each possible company and the quality of their work. You should also assess whether the financial investment(s) involved could produce sufficient return. Is there a real possibility that one (or more) will enhance your chances of acting work?

Note: It is very important that you have permission from the copyright-holders of any material that you intend to use, and some companies will help with this. It is also important to check the current charges of each company that interests you, as some will change during the lifetime of this edition.

Accent Bank
tel 020 7223 5160
email info@theaccentbank.com
website www.theaccentbank.com

Voicereel services: A voice-over portal distributed to an international market. Acts as a shop window for experienced voice-over talent specialising in authentic regional and international voices. "Accent Bank provides bespoke one-on-one coaching and workshops for those new to the business. We pride ourselves on a very personal service, using the best coaches and directors, original material and excellent production facilities to bring out the best in your voice. For more information, or to have a chat, contact us by phone or email."

Actor Showreels
51 The Cut, South Bank, London SE1 8LF
mobile 07766 066870

email post@actorshowreels.co.uk
website www.actorshowreels.co.uk
Key contact Hugh Montini Lee

Showreel services: The actor works with an editor to select the material from pre-existing clips. The edited material is uploaded online, so that the actor's agent can also view the edit. The editing/upload process continues until the actor is totally satisfied with the final edit. The average duration of a showreel is 3.5 minutes. Average cost per showreel is £175. Recent clients have included: Claire Goose (Independent), Gina Bellman (Independent), Tulisa (Cole Kitchenn), Kerry Ellis (Cole Kitchenn), Colin Salmon (Curtis Brown) and Jennifer Hennessy (Curtis Brown).

Actors Apparel
London based – travels to clients
email lulu@actorsapparel.com
website www.actorsapparel.com

Showreel services: Established in 2010. Tailor-made showreels; originally written scenes tailored to client's casting type and preference. Charges from £400 for a single scene. HD footage, montage clips, editing and high-quality sound. Online links and hard copies included, as well as online conversion for Spotlight and Mandy. Recent clients include: Max Fowler (Eamonn Bedford Associates), Katie Redford (Red Canyon Management), Verity Hewlitt (Hoxton Street Casting), Nick Lavelle (SCA Management), Cherice Mckenzie-Cook (Top Talent Agency), Thea Cantell (Sandra Boyce Management) and Carla Nicholls (Lynda Ronan Personal Management).

Crying Out Loud Productions

218 Chester House, 1-3 Brixton Road,
London SW9 6DE
mobile Simon: 07809 549887
mobile Marina: 07946 533108
email simon@cryingoutloud.co.uk
website www.cryingoutloud.co.uk
Key contacts Simon Cryer, Marina Caldarone

Voicereel services: Established in 1999. Charges from £325 plus VAT to produce a bespoke voicereel from scratch; this includes a face-to-face consultation with Marina Caldarone or Debbie Seymour to select material, studio time with both producer and director, full editing and production, a copy of the voice-only files, a two-minute megamix for online service and a 2-year archive.

Clients will record a selection of material consisting of a mixture of commercials, narrative, documentary, corporate, animation and drama as well as any other content they may wish to add to best suit their strengths.

The team are practitioners in the industry - Simon Cryer (Voice Director and Producer and owner of Damn Good Voices Agency) and Marina Caldarone (Director of BBC's *The Archers*). Limits recording sessions to 20 clients per month - demand is high so book early.

Pelinor

tel 020 7183 8568
email support@pelinor.com
website www.pelinor.com
Key contact Misha von Bennigsen

Showreel services: Established in 2003. Produces showreels from existing material only.

Website services: Offers a bespoke 'from scratch' package which includes designing and setting up a website. Package includes hosting and domain name registration, email addresses, search engine optimisation, and facility for clients to update their own site. Updates charged separately. Material is usually selected from existing headshots, biographies/CVs, publicity stills, showreels and voicereels.

Replay Film & New Media

25 Museum Street, London WC1 1ST
tel 020 7637 0473
email solutions@replayfilms.co.uk
website www.replayfilms.com

Showreel services: Established in 1991. Although Replay can record presentations and performances from scratch, for most clients the task is to produce a carefully constructed compilation of highlights from existing TV and film performances. Advises that the correct selection and juxtaposition of these clips is essential, and it is therefore vital that clients sit in on the editing process to ensure that they are happy with the final result. Most showreels last 4-7 minutes. Will supply scripts if requested, but does not organise for copyright clearance.

As most showreels take around 4 hours to edit, Replay has put together the following package for a fixed fee: up to 4 hours in the edit studio with the editor (digitising existing clips from VHS, capturing digitised clips onto an Avid editing suite, editing the captured clips and inserting titles where required). The digital master will be archived at 2 sites. Exact prices are available on application only. Discounted rates are available to actors, presenters, students and non-commercial theatre companies. Overtime (anything over 4 hours) is charged at approximately 50% of the commercial editing rate.

Recent clients include: Donald Standen, Julian Hanshaw, Justine Waddel, Michael Mears, Patsy Kensit, Shared Experience Theatre Company and Vicky Johnson.

Shine Showreels

71-75 Shelton Street, Covent Garden,
London WC2H 9IQ
tel 020 7205 2772
email jonathan@shineshowreels.co.uk
website shineshowreels.co.uk

Showreel services: Established in 2017. Recent clients include Michelle Gayle (independent), Bill Nash (Price Gardner) and Andrew Leung (Hamilton Hodell).

Shine Showreels offers 2 types of reel format – full and sizzle. With full showreels, the common aim is to showcase the performer as completely as possible in the briefest time possible. To make the opening 30 seconds as strong as possible and ensure the source video and audio is of the highest quality.

A slick mixture of fast cut sequences and short dialogue bites, a sizzle reel is a great way of attracting attention or as a taster before sending your full reel. Both are edited and re-edited until the client is completely happy. Flat rate with no extras.

Advises 'view and log your material first as this will save time'. Shine Showreels operates powerful search and retrieval tools to find material.

Charges: full showreel or sizzle reel £250; updates £35/hr; clip finding, video and audio enhancement, and file compression services £35/hr. Average duration of sizzle reels is 1 min; full reel as required but usually 3–5 mins.

The Showreel Ltd

Soho Recording Studios, 22-24 Torrington Place,
London WC1E 7HJ
tel 020 7043 8660
website www.theshowreel.com
Facebook www.facebook.com/groups/theshowreel
Twitter @theshowreel

Showreel services overview:

• Get started in voiceovers with our Intro Workshops
(from £195, studio or online)
• Release the voices in your head with our Character
Workshops (from £175/day)
• Learn to make money from home with our Home
Studio Workshop (from £195)
• One-to-one personal training plans to increase your
skills, such as personal voice over coaching and
development (from £85)
• Agents' Demo to get a voiceover agent
• Drama Demo for the BBC
• Character Demo for games and animation
• Audio Book Demo for RNIB, Audible, iTunes and
Amazon (from £175)

For other services, please visit the website.

Showreel Editing by Anthony Holmes

17 Knole Road, Crayford, London DA1 3JN
tel 020 8144 8835
email anthony@showreelediting.com
website www.showreelediting.com
Facebook www.facebook.com/showreeleditingservice
Twitter @showreelediting
Instagram @showreelediting
Key contact Anthony Holmes

Services: Showreel, voicereel and sizzle reel editing
service for talent with existing material. Clients
include many award-winning and household names.
Works directly with actors, talent management and
press agents/publicists (where relevant) to ensure
correct branding and career positioning. Charges £90
per hour billed in half-hourly increments (minimum
charge one hour). Showreel provided as a digital file
for direct upload to Spotlight or other casting
websites. Able to record material broadcast on
television on request, and to download/record
material from streaming services such as Netflix,
iPlayer and YouTube (where client has permission to
do so). Showreel material archived for easier updates.
Those who quote *Actors' and Performers' Yearbook*
when booking, will receive a 10% discount. Also
offers assistance with selection of material for existing
footage if required. Does not record voicereels, but is
able to edit from radio, animation and videogame
material and from existing voicereels if required.

Silver-Tongued Productions

tel 07468 492935
email silvertongued@mail.com
website www.silver-tongued.com
Twitter @STP_Voicereels

Voicereel services: With over 24 years of experience
recording and producing high-quality voicereels at a
competitive price. "We guide you through the whole
process of recording your voicereel, from choosing
your scripts to directing you during the recording
session, making it as simple and as easy as possible.
Our voicereels are truly bespoke, so are as individual
as you are." Visit the website for full details of
services.

Silvertip Films Ltd

20 Enterprise House, Foundry Lane, Horsham,
West Sussex RH13 5PX
tel (01403) 221068 *mobile* 07786 331502
email info@silvertipfilms.co.uk
website www.silvertipfilms.co.uk
Facebook www.facebook.com/silvertipfilms

Showreel services: Established in 2005.

Shoot and Edit 1: a half day shooting 3 scenes, either
monologue or duologue and editing the scenes for
the reel plus any existing material you have.

Shoot and Edit 2: as above but includes a full day
shooting up to 4 scenes plus editing, including any
existing material.

Editing existing material only: a half-day edit and
includes transfer of existing material on DVD or
from online, and editing the reel using either notes or
direct input from the client. The reel is sent to the
client for approval and any reasonable changes will be
made where possible.

Packages include reel in web HD format and HD data
file, as well as a DVD or BluRay copy. The average
length of a showreel is 3-4 minutes

Silvertip's previous clients include: Jessica Jay (cre8
talent), Alexis Peterman (United Artists), Dar Dash
(Hobsons), Heather Skermer (Red Hot
Entertainment) and Libby Gore (Imperium
Management).

SonicPond Studio

70 Mildmay Grove South, Islington, London N1 4PJ
tel 020 7690 8561
email martin@sonicpond.co.uk
website www.sonicpond.co.uk
Key contact Martin Fisher

Showreel services: Editing of existing material only.
Charges £200 (£180 for students) to edit a showreel
from existing material, uploaded directly to Spotlight
for you. The average duration of a showreel is 3-4
minutes. Clients include: Annie Cooper (Felix de
Wolfe); Zoe Lister (*Hollyoaks*) and Sid Owen
(*EastEnders*). Advises actors: "Don't worry that you
may not have enough material; you most likely do.
Less is truly more with showreels. Also, don't wait for
that copy of the student film you have been waiting
to be sent; think of the reel as an organic growing
thing which you will add to and change for the whole
of your career. Just get it started."

Voicereel services: Supplies scripts for actors to use if desired. Charges £365 to produce a commercial voicereel from scratch; working from existing material the rate is £65 per hour. Broadcast quality MP3s of all files are included in the package. Nine pieces recorded, commercial and narrative, with a 90-second montage included. Students: £325 for a full voicereel. Game or animation reels £345. Voice clients include: Bob Golding (Hobsons); Nicholas Keith (Yakety Yak); Kellie Bright (Sue Terry Voices); Sam & Mark (Harvey Voices); Ronan Vibert (Harvey Voices) and James Alexandrou (Earache). Advises actors: "Don't worry about the pieces, we will work together to find you the best material. It's much more about finding the tone for each piece, and material that suits you perfectly, rather than the best copy. In the meantime, listen to as much voice-over as possible, and think about why any particular voice is used for any piece."

Voiceover Kickstart

North London
website www.voice-reel.com
Key contact Guy Michaels

Voicereel services: All voiceover demos are recorded and produced remotely. Strict 2 client a week limit ensures a bespoke service.

Clients receive all full versions of the tracks in addition to the compilation. Full guidance/online client area. Sourcing and choosing material is a collaborative process. Scripts are written and tailor-made for gaming demos. Does not arrange copyright clearance.

Has clients worldwide and with all major agencies including Excellent Talent, Lip Service, Soho Voices, Rhubarb Voices, Sue Terry Voices and many more. Full voice-over training facility starting with 'The Recorded Voice' free programme at **www.voiceoverkickstart.com**.

Showreels: creation and maintenance

Anthony Holmes

What is a showreel, and why does an actor need one?

A showreel, also known as a demo reel or acting reel, is a short video showcase featuring an actor's best clips.

The key objective of a showreel is career development; a reel isn't a compilation of every character an actor has ever played, but a tool with which to help get cast. As such, your primary audience for a showreel should be casting directors, whose job it is to cast or shortlist actors in film and television. Always think of this audience when editing a showreel; will it help the casting director cast you? Have you used your best clips, and are they appropriate for the roles you're applying for? Think like a casting director. Your showreel should represent you as you are now, and reflect your current vital statistics and casting age. A showreel is successful if it fulfils the primary objective; helping the actor get more work. A showreel by itself won't necessarily secure an actor a role (although there have been many cases of actors being cast on the strength of their showreel alone), but it's a crucial part of the mix which leads to casting success.

Many actors have a main general-purpose showreel, and then additional reels to help them target specific roles, e.g. a commercials reel and a comedy reel, ensuring their reel is always relevant to the specific submission.

Once you have your showreel, how is it best used? Spotlight's interactive services have a near monopoly status for professional productions in the UK, although there are a number of other casting websites used, particularly by low budget or no budget productions, which are unlikely to have a casting director on board. Your agent will submit your application through Spotlight for a particular role, and the casting director will view your CV, headshot and showreel on Spotlight, and consider your suitability for the role. You can also send your Spotlight link directly to casting directors, but unless you're responding to a specific open casting call, please check first that the casting director accepts cold submissions. Never send the showreel file itself (or any other large file such as a headshot), but send a link to your Spotlight profile – large files clog up email inboxes and the last thing you want to do is annoy a casting director!

It's also becoming more important to have an active social media following; a large and active fan base will make you more attractive to producers, particularly for high-profile US-produced television shows and major features. Many actors like to promote their showreel on social media, although opinions among agents are mixed; some prefer to keep their clients' reels away from general public view, and prefer to keep them for the eyes of casting directors and other stakeholders only. Shorter clips or 'sizzle' reels are becoming increasingly popular, however, both with actors and agents, and can be used effectively on social media to help promote an actor's appearance in a film or television series, and help the actor to build and maintain a fan-base.

If you're just starting your career, you may not have much in the way of scenes from film and television to include in a showreel. It can be useful to increase the number of your showreel scenes by applying for lower budget short films and student films. These productions may not have a budget to employ a casting director, and you are likely to be applying directly to the director or producer.

Your headshot will persuade a casting director to look at your CV, and your showreel will persuade them to call you in for an audition. Once you're in the room, your performance and personality can persuade the casting director you're the right person for the job.

You will maximise your opportunities and your chances of being cast if you use the right selection of clips in the right way. A skilled and experienced showreel editor will be able to advise on this.

The general-purpose showreel

Your main showreel should showcase your range, a variety of different roles, and some different looks, but also bear in mind that consistency and suitability for type can be attractive to casting directors.

You may wish to demonstrate your ultimate acting ability by including a range of roles. You should certainly include a good contrast of scenes in your showreel, but bear in mind many casting directors are looking for a type, and you're making their job easier to cast you if you don't try to be all things to all people. This is a difficult balance to strike, especially if you do not wish to be known as a one-trick pony. Theatre casting directors may appreciate a greater contrast of roles than film or television directors, but I do not advise including filmed scenes of theatre work given than the greater part of actor employment is for the screen. If you pride yourself on being a good character actor, you could benefit from a separate reel for each type of character you know you can play, but a more common approach is to edit your general tape for specific submissions, including the most appropriate scenes for that job.

The duration of your main showreel will depend on the experience you have, and the footage you have. Many showreels are around two to three minutes. It's better to have a shorter and tighter showreel featuring the best of the best, rather than padding things out. Casting directors are busy people; if they don't see what they're looking for in the first few seconds, they'll move on – so make the most of your time!

Some actors present an opening montage of moments from the scenes that are to follow. This is generally not recommended. An opening montage to a general reel wastes valuable screen time and a majority of casting directors don't like them. Don't waste time at the start – jump straight into a substantial scene with dialogue. Remember that casting directors want to hear you and see you interact with others, so don't spend long on a moody visual opening shot. Always open with your strongest material. Make it clear who you are, and avoid any confusion; where possible, your showreel should open with a close-up of you rather than a group scene or a close-up of another actor, and be wary of opening your showreel with a scene including another actor of the same gender and age range.

Prioritise your higher profile footage and scenes with better production values. If you have the experience and material, casting directors prefer to see how you handle yourself in the real world, in a fully professional environment; be wary of using 'shot-for-showreel' scenes which often don't reflect a typical working environment, which are likely to have lower production values than even a typical student film, and in which you may be acting with less talented and less experienced actors, dragging down the tone of the showreel and making it less attractive to casting directors. Self-tapes are the way forward for individual castings, but don't belong in your general showreel.

A showreel, like your CV, is an on-going process; keep it up-to-date with your latest footage. If it's not getting you called in for appropriate castings, tweak the edit until it does. Your showreel is all about you. An existing scene can be re-edited to reduce the screen time of other actors, and refocus the scene more on you. Don't forget, though, that casting directors don't just want to see you act, they want to see you react to other actors.

It's important to always focus on your objective; getting cast. Different casting directors and different talent agents often have different preferences, tastes and expectations from a showreel – if you know you're applying for a specific job, and you know what that casting director likes, then tweak your showreel appropriately. Once again, this is where a specialist showreel editor can advise; a good editor will have experience of what is most likely to work best, and will be interacting with a network of agents and casting directors on an ongoing basis.

Specialist showreels

Action reel: this is often more visual, focusing on your physicality. It may be either full action scenes, or a montage of action clips set to music, depending on your skillset and experience.

Comedy reel: this showcases your physical and verbal comic timing and delivery, and may be appropriate if you would like to work in sitcoms and film comedy. Stand-up comedy may be included, but as the skill sets are quite different, with different target audiences, it may be advisable to keep stand-up in a separate reel.

Commercial reel: this includes clips from your commercials, and is crafted specifically to get more work in commercials. A commercials reel is often shorter than your main showreel, with a greater emphasis on visuals rather than dialogue, as would be expected. Creating the right mood both appropriate for and respectful of each brand included in the commercial reel is important, as your audience in this case is not just the casting director but the advertising agency commissioned to represent the brand.

Demo reel: a showreel is known as a demo reel in the US. Quite rapidly, the differences between US demo reels and UK showreels are narrowing, but if you're applying for roles in US-produced drama, your general showreel may benefit from some slight tweaks to make it more attractive to US productions, such as making it a little more 'glam', and emphasising your looks. A demo reel can be important for career development, as it opens you up to higher profile work. Even if you don't want to work in the US, many American productions are shot in the UK.

Dramatic reel: this is often less visually active than the general reel, and focused on character relationships.

Public reel or 'sizzle' reel: unlike your main reel and most other specialist reels, which are aimed primarily at casting directors, your public reel is used on your website or social media channels to help build and maintain a fan base. A sizzle reel can take many forms, but generally has more action than dialogue and is more fast-paced than other reels, often (but not always) well under a minute long. It can feature shortened scenes or short sound-bites (along the lines of a film trailer), or can be a visual montage set to appropriate music. This positive encouragement to consider sizzle reels should not be confused by the disapproval of montages at the beginning of general reels. The general/main reel and the sizzle reel serve very different purposes.

Voiceover reel: actors' use of audio voice reels for their narration/voiceover work is long established, but recently it has become more popular to have a video reel to place their work in context, and to show examples of their work as transmitted, though many casting directors still prefer voice reels. Examples of video voiceover reels include an animation, narration and videogame reels.

Actors can also use visual voiceover reels on their websites and social media to help build and maintain a fan-base. It's also easy to provide an audio-only MP3 file from a video voice reel to provide to casting directors who only want an audio reel; it's not easy to simply add video to an existing voice reel. Starting off with a video voice reel means you have a lot of flexibility for use.

You may prefer to specialise in a specific skillset, or develop latent ability as your career advances necessitating the creation of dance reels, modelling reels or presenting/hosting reels.

All rules are made to be broken! The advice given in this article is applicable to many situations, but there will often be occasions where individual situations require different approaches, particularly as the world of online casting is ever-changing. Your showreel editor will be able to advise on the best approach for your situation. To view some examples of the different styles of showreels and demo reels that are available to actors, visit **www.showreelediting.com.**

Anthony Holmes has nearly twenty years' experience as a specialist editor of showreels, working with actors, agents and casting directors in the UK, US, Canada and Europe. Anthony has edited reels for actors at every stage of their careers; from young actors (under 16s) and recent graduates, all the way to Emmy Award winners and Oscar nominees. A good showreel editor knows what works, and Anthony has helped to develop the television and film careers of hundreds of actors, from recurring roles on television to major roles in Academy Award-winning films.

Digital wellbeing for actors

Essentially, digital wellbeing is using the web to work better, not longer; making smart digital choices that work for you. Here, Sinead Mac Manus looks at some of the ways in which you can harness the power of the social web without suffering the burnout.

Getting a web presence

Having a dedicated web presence is increasingly important for any freelance actor. Your personal website can act as a central place on the web for potential employers or collaborators to find you. With free platforms such as WordPress[1], Posterous[2] or Flavors[3], it's never been easier to raise your profile online.

Your domain name

The first step before choosing a web platform is to register your own domain name. Even if you never use it, for the cost of a few pounds each year it is worth owning your own .com and retaining control of your name online. Use a site such as Netnames[4] to search for your professional name and check that it is available. 123-reg[5] is a company with a good reputation for domain name management in the UK, or you can buy your domain name with your web hosting package (see below).

Now you have your domain name secured, how can you build your web presence?

Building a WordPress site

WordPress's easy-to-use and powerful Content Management System (CMS) makes it perfect for freelance artists wanting to create their own website. The platform is free to install and adapt; the only expenses incurred are registering a domain name and paying for web hosting. The CMS of WordPress is easy to get to grips with: in fact, anyone at ease with Microsoft Word will be able to publish a website using WordPress.

Before you start building your site, have a think about what content you want on it. Suggested pages could be Biography, Photography, Credits, Reviews and Contact Me. With WordPress you can easily add a blog to your website with updates of your work.

For a practical step-by-step guide to using WordPress to build your web presence, do read my two-part series on WordPress written for the London Theatre Blog[6]. Part One covers the basics, and Part Two goes into more detail about design, themes, widgets and plug-ins.

Zen Tip: Use a WordPress approved web hosting service to install the WordPress software in one click, rather than going through the complicated manual process.

Do I need a blog?

Blogging can be a great way of building your personal brand as an actor. Through text, images, video or sound, you can demonstrate, reflect and comment on your artistic process. Writing a blog is also a powerful learning tool, promoting critical and analytical thinking, as well as being a powerful audience development and marketing tool.

Microblogging platforms such as Posterous[2] and Tumblr[7] are simple and free ways of starting a blog. Easier to set up than a WordPress blog, these platforms really come into their own when blogging on the go; perfect for freelance actors on tour. Both platforms allow you to post snippets of text, photos, quotes, links, dialogues, audio, video and slideshows from the web or direct from your smart phone.

For a look at the multimedia capabilities of Posterous in action, go to my blog *From Apps to Zen*.[8]

Zen Tip: Use the scheduling feature of Posterous or Tumblr to queue your posts for autoposting during busy tour periods.

Other platforms

Flavors[3] is a relative newcomer to the platform scene, but a fantastic way of creating a personal portal for all your online content in minutes. Simply register your Flavors name (or use you own custom domain), design your layout and background, and then add your choice of 30 social websites. You can pull in tweets from your Twitter Feed, your Wall activity from your Facebook Page, videos from YouTube or Vimeo, posts from your Posterous, Tumblr or WordPress blogs, or photos from Flickr or Instagram[9].

Have a look at some of the wonderfully creative sites on the Flavors' Directory[10] for inspiration.

Zen Tip: Use the Promote tab to add a Search Engine Optimised (SEO)[11] title and description of your page to ensure you are easily found in the search engines.

Using social media

There is a wide range of social media networks and platforms that you can use to communicate and connect with people in the creative industries. Social networks such as Facebook and Twitter, as well as multimedia platforms such as YouTube and Flickr, can help you market yourself, raise your profile and connect with potential employers.

Getting started on social media is relatively easy as the entry barriers are low, both technologically and financially. Social media also harnesses the most highly prized of the marketing methods: word of mouth. It allows you to exponentially expand your marketing potential and reach many more potential audience members or clients than you could using solely an offline approach.

All good so far … But if social media is so effective and easy to use, why isn't every artist jumping on board?

The number one reason why creative people do not get engaged with social media is lack of time, and specifically a fear that if they do engage, it will eat up large chunks of an already busy day. Questions to consider are: do you have the time to plan how you are going to use social media in your work? Do you have the time to set up profiles and start connecting with people? Do you have the time to maintain your online presences and maximise the return from these sites?

I think social media has a bad reputation for being a source of time-wasting. Many of us are guilty of having spent too much time on Facebook or YouTube when we could have been doing something more productive! However, social media does not have to be an unnecessary drain on your time. Rebecca Coleman, a Canadian PR consultant in the performing arts, has written an excellent guide to getting started in social media[12]. She recommends that artists create a Social Networking Marketing Plan, outlining what they want to achieve with social media; what platforms and tools they will focus on; and lastly, how much time they are going to dedicate to being online. Think of social media like email: a brilliant innovation which, when used strategically, can enhance your business and increase opportunity. Of the social media-savvy people I know, many deliberately limit their time online to one or two hours a day for this very reason.

LinkedIn

My first recommendation would be to set up a LinkedIn[13] profile for your professional name. LinkedIn is a popular social networking site for professionals, featuring high in the search engine rankings, so you can use it as an opportunity to shine.

Setting up a LinkedIn profile is easy. A great profile picture is essential, and an easy one for actors – you can use one of your headshots.

Next, add a juicy-sounding headline that highlights your talents, e.g. "Freelance Actor, Facilitator & Workshop Leader specialising in Site-Specific Theatre". Add Current and Past employments, bearing in mind that LinkedIn lists these in order of start date with the latest position appearing at the top. Claim your 'vanity' URL, i.e. http://uk.linkedin.com/in/yourname by clicking on the Edit link beside it.

Spend some time writing a Summary for your profile. Have a search for other actors on LinkedIn for inspiration. Highlight any noteworthy achievements or credits. Use the Specialities section to summarise any particular talents or skills that you have, e.g. workshop facilitating, fluent Spanish speaker, trained ballet dancer, mask skills, etc.

Recommendations on LinkedIn are a powerful example of what's called 'social proof' – proof to your potential clients that others have already gone before and had a positive experience working with you. No one wants to be the guinea pig!

Now you are ready to start connecting. Use the Add Connections button to find people through your email contacts or through LinkedIn's recommendations. I make a point of connecting on LinkedIn with people I meet socially or at networking events to keep them in my network.

LinkedIn can be a great way of getting introductions to a particular person, e.g. a director or agent that you want to connect with. The more you build your network on LinkedIn, the more likely it is that someone in your network might know them and can provide an introduction.

Twitter

Twitter is one of those social networking sites that divides opinion. To the Twitterarti, it's a way of keeping abreast of what's going on in their industry as well as a way to connect and boost their online profile. To everyone else, it seems like a complete waste of time! But its reach is growing exponentially.

Once you have set up a Twitter account by registering a Twitter name and posting some information about yourself, you can start 'tweeting'. Other users can choose to 'follow' your tweets – they are called 'followers', and you can search for and follow others using the Find People tab. The best way to learn how to use Twitter is to use it: get an account, search for people you think are interesting to follow, and watch and learn how people interact. The Arts Council England digital strategy programme AmbITion has a free Twitter for Beginners ebook[14] on their website, which is a great guide to getting started.

For me, the number one strategic use of Twitter is the constant sharing of valuable information. Following others in your industry or sector allows you to have a network at your fingertips to share ideas and conversations, to find answers or to keep updated on great blog posts and resources. The beauty of Twitter is the brevity of the medium. No essay-style blog posts here, just up-to-date, relevant and interesting conversation that can be skimmed through in minutes. Andrew Girvan[15] on his blog has a great article on 129 people to follow in theatre, crossing venues, companies, news feeds and commentators, and is a good place to start to build your Twitter community.

Zen Tip: Use a free Twitter application such as Tweetdeck[16] to provide a one-stop shop dashboard for managing all your social media use.

Video sharing

The practical application of being able to upload and share video on the web to someone working in theatre is fairly self-explanatory. With video cameras built into almost everything, it's inexpensive to make high-quality videos to showcase your talents.

There are many different video hosting and sharing sites, but a handful do stand out from the rest. YouTube[17] is the world's most popular video sharing site, and it is easy to see why. The site is free to use and, once you have set up an account, videos are easy to upload either singly or in batches. YouTube videos, now that the company is owned by Google, also rate highly in the Google search engine, and therefore clever tagging of your videos can help potential customers and audiences find your work. Another good video sharing site is Vimeo,[18] which features a lot of content from creative people.

The mobile office

An actor's life is sometimes a nomadic one, and therefore it is essential to be able to access your email and important documents wherever you go. I find a combination of Gmail[19] as my email client and file storing and sharing site Dropbox[20] fulfils all my needs when I am away from the office for any period of time.

Using Gmail on your smart phone can mean that you don't need to travel with a laptop and you can process your emails on the go. Similarly, with Dropbox, you can access all your important documents for reading, forwarding or printing direct from your smart phone.

Final thoughts

The social web can provide many benefits to the jobbing actor. It can provide an online showcase for your work, connect you to potential clients, and be used to manage your work.

With mobile computing so readily available, the social web is not going to go away. The smart actor can use these free tools to promote her/himself above the rest of the bunch.

[1]http://wordpress.org; [2]https://posterous.com; [3]http://flavors.me; [4]http://www.netnames.co.uk; [5]http://www.123-reg.co.uk; [6]http://www.londontheatreblog.co.uk/category/articles; [7]http://www.tumblr.com; [8]http://www.fromappstozen.com; [9]http://instagr.am; [10]http://flavors.me/directory; [11]http://en.wikipedia.org/wiki/Search_engine_optimization; [12]http://www.rebeccacoleman.ca; [13]https://www.linkedin.com; [14]http://www.getambition.com/resources/twitter-for-beginners; [15]http://andrewgirvan.com/100-theatre-people-to-follow-on-twitter; [16]http://www.tweetdeck.com; [17]http://www.youtube.com; [18]http://vimeo.com; [19]www.gmail.com; [20]www.dropbox.com

Sinead Mac Manus is founder of 8fold (**www.eightfold.org**), a digital well-being company that helps busy people work better. She writes about mindful 21st-century working at her blog *From Apps to Zen* (**www.fromappstozen.com**) and is the author of *From Apps to Zen: 26+ Ideas for Building a Business with Balance*. Sinead has worked for, consulted and provided training for organisations as diverse as the Independent Street Arts Network, London Metropolitan University, CreativeCapital and the Anne Peaker Centre for Arts in Criminal Justice. Sinead's activity in developing new business models around the idea of e-learning for creative entrepreneurs, using web 2.0 tools and social media, led her to be selected in 2009 as one of the Courvoisier: Future 500 to watch.

Building your personal brand on social media

Daniel Heale, CEO and Chief Strategy Officer, Way To Blue
Interview by Rob Ostlere

Daniel Heale is an award-winning marketer, and the CEO and Chief Strategy Officer of Way To Blue. Way To Blue's campaigns include major films and television series, alongside their work with actors; both established stars and up-and-coming performers. Here, Daniel explains how major projects are marketed and shares tips for performers at all levels of the industry.

Could you first give an overview of the work you do with Way To Blue?

We're an entertainment marketing agency that does the full marketing mix for film, television and talent. Often we're asked to deliver strategy for a TV series or a film; how to position a show in order to give it the best possible opportunity for success, particularly online. Then we look at how to use the marketing campaign to go about achieving those objectives; things like what platforms should they be on? The next level down would be what type of things should you be doing on those platforms? There's also a creative team that does everything from ideation right the way through to the production of content; from the static graphics you get on social to long-form video. For me, it's great that we work right the way through the lifecycle of a project; you build relationships with people on the production team and the talent.

What work do you do with the individual actors in a production?

I'll have a team of people rotating on set, spending hours and hours with the cast, pulling content either during shoot days or indeed when they're having downtime. We also advise the actors on how to develop and curate their own feeds, relevant to them but also to positioning themselves as stars of the show when it comes on air.

Does the size of their following matter?

Some of them could have a million followers, some a few hundred thousand and others much smaller numbers. But if you can do something interesting with that person – seed a piece of content that gets editorial coverage and pickup – it can really help them to grow their profile. Generally, it's not about the volume of followers you've got but the level of engagement with your content. You can have 5,000 followers be really engaged with what you do versus a million who don't have a clue who you are and never see any of your content. So, it's really useful for actors early on in their careers to think about that brand because when it comes to getting the job marketers can use that and that's only going to help the actor.

What are the first steps for performers who want to use social media in a more constructive way?

You can work with a professional and pay them a fee to help you. But you can just follow some basic guidance. Over and above everything, authenticity is the most important thing; remaining true to the values that you have as a person and the things that are interesting to you. Start with a "landscape analysis" on yourself: what are your hobbies, your interests, what would your perfect day look like, where would you'd be and what would you be doing, what are your favourite holiday destinations, what quotes inspire you, what do you do outside of work, are their causes that you are passionate about? These sorts of things can help you understand your sense of self, something that is real for you, your thing, your brand.

And that's the basis for content?

Yes, it's then about how that sense of self would be translated into posts and imagery. That could be something broad like what do you want to engage with most, or more specific like what's your colour palette? The idea is for some sense of both visual and copy tone-of-voice around you as an individual. The reason it's so important to get it right at the beginning is that it will become a long-term thing. The brands within the brand will obviously evolve over time but there needs to be threads that run through everything. People should look at your feed and say, "Oh yeah, I get a sense of who that person is and what their interests are."

What are some of the common mistakes you see on social media?

Generally, people can quite quickly sniff out something that isn't authentic. My advice is to be careful about how you position your alignment with something if you haven't been engaged with it or talked about it before. I've seen a lot of missteps happen in that way. People do go back and look, and if you start to grow some profile, it'll be journalists. They might see that one minute you're talking about things that feel very relevant and worthy but a few years ago you posted a photograph or a tweet that wasn't quite saying the same thing. We always advise people to go back, delete or archive things, to clean up their feed. If you are being authentic at all times, then it's likely you will be consistent too. One follows the other.

How do actors balance promoting themselves and their projects with not upsetting their employers?

For emerging actors, I think it is important to follow the rules. Those social media embargoes are in place for good reasons. I would always say as a blanket rule never post any pictures that you take on set unless you've got permission from the producer or from the studio to do to so.

Is there a mindset that perhaps can help actors to use social media more positively?

I think it's about seeing it as a tool that's going to be of benefit to you from a career perspective. Using it as personal brand building is using social for good purpose. It's something that people definitely look at more than ever before, so it needs to tell your story. Think about what that is and then get all of those building blocks in place.

15 key tips from Daniel Heale for building your social media presence

1   Your overall aims are to develop a well-balanced and curated feed, increase the quality and number of posts, and build followers and engagement.
2   Decide which platforms to focus on. For performers the starting point is often Instagram.
3   Think about what you want to portray to followers. Balance showing off your personality with reflecting your acting career.

4 Use your bio to give followers just enough info about yourself while keeping them wanting more.

5 The "About me" should be short, clever and direct. Add where you're from, plus links to your website or latest project.

6 Acting-related posts that tend to work well are: photos that include you; headshots/publicity photos; behind-the-scenes and cast photos and other project-related posts.

7 Archive any old posts that aren't well shot and/or don't fit in to the rest of the feed.

8 Improve the quality of photos with filters and editing. Planning can help you capture key moments.

9 Write engaging copy: short, sweet, clever and relatable.

10 Use hashtags that will draw followers to your account. Putting hashtags in the comment section will avoid cluttered captions.

11 Insights will show you the best times to post.

12 Stories are there to share the fun activities you're doing that day.

13 Engage with people who comment and like your posts.

14 Follow relevant accounts with large followings.

15 Increase the amount you post. Create an even mix of photoshoots, behind-the-scenes shots, project-promotion, events and everyday life.

And some advanced tips:

• Hire a photographer so you can have an existing bank of photos. Use the same photographer and have different shoots so you have a spread. Other photos can then be sprinkled in between.

• IG Live allows followers to get a real look into your life.

• Add polls to your stories or do a quick Q&A to create even more engagement.

To find out more about Way To Blue, visit **www.waytoblue.com**

Accountants

Alexander & Co

CHARTERED ACCOUNTANTS

Centurion House, 129 Deansgate,
Manchester M3 3WR
tel 0161 832 4841
email info@alexander.co.uk
website www.alexander.co.uk
Twitter @alexandercoMCR
LinkedIn www.linkedin.com/company/alexander-&-co-chartered-accountants
Accountants John McCaffery, Stephen Verber

Established in 1976, Alexander & Co is an Equity approved and recommended firm of chartered accountants and tax advisors who have looked after clients in the film, TV and theatre industry for many years.

The firm provides strategic planning advice to ensure that you make the most of the opportunities within the current tax system, and your business affairs are structured the most tax efficient way. Alexander & Co also provides more specialist advice as and when required, this includes tax advice on other income streams, such as property investments, crypto, shares and pensions.

Frequently used services include Self Assessment tax returns, limited company accounts, Theatre Tax Relief claims and business planning/restructuring.

Alexander James & Co.

Upper Deck, Admirals Quarters, Portsmouth Road,
Thames Ditton, Surrey KT7 0XA
tel 020 8398 4447
email info@alexanderjames.co.uk
website www.alexanderjames.co.uk
Accountant Andrew Nicholson

Established in 1991. Fees vary according to complexity and completeness of information supplied. Costs are on average between £375 and £500 per annum. First meeting is free, with ongoing support by phone and email and regular email newsletter. Entirely UK-based staff accustomed to working with media industry clients. Advisory work during the year is billed on completion; rates vary depending on requirements. Standard spreadsheet template provided, and online accounts support available. Around 10-15% of clientele are actors or other entertainment industry professionals. Home or workplace visits can be arranged.

Bambridge Accountants

London Office: 7 Henrietta Street, London WC2E 8PS
tel 020 3797 1432 (UK)
email info@bambridgeaccountants.com
New York Office: 442 Broadway, New York NY 10013, USA
tel +1 646 956 5566 (US)
website www.BambridgeAccountants.com
Facebook www.facebook.com/BambridgeAccountants
Accountants Alistair Bambridge, Callie Marles, Anna Heery

With over 10 years' experience, Bambridge Accountants is an award-winning creative industry tax accountancy firm based in London, New York and California. Bambridge employs their specialist knowledge to minimise the tax and maximise the profit of actors, performers and other creative professionals.

Breckman & Company

London office: 49 South Molton Street, London W1K 5LH
tel 020 7499 2292
email info@breckmanandcompany.co.uk
Brighton office: 95 Ditchling Road, Brighton BN1 4ST
tel 01273 929350
website www.breckmanandcompany.co.uk
Accountants Kevin Beale FCCA, Graham Berry FCCA, Richard Nelson FCCA

Established for more than 50 years. Costs are dictated by complexity and time spent. Initial meeting is free during which the fee structure will be discussed. Client support includes face-to-face meetings, phone and email.

Services include: audits, independent examinations, Theatre Tax Relief claims, limited company accounts, self-employed accounts, VAT and wages preparation.

P O'N Carden

56-58 High Street, Ewell, Surrey KT17 1RW
tel 020 8394 2957

Resources

email info@poncarden.com
website www.poncarden.com
Facebook www.facebook.com/poncarden
Accountants Philippe Carden, Mondane Carden, Andrew Fairmaner

Founded in 1977. Charges £400+VAT for a complete set of accounts and tax return for sole traders. "Time and complexity increase this. Tailor-made packages for complex cases and limited companies." Provides face-to-face meetings in-person or via Zoom. "Our actor clients make clear how much support they feel they need, and the programme of work is tailored accordingly." Provides Excel spreadsheets appropriate to the client's needs. 50% of clients are actors and performers; 35% are other entertainment industry professionals. The offices are not wheelchair accessible, but meetings can be held in wheelchair-accessible locations. Advises actors *not* to "just give your accountant bags of receipts. Provide information about why you are claiming particular expenses. Do be obssessive about keeping payslips and remittance advices".

Mark Carr & Co. Ltd

Mark Carr & Co
PART OF THE STREETS MEDIA GROUP

London office: Spaces Covent Garden, 60 St Martin's Lane, London WC2N 4JS
tel 020 3897 9384
email markcarr@streetsweb.co.uk
Brighton office: Century House, 15-19 Dyke Road, Brighton, East Sussex BN1 3FE
tel (01273) 778802
website www.markcarr.co.uk

"We are recognised as one of London's and the UK's leading specialist providers of accountancy, financial and tax services to actors, entertainers, agents, singers, musicians and dancers. In fact, anyone in or connected with the entertainment industry and the arts world.
     We are fully aware of the unique set of circumstances that those within the industry live and work in and the challenges of juggling income generating work with the need to ensure their financial affairs are in order."

ClearSky Accounting
Optionis House, 840 Ibis Court, Centre Park, Warrington WA1 1RL
tel (01925) 644861
email agency@clearskyaccounting.co.uk
website www.clearskyaccounting.co.uk

Established in 1995, has offices in Warrington, Reading, Hemel Hempstead and Edinburgh. ClearSky is very experienced in dealing with entertainment accountancy and provides advice and recommendations on all tax issues, ranging from completing a standard self-assessment return to dealing directly with agents regarding VAT and payments. There are a number of different packages available – details can be found on the website. The company offers support via telephone and email and is happy to provide Excel templates for book keeping, if required. The company's office is wheelchair accessible. "Our team of qualified experts have specialist knowledge of all Equity, PACT & BECTU rules and regulations – giving peace of mind that our work is fully compliant."

Count and See Ltd
219 Macmillan Way, London SW17 6AW
tel 020 8767 7882
email info@countandsee.com

Charges an annual fee of £300 (+ VAT) upwards, depending on the amount of work involved. "Before setting up my own practice, I worked for a number of firms specialising in the entertainment industry, so I have experience in advising such clients."

Dub & Co.
7 Torriano Mews, Torriano Avenue, London NW5 2RZ
tel 020 7284 8686
email office@dub.co.uk
website www.dub.co.uk
Accountants George Dub, Joyce Davies, Jaysukh Thakrar

Chartered, certified accountants established in 1979. Charges from £400 (+ VAT) for preparation of accounts for a tax return. Face-to-face meetings, phone and email support included in this fee. Does not provide software or spreadsheet templates to clients. Handles the tax and accountancy affairs of around 50 actors and 100 other entertainment industry professionals. The company's offices are wheelchair accessible.

Jonathan Ford & Co.
Maxwell House, Liverpool Innovation Park, 360 Edge Lane, Liverpool L7 9NJ
tel 0151 426 4512
email info@jonathanford.co.uk
website www.jonathanford.co.uk
Facebook www.facebook.com/JonathanFordandCo
Accountant Jonathan Ford

Premium services starting from £80/month (+ VAT), depending on the level of bookkeeping the client has done themselves. All fees are agreed in advance. Client service is comprehensive and includes face-to-face meetings, telephone and email support, all included within the fee. Supplies Excel spreadsheet templates, so MS Office is required; the software is suitable for all operating systems. Has around 10 actor clients and 40 other entertainment industry professionals. Offices are not wheelchair accessible. Advises actors to "see our 10 tax commandments".

Goldwins
75 Maygrove Road, London NW6 2EG
tel 020 7372 6494
email info@goldwins.co.uk
website www.goldwins.co.uk
Accountant Anthony Epton

Established in 1987. Specialises in the entertainment industry, handling the tax and bookkeeping affairs of around 200 actors. Price for preparing an actor's tax return can vary depending on the complexity of the job. Face-to-face meetings, phone and email support included in this price. Does not provide software or spreadsheet templates. The company's offices are wheelchair accessible.

Goodman Jones LLP
29/30 Fitzroy Square, London W1P 6LQ
tel 020 7388 2444
email info@goodmanjones.com
website www.goodmanjones.com
Partner Julian Flitter

Founded in 1934. "Each person is different and we tailor our support to the clients needs, so costs can range for more complex returns involving international aspects and multiple categories of income." This amount would include any support required in the form of face-to-face meetings, phone calls, letters and emails. "The range of services we offer includes tax compliance services from personal tax returns and VAT returns, advice on whether or not to incorporate as a limited company, when to register for VAT, how to deal with working abroad, bookkeeping services, preparation of financial accounts (limited company, sole trader, LLP or partnership) as well as full personal tax planning and company secretarial and payroll services." Can supply software templates to clients as required, but recommends "keeping it simple". Offices are wheelchair accessible.

H and S Accountants Ltd
90 Mill Lane, West Hampstead, London NW6 1NL
tel 020 3174 1905
email hstaxplan@gmail.com
website www.hstaxplan.com
Accountants David Summers, Chet Haria

Established in 1982. Charges start from £300 (+ VAT) for preparation of annual self-employed accounts and the self-assessment tax return. A quote is given at the initial meeting, which is free of charge. The services offered also include preparation of limited company accounts and corporate tax returns, VAT registration, payroll, tax-planning advice, etc. Client support includes face-to-face meetings, phone, email and dealing with day-to-day queries as they may arise (all included in the price). Approximately 10% of clients are actors or members of the entertainment industry.

Harvey Mead & Co. Ltd
167 Southborough Lane, Bickley, Kent BR2 8AP
tel 020 8467 1167

email harveymead@live.co.uk
website www.harveymead.co.uk

Established in 2008. Client support includes face-to-face meetings, telephone and email, as well as fee protection insurance and freepost record envelopes. Also offers accounts support and tax compliance. Supplies clients with MS Excel spreadsheet templates. 50% of the client base comprises actors, and 30% other entertainment industry professionals. Offices are wheelchair accessible.

Hogbens Dunphy Ltd
Third Floor, 104-108 Oxford Street, London W1D 1LP
tel 020 7016 2450
email anything@hogbensdunphy.co.uk
website www.hogbensdunphy.co.uk
Director Richard Wadhams

Established in 1921. Offers complete support to actors and other theatre professionals in dealing with their business, accounting and taxation needs. Prices are dependent on each individual client's needs.

Lees
Hogarth House, 136 High Holburn, London WC1V 6PX
tel 020 7242 1134
email a.mccarthy@leesaccountants.co.uk
website www.leesaccountants.co.uk
Accountants Mrs A. McCarthy, Mr P. Skinner, Mr G. Lyon

Established in 1925, charges from £450 to prepare actors' accounts for the tax return, depending on the complexity of the accounts. Provides a face-to-face initial meeting; support thereafter is as convenient to the client and this is included in the fee. Provides a complete range of accounting services – VAT, income tax, PAYE, business support, book keeping *et al.* Software and/or spreadsheets are provided to the client as required. Offices are wheelchair accessible.

MHA MacIntyre Hudson
6th Floor, 2 London Wall Place, Barbican, London EC2Y 5AU
tel 020 7429 4100
website www.macintyrehudson.co.uk
Twitter @MHUpdates
Accountants Neil Stern, John Coverdale

Established in 1880, MHA MacIntyre Hudson acts for over 2,000 individuals in the media and entertainment industry, with 12 national offices and extensive overseas support throughout the Baker Tilly International Network.

Offers a full accountancy service from cloud accounting advice to high-end tax solutions. A fee structure is set out at the first complimentary meeting when media and entertainment specialists will discuss tax needs; arrangements can include monthly payments. They are happy to support clients through face-to-face meetings, telephone or email. Offices are wheelchair accessible.

Nyman Libson Paul LLP
124 Finchley Road, London NW3 5JS
tel 020 7433 2400

Resources

email entertainment@nlpca.co.uk
website www.nlpca.co.uk

Over 75 years servicing the entertainment industry.

Performance Accountancy

6 Pankhurst Drive, Bracknell, Berks RG12 9PS
tel (01344) 669084
email louise@performanceaccountancy.co.uk
website www.performanceaccountancy.co.uk/Actors
Accountant Louise Herrington

Established in 2012. Charges from £350 +VAT for
early years tax returns based on the client's
bookkeeping records; if bookkeeping done by the
company then £55 +VAT per hour is charged. If
Equity number is quoted, then price starts at £245
+VAT for the return and £40+VAT per hour for
bookkeeping. For more established actors and
performers who may have more complex returns,
such as overseas income, the charge can go up to
£750 +VAT. Offers an e-book and support by phone,
Skype, webinars and video. Offers face-to-face
meetings when starting out, either in Bracknell or
Egham. First 30 minutes consultation is
complimentary. Offers monthly services to handle
bookkeeping and accounting requirements for the
self-employed or those who operate through a
company. This will help prepare for quarterly digital
accounts starting in April 2024. Range of services in
addition to personal self-assessment return include
company accounts and company tax, bookkeeping,
payroll, VAT, strategic planning and help with
managing your money. Investment advice not
offered. Excel workbook can be supplied to actors
and performers with typical categories of spend to
help with bookkeeping. Software offered works with
Windows, but not so well with Mac. Clients are
mainly actors, musicians and others in the
entertainment inductry. The company is
recommended by Equity and is the preferred supplier
of tax returns for the Incorporated Society of
Musicians.

Premises not suitable for wheelcahirs but face-to-face
meetings can be arranged in a wheelchair accessible
location.

Theataccounts Ltd
49 Greek Street, London W1D 4EG
tel 01905 706050
email info@theataccounts.co.uk
website www.theataccounts.co.uk

Twitter @theataccounts
Accountant Alex Dyer

Specialist Entertainment Industry Accountants
established in 1967. Charges are based on a sliding
scale according to each client's requirements. Basic
package can start from £150. Offers unlimited
support to clients through face-to-face meetings,
phone, email, Zoom, etc. No particular software is
provided unless required. All clients are actors and
other entertainment industry professionals.

Simia Wall LLP in association with Fisher Packman & Associates
Devonshire House, 582 Honeypot Lane, Stanmore,
Middlesex HA7 1JS
tel 020 8732 5500
email nik@simiawall.com
website www.simiawall.com
Accountant Nik Fisher FFA FCCA

Established in 2005. Charges between £250 and £750
on average, depending on the amount of work
involved. Offers actors face-to-face and email/phone
support: "as much as they require; our policy is to
teach actors how best to keep their books and
records, to save on accountancy fees." Provides
spreadsheet templates in Excel and for VAT analysis,
suitable for a range of software platforms. Around
15% of clients are actors, and 25% other
professionals in the entertainment industry.

Wise & Co. Chartered Accountants & Business Advisers
Wey Court West, Union Road, Farnham,
Surrey GU9 7PT
tel 01753 656770
email info@wiseandco.co.uk
website www.wiseandco.co.uk
Accountants Colin Essex, Mandy Cornelius, Tom
Mason

Established in 1972. Provides a full accounting
service, business advice plus tax returns and staff
payroll – "a personal, discreet and friendly service
tailored to the needs of each individual". Prices vary,
please phone to arrange a free initial consultation.
Office at Pinewood Studios as well as in Farnham,
Surrey. Works with Windows and MS Office, so
Excel is widely used; spreadsheet templates can be
provided if required. Offices at Farnham are
wheelchair accessible. Coffee shop and restaurant at
Pinewood.

Wyatts Partnership
247 Church Street, London N16 9HP
tel 020 7241 6779
email admin@wyatts.uk.com

Friendly and clear accounting service. Specialists with
actors, artists and performers. Reasonable and
transparent scaled fees and charges. Client base is
100% arts and entertainment industry professionals.
Offices are wheelchair accessible.

Tax and National Insurance for actors

Philippe Carden

Actors are treated as self-employed for income tax purposes, but can benefit from certain advantages not generally available. Many actors choose to instruct an accountant to benefit from those advantages and to avoid the attendant pitfalls.

The income tax advantages include being able to claim a deduction for expenses against income in arriving at taxable net profit (or allowable loss), provided that those expenses are incurred 'wholly and exclusively for the purposes of the trade'. The Equity Tax and National Insurance Guide, available free of charge to its members, provides a very helpful list of usually allowable expenses, with suitable notes to restrain the enthusiasm of actors to stretch definitions to their limits. Self-imposed restraint in claiming for expenses is sensible in minimising the risk of being selected for an enquiry by HM Revenue and Customs (HMRC). Some accountants produce their own list of generally allowable expenses.

It is helpful to assess the types of expense according to the risk of being challenged by the Revenue. Here are some examples:

Low risk or No risk
- Commission paid to agent (including VAT)
- Annual subscription to Equity
- Travel and subsistence on tour
- Photographs and publicity (repros, showreel, Spotlight entry)
- Classes to maintain skills, e.g. voice, movement
- Business stationery and postage
- Fee paid to accountant

Medium risk
- Professional library – scripts, books, CDs
- Publications – *The Stage, Empire magazine*
- Travel and subsistence when not on tour
- Visits to theatre and cinema

High risk
- Home as office unless making the standard simplified claim (Google home as office HMRC)
- Cosmetic dentistry

Very high risk
- Wardrobe – renewal, dry cleaning and repair
- Hairdressing and make-up – before auditions reduces the risk
- Gratuities to dressers and stage door-keepers
- Osteopathy and other treatments – lower risks for circus performers and stunt persons
- Gym membership – for a specific role or if you are ready to make a business case
- Television licence – a 50% business proportion?

As the risk rises, so too must the care taken in deciding which to claim and which to discard. Engaging an accountant to use his or her experience, skill and judgement in carrying out a review of expenditure claims is a source of considerable reassurance to many actors. It is worth noting that entertaining, as in paying a meal for another person (even if a casting director), and gifts are never allowed.

An accountant's review may also be key in calculating the business proportions of motor car expenses, landline and mobile telephone charges (including internet access), television and film hire, including subscriptions to Sky, Netflix etc. An accountant's help in computing capital allowances for expenditure on capital items (computer, motor car, musical instruments) is appreciated by all but the most self-confident.

The emphasis so far has been on the income tax advantages of being self-employed. Whilst many actors are happy to register themselves as self-employed, others enlist the help of an accountant, even at that stage, to help with form-filling and provide a buffer-zone between themselves and the HMRC. Once registration is done, a Unique Taxpayer Reference (UTR) will be issued, often still referred to as a Schedule D number except by the HMRC. This registration is also for payment of Class 2 National Insurance ('NICs') calculated at the weekly flat rate, currently £3.05 a week. This is paid as part of the self-assessment process administered by HMRC.

If an actor achieves only a very modest net profit from his or her self-employment, less than £6,475, the actor is not charged Class 2 NICs. It is important to remember, however, that paying Class 2 NICs is a cheap way of securing entitlement to certain basic state benefits such as maternity allowance and the state pension. If you are below the threshold at which you pay Class 2 NICs you can make voluntary payments via the tax return to preserve benefit entitlements.

For the sake of completeness, Class 4 NICS are payable by actors if their annual net profit rises above the threshold: currently £9,500. That class of NIC is the earnings-related charge borne by self-employed people in addition to the flat-rate Class 2. It confers no benefits to the payer and is collected by the HMRC as part of the self-assessment system.

The complexities of the NI regime, and especially the interaction of its different classes, encourage co-operation between actor and accountant almost as much as does the application of the criteria for acceptability of expenses for income tax purposes.

Core services provided by an accountant include the following:

- Annual income and expenditure account
- Capital allowances computations
- Completion of the annual Tax Return
- Preparing a tax calculation and checking the Revenue's version
- Applying to reduce income tax payments on account, if appropriate

Additional services would include completing quarterly returns for actors successful enough to be registered for VAT, and advice on the tax and NIC implications of performing abroad. Student loan repayments and tax credit deadlines can also be discussed and planned for. Universal Credit has replaced a whole range of means-tested benefits including tax credits (other examples are income-based jobseeker's allowance, income support, income-related employment support allowance). When applied to the self-employed, the

Department of Work and Pensions usually assumes an arbitrary amount of income called the 'Minimum Income Floor'. Equity provides expert advice in this difficult area.

Most accountants charge according to time spent and the seniority and expertise of the persons doing the work. Here is an example of how this might work in practice for a young actor: he would need five hours of a bookkeeper, an hour for a manager's review and tax return and finally half-an-hour of the principal's/partner's time for overall review and quality control. With perhaps a few telephone calls and shortish meeting, the annual fee would typically be £400 plus VAT, i.e. £480. Accordingly, careful sorting of expenses by expense type can save both time and money.

In my experience, as the cost of the initial meeting is rarely charged for, I make a loss in year one of a new client. I break even in year two, and only make a profit in year three and subsequent years. It is not a surprise, therefore, that I see my relationship with a client as a long-term one – one which has time and effort invested in it by both actor and accountant.

To an actor in the early years of his career, the accountant's annual fee of about £480 represents a significant expense. The decision to instruct an accountant is a personal one. Some actors are much more comfortable and confident than others in dealing with money matters, taxation and National Insurance. Others shy away from such a course of action and choose to have an ally in the form of an accountant.

In general terms, for an actor with gross earnings of less than £25,000 but who still makes a profit, having an accountant is optional. For one with smaller earnings and who makes a loss, having an accountant could be worthwhile to relieve that loss and seek a refund of income tax. For those with gross earnings in excess of £25,000, the choice is compelling. For those with low earnings and perhaps suffering hardship, advice from Tax Aid can be invaluable. Tax Aid is a charity which helps people on low incomes with their tax problems: **http://taxaid.org.uk**. Helpline 0300 200 3300.

Having made the decision to use an accountant, choose the firm carefully. The most desired method is word of mouth. A personal recommendation from another actor, from your drama school or indeed from the company manager works well. It is important that the accountant selected knows about the taxation and NIC of actors rather than being a general practitioner. It is also important that the accountant be a member of one of the professional bodies of accountants as an indication of quality – and just in case a dispute arises which cannot be resolved amicably. Most of the institutes have a system of arbitration for fee disputes, for example, which can be used as a last resort.

Another factor in the choice of accountant is the size of the firm. The range is huge: from a sole practitioner to a multinational firm employing thousands. The former will be suitable for an actor of modest means, while the latter might be a good match for a performer with very considerable earnings and royalties from several countries around the world. In between those extremes are smaller firms with one to five partners which specialise in the tax affairs of those who work in theatre, television and film, and larger firms which have an entertainment and media department with a similar specialism. The smaller firms are likely to provide a more personal service and lower fees. The larger are likely to have access to a greater breadth of related expertise (such as film finance, production accounting) but fees will be correspondingly higher.

Each accountant will have his or her favoured way for actors to keep records. The most important point is that an actor must co-operate with his or her accountant to save time and maximise the return on effort. Here are some guidelines and handy hints:

• Keep all agent's remittance advices, payslips and invoices.

• Only claim expenses incurred 'wholly and exclusively for the purposes of the trade'.

• Use the Equity list of usually allowable expenses for guidance and perhaps an Excel spread sheet to record them.

• Keep receipts for all expenses and write explanatory notes on them (for example, 'for audition with X') and consider using an App to help you.

• File carefully details of any other income such as interest or dividends received, P60/P45s from employments (for example, bar work), rental income as well as Gift Aid payments made and any other item which may be needed to complete your tax return.

• Deliver your accounts papers to your accountant *as soon as you can* after the end of the tax year (5th April) – never leave it until close to the 31st January deadline! The sooner your return is submitted, the earlier the warning of any tax liability payable 31st January and of any other payments on account due for the following year.

Watch this space! A glimpse into the future

HMRC introduced Making Tax Digital (MTD) in April 2019 for VAT registered businesses with an annual turnover exceeding the VAT threshold, currently £85,000. MTD for Income Tax will be introduced for accounting periods commencing 6 April 2023 for the self-employed and landlords, with income over £10,000. This will mean digital record keeping – something to start thinking about.

Philippe Carden is a chartered accountant specialising in the taxation of actors and other individuals working in theatre, film, television and dance, onstage and backstage, artistic and technical. He co-wrote *Investing in West End Theatrical Productions* (Robert Hale, 1992) and has written articles for the *Guardian*, *The Stage* and other publications.

Equity Pension Scheme

Andrew Barker @ First Act

Auto-Enrolment, what is it?

Since October 2012, new legislation has gradually applied to all UK employers to ensure that they provide a suitable pension product for their workers. This legislation includes actors and is calledAuto-Enrolment (AE). If you are aged over 22 and below State pension age there is a probability that any production company that you work for *will* auto-enrol you into their chosen pension scheme. They are legally bound to enrol you. You have no choice on being auto-enrolled, but you can choose to opt out afterwards. The nature of your occupation could result in you ending up with many separate pension pots over the time span of your career.

However, there is an alternative and a way to avoid AE: the Equity Pension Scheme (EPS). The EPS has been in existence since October 1997. Designed and administered by First Act (the preferred insurance advisers to Equity and its members), it has become the pension scheme of choice for actors. If you are engaged on an Equity Agreement, whether it be in theatre, television, film or radio, the production company has an obligation to contribute to the EPS on your behalf and at rates that are higher than those that apply to AE.

The EPS' status as a qualifying workplace pension scheme will ensure that if you are an EPS member, and you inform each company manager of the production companies you work for, they will *not* auto-enrol you into their AE scheme resulting in you having one pension receiving all your contributions.

The EPS provides access to a market-leading pension product for all those working in the creative arts sector (Equity membership is not required). It is the ideal way to start or improve your personal pension arrangements.

Here is how it works

If you are working under an Equity agreed contract you could get your manager to contribute to your EPS.

Current qualifying contracts are issued by: BBC, ITV, PACT & TAC, SOLT, UK Theatre Commercial, UK Theatre Sub Rep, ITC, RSC, RNT, Disney Theatrical, plus a number of in-house arrangements.

Equity Pension Scheme – questions and answers

Q How does the EPS work?

A The funds are managed by AVIVA, one of the UK's largest and most respected pension providers. The EPS has access to over 280 investment funds catering for all attitudes to investment risk, including ethical and sustainable funds.

You have total flexibility. You contribute when you are working, and when you are not, you can take a break. The EPS is penalty-free and currently has a base charge on the core funds of 0.7% cent per annum i.e. £0.70 for every £100 in your personal pot.

Q How do I make payments into the EPS?
A You can make contributions in several ways:
• You can make contributions related to your engagement only; this way you can pay in when you are working but freeze payments when you are not.
• You can make additional regular personal payments by direct debit on a monthly basis.
• You can make additional single personal contributions on-line or by cheque.

Q How does the EPS work in theatre?
A As an EPS member you benefit from a contribution paid by your employers, equal to a percentage of your weekly wage. To qualify, you agree to make a contribution from your weekly wage. The employer contribution is added to your wages and then deducted together with your personal contribution. The employer contributions are sent directly by the employer to First Act, for investment on your behalf. Once with Aviva, basic rate tax relief is added.

Q Which theatrical managers contribute to the EPS?
A Most theatrical employers now contribute to the scheme.

West End managers (SOLT), Disney Theatrical and Shakespeare's Globe
Managers will contribute an amount equal to 5% of your weekly rehearsal or performance wage up to a maximum of 5% of 1.75 x the minimum performance wage. Two years' continual employment with the same manager increases this to 7.5%, 10% after 5 years.
    You pay a 3% personal contribution, rising to 3.75% and 5%.

Subsidised repertory theatres (UK theatre)
The manager will contribute an amount equal to 5% of your weekly rehearsal or performance wage up to a maximum of 5% of 1.5 x the appropriate middle-range salary level (MRSL).
    You pay a 3% personal contribution.

Commercial theatre (UK theatre)
Managers contribute an amount equal to 5% of your weekly rehearsal or performance wage.
    You pay a 2.5% personal contribution.

Independent Theatre Council (ITC)
Managers contribute an amount equal to 5% of your weekly rehearsal or performance wage.
    You pay a 3% personal contribution.

Royal National Theatre
You have a choice of:
    1. RNT pay 5%; you pay 3%
    2. RNT pay 5.5%; you pay 4.5%
    3. RNT pay 6%; you pay 6%
    4. RNT pay 7.5%; you pay 7.5%

Royal Shakespeare Company
The RSC contribute an amount equal to 5% of your weekly rehearsal or performance wage.
    You pay a 2.5% personal contribution.

Q How does the EPS work in television?

A Basically, the scheme works in the same way in television as it does in theatre, but your contribution will be based on either your episode fee or weekly fee, whichever basis brings you the most benefit. It is the responsibility of the artist to notify the producer prior to the engagement that they are a member of the EPS and to provide their pension membership number in the space provided in the form of engagement.

Q Which TV and film managers contribute to the EPS?

A Most TV and film employers will contribute to the scheme.

BBC Television and ITV companies will contribute an amount equal to 5% of your engagement/episode fee or weekly fee.

You pay a 2.5% personal contribution.

PACT and TAC independent TV production companies will contribute an amount equal to 5% subject to a maximum per engagement/weekly/episode fee.

You pay a 2.5% personal contribution.

Film companies will contribute an amount equal to 6% of your fee, subject to a reviewable maximum per production.

You pay a 3% personal contribution.

BBC Radio will contribute an amount equal to 5% of your engagement/weekly/episode fee.

You pay a 2.5% personal contribution.

Details of the current minimum engagement fees/wages for your production company are available from Andrew Barker at First Act 020 8686 5050, by e-mail **eps@firstact.co.uk** or at **firstact.co.uk**.

Q How can I join the EPS

A On-line at firstact.co.uk, by email **eps@firstact.co.uk** or by telephone 0208 686 5050.

Andrew Barker is a Director of Hencilla Canworth Ltd (First Act). Hencilla Canworth is an independent insurance intermediary having facilities with the UK's leading insurers and underwriters. It specialises in insurance products for performing arts companies and groups. He was part of the original team that designed and introduced the EPS in 1997 and has continued to oversee its management to this day.

Resources

Physical and mental fitness for actors

Alex Caan

The instrument or tool of the actor is the body. Like a musical instrument, if it is left idle it will become out of tune and lose its ability to function effectively.

Actors need to constantly develop their instrument to get the best out of it. Unlike a musical instrument, we carry our tool with us every day. With good habits and practice we can alleviate many of the problems that need to be fixed before they start. The work required to have a positive ongoing effect is not as great or as demanding as one would expect. Before we look at what we can do to make our bodies outstanding, let's look at what our bodies really are.

In a person of average weight and build, 70 per cent of the mass of the body is muscle and bone. Therefore we can have a large effect on our bodies, by focusing on our muscles and bones. Before we can affect change in our muscles and bones we need to understand how they work and what relationships they have with each other.

The structure of the body is extremely complicated but can be viewed in quite a simplistic manner. Originally we would have walked on all fours, which is why our upper limbs have very similar corresponding joints to our lower limbs. Each hand has five digits, with a dominant thumb; our corresponding lower body part is the opposite foot, with the big toe as the dominant digit. The wrist and ankle are similar multi-directional joints, whereas the elbow and knee are both hinged joints. The shoulder and hip are ball and socket joints.

The upper and lower limbs are also connected by corresponding groups of muscles. The quads, which are in the front of the thigh, are related to the upper body through the triceps, which are in the back of the upper arm. The hamstrings, at the back of the upper leg, are related to the biceps. The gluteus or buttocks are related to the pectorals or chest muscles. So rather than looking at muscular activity in isolation, we must see muscles as groups working together.

When the body moves forward, the opposite arm and leg swing. The combination of muscles working together propels our bodies. Muscles move limbs by shortening.

Muscles work together synergistically, and in a healthy, well-maintained body are balanced. If bad habits occur, this simplicity of movement can lead to long-term health problems by over-use of some muscles, and under-use of others. This constant over-use/under-use will lead to a tired or sore body part in a specific area, often one side of the neck or lower back.

As we move forward, the chain of movements pass through the centre of the body. This passing through the centre is a clue to the focus of long-term fitness and wellbeing for the actor.

The centre of the body is the place where all life stems from. It is here that a baby is connected to its mother through the placenta, that later becomes the belly button. In the centre of the body is the diaphragm, from which, through correct training, all breath should originate.

The movement of our bodies creates heat and energy. Contrary to what some directors believe, we are not beings that live in our head or brain space. We live in our bodies, and movement produces powerful emotional responses. This is encapsulated in the phrase 'Motion creates Emotion'. This is why actors talk about getting the walk of the character, because this allows them to get into the body of the character, which in turn allows them to get into the personality of the character. Some actors do this instinctively, but it is and can be a learned skill.

Actors communicate thoughts in the vast majority by speaking. There are, of course, actors who use mime and dance to communicate, but mainly thoughts are communicated verbally, using speech or song. Words are merely a manipulation of breath using the tongue, mouth and vocal cords. Without breath we have nothing to carry our thoughts over large theatrical space.

Coincidentally, breath or oxygen is the most important nourishment our bodies need. Without food one can live for 40 days or more; without water one can live for 7-10 days; but if you don't breathe for five minutes you will die.

Using this as our guide, the focus of the actors' fitness should be built around the development of a robust powerful tool that can create large amounts of powerful breath. Not just large volumes of breath, but outstanding control of the mechanism that delivers that breath.

The mechanism that delivers the breath is the lungs and diaphragm and their supporting muscles. These muscles need to be strong, but also need to be mobile and have excellent endurance.

Lastly, the value of water cannot be underestimated. A 5 per cent drop in hydration can lead to mild dehydration, which can lead to a large drop in bodily function, both mental and physical. Even a 2 per cent drop in hydration can have a very damaging and negative effect on our voice. In temperate climates we lose 2.5 litres of water throughout an average day. If we are performing, rehearsing or undertaking strenuous physical activity we will use much greater amounts of water than this. Therefore we must monitor our bodies and increase water intake when needed. Passing clear urine is a good indicator of hydration – if not first thing in the morning, then definitely throughout the day.

So where does one start in the nitty-gritty of training the actor's body? Actors come in all shapes and sizes. I am not advocating that all actors try to become slim and pert: who would play all the non-slim, non-pert roles? Equally, I am not advocating that all actors develop muscular physiques. We need to be limber in the joints and muscles, but there is no point in the serious actor developing big muscles at the expense of range of movement. I believe that you can be tall, short, slim, rotund, lanky or squat and at the same time be very fit. Olympic shot putters are very large but all can run great distances and move like ballet dancers.

Fitness for actors doesn't require a massive overloading of the body. To reach Olympic-standard fitness we would need to break the body down systematically over a period of time, in order to allow the body to regenerate stronger than before. This regeneration occurs during periods of rest. But this overloading is not really needed for general fitness for actors.

In all of our fitness development we need to place breath control and posture at the forefront. The ideas and concepts of the Alexander Technique are pivotal to this. Its values are based on excellent posture and good use of muscles, rather than overuse and bad postural habits. So when performing any movement, be aware of the alignment of the

Resources

head, neck and back. Often actors strain their voices because they are tight in another part of their body, which pulls the head and neck out of alignment, resulting in a sore throat or strained voice. For those of you who are not familiar with the Alexander Technique, I would recommend that an awareness of posture and balance is vital to long-term fitness.

A simple starting point for general fitness for actors is walking. Walking is the most underused and undervalued exercise we can do. It involves a good pair of training shoes and a place to go! Between 20 and 60 minutes' continuous walking a day will increase lung capacity and make our heart a great deal stronger. I know many actors say that they walk at least that in a day – going shopping, walking to the bus or train, and so on. I am not discounting that, but I am advocating a steady brisk walk with arms swinging back and forth in time with the opposing leg. By doing this, the whole body is being exercised, and the core muscles through the centre of the body are activated. It is akin to the phase of human development that we know as crawling. The same benefits cannot be achieved through passive day-to-day walking.

Walking has a very effective return for the amount of effort expended, because there is little detrimental impact on the joints of the lower limbs. The swinging of opposing arms and legs also helps reinforce correct neurological pathways. This helps us to move our bodies more effectively and efficiently as a kinetic chain, rather than as disjointed isolated movements.

A walking regime three days a week is a good place to start. You will not only build your lungs and heart, but also the tissues around your joints in the legs, arms and back. These need time to adapt and grow to the new stresses being placed on them. Taking a day off in between will allow the tissues throughout your body to regenerate during the periods of rest.

If you are a fitness novice, then building up to an hour-long walk is an achievable goal. Start with a ten-minute walk that builds systematically over a period of between four and six weeks, rather than blazing into a brisk hour-long walk initially. Increasing your walks by three minutes each walk will let you achieve an hour-long walk from a ten-minute starting point in just six weeks. Three minutes may sound a lot, but since it requires adding just one and a half minutes to your outward journey, it is not an unrealistic amount.

Swimming is also an excellent way to work the heart and lungs without placing any stress on the joints, as it is a non-weight bearing form of exercise. However, it is important to swim using the front crawl and backstroke rather than predominantly using the breast stroke, so that we continue to move opposing upper and lower limbs to work our core muscles. A mixture of all swimming strokes would be best to work the greatest range of muscle groups and minimise the likelihood of housemaid's knee (a common breast stroke-related injury)! Learning to swim with your head partially submerged in the water is vital, in order to maintain correct alignment of the spine.

The same incremental approach to developing fitness through walking, as recommended above, should be applied when undertaking a swimming regime. Rather than using the increment of time, the number of lengths swum is a very simple starting point. Do bear in mind the length of each pool that you may swim in may vary! It is likely that the more often you swim, the quicker you will become. So increasing the number of lengths that you swim each session may require little or no extra time in the pool.

We have exercised the heart and lungs with walking and swimming. We need now to develop our range of movement and strength. Basic Yoga movements are also a simple and effective way to increase inner strength and develop range of movement and good posture. I am not looking at the more physical jumping around or sauna types of Yoga. I am advocating basic Yoga moves.

Yoga has many positive effects, which include large ranges of movement and mobility. By getting into certain Yoga positions, we are not only stretching the muscles, but also massaging the internal organs. Yoga also has the benefit of establishing excellent breath control. The breath floods into the centre of the body and has to be released with control and in a sustained manner. This has a very relaxing and meditative effect. This helps us switch off our overactive minds, the value of which cannot be underestimated.

Buying a book or DVD on Yoga or joining a Yoga class is an excellent place to start. If Yoga doesn't appeal to you, then Pilates is an excellent alternative. Both Yoga and Pilates are fantastic for developing breath control and posture control techniques.

Let us look at a sample week's exercise programme – for example, walking or swimming on Monday, Thursday and Saturday, with Yoga or Pilates on Tuesday and Friday. This gives you two days off, on Wednesday and Sunday, which follow either two or three days of activity. Rest is vital to regeneration. We only become fitter and stronger by allowing our bodies to recover and grow. These days off give the individual physical downtime, which can then be filled with mental stimulation of some kind, including meditation, vocal and singing practice, reading or other pursuits that aid the actor's development as a whole.

> **Further information**
>
> For more information about any of the suggested forms of exercise, see the websites listed below:
>
> Alexander Technique www.alexandertechnique.com
>
> Walking www.thewalkingsite.com
>
> Swimming www.britishswimming.org
>
> Yoga www.bwy.org.uk (British Wheel of Yoga)
>
> Pilates www.pilatesfoundation.com

This is a brief overview of the most suitable and simple exercises to cover what is required for the stresses and strains of most acting jobs. All of these suggestions can be carried out from home or on tour. The time and effort required to train in this manner will not be detrimental to the actor's performance. By starting small, and increasing gradually, the actor will feel more invigorated and energised from undertaking an exercise programme.

The actor's body should be viewed as a communication tool. Bodies require stimulation to develop. Without stimulus, the body and mind will deteriorate. Permitting this to happen is an injustice to the craft of acting. We all only have one body, and we need to look after it and maintain it for our specific needs.

Alex Caan was an international athlete before training at RADA for three years. Since graduation, he has worked extensively in theatre, TV and radio. As a consultant Alex teaches business people powerful communication through effective use of the body. As a sports coach Alex has coached Premiership football and rugby players to international level. He has coached sportsmen and women to Olympic and World level in a range of different athletic disciplines. He is currently National Event Coach for High Jump in the UK, and prepared the group of talented high jumpers for the London 2012 Olympics.

Mental health in the performing arts

Claire Cordeaux, Director of the British Association for Performance Arts Medicine
Interview by Rob Ostlere

Claire Cordeaux is the director of the British Association for Performance Arts Medicine (BA-PAM), a specialist healthcare charity supporting individuals and organisations in the performing arts. BAPAM provides free clinical services, expert training, essential resources and clinical leadership. In 2020, BAPAM worked in association with Equity to create a new dedicated 24/7 mental health helpline for union members throughout the UK, with individual assessments and up to six counselling sessions available.

Perhaps you could start by giving us an overview of the services BAPAM provides for performers and the industry?

BAPAM was set up about thirty years ago by a group of doctors initially, although we've added lots of different health care professionals since, including psychologists and psychotherapists. We focus on the health needs of performers and other creative practitioners – these can be quite specific because of the context they are working in. We offer free assessments with expert clinicians who are highly qualified, but also used to treating performing arts professionals so they understand where they're coming from and the demands of the job. The aim is very much to help people get back into work and learn strategies to manage conditions in an ongoing way to sustain their careers. Alongside that we also do a lot of health education. At the moment we're running a whole series of webinars on keeping mentally and physically healthy, preventing injuries and also focusing on vocal health. We want people to have the knowledge – hopefully before they've got a problem – on how to look after themselves so that they can prevent it from happening.

Another core part of BAPAM's work is researching mental health in the industry. One of the stats that stood out to me on your website is that nearly 75 per cent of performers report mental or physical health problems

The national average is about one in four people, so it is significantly higher in the performing arts than the general population. I think one of the key messages to take from that research is everybody in the industry should recognise that it is a normal thing to happen. If you haven't got those health issues yourself, you're likely to be working with somebody who has.

What can performers do to protect themselves and others' mental health?

Just having that knowledge – that it's quite likely that this is something you will come across – is important, particularly if you're starting out in your career. Then, think about ways of managing it; develop a mental health practice that you can draw on so that if a problem does occur, you've got resources and a plan of what to do. Take every opportunity to learn strategies. Learn about good mental health practise just as you would learn about your craft. And then, if there is an issue, get help – use the services available – as soon as you can. Support your friends and colleagues in creative communities by sharing resources and nurturing environments where communication and respect are priorities.

What steps are being taken more widely in the industry to address mental health issues, for example in drama schools and the training sector?

I work with drama schools and I know that mental health is very much at the forefront for educators and institutions. There's a lot more research now into what happens, what's likely to happen and what interventions are useful. It is essential that training teaches future professionals the skills they will need to sustain a very psychologically demanding career. Even if drama schools haven't got it perfectly right yet, what I'm pleased about is that the dialogue seems to be shifting to acknowledging problems and implementing improvements and interventions.

What about steps being taken to address mental health in workplaces; in rehearsal rooms, in theatres and on sets?

It's an ongoing dialogue which is had differently at different levels. The larger organisations often have infrastructure in place; they might have counsellors in or accessible through the theatre, which is fantastic. Obviously for smaller companies it's much harder; there isn't the budget necessarily and they're dealing with how they're going to wash the costumes and get the props from A to B. Where there's a bit more of a looser arrangement and not necessarily a plan in place, it's about trying to get a clearer understanding of what are healthy practices. BAPAM has been putting out information about that: is there a checklist we can look at and what should the organisers of an environment do to support people to keep healthy? Where do we signpost people for additional help? And we have a group that's currently working on trying to get areas of best practice highlighted so that people can see that, actually, it's not that difficult to do. We're trying to get the message out there: here's what you can do on a very low budget and it does make a difference.

And you work with industry organisations directly?

That's right; we currently have a collaboration with the Centre for Performance Science, which itself is a collaboration between Imperial College and the Royal College of Music, though they cover all art forms. We have a PhD student looking at all the risk factors that might cause health problems in a performer. Some of these are things that you can't necessarily do anything about but being aware of them is useful. There are risks that you carry yourself: that you're a certain age, a certain physique or you might have some mental health issues in your family background. Then there's the environmental factors: poor equipment or no breaks, for example. There are problems caused by prejudice or bullying. And then there might be the inciting event, which is the thing that's sort of the straw that breaks the camel's back: the long tour or the new show that is really very challenging. The aim of our work was to help people understand what are the things that actually causes health problems and how we as an arts community can work together to avoid them happening. We want it to be something that is much more of a can-do type of programme, that tries to create better environments by celebrating what's already good.

A problem for most performers is facing periods of unemployment. Is there advice on how to cope with the challenges that creates?

Well, if we use the lockdown as an example, then one of the things we worked on with performers was seeing the time as an opportunity to develop skills by setting goals and creating a routine that they follow every day. That included taking breaks, looking at when you do physical exercise, when you develop your mental practice, picking up skills that you wouldn't normally have the time to do, and socialising; to be your full human self as opposed to just your performance self. Of course, I'm totally aware that this is easier said than done. When you're not working, and it's not a situation of your choosing, you can feel quite paralysed I think about doing anything. It's quite hard to get motivated to do anything if you don't know what you're working towards. And it's difficult in a situation where you're not sure about your finances. We see lots of people trying to do things and they can't even begin to even think about it because other issues in their life are just so overwhelming. What one of our trainers on mental health was saying at a session the other day is try to think of one thing you can do that's achievable, however small. Then the fact that you do it is brilliant; you've met the goal and you celebrate that thing. That's as opposed to setting unrealistic goals and weighing yourself down with things that you're not going to be able to achieve.

BAPAM have been working with Equity on their new support system for performers. How has that been going?

Equity have a helpline number that you can call which is staffed by counsellors, and they can pick up a whole range of issues. So, if you're an Equity member and you recognise there's a problem, then you can call BAPAM and we will organise a free assessment with a clinician who is experienced working with creative artists. If you would then benefit from some counselling, up to six sessions are provided via Equity funding. If this approach isn't likely to be helpful for you, the clinical assessor will look at what else could be put in place. For many people it has and will be incredibly helpful, and we've got some amazing counsellors working with us on it.

That sounds like a hugely positive step for the industry

We have to try and be positive, to try and look for what can be done better. Not to minimise the problem but to reframe the discussion so that we're moving everything forward.

To learn more about BAPAM and the many resources and services they provide for performers, visit **www.bapam.org.uk**. To discuss your mental health in confidence you can call the Equity Mental Health and Wellbeing Helpline line on 0800 917 6470 (available 24/7; have your Equity number to hand).

Funding bodies

The competition for funding is so fierce that it is important to allow sufficient time for research, planning and proper presentation of your proposed project. It is well worth checking to see what information is available on the websites listed in this section. Many funding bodies are happy to advise on form-filling, what kind of projects stand a chance and what could constitute a realistic amount to ask for. Equally, it's becoming far more common for industry figures to offer guides on social media on how to apply for funding, or perhaps even one-on-one sessions to help guide your specific application - keep an eye out online! It is also well worth going on one (or more) of the Independent Theatre Council's (ITC; see page 425) courses for assistance in the complex world of funding applications.

Bodies that offer individual funding should be approached with similar care and attention.

NATIONAL ARTS COUNCILS

Arts Council England
The Hive, 49 Lever Street, Manchester M1 1FN
tel 0161 934 4317
email enquiries@artscouncil.org.uk
website www.artscouncil.org.uk
Facebook www.facebook.com/artscouncilofengland
Twitter @ace_national

Arts Council England champions, develops and invests in artistic and cultural experiences that enrich people's lives. It supports a range of activities across the arts, museums and libraries, from theatre to digital art, reading to dance, music to literature, and crafts to collections. "Great art and culture inspires us, brings us together and teaches about ourselves and the world around us. In short it makes us better."

Between 2018 and 2022, they invested £1.45 billion of public money from government and £860 million from the National Lottery to help create these experiences for as many people as possible across the country.

Application forms, guidance notes and information sheets can be downloaded from the website. A wide range of resources, publications, links and information about other funding sources is also accessible on the website.

Arts Council of Northern Ireland
Linen Hill House, 23 Linenhall Street, Lisburn BT28 1FJ
tel 028 9262 3555
email info@artscouncil-ni.org
website www.artscouncil-ni.org

The prime distributor of public support for the arts, the Arts Council of Northern Ireland is committed to increasing opportunities for artists to develop challenging and innovative work. In addition to funding schemes for organisations and community groups, the council has developed a special programme of schemes to extend support for the individual artist. This programme includes the General Arts Award, which provides funding for specific projects, specialised research and personal artistic development; and the Major Individual Award, which supports established artists in the development of ambitious work.

Arts Council of Wales
Bute Place, Cardiff CF10 5AL
tel 0330 124 2733
email grants@arts.wales
website www.arts.wales

Responsible for funding and developing the arts in Wales, using money from Welsh Government and the National Lottery. Provides arts organisations and individuals in Wales with the opportunity to apply for funding towards clearly defined arts-related projects. Scheme Guidelines for the funding programmes are available on the website.

Creative Scotland
Edinburgh office: The Lighthouse, Mitchell Lane, Glasgow G1 3NU
tel 0330 333 2000
Glasgow office: Waverley Gate, 2-4 Waterloo Gate, Edinburgh EH1 3EG
website www.creativescotland.com

The public body that supports the arts, screen and creative industries across all parts of Scotland on behalf of everyone who lives, works or visits there. Through distributing funding from the Scottish Government and the National Lottery, Creative Scotland enables people and organisations to work in and experience the arts, screen and creative industries in Scotland by helping others to develop great ideas and bring them to life. Creative Scotland supports film and theatre professionals based in Scotland through a range of funds and initiatives.

It helps "Scotland's creativity shine at home and abroad... We invest in talented people and exciting ideas. We develop the creative industries and champion everything that is good about Scottish creativity."

REGIONAL ARTS COUNCIL OFFICES

Arts Council England, East Midlands
Rooms 005 & 005A, Arkwright Building, Nottingham Trent University, Burton Street, Nottingham NG1 4BU

Area covered: Derbyshire, Leicestershire, Lincolnshire (excluding North and North East Lincolnshire), Northamptonshire, Nottinghamshire, Rutland.

Arts Council England, London
Bloomsbury Street, Bloomsbury, London WC1B 3HF

Area covered: Greater London.

Arts Council England, North East
Central Square, Forth Street, Newcastle upon Tyne NE1 3PJ
First Floor South, Marshall's Mill, Marshall Street, Leeds LS11 9YJ

Area covered: Newcastle office: Darlington, Durham, Gateshead, Hartlepool, Middlesbrough, Newcastle upon Tyne, North Tyneside, Northumberland, Redcar & Cleveland, South Tyneside, Stockton-on-Tees and Sunderland; Leeds office: Barnsley, Bradford, Calderdale, Doncaster, East Riding of Yorkshire, Kingston upon Hull, Kirklees, Leeds, North East Lincolnshire, North Lincolnshire, North Yorkshire, Rotherham, Sheffield, Wakefield and York.

Arts Council England, North West
49 Lever Street, Manchester M1 1FN

Area covered: Blacburn with Darwen, Blackpool, Bolton, Bury, Cheshire, Cumbria, Halton, Knowsley, Lancashire, Liverpool, Manchester, Oldham, Rochdale, Salford, Sefton, St Helens, Stockport, Tameside, Trafford, Warrington, Wigan and Wirral.

Arts Council England, South East
Unit A, Level 4, New England House, New England Street, Brighton BN1 4GH
Brooklands, 24 Brooklands Avenue, Cambridge CB2 8BU

Area covered: Brighton office: Bracknell Forest, Brighton and Hove, Buckinghamshire, East Sussex, Kent, Medway and Milton Keynes ; Cambridge office:

Bedfordshire, Cambridgeshire, Essex, Hertfordshire, Luton, Norfolk, Peterborough, Southend-on-Sea, Suffolk and Thurrock.

Arts Council England, South West
Fourth Floor, 66 Queen Square, Bristol BS1 4JP

Area covered: Bath & North East Somerset, Bournemouth, Bristol, Cornwall, Devon, Dorset, Gloucestershire, Hampshire, Isles of Scilly, Isle of Wight, North Somerset, Plymouth, Poole, Portsmouth, Southampton, Somerset, South Gloucestershire, Swindon, Torbay and Wiltshire.

Arts Council England, West Midlands
The Foundry, 82 Granville Street, Birmingham B1 2LH

Area covered: Birmingham, Coventry, Dudley, Herefordshire, Sandwell, Shropshire, Solihull, Staffordshire, Stoke-on-Trent, Telford & Wrekin, Walsall, Warwickshire, Wolverhampton and Worcestershire.

NATIONAL FILM AGENCIES

Northern Ireland Screen
3rd Floor, 21 Alfred House, Belfast BT2 8ED
tel 028 9023 2444
email info@northernirelandscreen.co.uk
website www.northernirelandscreen.co.uk
Facebook www.facebook.com/northernirelandscreen
Twitter @NIScreen
Instagram @northernirelandscreen

Northern Ireland Screen is the national screen agency for Northern Ireland. Its aim is to accelerate the development of a dynamic and sustainable screen industry and culture in Northern Ireland.

REGIONAL FILM AGENCIES

Film London
The Arts Building, Morris Place, London N4 3JG
tel 020 7613 7676
email info@filmlondon.org.uk
website www.filmlondon.org.uk

Film London is the capital's public agency for feature film, television, commercials and other interactive content, including games. "Our aim is simple: to ensure that London has a thriving film sector that enriches the capital's businesses and its people." The government has charged Film London with developing and managing a national strategy to generate inward investment through film production via a public-private partnership with key industry bodies.

North East Screen
The BIS, 17 Whitby Street, Hartlepool TS24 7AD
tel 0191 440 4940

email hello@northeastscreen.org
website www.northeastscreen.org
Facebook www.facebook.com/northeastscreen
Twitter @nescreen
Instagram @nescreen

North East Screen is the screen agency for the North East of England. "Our vision is to create a strong commercial creative economy in the North East, by investing in talent and ideas."

Screen South

Digital Hub, The Glassworks, Mill Bay, Folkestone, Kent CT20 1JG
tel (01303) 259777
email info@screensouth.org
website www.screensouth.org

Screen South is the film and media agency for the South East of England. "We aim to be a resource that helps people get their ideas off the ground, whether they want to make a short film, learn how to write successful scripts, set up a film festival or shoot a major movie here. We promote talent, preserve our film heritage and find ways of presenting exciting film to new audiences. Screen South is a Lottery distributor."

Screen Yorkshire

Studio 30, 46 The Calls, Leeds LS2 7EY
tel 0113 236 8228
email info@screenyorkshire.co.uk
website www.screenyorkshire.co.uk
Twitter @screenyorkshire

Screen Yorkshire champions the film, TV, games and digital industries in Yorkshire and the Humber. Screen Yorkshire offers production financing through its Yorkshire Content Fund. Since it launched in February 2012, Screen Yorkshire has invested in 50 film and TV projects including: *The Duke, Ali & Ava, Official Secrets, Ghost Stories, Yardie, Hope Gap, National Treasure, Dad's Army, Sawallows and Amazons, Dark Angel, Journeyman, Dark River, Black Work, The Great Train Robbery, Peaky Blinders, Jonathan Strange and Mr Norrell* and *Testament of Youth*. Screen Yorkshire develops talent by designing and delivering industry schemes, and also provides film office services for productions filming in Yorkshire, including crew and facilities and location services.

OTHER SOURCES OF FUNDING

Additional information about various entertainment charities and benevolent funds can be found on the website of The Actors' Charitable Trust **www.tactactors.org**. Unless explicitly mentioned, most of the organisations listed below and on the TACT website do not provide assistance with drama school fees or maintenance.

Actors' Benevolent Fund

6 Adam Street, London WC2N 6AD
tel 020 7836 6378

email office@abf.org.uk
website www.actorsbenevolentfund.co.uk

Since 1882 the Actors' Benevolent Fund has provided support to professional actors, actresses and stage managers unable to work due to poor health, an accident or old age.

Equity Charitable Trust

Plouviez House, 19-20 Hatton Place, London EC1N 8RU
tel 020 7831 1926
email info@equitycharitabletrust.org.uk
website www.equitycharitabletrust.org.uk

The Equity Charitable Trust provides educational bursaries to performers and industry professionals with a minimum of 10 years' professional adult experience who are looking to retrain, develop new skills and obtain valuable new qualifications. Depending on your circumstances, grants can cover a portion of your course costs.

Also provides benefit and debt advice to industry members who are experiencing a financial or medical setback and who may qualify for a one-off financial grant. For information and to download an application form for either a Welfare or Education Grant please visit the website.

Evelyn Norris Trust

Plouviez House, 19-20 Hatton Place, London EC1N 8RU
tel 020 7831 1926
email info@equitycharitabletrust.org.uk
website www.equitycharitabletrust.org.uk/other-grants/evelyn-norris-trust/
Facebook www.facebook.com/Equity-Charitable-Trust-264371367256456
Twitter @ECT_performer

The Evelyn Norris Trust is a charity that accepts applications for grants from members of the concert and theatrical professions. The Trust aims to help with the cost of convalesence or a recuperative holiday following illness, injury or surgery.

The Foyle Foundation

Rugby Chambers, 2 Rugby Street, London WC1N 3QU
tel 020 7430 9119
email info@foylefoundation.org.uk
website www.foylefoundation.org.uk

The Foundation operates a Main Grants Scheme supporting charities with a core remit of Arts or Learning and a Small Grants Scheme covering small charities in all fields. It has supported tours, festivals and education projects and helped to develop new work. It will also consider funding the building or updating of arts facilities. The majority of main grants are in the range of £10,000 to £50,000. Capital projects seeking more than £75,000 are normally considered twice a year. Guidelines are available to download from the website.

Jerwood Trust

171 Union Street, London SE1 0LN
tel 020 7261 0279
email info@jerwood.org
website www.jerwood.org

The Jerwood Trust is dedicated to imaginative and responsible revenue funding of the arts, supporting professional artists to develop and grow at important stages in their careers. It works with artists across art forms, from dance and theatre to literature, music and the visual arts.

The Oxford Samuel Beckett Theatre Trust Award

PO Box 2637, Ascot, Berks SL5 8ZN
email OSBTTA@barbican.org.uk.com
website www.osbttrust.com
website www.barbican.org.uk/theatre/abouttheatre/award

The purpose of this bi-annual award is, in particular, to help the development of emerging practitioners in the field of innovative theatre/performance and, in general, to encourage the new generation of creative artists. Artists from all disciplines are encouraged to apply.

The award is for a company or individual to create a show either for the Pit Theatre, Barbican, London, or a site-responsive, non-traditional show to take place in London. The winning show, either at the Pit or, if site-responsive, elsewhere, will be part of the Barbican Theatre season.

The Royal Theatrical Fund

11 Garrick Street, London WC2E 9AR
tel 020 7836 3322
email admin@trtf.com
website www.trtf.com
Facebook www.facebook.com/theRTF1839
Twitter @theRTF1839
Instagram @royaltheatrefund

The Royal Theatrical Fund helps people from *all* areas of the entertainment industry. The Fund makes grants which will alleviate the suffering, assist the recovery, or reduce the need, hardship or distress of those in the entertainment industry or their families/dependants. To be eligible to receive a grant, a person must be unable to work due to illness, injury or infirmity, and to have professionally worked in the theatrical arts (on stage, radio, film or television) for a minimum of 7 years.

Sophie's Silver Lining Fund

email office@sslf.org.uk
website www.sslf.org.uk

Provides assistance with the cost of their training to needy acting and singing students. "Please note that regretfully, we are no longer able to accept applications for funding from individual students. Awards are only made to students put forward by a small number of drama and music colleges selected by the trustees."

The Wellcome Trust

Gibbs Building, 215 Euston Road, London NW1 2BE
email contact@wellcome.ac.uk
website www.wellcome.org/grant-funding

The Wellcome Trust Arts Awards is the Trust's funding scheme that supports arts projects which engage with biomedical science.

The Arts Awards provide funding for a range of projects that bring together any art form and any area of biomedical science. Projects must involve the creation of new artistic work and have biomedical scientific input into the process, either through a scientist taking on an advisory role or through direct collaboration. 2 levels of funding are available – small- to medium-sized projects (up to and including £30,000) and large projects (above £30,000) – primarily for artists or organisations with an existing track record with the Wellcome Trust or Wellcome Collection. Full details are available on the website, including details of pending deadlines for large and small grants, application guidelines, examples of previously funded projects, and the online application portal.

Publications, libraries, references and booksellers

This section lists the major sources for scripts and sheet music – and routes to finding that elusive script or score. While the Internet can be extremely useful in such a quest, it sometimes requires some lateral thinking to find what you want. It is possible to find out-of-print plays via libraries or book-finding services, and by combing second-hand bookshops. Some publishers (even a few playwrights' agencies) will organise a photocopy – for a fee. Also, the British Library (in theory) has a copy of every play ever performed in this country, but there can be complications in actually getting hold of a copy. Start with your local library if you're determined to find a specific play; if they don't have it, they may well be able to get it from another library (via the inter-library loan system), but be prepared for it to take a long time. Another route is to try to find a theatre at which the play has been performed: they may be able to help.

AbeBooks.com
website www.abebooks.com

Excellent website which will search the catalogues of hundreds of second-hand booksellers in this country and around the world.

Actorsandperformers.com

Actors & Performers is a professional networking site for the acting community, containing must-have career information, and with authors, casting directors, actors and industry practitioners such as Richard Eyre appearing as guest bloggers and contributors, offering advice and insight into the profession.

Actors & Performers provides a community for actors to share events, ask questions, network, comment on blogs and events, and obtain career advice for free.

Register free for Actors & Performers at **www.actorsandperformers.com**.

Amazon.co.uk & Amazon.com
website www.amazon.co.uk or www.amazon.com

Remarkably useful not just for what is currently in print, but also for links to second-hand retailers who may have that out-of-print play or score you are seeking.

Barbican Library
Barbican Centre, London EC2Y 8DS
tel 020 7638 0569
website www.barbican.org.uk/your-visit/during-your-visit/library

Situated on level 2 of the Barbican Centre, this is the largest lending library in the City of London. In addition to the general library, the strong arts and music sections reflect the Barbican Centre's emphasis on the arts. The library is fully accessible to wheelchair users. *Opening hours*: Monday and Wednesday: 9.30am–5.30pm; Tuesday and Thursday: 9.30am–7.30pm; Friday: 9.30am–5.30pm; Saturday: 9.30am–4pm.

Bookbarn International
Units 1-2, Hallatrow Business Park, Hallatrow, Bath & Avon BS39 6EX
tel 01761 452178
website www.bookbarninternational.co.uk

"The UK's largest used book warehouse," with many thousands of cheap second-hand scripts and a searchable catalogue online.

The British Library
St Pancras Building, 96 Euston Road, London NW1 2DB
tel 0330 333 1144 (switchboard)
Legal Deposit Office: The British Library, Boston Spa, Wetherby, West Yorkshire LS23 7BQ
tel (01937) 546268
email legal-deposit-books@bl.uk
website www.bl.uk
Facebook www.facebook.com/britishlibrary
Twitter @britishlibrary

The British Library is the national library of the United Kingdom and contains a substantial collection of plays and manuscripts from the UK and Ireland, as well as from other parts of the world. The sound archive also includes just about everything from the sound of Amazonian tree frogs to classic recordings of Shakespeare's plays. Users need a Reader's Pass (details on how to acquire same are on the website)

Resources

to access and read particular publications. The library will, for a fee, allow photocopying – subject to copyright legislation.

Contacts

See the entry for Spotlight under *Spotlight, casting directories and information services* on page 351.

Doollee.com

website www.doollee.com

An excellent online guide to modern playwrights and theatre plays which have been written, or translated, into English since the production of *Look Back in Anger* in 1956. It costs £5 per week for access or £25 for a year.

Dress Circle

tel 020 7240 2227
email sales@dresscircle.london
website www.dresscircle.london/

Dress Circle formerly had a shop in London's Covent Garden; it now operates online only. It aims to supply the widest selection of musical theatre and cabaret-related products from around the world – CDs, DVDs, posters, cards, mugs, collectibles and more. "If we can't get it – no one can!"

Fourthwall (incorporating The Drama Student)

3rd Floor, 207 Regent Street, London W1B 3HH
tel 020 3371 0995
email editor@fourthwallmagazine.co.uk
website www.fourthwallmagazine.co.uk
Editorial Director Phil Matthews *Editor* Josh Boyd-Rochford

Fourthwall covers the whole journey, from auditioning for drama school through to graduation and beyond. Believes that to succeed in this industry, it is important that we constantly challenge ourselves, and often that means the training never leaves us. *Fourthwall* is at the forefront of that passion, delivering a magazine that is informative, amusing, intelligent, thought provoking, accessible and challenging. "Above all, we're a publication that is passionate about careers in the performing arts."

Samuel French Bookshop at the Royal Court Theatre

Sloane Square, London SW1W 8AS
tel 020 7565 5024
email bookshop@royalcourttheatre.com
website www.royalcourttheatre.com/your-visit/bookshop
website www.concordtheatricals.co.uk/resources/royal-court-bookshop/

Offers a diverse selection of contemporary plays as well as publications on the theory and practice of modern drama. The staff specialise in assisting with

the selection of audition monologues and scenes. Playtexts for current Royal Court productions typically cost just £4 and past production texts cost £5. The Bookshop is situated on the first floor. *Opening Hours*: Monday to Saturday: 11.30am–7.45pm. On performance nights, there is a smaller bookstall in the downstairs bar from 6pm until curtain.

Nick Hern Books

tel 020 8749 4953
email info@nickhernbooks.co.uk
website www.nickhernbooks.co.uk

Nick Hern Books is the UK's leading specialist performing arts publisher, with plays by writers including Mike Bartlett, Caryl Churchill, debbie tucker green, Lucy Kirkwood, Conor McPherson, Rona Munro, Jack Thorne and Enda Walsh. Also publishes practical books by renowned practitioners such as Mike Alfreds, Peter Brook, Declan Donnellan, Richard Eyre and Harriet Walter.

Offers online discounts and special promotions, plus downloadable extracts, exclusive signed editions and more. Enquiries for performing licences to their plays can also made online. The online Play Finder allows searches by genre, cast size, length and more.

Useful series for actors include *The Good Audition Guides*, which offer classical, Shakespeare and contemporary monologues and duologues as well as guidance on how to perform them; the *So You Want To...?* career guides, giving advice on a range of careers in the performing arts, written by practitioners with a wealth of knowledge and expertise in their field, and *Drama Classics*, offering great plays from around the world by dramatists including Chekhov, Euripides, Ibsen, Lorca, Molière and Wilde, with introductions, plot synopses and author biographies.

Nick Hern Books publishes plays in the English language alongside major professional productions on stage in the UK or Ireland. Submissions can be emailed to the Commissioning Editor at submissions@nickhernbooks.co.uk.

Internet Movie Database (IMDb)

website uk.imdb.com

A comprehensive database and news round-up of film and television around the world.

The Knowledge

Cally Yard, Unit 4D, 445 Caledonian Road, London, N7 9BG
tel 020 8102 0931
email alexandra.zeevalkink@mbi.london
website www.theknowledgeonline.com
Twitter @TheKnowledgeUK

Covering all aspects of production, The Knowledge Online contains contacts and services for the UK film, television, video and commercial production industry. The website features around 18,000 contacts, is free to use and does not require registration. Its new subscription service Production Intelligence features contact details of casting directors and line producers for forthcoming productions.

London Arrangements

tel 020 7096 1801
email enquiries@londonarrangements.com
website www.londonarrangements.com
Facebook /londonarrangements
Director Stephen Robinson

London Arrangements specialise in the production of professional backing tracks ranging from stage and screen, swing and jazz, to classical and easy listening genres. Samples of all tracks can be listened to online, and the majority may be ordered in any key at no extra charge. We also produce bespoke backing tracks, piano rehearsal tracks and piano/vocal sheet music.

London Theatre

website www.londontheatre.co.uk

A website containing news, reviews, events, booking information and seating plans for London's theatre scene plus maps, hotels and general tourist information.

Methuen Drama

50 Bedford Square, London WC1B 3DP
tel 020 7631 5600
website www.bloomsbury.com/uk/academic/academic-subjects/drama-and-performance-studies/
Twitter @MethuenDrama

Methuen Drama covers a wide range of books that examine the works of key practitioners and playwrights including Stanislavsky, Chekhov, Laban, Bertolt Brecht, Noël Coward, Simon Stephens, Caryl Churchill, Edward Bond and many more. Also publishes books that run the gamut of theatre and performance studies: from movement to directing, voice to playwriting, the list features original material for everyone with an interest in drama, whether a student or a professional. The popular series Student Editions and Student Guides make the most prominent plays and playwrights accessibe to students studying theatre at A level through to undergraduate, whilst Modern Classics, Modern Plays and play anthologies feature the best in new writing and classic contemporary theatre.

Accepts unsolicited play scripts and are pleased to consider proposals for theatre and performance studies textbooks and monographs. For submission details go to the website **www.bloomsbury.com/uk/company/contact-us/**

Music Theatre International

website www.mtishows.com

A great resource for researching songs – some of which can be partially listened to and read about on this site.

Musicroom

email info@musicroom.com
website www.musicroom.com

The world's largest online retailer of sheet music, tutor methods, instructional DVDs & videos, music software and instruments & accessories.

National Theatre Bookshop

National Theatre, South Bank, London SE1 9PX
tel 020 7452 3456
email bookshop@nationaltheatre.org.uk
website www.shop.nationaltheatre.org.uk/
Twitter @ntbookshop
Instagram @ntbookshop

Britain's leading specialist theatre bookshop. An inspiring selection of books, plays and design-led gifts. *Opening Hours*: Monday to Saturday: 9.30am – 10.45pm (this varies on certain public holidays); 12pm – 6pm on Sundays when there is a performance.

PlayDatabase.com

website www.playdatabase.com

US site that helps theatre-lovers find monologues and plays for production.

Project Gutenberg

website www.gutenberg.org

An online library of more than 18,000 books – and many classic plays – which have gone out of copyright in the US. Also a growing collection of music recordings and scores. Possibly the largest of its kind in the world.

Screen International

Greater London House, Hampstead Road, London NW1 7EJ
tel 020 7728 5000
website www.screendaily.com

International news and features on the film business. Subscriptions cost £175 per annum for:

- Screen International – 12 monthly issues delivered to your door
- ScreenDaily.com – instant access to the latest news, reviews and industry moves available online
- Global box office data available online – structured by territories, films and distributors
- Screen Base – the new online, interactive database providing vital production and financing information for the top five European territories

Script Websites

Although subject to rules on copyright, a number of websites make the scripts for films and television shows and suggestions for audition speeches available online. These sites tend to come and go, but here are some that are current at the time of going to press:

- www.script-o-rama.com
- www.sfy.ru

- www.imsdb.com
- www.playscripts.com
- www.simplyscripts.com
- www.whysanity.net/monos
- www.singlelane.com
- www.filmsite.org/bestspeeches.html

The Sheetmusic Warehouse

email pianoman@sheetmusicwarehouse.co.uk
website www.sheetmusicwarehouse.co.uk

Specialists supplying old music, rare music, music from the shows, musicals and operetta, popular music, wartime music, jazz music, Deep South American music, music hall music, classical music, modern music . . . "You name it, we've probably got it. Music to play, music to sing to or music to frame and hang on your wall!"

Shooting People

PO Box 51350, London N1 6XS
email contact@shootingpeople.org
website www.shootingpeople.org

Shooting People allows thousands of people working in independent film to exchange information via a range of daily email bulletins. These include:

- Daily UK Filmmakers Bulletin – for directors, producers and crew to share information on the latest technologies, get advice, find crew, locations, production deals, events & screenings, training and more. Currently more than 22,000 members
- Daily UK Screenwriters Bulletin – writers all over the UK use this email network to discuss writing, share ideas and hear about competitions, opportunities and training. Currently more than 13,000 members
- Daily UK Casting Bulletin – for actors to discuss their craft and receive casting calls from directors, producers and casting directors. Currently more than 14,000 members
- Weekly UK Script Pitch Bulletin – a weekly collection of script pitches offered to producers and directors by the writers on the Screenwriters Network. Currently more than 11,000 members

Both part- and full-membership are available. Part-membership allows subscribers to receive email bulletins only, and is free. Full-membership costs £20 per year and entitles users to a range of other services. Full-members can create an actor's personal profile with a photograph and be listed in the online directory, post to any bulletin and download guides on various confusing aspects of film-making such as actor contracts, health and safety and distribution. They are also entitled to create member cards and to browse other member cards to find potential local collaborators.

Shooting People also organises a number of parties, screenings, workshops and other events for which full members receive advanced notice.

Skoob Books

66 The Brunswick, Marchmont Street,
London WC1N 1AE
tel 020 7278 8760
website www.skoob.com

An excellent resource for the peforming arts. Large collection of second-hand plays, including many translated works and as-new titles at half RRP. Strong theatre, film, music and TV sections in a very large basement bookshop. All academic areas covered, and masses of paperback fiction. Lift access and knowledgeable, friendly staff. More/different books are available to buy on line via the website. Skoob is the leading UK supplier of books to TV, film and theatre productions; please contact our Didcot office for hire enquries at skoobhire@psychobabel.co.uk.

The Stage Media Company Ltd

47 Bermondsey Street, London SE1 3XT
tel 020 7403 1818
email reception@thestage.co.uk
website www.thestage.co.uk

Online and weekly print publication for the entertainment industry. Established in 1880. Advice, news, reviews, features and recruitment for theatre, entertainment, opera, dance, TV, radio, backstage and technical, management, education and training. *The Stage* is also available on iPad, Android, Kindle and other tablet devices.

Theatre Record – The continuing chronicle of the British Stage

Southernhay, 22 Carlton Road South,
Weymouth DT4 7PR
mobile 07777 697270
email editor@theatrerecord.com
website www.theatrerecord.com

Established in 1981 as *London Theatre Record*, the website also incorporates www.doolee.com. theatrerecord.com collates the complete, unabridged reviews of all new shows in the UK covered by national press, leading magazines and the internet. As well as reviews, each show is represented by a full listing of cast, technical credits and, usually, production photographs. Updated daily, the search feature enables in-depth research on all archive productions to 1981.

Theatrevoice

website www.theatrevoice.com

The leading site for audio content about British theatre, featuring journalists from across the UK press, and practitioners from across the theatre industry. It was set up in 2003 to see if theatre could be talked about in a new way – critics to be more expansive than what the usual space constraints of the print media allowed; to enable actors, writers, directors and designers to be heard talking in detail and at length about their work; and to help members of the public interact more directly with theatre-makers and commentators. The Theatre Museum, now V&A Theatre Collections, which provided technical assistance and a place for recording from the site's inception, assumed management responsibilities for the site in the summer of 2005, to ensure that Theatrevoice's growing archive of material would be preserved for posterity. In April 2008, V&A Theatre Collections and Rose Bruford College agreed to support the site in partnership. Theatrevoice acknowledges with gratitude all the input that has been and still is freely given.

Theatricalia

website theatricalia.com

Theatricalia is aiming to become "the repository of theatre productions on the Internet". In doing so, it will enable people to discover theatre that is going on around them, follow actors they have seen in previous productions and record memorable events of productions they have seen.

UK Theatre Network

Admiralty Way, Teddington TW11 0NL
0203 652 7453
email editor@uktheatre.net
website www.uktheatrenetwork.com
Facebook @uktheatrenet
Twitter @UKTheatreNet

Established 2001. A theatre community with a UK-wide team of reviewers who attend the best of regional theatre and share their experience and ticket information. New members can join by visiting the website and subscribing.

Virtual Library of Theatre & Drama

website www.vl-theatre.com

Lists online versions of plays and resources in more than 50 countries.

Westminster Reference Library

35 St Martin's Street, London WC2H 7HP
tel 020 7641 6200
website www.westminster.gov.uk/libraries-opening-hours-and-contact-details#westminster-reference-library

A West End public library with an art and design and music collection of national significance, along with a performing arts collection, Access to these collection is free and open to all. There are regular talks, workshops, performances in support of the collections, with the library open to suggestion for future events. Opening Hours: Monday to Friday: 10.00am – 8.00pm; Saturday: 10.00am – 5.00pm.

Wikipedia

website en.wikipedia.org

A free, online encyclopedia with over 1 million articles. Originally created by an army of volunteers in 2001, it can be added to or edited by anyone at all – a very democratic publication. This democracy can sometimes mean that contentious or politically sensitive issues are not always presented in the most balanced way, although some measures are in place to prevent flagrant abuse of the system. Occasionally the editing process makes for some slightly disjointed articles. However, as a free source of information on just about any topic, it is unsurpassed. The theatre section can be accessed via: **en.wikipedia.org/wiki/Theatre**.

Organisations, associations, societies and contacts

This section contains details of all kinds of ways (not listed elsewhere) of getting involved, sourcing useful information, learning, finding interesting lectures, networking, and simply keeping in touch with what's going on. It is important for the 'jobbing' actor to keep up-to-date with developments within the industry, and getting involved in related activities can pay dividends in the future.

The Actors' Guild of Great Britain
The Actors' Guild Hub at Spotlight, 2nd Floor, 7 Leicester Place, London WC2H 7RJ
tel 020 7112 8458
email mail@actorsguild.co.uk
website www.actorsguild.co.uk
Twitter @ActorsGuildGB
Instagram @actors_guild

The Actors' Guild is a community of professional actors who meet with leading acting tutors, casting directors, directors, artistic directors, producers and agents to develop their craft, maximise their career development and benefit from the professional networking opportunities that membership brings.

The Guild was formed as an antidote to the increasing number of enterprises that seemed to be taking advantage of actors. Providing a haven, a support network and the opportunity to work with the very people you meet in the audition room.

"Our unique set-up means we are able to swing the pendulum of power firmly back to the actor. Our programme is dictated purely by feedback from our membership; we never ask you to book casting director workshops in 'blocks', and believe quality does not have to cost the earth – workshops start at just £24 and are run both on Zoom and in person.

"We also offer an exclusive range of industry discounts for members and a support network that brings this often disparate, nomadic community together."

ASSITEJ (International Association of Theatre for Children and Young People)
Preradoviceva 44, 10000 Zagreb, Croatia
tel +385 (0) 1 4667034
email sec.gen@assitej-international.org
website www.assitej-international.org

ASSITEJ International (Association Internationale du Theatre pour l'Enfance et la Jeunesse) states: "Since the theatrical art is a universal expression of mankind, and possesses the influence and power to link large groups of the world's people in the service of peace, and considering the role theatre can play in the education of younger generations, an autonomous international organisation has been formed which bears the name of the International Association of Theatre for Children and Young People." Also see Theatre for Young Audiences (TYA), below.

ASSITEJ UK (International Association of Theatre for Children and Young People)
PYA-UK Centre of ASSITEJ, c/o the egg, Theatre Royal Bath, Sawclose, Bath BA1 1ET
email info@tya-uk.org
website www.tya-uk.org
Twitter @ASSITEJ

TYA-UK (UK Centre of ASSITEJ) is a network for makers and promoters of professional theatre for young audiences, linking the UK to theatres, organisations and individual artists around the world. Works for a fuller awareness of the value of theatre for young audiences.

AudioUK
c/o Unit 2, Olympic Court, Boardmans Way, Whitehills Business Park, Blackpool FY4 5GU
email admin@audiouk.org.uk
website www.audiouk.org.uk
Twitter @WeAreAudioUK

AudioUK is the trade association for UK audio production companies, with over 120 members across the UK, making high-quality award-winning podcasts, radio and audiobooks. Offers business affairs support for members and negotiates terms of trade with the BBC as well as liaising with talent unions. Also runs the Audiotrain skills programme and organises the annual Audio Production Awards. AudioUK jointly oversees the Government-financed Audio Content Fund.

Steve Bennett of Chortle
tel 020 8281 5204
email steve@chortle.co.uk
website www.chortle.co.uk

Established in 2000 with the aim of being the most comprehensive, critical and up-to-date guide to all aspects of comedy in Britain. Today, the site is the premier source of comedy news, reviews and listings and attracts around 180,000 unique visitors every month.

BAFTA

195 Piccadilly, London W1J 9LN
tel 020 7734 0022
email reception@bafta.org
website www.bafta.org
Chief Executive Officer Amanda Berry OBE

Founded in 1947, BAFTA is the UK's pre-eminent independent charity bringing the very best work in film, games and television to public attention, and supporting the growth of creative talent in the UK and internationally. BAFTA does this by identifying and celebrating excellence, discovering, inspiring and nurturing new talent, and enabling learning and creative collaboration. BAFTA's awards are awarded annually by its members to their peers in recognition of their skills and expertise. In addition, BAFTA's year-round learning programme offers unique access to some of the world's most inspiring talent through workshops, masterclasses, lectures and mentoring schemes, connecting with audiences of all ages and backgrounds across the UK, USA and Asia.

British Association for Performing Arts Medicine (BAPAM)

7-9 Breams Buildings, London EC4A 1DT
tel 020 7404 8444
website www.bapam.org.uk

The British Association for Performing Arts Medicine is a unique medical charity helping performing arts professionals and students with work-related health problems, both physical and psychological.

BAPAM provides:

• Free confidential clinical advice from medical practitioners who have specialist understanding of industry professionals' needs
• Directory of Performing Arts Medicine Practitioners – a list of clinical specialists and practitioners in many branches of healthcare who have an interest in treating performing arts professionals
• Health-information resources enabling you to understand what you can do to keep in peak condition throughout a demanding career
• Healthy Performance talks and training for a wide range of audiences, including introductory sessions for student groups and educational institutions. Bespoke sessions for clients including performers, teachers, clinicians and employers.

British Council

Belfast office: Norwich Union House,
7 Fountain Street, Belfast BT1 5EG
tel 028 9024 8220

Edinburgh office: British Council Scotland, Waverley Gate (Fourth Floor), 2-4 Waterloo Place, Edinburgh EH1 3EG
tel 0131 524 5714
Cardiff office: 1 Kingsway, 2nd Floor, Cardiff CF10 3AQ
website www.britishcouncil.org/arts

The British Council is the UK's public diplomacy and cultural organisation, and works in 100 countries, in arts, education, governance and science. The Arts Group supports around 2,000 arts events every year, encouraging international collaborations, performances and exchanges with some of the top UK artists. In addition they support arts-based workshops, seminars and online events.

The form of support which is offered varies according to the project. In most cases the Council acts as an advisory body, and brokers partnerships with overseas contacts such as artistic programmers and producers, venues, choreographers and festival directors. Although most work is geared towards young people aged 16-35, this isn't an exclusive emphasis, and classic or traditional work is supported, especially if it has a modern slant.

Resources available on the website include an annual directory of UK drama, dance, live art and street art companies that have work suitable for overseas touring; specialist information about drama/performing arts education in the UK; and *Britfilms* **www.britfilms.com** – a portal site for the UK film industry with information about international film festivals, UK film directors and films, making a film in the UK, training and careers advice.

Not open to the public except by appointment. Write, phone or email to establish contact, or get in touch with an artform specialist.

British Film Institute (BFI)

21 Stephen Street, London W1T 1LN
tel 020 7255 1444
BFI Southbank, Belvedere Road, South Bank, Waterloo, London SE1 8XT
tel 020 7928 3535
website www.bfi.org.uk

Established in 1933, the BFI strives to increase the level of understanding, appreciation and access to film and television culture. In addition to the BFI Reuben Library, which provides access to the largest collection of written material on film, television and the moving image in the word, the organisation runs the BFI National Archive, BFI Southbank (formerly the National Film Theatre), BFI Flare: London LGBTIQ+ Film Festival and the London Film Festival (see entry under Media festivals). It also publishes books, releases films in cinemas, on DVD and via its VOD platform BFI Player, runs educational programmes, and has one of the largest collections of film stills and film posters in the world. The BFI also awards Lottery funding to film production,

Resources

distribution, education, audience development and market intelligence and research.

British Music Hall Society

email contact@britishmusichallsociety.com
website www.britishmusichallsociety.com
Facebook www.facebook.com/
BritishMusicHallSociety
Twitter @musichallsoc

Founded in 1963, the society aims to preserve the history of music hall and variety, to recall the artistes who created it and to support entertainers working today. Members receive copies of the society's quarterly magazine *The Call-Boy* containing news, views and information about the sector; they also have the opportunity to attend evening 'In the Limelight' talks. Arranges live theatre shows, and it is possible for members to take part in such performances on these occasions. Organises #MusicHallVarietyDay on the 16th of May each year.

Casting Directors Guild of Great Britain and Ireland

website www.thecdg.co.uk
Twitter @CDGNews

A professional organisation which represents casting directors working in film, television, theatre and commercials. The Casting Directors Guild aims to standardise professional working practice and to enable the exchange of information and ideas between members.

Election to the Guild is at the discretion of the Committee. Full members must have worked in one or more areas of the industry for at least 5 years, and are entitled to use the initials CDG after their name. Probationary members must have worked as an assistant to a casting director for 3 years.

Members are listed on the website with information about their areas of work and recent credits.

Co-operative Personal Management Association (CPMA)

email cpmauk@yahoo.co.uk
website www.cpma.coop

Founded in 2002, the CPMA works to further and promote the interests of its members, who are acting agencies located across the UK. Backed by Equity, it seeks to raise the profile of co-ops with both employers and actors, and to represent the interests of co-ops with external bodies. Also works with members to identify and assist in solving the unique problems of a co-operative, to enourage good practice, to develop training skills and opportunities, and to act as an advocate for co-operative working.

Directors UK

4th Floor, 22 Stukeley Street, London WC2B 5LR
tel 020 7240 0009
email info@directors.uk.com
website www.directors.uk.com
Facebook www.facebook.com/DirectorsUKcmo
Twitter @Directors_UK

Directors UK is the professional association for screen directors in the UK. It is a membership organisation representing the creative, economic and contractual interests of over 8,000 members - the majority of working TV and film directors in the UK. Directors UK negotiates rights deals and collects and distributes royalties to its members. It also campaigns and lobbies on its members' behalf and provides a range of services including legal advice, events, training and career development. Directors UK works closely with fellow organisations around the world to represent directors' rights and concerns, promotes excellence in the craft of direction and champions change to the current lanscape to create an equal opportunity indusry for all.

Drama Association of Wales

The Old Library, Singleton Road, Splott, Cardiff CF24 2ET
email office@dramawales.org.uk
website www.dramawales.org.uk
Facebook www.facebook.com/
DramaAssociationOfWales?
Twitter @DramaWales

Founded in 1934 and a registered charity since 1973, the Drama Association of Wales aims to increase opportunities for people in the community to be creatively involved in high-quality drama.

Its main activities include a mail-order library service for DAW Publications and training courses in all aspects of theatre, including a 5-day residential summer school.

Also runs a playwriting competition and workshops. Organises the Wales National Drama Festival from March to June, culminating in the Wales Final Festival of One Act Plays at the beginning of June.

UK membership costs £15 per year for individuals and £25 for groups, both professional and amateur. Overseas members are very welcome: contact Shirley Betts for details.

Dramaturgs' Network

c/o Old Coghurst Farm, Rock Lane, Hastings TN35 4NX
email info@dramaturgy.co.uk
website www.dramaturgy.co.uk
Facebook www.facebook.com/dramaturgsnetwork/
Twitter @dramaturgs_net

Founded in 2001, the Dramaturgs' Network is an organisation for UK theatre practitioners committed to developing dramaturgy and supporting practitioners' development in the field. A volunteer arts organisation, it was created to share ideas, knowledge, resources and skills in current dramaturgical practices. The network aims to provide support for theatre makers functioning in the role of dramaturg and/or literary manager and educational professionals involved in dramaturgical practice. Every other year it bestows the Kenneth Tynan Award, which recognises excellence in the field of dramaturgy.

Federation of Scottish Theatre

c/o Royal Lyceum Theatre, 30ʙ Grindlay Street, Edinburgh EH3 9AX
tel 0131 248 4842
email info@scottishtheatre.org
website www.scottishtheatre.org

The Federation of Scottish Theatre is the membership and development body for professional dance, opera and theatre in Scotland, bringing the sector together to speak with a collective voice, to share resources and expertise, and to promote collaborative working.

Independent Theatre Council (ITC)

c/o The Albany, Douglas Way, London SE8 4AG
tel 020 7403 1727
email admin@itc-arts.org
website www.itc-arts.org

Founded in 1974, the Independent Theatre Council (ITC) is the management association and political voice of around 450 performing arts professionals and organisations. ITC provides its members with legal and management advice, training and professional development, networking, regular newsletters and a comprehensive web resource.

Working across a variety of art forms, including drama, dance, opera, music theatre, puppetry, mixed media, mime, physical theatre and circus, ITC members usually operate on the middle- and small-scale, and are dedicated to producing innovative work, often in unconventional performance spaces.

ITC has commissioned a wide range of publications which offer guidance on potentially difficult aspects of working in the performing arts, advice on good practice and further sources of information. For more than 20 years the Independent Theatre Council has been organising training for managers and staff across the performing arts.

For details of how to join and other benefits available to members, consult the website.

International Casting Directors Network (ICDN)

website https://theicdn.com

The idea for an informal international network was floated during a meeting of casting directors during European Film Promotion's ShootingStars event at the Berlinale. Until then, casting directors had only been organised in national associations, but ICDN offers them the opportunity to network, connect, share information and raise the profile of the profession. Members include the most influential and high-profile casting directors in film and television.

International Federation of Actors (FIA)

Rue Joseph II 40, Box 4, B-1000 Brussels
tel +32 (0) 2 234 56 53 / +32 (0) 2 235 08 65 / +32 (0) 2 235 08 74
email office@fia-actors.com
website www.fia-actors.com

The FIA currently represents 90 performers' unions and guilds in 66 countries around the world. Membership is limited to unions, guilds and professional associations – individual actors may not join. FIA works internationally to represent and co-ordinate the interests of performing artists and their professional organisations.

Services: Lobbying at European and international level on behalf of performers; defence of artists' freedom; trade union development; information exchange through conferences and meetings; networking.

Objectives: To promote a better understanding of performers' concerns and challenges around the world; to ensure that all main decision-making processes take due consideration of the specific needs of performers; to contribute to improve the social and professional conditions of performers worldwide; to facilitate the sharing of knowledge and experience on all issues of common interest between member organisations.

Irish Theatre Institute

17 Eustace Street, Temple Bar, Dublin 2, D02 F293 Republic of Ireland
tel +353 (0)1 670 4906
email info@irishtheatreinstitute.ie
website www.irishtheatreinstitute.ie

Irish Theatre Institute is a resource organisation that nurtures, promotes and drives the ambition of Irish theatre makers and Irish theatre, from its grassroots beginnings to its presentation on the world stage.

Mirth Control

tel 07974 674133
email geoff@mirthcontrol.org.uk
website www.mirthcontrolcomedy.com/
Twitter @MirthControl

The UK's largest independent comedy bookers. Books for over 100 comedy clubs in the UK and Europe and holds a database of over 1,500 comedians. Also manages clients.

The Mono Box

email hello@themonobox.co.uk
website www.themonobox.co.uk
Facebook www.facebook.com/TheMonoBox/
Twitter @TheMonoBox

Instagram @The_mono_box
Editor Executive Creative Director Blayne George
Editor & Co-founder Polly Bennett *Co-founder* Joan Iyiola

The Mono Box is a well-established theatre education programme that plays an important leadership role in advancing the education and career development for thousands of theatre artists. The Mono Box provides access to affordable and continual training, writing, performing and wider creative opportunities as well as inspirational live and digital events and content that reach people around the world.

It has become a go-to resource for those looking for alternative routes of training, those searching for a like-minded working community and those looking to enhance their skills as they navigate their way through the industry. In 2019, The Mono Box became an Associate Company of Hampstead Theatre.

At the heart of The Mono Box's work is the belief that creativity is not limited to age, race, religion, sexuality or background and it is committed to ensuring everyone has regular access to the performing arts and the ability to express themselves through storytelling in a safe, welcoming and creative environment. The Mono Box supports artists of all ages, at all stages of their career. By encouraging engagement at a professional, personal and social level through workshops, classes, free talks, mentorships, creative opportunities and ticket offers, the Mono Box is helping to ensure the performing arts are accessible to people from all walks of life.

Workshops are single sessions and long courses and cost between £5–£100. Bursary places are available.

National Campaign for the Arts
email hello@forthearts.org.uk
website www.forthearts.org.uk
Facebook www.facebook.com/weareforthearts
Instagram @weareforthearts

The National Campaign for the Arts is the UK's only independent organisation campaigning for all the arts. Since 1985 they have worked to protect and promote the UK's world-class arts scene and acted as a powerful and effective advocate for the sector, able to influence the people who matter. With a growing UK-wide membership, the NCA is driven by the needs of the arts sector. "We believe that only by speaking with a united voice can the arts truly be heard."

National Rural Touring Forum (NRTF)
email admin@nrtf.org.uk
website www.ruraltouring.org

The NRTF is the organisation that represents a number of mainly rural touring schemes and rural arts development agencies across the UK. "Our touring scheme members work with local communities to promote high-quality arts events and experiences in local venues."

North American Actors Association (NAAA)
mobile 07873 371891
email admin@naaa.org.uk
website www.naaa.org.uk
Administrator Kelly Jeffreys

The North American Actors Association is an association promoting and supporting North American actors based in Britain, and is the largest non-Americas-based casting resource and database of genuine North Americans for the entertainment industry.

Membership is open to genuine North American professional actors who can work on both sides of the Atlantic without restriction, are full members in good standing of at least 1 entertainment union and have proof of professional contracts. Not an agency, but through the website provides agent and other contact details.

Pact (Producers Alliance for Cinema and Television)
3rd Floor Fitzrovia House, 153-157 Cleveland Street, London W1T 6QW
tel 020 7380 8230
email info@pact.co.uk
website www.pact.co.uk
Twitter @PactUK
Chief Executive John McVay

The UK trade association that represents and promotes the commercial interests of independent feature film, television, animation and interactive media companies. Headquartered in London, it has regional representation throughout the UK in order to support its members, including an office in Leeds. An effective lobbying organisation, it has regular and constructive dialogues with government, regulators, public agencies and opinion-formers on all issues affecting its members, and contributes to key public policy debates on the media industry, both in the UK and in Europe. It negotiates terms of trade with all public service broadcasters in the UK and supports members in their business dealings with cable and satellite channels and streaming services. It also lobbies for a properly structured and funded UK film industry and maintains close contact with other relevant film organisations and government departments.

Personal Managers' Association (PMA)
tel 0845 602 7191
email info@thepma.com
website www.thepma.com

Established in 1950, the PMA is a membership organisation for agents who represent actors, writers and directors working mainly in film, television and theatre. The PMA aims to encourage good practice among agents by encouraging better communication between agents and better communication from agents to the industry – an ethos that remains true to this day.

Royal Television Society (RTS)

3 Dorset Rise, London EC4Y 8EN
tel 020 7822 2810
email info@rts.org.uk
website www.rts.org.uk

Provides the leading forum for discussion and debate on all aspects of the television industry, with opportunities for networking and professional development for people at all levels and across every sector. The RTS has 14 national and regional centres in the UK, which draw up an annual programme to suit the needs of their members.

Events organised by the RTS include dinners, lectures, conventions, conferences and awards ceremonies. In addition it produces a monthly magazine, *Television*, outlining key industry debates and developments.

Scene & Heard

128A Chalton Street, London NW1 1RX
tel 020 7388 9009
email mail@sceneandheard.org
website www.sceneandheard.org
Twitter @SceneandHeardUK

Scene & Heard is a unique mentoring project that partners the inner-city children of Somers Town, London, with volunteer theatre professionals. Scene & Heard gives children an experience of quality one-to-one adult attention enabling them to write plays to be performed by professional actors.

The fundamental purpose of the project is to boost the self-esteem and raise the aspirations of the children by giving them a public platform for their voice and providing a personal experience of success.

Only accepts enquiries from professional actors, directors and writers. The best way to get in touch is to see a performance.

The Society of Teachers of the Alexander Technique (STAT)

PO Box 78503, London N14 9GB
tel 020 8885 6524
email info@alexandertechnique.co.uk
website www.alexandertechnique.co.uk
Facebook www.facebook.com/AlexanderTechUK
Instagram @alexandertechuk

The Alexander Technique has been taught for more than 100 years. In 1958, the Society of Teachers of the Alexander Technique (STAT) was founded in the UK by teachers who were trained by FM Alexander. STAT's first aim is to ensure the highest standards of teacher training and professional practice.

Teaching members of STAT are registered (MSTAT) to teach the Technique after completing a 3-year, full-time training course approved by the Society or one of the Affiliated Societies overseas; they are also required to adhere to the Society's published *Code of Professional Conduct and Competence* and are covered by the professional indemnity insurance.

There are currently more than 2,500 teaching members of STAT and its affiliated societies worldwide. Graduates of STAT training courses are assessed by a system of external moderation; the Society also runs a postgraduate programme of Continuing Professional Development. STAT's further aims are to promote public awareness and understanding of the Alexander Technique, and to encourage research. The Society publishes a regular newsletter, *STATNews*, and *The Alexander Journal*.

Society of London Theatre (SOLT)

32 Rose Street, London WC2E 9ET
tel 020 7557 6700
email enquiries@soltukt.co.uk
website www.solt.co.uk

Founded in 1908 by Sir Charles Wyndham, the Society of London Theatre is the trade association which represents the producers, theatre owners and managers of the major commercial and grant-aided theatres in central London.

Today the Society combines its long-standing roles in such areas as industrial relations and legal advice for members, with a campaigning role for the industry, together with a wide range of audience-development programmes to promote theatre-going.

The Stephen Sondheim Society

44 Little Lane, Kimberley, Nottingham NG16 2PE
tel (01158) 882667
email sondheimsociety@sondheim.org
website www.sondheim.org
Chairman Craig Glenday *Administrator* Lynne Chapman

The Stephen Sondheim Society is a registered charity promoting the works of the composer and lyricist Stephen Sondheim. Keeps track of all productions (professional and amateur) of Sondheim's musicals, publishes a newsletter, arranges theatre visits, runs an annual student competition and has an extensive archive housed at Kingston University.

At the time of writing, UK membership is £27 (single), £22 (concession) or £32 (joint), £17 (student/Equity/MU/ISM) and £40 (for international membership) but please consult the website for the latest rates.

Stage Directors UK

Exchange at Somerset House, South Wing, Strand, London WC2R 1LA
tel 020 7112 8881
email info@stagedirectorsuk.com
website www.stagedirectorsuk.com
Facebook www.facebook.com/StageDirectorsUK
Twitter @StageDirectors

Stage Directors UK is the professional trade association for stage directors, choreographers and movement directors across the UK. SDUK represents the interests of stage directors, campaigning and lobbying for better rights and working conditions. SDUK provides a sense of community and a unifying network for its members, and offers support, training and professional development, directing culture towards a greater spirit of collaboration and mutual support.

The Ten
mobile 07415 009639
email office@thetentalent.co.uk
website www.thetentalent.co.uk
Twitter @thetentalent
Instagram @thetentalent
Editor Head of Talent Mark Weinman

The Ten is passionate about improving the way the industry can help support one another. At the core is their not-for-profit year-long mentorship initiative offering free coaching and representational support to 10 young actors aged between 18–25. Their aim is to improve access, champion inclusive practice and promote equal opportunities in the performing arts.

They are keen to meet anyone who feels they would benefit from the opportunities offered by The Ten, though they should stress that their primary aim is to discover acting talent among disadvantaged and under-represented communities around the UK.

Services offered: In addition to the mentorship programme, free online acting workshops are also offered to the general public as part of Ten Teach.

As a company, The Ten also offers a mobile self-tape support service YourTape, acting coaching, drama school tuition, bespoke acting workshops, line reading services and headshot/portrait photography.

The Ten specialises in acting, ensemble, monologue preparation, audition technique, improvisation, character, self-tape, acting for screen, creative writing, duologues, scene studies and sight reading.

The Ten mentorship programme and online workshops are free to participants. Donations towards expenses are welcome but are not obligatory. Fees are charged only for services such as self-tape support, private acting coaching and bespoke workshops. For more details on fees and contributions, please visit the website.

The Ten are only able to accept submissions from those aged 18+.

Theatre Chaplaincy UK
St Paul's Church, Bedford Street, London WC2E 9ED
tel (07501) 829491
email info@TheatreChaplaincyUK.com
website www.theatrechaplaincyuk.com
Facebook www.facebook.com/TCUKchaplains
Twitter @TCUKchaplains
Senior Chaplain Reverend Lindsay Meader

Provides pastoral support for all members of the entertainment world, regardless of beliefs. Runs a network of voluntary chaplains for theatres, clubs and studios, in the UK and overseas. Also runs a charitable trust for children of parents in entertainment.

Theatres Trust
22 Charing Cross Road, London WC2H 0QL
tel 020 7836 8591
email info@theatrestrust.org.uk
website www.theatrestrust.org.uk
Twitter @TheatresTrust

National Advisory Public Body for theatres, we are a statutory consultee on theatres in the planning system, and also operate as a charity. Champions the future of live performance by protecting and supporting excellent theatre buildings which meet the needs of their communities. They do this by providing advice on the design, planning, development and sustainability of theatres, campaigning on behalf of theatres old and new, and offering financial assistance through grants.

They promote the quality and design of existing and new theatres and protect important historic theatres so that they can be used as theatres in the future. The Trust also advises to ensure theatre buildings meet the current needs and demands of the theatre industry and the audiences they serve.

UK Theatre Association (TMA)
32 Rose Street, London WC2E 9ET
tel 020 7557 6700
email enquiries@soltukt.co.uk
website www.uktheatre.org
Interim Chief Executive Martin Scott *Head of UK Theatre & Workforce* Sebastian Cater

The UK Theatre Association is a membership organisation representing approximately 240 theatres, concert halls, dance companies, producers and arts centres throughout the UK. Also operates as a professional association, supporting over 1,400 individuals working professionally in theatre and the performing arts in the UK. Members benefit from access to a range of services, high-quality training and events, resources and initiatives, and networking opportunities. As well as running the only awards scheme to recognise excellence in theatre throughout the UK, UK Theatre promotes excellence, professional development and campaigns to improve resilience and increase audiences across the sector.

University of Bristol Theatre Collection
Wickham Building, Cantocks Close, Bristol BS8 1UP
tel 0117 331 5045
email theatre-collection@bristol.ac.uk
website www.bris.ac.uk/theatrecollection

The University of Bristol Theatre Collection is one of the world's largest and most significant collections relating to the history of British theatre. It is an Arts Council England Designated Collection, an Accredited Museum and an Accredited Archive Service. It is a research facility that is open to the public. Its collections cover all aspects of theatre from the seventeenth century up to the present day and includes original documents, photographs, artwork and artefacts.

V&A Theatre & Performance Collections

email tmenquiries@vam.ac.uk
website www.vam.ac.uk/collections/theatre-performance

The V&A's Theatre and Performance Collections comprise over 80,000 objects and 600 archives exploring the practice, process and history of performance in the UK since Shakespeare's day, covering theatre, dance, popular entertainment, music and film. In 2009, permanent Theatre & Performance Galleries opened at the V&A, replacing the Theatre Museum in Covent Garden which closed in 2007. From 2024, the Theatre & Performance Collections will be available to access at V&A Storehouse, the museum's new Collections and Research Centre opening in Stratford, East London.

Women in Film and Television (UK) (WFTV)

CMS Cameron McKenna Nabarro,
78 Cannon Street, London EC4N 6AF
tel 020 7287 1400
email admin@wftv.org.uk
website www.wftv.org.uk

Women in Film and TV (UK) is the leading membership organisation for women working in creative media in the UK and part of an international network of over 12,000 women. Members come from a broad range of professions spanning the entire film and television industry. WFTV hosts a variety of online and in person events throughout the year, presents a prestigious awards ceremony every December and runs a four nations mid-career mentoring programme for women. WFTV also collaborates with industry bodies on research projects, runs bursary initiatives and lobbies for women's interests.

WGGB (Writers' Guild of Great Britain)

First Floor, 134 Tooley Street, London SE1 2TU
tel 020 7833 0777
email admin@writersguild.org.uk
website www.writersguild.org.uk
General Secretary Ellie Peers

WGGB is a trade union for professional and aspiring writers in TV, radio, film, theatre, books, poetry, comedy, animation and video games with 2,600 members; affiliated to the Trades Union Congress. WGGB negotiates collective minimum terms agreements with the main broadcasters and trade bodies for film, TV, radio and theatre – these cover fees, advances, royalties, residuals, pension contributions, rights, credits and other matters. WGGB members have access to free contract vetting, legal advice and representation in work-related disputes (depending on their membership level), and the Writers' Guild Welfare Fund gives emergency assistance to members in financial trouble. Members receive a weekly email bulletin containing news and work opportunities. WGGB has recently introduced a student membership package for £30 per year.

Resources

Bibliography

Books for aspiring, student and young actors

Margo Annett, *Actor's Guide to Auditions and Interviews* (Methuen Drama, 2004). Now in its third edition, this useful guide outlines the techniques needed to achieve success in the challenging process of getting work, covering all aspects of casting, including gaining a place on a drama course, landing a part in film, TV, commercials or theatre, and becoming a radio or TV presenter.

Clive Barker, *Theatre Games* (Methuen Drama, 2010). A guidebook to improvisational games for actors, and a comprehensive exploration of acting techniques.

Tom Cantrell and Christopher Hogg (eds.), *Exploring Television Acting* (Methuen Drama, 2018). A collection of eleven essays from internationally distinguished researchers, actor trainers and early-career advisers bring together scholarly and practical perspectives on acting for television for the first time.

Louise Dearman and Mark Evans, *Secrets of Stage Success* (Nick Hern Books, 2015). Two of the biggest musical-theatre stars working today offer advice on training, auditions, finding an agent, building your career, staying healthy and more

Simon Dunmore, *Alternative Shakespeare Auditions for Men* (A & C Black, 1997). A collection of 50 less-well-known speeches for men.

Simon Dunmore, *Alternative Shakespeare Auditions for Women* (A & C Black, 1997). A collection of 50 less-well-known speeches for women.

Simon Dunmore, *MORE Alternative Shakespeare Auditions for Men* (A & C Black, 2002). Another collection of 50 less-well-known speeches for men.

Simon Dunmore, *MORE Alternative Shakespeare Auditions for Women* (A & C Black, 1999). Another collection of 50 less-well-known speeches for women.

Vanessa Ewan with Kate Sagovsky, *Laban's Efforts in Action* (Methuen Drama, 2018). An accessible textbook for students and teachers looking for new ways to facilitate the creation of embodied and physically ambitious performance.

Niki Flacks, *Acting with Passion* (Methuen Drama, 2015). A revolutionary new approach to the age-old problems of the actor: dealing with nerves, engaging the body, quieting the inner critic, auditioning, creating a character, and even playing comedy.

Helen Freeman, *So You Want To Go To Drama School?* (Nick Hern Books, 2012). A clear and honest guide, written by a teacher and audition panellist with a lifetime's experience of the audition process.

Alison Hodge (ed.), *Twentieth Century Actor Training* (Routledge, 2000). A valuable introduction to the lives, principles, and practices of fourteen of the most important figures in twentieth-century actor training.

Kelly Hunter, *Cracking Shakespeare* (Methuen Drama, 2015). A book that demystifies the process of speaking Shakespeare's language, offering hands-on techniques for drama students, young actors and directors who are intimidated by rehearsing, performing and directing Shakespeare's plays.

Andy Johnson, *The Excellent Audition Guide* (Nick Hern Books, 2013). An engaging, upbeat guide for any student thinking of applying to drama school, this book demystifies the often scary-looking process, leading you through every step with reassurance and encouragement.

Ellis Jones, *Teach Yourself Acting* (Hodder & Stoughton Ltd, 1998). A good overview of acting and the profession.

Samantha Marsden, *100 Acting Exercises for 8–18 Year Olds* (Methuen Drama, 2019). Offers acting exercises to be used with young people in the classroom or by individuals, many based on the teachings of Meisner, Stanislavski and Brecht.

John Matthews, *Training for Performance* (Methuen Drama, 2011). An innovative introduction to the concept of 'askeology' – a field of study that dissolves divisions between disciplines and their exercises – and identifies four meta-disciplinary categories in the process of training that are common to all institutional contexts: vocation; obedience; formation and automatisation.

Jennifer Reischel, *So You Want to Tread the Boards: The Everything-you-need-to-know, Insider's Guide to a Career in the Performing Arts* (JR Books Ltd, 2007).

Anna Scher, *Desperate to Act* (Lions, 1988). Brilliant, basic advice for those so 'desperate', from a lady who should know.

William Shakespeare, *Hamlet, Prince of Denmark.* Especially Hamlet's advice to the players (Act 3, scene 2), which is some of the best advice on acting ever given.

Malcolm Taylor, *The Actor and the Camera* (A & C Black, 1994). Another good 'primer' for the beginner.

Other career advice books for actors

Laura Barnett, *Advice from the Players* (Nick Hern Books, 2014). A host of tips and guidance on every aspect of the actor's craft, direct from some of the best-known stars of stage and screen, including Zawe Ashton, Jo Brand, David Harewood, Mark Gatiss, Lenny Henry, Lesley Manville, Simon Russell Beale and Julie Walters.

James Calleri and Robert Cohen, *Acting Professionally* (7th edition, Palgrave Macmillan, 2009). The first edition was published in 1972, and is now regarded as godfather of this genre in the USA.

Paul Clayton, *The Working Actor* (Nick Hern Books, 2016). A guide to putting yourself in the best possible position to get work, to keep getting it, and to make a living from it. Written by the Chairman of the Actors Centre, with over forty years' experience as an actor himself.

Jane Drake Brody, *Actor's Business Plan* (Methuen Drama, 2015). A smart approach that offers a method for the achievement of dreams through a five-year life and career plan giving positive steps to develop a happy life as an actor and as a person.

Simon Dunmore, *An Actor's Guide to Getting Work* (5th edition, Methuen Drama, 2012). Honest, humorous and thorough, this practical, comprehensive guide draws on the author's rich experience in the field and offers invaluable information and advice to enable actors to succeed in the business.

Ed Hooks, *The Audition Book* (3rd edition, Back Stage Books, 2000). Excellent reading if you're thinking of trying your hand in the USA. It's also worth looking at Ed's website for his excellent 'Craft Notes' (www.edhooks.com).

Felicity Jackson and Lianne Robertson, *Surviving Actors Manual* (Nick Hern Books, 2015). A no-nonsense breakdown of the day-to-day essentials you need to succeed in the industry – including establishing a personal brand and business plan, dealing with agents and casting directors, networking and managing your money – from the team behind the internationally successful Surviving Actors conventions.

Peter Messaline and Miriam Newhouse, *The Actor's Survival Kit* (3rd edition, Simon & Pierre, 1999). Well worth reading if you're thinking of trying your hand in Canada.

Andy Nyman, *The Golden Rules of Acting* (Nick Hern Books, 2012). An honest, witty and direct treasure trove of advice, support and encouragement that no performer should be without.

Robert Ostlere, *The Actor's Career Bible* (Methuen Drama, 2019). A career guide for the modern actor filled with wisdom and inside knowledge from industry experts: key organisations, casting directors, agents, producers, directors and most importantly, actors, at different stages in their careers. Backed by online resources.

Jon S. Robbins, *The Actor's Survival Guide* (Methuen Drama, 2019). Completely revised and updated, this new edition is the perfect business handbook and guide to living and working in Hollywood.

Donna Soto-Morettini, *Mastering the Audition* (Methuen Drama, 2012) and *Mastering the Shakespeare Audition* (Methuen Drama, 2016). These thorough handbooks coach the actor to master the audition experience for contemporary and classical speeches, allowing them to master their fear and gain a deeper understanding of the ideas and skills involved.

Books for any actor

Mike Alfreds, *Different Every Night* (Nick Hern Books, 2007). A top ranking director sets out his rehearsal techniques in this vital masterclass.

Glenn Seven Allen, *The Singer Acts, The Actor Sings* (Methuen Drama, 2019). An essential handbook for actors and singers looking to combine great acting with great singing technique.

Brian Bates, *The Way of the Actor* (Century Hutchinson, 1986). Very interesting insights into the inner workings of the actor's psyche.

Nancy Bishop, *Secrets from the Casting Couch* (Methuen Drama, 2009). A practical workbook written from the point of view of a very experienced casting director.

Giles Block, *Speaking the Speech* (Nick Hern Books, 2014). An authoritative, comprehensive book on understanding and performing Shakespeare's language, by the 'Master of Words' at Shakespeare's Globe. Foreword by Mark Rylance.

Peter M. Boenisch, Thomas Ostermeier, *The Theatre of Thomas Ostermeier* (Routledge, 2016). The German director presents his advanced contemporary directorial approach to staging texts, for teh first time.

Anne Bogart and Tina Landau, *The Viewpoints Book* (Nick Hern Books, 2014). The Viewpoints are an improvisation technique: a set of names given to certain principles of movement through time and space – they constitute a language for talking about what happens on stage.

Bertolt Brecht, *Brecht and the Writer's Workshop: Fatzer and Other Dramatic Projects* edited by Tom Kuhn and Charlotte Ryland (Methuen Drama, 2019). A collection of previously uncollected texts from major unfinished dramatic projects dating from all periods of Brecht's creative life.

Bill Britten, *From Stage to Screen* (Methuen Drama, 2014). A handbook for the professional actor packed with advice on how to make the transition from theatre and fully prepare for a film role.

Peter Brook, *The Empty Space* (Penguin, 1990). Written in the 1960s, but still essential reading.

Adrian Cairns, *The Making of the Professional Actor* (Peter Owen Publishers, 1996). A fascinating study of the history, and possible future, of the art of acting.

Simon Callow, *Being an Actor* (Penguin, 1995). Autobiographical books by famous actors are generally useless in terms of practical career advice. However, this one – part autobiography and part advice – has a great deal of down-to-earth common sense. His famous 'manifesto' on directors' theatre is spot on.

Dee Cannon, *In-Depth Acting* (Oberon Books, 2012). An essential guide to mastering the Stanislavski technique, filtering its complexities and offering a dynamic, hands-on approach.

David Carey and Rebecca Clark Carey, *The Shakespeare Workbook* (Methuen Drama, 2015). A unifying approach to acting Shakespeare that is immediately applicable in the rehearsal room or classroom.

David Carey and Rebecca Clark Carey, *The Dramatic Text Workbook and Video* (Methuen Drama, 2019). A new edition of The Verbal Arts Workbook, now featuring detailed online supplementary video.

Mel Churcher, *Acting for Film: Truth 24 Times a Second* (Virgin Books, 2003). Invaluable insights into the specific techniques involved.

Mel Churcher, *A Screen Acting Workshop* (Nick Hern Books, 2011). An excellent and comprehensive training course in screen acting which includes a DVD showing the work in action.

Alex Clifton, *The Actor's Workbook* (Methuen Drama, 2016). Essential and clear, this workbook for actors, actors in training and teachers of acting and drama provides a step-by-step guide to learning techniques in acting through a system of exercises which will develop core acting skills and offer techniques for developing an authored role and models for devising new work.

Michael Clune, *Gamelife: A Memoir of Childhood* (Text Publishing, 2016). This is a history of an intellectual awakening told through the medium of video games.

Martin Constantine, *The Opera Singer's Acting Toolkit* (Methuen Drama, 2019). A step-by-step guide detailing how to create character, from auditions through to rehearsal and performance and formulate a successful career.

Declan Donnellan, *The Actor and the Target* (Nick Hern Books, 2005) A fresh approach to the actor's art from the artistic director of Cheek by Jowl.

Daniel Dresner, *A Life-coaching Approach to Screen Acting* (Methuen Drama, 2018). This handbook combines effective life-coaching techniques with screen acting tools to enable actors to approach their characters and their work with self-confidence.

David Edgar, *How Plays Work* (Nick Hern Books, 2009). The distinguished playwright examines the mechanisms and techniques, which dramatists throughout the ages have employed to structure their plays and to express their meaning.

Paul Elsam, *Acting Characters* (Methuen Drama, 2011). Fundamentally practical, this introductory handbook for the aspiring actor helps them create, present and sustain a believable character using different voice and body language.

Vanessa Ewan, *Actor Movement* (Methuen Drama, 2014). A textbook and video resource for the working actor, this book inspires confidence in the actor to make fully owned physical choices and develop a love for movement.

Gabriella Giannachi and Mary Luckhurst, *On Directing* (Faber & Faber, 1999). Twenty-one directors with very different styles, all working in the UK are interviewed to ascertain how they begin work on a play or performance, what methods they use in rehearsal and answer the question: 'is the modern director an enabler, collaborator or dictator?'

John Gillett, *Acting Stanislavski* (Methuen Drama, 2014). Offering a clear, accessible and comprehensive account of the Stanislavski approach, this book demsytifies the practitioner's key words and concepts from the actor's training to final performance.

Bernard Graham Shaw, *Voice-Overs, A Practical Guide* (A & C Black, 2000). A useful guide which explains and teaches the skills of voicing radio and television commercials.

Uta Hagen, *A Challenge for the Actor* (Macmillan, 1991). One of the best books on acting ever written.

Paul Harvard, *Acting Through Song* (Nick Hern Books, 2013). Takes the techniques of modern actor training – including the theories of Stanislavsky, Brecht, Meisner and Laban, amongst others – and applies them to the fundamental component of musical theatre: singing.

Julie Hesmondhalgh, *A Working Diary* (Methuen Drama, 2019). Reveals the numerous projects and preoccupations of a year in the life of one of Britain's best-loved actresses.

Sidney Hoffman and Brian Rhinehart, *Comedy Acting for Theatre* (Methuen Drama, 2018). A textbook for actors and acting students seeking to learn how to be funny on stage.

Stephen Jeffreys, *Playwriting: Structure, Character, How and What to Write* (Nick Hern Books, 2019). For over two decades, Stephen Jeffreys's remarkable series of workshops attracted writers from all over the world and shaped the ideas of many of today's leading playwrights and theatre-makers. Now, with this inspiring, highly practical book, you too can learn from these acclaimed Masterclasses.

Angela V. John, *The Actors' Crucible: Port Talbot and the Making of Burton, Hopkins, Sheen and all the Others* (Parthian Books, 2015). Dr John presents the emergence of these famous actors as part of a rich culture and commitment to drama long embedded in the town's history.

Keith Johnstone, *Impro: Improvisation and the Theatre* (Faber & Faber, 1979); and *Impro for Storytellers* (Faber & Faber, 1999). Keith Johnstone suggests a hundred practical techniques for encouraging spontaneity and originality by catching the subconscious unawares.

Paterson Joseph, *Julius Caesar and Me: Exploring Shakespeare's African Play* (Methuen Drama, 2018). A casebook of the RSC's African production of *Julius Caesar*, with audience reactions and a detailed evaluation of the position of ethnic minority actors in Shakespeare productions in general.

David Mamet, *True and False* (Faber & Faber, 1998). This book cuts through much of the mythology that surrounds acting.

Lorna Marshall, *The Body Speaks: Performance and Expression* (Methuen Drama, 2001). Lorna Marshall enables actors and performers to recognise and lose unwanted physical habits and discover new possibilities for the body.

John Matthews, *The Life of Training* (Methuen Drama, 2019). In this follow-up to *Anatomy of Performance Training* (2014) John Matthews makes a compelling argument that training not only takes time, but also makes time. Employing the mature philosophy of Hannah Arendt.

Dick McCaw, *Training the Actor's Body* (Methuen Drama, 2018). A practical book that draws on recent research into neurophysiology to illuminate key principles in the movement training of actors.

Kelly McEvenue, *The Alexander Technique for Actors* (Methuen Drama, 2001). The Alexander Technique is a method of physical relaxation that reduces tension and strain throughout the body. F.M. Alexander (1869-1955) was an actor who developed this technique to conquer his habit of straining his voice. This book's exercises are linked to accurate anatomical drawings, showing where stress is most pronounced in the body.

Ros Merkin (compiler), *The Liverpool Everyman Theatre: Liverpool's Third Cathedral* (Liverpool and Merseyside Theatres Trust Limited, 2004). This book offers brief encounters with some of the people, the plays, the on-and-off stage dramas of the Everyman's first 40 highly eventful years.

Ros Merkin (ed.), *Liverpool Playhouse: A Theatre and its City* (Liverpool University Press, 2011). From its opening in 1911, Liverpool Playhouse has reflected the history of Liverpool – and at times the city itself has appeared on stage as a key character.

Bella Merlin, *Facing the Fear* (Nick Hern Books, 2016). An insightful, empowering and reassuring guide to stage fright: why it happens, how it manifests itself, and how to overcome it.

Jeannette Nelson, *The Voice Exercise Book* (National Theatre Publishing, 2015). The Head of Voice at the National Theatre shares the voice exercises she uses with many of Britain's leading actors to help to keep their voices in shape.

Patrick O'Kane (ed.), *Actors' Voices: The People Behind the Performances* (Oberon Books, 2012). Twelve experienced actors share their process, comment on their experiences and consider their role as theatre artists in the broader spectrum of Art and Culture.

Chris Palmer, *Voice and Speech for Musical Theatre* (Methuen Drama, 2019). A workbook with online video resources, which combines traditional voice training for actors and musical training, allowing performers to train their spoken voice specifically for musicals.

Simon Parkin, *Death by Video Game* (Serpent's Tail, 2016). The writer and games critic Simon Parkin offers an enlightening and well-informed survey of developments in the medium, attempting to explain what it is that drives people to these virtual worlds and what keeps their interest when they get there.

Litz Pisk, with introduction by Ashe Taskiran, *The Actor and His Body* (Methuen Drama, 2017). In this seminal book, Pisk quests to find expression for the inner impulse that motivated actors to move and subsequently offer insight on the specific craft of the actor and the relationship between movement and imagination.

Theresa Robbins Dudeck, *Keith Johnstone: A Critical Biography* (Methuen Drama, 2013). A fascinating account of Keith Johnstone's early years at the Royal Court Theatre and teaching at RADA, and a good assessment of his approach and contributions to theatre and improvisation.

Resources

Patsy Rodenberg, *The Actor Speaks* (Methuen Drama, 2019). A brand new edition of legendary voice coach's work on voice for actors with excellent advice and exercises to develop the performer's voice.

Sinéad Rushe, *Michael Chekhov's Acting Technique* (Methuen Drama, 2019). Provides a complete overview of Michael Chekhov's method, offering clear explanations of the principles, practical exercises and application of the exercises to dramatic texts.

Neil Rutherford, *Musical Theatre Auditions and Casting* (Methuen Drama, 2012). A performer's guide viewed from both sides of the audition table.

Michael Sanderson, *From Irving to Olivier – A Social History of the Acting Profession* (Athlone Press, 1984). A very expensive, but nevertheless fascinating, study of the actor's world over the last century.

Edda Sharpe and Jan Haydn Rowles, *How to Do Any Accent: The Essential Handbook for Every Actor* (Oberon Books, 2007).

Michael Shurtleff, *Audition* (Walker & Company, 1984). An American book which should be read. It contains brilliant insights and thoughts to help any actor.

Spotlight, *Contacts* (Spotlight, annually in October). Contact details for everything you can think of (and more) that relates to actors and performers.

Jane Streeton and Phillip Raymond, *Singing on Stage: An Actor's Guide* (Methuen Drama, 2014). Singing should be an essential part of every actor's toolkit. This book encourages each actor to explore their own authentic voice as opposed to offering a 'one-size-fits-all' or 'quick fix' approach.

Steve Waters, *The Secret Life of Plays* (Nick Hern Books, 2010). Covers the key elements of dramatic writing – scenes, acts, space, time, characters, language and images – to show how a play is more than the sum of its parts.

Victoria Worsley, *Feldenkrais for Actors* (Nick Hern Books, 2016). A fascinating guide to the Feldenkrais Method, and how it can help actors with presence and posture, emotion, voice and breath, avoiding injury and more.

Webography

What follows is a selected collection of the most important websites for aspirants and professionals, and some others which the editors have found extremely useful, but don't quite fit elsewhere in this book.

Important websites for aspirants and professionals

www.bbc.co.uk – BBC homepage

www.bbc.co.uk/soundstart – advice on how to get work in radio drama

www.thecdg.co.uk – Casting Directors Guild

www.cpma.coop – The Co-operative Personal Management Association

www.cukas.ac.uk – Conservatoires UK Admissions Service (CUKAS) provides the facilities to research and apply for practice-based music, dance and drama courses at some UK conservatoires

www.edfringe.com – Edinburgh Festival Fringe

www.eif.co.uk – Edinburgh International Festival

www.equity.org.uk – Equity

www.federationofdramaschools.co.uk – Federation of Drama Schools

www.imdb.com – Internet Movie Database; catalogues all sorts of information on more than 250,000 films and the 900,000 people who helped to make them

www.itc-arts.org – Independent Theatre Council homepage with links to member companies' websites

www.thepma.com – Personal Managers' Association

www.sevendialsplayhouse.co.uk – Seven Dial's Playhouse

www.spotlight.com – Spotlight publishes the most important actors' directories

www.thestage.co.uk – *The Stage*, contains news, information and job advertisements which are updated each Thursday

www.ucas.ac.uk – UCAS, the central organisation that processes applications for·full-time undergraduate courses at UK universities and colleges

Other useful websites

http://accent.gmu.edu – the speech accent archive uniformly presents a large set of speech samples from a variety of language backgrounds

www.companieshouse.gov.uk – Companies House: useful for checking background details (like date of foundation) of individual companies

www.dialectsarchive.com – the International Dialects of English Archive (IDEA) is a useful collection of English-language dialects and English spoken in the accents of other languages

www.edhooks.com – contains some interesting articles on acting

www.excellenttalent.co.uk – information and advice for voice-over artists with examples of good voicereels online

film.britishcouncil.org – lots of articles, reviews and links about British theatre

www.its-behind-you.com – seemingly a comprehensive list of pantomimes and their producers

www.officiallondontheatre.com – Society of London Theatre website with news, reviews and booking information

www.shakespeare-online.com – electronic copies of the plays and poems, along with other related material of interest. These copies of the texts should be checked against published editions before use in audition or performance, in order to gain the benefit of modern scholarship

www.shakespeareswords.com – an excellent resource for understanding Shakespeare

http://sounds.bl.uk/Accents-and-dialects – the British Library's archive of accents and dialects

www.theatredigsbooker.com – a site aimed solely at touring professionals within the UK entertainment industry

www.uktw.co.uk – UK Theatre Web, with information, events and tickets for theatre in the UK

www.usefee.tv – a site which lets performers, their representatives and employers quickly calculate the appropriate use fee for featured players in TV commercials based on the established, industry-endorsed method approved by the Personal Managers' Association, the Association of Model Agents and Equity

www.vocalist.org.uk – a site for singers, vocalists, singing teachers and students of voice of all ages, standards and styles. The site contains useful information on aspects of singing, performance, plus free online singing lessons and articles for vocalists related to singing and getting into the music industry

www.voiceovers.co.uk – a forum for voice-over artists to advertise themselves

www.whatsonstage.com – a UK theatre listing service with search facilities, a ticket-ordering service, reviews, news and debate

Index